THE ART AND LIFE OF

WILLIAM SHAKESPEARE

Mr. WILLIAM
SHAKESPEARES

COMEDIES,
HISTORIES, &
TRAGEDIES.

Publiſhed according to the True Originall Copies.

Martin Droeshout ſculpsit London.

LONDON
Printed by Iſaac Iaggard, and Ed. Blount. 1623.

THE ART AND LIFE OF

WILLIAM SHAKESPEARE

BY HAZELTON SPENCER

*Ce qui fait les hommes de génie, ou plutôt
ce qu'ils font, ce ne sont pas les idées
neuves; c'est cette idée, qui les possède, que
ce qui a été dit ne l'a pas encore été assez.*

BARNES & NOBLE, Inc.   NEW YORK

Publishers   Booksellers   Since 1873

Reprinted, 1970

by Barnes & Noble, Inc.

SBN 389 01164 9

TO

ROSETTA MUNROE SPENCER
AND THE MEMORY OF
GEORGE HAZELTON SPENCER

FOREWORD

I'VE had," said Lawrence of Arabia, "no pity on myself
writing it, nor on my readers reading it." Wiser, yet less
wise than languid, was an earlier voice from the East,
more considerate than the run of Ancient Mariners, willing
to concede that "much reading is a weariness of the flesh."
Both these sages had a virus in their blood streams. It may
have killed Lawrence. But the author of Ecclesiastes, equally
self-conscious, equally set on nailing the fact with words,
was merely goaded to a smiling, theological acceptance of
the death sentence pronounced on nearly all artists. "Of
making many books there is no end."

If he had known how many were going to be made about
Shakespeare, he might have flung down his pen at "vanity
of vanities," and let it go at that. Of books and articles on
Hamlet alone, the last half-century has spawned upwards of
two thousand. Fortunately (since he was among the few who
still defy the Hangman's best efforts), the Preacher refused
to be intimidated by his own eloquence. He decided not to
burn the manuscript after all.

But what of the man who, instead of carnal lassitude, finds
in reading a joy active yet durable? How is he to stem the
avalanche of books amid the thunder of the presses printing
more? If he has read and loved Shakespeare, and wants to
know more about him, how is he to choose? What chance
has he of discriminating between sense and nonsense, when
both are served up with equal solemnity and, as far as he
knows, with equal authority?

Though millions fall every year into the clutches of the
English Department, there is an appalling time lag, at any
rate in this country, between the exertions of our literary
historians and any sort of public consciousness of what their
game is. When, for example, *Hamlet* is revived, journalistic
criticism is likely to betray a certain lack, not of intelligence,
nor of taste, but of information. Most Shakespeareans no
longer believe in the moony creature invented by the Roman-

tic critics, yet popular allusions to the Prince still assume that he spinelessly procrastinates or even that his wits are addled. Reports of an unexpected biographical hit will trickle back from the firing line of scholarship, but as fine an intelligence as the late John Jay Chapman could spray the professors with picturesque invective from behind a shield of innocence seldom pierced save by something really shocking, like the unimportant but overrelished news that Wordsworth had an illegitimate daughter.

An ivory tower is a fine place to work in; it often affords a larger view of things, and some very great books would not have been written anywhere else. But in our threatened times the strategic value of such posts is increasingly under suspicion. Whatever their tactical strength, they are practically useless for holding lines of communication. This book will not, I earnestly hope, be without interest to fellow workers in the vast and international and increasingly co-operative undertaking on which we are all engaged together; and I hope, too, that it may prove serviceable to less experienced students; but I have kept the inquisitive layman in mind all the way along, the man, that is, or the woman, who, while not particularly interested in the *modus operandi* of scholarship, *is* curious about the results and would rather have the truth, however imperfect its outline, than an "imaginary portrait," however bizarre or stunning its color. In fact, the notion of writing this book was partly inspired by the manifest eagerness of readers or spectators who have asked me what scholars now think of this or that point in Shakespeare studies. One is repeatedly struck with the acuteness of such questions. They are frequently harder to answer than the kind one's docile pupils ask.

For such inquirers I have woven in a good deal more about Shakespeare's art than appears in the thumbnail sketches of Chapter 2, preferring to handle the uses of the soliloquy or the Senecan influence where the topic naturally arises in discussing the several plays. The reader will find a fair number of cross references in the notes (which follow the final chapter); but if, instead of going straight through the book, he wishes to read a play and then turn directly to the section that treats it, he may be stumped occasionally by an unfamiliar name or term. If he will resort to the Index, which is very full, such difficulties will disappear.

Naturalism on our stage has gone about as far as it can go. Expressionism made a valiant attempt to find a way out; but however the other arts may seek to approximate music, drama can never become abstract so long as its medium is the living voice and flesh. Yet it is evident that our theatre, now (if we include the screen) a more direct social force than ever before in modern times, has already taken, at least on its serious and artistic flank, a new turning which is really an old one. While it is impossible to believe we shall ever revert to the windy Romanticism of nineteenth-century "poetic" drama, we are already less preoccupied than we were with surface realisms. The most impressive thing in the theatre, as in life, is the human spirit. Whenever, during the last two hundred years, literature has returned to that for its inspiration, Shakespeare has come to the front again. That is what is happening today. Once more his players stalk our boards, while screen and radio are beginning to recognize his availability.

The return to Shakespeare has not always been an unmixed blessing. In its time, Mr. Shaw's iconoclasm was as salutary as it was smart; for the second renascence of British drama became possible only after an exposé of the futility of fake Elizabethanism. Shaw was a sounder Shakespearean than the bardolaters; and he did his work so well, both as critic and as playwright, that the most elaborate program of revival is unlikely to hamstring dramatic art again. If anything is clear now, it is that any of the best examples of classical, neoclassical, romantic, realistic, naturalistic, impressionistic, or expressionistic drama is more like the best work of the other schools than it is like the inferior work of its own school. For the great things, whether in verse or prose, all have poetry — which is rarely present in the wooden-statuary department of neoclassicism, the tawdry heroics of a *Cyrano*, or the shallow naturalism of the timid, unimaginative, and

merely realistic. Whatever happens, drama that expects to
be taken seriously can never be again what it was before Ibsen,
Shaw, Chekhov, and Hauptmann. The social note has come
to stay; but it may not continue much longer to be the tonic
of the dramatic chord.

Although, quite aside from recent important discoveries of
fact and revisions of opinion, the time therefore seems ripe
for a new book on Shakespeare, this one is not intended for
an essay on his art as the supreme example of what man's
genius can rise to. It is first and foremost a sober compilation
and selection from a large body of fact and inference. I have
not written it around a theory, nor ground any axes. It gives
my views, but by and large these happen to approximate the
conclusions generally held by those best qualified to draw
them. Where mine differ, I have said so and have directed
the reader to the orthodox theory, if there is one. Where, as
is sometimes the case, there is no agreement among scholars,
I have said that. I can not pretend that I have conducted a
formal poll of opinion. On some points, but not I think on
many, my estimate of where the present weight of expert
testimony rests may be wrong. Obviously, too, a majority
decision is not necessarily the right one. The most learned
one always is. But to state that principle is only to raise the
question of what constitutes learning. For a corrective to the
extreme views of Dr. Dryasdust, *Love's Labour's Lost* is available and pertinent, but equally extreme.

Here, then, is no attempt at high-flying in a critical plane
launched from Shakespeare's catapult, though I confess and
warn that my machine belongs to the heavier-than-air type.
This is not, except in a minor way, a book on What Shakespeare Means to Me. There are many of that stripe, some
quite preposterous, others of absorbing interest, not because
they tell us much about the poet, but for the light they throw
on the remarkable minds that produced them. There is only
one better key to the heart of any man's mystery than what
he makes of Shakespeare. But that is not why this book was
written.

Of all the admirable works on this subject many hit their

marks better than I have any reason to hope I have hit mine. Yet none seems to me to do precisely what is attempted here. There are excellent general studies which string everything on the thread of biographical fact. The trouble with that resides in our having more beads than string. I have adopted a simpler plan of organization, separating biography from analysis and criticism, though the chapter on the Life includes a brief consideration of the poems, partly because they are inseparable from biographical problems, partly because my main concern is with the dramatic works. The one great and indisputable fact about Shakespeare is the existence of his plays, and that fact I have tried not to lose sight of for a single instant while I wrote. It is one of the most substantial facts in the world's history.

Some indispensable books about Shakespeare have, naturally, proved more useful to the specialist than to general readers or even to most teachers and students. Commonly, though there are splendid exceptions, readability varies in inverse ratio to the degree of technical competence. A number of once invaluable contributions are no longer trustworthy because so much of importance has appeared within the last few years. Others, helpful at certain points, are marred by speculative sentimentalism, loose sallies of the undisciplined imagination, or insensitiveness to art.

I offer no apology for trying to grapple with the aesthetic in mine. It is the most important of all considerations in Shakespeare study, and most often the worst handled. On the one side, we have the dilettante, sometimes amazingly industrious, but unversed in historical techniques and often too naive or too lazy to plow through the professional journals and monographs. Occasionally shameless, but ordinarily oppressed by a secret sense of sin, he finds his best defense in a vigorous offensive; hence the stereotyped preface in which he explains that the apparatus of scholarship is beneath his notice. On the other side, while there is nothing in the superstition that doctoral studies are bound to harden the aesthetic arteries, there is in degree of guilt little to choose between those who profess the literary branches of humanistic learning and their scientific colleagues. Undeniably our end of the shop has turned out a good many Ph.D.'s who, well equipped as technicians, have never experienced poetry. In the sciences such men become laboratory experts instead of scientists. In the humanities, they operate (as Emerson puts it) "as spectators merely," without being "parties and possessors of the fact." "It is of no use," he continues, "to preach to me from without." But unless one is willing (as many are) to surrender everything to feeling, and equate one's own visceral reactions with Shakespeare's intellectual process, aesthetic interpretation, if it is to make any sense, must rest on the knowledge scholarship has accumulated and interpreted concerning the Renaissance and its classical and medieval backgrounds, the Early Modern English language, Elizabethan and Jacobean literature, the origins and development of European drama, and the resources and limitations of the theatre Shakespeare wrote for.

Aside from the scanty manuscript records of his life, fortunately available in photographs, I have been able to use original materials pretty consistently; yet to name the scholars on whose works I have repeatedly drawn would be to call the roll of living Shakespeareans. One name must be cited. It will be a long time before the preface to a treatise like this can with propriety neglect to mention Sir Edmund Chambers's expert organization of the materials for studying Tudor and early Stuart drama. To *The Elizabethan Stage* and *William Shakespeare: A Study of Facts and Problems* the reader whose curiosity is not satiated by the work in hand should turn for guidance on nonaesthetic puzzles not mentioned in my Bibliography, where only the next steps *for students* are indicated. The titles I list there suggest the scope of my indebtedness, which I have not always acknowledged in direct connection with the text. Most of what we *know* about Shakespeare, however variously it has been interpreted, has long been common property; in many cases one can not tell where one first encountered it. Even if one could, the attempt to specify would subordinate text to notes in any serious work on this subject. For the subject is so large, as large as Shakespeare's

mind, and the study of it is now so parceled out into the
keeping of subspecialists, that only the most impressionistic
book can pretend to stand alone. I know, moreover, only
too well — every editor of a philological journal is dismally
reminded of it with each mail that brings him a "new"
contribution on Shakespeare — that somewhere the notion
one thought original may lurk in print.

These deprecatory remarks do not, of course, exhaust the
possibilities; but I will add only one more. The aim in the
little sketches of each play's stage history is not to achieve
completeness, but merely to give the reader some idea of its
fortunes. No attempt has been made to list all the rôles assumed by even the most eminent of the players. Like others
on textual matters and on sources, such paragraphs can easily
be skipped by those to whom there is no magic in the names
of Betterton, Garrick, Siddons, Kean, Booth, and Terry.

I assume that no one is likely to read my pages who has not
read a good many of Shakespeare's first. I hope not. A not too
painful course for the general reader desirous of making up
for lost opportunities would be: first, Chapters 1 and 2 on the
Life and Medium; then the plays themselves in an edition
with a good glossary, starting with the Four Great Tragedies,
the Later Histories, and the Best Comedies; and after each
play the appropriate section of this book, to be followed by
immediate rereading of the play. There is no guarantee that
adoption of this program will make any man wise. But it
will give him a rudimentary knowledge of Shakespeare, and
in the experience of many that has been a step toward wisdom.

I do not mean that Shakespeare will provide you with the
tools of a trade or a system of philosophy. What he will do
is the best thing one human being can do for another — the
thing that, because artists do it best, makes theirs a contribution beyond price: he will stir you up; he will open your eyes
wider to the world's beauty and wonder; he will remind you
that you also are a man or a woman, its heir, with dimensions
and scope not equal but not incomparable to the enchanting
creatures on his canvas; he will say for you what you have
dimly thought but could not bring yourself to utter; if you

have not yet learned to loathe the pretentious and see through the pompous, he will accelerate your education; if you are too slow, he will quicken you; if you are too cold, he will warm you; if you have anything in you at all, you will not be the same after reading him, for to read him is, at "one remove, though dread," little less joyous and terrible than to live.

Quotations in this book from his plays and poems agree with the best one-volume edition, by G. L. Kittredge, since it seems inadvisable to risk disturbing readers used to modernized texts and hence unaccustomed to Elizabethan spelling and punctuation. But the less familiar extracts and titles I have kept as faithful as I could to the original editions, glossing here and there when driven to it. If a "u" or a "v," or an "i" or a "j," looks queer, all you have to do is substitute the other letter. This trick of our forefathers' orthography is not so exasperating as it may appear to a novice; it will soon cease from troubling.

My thanks are due to many libraries, especially to the Harvard College Library, the Library of Congress, the Enoch Pratt Free Library of Baltimore, and the libraries of Duke University, the University of North Carolina, and the Johns Hopkins University. Above all I am indebted to the matchless resources and the brilliant staff of the Folger Shakespeare Library. There the knowledge and amiability of Dr. Giles E. Dawson and Dr. James G. McManaway have shortened many a search. A contribution by the Rockefeller Foundation has assisted in the preparation of these materials for publication. For permission to use pictures and books I am grateful to the institutions and persons mentioned in the List of Illustrations, and especially to the Director of the Folger Shakespeare Library, Dr. Joseph Quincy Adams, for both permission and very generous help in securing photographs. The quotations from the poems of Vachel Lindsay and of John Masefield I owe to the liberality of the Macmillan Company, and the virtual reprinting of several pages of my edition of *Richard the Third* to the kind permission of Messrs. D. C. Heath and Company. These acknowledgments would be incomplete if they did not include profound respect and gratitude for the innumerable workers who have brought in their reapings and gleanings and stacked them where others could find and use them. What a labor of love two centuries saw, and now a third is seeing! For the end is not yet.

The Preacher to the contrary notwithstanding, I for one hope it never will be. The day will come when every discoverable fact will have been discovered. Even then there will be more books. As the age of Elizabeth recedes in time, things that require no explanation now will need it. And every new age will offer praise in its own way, if Ben Jonson was right when in 1623 he predicted his friend's survival:

> Thou . . . art aliue still, while thy Booke doth liue,
> And we haue wits to read, and praise to giue.

H. S.

The Johns Hopkins University
Baltimore, Maryland
July 22, 1939

CONTENTS

ILLUSTRATIONS

THE ART AND LIFE OF

WILLIAM SHAKESPEARE

Chapter 1

HIS LIFE

THE LAUREL ROOT

WHY the wind that bloweth where it listeth veered in the spring of 1564 toward the small market town of Stratford-on-Avon is not explained by the handful of biographical fact which is all we have of Shakespeare — except his works. He left neither journals nor letters. He published no prefaces. His two dedications are conventionally abject, and unenlightening. Though several competent contemporaries jotted down impressions, and we are left in no doubt that his was a personality of great charm, it is from the plays and poems he wrote that we are bound to infer what manner of man he was. More than most writers he lives in his book.

Every reader adds a picture to his private gallery when he turns the last leaf of a major author; but there is no life portrait of Shakespeare on canvas nor anywhere else.[1] Was there in the face of this sensitive artist some clue to the mind's delicacy, some sign of the inner flame? Did features, voice, or gesture anywhere betray the spiritual toughness of the imperious creator or the slyness of ambition or the coarseness, cynical or naive, of the showman? Was he, like John Webster, generous to his brother poets in thought and utterance? Are we right in assuming that he loved laughter, or was he of the company who laugh that they may not weep? Did his hand fly to his pocket, or could he steel his heart, when misery in Shoreditch rags told a hard-luck story and held out a shaking claw? How much of the wisdom in the plays was his own experience and how much acquired vicariously or from the mysterious windings and unwindings of a poet's imagination? Was he ever deeply in love? Did he know how

3

it feels to be hungry and penniless? Was he hit hard or lightly when his parents died, and his little son?

These are all questions to be asked; but since they can not be answered, too much must not be expected of this chapter. For if the sonnets are an autobiography, no one has been able to read it. And as for the plays, the largest part of his work and the best, they are a snare and a delusion. Their truth is inescapable, but it is the truth of inspired fiction. We had better read them for what they are, which is ample enough. This Shakespeare, it seems reasonably clear, was a dramatist, and more than that a poet; and at will he could identify himself, whatever that self may have been, with any biological form in which the human spirit ever took flesh. If we are lovers no less of truth than of Shakespeare, we shall be cautious about our inferences from the lines he wrote for his walking shadows.

There is nothing in his environment, nor in his parentage and ancestry as far as these are known, to account for the emergence of the world's premier genius in Elizabethan Warwickshire. Stratford is now the Benares of the English-speaking peoples, though a ceremonial dip in the Avon is not as yet *de rigueur*. Our chambers of commerce and collectors of first editions do not know it, and living artists can starve while they watch the rites for the great departed; but the gift of a poet to the world is enough to dignify a town for ever. Few today are sufficiently recalcitrant (or mad) to deny the claims of Stratford.[2] Yet if Shakespeare had remained there, we might never have heard of him. He might have lived mute and died inglorious, and been anonymously elegized by Gray. Doubtless the most important thing that happened to him by way of external experience was that he got to London, where the English Renaissance was flowering and the theatres were ordering plays from anyone who could write at all. How and when he got there we do not know. But an early manifestation of his remarkable character must have been the decision to leave home.

That is not to say he owed nothing to Stratford. A royal borough since 1553, it had a population of about two thousand when Shakespeare was born there. It lay on the right bank of the Avon, south of the northern woodlands of Warwickshire known as the Arden, and off the main western highway to Shrewsbury and Chester; but two routes from London met at the stone arches which still bridge the pleasant stream. Stratford was no mean town, as minor provincial centers went; there were handsome timbered houses, gardens, and noble elms. There was the river. The master of its excellent school drew a stipend well above the average — a pretty reliable measure of what a municipality amounts to.

For its profusion of birds and flowers, its county evoked from that fine but now neglected poet Michael Drayton, also a poor boy from Warwickshire, glowing verses in his *Poly-Olbion*. Only two of the shire towns outranked Stratford. Warwick itself, seven miles away, was full of history and legend. About as far again stood Coventry, long a head-quarters for religious and guild pageantry. Also within easy walking distance was Kenilworth, with its famous castle, where the Earl of Leicester magnificently entertained his Queen in the summer of 1575, when Shakespeare was eleven.[3] Castles, pageants, and Biblical plays, as well as visits to Stratford by professional companies, may have fired the child with his lifelong delight in history's dramatic moments; and the lovely countryside must have impressed him with that tender affection for natural beauty which was never to leave him.

The name he bore [4] was common in the county in the fifteenth and sixteenth centuries. But his paternal line has not been traced beyond his grandfather, who was almost certainly Richard Shakespeare, a tenant farmer in Snitterfield, an hour's walk from Stratford. Richard probably died in 1560; early the next year administration of the estate was granted to a son John, described in his bond as a Snitterfield farmer.[5]

John Shakespeare of Stratford, if he was Richard's son as well as the poet's father, had moved there by 1552. For a while, at least, after Richard's death, he evidently continued management of the farm in Snitterfield. His principal business was making gloves in Stratford; perhaps he had been apprenticed to a craftsman there long before 1552. He is termed a glover in contemporary records, and also a whittawer, that is, a dresser and whitener of the soft skins used for gloves and light leather goods. Other references show him dealing in wool, timber, and grain. Slaughtering might easily have been allied with these activities; but he is first called a butcher in *Brief Lives*, a set of incomplete and disorderly manuscript jottings by the "shiftless . . . roving and magotie-headed" John Aubrey,[6] who adds to his note on the poet:

I have been told heretofore by some of the neighbours, that when he was a boy he exercised his fathers Trade, but when he kill'd a Calfe, he would doe it in a *high style*, & make a Speech. There was at that time another Butchers son in this Towne, that was held not at all inferior to him for a naturall witt, his acquaintance & coetanean, but dyed young.

Possibly Aubrey had got hold of an authentic tradition; but the question is complicated by the existence of an old humorous act or turn called "Killing the Calf." It seems to have been a stand-by with amateur and professional entertainers alike. Aubrey may have misunderstood an allusion to it. He had, however, been in Stratford, and about 1681 was in touch with William Beeston, a London theatrical manager, whose father (Christopher) had been an actor in Shakespeare's company. In a private letter of April 10, 1693, a visitor to Stratford corroborates the butcher story:

the clarke that shew'd me this Church is aboue 80 yrs. old he says that this Shakespear was formerly in this Towne bound apprentice to a butcher; but that he Run from his master to London & there was Recd Into the play house as a servture, & by this meanes had an oppertunity to be wt. he afterwards prov'd.[7]

There is nothing to bar these possibilities. But the testimony of William Castle, the aged clerk, is not decisive.

The first serious attempt at a Life of the poet was made by Nicholas Rowe for his edition in 1709, nearly a hundred years after Shakespeare's death. Thomas Betterton, the leading actor of the time, had made a pious journey to Stratford in quest of biographical evidence, which he turned over to

Rowe. He must have heard that John Shakespeare was "a considerable Dealer in Wool." Confirmation of this statement has recently been discovered,[8] and the respectability of tradition correspondingly enhanced; but it is seldom safe to conclude either that Aubrey's and Rowe's assertions are true or that there is nothing in them. An occasional biographer still takes the old primrose path and composes a floral tribute by ignoring the blooms which clash with his preconceived color scheme; but many writers on Shakespeare are now scrupulous in distinguishing documented fact from hearsay and both from tradition, and honest in accepting the existence of irreconcilable possibilities.

John Shakespeare makes his debut in the Stratford documents on April 29, 1552, when he is fined for leaving a "sterquinarium" in front of his house on Henley Street. There is nothing portentous about this dunghill; it would be unjust to infer that the Shakespeares were aesthetically more limited than their neighbors. Others were fined on the same occasion for the same delinquency. By October 2, 1556 John is making money; he buys two houses, one on Greenhill Street, the other on Henley Street. The latter is doubtless the eastern half of the present double house, almost completely "restored," on the north side of the street. It may be the dwelling he occupied in 1552. He bought two more, sites unknown, in 1575. One of these was very likely the western of the two adjoining houses he owned on Henley Street by 1590. He was living in the western half in 1597. That side of the present house is shown to visitors as the poet's birthplace, but there is no evidence that he was born at Henley Street. The eastern side, now called the wool shop, is the likelier possibility. On his father's death in 1601 William presumably inherited the property, though no document has been found.

It was probably in 1557 that John Shakespeare married a daughter of his father's landlord,[9] Robert Arden of Wilmcote in the parish of Aston Cantlow, half an hour's walk or more from Stratford. Arden owned several small properties, farming some of the land himself like any yeoman and parceling out the rest. Since, farmer though he was, it is fairly certain he sprang from a junior branch of an old landed family, the Ardens of Park Hall, those who think better of a poet for being genteel can take comfort in reflecting that the Shakespeares are only half the story. Mary Arden was the youngest of eight daughters, and an heiress; her father's death in 1556 left her, among other bequests, an estate called Asbies, in Wilmcote. She married John not long before Queen Elizabeth's accession; her first baby was baptized on September 15, 1558. She bore eight in all, of whom the third child and eldest son was to become, in the judgment of later generations, the chief glory of the great reign.[10] Documentary evidence of his existence is scanty till he is a success in London, but there is enough to identify him. The first record is the entry of his baptism at the Church of the Holy Trinity on April 26, 1564: "Gulielmus filius Johannes Shakspere." Baptism normally followed birth by a very few days.[11]

Of the parents' personalities nothing is known. John was evidently a small-town trader, perhaps a shrewd man who could drive a bargain and was not backward about resorting to the law when there was money to gain by it. If such a flair was responsible for his rise, it failed to save him from adversity later on, the cause of which may have been the decline of Stratford's woolen industry. This misfortune brought on a local business depression and much unemployment. Possibly John was merely lucky for a time, and not a grasping soul at all. He seems to have had a strong sense of civic responsibility. He made generous contributions to worthy causes. In some manuscript notes about the middle of the seventeenth century Archdeacon Thomas Plume of Rochester says that Admiral Sir John Mennes once saw Shakespeare's "old F[athe]r in h[is] shop — a merry Cheekd old man — [tha]t s[ai]d — Will was a g[oo]d Hon[est] Fellow, but he durst h[ave] crackt a jeast w[i]th him at any time." This description, such as it is, would be more interesting if its gallant author had been a little older when John Shakespeare died — he was then in his third year. His brother, Sir Matthew, was old enough to remember such an episode, supposing it occurred. If this anecdote about her husband is unauthenticated, there is none at all for the poet's mother. What part she played in bending that amazing twig, the mind of her eldest son, we shall never know.

John was reckoned a successful man during William's childhood. He was not accustomed to sign his name on official documents; but though only his mark has survived, his literacy remains an open question. We know that literate men sometimes attested documents with a mark. John's was usually a neatly drawn pair of glovers' dividers. As early as 1557 he began to play a modest part in the borough government. It was paternalistic to a degree unknown in modern democracies, and young William probably heard much talk about Stratfordians' private lives as well as the Corporation's business. Eventually John became an authority on municipal affairs, having been juror, constable, affeeror (assessor of fines for minor delinquencies), taster (inspector of malt liquors and bread), chamberlain (co-treasurer), capital burgess (councilman), alderman (from 1565 on), and finally bailiff (mayor) in 1568. But in 1577, though still an alderman, he quit attending council meetings. In 1578 his quota for poor relief was remitted and his tax for military equipment halved, which looks like financial embarrassment. The Arden inheritance began slipping through his fingers; William's name appears in a document of 1588 concerning unsuccessful attempts to recover a mortgaged portion of it. A distressing and costly experience is recorded in 1580, when John was summoned to the Court of Queen's Bench at Westminster to be bound over to keep the peace. Why is unknown. He failed to appear and was heavily fined. In 1586 the Corporation took official notice of his inability to carry on and chose another alderman in his place.[12] Yet he retained his fellow townsmen's good will.

There is no use in speculating whether these troubles, which began when William was about thirteen, cast a shadow over his adolescence, though we should like to learn whether he had hoped to complete his education at Oxford or was glad his schooldays were over. About his boyhood we know nothing. Imagery in *Venus and Adonis* and some of the early plays encourage the supposition that he loved the woods

and fields and ranged them with an observant eye, and numerous allusions to village games suggest (but do not prove)
that he was active in them. On the other hand, who can
doubt he was a great reader? It is safe enough to assume that
he attended the local school, founded by the Guild of Holy
Cross at least as early as the thirteenth century, and endowed
toward the end of the fifteenth for the free instruction of the
burgesses' sons. Under Edward VI, Guild and school had
been abolished; but when Stratford secured its charter in
1553, the Crown granted part of the Guild's confiscated property toward the support of school, almshouse, and church.

Little Will probably prepared under an usher attached to
the school. After he entered, Latin was no doubt his major
study and William Lily's famous grammar his principal text-
book; but the curriculum has not survived. The successive
masters were well-trained men; whether Simon Hunt, an able
B.A. of Oxford, afterward a Jesuit, helped kindle the poet's
mind we have no means of knowing. Nor can we tell how
long his formal education continued. While still in school he
probably read far enough to make the acquaintance of Virgil
and to fall in love with Ovid, his favorite classical poet.
Perhaps he also met those second-rate but influential playwrights Seneca and Plautus. The chances are he read little if
any Greek, but he seems to have picked up some French and
Italian. When is not known; probably it was after he went to
London. He was doubtless more fluent in Latin than most of
us, yet he read some of his Roman authors in translation, too.
Ben Jonson's allusion to his "small *Latine*, and lesse *Greeke*"
tells us nothing except that he was no scholar. One of his
most important books was certainly the Bible, in the Genevan
version (1560). His writings are full of allusions to it.

Relying, no doubt, on Betterton's fact-finding pilgrimage,
Rowe says that John had to take the boy out of school on
account of "the narrowness of his Circumstances, and the
want of his assistance at Home." Though made more than
a century after the event, this statement agrees with the
documentary evidence of John's reverses. William was probably through or nearly through "grammar" school and about

WARWICKSHIRE FROM STRATFORD TO COVENTRY

from a map probably of 1603

JOHN SHAKESPEARE'S HOUSE ON HENLEY STREET, STRATFORD

THE HATHAWAY COTTAGE AT SHOTTERY

THE GUILD CHAPEL, STRATFORD-ON-AVON

One corner of the site of New Place appears in the left foreground; on the right of the Chapel is the grammar school Shakespeare presumably attended.

CLOPTON BRIDGE

HOLY TRINITY CHURCH, STRATFORD-ON-AVON

ready for the university. Rowe's account is really all there is
to fill the gap between Shakespeare's baptism and his marriage
in 1582, in his nineteenth year. He may have gone to work
for his father; he may have been bound apprentice to someone
else.

What Shakespeare actually thought of sexual love we do
not know. In his plays and poems he was to express nearly
every variety of it, from the saddest of degradations to that
"marriage of true minds" which is "not Time's fool." Like
many another man's, his ideas may have changed. It is impossible to tell from what he wrote, as it *is* possible to tell
from the works of some authors, not merely whether he had
encountered love but whether he had direct knowledge of it
on the plane which even the most highly gifted man can not
reach alone. As Dr. Gogarty sings, "There's no good love
without good luck." Many whose deep desire ought to be
rewarded never catch more than a glimpse of it, and live out
their lives aware of its existence but unable to realize it. One
can hardly suppose Shakespeare lacked what goes to make
up a lover, but whether his experience equaled his dreams
depended also on the women he loved. There is no telling to
what extent his various phrases reflect his own happiness.
For to the dramatic artist is granted the power of taking short
cuts and of writing authoritatively concerning things that
lie outside his personal scope. Why Shakespeare was attracted
to Anne Hathaway and got her with child three months before their wedding, and whether he married her willingly,
we can not know. It may all have been very beautiful. Or
it may not.

She was seven or eight years older than he. Her father,
Richard Hathaway, was a substantial yeoman; and the "Cottage" still standing, though much altered, at Shottery, a
mile across the fields from Stratford, was his farmhouse.[13]
He died a few months before the marriage. No record of its
solemnization has been found, despite microscopic search in
the extant parish registers of the diocese. On November 27,
1582, an entry in the episcopal register at Worcester records
the issue of a marriage license to "Willelmum Shaxpere et

Annam Whateley de Temple Grafton." The next day [14] two yeomen of Stratford, friends of the Hathaways, agree to pay £40 in case legal consideration arises to prevent the marriage of "william Shagspere" and "Anne hathwey of Stratford in the Dioces of worcester maiden." Such bonds were part of the required procedure when a marriage was expedited. Here the bishop permits the marriage to proceed after a single reading of the banns. The normal program was to read them thrice in successive weeks, in order to advertise the contracting parties' intentions and thus allow time for the disclosure of any impediment. Since the church prohibited weddings during certain seasons, one of which began in 1582 almost immediately after the license was issued, and lasted until January 13, 1583, the ordinary practice would have entailed a delay of almost exactly two months. The "Whateley" of the license entry is probably the clerk's mistake for the "hathwey" of the bond. He made other mistakes in proper names, and "Hathaway" is the traditional name of Shakespeare's wife. Rowe gives it, and neither he nor Betterton knew anything about the bond at Worcester. Temple Grafton, a village five miles from Stratford, is rather a mystery. Its specification in the license entry, instead of the bride's parish as was regular, may reflect a hope of avoiding publicity; it is also possible that after her father's death Anne had gone there to live. Unfortunately the marriage register of Temple Grafton has not survived; nor has that of Luddington, another possibility near Stratford.[15] On May 26, 1583,[16] the christening of "Susanna daughter to William Shakspere," was recorded in the baptismal register at Stratford.[17] On February 2, 1585 twins were christened Hamnet and Judith, no doubt for the Sadlers. Hamnet or Hamlet Sadler was a lifelong friend; he witnessed the poet's will. The coincidence of the boy's name and that of his father's most famous character is purely fortuitous.[18] These are all the children Shakespeare is known to have had.

And now we part company with contemporary records till we pick up the rising young dramatist in London. The legal document of 1588 [19] merely mentions him as an interested

party in 1587; it does not help determine when he left Stratford. That question, and its associates, how and why he left,
remain unanswered. From 1585 to 1592 we have nothing to
go on except accounts written long after, always bearing in
mind that they neither prove anything nor are to be waved
aside as utterly negligible.

Aubrey, to whom we owe Shakespeare's original style in
calf killing, continues:

This W^m. being inclined naturally to Poetry and acting, came to
London I guesse about 18. and was an Actor at one of the Playhouses and did act exceedingly well: now B. Johnson was never a
good Actor, but an excellent Instructor. He began early to make
essayes at Dramatique Poetry, wch at that time was very lowe; and
his Playes tooke well: He was a handsome well shap't man: very
good company, and of a very readie and pleasant smooth Witt. . . .
Though as Ben: Johnson sayes of him, that he had but little Latine
and lesse Greek, He understood Latine pretty well: for he had been
in his younger yeares a Schoolmaster in the Countrey.

As his authority for the last statement Aubrey cites Beeston,[20]
who probably knew as much about Shakespeare as any man
alive under the Restoration. Was the poet ever a schoolmaster? Some think he was hardly qualified; but he could well
have been an usher, such as the Stratford school maintained
to teach young children reading and writing. And indeed, as
Thomas Fuller complains, men did "commence schoolmaster
in the country" without a university degree. Beeston's statement was intended to refute aspersions on Shakespeare's Latinity, and thus points to actual mastership of a grammar
school.

The extent of the poet's learning has been much debated.
He was certainly a wide reader; but those who suppose he
had a scholar's mastery of any field betray their ignorance
of how artists work. The creative genius owns a sixth sense
for essentials and a spongelike faculty of absorbing them.
Shakespeare was the world's most adroit snapper-up of both
the unconsidered trifles and the laborious conclusions of other
men. This is not to belittle his mind. No doubt he could

have applied it with success to various branches of learning. But he did not, having, fortunately for us, other notions of what to do with his time. They but confuse the form and substance of good manners who, not so much troubled by the poet's superficial acquaintance with many subjects as puzzled by a countryman's exquisite feeling for courtesy, think he must have been reared in some noble household. Any clever person, whatever his antecedents, can learn the form if he has opportunities and is willing to put his mind on it; the substance is an inward matter and is found in all strata of society. It springs perhaps chiefly from a genuine interest in one's fellow creatures; and no man ever had that more than Shakespeare.

The manuscripts of William Fulman in the library of Corpus Christi College, Oxford, contain some notes on Shakespeare written in another hand, that of Richard Davies, into whose possession the papers passed after Fulman's death in 1688. Both men were parsons. Davies, who died in 1708, was for a time rector at Sapperton in Gloucestershire and later Archdeacon of Coventry. Neither place is far from Stratford. To Fulman's note on Shakespeare's birth Davies adds that he was

much given to all unluckinesse in stealing venison & Rabbits particularly from Sr Lucy who had him oft whipt & sometimes Imprisoned & at last made Him fly his Native Country to his great Advancem^t. but His reveng was so great that he is his Justice Clodpate and calls him a great man & y^t [i.e., that] in allusion to his name bore three lowses rampant for his Arms.

Whether this story is true no one knows. In any case the details can not be entirely accurate; for example, the statute against poaching did not prescribe whipping. *The Merry Wives of Windsor* begins with the arrival of the rustic justice and his threats to have the law on Falstaff. The countryman and his family are lauded by his cousin Slender: "They may give the dozen white luces in their coat [of arms]." The luce is a fish, a full-grown pike, rather common in heraldry. The joke comes in a play on "luce" and another on "coat" when Parson Evans, the Welshman who (as Falstaff complains) "makes fritters of English," chimes in: "The dozen white louses do become an old coat well. It agrees well passant. It is a familiar beast to man and signifies love." The play on "luce" and "louse" was probably not literary in origin. Nor is it likely that Justice Shallow is set up for a portrait of Sir Thomas Lucy. That was not Shakespeare's way. But there were three luces in Sir Thomas's coat-of-arms, and the dramatist may be indulging in a quiet laugh of his own in addition to the obvious humor of the passage.

In 1709, after telling how Shakespeare had to leave school and toil for his father, Rowe mentions his marriage and proceeds:

In this kind of Settlement he continu'd for some time, 'till an Extravagance that he was guilty of, forc'd him both out of his Country and that way of Living which he had taken up; and tho' it seem'd at first to be a Blemish upon his good Manners, and a Misfortune to him, yet it afterwards happily prov'd the occasion of exerting one of the greatest *Genius*'s that ever was known in Dramatick Poetry. He had, by a Misfortune common enough to young Fellows, fallen into ill Company; and amongst them, some that made a frequent practice of Deer-stealing, engag'd him with them more than once in robbing a Park that belong'd to Sir *Thomas Lucy* of *Cherlecot* [Charlecote], near *Stratford*. For this he was prosecuted by that Gentleman, as he thought, somewhat too severely; and in order to revenge that ill Usage, he made a Ballad upon him. And tho' this, probably the first Essay of his Poetry, be lost, yet it is said to have been so very bitter, that it redoubled the Prosecution against him to that degree, that he was oblig'd to leave his Business and Family in *Warwickshire*, for some time, and shelter himself in *London*.

It is at this Time, and upon this Accident, that he is said to have made his first Acquaintance in the Play-house. He was receiv'd into the Company then in being, at first in a very mean Rank; But his admirable Wit, and the natural Turn of it to the Stage, soon distinguish'd him, if not as an extraordinary Actor, yet as an excellent Writer. . . . Besides the advantages of his Wit, he was in himself a good-natur'd Man, of great sweetness in his Manners, and a most agreeable Companion; so that it is no wonder if with so many good Qualities he made himself acquainted with the best Conversations of those Times.

The motif of deer stealing, not seriously reprehensible in the eyes of our forefathers, except to the owner of the deer, turns up with variations in several other writers. This does not prove its authenticity, but it was evidently a tradition in Stratford by the end of the seventeenth century. An alleged stanza of the alleged ballad is given by the antiquarian William Oldys toward the middle of the eighteenth century, and again by Edward Capell (1780). Oldys says he obtained it from a relative of an acquaintance of "a very aged gentleman living in the neighbourhood of Stratford, (where he died fifty years since)," who had heard it "from several old people in that town." It has no literary merit.

Halliwell-Phillipps [21] transcribes a "manuscript note preserved in the University Library, Edinburgh, written about the year 1748"; its author retails it on, but not directly on, the authority of Sir William D'avenant, the Caroline poet laureate:

Shakespear, when he first came from the country to the play-house, was not admitted to act; but as it was then the custom for all the people of fashion to come on horseback to entertainments of all kinds, it was Shakespear's employment for a time, with several other poor boys belonging to the company, to hold the horses and take care of them during the representation; — by his dexterity and care he soon got a great deal of business in this way, and was personally known to most of the quality that frequented the house, insomuch that, being obliged, before he was taken into a higher and more honorable employment within doors, to train up boys to assist him, it became long afterwards a usual way among them to recommend themselves by saying they were Shakespear's boys.

The horseboy story is repeated by several eighteenth-century writers, including Robert Shiels (or Shields) who worked on *The Lives of the Poets* (1753) for Theophilus Cibber. It was recounted by "a gentleman, who heard it" from "Dr. Newton, the late editor of Milton," who was "told it" by Pope, who had it from Rowe, who had it from Betterton, who had it from D'avenant. Rowe did not see fit to include it in his own Life. Dr. Johnson adds the very words the horseholders used: "I am *Shakespeare*'s boy, Sir."

There is nothing for the biographer to do but rehearse these stories. Any of them may be true. All of them may be false. Shakespeare may or may not have left Stratford under a cloud. He may have left in the early, middle, or late eighties. He may or may not have served a term or two as a country schoolmaster. He may or may not have done odd jobs in London before he went on the stage. One fact is certain, and it is more important than any of these: up to London he went.

To leave the realm of fact and formulate a reasonable conjecture, the departure from Stratford was probably about 1585. Whether he went up directly is not worth even a guess. Beeston's authority for the schoolteaching is better than most of the Restoration assertions; but if Shakespeare held such a post, it may have been prior to or after his marriage. Very likely he assaulted the city more than once, before it began to think of capitulating. Since by 1592 he was cutting so wide a swath that he stirred the spleen of one of London's best-known men of letters, we are fairly safe in concluding he had been there several years.[22] It may be that on and off from about 1585 to about 1590 he was struggling to find himself in the metropolis, and that rewards began to come his way just before the century's last decade opened. One would like to know where he was and what he was doing in the summer and fall of 1588, when England girt herself to meet the Spanish attack and then watched the Atlantic gales finish the work Howard and Drake had begun.

How Mistress Shakespeare and her babies got on in the meantime is not a matter of record. Everything points to their remaining in Stratford even after William prospered. There were no more children — strong evidence, in those days, for the spouses' separation. Yet apparently the poet's native town always meant home to him. There he invested much of the capital he accumulated. Tradition has it that at least eventually he spent his vacations there. And at the height of his success he turned his back on the world he had conquered and, obediently to the homing instinct of the English and their passion for country gardens, settled down for good in Stratford.

THE WINNING OF LONDON

By the summer of 1592 Shakespeare must have known the battle was won. Either a substantial amount of competent work by him, whether or not his name meant anything to the public, had convinced the established dramatists that the actor from Stratford would have to be reckoned with as a writer, or else one of his plays had scored a decisive hit. For on September 3 died Robert Greene, a brilliant but erratic jack-of-all-literary-trades, including drama. Unhappily for his reputation, he was a poseur, addicted to public renunciation of his shortcomings and excesses; and his remorse took the form, not of amended conduct, but of hortatory pamphlets. His *Groats-worth of witte, bought with a million of Repentance* was entered in the Stationers' Register [23] on September 20. Greene had finished it on his deathbed, whence he added a valedictory warning

To those Gentlemen his Quondam acquaintance, that spend their wits in making plaies, R.G. *wisheth a better exercise, and wisdome to preuent his extremities.* . . . Base minded men all three of you, if by my miserie you be not warnd: for vnto none of you (like mee) sought those burres to cleaue: those Puppets (I meane) that spake from our mouths, those Anticks garnisht in our colours. Is it not strange, that I, to whom they all haue beene beholding: is it not like that you, to whome they all haue beene beholding, shall (were yee in that case as I am now) bee both at once of them forsaken? Yes trust them not: for there is an vpstart Crow, beautified with our feathers, that with his *Tygers hart wrapt in a Players hyde* supposes he is as well able to bombast out a blanke verse as the best of you: and beeing an absolute *Iohannes fac totum,* is in his owne conceit the only Shake-scene in a countrey. O that I might intreat your rare wits to be imploied in more profitable courses: & let those Apes imitate your past excellence, and neuer more acquaint them with your admired inuentions. . . . [F]or it is pittie men of such rare wits, should be subiect to the pleasure of such rude groomes.

The trio thus preached at are probably Christopher Marlowe, George Peele, and either Thomas Nashe or possibly Thomas Lodge. The "puppets" are the actors, dumb till the playwrights give them speech. This is the old grudge of the creative artist against the interpretive artist, of the composer against the stellar soloist or virtuoso conductor, to whom falls the lion's share of the applause and the emoluments. For Greene *was* a poet, and the implication that he had touched the actors for a loan or an advance and been turned down adds a grotesque overtone to the bitter protest of a disappointed and dying man. Under the circumstances we can forgive him for the direct insult to Shakespeare, with its parody of "O tiger's heart wrapp'd in a woman's hide!" in *Part 3* of *Henry the Sixth* (I, iv, 137), its "absolute Jack-of-all-trades" for the actor turned playwright, and the sneering "Shake-scene." "In his owne conceit" means "according to his own notions"; this phrase may reflect something Shakespeare had said or done. Possibly, in 1592, not yet thirty but tasting the strong wine of success, he was a little heady with new knowledge that the power was already his and the glory certain to come. This, of course, is mere speculation; Greene's jealousy may have had nothing to feed on but itself, though there is a superb self-confidence in

> Vilia miretur vulgus: mihi flauus Apollo
> Pocula Castalia plena ministret aqua.[24]

These proud words of Ovid Shakespeare was to set as a motto on the title page of his first published poem before a year had passed.

Greene's mocking quotation looks as if the Henry VI trilogy had already marked Shakespeare as the coming man. We have another clue to its popularity. In this same year of 1592 Nashe exclaims in *Pierce Penilesse his Supplication to the Diuell:*

How would it have ioyd braue *Talbot* (the terror of the French) to thinke that after he had lyne two hundred yeare in his Toomb, he should triumph againe on the Stage, and haue his bones new embalmed with the teares of ten thousand spectators at least, (at seuerall times) who in the Tragedian that represents his person, imagine they behold him fresh bleeding.

This reference is almost certainly to *Henry the Sixth, Part 1.*

Greene's attack has often been misinterpreted; indeed it was misunderstood within two years, when one R.B., otherwise unknown to history, takes up the cudgels in *Greenes Funeralls* (1594):

> *Greene*, gaue the ground, to all that wrote vpon him.
> Nay more the men, that so Eclipst his fame:
> Purloynde his Plumes, can they deny the same?

It was not, however, plagiarizing authors, but the actors, helpless without dramatists, whom Greene calls clowns "garnisht in our colours." Shakespeare is of them, being neither a university wit nor a properly cultivated poet. As a dramatist he is therefore an upstart.

In another passage Greene is also sharp with Marlowe, and both Shakespeare and the fiery Christopher resented the attack. Soon after its appearance, Henry Chettle, a printer and later a prolific hack-poet-dramatist, who had edited Greene's manuscript, refused an apology to Marlowe but made amends to Shakespeare in an Epistle published with his *Kind-Harts Dreame*.

About three moneths since died M[aster]. *Robert Greene*, leauing many papers in sundry Booke sellers [i.e., publishers'] hands, among other his Groats-worth of wit, in which a letter written to diuers play-makers, is offensively by one or two of them taken, and because on the dead they cannot be auenged, they wilfully forge in their conceites a liuing Author: and after tossing it two and fro, no remedy, but it must light on me. . . . With neither of them that take offence was I acquainted, and with one of them I care not if I neuer be: The other, whome at that time I did not so much spare, as since I wish I had, for that as I haue moderated the heate of liuing writers, and might haue vsde my owne discretion (especially in such a case) the Author beeing dead, that I did not, I am as sory, as if the originall fault had beene my fault, because my selfe haue seene his demeanor no lesse ciuill than he excelent in the qualitie he professes [i.e., acting]: Besides, diuers of worship [i.e., various persons of position] haue reported his vprightnes of dealing, which argues his honesty, and his fa[ce]tious grace in writting, which aprooues his Art [i.e., demonstrates his artistry].[25]

This passage is among the few important bits of evidence for Shakespeare's personal standing. Possibly a friend or patron

had taken Chettle to task; perhaps Shakespeare himself called
and protested. Marlowe only gets another cut from Chettle.
His splendid verse had failed, in the eyes of the respectable,
to offset his wild plunge into *la vie de Bohème* and his "atheistic" witticisms at the expense of Trinitarian orthodoxy. The
man from Stratford had not enjoyed the advantages of a
higher education; but he was decent or canny enough to keep
off the shoals on which some of his most hopeful contemporaries wrecked their careers. Evidently he was considered in
1592 steady as well as brilliant, and had won the liking of
several persons whose good opinions were worth having. It
has been urged that Chettle's lack of acquaintance with him
in the early fall of that year shows that he had not been
writing plays very long; but Marlowe was certainly no new-
comer, and Chettle did not know him either. The episode has
no bearing on the date of Shakespeare's arrival in the metropolis.

For two years, beginning in the summer of 1592, the theatres
were subjected to an almost unbroken suspension by a fright-
ful outbreak of London's periodic scourge, the bubonic
plague.[26] To what extent the collapse of his market em-
barrassed the young actor-dramatist is unknown. He may have
toured the provinces with his company, but there is no evidence for his whereabouts and indeed nothing to determine
which of the troupes he was then attached to. He may have
found a noble patron and lived under his roof, in constant
expectation of a speedy reopening. Wherever he was, he
probably went on with his playmaking.

Certainly he wrote some nondramatic poetry. Before the
theatres got under way again in 1594, he made frank bids for
a literary reputation, not as yet accorded to mere dramatists,
with *Venus and Adonis* and *Lucrece*. The first of these graceful
exhibition pictures was registered on April 18, 1593 and the
second on May 9, 1594. The latter entry entitles the poem
"the Ravyshement of Lucrece"; the quarto title page has
simply *Lvcrece;* the quarto's running title is "The Rape of
Lvcrece." In the dedication of *Venus and Adonis* Shakespeare
calls it his first poetic offspring, and some have inferred that

it antedates his earliest plays and even that he wrote it in the country and brought it along with him to London as a kind of literary passport. It seems more likely that in styling it his eldest brain-child he is thinking of publication and his literary aspirations. There is no evidence, until their registration, for the date of either poem. Presumably Shakespeare published them as soon as he finished them. If so, the winter of 1592–93 probably saw the composition of *Venus*.

The first edition of each of these works was printed by Richard Field, at whose establishment Shakespeare very likely read the proofs himself. There is no evidence, internal or external, that he ever felt such solicitude again. The world would gladly exchange the excellence of these texts for a single act of one of the great plays, purged by its author of accretions from "that sink of corruption," the prompt book, and of blunders, "improvements," normalizations, hasty "corrections," and other bright ideas acquired in those dens of only less miasmatical iniquity, the composing and press rooms. For, despite the current fashion of regarding the Elizabethan printer as a sainted hero, the havoc of his hand, drunk or sober, confronts us again and again when it was merely a matter of setting up and running off a sixpenny play quarto. A play belonged to the acting company, not to the author, whom there was no need of consulting when its publishing rights were sold. At any time the company could hire another writer to revise it; neither company nor publisher felt any remarkable obligation to preserve the original text. Not yet had English plays come to be taken seriously as a department of literature. When Jonson published his in 1616, he was laughed at for calling them Works. Field, however, did well by Shakespeare's maiden books. He was the son of a Stratford tanner and about three years older than the poet. In 1579 he, too, had struck out for the metropolis; he was now rapidly making his way to the top of his trade, having acquired a well-equipped shop by the popular method of marrying his employer's widow. Of *Venus* Field was publisher as well as printer; but next year he assigned his rights to John Harrison, the publisher of *Lucrece*.

Both poems were dedicated to one of the most gilded youths of the day, Henry Wriothesley, third Earl of Southampton. Whether Shakespeare was introducing himself or had already been encouraged is uncertain. Southampton was a great theatregoer; they may have met backstage. If our sense of the fitness of things is offended by the spectacle of the world's finest artist humbling himself to a lord, we must remember that patronage of the arts was among the noblest obligations of Renaissance aristocracy; that Shakespeare's phraseology, however sincere, conforms to convention; and that, in the corrupted currents of this world, a graceful deference to a titled patron compares not unfavorably with the truckling of many a modern author to a master that is no worthier for being many-headed.

To the Right Honorable Henrie Wriothesley, Earle of Southampton, and Baron of Titchfield.

Right Honourable, I know not how I shall offend in dedicating my vnpolisht lines to your Lordship, nor how the worlde will censure mee for choosing so strong a proppe to support so weake a burthen, onelye if your Honour seeme but pleased, I account my selfe highly praised, and vowe to take aduantage of all idle houres, till I have honoured you with some grauer labour. But if the first heire of my inuention proue deformed, I shall be sorie it had so noble a god-father [this sounds as if the dedication was by permission]: *and neuer after eare* [plow] *so barren a land, for feare it yeeld me still so bad a haruest, I leaue it to your Honourable suruey, and your Honor to your hearts content which I wish may alwaies answere your owne wish, and the worlds hopefull expectation.*

Your Honors in all dutie,
William Shakespeare.

Thus Shakespeare in 1593. Next year his dedication of *Lucrece*, no doubt the "graver labor," is couched in warmer terms:

To the Right Honourable, Henry Wriothesley, Earle of Southampton, and Baron of Titchfield.
The loue I dedicate to your Lordship is without end: wherof this Pamphlet without beginning is but a superfluous Moity. The warrant I haue of your Honourable disposition, not the worth of my vntutord Lines makes it assured of acceptance. What I haue done

is yours, what I haue to doe is yours, being part in all I haue, deuoted yours. Were my worth greater, my duety would shew greater, meane time, as it is, it is bound to your Lordship; To whom I wish long life still lengthned with all hapinesse.

Your Lordships in all duety.
William Shakespeare.

These poems, the only works we can be certain he ever gave the press himself, were enthusiastically welcomed by the reading public. A new edition of *Venus* appeared in each of four consecutive years, and in all at least ten editions of *Venus* and five of *Lucrece* were printed before 1616.

Venus, no doubt, especially pleased the Earl, belonging as it does to an erotic genre then much in favor with young sophisticates. The sage and serious Spenser had given a great impetus to narrative poetry; but Marlowe's *Hero and Leander*, Lodge's *Scillaes Metamorphosis*, and Nashe's rather stupidly sensual *The Choise of Valentines* all reflect the fleshly side of the Renaissance. There is much of that side in Shakespeare, and we would not have it otherwise. But just as the good life merges flesh and spirit, Shakespeare's art was not to be dualistic. His concern with spiritual values is not evident in *Venus and Adonis;* yet, for all we know, it may have been his own taste that led him in his next poem to adopt a heroine famous for her noble purity, and not some critical scolding he had listened to. Lucrece, as Mrs. Pearson notes, is "a typical Petrarchan heroine, chaste, beautiful, without a flaw." No early stricture on *Venus* has survived, though it came in for an occasional rebuke a few years later. As for the immediately favorable reception of *Lucrece*, that is attested by verses in *Epicedium* by "W. Har" (not certainly identified), in *Willobie his Avisa* by an anonymous writer of a commendatory poem,[27] and possibly by an allusion in Drayton's *Matilda*. All three of these references appeared in 1594, though Drayton's may be to some lost play.

Neither *Venus and Adonis* nor *Lucrece* is a great poem; but even in this minor department it was easy for Shakespeare to outdo all his contemporaries, except Marlowe. To it he carries over the vigorous sense of fact which is among his sources of strength as a dramatist. Neither piece is comparable to the plays or the sonnets in imaginative force or emotional integrity; but *Venus*, at least, repeatedly exemplifies Shakespeare's superb descriptive powers, whether in a tour de force like the horse or poor Wat the hare, or in an exquisitely fresh detail like "these blue-vein'd violets," or the divedapper peering through a wave, or the hurt snail. An extensive search for the sources of his imagery in Latin, French, and English poetry has left no doubt that, although much of the *Venus* tapestry is woven from stock materials such as the Theocritan conceit of the boar's kiss and the endless Renaissance blending of lilies and roses on damask cheeks, the proportion of allusions reflecting the poet's firsthand experience with Nature is extraordinarily high. The artist can deceive us, of course. But even when every doubtful case is relegated to a neutral category of workyday expressions scarcely felt as figurative at all, the statistics are impressive. Inevitably, the neutral class is overwhelming numerically, though it has a much slighter *figurative effect* than either of the others. According to my estimate, more than one-eighth of the poem's metaphors and similes appear to reflect Shakespeare's direct observation, nearly two and a half times the number derived from books. Quite as striking is the proportion of figurative expressions relating to the out-of-doors. Of the total of all classes, neutral, bookish, and apparently original, more than one-fourth draw on birds, animals, plants, heavenly bodies, atmospheric conditions, other natural phenomena, hunting, and fishing. A statistical treatment of such data can at best only approximate accuracy; but it confirms a reader's impression that *Venus and Adonis* is neither merely an icehouse, as Hazlitt calls it, nor wholly a conventional Renaissance hothouse: among its major sources are the fields and woods of Warwickshire.

None the less, like *Lucrece*, it remains essentially a salon piece. In it Shakespeare elaborates, deliberately and a little too coolly (as Hazlitt perceived), the charming and pathetic story, much handled by Renaissance poets and painters, as he finds it in the tenth book of the *Metamorphoses* (lines 519–59, 708–39). He makes one fundamental change, for Ovid's Adonis is older and bolder. Shakespeare was not, however, the first to introduce the boyish reluctance; when this got attached to the myth no one knows. It appears, for example, in a reference to Adonis in Marlowe's *Hero and Leander*, though with a difference; and it is implied by two lyrics in Greene's novels, *Neuer too late* and *Perimedes The Blacke-Smith*. Shakespeare's depiction of it was probably influenced by two other books of the *Metamorphoses*, for there is shy young masculinity in the stories of Salmacis and Hermaphroditus (IV, 285–388) and of Echo and Narcissus (III, 341–510). Lodge's *Scillaes Metamorphosis* (1589), or *Glaucus and Scilla* according to its running title, uses the same six-line stanza as Venus. The sixain was common, but Shakespeare may be somewhat indebted to the reluctance of Glaucus. The description of the boar comes from the Calydonian hunt in the eighth book of the *Metamorphoses* (lines 267 ff.). Whether Marlowe's brilliant poem inspired Shakespeare to emulation is impossible to say. *Hero and Leander* was left unfinished when Marlowe died on May 30, 1593. It was not printed till five years later; George Chapman supplied a continuation. Perhaps Shakespeare read Marlowe's verses in manuscript; or the other hand, Marlowe's poem may be later than his. Certainly Ovid is Shakespeare's main source, and no doubt he had read the Latin text. For some passages, however, it is certain (though the point has been disputed) that he had either on his desk or precisely filed away in his memory portions of the translation of Arthur Golding.

The story of Lucrece likewise comes from Ovid (*Fasti*, II, 711–852) and also from Livy (I, 56–60). It was an old favorite, and where Shakespeare went for it is still debated. He may have read it in both these Latin versions, in Chaucer's *Legend of Good Women*, in William Painter's *The Palace of Pleasure*, in a *novella* by the famous Italian storyteller Matteo Bandello, and in François de Belleforest's French translation of Bandello in his *Histoires Tragiques*. As Professor Rollins observes, the popularity of the story, still evinced by its frequent adoption as a literary or dramatic subject, "is a sufficient reply to those numerous critics who object to Shakespeare's using such a 'morbid' and 'unpleasant' theme." For his version Shakespeare chose the seven-line stanza known as rhyme royal. Though no one since Chaucer had handled it so effectively, Samuel Daniel had employed it in *The Complaint of Rosamond* (1592), which may have had some slight influence on Shakespeare's poem. On the whole, *Lucrece* is a less agreeable exercise than *Venus;* but it has more of genuine feeling in it and occasionally breaks away from the merely decorative into the dramatic.

A vast deal of speculation has played about the extent to which Southampton, who was nine years Shakespeare's junior, helped establish him. Some believe the poet was actually attached to the Earl's household, and profess to find his plays full of topical hits at the enemies of Southampton and his idolized friend, Robert Devereux, second Earl of Essex. The case for this theory is not impressive. Neither is the suggestion that Shakespeare was a Catholic because Southampton leaned toward Rome. If the poet had a religious life, he kept it to himself, as far as the surviving evidence goes. Rowe records D'avenant's assertion that the Earl once gave Shakespeare a thousand pounds "to enable him to go through with a Purchase which he heard he had a mind to"; but this is an incredibly tall figure, larger than the sum of all Shakespeare's known purchases.[28] Southampton did have a reputation for lavish generosity. Nothing, however, is certain save that Shakespeare found a patron in him. How long their friendship continued is unknown.

When Shakespeare began sonneteering is likewise unknown. Most of his biographers assume it was not till the 1590's. But Wyatt and Surrey had domesticated the form under Henry VIII; and the best English poets of the century's early years were included in *Tottel's Miscellany*, that is, the *Songes and Sonettes* brought out by the printer Richard Tottel, the first of many remarkable collections of Tudor poetry. It appeared in 1557, and went through numerous editions. Shakespeare grew up in England with the sonnet, and he may have tried his hand at writing it while still a boy. His repeated success in adjusting his impetuous flow to the difficult requirement of stating a theme, developing it, getting somewhere with it in fourteen lines, and concluding the treatment with an effect instead of just dropping it, should have given pause to the eighteenth-century critics who thought he could not control his genius.

Shakespeare's sonnets are part of the vogue of Petrarchism in Elizabeth's England; but, like the greatest examples of any art form, they can not be classified so simply as the products of mere talent. First and foremost they are lyric poems by Shakespeare; as such, they frequently transcend the boundaries of genre and school. The French sonneteers had some influence on the vogue; but the fourteenth-century Italian who sang of Laura was still high priest of love and its expression or simulation in verse. Unfortunately, most of Petrarch's imitators were more successful in copying his mannerisms than in communicating his spirit. The Petrarchan "conceit" was worked to death by them. These metaphors, similes, and graphic symbols of emotion are sometimes moving, but too often they are limp and shopworn from endless repetition. Good taste was consistently violated by writers who tried to avoid too frank an indebtedness; ingenuity and cleverness were thought to justify the most farfetched extravagance. To illustrate, there is the conceit that the poet's tears will soften the flinty heart of his mistress, just as drops of water eventually wear away the hardest stone. From Petrarch to Shakespeare, and of course long after, everyone employs that comparison. Perhaps it was lovely once; perhaps it still seemed so when Shakespeare used it. It can not touch us now. We gratefully turn away from Sonnet 46, where Shakespeare's heart and eye are plaintiff and defendant in a jury trial over the legal title in "thy picture's sight," to the anti-Petrarchism of Sonnet 130:

> My mistress' eyes are nothing like the sun;
> Coral is far more red than her lips' red;
> If snow be white, why then her breasts are dun;
> If hairs be wires, black wires grow on her head,

or to Falstaff's matching of unsavory similes with his "most comparative, rascalliest, sweet young prince." If we *remain* away, we shall miss some uncommonly fine poetry, not in Sonnet 46, but in those of its companions in which Shakespeare was able to master convention.

Petrarchism was a cult. Naturally, there was also a cult of opposition. It was probably not so well organized nor so conscious of a Mission as some historians have supposed, and it was in existence long before John Donne appeared on the literary scene. This once neglected but lately overrated poet took the lead against Petrarchism shortly before the turn of the century. His school, for he had followers then as well as now, rejected the sonnet conventions in style, structure, and ideas. Donne sometimes announces an exclusive interest in the soul of the beloved, protesting (rather too much, perhaps) indifference to her outward charms. Yet some of his poems are a queer blend of Christian sublimation and Ovidian sensuality. His sincerity is a much debated question, into which we shall not venture here. To some extent, anti-Petrarchism was merely another swing in the inevitable and necessary oscillation of art between acceptance of convention and rebellion against it. Partly it was a conscious search for novelty and notoriety. Donne made the same mistake certain statesmen have made: he thought he was being realistic. His deliberate revolt against Petrarchism has little in common with Shakespeare's momentary revulsion. For, however disillusioned the air of the quatrains in Sonnet 130, its couplet winds up with the roundest of declarations:

> And yet, by heaven, I think my love as rare
> As any she belied with false compare;

and it is plain to see that Shakespeare is not a rebel at all: on the contrary, he is cleverly inverting Petrarchan conventions for the sake of a novel restatement of Petrarchan orthodoxy. Donne, to be sure, reverts to Petrarchism in some of his better poems, but never with anything like Shakespeare's passion or Shakespeare's grace. Donne's somewhat artificially stimulated twentieth-century reputation has long passed its peak; his critical "kidnappers," as Professor Hughes has wittily dubbed them, exacted a substantial ransom in their day; but their day is over. Their victim is now a very interesting figure rather than a great one; but in his way Donne was a true poet — occasionally a line flashes with pure radiance, — and his works are worth reading for their own sake as well as in order to sample a variety of aggressive intellectualism, contemplating which a man who was all artist like Shakespeare must sometimes have felt his heart chilled and his pen stayed.

Thus far we have been considering the sonnet as a lover's lute. Such it was when Petrarch swept its strings; such it remained under the clever fingers of the insular performers, at least throughout the age of Shakespeare. The next great English sonneteer increased the instrument's range and changed its tone; for, as Wordsworth says, in Milton's hand "the Thing became a trumpet," its use no longer restricted to the melodious voicing of amorous wonders and complaints. In rhyme scheme (though not in his failure to observe the customary pauses within the sonnet), Milton reverted to the Petrarchan norm. The "Italian" sonnet broke its fourteen lines into an octave and a sestet, rhymed respectively *abbaabba* and *cdcdcd* (or, if you preferred, *cdecde* or with another of several permissible variations). Why this example of Mediterranean subtlety should have provided a frame for some of England's noblest poetry remains almost as complete a mystery as genius itself. The Elizabethans, however, made the form somewhat less exacting, though they did write a few "Italian" sonnets. The "English" or "Shakespearean" variety consists of three quatrains rhymed alternately, followed by a rhyming couplet: *abab cdcd efef gg*.

The vogue in England reached its height after 1591, when Sir Philip Sidney's *Astrophel and Stella* was posthumously printed, against the wishes of the family. Publication was not quite the thing, since a sonnet seems to pin the heart upon the sleeve. A substantial number of Shakespeare's had been written by 1598, when Francis Meres's *Palladis Tamia* mentions their private circulation, of course in manuscript.

With two exceptions, to be noted later, they were not published till 1609, when they appeared as *Shake-speares Sonnets*, in a text not very badly printed, but badly enough to absolve the author of the proofreading. Thomas Thorpe, their publisher, registered the book in due form on May 20. With its publication Shakespeare evidently had nothing to do. The quarto carries an enigmatical dedication by Thorpe: "To the onlie begetter of these insving sonnets Mr. W.H. all happinesse and that eternitie promised by ovr ever-living poet wisheth the well-wishing adventvrer in setting forth. T.T." Put into normal order, this may be paraphrased: "Thomas Thorpe, the well-meaning undertaker of this publishing venture, extends to Master W. H., the sole begetter of the following sonnets, his wishes for all happiness and the immortal fame which is promised by the immortal poet who wrote them." It is often assumed that Thorpe is endorsing a promise of immortality already made to W.H. by Shakespeare, but such is not necessarily the case. Thorpe wishes for W.H. either (1) the fruition of the promise Shakespeare makes him in these sonnets, or (2) a slice of the same luck, that is, the immortality which Shakespeare promises some unspecified person in these sonnets.

It is strange that the favorite expansion of "W.H." has been into Henry Wriothesley; for there is nothing to connect Shakespeare with the Earl of Southampton after the spring of 1594, and "W.H." does not equal "H.W." William Herbert is another and a more plausible guess, though only that. Herbert became third Earl of Pembroke in 1601, and lord chamberlain in 1615. He loved plays and players, and the dedication of the First Folio leaves no doubt that he had been a patron of Shakespeare's. Yet Thorpe's "*Master* W.H." weights the scale against the identification of any belted earl with the recipient of this volume of 1609. His meaning remains unpenetrated. Since he had obviously got hold of a manuscript without Shakespeare's consent, as likely a conjecture as any suggests that the "begetter" of the sonnets was not the man who inspired them but the thief who stole them. We know from Meres that they had been passed about among Shakespeare's friends, and no doubt among his friends' friends. In those days gentlemen kept commonplace books and transcribed poems that pleased them. If such was the source of Thorpe's text, we have no assurance that all the sonnets have been preserved or that all those he printed are Shakespeare's. Nor, since some of them are addressed to one or more women, is "only begetter," even if it does mean "sole inspirer," an appropriate epithet for Master W.H. Whatever "begetter" means, it is probably not "inspirer." To beget is to conceive, and obviously Thorpe is not dedicating the book to its author. Another meaning of the verb was "to acquire." Quite possibly W.H. was some gentleman, but surely no lord, who conceived the idea of bringing out an unauthorized edition of the much praised lyrics, got Thorpe interested, and agreed to secure a copy of them. On virtually nothing, however, which pertains to the Sonnets is there any agreement among scholars, save that the best are among the finest poems in our language.

Opinion is at present sharply divided between those who think the Sonnets are a coherent sequence, in which Shakespeare's private life can be traced, and those who hold that, like *Venus* and *Lucrece*, they are nothing more than poetic exercises. The truth probably lies between these extreme views. Some of the poems are addressed to a young man who is averse to marriage. The poet admires him, extravagantly compliments him on his beauty, and urges him to perpetuate it by the procreation of children. This group may be addressed to Southampton, who was balky under the matrimonial injunctions of his widowed mother and their friends; but Herbert was also reluctant. Efforts to read the whole cycle as an autobiography have failed before a series of obstacles, not one of which has been surmounted.

In the first place, these poems can not be dated. Some think they were all written by 1596 because after that year the vogue of the sonnet cycle declined. It had been great while it lasted. English literature had been permanently enriched by Sidney's *Astrophel and Stella*, Spenser's *Amoretti*, Daniel's *Delia*, and Drayton's *Ideas Mirrour* (though Drayton's best were later), to mention only the most gifted sonneteers. But some of the poets, in dogged defiance of the timetables destined to be devised by literary historians, kept on after '96. There is no evidence that Shakespeare was not among them.

A second obstacle to the biographical interpretation is the absence of any clue to the right sequence of his sonnets. We have no reason to suppose that their appearance in 1609 was in either the chronological order of their composition or the arrangement the author would have adopted. Various schemes of rearrangement have been proposed, some rather ingenious, some downright silly. None convinces.

A third obstacle is the impossibility of determining, for many of the poems, not only the identity but even the sex of the recipient. Despite frequent assertions to the contrary, the sequence does not break into two main divisions, one addressed to a man, the other to a woman. Some of the "procreation" sonnets are certainly addressed to a man. There is no hint of homosexuality in them, not even in Sonnet 20; that suspicion arose from unfamiliarity with Elizabethan convention. Men expressed mutual affection in more ardent terms than is now considered good form in the United States, Great Britain, and the British Dominions. The exalted ideal of masculine friendship is frequently reflected in Shakespeare's plays — in *The Two Gentlemen of Verona*, for example, and in the beautiful relationship of Hamlet and Horatio. If "Let me not to the marriage of true minds" (Sonnet 116) really was addressed to a male friend or patron, the subject, whatever its immediate inspiration, becomes a general glorification of idealistic love. Moreover, mixed in with the procreation group, with which the cycle opens, are several poems that may not belong to it at all; and the truth is that, while some of the sonnets are evidently directed to a man and others no less plainly to a woman, many may be to either and some may not be intended for any individual.

The last of these possibilities brings us to the fourth obstacle, thus summarized by Professor Kittredge:

A sonnet (if it would not fail of its purpose, would not falsify the end for which it comes into being) must seem to be veracious and actual; it must seem to express authentic emotion, and (most pernicious of qualities!) it must speak in the first person. In a word, a sonnet must be either patently artificial, and then it is *bad*—or *good*, and then it sounds like autobiography. There is no escape; a good sonnet appears to be a confession.[29]

That Shakespeare's are *in part* responsive to the fashion set by Sidney's is obvious. If he had lived under Queen Anne he would probably have written many plays but no sonnets. Yet to recognize their conventionality need not exclude admiration for their beauty and their sincerity. The same passionate and imaginative nature that gives us the great moments of the plays finds no such scope in the sonnet's scanty plot of ground; but it finds a good deal — more, in fact, than most poets have been able to make use of in any genre, concise or discursive. Some of the sonnets are little more than graceful sets of variations on familiar themes for the fashionable instrument. But many are hot from "the burning core," as Emerson called the authentic process of artistic combustion. The assumption that Shakespeare threw down his sonnet tools when the whistle blew in 1596 or 1597 does not seem to me a happy one. It is far more likely that many a midnight mood continued to be distilled in fourteen exquisite lines all through the years when he was writing the romantic comedies and the greatest tragedies.

I have no arrangement to propose, nor any pattern of dates and identifications. A dozen men and women may have been honored with sonnets from Shakespeare. Besides the golden lad of the procreation group, there is a friend (it may be the same person) who has stolen the love of the poet's mistress. But it is in a suspiciously conventional style that the sonneteer indites a quibbling forgiveness and exalts friendship for the man above love for the woman. Then there is a dark lady, that is, a brunette, who seems to have led the poet a merry dance. She has not been identified. A rival poet half emerges from the shadows. In the affections of a beloved friend (perhaps the golden lad again) he has won, possibly with "the proud full sail of his great verse," a place that wounds the sonneteer with jealousy. Some think he was George Chapman, but there is no evidence.

The Sonnets puzzle intrigues everyone — scholars, brilliant amateurs, not-so-bright amateurs, charlatans, and cranks. Even if it continues to attract any number of busy or idle minds for another three hundred years, we may be confident it will remain unsolved — unless external evidence is turned up. For no better (and no madder) brains will be applied to the internal evidence than have already tackled it. If new documents are discovered, it will be they, and not the sonnets, that will give us the facts. The sonnets will only tell us how Shakespeare felt about the facts. And that they tell us now — how, that is, Shakespeare chose *as an artist* to express and communicate certain moods of joy, longing, wonder, doubt, and despair. The truth and value of these beautiful poems do not wait upon the results of further research. He who runs may read them. He who has loved may rejoice in them. He who has suffered may be lifted up by them.

As if the problems raised by the sonnets of Thorpe's 1609 quarto were not sufficiently exasperating, the enterprising publisher blithely included another poem, which he ascribes to "William Shake-speare." It is a substantial piece of 329 lines, entitled "A Lover's Complaint." There is no external evidence for the date of composition, and no decisive evidence of any kind for its authorship. On neither question is scholarly opinion agreed. The sceptics are at present in the majority, but nothing precludes the possibility that Shakespeare wrote these stanzas. They may be an early and unfinished essay in narrative poetry which he had the good sense not to publish, but which Thorpe secured surreptitiously from the same source his text of the Sonnets came from. Possibly we have here a sample of the kind of verses Shakespeare brought along to London about 1585 or 1586. On the other hand, there is no virtue in Thorpe; his reputation was shady; his ascription is not proof. And the verses are neither good enough nor bad enough to settle the question. A few of them are well worthy of Shakespeare in his novitiate. The poem is certainly not

Spenser's, but its gentle pastoralism may have been inspired by him. The possibility must also be entertained that an imitator of Shakespeare wrote "A Lover's Complaint," after the publication of *Venus* and *Lucrece*.

By the end of the year, 1594, in which appeared the first testimony to Shakespeare's new fame as a poet, he was a leading member of the principal company of players, the Lord Chamberlain's Men. The accounts of the treasurer of the Chamber record on March 15, 1595 a payment for performances before the Queen at Greenwich Palace on December 26 and (probably) 27, 1594. The actors who drew it were William Kempe the chief comedian, William Shakespeare, and Richard Burbage the great tragedian.

Now if Shakespeare did not reach London till the early nineties, this rise to a major theatrical position, this progress in making friends with the great, this winning of fame as a playwright, must have been extraordinarily rapid. More than one of the other dramatists seems to have risen to company membership as quickly; but the payment just cited is the first record of Shakespeare's connection with any theatrical organization — and we find him in the front rank of the best troupe. *Venus and Adonis* was the first poem he published. And as for the plays, it is asking too much to expect us to believe that all the young genius from Stratford had to do was take pen in hand and dash off a hit. It is a far cry from *Henry the Sixth* to *Henry the Fourth*, from the experimental comedies to *Twelfth Night*, from *Titus Andronicus* to *King Lear*. All through the nineties we shall follow in his successive dramas his growing mastery of technique and the waxing power of his imagination. None of his fellow dramatists went so far beyond early work as he did. Yet all those early plays of his are on the whole better plays than were being turned out by the others in the late eighties and early nineties, with the possible exception of one or two by Marlowe. Perhaps there were prentice pieces before *Henry the Sixth*, *Titus Andronicus*, and *The Comedy of Errors*. If so, they have not survived. Perhaps the young actor merely did hack work for the company when old plays were revived. A once popular theory that he began by collaborating with leading dramatists has been abandoned. But surely there must lie behind the first plays of his that ever got into print years of experience of some sort, if not in dramatic writing then at least in acting, probably as a "hireling," that is, a salaried employee, not a full-fledged profit sharer. We have already faced the long hiatus in the record from 1585 to 1592,[30] and now we are speculating again. Perhaps there was a year or more as a country schoolteacher, which may have come before or after the twins were born; but though there is no scholarly agreement on this point, the best guess is that Shakespeare laid siege to the capital about 1585–86 and, whether consciously or not, prepared for his great career by experiencing his medium, the London stage, at first hand, as an actor, over a considerable period of time, before he wrote successfully for it. Moreover, it is inconceivable that this teeming imagination brought forth nothing till its owner was nearly thirty. It is much more likely that Shakespeare was writing verses in his late teens and verses and perhaps plays in his early and middle twenties. Quite possibly neither were very remarkable, at any rate in comparison with what was to come.

The first surviving plays can not, unfortunately, be precisely dated. *Titus Andronicus* is certainly the earliest of the tragedies. Ben Jonson mentions it in the Induction to *Bartholomew Fayre* (acted 1614): "Hee that will sweare, *Ieronimo* [Kyd's *The Spanish Tragedie*], or *Andronicus* are the best playes, yet, shall passe vnexcepted at, heere, as a man whose Iudgement shewes it is constant, and hath stood still, these fiue-and-twentie, or thirtie yeeres." If Jonson is accurate, this dates *Titus* not later than 1589; but we can not assume his accuracy, though it is probable. The obvious classical influence on this play has led some to lump it with *The Comedy of Errors* as the earliest work of the country schoolmaster. But *Titus* shows the future author of *King Lear* a little absurdly under the spell, not only of Seneca, the prime inspiration of the Elizabethan tragedy-of-blood, but also of that inferior poet yet robustly passionate playwright Thomas Kyd. And that is what we should expect. The most popular play in

London was *The Spanish Tragedie* (*c.* 1586). Shakespeare was trying his prentice hand at the same blood-and-thunder game. In *Henry the Sixth* he draws for the first time, as far as we know, on a book that never lost its fascination for him, the *Chronicles* of Raphael Holinshed, another Warwickshire man. Plays on British history were relished by an audience which the defeat of the Armada in '88 made more conscious than ever of England's greatness. Shakespeare catered to that appetite more successfully than anyone else. Hence Greene's outburst. In *An Apology For Actors* (1612) Thomas Heywood seriously makes the point that such pieces serve the useful function of teaching English history to the illiterate. Less skill in construction was required in this kind of drama. While the aim was to include all the striking episodes of a reign, the recorded facts, not so amenable to cavalier modification as the materials of fiction, often stood in the way of structural unity. Historical plays had long been on the stage, but as a genre the chronicle drama was slow to detach itself from the older morality type. Shakespeare may have given his theatre something distinctly new with the three parts of *Henry the Sixth*, which were probably followed up at no long interval by *Richard the Third*. It is, however, impossible to date many contemporary plays by the other dramatists. In the light of present information there is not much use in trying to assign priority, though in his *Edward the Second* Marlowe is probably following, not leading, Shakespeare.

On the lighter side Shakespeare was to have his most enduring success in romantic rather than pure comedy, that is, in humorous yet sympathetic narratives of trials and tribulations that end happily. He is never really easy in critical comedy. He is a skilful delineator of manners, but he never wrote a comedy-of-manners scene equal to many by Jonson, Congreve, Sheridan, and Shaw, to say nothing of Molière. He was a long time finding his true vein, which is rather curious when we consider how the humorous point of view permeates his work. In his early comedies he mounts a borrowed horse and rides off in several directions. *The Comedy of Errors* is based on Plautus; it is an artificial thing, really a farce, which mildly pleases by adroit manipulation of plot. It is the only one of his plays that a stay-at-home countryman might conceivably have managed to write; but it is likelier, on the face of it, that Shakespeare had been an actor before he wrote plays at all. In either case he turned for a theme to an author he had very likely read in school. *The Taming of the Shrew*, rollicking farce that it is, betrays constantly in the main plot the hand of the experienced actor, and may even have been written later than *The Two Gentlemen of Verona* and *Love's Labour's Lost*. The best guess, however, puts it second among the comedies. In part the subplot is adapted directly from George Gascoigne's *Supposes*, a translation of Ariosto's *Suppositi*. The classical influence reached the English dramatists directly and also through the Italian and French playwrights.

Any attempt to date these nine early plays even approximately is inseparable from the thorny problems of Shakespeare's theatrical connections, which we shall consider in Chapter 2. There is still much dispute; but it seems probable that *Titus*, the three Henry VI histories, and perhaps *Errors* had all been composed by June, 1592, and very likely earlier. Certainly *Errors* and probably *Richard the Third*, *The Shrew*, *The Two Gentlemen*, and *Love's Labour's Lost* all came at least before the end of 1594, when we take up the story once more from documentary evidence.

SOUL OF THE AGE: 1594–1603

For the rest of Elizabeth's reign Shakespeare also reigned. Marlowe, Greene, and Kyd were dead. Lyly was still a great name; but his Muse, never fecund, was now sterile. With one exception, none of the others could challenge Shakespeare at any kind of writing for the theatre. In 1598 Ben Jonson's *Every Man in his Humor* was to set a rival fashion in comedy, and for a while dramatic satires excited the *cognoscenti;* but Jonson's best work came later. Recalling, in the Shakespeare Folio of 1623, how thirty-odd years earlier the new planet had swung over the horizon, "I, therefore will begin," says Ben:

Soule of the Age!
The applause! delight! the wonder of our Stage!
My *Shakespeare*, rise. . . . .
For, if I thought my iudgement were of yeeres,
I should commit thee surely with thy peeres,
And tell, how farre thou didst our *Lily* out-shine,
Or sporting *Kid*, or *Marlowes* mighty line. . . .
He was not of an age, but for all time!
And all the *Muses* still were in their prime,
When like *Apollo* he came forth to warme
Our eares, or like a *Mercury* to charme!

Most of Shakespeare's mightiest works were composed after
the accession of James; but by then there were new playwrights, great ones, and beginning with Heywood's *A Woman
Kilde with Kindnesse* (1603), Chapman's *Bussy D'Ambois*
(?1604), Dekker's *The Honest Whore* (1604), Marston's *The
Malcontent* (?1604), Middleton's *A Tricke to Catch the Old-one*
(*c.* 1605), Jonson's *Volpone* (1606), and Beaumont's *The Knight
of the Burning Pestle* (*c.* 1607), came masterpiece upon masterpiece; while from 1594 to at least the turn of the century,
Shakespeare bestrides the narrow stage like a colossus.

In *The Two Gentlemen of Verona* and *Love's Labour's Lost* he
is still groping his way. The latter used to be taken for his
first play and even assigned to the rural schoolmaster's leisure
hours, but it is much too alive to literary gossip for the work
of an author still unacquainted with the metropolitan co-
teries. Shakespeare could have acquired its smart light touch
from the comedies of John Lyly, which enjoyed, during his
early years in London, a great vogue among connoisseurs.
He may have written it while the plague of 1592–94 kept the
theatres closed; [31] perhaps it was one of the first pieces he
gave the Lord Chamberlain's Men when they reorganized in
'94. Very likely another was *The Two Gentlemen*, in which,
though as usual he borrows his plot, he begins to find his
own feet as a comic dramatist. Despite some brilliant things,
it is not a very good play; but at last he strikes into the vein
of romantic comedy. Both these pieces are doubtless earlier
than *A Midsummer Night's Dream*, written about the middle

of the decade. This was Shakespeare's first comic masterpiece, though he is still experimenting and the play is a mixture of several kinds of comedy.

His first good tragedy, *Romeo and Juliet*, was probably written about the same time, in his so-called lyrical period. Meanwhile he had made the Henry VI trilogy into a tetralogy by adding *Richard the Third*, composed either just after *Henry the Sixth, Part 3* or during the suspension of acting. He goes on with his histories in the "lyrical period." Whether *King John* or *Richard the Second* came next is uncertain. Parts of the latter are very lyrical for a chronicle play; but it is likelier that *King John* had intervened between it and *Richard the Third*, since Shakespeare's next history was to carry on the story of usurping Bolingbroke in the second member of a new tetralogy of which *Richard the Second* is the opening piece. All these plays were probably on the boards by 1596, and the Burbage repertory was now equipped with two stunning successes and several others only less sensational. Of the remainder, *Love's Labour's Lost* and *A Midsummer Night's Dream* may have been staged privately first. *Richard the Third* and *Romeo and Juliet* were the *pièces de résistance*.

In the summer or fall of 1594 Shakespeare's company had probably begun acting in Shoreditch, a northern suburb, at the Theatre, the oldest of the London playhouses.[32] It is rather likely that they played that winter and the next in the city itself, at the Cross Keys Inn, on Gracechurch or "Gracious" Street. The troupe probably had nine members, who shared the profits, besides boys and "hirelings." From 1594 on, the sharers included Richard Burbage, William Shakespeare, William Kempe, Thomas Pope, John Heminge (or Heminges), Augustine Phillips, and George Bryan. The membership of William Sly and Henry Condell is probable though not actually demonstrable so early as this. Christopher Beeston and John Duke, as well as Condell and Sly, were important players by 1598; whether Beeston and Duke were ever sharers is not known. They afterwards left the company, along with Kempe, and joined Worcester's Men. Most of the rôles were taken by members, doubtless with some doubling.

Richard Burbage was a highly accomplished man, a painter as well as a player. He was evidently a great actor. Several tributes to him have survived, though the expanded version of an elegy listing his rôles is one of the forgeries of John Payne Collier. Burbage made a special hit as Richard III. In his *Iter Boreale* Bishop Richard Corbet (d. 1635) describes a visit to Bosworth Field:

> Mine Host was full of *Ale* and *History*. . . .
> Upon this hill they mett. Why he could tell
> The inch where *Richmond* stood, where *Richard* fell:
> Besides what of his knowledge he can say,
> He had Authenticke notice, from the Play. . . .
> For when he would have sayd, King *Richard* dyed,
> And call'd, a horse, a horse; he, *Burbidge* cry'de.

Shortly after the death of this famous actor in 1619, a letter of the Earl of Pembroke tells how a group of his friends adjourned from a supper party to the play, "which I being tender harted could not endure to see so soone after the loss of my old acquaintance Burbadg." Presumably he played all the principal tragic rôles; but the only Shakespearean ones for which evidence has survived are Richard III, Hamlet, Othello, and Lear. Kempe left the company early in 1599, and Robert Armin came in to act the Fools.[33] Some of the players specialized in types; but it seems likely that versatility, Colley Cibber's acid test of the accomplished actor, was a prime requisite for most members of an Elizabethan repertory company. As for Shakespeare, Rowe says he was not an "extraordinary" actor and that evidence concerning his rôles had not survived except for the Ghost in *Hamlet*, which was "the top of his Performance." Aubrey, on the other hand, asserts that he acted "exceedingly well." Oldys tells a story about one of the dramatist's "younger brothers" who used to visit London; in his old age all he could remember was seeing William play

a part in one of his own comedies, wherein being to personate a decrepit old man, he wore a long beard, and appeared so weak and drooping and unable to walk, that he was forced to be supported

THE CHANCEL OF HOLY TRINITY CHURCH

Shakespeare's grave is inside the rail, at the left; his monument
is above it, the first on the left wall, beyond the door.

THE SHAKESPEARE MONUMENT

Holy Trinity Church

THE MONUMENTAL BUST

THE BUST IN PROFILE

and carried by another person to a table, at which he was seated
among some company, who were eating, and one them sung a song.

This is the part of Adam in *As You Like It*, but the authenticity
of the anecdote is dubious.[34] In 1610 John Davies of Hereford
addressed some lines "*To our English Terence, M*ʳ. Will: Shakespeare":

> Some say (good *Will*) which I, in sport, do sing)
> Had'st thou not plaid some Kingly parts in sport,
> Thou hadst bin a companion for a *King*.

With the Burbage troupe Shakespeare remained throughout
the rest of his career. When their patron, Henry Carey, the
lord chamberlain, died on July 23, 1596, his son George became Lord Hunsdon and their sponsor. On March 17, 1597
he succeeded to his father's high office at court. As an actor
in this company and its chief writer, Shakespeare led an
existence crowded with the hard, joyful work of creation
and interpretation — a life in art if there ever was one. The
daily change of bill entailed setting aside many hours for
memorizing new rôles, and frequent rehearsals must have been
indispensable. An Elizabethan actor faced the same task an
ambitious opera singer does now; he had to increase his
repertory and keep it all fresh in his mind, since a new play
that was well received went into the stock from which the
subsequent program was selected. This requirement was a
constant one, a harness from which an actor could never
escape while the season lasted. Shakespeare alludes to it in
Sonnet 23, which begins with a player who has failed to
memorize all his lines:

> As an unperfect actor on the stage
> Who with his fear is put besides his part. . . .

There were daily matinees, except on Sundays; and occasionally the company acted in the evening, too, for the entertainment of the guests at some great house.

Another responsibility — it rested on Shakespeare's shoulders with double weight — was the necessity of pleasing.
Unlike a lyric poet, the playwright and the actor can not

disdain the present and appeal to posterity's verdict. They must score immediately. The Elizabethan audience was exacting, and the theatre was not the decorous institution we know. If the spectators disliked anything they said so. Sometimes they threw things. Yet, despite such moods as Sonnet 110 reflects,

> Alas, 'tis true I have gone here and there
> And made myself a motley to the view,
> Gor'd mine own thoughts, sold cheap what is most dear,

Shakespeare was apparently content to let the theatre absorb him. Even after he left off acting important rôles, he wrote almost exclusively for it; no large poetic design, no series of lyric volumes, came from his pen. Into his dramas he poured the richness of his spirit; and, beautiful as the sonnets are, his finest lyricism is in his plays. The so-called lyrical period is something of a misnomer. Several of the plays are more consistently lyric than the rest, but Shakespeare's own moods found expression again and again throughout his career. Only, these lyrical outbursts are adjusted to the exigencies of plot and character; so they are dramatic as well as lyric, and we must be wary of putting our finger on a passage and saying, "This is what Shakespeare really thought." If his enslavement to his stage strikes us as the fettering of a spirit that ought to have been free, we must remember it did not circumscribe him as a poet. Some artists thrive on set tasks. Shakespeare certainly did. And this absorption kept his work as a poetic dramatist the very stuff of the theatre. A first-rate play is written only by a man who is a double master: he must be literary artist and theatrical technician. Shakespeare knew his medium inside out. Like his great peer Molière, he learned it as a player.

The activities of the company included not only their regular public appearances but also private ones, most notably at court. They acted in Elizabeth's palace at Greenwich on December 26 and (probably) 27, 1594; the next night they were at Gray's Inn, playing *The Comedy of Errors* for the young gentlemen who were supposed to be studying law there. The

Inns of Court, where the scions of the country squires came up from the universities, or even straight from grammar school, to acquire a legal smattering for later use as justices of the peace, and where many a man found literature a more charming mistress and turned author, furnished a sizable portion of the regular audiences and occasionally sponsored performances in their own halls. Before the royal court at Richmond Shakespeare's company played five times in the winter of 1595–96, and at Whitehall six times the next winter. These engagements, mostly during the Christmas holidays, are typical of the remaining years of Elizabeth's reign.

We still have with us those who attempt to trace Shakespeare's domestic as well as artistic life in his plays. Do the lamentations for the boy Arthur in *King John* reflect the grief of the poet and his wife over the death of their son in 1596? We have no reason to suppose so. Every pang and joy that Shakespeare knew deepened his experience, made his life fuller. He writes out of his own experience, of course. But the sensitiveness of an artist is impressed by the far as well as the near, by the sorrows and ecstasies of others, and by the mysterious destiny of mankind. Shakespeare unlocks many hearts; he does not tell us which key fits his.

> Others abide our question. Thou art free.
> We ask and ask — Thou smilest and art still,
> Out-topping knowledge. For the loftiest hill,
> Who to the stars uncrowns his majesty,
> Planting his stedfast footsteps in the sea,
> Making the heaven of heavens his dwelling-place,
> Spares but the cloudy border of his base
> To the foil'd searching of mortality;
> And thou, who didst the stars and sunbeams know,
> Self-school'd, self-scann'd, self-honour'd, self-secure,
> Didst tread on earth unguess'd at. — Better so!
> All pains the immortal spirit must endure,
> All weakness which impairs, all griefs which bow,
> Find their sole speech in that victorious brow.

This superb tribute by Matthew Arnold correctly states the biographer's difficulty, but is wrong in assuming that Shakespeare's genius went unrecognized. He probably had a good schooling; as a colleague of Ben Jonson he doubtless received many a friendly but incisive "scanning"; and he was not only honored, he was loved, by his associates. The implication of Arnold's line is none the less sound. Too much has been made of the "gentle" Shakespeare; an uncommonly sweet nature his seems to have been, but there was plenty of iron in him. "Next to God," says Dumas *fils*, "Shakespeare created most." Robert Browning expands that thought in another sonnet:

> Shakespeare! — to such name's sounding, what succeeds
> Fitly as silence? Falter forth the spell, —
> Act follows word, the speaker knows full well,
> Nor tampers with its magic more than needs.
> Two names there are: That which the Hebrew reads
> With his soul only: if from lips it fell,
> Echo, back thundered by earth, heaven and hell,
> Would own "Thou didst create us!" Naught impedes
> We voice the other name, man's most of might,
> Awesomely, lovingly: let awe and love
> Mutely await their working, leave to sight
> All of the issue as — below — above —
> Shakespeare's creation rises: one remove,
> Though dread — this finite from that infinite.

Making that cosmos out of nothing was never the work of a weakling nor of one who shrank from life. The very faults of his writings, as the neoclassicists of the eighteenth century held them to be, are the sallies of a strong, adventurous spirit. The confident aspiration of the Renaissance is reflected again and again in what Shakespeare wrote, but never thoughtlessly. The imminence of death was no less omnipresent in Renaissance thinking and expression. Of some men it exacted "a trembling walk with God." In Shakespeare it kindled passionate admiration for the human spirit, and a deep pity for the lot of man.

In 1596 he began, perhaps, to think more seriously of ultimate retirement to Stratford. He knew he was going to make money, and he wished to return as one of the gentry. He was not alone among the actors who aspired to a coat of arms. When John Shakespeare was bailiff of Stratford he had made motions; the granting of arms would take him out of the yeoman class. Now he applied again, probably at his son's instigation. Some play was made with the pleasant fiction, for such it seems to be, that John's ancestors had done valiant and faithful service to Henry VII. Fees outweighed genealogies in the estimation of some heralds, and William Dethick, Garter King-of-Arms, was not one to strain at a gnat or even a camel of normal dimensions. A draft of October 20, 1596 has survived in the Herald's College. It assigns *Or on a bend sable a spear of the first steeled argent* and a crest of a falcon bearing a spear. Arms and crest are sketched in the margin.[35] There is also a later draft, of 1599–1600, in response to a request for an exemplification of a grant already made. This draft adds John's right to impale and his descendants' to quarter "the Auncyent Arms of . . . Arden of Wellingcote"; but though the arms appear on Shakespeare's monument in the church at Stratford, they lack the Arden quartering, which was apparently not granted. A little later the assignment was among points of attack when the heralds were accused of making grants too liberally. Their defence was the eminence of John Shakespeare as a civic dignitary.

What contact Shakespeare had maintained with his parents and with his wife and children in the years between his coming to London and this of 1596 is quite unknown. Some have conjectured that his immediate family was with him, others that he had been for about eleven years absent from Stratford. Perhaps there had been visits in the summer and a steady correspondence; but all the evidence we have for these years connects the family with Stratford and the poet with London. Whatever he had done or left undone, he is certainly in touch in 1596–97.

He had been living in St. Helen's parish, Bishopsgate, not far from Shoreditch where he acted. He is named in a certificate of November 15, 1597 among certain persons "ether dead, departed, and gone out of the sayde warde or their goodes soe . . . conveyd out of the same" that taxes "nether mighte nor coulde . . . be levyed of them." The taxes were an installment on a subsidy granted by the parliament of 1593. Shakespeare had failed to make, on an assessment fixed in October, 1596, the payment due the following February; for, as Hales inferred (see Bibliography), he had moved from Bishopsgate to the Bankside in Surrey. Professor Hotson has found a writ returnable on November 29, 1596, the Latin text of which shows that one William Wayte craved sureties of the peace against William Shakspere, Francis Langley, Dorothy Soer wife of John Soer, and Anne Lee, "for fear of death, etc." These women have not been identified, but Langley was the real-estate man who built the Swan Theatre on the Bankside in 1594–95. It stood in the Manor of Paris Garden, to the west of Philip Henslowe's Rose. A new company under the patronage of the Earl of Pembroke was acting at the Swan in the late winter of 1596–97. Who preceded them was a mystery till Hotson suggested that Shakespeare changed his residence because his company had shifted to the new house. As we have seen, the first Lord Hunsdon died in the summer of 1596. His immediate successor as lord chamberlain, William Brooke, Lord Cobham, had no love for players; and since the municipal authorities at once banned acting in the city, the Cross Keys Inn was no longer available. The Burbages were deeply involved in a dispute with the lessor of the land on which their Theatre stood. Both it and the Curtain, the second of the London houses, also in the hands of the Burbages, were now old; while the Rose was occupied by the Admiral's Men. An allusion in Thomas Dekker's *Satiro-mastix* (acted in 1601) links the Hunsdon company with the Swan: "my name's Hamlet reuenge: thou hast been at Parris garden hast not?" Since Hotson's brilliant discovery links Shakespeare with Langley, the owner of the Swan in Paris Garden, it seems probable that his company was acting there.

Another document found by Hotson shows that, earlier in this same month of November, 1596, Langley had sworn the peace against William Gardiner and Wayte, the complainant of the 29th. Gardiner was a wealthy justice of the peace on the Surrey side; Wayte was his stepson. About the same time

Gardiner brought three actions for slander against Langley, whom he charges with calling him among other things "a perjured knave." How Shakespeare was involved is not known. You swore the peace by giving a justice reason to suppose you were threatened with bodily injury. The offender was then required to produce surety against an act of violence.

Shakespeare was assessed again in St. Helen's parish in October, 1598, on goods valued at £5, but once more the tax-gatherers reported the item uncollectable. The case seems to have been referred first to the sheriff of Sussex and Surrey, and then to the Bishop of Winchester; Shakespeare apparently had to pay up. The Bishop comes into the picture because he had jurisdiction over the Liberty of the Clink, a portion of the Bankside devoted to theatrical and other amusements even less staid. There stood the Bear Garden, where the Elizabethans enjoyed fights between bears (or bulls) and bulldogs, and the even more shockingly cruel sport of whipping the blind bear. There stood also a congeries of brothels and gambling joints, from which the good Bishop derived a handsome revenue. On the Bankside the Chamberlain's Men were soon to erect their own theatre. It was a gaudy district, the rendezvous of sporting men and ladies; yet a number of theatrical worthies lived there, among them such respectable persons as Henslowe, the owner of the Rose, and Edward Alleyn, the Admiral's chief player. So did several members of Shakespeare's company. Beaumont and Fletcher later set up their famous partnership there. Shakespeare was doubtless residing in the Liberty of the Clink late in 1596. The new evidence, like that of Hales, corroborates a document belonging to Alleyn, now lost but seen in 1796 by Malone, who says it shows that in 1596 the poet lived "in Southwark, near the Bear-Garden."

Next summer (1597) all the actors were in trouble because Pembroke's company, now at the Swan, had acted Nashe's *The Isle of Dogs*, in which some unidentified persons of high degree were attacked. On July 28 the Privy Council ordered the justices of Middlesex, which included Shoreditch, and of Surrey, which embraced the Bankside, to suppress acting within three miles of the city and to require owners of theatres to dismantle them. The last injunction was not carried out; acting was resumed at least as early as October, and the ban was lifted on November 1. The Privy Council then limited playing to two houses, the Curtain and the Rose. Shakespeare's troupe occupied the former, which stood near the Theatre outside the northern walls. Whether he had moved out there or back into town is unknown. Malone mentions "Another curious document in my possession, which . . . affords the strongest presumptive evidence that he continued to reside in Southwark to the year 1608." This great scholar died before he finished his biography, and the document is unknown except by this brief allusion. We shall come, in the next section, to some evidence that Shakespeare was not, in 1604, a resident of Southwark. During the suspension of 1597 his company made its only extensive provincial tour during these years. Whether he accompanied it is not recorded.

On May 4, 1597 he had purchased New Place in Stratford, apparently for £60, and presumably soon established his wife and daughters there. It was a corner house across the lane just north of the old chapel of the Guild. Sir Hugh Clopton, restorer of the town's fine bridge, had built New Place about a century before. With one exception it was the largest dwelling in Stratford when Shakespeare acquired it. The Corporation bought a load of stone from him soon after he took title. They used it to mend the bridge; perhaps it was left over from repairs on the house. To New Place the poet afterwards retired, and it was in Lady Bernard's possession when, the last of Shakespeare's descendants, she died in 1670. The house was rebuilt about 1700 and stood till 1759, when its owner, the Reverend Francis Gastrell, demolished it to spite the town. It was described about 1540 in the *Itinerary* of John Leland as "a praty howse of brike and tymbar," and it had a large garden. Shortly after the purchase of New Place, the Shakespeares again brought suit, this time in Chancery, to recover the Arden inheritance. Record of the court's presumably adverse decision has not survived.

In 1598 the poet may have considered investing in real

estate near Stratford. This we learn in a letter of January 24 from Abraham Sturley of Stratford to his fellow townsman Richard Quiney, Judith Shakespeare's future father-in-law, who was on a business trip to London, where he made several long sojourns between 1597 and 1601. On October 25, 1598 Quiney wrote the only letter to Shakespeare which has been preserved, though whether the poet actually received it is uncertain, since it was found among Quiney's papers. Very likely an interview made its dispatch unnecessary. It is addressed "To my Loveinge good ffrend & contreymann m^r w^m Shackespere." This and other letters in Quiney's correspondence indicate that he wanted Shakespeare to lend him money for his personal needs and also to provide capital for some investment. Whether these hopes were realized is unrecorded. Stratford was in a bad way. There had been disastrous fires and scanty harvests — Shakespeare probably refers to the long spell of ruinous weather in *A Midsummer Night's Dream* (II, i). The rising price of grain faced the poor with the prospect of going breadless, and the slump in the woolen trade had thrown many out of work. Evidently Shakespeare was regarded by his native town as a rich man. On February 4 of the same year a Stratford inventory lists him as owner of eighty bushels of grain and malt. Householders were accustomed to do their own brewing. The Privy Council tried to check the use of barley for this purpose, and local authorities were ordered to make inventories to discover hoarders and maltsters. Shakespeare's stock was one of the largest in Stratford.

By 1598, then, we have ample evidence that Shakespeare had prospered to an extent denied most creative spirits, who as a rule are, and have to be, disinclined to make the sacrifices and adopt the preoccupations of those who find the ownership of things supremely interesting. There seems to have been no clash between his acquisitiveness and his art. The latter steadily deepens, and this year finds him well past the period of experimentation and on the threshold of his greatest achievements. Allusions to his works are now more frequent. Important ones occur in Francis Meres's *Palladis Tamia. Wits*

Treasvry, entered in the Stationers' Register on September 7, 1598. Meres was a young parson; he was living in London when his volume appeared. Its critical value is negligible — the method is "A comparatiue discourse of our English Poets, with the *Greeke, Latine, and Italian Poets*" — but this part of the book shows that Shakespeare was now a well-known author. His name begins to appear on the title pages of play quartos in this year, and Meres's list of his works is helpful in establishing their chronology:

the English tongue is mightily enriched, and gorgeouslie inuested in rare ornaments and resplendent [h]abiliments by sir *Philip Sidney, Spencer, Daniel, Drayton, Warner, Shakespeare, Marlowe* and *Chapman*. . . . As the soule of *Euphorbus* was thought to liue in *Pythagoras:* so the sweete wittie soule of *Ouid* liues in mellifluous & hony-tongued *Shakespeare*, witnes his *Venus* and *Adonis*, his *Lucrece*, his sugred Sonnets among his priuate friends, &c. As *Plautus* and *Seneca* are accounted the best for Comedy and Tragedy among the Latines: so *Shakespeare* among yᵉ English is the most excellent in both kinds for the stage; for Comedy, witnes his *Gentlemen of Verona*, his *Errors*, his *Loue labors lost*, his *Loue labours wonne*, his *Midsummers night dreame*, & his *Merchant of Venice:* for Tragedy his *Richard the 2. Richard the 3. Henry the 4. King Iohn, Titus Andronicus* and his *Romeo* and *Iuliet*. As *Epius Stolo* said, that the Muses would speake with *Plautus* tongue, if they would speak Latin: so I say that the Muses would speak with *Shakespeares* fine filed phrase, if they would speake English.

Love's Labour's Won is an unsolved mystery. If it is an earlier title of any of the surviving plays, it best fits *All's Well that Ends Well*, though it may allude to the subplot of *The Shrew*. Meres also includes Shakespeare among "the best Lyrick Poets," "our best for Tragedie," "the best for Comedy," and "the most passionate among vs to bewaile and bemoane the perplexities of Loue."

In the same year John Marston writes in *The Scovrge of Villanie:*

> *Luscus* what's playd to day? faith now I know
> I set thy lips abroach, from whence doth flow
> Naught but pure *Iuliat* and *Romio*.

Sometime between 1598 and 1601 Gabriel Harvey, the Cambridge scholar, mentions Shakespeare in some manuscript notes as one of nine of "owr florishing metricians." With a university teacher's properly conservative interest in the boys' outside reading, Harvey also observes that "The younger sort takes much delight in Shakespeares Venus, & Adonis: but his Lucrece, & his tragedie of Hamlet, Prince of Denmarke, haue it in them to please the wiser sort." In 1599 the Countess of Southampton alludes to Falstaff in a letter to the Earl. Also in 1599, John Weever in his *Epigrammes* begins a sonnet "Ad Gulielmum Shakespeare":

> Honie-tong'd *Shakespeare* when I saw thine issue
> I swore *Apollo* got them and none other.

He mentions "Rose-checkt *Adonis*," "fire-hot *Venus*," "Chaste *Lucretia*," "lust-stung *Tarquine*," "*Romea*," and "*Richard*," and urges Shakespeare to create more such characters. Brutus, Cæsar, and Antony are mentioned in the same author's *The Mirror of Martyrs*, probably composed in 1599.

In *Part 1* of *The returne from Parnassus*, acted at St. John's College, Cambridge, about 1599–1600, there are allusions to Shakespeare. In his third act the anonymous author lifts several passages from *Venus and Adonis*, for example (cf. lines 5–6):

Gullio. Pardon faire lady, thoughe sicke thoughted Gullio maks amaine vnto thee, & like a bould faced sutore gins to woo thee.
Ingenioso. We shall haue nothinge but pure Shakspeare, and shreds of poetrie y^t [i.e., that] he hath gathered at the theators.

He knew *Romeo and Juliet* (cf. II, iv, 42 ff.): "ye moone in comparison of thy bright hue a meere slutt, *Anthonies* Cleopatra a blacke browde milkmaide, Hellen a dowdie[.] Marke Romeo, and Iuliet. o monstrous theft. . . ." After reverting once more to *Venus and Adonis*, Gullio continues: "O sweet Mr. Shakspeare, Ile haue his picture in my study at the courte." And again (IV, i): "let this duncified worlde esteeme of Spencer and Chaucer, Ile worshipp sweet Mr. Shakspeare, and to honoure him will lay his Venus, and Adonis vnder my pillowe." It can not be maintained that Shakespeare is much honored in these allusions, but they leave no doubt that he was famous. In *Part 2* of *The Retvrne* there are references to both the narrative poems and to *Richard the Third;* Judicio testifies to Shakespeare's popularity and wishes he would turn from love to a "grauer subiect."

His name was now worth money on a title page. In 1599 William Jaggard published in a diminutive octavo *The Passionate Pilgrime*, "By W. Shakespeare"; but it is unlikely that more than a few of the poems are his. Two are from his sonnet cycle and three from *Love's Labour's Lost*.[36] A "newly corrected and augmented" edition in 1612 added nine pieces lifted from Thomas Heywood's *Troia Britanica* (1609). Heywood, already infuriated with Jaggard by a quarrel over that book, which Jaggard had published, rushed to attack him for printing the nine pieces from it in *The Pilgrim*

vnder the name of another [Shakespeare], which may put the world in opinion I might steale them from him; and hee to doe himselfe right, hath since published them in his owne name [there can be little doubt that Heywood is making an unwarranted assumption] but as I must acknowledge my lines not worthy his patronage . . . so the Author [Shakespeare, still] I know much offended with M. *Iaggard* (that altogether vnknowne to him) presumed to make so bold with his name.

This piece of righteous indignation was appended to Heywood's *An Apology For Actors* (1612). Shakespeare himself may have brought powerful influence to bear on Jaggard. At any rate, the mendacious title page seems to have been canceled in the unsold sheets and replaced by one that omits Shakespeare's name.

In 1601 appeared some strange verses by Shakespeare on "The Phoenix and the Turtle"; they form one of several appended poems in Robert Chester's *Loves Martyr: Or, Rosalins Complaint. Allegorically shadowing the truth of Loue, in the constant Fate of the Phoenix and Turtle*. These additional effusions are introduced by a separate title page: "Hereafter Follow Diverse Poeticall Essaies on the former Subiect; viz: the Turtle and Phœnix. Done by the best and chiefest of our moderne writers [others are Jonson, Chapman, and Marston] . . . consecrated by them all generally, to the loue and merite of the true-noble Knight, Sir Iohn Salisburie." Shakespeare's contribution is a poor thing, but no doubt his own. (It has been praised by some very sensitive critics.) There is no evidence for its date; presumably it was written to order for Chester's volume. What it is about no one knows. There is, accordingly, little to be gained by invoking Petrarchism or Platonism. The poem is unlike anything else in the Shakespeare canon. Perhaps its cryptic obscurity is an effect of the same thing that ruined the literary digestion of some twentieth-century poets — an overdose of John Donne. If so, the difference is that our metaphysical contemporaries suffered from a fundamental misconception of the nature of poetry, and the remedy they took is even worse than the disease; while it is likely enough that Shakespeare wrote "The Phoenix and the Turtle" with his tongue in his cheek, partly to amuse himself in the new crabbed style and partly to see what the world would make of it.

As for his dramatic work during these years (1596–1603), it includes most of his finest comedies, the best of his histories, and the first of his greatest tragedies. *The Merchant of Venice* was probably written in 1596, and then followed the matchless romantic comedies: *Much Ado about Nothing* (1598–99), *As You Like It* (*c*. 1599), and *Twelfth Night* (*c*. 1600–1602). *The Merry Wives of Windsor* (*c*. 1600–1601) probably came just before or just after *Twelfth Night*. About the same time is the likeliest date for the first two of the more realistic comedies, *Troilus and Cressida* (*c*. 1601–1602) and *All's Well that Ends Well* (*c*. 1602). Meanwhile Shakespeare had exploited a new vein, the historical-comical, in the two parts of *Henry the Fourth* (1597–98) and in *Henry the Fifth* (1599), which complete the tetralogy begun in *Richard the Second* and bring his dramatic chronicling down to the reign he had started with in *Henry the Sixth, Part 1*. The two tetralogies cover English history from 1398 to 1485, precisely the period of Halle's chronicle. Hard upon the completion of this remarkable panorama, he

turns to Roman history in *Julius Cæsar* (1599). Either the last
year of the old century or the first of the new (i.e., 1600–1601)
probably saw the original performance of his *Hamlet*, the
earliest of the works on which rests his title to supremacy.
It gave a great impetus to the current vogue of the revenge
tragedy. *Hamlet* leaped at once into universal favor, which it
has never lost. The most striking early evidence of its popularity is not its performance at both the universities, nor
Anthony Scoloker's statement in 1604 that Prince Hamlet
pleased all,[37] but two of the following items from the journal
of Captain William Keeling, master of the East Indiaman
Dragon. In September of 1607 the ship was off Sierra Leone.
On the fifth "we gaue the tragedie of Hamlett." On the
thirtieth "my companions acted Kinge Richard the Second."
On March 31, 1608, "I envited Captain Hawkins to a ffishe
dinner, and had Hamlet acted abord me: w[hi]ch I permitt
to keepe my people from idlenes and vnlawfull games, or
sleepe."

All this while Shakespeare was sharing the fortunes of
the Chamberlain's Men. Both their playhouses, the Curtain
and the Theatre, were antiquated. The land on which the
former stood was leased by the Burbages, and they had long
been quarreling with the owner over terms of renewal. James
Burbage, the first English theatrical proprietor, had died early
in 1597, leaving to his sons, Cuthbert and Richard, the Theatre
in Shoreditch and also the Blackfriars in the city. The latter
was a "private" theatre, remodeled out of part of the old
monastery. Aristocratic neighbors objected to its use as a
regular playhouse, and the Privy Council backed them up.
It was now the home of a children's troupe, to which the
Burbages had leased it and from which the adult companies
were getting lively competition about the turn of the century.

The Chamberlain's Men were playing at the Curtain. The
Burbage brothers now conceived the idea of taking down the
older of the two northern houses, both of them inferior to the
Swan and the Rose, and reconstructing it on the Bankside.
The ground owner was threatening to seize the building, his
lease to the Burbages having expired. So, despite his protests,

the Theatre was wrecked on December 28, 1598; and its timbers were carted across the town to a site on, as some argue, the south side of Maid Lane, a little east of the Rose and Bear Garden, not far from St. Saviour's, the great medieval church (also known as St. Mary Overy's), the present Southwark Cathedral. And at this point begins the history of the most famous of Elizabethan playhouses, the Globe. Though it stood on ground so marshy that piles had to be driven for a foundation, it was easily the finest theatre England had seen. Jonson calls it "the Glory of the *Banke.*" It seems to have been a circular structure with a polygonal exterior wall. It was probably completed by the early summer of 1599; meanwhile the company continued at the Curtain.

For the new undertaking a syndicate was formed. There were ten shares, the two Burbages holding five between them, and five players one apiece. These five, who thus became "housekeepers" owning ten per cent each of the building itself, were Shakespeare, Phillips and Pope (eminent players), Heminge (actor and apparently business manager of the acting company), and Kempe (the star low-comedian). The syndicate maintained the theatre and shared receipts assigned by the company in return for occupancy. It got half the gallery money, the other half and the admissions at the door going to the company. Thus all the members of the housekeepers' syndicate except Cuthbert Burbage were also members (sharers) of the company; and six members of the company shared again as members of the syndicate. Shakespeare's income was chiefly derived from these two sources, at the Globe and afterwards at the Blackfriars as well. He probably received additional payments outright for his plays. The Reverend John Ward, who came to Stratford as vicar in 1662, asserts in his diary, now in the Folger Shakespeare Library:

I haue heard y^t. M^r. Shakespeare was a natural wit without any art at all. hee frequented ye plays all his younger time, but in his elder days liud at Stratford: and supplied ye stage with 2 plays euery year and for y^t. had an allowance so large y^t. hee spent at ye Rate of a 1,000 l. a year as I haue heard.

The last figure must be vastly exaggerated.

Kempe soon withdrew. Pope died in 1603 or 1604, and Phillips in 1605. Some of the housekeeping shares passed into the hands of persons unconnected with the acting company. Of the players, Condell and Sly were later admitted as housekeepers, and still later William Ostler. When Kempe left, the shares were divided again; Shakespeare now had an interest of one-eighth in the house. He had one-twelfth after Condell and Sly came in (1605–1608), and one-fourteenth after Ostler was admitted (1612). In 1609 the company began acting in the winter months at their own house in the city. A similar syndicate of housekeepers was formed at the Blackfriars, Shakespeare's share fluctuating between one-sixth and one-seventh. He long remained a shareholder, perhaps to the end, though the shares are not mentioned in his will; whether he had sold out is unknown.[38]

The best index to Shakespeare's prosperity is the fact that he had money to invest. On May 1, 1602 he purchased for £320 one hundred and seven arable acres chiefly in the fields of Old Stratford outside the borough. The conveyance was delivered to Gilbert Shakespeare, doubtless because of his brother's absence in London. On September 28 the poet also bought a cottage and garden across the lane from New Place, perhaps for his gardener. He was the head of the family now; John Shakespeare died in September, 1601.

To return to the Globe. The Jonson Folio of 1616 gives the names of the actors in his plays, though unfortunately not their rôles. Shakespeare played in *Every Man in his Humor* (1598) and in *Sejanus* (1603). Since he is not listed for Jonson's subsequent plays, he may have given up acting by 1606, when *Volpone* was produced by his company, though he is not listed for *Every Man Out of His Humor* in 1599. We have no information about the company's rehearsals. Someone directed new productions; no doubt it was often the author, but that all the playwrights were qualified is very unlikely. There must have been a permanent director of some sort, and it is just possible that the exacting duties of this key position were responsible for Shakespeare's withdrawal from the acting of important rôles — if, indeed, he did withdraw. This is the merest guess, but no one could have been better equipped. Since the Jonsonian casts give only the names of the principal players, Shakespeare may have continued to walk on in minor rôles, as was the custom of many a veteran actor and stage manager in our stock companies a generation ago. At any rate, it is hard to believe that the last third of his career in London was spent outside the theatre.

Rowe records a pleasant tradition that the friendship of the age's foremost writers

began with a remarkable piece of Humanity and good Nature; Mr. *Johnson*, who was at that Time altogether unknown to the World, had offer'd one of his Plays to the Players . . . and the Persons into whose Hands it was put, after having turn'd it carelessly and superciliously over, were just upon returning it to him with an ill-natured Answer . . . when *Shakespear* luckily cast his Eye upon it, and found something so well in it as to engage him first to read it through, and afterwards to recommend Mr. *Johnson* and his Writings to the Publick.

"Many," says Thomas Fuller,[39]

were the *wit-combates* betwixt him and *Ben Johnson*, which two I behold like a *Spanish great Gallion*, and an *English man of War;* Master *Johnson* (like the former) was built far higher in Learning; *Solid*, but *Slow* in his performances. *Shake-spear* with the *English-man of War*, lesser in *bulk*, but lighter in *sailing*, could turn with all tides, tack about and take advantage of all winds, by the quickness of his Wit and Invention.

This is sufficiently apt, though it has more the air of fancy than of tradition. In the winter of 1618–19 Jonson visited the Scottish poet, William Drummond of Hawthornden, who put future generations in his debt by keeping notes of their conversations: "his Censure of the English Poets was this . . . That Shaksperr wanted Arte. . . . Sheakspear jn a play [*The Winter's Tale*] brought jn a number of men saying they had suffered Shipwrack jn Bohemia, wher y^r [i.e., there] is no Sea neer by some 100 Miles." In the Prologue [40] to *Every Man in his Humor* Jonson gibes at several of Shakespeare's successes:

Though neede make many *Poets*, and some such
As art, and nature haue not betterd much;
Yet ours, for want, hath not so lou'd the stage,
As he dare serue th'ill customes of the age:
Or purchase your delight at such a rate,
As, for it, he himselfe must iustly hate.
To make a child, now swadled, to proceede
Man, and then shoote vp, in one beard, and weede,
Past threescore yeeres: or, with three rustie swords,
And helpe of some few foot-and-halfe-foote words,
Fight ouer *Yorke*, and *Lancasters* long iarres :[41]
And in the tyring-house bring wounds, to scarres.
He rather prayes, you will be pleas'd to see
One such, to day, as other playes should be.
Where neither *Chorus* wafts you ore the seas ;[42]
Nor creaking throne comes downe, the boyes to please . . .[43]
But deedes, and language, such as men doe vse. . . .

In his "Ode to Himselfe" Jonson calls *Pericles* a "mouldy tale"; and in the Induction to *Bartholomew Fayre* he jeeringly lumps *Titus Andronicus* with the old-fashioned melodrama of *The Spanish Tragedie*, laughs at bringing on "a *Seruant-monster*," and declares he "is loth to make Nature afraid in his *Playes*, like those that beget *Tales*, *Tempests*, and such like *Drolleries*." Far more important than such rough-and-tumble theatrical allusions is Jonson's note in his *Timber: or, Discoveries:*

I remember, the Players have often mentioned it as an honour to *Shakespeare*, that in his writing, (whatsoever he penn'd) hee never blotted out line. My answer hath beene, would he had blotted a thousand. Which they thought a malevolent speech. I had not told posterity this, but for their ignorance, who choose that circumstance to commend their friend by, wherein he most faulted. And to justifie mine owne candor, (for I lov'd the man, and doe honour his memory (on this side Idolatry) as much as any.) Hee was (indeed) honest, and of an open, and free nature: had an excellent *Phantsie* [i.e., imagination]; brave [fine] notions, and gentle expressions: wherein hee flow'd with that facility, that sometime it was necessary he should be stop'd: *Sufflaminandus erat;* as *Augustus* said of *Haterius*. His wit was in his owne power; would the rule of it had beene so too. Many times hee fell into those things, could not escape laughter:

As when hee said in the person of *Cæsar*, one speaking to him; *Cæsar thou dost me wrong*. Hee replyed: *Cæsar did never wrong, but with just cause:* and such like; which were ridiculous. But hee redeemed his vices, with his vertues. There was ever more in him to be praysed, then to be pardoned.

This single passage is enough to dispose of the notion that Shakespeare's greatness went unrecognized. Evidently he was idolized; but different as the two geniuses were in temperament, and bored or cut as Jonson must often have been when, struggling gamely against sickness, poverty, and old age, he had to listen politely while Shakespeare was posthumously extolled, his is no grudging praise. That Shakespeare helped him to his first success is incapable of proof; but for a good many years, while Jonson was being produced by the Chamberlain's Men at the Curtain and the Globe, they must have been closely associated.

There is every reason to suppose that this company of actors professed their art together in loyal harmony. The tone of Heminge and Condell, in the preliminaries of the First Folio, where they invent the familiar "our Shakespeare," is one of admiration and affection. The opening of the Globe gave them a still longer lead over the Admiral's Men, their chief rivals; and in 1600 Henslowe [44] responded by building the Fortune, north of what was then the west end of the city, outside Cripplegate, in the parish of St. Giles. The contract with the carpenter, the same who built the Globe, has survived at Dulwich College, among the papers of its founder, Edward Alleyn. Though the new house was square (its sides measured eighty feet each), the contract is full of stipulations for duplicating details of the Globe. It does not help us much in reconstructing the Fortune. There the Admiral's Men played throughout the rest of Shakespeare's lifetime. On the accession of James they became Prince Henry's Men; and after the death of that promising boy in 1612, their patron was the King's son-in-law, the Elector Palatine.

About the time Henslowe built the Fortune, the children's companies, once very popular but of late less active, flared up again; and the boys of St. Paul's, and the Children of the

Chapel Royal (who had leased the Blackfriars), gave the adult companies a hard run for their money. Trained singers, the boys could lard their performances with more music than the Globe or Fortune commanded. Some of the best dramatists wrote for them. The Chamberlain's Men also had competition almost on their doorstep when, probably in 1602, a new company began acting at the Rose. This was the reorganized Worcester's, augmented from Oxford's Men, and adorned by Will Kempe. Christopher Beeston and the famous John Lowin were also members. The latter transferred to Shakespeare's company in 1603. Thomas Heywood was principal writer for Worcester's. Under King James, this company became the Queen's players and eventually moved from the Rose to the Red Bull, a larger theatre erected about 1605 northwest of the city in Clerkenwell. Meanwhile they seem to have acted at the Curtain. Thus toward the end of the decade of 1594–1603 there were three adult companies and two of children bidding for public favor.

There was, however, only one Shakespeare. He lived his own life, pursued his own thoughts, and stuck to his wonderful last. For his industry there is eloquent testimony in the sheer bulk of his writings, but of his private concerns almost nothing has survived. On March 13, 1602 John Manningham sets down an unsavory anecdote in his diary, apparently on the authority of Edward Curle, a fellow student at the Middle Temple.

Vpon a tyme when Burbidge played Rich. 3, there was a citizen greue soe farr in liking with him, that before shee went from the play shee appointed him to come that night vnto hir by the name of Ri: the 3. Shakespeare overhearing their conclusion went before, was intertained, and at his game ere Burbidge came. Then message being brought that Rich. the 3ᵈ. was at the dore, Shakespeare caused returne to be made that William the Conquerour was before Rich. the 3.

This story has every appearance of the sort of smart gossip that is always being fabricated about persons much in the public eye. There is no means of proving either its truth or its falsity.

One more allusion claims our attention before we turn to Shakespeare's life under the new reign. It pertains to that lively episode, the War of the Theatres. Over a period of several years, beginning about 1599, Jonson's plays contained attacks on Dekker and Marston, who retaliated in kind. In 1601 Ben's *Poetaster* brought his adversaries to the bar of aesthetic justice, where for Marston he prescribes an emetic which relieves that satirical innovator of the long, outlandish words he has ventured to swallow in the course of stylistic experiments. Jonson told Drummond he "beate Marston and took his pistoll from him." They were at least temporarily reconciled by 1604. In this *poetomachia*, as Dekker calls it, Shakespeare may have been involved. How or why no one knows, though Jonson, who was now produced by the children, had indulged in witticisms at the expense of the adult actors. In *Part 2* of the anonymous *The Retvrne from Pernassvs* (*c.* 1601–1602) Will Kempe appears as a character and observes (IV, [iii]):

Few of the vniuersity pen plaies well, they smell too much of that writer. *Ouid*, and that writer *Metamorphosis*, and talke too much of *Proserpina* & *Iuppiter*. Why heres our fellow *Shakespeare* puts them all downe, I [ay] and *Ben Ionson* too. O that *Ben Ionson* is a pestilent fellow, he brought vp *Horace* giuing the Poets a pill, but our fellow *Shakespeare* hath giuen him a purge that made him beray his credit.

What that purge was remains a mystery. Ajax in *Troilus and Cressida*, Corporal Nym in *Henry the Fifth* and *The Merry Wives*, and Jaques in *As You Like It* have all been proposed, with little cogency. Chambers plausibly suggests Dekker's *Satiromastix* (1601), which is not without cathartic properties. It was acted by Shakespeare's company; possibly the student author of *The Retvrne* thought he had written it.

Of politics Shakespeare seems to have steered clear. In "The Lost Leader" Browning claims this court as well as public dramatist for the Liberals, but at least by implication Shakespeare repeatedly endorses the strong-monarchy policy of the Tudors and Stuarts. He stands firm for order and gradation. He was pretty clearly a Little Englander, proud of the

tight little island and as dubious as the Queen herself about
the incipient imperialism of the English voyagers. If he had
any Whiggish misgivings under the first Stuart, he failed to
express them in his works. On the other hand, he was not
blinded by the dazzle of ceremony, which still impresses the
English so powerfully that governments spend huge sums on
its stabilizing effects. Shakespeare always saw the man in
the monarch. There is nothing mystical in his conception of
leadership, and attempts by certain German writers to dress
him up in the bloodstained shirt of Fascism are utterly unconvincing. Since we are dealing with the greatest of artists,
more especially with a writer remarkable for powers of observation, largeness of heart, and an imagination that seems to
have functioned comprehensively, sympathetically, and at the
same time with professional objectivity, a writer moreover
to whom a thoroughly dramatic mode of expression seems
to be so native that it is not shattered but only intensified
by the pressure of a lyric impulse as forceful as any purely
lyric poet was ever endowed with, anyone who is naive or
unscrupulous enough to select materials for a pattern of half-
truths can find in Shakespeare enough to prove almost anything he pleases. He can also, if he will, find as much to
prove the opposite.

Attempts have been made to align Shakespeare with the
partisans of Robert Devereux, second Earl of Essex, whose
foolish rebellion on February 8, 1601 brought him to the
block. The compliment to this peer, as the Queen's general,
in a Chorus of *Henry the Fifth* two years earlier, has no political significance. An affiliation between him and Shakespeare is inferred by some from the friendship of both men
for the Earl of Southampton; but though Southampton had
evidently been gracious to the poet in and about 1593, and
though he was implicated in the Essex conspiracy, his treason
proves nothing about Shakespeare's opinions in 1601. The
Queen spared Southampton's life, but kept him in the Tower.
For the notion that the tragic intensity of Shakespeare's
greatest plays was engendered by his disapproval of the execution of Essex there is not a shred of evidence. If he felt strongly

on the subject, the chances are he thought England safer with the Earl out of the way. It is true that his company was hired by some of the conspirators to act *Richard the Second*, with its deposition of an English monarch, as a curtain raiser to the revolt. The players were evidently innocent tools; and, though they were called on the carpet for it, their performance did them no harm. Concerning it Augustine Phillips was examined on February 18. On the 25th Essex lost his head, but the Chamberlain's Men were playing at Whitehall on the 24th. They appeared before the Queen as usual during the next Christmas season. Hunsdon was her cousin; she liked his troupe of players.

She died on March 24, 1603, leaving in one of them, though she did not know it, her reign's most precious legacy. What his emotions were as the old epoch closed and the new began he does not tell us. Faction was rife, and the politico-religious struggle which was to strike off the head of his new patron's son was already bitter. If the sixteenth century was the prologue to the modern world, the seventeenth was Act I. The advance of science was already under way. Shakespeare seems to have given no heed to it. His business was not analyzing a cosmos but making one. And the great Queen died and was buried without one elegiac line from his facile pen.

THE LAUREL BOUGH: 1603–1611

James was even fonder of plays than Elizabeth; at any rate it cost this royal Scot fewer pangs to see money spent on them. By 1616 the Burbage troupe had acted at the Stuart court upwards of 175 times, much more frequently than all the other companies put together. In the winter of 1603–1604 they gave nine performances for royalty,[45] and in the fall and winter of 1604–1605 eleven. A much discussed manuscript in the accounts of the Revels Office [46] lists, among others, the following plays during the second of these seasons: "The Moor of Venis," "the Merry wiues of winsor," "Mesur for Mesur," "The plaie of Errors," "Loues Labours Lost," "Henry the fift," and "The Martchant of Venis" (twice).

This document has been attacked as a forgery, but most scholars now regard it as probably genuine.[47]

In addition to professional performances, the court delighted in amateur theatricals, especially in the form of masques, on a long series of which Ben Jonson collaborated with the eminent architect Inigo Jones. They were semidramatic entertainments of dialogue, pageantry, music, and dancing. As far as we know, Shakespeare supplied none of these; but he occasionally yields to the vogue and introduces masquelike passages in his plays.[48]

Soon after the accession of James, the London companies passed under royal patronage. The Chamberlain's Men became the King's; the Admiral's, Prince Henry's; Worcester's, the Queen's. On May 19, 1603 a royal license was issued to

aucthorize theise our Servauntes lawrence ffletcher William Shake-speare Richard Burbage Augustyne Phillippes Iohn heninges henrie Condell William Sly Robert Armyn Richard Cowly and the rest of theire Assosiates freely to vse and exercise the Arte and faculty of playinge Comedies Tragedies histories Enterludes moralls pastoralls Stageplaies and Suche others like as theie haue alreadie studied or hereafter shall vse or studie aswell for the recreation of our lovinge Subjectes as for our Solace and pleasure when wee shall thincke good to see them duringe our pleasure.

With one exception, these players were the surviving members, still active and in good standing, of the Lord Chamberlain's company. Fletcher's relations with them are uncertain. The general assumption that his was a purely honorary appointment to the newly licensed King's Men is very likely correct; for his name does not appear in the Folio of 1623, which gives a list of the twenty-six "Principall Actors in all these Playes," and there is no evidence that he ever took any rôle at the Globe or Blackfriars. Yet the possibility remains that he served the company in some other capacity, or that favoritism impelled the King to stipulate a share in the profits for him. He had already performed before James in Scotland.

Besides the members, who held the patent licensing them

and their associates to act, there was, in addition to their apprentices, a large group of nonsharing employees. These "hirelings" may have numbered a score or more. A few were primarily actors; but most of them were musicians, stage-hands, and "gatherers," that is, collectors of the admission and gallery fees. Doubtless anyone might be required to walk on as a supernumerary; and the musicians, at least, sometimes played bits. Other hirelings were the "tireman" or ward-robe master, and the "book-keeper" or prompter.

The nine names in the patent of 1603 are repeated about March 15, 1604 in a list of persons granted at the King's expense four and a half yards each of red cloth. This was for liveries; it was issued on the grand occasion of the coronation procession, which the severity of the plague had postponed. Apparently the actors were not among the marchers; but, like everyone who held a court post however humble, they were given means of appearing in festive array. From time to time thereafter His Majesty's players drew similar allotments of bastard scarlet and crimson velvet; for they now had the status of Grooms of the Chamber, under the authority of the lord chamberlain. This post was filled by Admiral Thomas Howard, first Earl of Suffolk (1603–14); the ill-fated Robert Carr, Earl of Somerset (1614–15); and William Herbert, third Earl of Pembroke, patron of letters and friend of Shakespeare and Jonson (1615–26). As Grooms the duties of Shakespeare and his fellows were ordinarily nominal. But in August, 1604, they were in attendance for eighteen days on the Span-ish Ambassador. He had come on a treaty-making mission and was magnificently lodged by the King at Somerset House. Presumably the royal players were idle and, a number of them at least, in London that summer. For this special assignment the accounts of the treasurer of the Chamber record fees to twelve of His Majesty's "Groomes of the chamber, and Play-ers," though only Phillips and Heminge, who received the payment, are named. Whether Fletcher was among the "tenne of theire ffellowes" is unrecorded. If he was, and if "fellows" means "fellow members," and if none but sharers had been pressed into service, the number of members constituting the licensed company had by this time been raised from nine to twelve. Whether Shakespeare was on hand that summer is unknown, though likely enough. Probably, as Law suggests, "the main function" of the Grooms was "to stand about and try to look pleasant."

Attempts to establish the chronology of membership are necessarily more or less conjectural. Professor Baldwin, our leading authority, observes that while livery lists "at times name others than members, they also fail at times to include all members." Obviously, however, three of Shakespeare's old associates in the Chamberlain's Company are quite accountably missing from the patent of 1603 and the livery list of March, 1604. Bryan had dropped out, probably by 1598; so had Kempe, probably in 1599. Pope had doubtless resigned; he died soon after the company became the King's Men, perhaps in the summer of 1603. Kempe's place was more than filled by Armin. The change is immediately reflected in Shakespeare's plays. Beginning with *As You Like It*, the Fool's rôle becomes less clownish, till it culminates in the matchless jester of King Lear. Cowley was another replacement, before the company increased its membership; he had come in as a sharer not later than 1601. Who the third was is doubtful.

As for the three new sharers, who seem to be indicated by the payment to twelve Grooms in the summer of 1604, two of them were presumably John Lowin and Alexander Cooke. Lowin created a number of important Shakespearean rôles, for he became the company's second actor. He and Cooke are listed with Burbage, Shakespeare, Phillips, Sly, Heminge, and Condell as the leading players in Jonson's *Sejanus* in 1603.[49] On the other hand, either Lowin or Fletcher may have entered to take the place of Pope, and not as a result of the company's expansion from nine to twelve. Membership seems to have stood at twelve throughout the rest of Shakespeare's connection with it, and indeed long after. Among his fellows was Nicholas Tooley, who was a sharer by 1605, when Phillips died. The latter's will is precise in distinguishing the members from the remainder of the staff at the Globe.

Apprentices are mentioned, and also "the hyred men of the Cnmpany which I am of"; and Phillips repeatedly prefixes the names of other legatees with the words "my Fellowe." Among the recipients is Shakespeare. Fletcher is also mentioned, on even terms with such pillars of the company as Armin and Cowley.[50]

Beginning in 1609, the troupe played during the winter months at the Blackfriars. The boy actors there had hanged themselves with a saucy series of topical hits, some of which had not spared the King himself. A new syndicate of housekeepers was now organized, and Shakespeare henceforth shared in the profits of this theatre as well as in the Globe's. The Blackfriars came gradually to be the King's Men's headquarters. Performances there were fashionably attended. Their success continued long after Shakespeare's connection with the company had ceased; and when the Puritans suspended all the houses at the outbreak of the fighting in 1642, the leading London theatre was still the Blackfriars. There are many allusions to it under the Restoration, when it was regarded as the standard pre-Wars establishment.

For several years before the company began at the Blackfriars the plague often interrupted public acting, and the King's Men occasionally took to the road. There is no evidence for Shakespeare's presence or absence on any of these jaunts. There are, however, further indications about this time of his interests in Stratford and, curiously enough, records of his activity as a matchmaker in London. Professor Wallace discovered a deposition by him in a suit brought in 1612 by Stephen Belott against his father-in-law, Christopher Mountjoy, a French Huguenot who lived at the northeast corner of Silver and Monkwell streets in St. Olave's parish, Cripplegate ward, near the northwest corner of the city wall. Mountjoy was a tire-maker, that is, a manufacturer of women's headdresses. Jonson refers to the locality in *Epicoene, or The silent Woman* (IV, ii): "All her teeth were made i' the Blacke-*Friers:* both her eye-browes i' the *Strand*, and her haire in *Siluer-Street*." Originally apprenticed to Mountjoy, Belott had married his employer's daughter Mary in 1604, had set up his own shop, and now charged failure to execute a promised financial settlement. A former servant of Mountjoy's deposed that "the def[endan]t did send and perswade one Mr Shakespeare that laye in the house to perswade the pl[ain]t[iff] to the same Marriadge." Another witness alleged that "he herd one W^m: Shakespeare saye that the def[endan]t . . . did move the pl[ain]t[iff] by him the said Shakespeare" to marry Mary "And for that purpose sent him the said Sh[akespeare] to the pl[ain]t[iff] to perswade the pl[ain]t[iff] to the same . . . wch was effected and Solempnized vppon promise of a porcion wth her." Witness added that Belott bade him inquire of Shakespeare what settlement Mountjoy would make. "And askinge Shakespeare th^rof, he Answered that he [Mountjoy] promised . . . about the some of ffyftye pound in money and Certayne Houshould stuffe."

On May 11, 1612 was examined "William Shakespeare of Stratford vpon Aven . . . gen[tleman] of the Age of xlviij yeres or thereabout." He acknowledged having known Mountjoy and Belott for some ten years, gave the plaintiff a good character for industry and honesty, and testified that at the request of Mountjoy's wife he had helped persuade Belott to the marriage. But on the crucial point of the financial terms either his memory failed him or he was loth to commit himself. A subsequent deposition repeats the allegation that Shakespeare had mentioned a portion, and adds that the couple were betrothed by him. For want of explicit corroboration by Shakespeare the court was evidently unsatisfied; the case was referred to the overseers and elders of the Huguenot church in London, who found for Belott.

Evidently, then, Shakespeare was lodging with the Mountjoys in 1604; but how long he lived in Silver Street is unknown. According to Aubrey, he was once a resident of Shoreditch; and we have seen that for a while he lived on the Bankside, and before that in the parish of St. Helen's, Bishopsgate. Since he is described in 1612 as a Stratfordian, he was doubtless then without a London address.[51]

As for the Stratford connections, ours was probably the Shakespeare who about 1604 takes, in the local court of record,

legal action for small debts against Phillip Rogers, a Stratford apothecary, and in 1608–1609 against one John Adden-
brooke and Thomas Horneby, his surety. Horneby was a
Henley Street blacksmith. In 1605 Shakespeare purchased for
£440 a half interest, valued in 1611[52] at £60 a year, in the
lease of those tithes of the parish of Stratford which, confiscated at the dissolution of the religious houses, had been
granted to the Corporation in the royal charter of 1553.

According to Aubrey, he "was wont to goe to his native
Country once a yeare." Elsewhere Aubrey adds that on these
journeys he commonly stopped in Oxford at the Crown,
"where he was exceedingly respected." This establishment
was, however, a tavern, not an inn; and it was not called
the Crown till after Shakespeare's time. It stood next door to
an inn, the Cross. The tavern was kept by the father of
Sir William D'avenant, who, according to an old but un-
verifiable tradition, was Shakespeare's godson.

His father was John Davenant a vintner there, a very grave and
discreet Citizen: his mother was a very beautifull woman, & of a
very good witt and of conversation extremely agreable. . . . Now
Sr. W^m would sometimes when he was pleasant over a glasse of wine
with his most intimate friends e.g. Sam: Butler (author of Hudibras)
&c. say, that it seemed to him that he writt with the very spirit
that Shakespeare, and was ["seemed" interlined] contentended
enough to be thought his Son.

In his *Athenae Oxonienses* (1692) Anthony à Wood tells the
story more discreetly; his version may rest on his own investigations, but its phraseology at several points resembles Aubrey's. Wood asserts that of Mrs. Davenant's children only
William had her "wit and conversation." Thomas Hearne,
another Oxford antiquarian, gives the yarn the final touch in
1709:

ye said M^r. Shakespear was his [Sir William's] God-father & gave
him his name. (In all probability he got him.) 'Tis further said that
one day going from school a grave Doctor in Divinity met him, and
ask'd him, *Child whither art thou going in such hast?* to wch the child

reply'd, O Sir *my God-father is come to Town, & I am going to ask his blessing*. To wch the Dr. said, *Hold Child, you must not take the name of God in vaine*.[53]

It is certainly possible that truth was vouchsafed traditionally to these diligent Oxonians. But the successive stages in which the story seems to have been built up recommend it as little as the poetical attainments of Jonson's successor in the laureateship encourage the theory that he inherited them from Shakespeare. And there is some evidence that the marriage of the Davenants was a happy one.

On June 5, 1607 Shakespeare's daughter Susanna married the Stratford physician John Hall. He was an able and intellectual person, much in demand throughout the county. The poet's brother Edmund, the actor, died at the end of the same year and was buried on the Bankside. Elizabeth Hall, Shakespeare's first grandchild, was baptized on February 21, 1608. His mother died that September. During these and the years immediately after, the bonds with Stratford doubtless tightened, while those with London began relaxing. Thomas Greene, a kinsman of some sort, had been living at New Place. He was a lawyer and town clerk of Stratford. Whether he leased the house or merely lodged there is uncertain. On September 9, 1609 a memorandum shows he expected to stay there one more year. He bought a house about May, 1611. Precisely when Shakespeare retired to New Place is unknown. The abdication may have been gradual. Unless illness drove him from the theatre earlier in 1610–11, the end of that season may have witnessed his departure from the London scene. There is, however, no real evidence. Meanwhile, in 1609, the Sonnets had been published.

These are the biographical facts (and the gossip that became tradition) about Shakespeare while he was still active as a King's Man. The really important facts of this period have yet to be mentioned. They include three of his greatest plays and at least two others that differ from them only as one star differs from another star in glory. Probably in 1604 were composed the last of the realistic comedies and the second of the greatest tragedies; both *Measure for Measure* and

Othello were acted at court in that year.[54] Whether *King Lear* or *Macbeth* (1605–1606) was the next tragedy is uncertain. The superb pageant of *Antony and Cleopatra* (*c.* 1606–1607) came next, and the attraction of Roman history for Shakespeare is further exemplified by *Coriolanus* (*c.* 1608). *Timon of Athens* (*c.* 1605–1608) was evidently never completed. There is a falling off in these plays of 1608 or thereabouts, as if in the work of the great tragic period ending with *Antony and Cleopatra* the author had said his say in that genre.[55] His next work was to assume a new form, the dramatic romance. It has long been held that in it he followed the fashion set by Francis Beaumont and John Fletcher, who began writing for the King's Men about 1608–1609. Their *Philaster* is at once lyrical, melodramatic, and comic. In this and other plays of the species the austere mood of tragedy is not present. There is violence; there may be deaths; but the plots end happily with reconciliations and often amid the chime of wedding bells. Shakespeare's contributions to the new genre are not, however, marked by a sharp break with his past. At one point or another all his romantic comedies skirt the brink of violent disaster.

Unfortunately neither *Philaster* (*c.* 1608–10) nor *Pericles* (*c.* 1607–1608) and *Cymbeline* (*c.* 1609–10) can be precisely dated. *Pericles* was an immediate hit; the reception of *Cymbeline* is unrecorded. Far too much has been made of the notion that Shakespeare lacked original force, that he habitually trimmed his sails in the wake of bolder venturers. The new fashion of playwriting may have been set by him, or the two famous collaborators may have set it, or it may have been an inevitable turn of the drama in a search for novelty after Shakespeare had carried tragedy to a peak that no one, not even he, could hope to top. *Hamlet, Othello, King Lear*, and *Macbeth* are not, like the tragedies of Sophocles, resigned. They are not Christian. They are not meek. They are not full of hope, despite their vindication of the noble fortitude of which the human spirit is capable. Perhaps toward the end Shakespeare mellowed a little in his estimate of what life amounts to. But speculation is useless, since the decisive factor may have been, not a simple desire to emulate or to show the way to brilliant new writers, but some episode of which we know nothing. Love, illness and recovery, bereavement, or some great joy — any of these may have been the vital cause of the new and serene mood, if not of the new form. These suggestions by no means exhaust the possibilities. Court influence, now stronger than ever, favored the elegant and light above the weighty and profound. The change was already under way that was to make Restoration drama less national and popular, and more the reflection of coterie tastes. Tragicomedy was much admired by the Jacobeans; it was pleasanter and easier on the mind than the great tragedies. As Mr. Bonamy Dobrée complains, the result in Beaumont and Fletcher is

a prettification of the drama; even tragedy . . . was prettified; the sentiments are 'literary' in the bad sense of the word, 'poetic' in the same bad sense, 'poetry' being added as a 'beauty,' instead of being the life-blood of the whole thing.[56]

There is also a relaxation of moral integrity in the new drama. Shakespeare is full of ribaldry of a coarse, hearty, Rabelaisian kind. The New Obscenity was the sly, self-conscious sort which, essentially less moral than mere coarseness of phraseology, is on our own stage more successful in getting by the censor.

Shakespeare alone avoided these weaknesses in his best dramatic romances. They are more than "pretty." Either just before or just after his retirement he wrote *The Winter's Tale* and *The Tempest* (c. 1611), and the latter is in its own way quite as wonderful a performance as any that went before it.

> We are such stuff
> As dreams are made on, and our little life
> Is rounded with a sleep.

On that quiet chord in minor, Shakespeare played himself off the stage he had graced above all its servants.

THE GRAVE AND THE BOOK

Of his life there is little more to tell. The great work was finished, the enchanting staff of Prospero broken.

> These our actors,
> As I foretold you, were all spirits and
> Are melted into air, into thin air;
> And, like the baseless fabric of this vision,
> The cloud-capp'd towers, the gorgeous palaces,
> The solemn temples, the great globe itself,
> Yea, all which it inherit, shall dissolve,
> And, like this insubstantial pageant faded,
> Leave not a rack behind.

One would like to know what Shakespeare's reflections were, as in retrospect he surveyed the world of shadows he had created. Evidently the world of phenomena did not seem to him a whit more stable. There was no reason for writing these lines unless he meant them; no necessary question of the play is handled in them. This is the mood of the lyric poet, of the idealist profoundly sceptical of the reality of the physical universe but without illusions concerning the indestructibility of personality. "Our little life is rounded with a sleep."

Two more plays were still to be made, but now he collaborates with the star that rose as his own began setting, John Fletcher, who took his place as chief writer for the King's Men. Another dramatic romance, *The Two Noble Kinsmen*, and the last history, *King Henry the Eighth*, were probably finished in 1613. Whether Shakespeare maintained any other connection with his company is unknown. It was much in demand at court in the winter of 1612–13. The country was shocked on November 6 by the untimely death of the young Prince of Wales, Henry, hope of England and flower of the house of Stuart; but on December 27 his sister, the beautiful Princess Elizabeth, was betrothed to Frederick, Elector Palatine and future king of Bohemia. They were married on February 14, and left the capital on April 10. The King's players were prominent in the long program of festivities. They acted twenty times, and among their offerings were *Much Ado*, *The Tempest*, *The Winter's Tale*, and "*The Moore of Venice.*" Presumably a "Caesars Tragedye" is *Julius Cæsar*. A "Benedicte and Betteris" is doubtless *Much Ado* again; the accounts of payments to Heminge also list twice a Beaumont and Fletcher play, once as "Filaster" and again under its subtitle, "Love lyes a bleedinge." "Sir John Falstaffe" may be any of the three plays in which he appears; "The Hotspur" is presumably *Henry the Fourth, Part 1*. Neither of the two new plays by Shakespeare and Fletcher appears in these lists. *Henry the Eighth* was acted at the Globe on June 29, 1613. During the performance the theatre was destroyed by fire,[57] greatly to the edification of the Puritans. It was rebuilt in even more splendid style and reopened early in the following summer. If Shakespeare was still a shareholder he had to pay a heavy assessment for the reconstruction, which included replacing the inflammable thatched roof with tiles. Whether he had felt a renewed urge to compose and was glad to lean on Fletcher, or whether Beaumont's retirement about 1612–13 left the more volatile Fletcher in need of a steadier hand, is impossible to say. It may be that Shakespeare spent in London the winter of 1612–13 and the following spring, perhaps through June. John Downes, for half a century prompter of Betterton's company, writes in his *Roscius Anglicanus* (1708) that John Lowin was instructed in the title rôle of *Henry the Eighth* by Shakespeare himself. This fact, if it be a fact, Downes would have learned (perhaps through Betterton) from D'avenant, who had seen Lowin's later performances and coached Betterton in the part.

Illness has by some been held responsible for Shakespeare's retirement; his putative inability to remember, when examined in 1612, the details of the alleged promise of Mountjoy has been thought to show that he was failing. Nothing else suggests this, and he may have been reluctant to take sides at the trial. He was apparently in London on March 31, 1613, when the steward of Francis Manners, sixth Earl of Rutland, records a payment to "M[r] Shakspeare . . . about my Lorde's impreso" and to "Richard Burbage for paynting and making yt." An *impresa* was a painted paper shield; this one was for display at a tilt on March 24, the anniversary of King James's accession. *Imprese* were symbolic and bore mottoes; evidently Shakespeare and Burbage collaborated on Rutland's. On the tenth of the same month Shakespeare bought for £140 and immediately mortgaged to the seller for £60 a "dwelling house or Tenement" in Blackfriars "abutting vpon a streete leading downe to Pudle wharffe . . . part of which . . . is erected over a great gate." Oddly enough, as Chambers has shown, this house had been a center of Catholic intrigue. Richard Davies, in his additions to Fulman's note on Shakespeare's death,[58] adds that he "dyed a papist." The evidence on this point is not sufficient to warrant any conclusion.

That Shakespeare was in London again on November 16, 1614 is evident from a memorandum the next day by Thomas Greene about a projected enclosure near Stratford. Such attempts of landowners to fence or ditch off open land in areas tilled by villagers in common or used communally for grazing caused bitter controversy.

my Cosen Shakespeare comyng yesterday to towne I went to see him howe he did he told me that they assured him they ment to inclose noe further then to [certain landmarks].

The surviving documents fail to indicate Shakespeare's attitude toward this burning economic question.[59]

Rowe declares:

The latter Part of his Life was spent, as all Men of good Sense will wish theirs may be, in Ease, Retirement, and the Conversation of his Friends. He had the good Fortune to gather an Estate equal to his Occasion, and, in that, to his Wish; and is said to have spent some Years before his Death at his native *Stratford*. His pleasurable Wit, and good Nature, engag'd him in the Acquaintance, and entitled him to the Friendship of the Gentlemen of the Neighbourhood.

Unlike his father, he played no part in the affairs of the Corporation. He was on friendly terms with the burghers and local gentry, especially with the Combes. John Combe, a

wealthy moneylender, died in July, 1614, leaving Shakespeare five pounds. Tradition twenty years later has the poet
perpetrating a satirical epitaph on his usurer friend some time
before the latter's death. There was hospitality at Shakespeare's house; the records of the Corporation note payment
for a quart of sack and another of claret for "a precher at the
newe place."

A few domestic episodes are recorded. On February 3, 1612
Gilbert Shakespeare, presumably the poet's brother, was
buried at Stratford; and on February 4, 1613 his last surviving
brother, Richard, was also buried there. In July, 1613 his
daughter Susanna Hall brought an action for slander in the
consistory court at Worcester, charging that John Lane, Jr.
of Stratford had said she had "the runninge of the raynes"
and had been indiscreet with Ralph Smith, a Stratford hatter.
Her character was vindicated by this ecclesiastical court; it
excommunicated the defendant, who had failed to appear.
On February 10, 1616, in her thirty-second year, Judith Shakespeare married Thomas Quiney, a Stratford vintner, that is,
a tavern keeper; he was four years her junior. The wedding
was celebrated during one of the prohibited seasons, another
of which in 1582 was a cause of her parents' hasty marriage.
Judith and her husband were at least threatened with excom-
munication by the consistory court, whether before or after
William Shakespeare's death is uncertain. The poet's brother-
in-law William Hart was buried on April 17, 1616.

It is likely that Shakespeare knew he had not long to live
when on March 25, 1616 he signed his will, in a clerk's copy,
with interlineations and deletions. It was originally drafted
some weeks earlier, probably in January, and then copied,
Shakespeare's revisions being incorporated when he signed it.
The first of its three sheets seems to have been written last,
a consequence of changes too extensive for mere correction of
the original. Judith's marriage on February 10 was no doubt
the cause of these alterations. Had Shakespeare been in health
a fair copy of the whole will would presumably have been
made. He was perhaps unable to remember the name of one of
Jano Hart's three boys, his nephews. His signatures on each of

the three pages are somewhat shaky. They are not, however, examples of inferior penmanship. The popular impression that Shakespeare wrote a bad hand arises from unfamiliarity with Elizabethan documents. Most of Shakespeare's contemporaries habitually used the Old English or Secretary hand, which looks more like the present German script than like the Italian hand now universal in writing English.

Michael Drayton, author of the ode "To the Virginian Voyage," the "Ballad of Agincourt," and other famous poems, used to spend vacations near Stratford. John Ward, formerly a medical student, who was vicar of Stratford from 1662 to 1681, notes in his diary that "Shakespear Drayton and Ben Jhonson had a merry meeting and it seems drank too hard for Shakespear died of a feavour there contracted." Judith Quiney died the year Ward became vicar; he could have learned the facts directly enough. His account is not conclusive; it is long after the event. But it may give the gist of the matter.[60] We can not, however, suppose that Shakespeare was a sot. Against the possibility of that are his financial success, the quantity of his published work, most of it written during a crowded life as actor and theatrical proprietor, and Aubrey's statement on Beeston's authority that he was "the more to be admired" because "he was not a company keeper [and though he] lived in Shoreditch, wouldnt be debauched, & if invited to writ: he was in paine." [61] If Aubrey's phraseology also means that the whores of Shoreditch did not interest Shakespeare, we may accept a further vindication of his character. It is, however, too much to suppose that this sensitive poet, apparently long separated from a wife for whom it is improbable that he entertained a grand passion, had no love affairs in London. This is not to attach much importance to such gossip as got recorded, nor to read autobiography into the Sonnets; the question is one of general probability. Aubrey says he was "a handsome well shap't man: very good company, and of a very readie and pleasant smooth Witt." Shakespeare's convivial potentialities can hardly be doubted, but his tastes and habits are not recorded. It is a curious fact that none of his published works

contains a reference to tobacco. That he loved music is certain
from the way he writes about it. That he heartily disliked
affectation is also certain.

The will, preserved at Somerset House in London, opens
with conventional declarations concerning health, memory,
God, Christ, and immortality. It leaves £300 to Judith: £100
as a marriage portion, £50 in consideration of her willingness
to surrender certain rights to Susanna, and the interest on the
remaining £150 (without consideration) to her and her children. To his sister Joan Hart the poet leaves £20, all his
clothes, and a life interest in one of the houses (probably the
western) in Henley Street, at the nominal rent of a shilling
a year. To each of her three sons £5 is bequeathed. To his
granddaughter Elizabeth Hall he leaves all his plate, "except
my brod silver & gilt bole"; to the poor of Stratford £10;
to Thomas Combe, John's nephew, "my Sword"; to Thomas
Russell, £5; and to Francis Collins, the lawyer who drew
the will, £13 6s. 8d., no doubt covering the fee and expenses. Other bequests specify small sums of money to his
godson William Walker and to friends, some for the purchase
of mourning rings; among the latter items are 26s. 8d. each
to "my ffellowes John Hemynge Richard Burbage & Henry
Cundell." Shakespeare's interests in the Stratford tithes and
in the theatres are not mentioned. To Susanna are bequeathed
New Place, the two houses in Henley Street, the house in
Blackfriars, and "all other my landes ten[emen]tes and here-
ditam[en]tes whatsoever." These properties are to go after her
death to her eldest son, or in default of surviving male issue
to Elizabeth Hall, and, in the event of the latter's leaving no
male heir, to Judith Quiney and her male issue. Having recited these bequests Shakespeare leaves, in an interlined clause,
"vnto my wief my second best bed with the furniture," that
is, the curtains, mattress, and bedding. The bowl already
excepted goes to Judith. The residuary legatees are "my
Sonne in Lawe John Hall gent and my daughter Susanna his
wief," who are named executors, with Russell and Collins
as overseers.

Though badly drawn, the will is a businesslike document

and contains no expressions of affection. The entail of the bulk of the estate is evidence of the poet's desire, not to be fulfilled, of founding a family of landed gentry. The bequest to Judith provides for outright payment of the final £150 to her husband if he "assures" her in land to the same value.[62] It is likely that Shakespeare was not greatly pleased with the marriage, though this stipulation may mean nothing more than a cautious safeguarding of his younger daughter's future. As a matter of fact, Thomas Quiney did not turn out well. The much discussed second-best bed has no significance for us. To Anne Shakespeare it probably had; and, moved by sentiment, she doubtless asked to have it mentioned. Her future was secure. By common law she had a dower interest of one-third for life in the real estate (except the Blackfriars house, from which it had been excluded — why we do not know) and the right of residence at New Place. She may have had by local custom right to a third of the personal property. Specification of such rights in a will was not material and was often omitted. The document thus affords no basis for conjectures concerning Shakespeare's domestic happiness. A Stratford tradition recorded in 1693[63] maintains that no one "Dare Touch his Grave stone," guarded by the well-known curse,[64] "tho his wife and Daughters Did Earnestly Desire to be Layd in the same Graue wth. him." Nor, since books are not mentioned but would come under the residuary bequest, does the will enable us to estimate the size of Shakespeare's library. What eventually became of his books and papers is unknown.[65]

He died on April 23, 1616 and was buried two days later in the chancel of the Stratford church.

As we have seen, voices had occasionally been raised. As far as we can tell from printed books, Robert Greene's was the earliest, in 1592. Chettle's was the first to praise man and author. Meres's was the first to eulogize with any particularity. The first actual tribute in verse is Richard Barnfield's, also in 1598, which mentions Shakespeare's "hony-flowing Vaine"; but it is undistinguished verse. John Weever's in 1599, already cited, is better, but far from breath-taking. And there were other notes of praise, among them John Davies's and William Camden's and William Barksted's.[66]

Not till 1612 does a really great name appear among the applauders, most of whom merely mention Shakespeare as one of a number of excellent writers. John Webster, author of two superb Jacobean tragedies, *The White Divel* and *The Dvtchesse Of Malfy*, writes in an address to the reader of the first:

> Detraction is the sworne friend to ignorance: For mine owne part I haue euer truly cherisht my good opinion of other mens worthy Labours, especially of that full and haightned stile of Maister *Chapman:* The labor'd and vnderstanding workes of Maister *Johnson:* The no lesse worthy composures of the both worthily excellent Maister *Beamont* & Maister *Fletcher:* And lastly (without wrong last to be named) the right happy and copious industry of M. *Shakespeare,* M. *Decker,* & M. *Heywood,* wishing what I write may be read by their light: Protesting, that, in the strength of mine owne iudgement, I know them so worthy, that though I rest silent in my owne worke, yet to most of theirs I dare (without flattery) fix that of *Martiall. — non norunt, Hæc monumenta mori.*[67]

This is not the left-handed compliment it appears at first glance. In 1612 Fletcher was rising, while Chapman and Jonson were still going strong; but Heywood was immersed in the extravagances of his *Ages* plays, Dekker was petering out, and Shakespeare had presumably retired.

In *Runne, And a great Cast* (1614) Thomas Freeman writes an uninspired but not ungraceful sonnet "To Master W:Shakespeare":

> Vertues or vices theame to thee all one is . . .
> Besides in plaies thy wit windes like *Meander:*
> Whence needy new-composers borrow more
> Then *Terence* doth from *Plautus* or *Menander.*
> But to praise thee aright I want thy store:
> Then let thine owne works thine owne worth vpraise.

This is good and valiant praise.

The next important voice seems to be Francis Beaumont's,

in a poetic epistle (*c.* 1615) to Ben Jonson, which has survived in seventeenth-century manuscript anthologies of uncertain date. Though the following lines of this poem are not in public eulogy, they are interesting for Beaumont's opinion of Shakespeare's lasting worth:

> . . . heere I would let slippe
> (If I had any in mee) schollershippe,
> And from all Learninge keepe these lines as [cl]eere
> as Shakespeares best are, which our heires shall hear.

The allusion to lack of learning may reflect Jonson's freedom on this subject in private conversation; Beaumont, as one of the "sons of Ben," is probably alluding to sage remarks his master had let fall. Beaumont died on March 6, 1616 and was buried in Westminster Abbey. Seven weeks later Shakespeare died. The event evoked no chorus of praise. That does not begin till 1623.

Meanwhile a blunt commercial statement reveals Shakespeare as an exception to the general rule that after the obituary eulogies a writer's reputation languishes, often for many years, till his merits are rediscovered by some enterprising critic. Publishing the *Othello* quarto in 1622, Thomas Walkley in a note to the reader declines to praise the play "because the Authors name is sufficient to vent [sell] his worke."

One more of the scattered voices requires quotation. Sometime between Shakespeare's death and the appearance of the First Folio, William Basse wrote an elegy which has survived in several versions; it begins:

> Renowned Spencer, lye a thought more nye
> To learned Chaucer, and rare Beaumont lye
> A little neerer Spenser to make roome
> For Shakespeare in your threefold fowerfold Tombe.
> To lodge all fowre in one bed make a shift
> Vntill Doomesdaye, for hardly will a fift
> Betwixt this day and that by Fate be slayne
> For whom your Curtaines may be drawn againe.

It is to this poem that Jonson alludes in lines 19–21 of his magnificent tribute, to which we now come and with which this account of the life must end.

For no biography of Shakespeare can end with April 23, 1616. If the most important of the facts about Shakespeare is the existence of his dramatic works, his mortal life's story closes with the publication of the First Folio. By it his immortality was assured. That book, in which all his unaided plays were first collected and without which many of them would have perished, is by the suffrage of the English-speaking nations, leaving out of account the sacred writings of the great religions, the most precious book in our possession and the world's. Some of the quartos are textually valuable for the works which appeared in quarto, but the First Folio is invaluable. On it rests every subsequent edition of Shakespeare's plays.

When we consider how much poorer humanity would be without this volume, the names of John Heminge and Henry Condell take on new lustre. They introduce it in two epistles. The first is to a pair of noble brothers, William and Philip Herbert, Earls of Pembroke and Montgomery; the former was then lord chamberlain. It acknowledges their Lordships' favor, indulges in conventional depreciation of the work in hand, and continues:

But since your L.L. haue beene pleas'd to thinke these trifles something, heeretofore; and haue prosequuted both them, and their Authour liuing, with so much fauour: we hope, that (they outliuing him, and he not hauing the fate, common with some, to be exequutor to his owne writings) you will vse the like indulgence toward them, you haue done vnto their parent. There is a great difference, whether any Booke choose his Patrones, or finde them: This hath done both. For, so much were your L L. likings of the seuerall parts, when they were acted, as before they were published, the Volume ask'd to be yours. We haue but collected them, and done an office to the dead, to procure his Orphanes, Guardians; without ambition either of selfe-profit, or fame: onely to keepe the memory of so worthy a Friend, & Fellow aliue, as was our *Shakespeare*, by humble offer of his playes, to your most noble patronage . . . we most humbly consecrate to your H.H. these remaines of your seruant

Shakespeare; that what delight is in them, may be euer your L.L. the reputation his, & the faults ours, if any be committed, by a payre so carefull to shew their gratitude both to the liuing, and the dead, as is

> *Your Lordshippes most bounden,*
> Iohn Heminge.
> Henry Condell.

The second epistle is "To the great Variety of Readers."

From the most able, to him that can but spell: There you are number'd. We had rather you were weighd. Especially, when the fate of all Bookes depends vpon your capacities: and not of your heads alone, but of your purses. Well! It is now publique, & you wil stand for your priuiledges wee know: to read, and censure. Do so, but buy it first. That doth best commend a Booke, the Stationer saies. Then, how odde soeuer your braines be, or your wisedomes, make your licence the same, and spare not. . . . But, what euer you do, Buy. . . . And though you be a Magistrate of wit, and sit on the Stage at *Black-Friers,* or the *Cock-pit,*[68] to arrainge Playes dailie, know, these Playes haue had their triall alreadie, and stood out all Appeales. . . .

It had bene a thing, we confesse, worthie to haue bene wished, that the Author himselfe had liu'd to haue set forth, and ouerseen his owne writings; But since it hath bin ordain'd otherwise, and he by death departed from that right, we pray you do not envie his Friends, the office of their care, and paine, to haue collected & publish'd them; and so to haue publish'd them, as where (before) you were abus'd [swindled] with diuerse stolne, and surreptitious copies [i.e., quartos], maimed, and deformed by the frauds and stealthes of iniurious impostors, that expos'd them: euen those, are now offer'd to your view cur'd, and perfect of their limbes; and all the rest, absolute in their numbers, as he conceiued them. Who, as he was a happie imitator of Nature, was a most gentle expresser of it. His mind and hand went together: And what he thought, he vttered with that easinesse, that wee haue scarce receiued from him a blot in his papers. But it is not our prouince; who onely gather his works, and giue them you, to praise him. It is yours that reade him. And there we hope, to your diuers capacities, you will finde enough, both to draw, and hold you: for his wit can no more lie hid, then it could be lost. Reade him, therefore; and againe, and againe: And if then you doe not like him, surely you are in some manifest danger, not to vnderstand him. And so we leaue you to other of his Friends,

whom if you need, can bee your guides: if you neede them not, you
can leade your selues, and others. And such Readers we wish him.

Iohn Heminge.
Henrie Condell.

   The volume in hand is intended to help readers of Shakespeare; but the injunction of his fellows is as sound today as
when it was written. Read *him*, therefore; and again and
again. The "other of his Friends" are the poets whose commendatory verses follow the epistles. Among them Hugh
Holland laments that

> His dayes are done, that made the dainty Playes,
> Which made the Globe of heau'n and earth to ring.

Leonard Digges, son of the great mathematician, declares:

> Nor shall I e're beleeue, or thinke thee dead
> (Though mist) vntill our bankrout Stage be sped
> (Impossible) with some new straine t'out-do
> Passions of *Iuliet*, and her *Romeo;*
> Or till I heare a Scene more nobly take,
> Then when thy half-Sword parlying *Romans* spake.

   Ben's was the noblest tribute, and remains so. For, unlike
Arnold and Browning, Jonson knew Shakespeare, man as well
as book, and his praise is discriminating, and of all the
Elizabethan and Jacobean writers he was best qualified by
critical bent and creative fire to appraise a peerless colleague
worthily. He rose superbly to a great opportunity. The lines
which follow are doubly a tribute to Shakespeare, whose
memory evoked the best occasional poem in our language.

To the memory of my beloued,
The AVTHOR
Mr. WILLIAM SHAKESPEARE:
AND
what he hath left vs.

> To *draw no enuy* (Shakespeare) *on thy name,*
>   *Am I thus ample to thy Booke, and Fame:*
> *While I confesse thy writings to be such,*
>   *As neither* Man, *nor* Muse, *can praise too much.*

'Tis true, and all mens suffrage. But these wayes
  Were not the paths I meant vnto thy praise:
For seeliest Ignorance on these may light,
  Which, when it sounds at best, but eccho's right;
Or blinde Affection, which doth ne're aduance
  The truth, but gropes, and vrgeth all by chance;
Or crafty Malice, might pretend this praise,
  And thinke to ruine, where it seem'd to raise.
These are, as some infamous Baud, or Whore,
  Should praise a Matron. What could hurt her more?
But thou art proofe against them, and indeed
  Aboue th'ill fortune of them, or the need.
I, therefore will begin. Soule of the Age!
  The applause! delight! the wonder of our Stage!
My Shakespeare, rise; I will not lodge thee by
  Chaucer, or Spenser, or bid Beaumont lye
A little further, to make thee a roome:
  Thou art a Moniment, without a tombe,
And art aliue still, while thy Booke doth liue,
  And we haue wits to read, and praise to giue.
That I not mixe thee so, my braine excuses;
  I meane with great, but disproportion'd Muses:
For, if I thought my iudgement were of yeeres,
  I should commit thee surely with thy peeres,
And tell, how farre thou didst our Lily out-shine,
  Or sporting Kid, or Marlowes mighty line.
And though thou hadst small Latine, and lesse Greeke,
  From thence to honour thee, I would not seeke
For names; but call forth thund'ring Æschilus,
  Euripides, and Sophocles to vs,
Paccuuius, Accius, him of Cordoua dead,
  To life againe, to heare thy Buskin tread,
And shake a Stage: Or, when thy Sockes were on,
  Leaue thee alone, for the comparison
Of all, that insolent Greece, or haughtie Rome
  sent forth, or since did from their ashes come.
Triúmph, my Britaine, thou hast one to showe,
  To whom all Scenes of Europe homage owe.

He was not of an age, but for all time!
And all the Muses *still were in their prime,*
When like Apollo *he came forth to warme*
Our eares, or like a Mercury *to charme!*
Nature her selfe was proud of his designes,
And ioy'd to weare the dressing of his lines!
Which were so richly spun, and wouen so fit,
As, since, she will vouchsafe no other Wit.
The merry Greeke, *tart* Aristophanes,
Neat Terence, *witty* Plautus, *now not please;*
But antiquated, and deserted lye
As they were not of Natures family.
Yet must I not giue Nature all: Thy Art
My gentle Shakespeare, *must enioy a part.*
For though the Poets *matter, Nature be,*
His Art doth giue the fashion. And, that he,
Who casts to write a liuing line, must sweat,
(such as thine are) and strike the second heat
Vpon the Muses *anuile: turne the same,*
(And himselfe with it) that he thinkes to frame;
Or for the lawrell, he may gaine a scorne,
For a good Poet's *made, as well as borne.*
And such wert thou. Looke how the fathers face
Liues in his issue, euen so, the race
Of Shakespeares *minde, and manners brightly shines*
In his well torned, and true filed lines:
In each of which, he seemes to shake a Lance,
As brandish't at the eyes of Ignorance.
Sweet Swan of Auon! *what a sight it were*
To see thee in our waters yet appeare,
And make those flights vpon the bankes of Thames,
That so did take Eliza, *and our* Iames!
But stay, I see thee in the Hemisphere
Aduanc'd, and made a Constellation there!
Shine forth, thou Starre of Poets, *and with rage,*
Or influence, chide, or cheere the drooping Stage;
Which, since thy flight from hence, hath mourn'd like night,
And despaires day, but for thy Volumes light.

Chapter 2

HIS MEDIUM

THE STAGE

NO ONE goes to a symphony concert to look at the players. If your aesthetic experience springs from the
gesticulations of a virtuoso conductor, you might as
well be sitting at a ball game watching the wind-up of a
virtuoso pitcher. Concert halls are built for people to hear
in, and so are theatres. The eye has no function at an orchestral performance, little at a recital, more at an opera, and a
good deal more at a play. But even in the theatre the ear
beats the eye.[1] That is still true in our playhouses; it was
doubly true in Shakespeare's.

Elizabethan drama was acted in inn yards before there
were theatres in England, and sometimes even after. The audience stood in the yard and sat or stood on the surrounding
balconies, from which the bedrooms opened. Inns were often
built around a double courtyard. At such houses it was easy
to lay a stage on trestles in front of the entrance to the inner
yard, which could be closed off by a curtain or screen. The
spectators were ranged on three sides of the rectangular outer
court; to the inner the actors retired when they left the stage.
The gallery at the rear of the stage and above the entrance to
the inner yard was available for balcony and battlement
episodes. Scenery was quite out of the question; and the first
thing the modern reader must do when he tries to visualize
the Elizabethan stage is to forget proscenium arch, painted
canvas, and artificial light. When the curtain goes up in our
theatres there is always something to see. The attention of
the audience is caught at once by an unfamiliar picture. When
a play began at a London inn, there was nothing there but
the same old inn, except some boards and perhaps a curtain

to mask the rear entrance. The actor comes forward; he must hush the audience, and his most effective instrument is his voice.

When the Theatre, the Curtain, the Rose, the Swan, the Globe, the Fortune, the Red Bull, and the Hope were built, the general arrangements of the inn yard were retained. Usually circular or polygonal, though the Fortune was square,

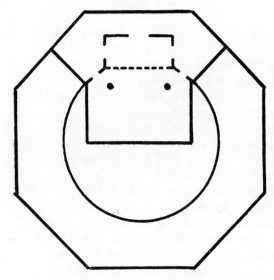

THE GLOBE THEATRE

A Conjectural Ground Plan

a high but shallow tier (normally of three galleries) enclosed the yard, as it was still called. In some theatres, there were galleries divided into boxes. The top of the tier was roofed with thatch or tiles; the yard was unroofed. Old pictorial maps exaggerate the height of the galleries, perhaps to emphasize the theatre's location. The Fortune was eighty feet square outside, and the height of the gallery roof probably not much more than half that.[2] Inside, the structure was fifty-five feet square.

Out into the middle of the yard thrust the principal feature of the stage, a large rectangular platform, both wide and deep — 43 by 27½ feet at the Fortune. On it most of the action proceeded, though the players were often incommoded by the presence of gallants who hired stools and sat on stage,

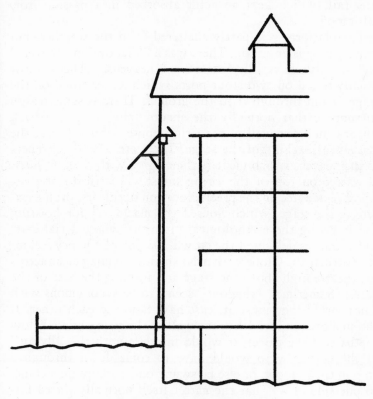

THE STAGE OF THE GLOBE
A Conjectural Cross Section

smoking, criticizing, and preening their fine feathers in full view of the audience.³ These were the wits — and the Witwoulds. In the yard below them, down on the level of Mother Earth, stood the "groundlings," who had paid least of all for their places. They were the butt of many a good-natured gibe from the dramatists, most of whom, however, seldom failed to throw in an occasional speech of rattling rhetoric or fustian unashamed, expressly designed to rouse to cheers this humble section of the "auditory." The front and sides of the platform were usually boarded up. Around the edge ran a low rail, which kept an actor absorbed in a passion from falling off.

The platform was partly sheltered from the weather, but exactly how is uncertain. There was a "shadow" or "cover," and we also have allusions to a "heavens." The shadow usually rested on two stout posts which either stood on the stage or ran through it to the ground. There is some reason to suppose that normally the shadow sloped up and back toward the front wall of the tiring house, which formed the permanent backing of the stage. There are several references to the heavens which identify that region with the hut, huts, or garret on top of the tiring house. Theatrical antiquarians do not agree on the precise location of this important feature of the stage, which housed the machinery for hoisting and lowering the mythological divinities whose aerial exits and entrances delighted the crowd. Dr. Joseph Quincy Adams reconstructs the Globe with a flat shadow running clear across the theatre high above the stage and forming the base of the garret. Sometimes "shadow" seems to be synonymous with "heavens"; they must at least have adjoined each other. If the shadow ran into the front wall of the tiring house below the base of the garret, it would interfere with the "flying" of the deities, who would have to come down through a trap in the shadow, or else be swung out, perhaps on a crane, to one side of it. That the garret itself normally jutted forward and partly overhung the stage seems more likely. If such was the arrangement, we could still have a sloping shadow, running, not all the way to the tiring house wall, but up to the front edge of the garret floor. Possibly some shadows were much shorter than they are usually shown in conjectural reconstructions, and hung from posts whose main function was to support the garret.

Our present knowledge, however, is not sufficient to warrant any dogmatism on these points. For the Hope (1613) the carpenter's contract specifies a heavens built "all over" the stage without supporting posts, while the stage itself is to be removable, the reason being that this house was for bear baiting as well as plays. This requirement implies that the regular thing was a stage only partly covered; and certainly a roof all the way across would make the inner stage that much darker. Posts for the canopy, whatever it was, were usual; they played their part in stage business. A soliloquizer or malcontent might lurk or step aside around a post. Orlando could use one for a tree and hang his verses on it.

The rear of the theatre was called the tiring house; its yard-side façade formed a permanent setting for the stage. Part of its lower floor was directly behind the platform and served as the "study," an inner stage separable from the platform by sliding curtains, called the "traverse." Its floor was strewn with rushes, as was usual in Elizabethan houses. Above it was yet another curtained stage, on the gallery. In exterior scenes the curtains had no significance; the audience ignored them as part of the familiar appearance of the stage. In interior scenes played on the outer platform they often represented the arras or painted cloth with which Elizabethan rooms were hung, and behind them eavesdroppers below or above could listen to their heart's content and the complication of many a plot. The traverse was used frequently, both at the end of a scene and within it. A scene with a character in bed or a group around a council table often begins with the opening of the study. Sometimes the stage direction is "Enter," even though the actors are "discovered."

Attempts to reconstruct a typical Elizabethan theatre differ in details but agree on the general relation of the three stages: a large platform, an inner stage behind it, and a gallery stage above that. All such attempts rest on early pictures, surviving contracts, and stage directions. Unfortunately, the builders' contracts are not precise enough to clear up a number of doubtful points. The early pictures are untrustworthy. The Dutch drawing of the Swan stage was made by Arend van Buchell either from a sketch or from the mere recollection of his

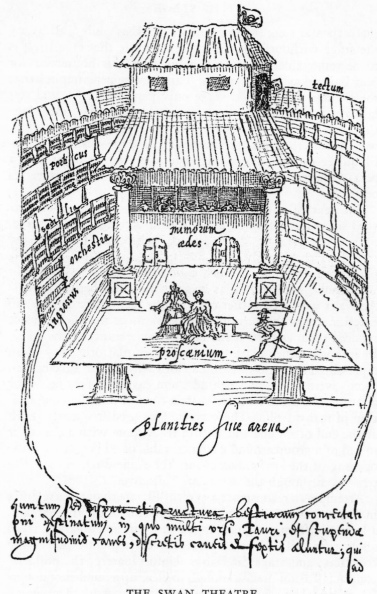

THE SWAN THEATRE
According to the Dutch Sketch

friend Johannes de Witt, who had visited London. It shows platform, shadow, and gallery, but not inner stage and curtains. The platform is unrailed. This drawing is not without interest; it is a chief source for our conception of the shadow. But we can not suppose it is accurate even for the stage of the Swan, to say nothing of its fidelity to type. Nor can we accept the often cited frontispiece to *The Wits* (1662) as a true picture of any Elizabethan stage. It is certainly not, as is often alleged, the Red Bull. The frontispieces of William Alabaster's *Roxana* (1632) and Nathaniel Richards's *Messallina* (1640) are likewise almost useless. The first of these plays was acted at Trinity College, Cambridge, and thus throws no light on Shakespeare's theatre. *Messallina* was acted publicly in London; but the two pictures are essentially alike, both appeared long after Shakespeare's career was ended, and they may be conventionalizations for the exigency of frontispieces. Whether or not in a crude effort to show perspective, both give us a stage tapering toward the front. This was almost certainly not typical, though the general relation of platform, inner stage, and gallery is about right. Possibly the *Messallina* and *Roxana* stages represent the alteration of halls for theatrical purposes, with platforms tapered to make more room for the audience. The conjectural reconstructer's safest reliance is on stage directions; and while these do not solve all problems, they leave the essential arrangements reasonably clear.

Most of the acting was doubtless on the outer platform. The gallery behind and above could be used for any scene needing an upper level — the gallery of a hall, the battlements of a beleaguered city, a hill, a rock, or even a tree. When the action required a second stage more sharply distinguishable from the platform than the study, the gallery could be used even if the essential point was not two levels. Platform and gallery could, for example, be the decks of separate ships. When the gallery was not needed for the action, spectators may have sat there. Dr. W. J. Lawrence argues that it was also the music room, though others would put the players of lute, viol, recorder, and oboe on a third level, above the gallery stage. That the music was somewhere "above" is certain; it did not come downstairs till after the Restoration, when scenery and opera contaminated and demoralized drama. We also have references to a "lords' room." This was doubtless either part of the gallery stage or some kind of box beside it.

On the inner stage heavy properties could be shifted behind the curtain by the "stage-keepers" while the action continued on the outer platform. The use of such properties, however, was not confined to the study. Sometimes the study is a shop, prison, tent, cave, cell, or tomb. Sometimes it is thrown into one with the platform, which thereupon assumes its character. The last scene of *Othello* begins with the opening of the curtain, Desdemona being "discovered" on the inner stage, in bed and asleep. Othello doubtless enters, not the study, but the platform. As soon as he looks up at the bed the audience accepts the two stages as one. His first speech is probably delivered from the platform till "I'll smell it on the tree," when he goes up stage to Desdemona. Emilia's clamorous entrance is also directly onto the platform. The use of the inner stage for cumbersome properties helped keep a play of many scenes moving swiftly. Not always, however, does the opening of its curtains throw the inner and outer stages together. Simultaneously they can be an interior and an exterior, as in *The Tempest*, V, i. Prospero, in an outdoor scene acted on the platform, suddenly shows Alonso the inside of his "cell," where Ferdinand and Miranda are discovered playing chess. Whether the inner stage was actually a three-walled room or simply a wide corridor is uncertain. It could be entered at the sides and at a rear door.

The ordinary entrance to the platform was through one of two downstage doors opening from the tiring house immediately upon it. Whether they faced the audience directly or obliquely is unknown; there may have been no uniformity among the theatres, but oblique construction would accord better with stage directions for movements across the platform. These unrealistic doors survived into the nineteenth century; long after the proscenium arch framed a scenic picture, the actor stepped into the Forest of Arden, not amid the scenery behind the proscenium, but on the "apron" in front of it. Our own stage, which became pictorial under the Restoration, is historically a progressive enlargement of the Elizabethan inner stage. Not till very recently did the last trace of the old platform-apron disappear.

Above the Elizabethan downstage doors there were probably windows; and there may have been a lower window between each of the doors and the study. Doubtless these and other features differed in various playhouses. One other means of entrance and exit should be mentioned, the trap doors. Slowly and majestically the ghost rose from the cellarage on an elevator, cranked up much like the small platform lifts that bring ash cans to the sidewalk level today. A stage direction in Marlowe's *The Jew of Malta* (V, vi) shows that a trap was sometimes used in the gallery.

Besides the study and the gallery stage, the tiring house must have contained lounging, dressing, and storage rooms and the library. In its top story, probably overhanging the platform to some extent, was the hut or garret already mentioned. Some of the dramatists went in for exploiting its mechanical resources, which were considerable. In the *Ages* plays of Thomas Heywood appear the following stage directions:

Sound a dumbe shew. Enter the three fatall sisters, with a rocke, a threed, and a paire of sheeres; bringing in a Gloabe, in which they put three lots. *Iupiter* drawes heauen: at which *Iris* descends and presents him with his Eagle, Crowne and Scepter, and his thunderbolt. *Iupiter* first ascends vpon the Eagle, and after him *Ganimed*. — Thunder and lightning. *Iupiter* discends in a cloude. — *Iupiter* appeares in his glory vnder a Raine-bow. — Mercury flies from aboue. — Earth riseth from vnder the stage. — Thunder, lightnings, *Iupiter* descends in his maiesty, his Thunderbolt burning. — As he toucheth the bed it fires, and all flyes vp, *Iupiter* from thence takes an abourtiue infant. — Iupiter taking up the Infant, speakes as he ascends in his cloud. — *Hercules* sinkes himselfe: Flashes of fire; the Diuels appeare at euery corner of the stage with seuerall fire-workes. . . . fire-workes all ouer the house. — Enter *Pluto* with a club of fire, a burning crowne, *Proserpine*, the Iudges, the Fates, and a guard of Diuels,

all with burning weapons. — *Hercules* . . . kils *Busyris* and sacri-
ficeth him vpon the Altar, at which there fals a shower of raine. —
Two fiery Buls are discouered, the Fleece hanging ouer them, and
the Dragon sleeping beneath them: *Medea* with strange fiery-workes,
hangs aboue in the Aire in the strange habite of a Coniuresse. —
Enter Hercules from a rocke aboue, tearing downe trees. — All the
Princes breake downe the trees, and make a fire, in which *Hercules*
placeth himselfe. — Iupiter aboue strikes him with a thunder-bolt,
his body sinkes, and from the heauens discends a hand in a cloud,
that from the place where Hercules was burnt, brings up a starre,
and fixeth it in the firmament.

The last of these effects certainly beats the swan and dove in
Lohengrin. Precisely how the creaking throne came down the
boys to please, as Jonson jeeringly describes the operation,
we do not know.

There was a good deal of music, and also an elaborate
technique for the production of nonmusical off-stage noises.
From the roof of the garret flaunted the flag, an eyesore to
the Puritans, since it announced that the theatre was playing.
From it, too, a trumpet warned late-comers; at the third
sounding the Prologue walked on and the play began. Its
title had been announced at the preceding performance, and
bills of advertisement had been posted.[4]

As long as the platform remained much larger than the study,
scenery was as impossible in the theatre as it was in the inn
yard. Performances were in the afternoon, beginning about
two o'clock, after dinner. Artificial light was not employed,
and the stage could not be darkened. When torches and
candles were used, the audience accepted them as conventional indications of a night scene. Though, judging by Henslowe's inventories and the notations in surviving prompt
books, properties were numerous and elaborate, pictorial
effect in the Elizabethan theatre was chiefly dependent on
costume, which was gorgeous. It was usually, though not
invariably, Elizabethan. A few stage directions indicate
that sometimes trees or bushes were actually brought on
stage, but they are treated more as properties than as scenery.
The hordes of supernumeraries employed, sometimes dis-

astrously, by modern producers who try to create the illusion by overwhelming an audience with quantity, were not available to an Elizabethan play director. This important member of the staff seems normally to have been the author. A talent for playwriting does not, however, necessarily include aptitude for the actual working out of business, grouping, and stage effects. That Shakespeare directed his own plays seems likely, but there is no evidence. It is clear that as a poet he was sometimes appalled by the limitations of his medium. In the Choruses of *Henry the Fifth* his tone is apologetic; repeatedly he appeals for imaginative support from the audience:

> But pardon, gentles all,
> The flat unraised spirits that have dar'd
> On this unworthy scaffold to bring forth
> So great an object. Can this cockpit hold
> The vasty fields of France? Or may we cram
> Within this wooden O the very casques
> That did affright the air at Agincourt?
> O, pardon! since a crooked figure may
> Attest in little place a million,
> And let us, ciphers to this great accompt,
> On your imaginary forces work. . . .
> Piece out our imperfections with your thoughts:
> Into a thousand parts divide one man
> And make imaginary puissance.
> Think, when we talk of horses, that you see them
> Printing their proud hoofs i' th' receiving earth.
> For 'tis your thoughts that now must deck our kings.

But any stage would be inadequate for this ambitious program, and the glory of the Elizabethan was that it seems to have served Shakespeare rather well. In general, he wisely refrains from straining its resources by overrealistic demands; his method is consistently impressionistic. In the first scene of *The Tempest* he actually stages a shipwreck, a very successful and thoroughgoing one, though we eventually learn that part of it was only an illusion. It is all accomplished in words. In 1670 was published the D'avenant-Dryden adaptation of this play. The "improvers" attempt to straighten out the storm, which they provide in due neoclassical style with a beginning, middle, and end. But though their scene is clearer, it fails to create the *impression* that Shakespeare secures by fragments of conversation, the bawling of orders, and the wild cry "We split!"

The pictorial weakness of the Elizabethan stage placed an added burden on the dramatist, and with it offered a literary opportunity. When the curtain rises in our theatres we *see* whether we are in Orsino's palace or on the Illyrian seashore, and whether the hour is noon or midnight. Shakespeare had to set his stage with the words his actors spoke; and that allowed him glowing descriptive passages which are out of place in a theatre where the carpenter, scene-painter, and electrician replace the poet. Carl Sandburg once declared, "Don't ask me how I write my poetry! I just take words and lay down a barrage hoping to create a mirage!" When Shakespeare wants to create a scenic mirage that is exactly what he does:

> Light thickens, and the crow
> Makes wing to th' rooky wood.
> Good things of day begin to droop and drowse,
> Whiles night's black agents to their preys do rouse.

No reliance on scenic materials can recapture that ominous crow. Shakespeare's plays reek with atmosphere. He uses it dramatically. We do not see it, but we feel it — which is the essential thing. In a modern play the electrician throws his switches, but never so effectively as when Horatio turns on the dawn in *Hamlet* at the end of a short scene that begins at midnight:

> But look, the morn, in russet mantle clad,
> Walks o'er the dew of yon high eastward hill.

Often, however, there is no need of specifying a scene's location or hour. It is needful for two characters to converse; it makes no difference where they talk — upstairs, downstairs, or in my lady's chamber, or in her garden, or on a city square. In such scenes the painstaking tags of the editors are really an impertinence. Few of the scenes are definitely placed by headings in the original texts. Many are deftly fixed by allusions in the dialogue, but some should be frankly tagged in modern editions "unlocated." When Shakespeare wants to give us an impression of time or place, he drops a hint or two into the speeches. He is writing a score for the players, and his control of the audience's impression is masterly and economical. He addresses it chiefly to ears, not eyes. Since his medium is, then, essentially sound, the modern reader should read him aloud; and the modern producer should cut away all the scenic lumber he dares, and stake the success of the play, as Shakespeare staked it, on well-spoken words.

We have been considering the public playhouse, for that was the norm. Staging at the so-called private theatres, such as the Blackfriars, seems not to have differed very much in Shakespeare's lifetime, though these houses were completely roofed, the entire audience was probably seated, and the performance was under artificial light. The prices were higher and the spectators more select. Productions at court were somewhat more pictorial. Scenery was lavishly employed there in the masques, which under James I commandeered the decorative genius of Inigo Jones. Lyly's plays for the boys' companies in private theatres had called for the old multiple setting, with façades of houses before which, however separated by imagined distances suggested in the dialogue, all the action takes place without any scene-shifting. The advent of the romantic drama changed all that. Words were certainly paramount on all stages. Even in the plays Shakespeare seems to have written for original production under private auspices, there are some differences in emphasis but not in technique.

When the words ceased, the spell was broken. Mounted in our theatres, Shakespeare's plays often seem scrappy. The modern producer's aim should be to keep the scenes flowing on at high speed. Elizabethan performances on the public stages were probably continuous. Whether the playwright even thought in acts is a moot question. In the two hours that were the normal length of a performance it is not likely the action was broken more than once, if indeed it was interrupted at all, at least till fairly late in Shakespeare's career. Eventually music was provided between acts. It was a special attraction at the private houses where the boys' companies flourished; there a concert sometimes preceded the play. In the public theatres the epilogue, which made no bones about asking for a *plaudite*, was regularly followed with a "jig," at first a mere vaudeville turn, often pretty coarse, with song, dance, and clowning. It developed into an afterpiece of music and farce, virtually a crude form of comic opera.

ACTING

Acting in the inn yards was often boisterous, and at the public theatres was probably less restrained than at the private ones. The latter were smaller and the audiences there more decorous. At court the actors doubtless used more finesse. When Shakespeare wrote a play he must have had all three publics in mind, and his own satisfaction as well. The requirement of pleasing all, from the apprentices in the yard at the Globe to the exquisites at Greenwich, Whitehall, or Hampton Court, may have had something to do with the survival of his best plays and the universality of their appeal.

The leading actors were accomplished men. There was probably not so high a standard of ensemble as we expect in our leading theatres today; but there were geniuses among the players, and we have every reason to suppose that the major rôles in Shakespeare's dramas were superbly handled. The audience knew the difference. York in *Richard the Second* (V, ii) compares Bolingbroke's and the King's reception by the citizens to the attention of spectators at a play:

> As in a theatre the eyes of men,
> After a well-grac'd actor leaves the stage,
> Are idly bent on him that enters next,
> Thinking his prattle to be tedious. . . .

The actor's principal job was to speak words, and such it remains even on our pictorial stage. Elizabethan art was more rhetorical than ours. Part of the dramatist's task was to provide the leading performers with elocutionary arias. Many of

Shakespeare's soliloquies serve that purpose and that alone. "Business" was probably less elaborate on the Elizabethan stage. It would amaze us to see a soloist omit the cadenza from a violin concerto and supply its place with pantomime expressive of the composer's mood. The low comedians of the Elizabethan troupes were not noted for sticking to the provided score; but though they doubtless made funny faces, sometimes at inappropriate moments, it is their gagging or "ad libbing" that Shakespeare denounces in Hamlet's advice to the players.

For practically everything in his theatre was accomplished by the spoken word. A great deal of unwise commentary on his plays betrays the critic's failure to grasp the principle that the dramatist leaves nothing to be inferred. If it is not expressed in the score, that is, in the dialogue, it does not exist. Many of our naturalistic actors seem, when they essay Shakespeare, afraid of the words. They give intelligent, carefully studied picturizations of their rôles; but too often they fail to abandon themselves to the glory of the sound — wary of ranting, they refuse to follow the indicated curve of emotional and verbal flamboyance. Shakespeare's effect often depends on the contrast between passages of rhetorical outburst and of deadly quiet. Macbeth's alternations in the fifth act are a case in point. Hamlet's rôle likewise abounds in sharp contrasts, which should produce an almost orchestral effect.

As we have seen, the principal parts were played by the sharers. The "hirelings" were salaried actors, whose work was mostly "general utility." Occasionally, however, an important player may have preferred a salary to a share; certainly that sometimes happened later in the seventeenth century. There were also minor hirelings, used as supers or even perhaps to play occasional bits. Their work was chiefly off stage, but no doubt every available man and boy about the theatre was pressed into histrionic service when needed. There is a significant stage direction in *Titus Andronicus:* [5]

Sound Drums and Trumpets, and then enter two of Titus *sonnes, and then two men bearing a Coffin couered with black, then two other sonnes, then*

Titus Andronicus, *and then* Tamora *the Queene of Gothes & her two sonnes* Chiron *and* Demetrius, *with* Aron *the More, and others as many as can be.*

The sympathy sometimes extended to Shakespeare because Sarah Siddons and Ellen Terry were not members of his troupe is on the whole gratuitous. There can be no doubt that his heroines were well acted. There is always drama where children are playing, and the natural aptitudes of the boys were fostered by sound instruction from the master actors to whom they were apprenticed. Their voices were trained, and by the time a boy had served several years he was likely to be a proficient player and a well-schooled singer. On our motion-picture screens, it is true, we often see brats of nauseating artificiality; but sometimes we see straightforward, unaffected playing, and occasionally even genius. Such children can move us now; they moved highly critical personalities then. In a charming lyric in his *Epigrammes*, Ben Jonson applauds the talent of Salathiel Pavy. This boy belonged to a children's company; his specialty was old men.

EPITAPH ON S. P. A CHILD OF Q. EL. CHAPPEL.

Weepe with me all you that read
    This little storie:
And know, for whom a teare you shed,
    Death's selfe is sorry.
'Twas a child, that so did thriue
    In grace, and feature,
As *Heauen* and *Nature* seem'd to striue
    Which own'd the creature.
Yeeres he numbred scarse thirteene
    When *Fates* turn'd cruell,
Yet three fill'd *Zodiackes* had he beene
    The stages iewell;
And did act (what now we mone)
    Old men so duely,
As, sooth, the *Parcæ* thought him one,
    He plai'd so truely.
So, by error, to his fate
    They all consented;

> But viewing him since (alas, too late)
>   They haue repented.
> And haue sought (to giue new birth)
>   In bathes to steepe him;
> But, being so much too good for earth,
>   Heauen vowes to keepe him.

Unimpeachable testimony to the success of the boys as heroines comes from the Restoration, when audiences, one might expect, would be less patient with surviving Elizabethan practices. It was between November 21 and December 15, 1660 that professional English actresses made their bow on the legitimate public stage; but it took some time to supplant the boys completely, and men long continued acting the strong feminine "character" rôles, such as Mrs. Quickly, and the Nurse in *Romeo and Juliet.* On August 18, Samuel Pepys had seen Fletcher's *The Loyal Subject,* "where one Kinaston, a boy, acted the Duke's sister, but made the loveliest lady that ever I saw in my life." That is a good deal, coming as it does from one who plumed himself on being a connoisseur. On January 7, 1661 Pepys saw this actor in the title rôle of Jonson's *Epicoene, or The silent Woman* and thought him "clearly the prettiest woman in the whole house." In his *Roscius Anglicanus* (1708) John Downes also pays a remarkable tribute to Edward Kynaston, who

being then very Young made a Compleat Female Stage Beauty, performing his Parts so well . . . being Parts greatly moving Compassion and Pity; that it hath since been Disputable among the Judicious, whether any Woman that succeeded him so Sensibly touch'd the Audience as he.

There is no reason to suppose the Elizabethan stars were less brilliant. It is impossible to believe that a youth ever played Lady Macbeth with anything like the awful grandeur Mrs. Siddons was to bring to the rôle. But however great the interpretation, the score itself is greater. Moreover, Shakespeare's heroines are chiefly distinguished for their charm. Portia, Rosalind, and Ophelia, to cite almost at random a few representative names, would easily come within the scope of the most talented of the boys. And it would probably be a lad in his late teens or early twenties who would be cast in the heavy tragic rôles like Lady Macbeth and Cleopatra.

EARLY COMPANIES AND THEATRES

We have seen that for the first record of Shakespeare's theatrical connections we have to wait till the end of 1594, when we find him at the top of the tree as a leading member of the Burbage troupe. That he had previously free-lanced is conceivable; but any such hypothesis also assumes that he introduced himself as a dramatist before he won his spurs as an actor, and it is more likely that in one Thespian capacity or another he had joined some company years before. The question is, which? Was his theatrical novitiate passed with the Burbages, or not? This problem has not been solved. It may never be. The evidence is scanty and in part contradictory, and students of Elizabethan stage history are still unable to reconcile their views. This section may therefore be skipped, unless the reader is naturally curious or insatiable. It has been withheld from the preceding chapter because one is obliged to deal almost exclusively with hypotheses. On the other hand, the theatrical background of Shakespeare's early years in London will be more vivid to him who perseveres.

When the actors began playing Stratford no one knows, but it was certainly long before their first appearance in the surviving local records. That was when Shakespeare was four or five years old, and his father, as bailiff, authorized payment from the town treasury. According to a contemporary, recalling a childhood in Gloucester, a strolling troupe was expected to give their first performance before the mayor and corporation. It would be a free show, but the authorities would grant the company a donation. "At such a play, my father tooke me with him and made mee stand betweene his leggs, as he sate upon one of the benches where wee saw and heard very well." [6] If small fry in Stratford were as lucky as Gloucester boys, some performance in the Guildhall,

THE BEAR GARDEN AND THE GLOBE

from Visscher's View of London, 1616

MESSALLINA STAGE   ROXANA STAGE

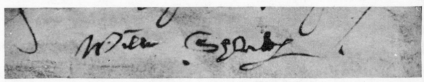

Deposition in Mountjoy Case.

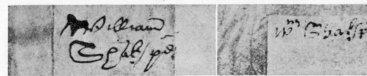

Conveyance of Blackfriars House.   Mortgage of Blackfriars House.

Will, page one.

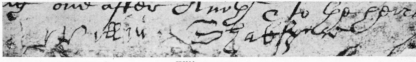

Will, page two.

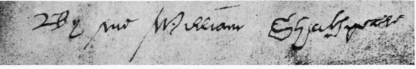

Will, page three.

SHAKESPEARE'S SIGNATURES

THE STAGE OF THE GLOBE
from a model of the Globe Theatre by Dr. John C. Adams

RICHARD BURBAGE

WILLIAM SLY

JOHN LOWIN

JOHN FLETCHER

whether in 1569 or later, was probably William Shakespeare's first taste of the theatre. If so, the chances are it was a "moral interlude" that he saw. His plays are full of allusions to this type of drama. There was, in fact, not much else a country boy could see till about the time Shakespeare left for London. After 1569, the actors' visits were frequent. Between Shakespeare's sixteenth and twenty-fourth years, from one to five companies came every year but one. It is therefore quite possible that he struck up an acquaintance with London actors in Stratford and applied to them when he arrived in the metropolis.

To the eight noble volumes of Chambers on *The Mediaeval Stage*, *The Elizabethan Stage*, and *William Shakespeare*, the reader should turn who wishes to follow the development of English drama in detail. Beginning in the ritual of the medieval church with dramatizations of Biblical narrative ("mystery" plays), the didactic aim continued in pieces devoted to the struggle between personified virtues and vices for the soul of Mankind ("morality" plays) and in many of the semi-"moral" "interludes" of early Tudor times. By the middle of the sixteenth century, drama had been revitalized by much revival and imitation of Roman plays in the universities and schools, and by the new intellectual movement known as humanism. Originally in the hands of the clergy and then of the medieval trade guilds and wandering minstrels, dramatic performance had become a profession when employees or protégés of the monarch and nobility began playing not only in palaces but also for the public, at first in the yards of London inns, and after 1576 in both inn yards and theatres. They often went on the road, especially in the summer; here their dependence on their patrons was of prime importance. For there were also troupes of strolling entertainers whose irresponsibility made them unwelcome to local authorities. The company that could show a letter from a great lord was sure of a better reception for his servants, as the actors were called. Performances were also given at court, and at certain periods in public theatres, by child actors who received their training in connection with the Chapel Royal. The choir of St. Paul's likewise littered a children's company. For public favor these boys were sometimes serious contenders with the adult companies; the conversation of Hamlet and the spying courtiers about the "little eyases" (II, ii) reflects that rivalry toward the end of Elizabeth's reign.

The Queen herself long sponsored an adult troupe, and there were numerous command performances at her court by others. Some believe Shakespeare may have been taken on by the Queen's Men. In 1583 a new royal company had been recruited from several others; its members were appointed Grooms of the Chamber. Acting at court was necessarily a small part of their work; they became for at least five years the principal London company. There is, however, no evidence that Shakespeare ever joined them, though if he came to London about 1586 they would have been a likelier market for his wares, literary or histrionic, than either of the companies we shall consider in more detail. After the death of their famous comedian Dick Tarlton, in 1588, the Queen's Men declined.

Acting by the Children of the Chapel Royal was one of Elizabeth's favorite diversions. The drama produced especially for the court doubtless had a civilizing influence on the public theatres, but it was likely to be pretty and overliterary. It was out of the inn yards that the admirable robustness of the main current of Elizabethan drama flowed. It was often too robust for the city fathers. London was increasingly Puritan throughout Shakespeare's lifetime. The wickedness of plays was a favorite theme of sectarian moralists, and every now and then some jack in office tried to run the actors out of town. Nevertheless, five London inns became to all intents and purposes theatres, the players and the owners splitting the proceeds. The opposition was not entirely fanatical. Theatres and theatrical inns were disorderly places; they bred riots and spread the plague, and it was not till Macready's time, early in the nineteenth century, that the playhouses ceased to be a recognized rallying ground for the London whores. The noble patrons of the companies often brought effective pressure to bear on the city government in their behalf, and the Privy Council itself sometimes interceded for them; but the theatre proper had to go outside the walls, where the municipal jurisdiction did not run.

James Burbage, Richard's father, originally a carpenter, became an actor and head of the Earl of Leicester's Men. On borrowed capital he built the Theatre in 1576, the first in England. The Curtain was erected a year later. Both stood in the notorious district of Shoreditch, north of Bishopsgate, on the edge of Finsbury Field, a favorite recreation spot of the citizens. When Shakespeare turns up in 1594 as a member of the Burbage organization, he is presumably at the Theatre in the summer and the Cross Keys within the city during the winter. Across the river at Newington Butts, about a mile from London Bridge, a third theatre was probably playing by 1580, but not much is known about it. In 1587 Philip Henslowe, not an actor, built the Rose on the Bankside in Surrey. Thus there were, besides city inns like the Cross Keys, at least three fine playhouses in the suburbs about the probable time of Shakespeare's arrival in London. The city had over 100,000 inhabitants; including the suburbs and Westminster, then a separate town, the metropolitan population numbered about 200,000.

Whether Shakespeare gravitated directly to the stage is unknown. The repertory system, the daily change of bill, the relatively small size of the theatregoing public (respectable women did not frequent the larger playhouses), and the competition between the companies — all these made writing for the stage as inevitable a resource of the aspirant for literary fame and a bread-and-butter job in the meantime as journalism offers today. Richard Field, who became a freeman of the Stationers in 1587, and by marrying the widow of his employer Thomas Vautrollier the following year took over one of the best printing offices in London, may have introduced his old schoolmate, as Shakespeare probably was, to theatrical circles. Some think the poet Fulke Greville, first Lord Brooke, who was Warwickshire born and had connections with Stratford, may have been his sponsor; but though Greville is alleged to have declared, long after, that he had been Shake-

speare's master, and Jonson's too, neither the truth of this
boast nor any certainty that Greville uttered it is capable of
proof. Perhaps the young genius already had manuscripts that
proved his knack with a pen. Writers who had yet to master
dramatic technique got plays produced. Marlowe's *Tamburlaine* (1587–88) has passages of great poetic merit but is not
well worked out theatrically. Some believe *The Comedy of
Errors* was written in the country — it is somewhat school-
masterish. But even that seems too good for a first play by an
author not yet conversant with the theatre.

It is more likely that Shakespeare had verses to show, and
that he was hired by the actors to play small rôles while he
learned how to write for them. He may have broken the ice
by a natural aptitude for acting, without any literary evidence to recommend him. His eventual mastery of his stage,
for which his best plays show perfect tact, suggests that he
may have made himself useful as stage-manager and after
that as director, before he came forward with the works we
know. But all this is almost mere guessing. Almost, but not
quite; for, as we have seen, Dowdall and Betterton had heard
that Shakespeare's first theatrical job was a minor one. Bagehot acutely remarks that

a play by Shakespeare reads as if it were written in a playhouse.
The great critics assure you that a theatrical audience must be kept
awake, but Shakespeare knew this of his own knowledge. When
you read him, you feel a sensation of motion, a conviction that there
is something 'up,' a notion that not only is something being talked
about, but also that something is being done. We do not imagine
that Shakespeare owed this quality to his being a player, but rather
that he became a player because he possessed this quality of mind.

As for the willingness of the companies to engage promising
but inexperienced young men to act, in hope of their proving
useful as writers, we have the testimony of *Part 2* of *The
Retvrne from Pernassvs*, in which Richard Burbage, who appears as a character, is made to say that although "these
schollers" may be inexpert, a "little teaching will mend these
faults, and it may bee besides they will be able to pen a part."

One must concede, however, that *The Retvrne* is a university play, and on this point the wish may be father to the thought.

The company Shakespeare belonged to by the end of 1594 was known as the Lord Chamberlain's Men from the high office held by their patron, Henry Carey, Lord Hunsdon. They had begun that year under another patron, Ferdinando Stanley, Lord Strange, who on September 25, 1593 had succeeded to the earldom of Derby, the style of the company changing with his new title. He died on April 16, 1594. For a time the troupe carried on as the Countess of Derby's players, but not for long; by summer they had secured their new sponsor, and perhaps reorganized.

As Lord Strange's Men, their recorded history does not go back very far. It is often asserted that Kempe, Bryan, and Pope were members as early as 1588 or soon after, on the theory that these actors, who like John Heminge may have been members of the Earl of Leicester's old company (Kempe probably was) and appear later with the Strange-Chamberlain troupe, transferred to it directly after Leicester's death in 1588. This hypothesis has encouraged the assumption that Shakespeare joined Leicester's Men when they played Stratford in 1586–87, and went to Strange's Men the year after. But proof is lacking of membership in Leicester's company at that time for any of these men, though all were afterwards associates of Shakespeare.

On November 5, 1589 Strange's Men defied the Lord Mayor of London, as he protests in a letter the next day, by performing at the Cross Keys Inn. Probably they were acting in 1590–91 at the Theatre or the Curtain or both under the management of James Burbage, in some sort of league with the Admiral's Men. Between December 27, 1591 and February 8, 1592 they gave six performances at court. Precisely when they transferred to Henslowe's management is not known, nor is it clear just what their relations with the Admiral's Men were either then or under Burbage. They were acting at Henslowe's house, the Rose, from February 19 to June 23, 1592, and may have gone there by the preceding summer. Henslowe lists the play for each day, with a sum which probably represents his share of the proceeds. They opened this spring season of 1592 with *fryer bacvne*, that is, Greene's *The Honorable Historie of frier Bacon, and frier Bongay*. Henslowe writes "ne" (i.e., new) [7] against certain plays, among them *harey the vj* on March 3. This is almost certainly Shakespeare's *Henry the Sixth, Part 1*. It was repeated either thirteen or fourteen times before the season ended on June 23. That meant in our parlance a smash hit. This is unquestionably the play Nashe alludes to in the passage about the spectators' tears for Talbot.[8] The next play marked "ne" is *tittus & vespacia* on April 11, 1592. It was repeated six times and made Henslowe more money *per diem* than any other that spring. This may be Shakespeare's *Titus Andronicus*.

Also in the repertory during this season at the Rose were plays of the Admiral's company; Marlowe's *The Jew of Malta* was acted ten times. For some of the Admiral's Men were also there, among them Edward Alleyn, a giant of a man, the Admiral's foremost player, who had not joined a number of his colleagues in touring the Continent. This temporarily divided company, under the patronage of Charles Howard, Baron Howard of Effingham, Lord High Admiral, and afterwards Earl of Nottingham, was destined to be the principal rival of Shakespeare's. Alleyn, the creator of Tamburlaine and other Marlovian rôles, married Henslowe's stepdaughter on October 22, 1592 and in alliance with his father-in-law proceeded to make a fortune. He conferred a lasting benefit on students of Elizabethan drama by founding Dulwich College, where some of our most important sources of documentary information are preserved. Henslowe left an account book, his so-called *Diary*, the spelling of which is amazing, even for an Elizabethan, who was allowed a good deal of latitude. It is invaluable for facts about the early companies and theatres.

Among the actors at the Rose in 1592 who were then or afterwards Shakespeare's associates were Richard Burbage, Augustine Phillips, Thomas Pope, George Bryan, William Sly, and Richard Cowley. Will Kempe and John Heminge were probably members of this company at this time, though their names do not appear in a cast, usually but not certainly dated 1592, given in a "plat" [9] of *Part 2* of *The Seven Deadly Sins*. They are, however, listed in a license to travel issued next May to the "servants" of Lord Strange.[10] Alleyn is described in the license as an Admiral's man; but the whole group, which also included Pope, Phillips, Bryan, and Cowley, are "al one companie."

The Rose's spring season of 1592 lasted through June 23, when the theatres were ordered to shut down. There had been a riot of the prentices on June 11. Before the term of the penalty expired the plague broke out, prolonging the suspension till the end of December. There was to be little acting in London till the summer of 1594. Strange's Men had been granted, precisely when is uncertain, temporary permission to act three times a week at Newington Butts; this house was so far from the river that the watermen, who had a steady trade when the Rose was playing, were much distressed. The company finally went on the road. They resumed at the Rose on December 29, and continued through January, 1593. *Titus*, as Henslowe now calls it, was played three times and *harey the vj* once. On January 5, 1593 a "ne[w]" play was acted, *the gelyous* [jealous] *comodey*. It was not repeated. Some think this was *The Comedy of Errors*.

To sum up, the following plays of Shakespeare may have been acted between March 3, 1592 and January 31, 1593 by a Henslowe company largely composed of Lord Strange's Men: probably *Henry the Sixth, Part 1;* perhaps *Titus Andronicus;* possibly *The Comedy of Errors*. Since none of these identifications is certain, the evidence that Shakespeare was ever with Strange's Men is inconclusive.[11] Moreover, his name does not appear in any of the Henslowe-Alleyn papers nor in the cast of *The Seven Deadly Sins, Part 2*. There are, however, two important rôles for which no casting is given. Nor does his name appear in the traveling license of 1593. He could, of course, have belonged to the company and not gone on tour. A vacation in Stratford is not beyond the bounds of possibility.

It is, in fact, impossible to determine which company

Shakespeare joined first. He may have belonged to more than one before we find him with the Chamberlain's in the season of 1594–95. A strong but not conclusive case has been made out for yet another troupe, the Earl of Pembroke's. Unfortunately, little of its history is known; but several of Shakespeare's plays had been acted by it before it collapsed in 1593. A Pembroke company was traveling in the provinces in 1575–76, but no connection has been established between it and the London organization we have now to deal with. When the latter came into existence is unknown. It may have broken off from the combined Strange-Admiral's company in 1592; Henslowe was advancing money to Pembroke's in 1592–93. On the other hand, it may be several years older.

Thomas Kyd, the pioneering dramatist whose example seems to have helped formulate Shakespeare's technique, was arrested on May 12, 1593 on suspicion of "atheism." In a letter to Lord Keeper Sir John Puckering, Kyd attempts to shift the blame to Marlowe for certain papers, his own possession of which he attributes to their having been "wrytinge in one chamber" two years before.

My first acquaintance wth this Marlowe, rose vpon his bearing name to serve my Lo[rd]: although his L[ordshi]p never knewe his service, but in writing for his plaiers, ffor never cold my L. endure his name, or sight, when he had heard of his conditions.

Kyd continues that he hopes he may still "reteyne the favo^{rs} of my Lord, whom I haue servd almost theis vj ^{12} yeres nowe." This letter was written after Marlowe's death. The great question is, of course, the identity of "my Lord." It may have been Pembroke, though the Earl of Sussex and Lord Strange have also been suggested. Marlowe had originally written *Tamburlaine* (1587–88), *Doctor Faustus* (*c.* 1589), and *The Jew of Malta* (*c.* 1590), for the Admiral's Men. But his *Edward the Second* (*c.* 1591–92) was acted, according to the Quarto of 1594, by Pembroke's company. Perhaps, then, this troupe had enlisted Marlowe, after Kyd's term of service to "my Lord" had begun. Did they also enlist Shakespeare when Marlowe came in, or earlier? Or did he join them to replace Marlowe? In another letter Kyd asserts that he kept away from Marlowe at "my Lord's" express bidding. Presumably Marlowe had left this nobleman's employ before January 26, 1593, when Henslowe notes the performance of a new play by his own company at the Rose: no doubt *the tragedey of the gvyes* (i.e., Guise) is Marlowe's *The Massacre at Paris*.[13]

Pembroke's company is known to have played at court twice during the Christmas holidays of 1592–93; Strange's Men acted three times. These performances, like the public season of Strange's already mentioned, came during a brief revocation, in the dead of winter, of the ban on plays which had been in force from June 24 to the end of December, 1592. The prohibition was renewed about February 1, 1593 and continued, again with the exception of a short midwinter season, until June, 1594; for 1593 was a terrible year of plague. This long interruption was a shocking blow to the actors, and consequently to the dramatists. It wrecked Pembroke's company. In the summer of 1593 both Pembroke's and Strange's Men went off on provincial tours. Toward the end of August, having failed to make expenses, Pembroke's gave up and returned to London. They had been obliged to pawn costumes; now they sold at least some of their plays. They may have reorganized subsequently, for provincial performances are on record in 1595–96, though it may be a new Pembroke company that we find in London in 1597. While on the road in 1593 they would not stand in need of new plays.

During this time (1592–94) of hard sledding for Thespians, Shakespeare's doings and whereabouts are unrecorded, and we do not even know whether he went on tour with whatever company it was that he belonged to. He may have put in his time cultivating the Earl of Southampton; no doubt he worked on *Venus and Adonis* and *Lucrece*, and perhaps on the Sonnets and one or more plays. It has been plausibly suggested that he got a lot of reading done. Whether he remained in London is unknown. Foreign travel has also been prescribed for him, particularly in Italy. There is no evidence for it. Others believe the comparative leisure of these years was partly devoted to an amour. In *Willobie his Avisa* (1594), a poem of uncertain authorship, Avisa is the beautiful, witty, chaste wife of an innkeeper. She has many wooers, including some of the nobility. An unhappy lover, one H.W., whom some would like to identify with Henry Wriothesley, Earl of Southampton, has a "familiar frend W.S. who not long before had tryed the curtesy of the like passion, and was now newly recouered of the like infection." This friend, "vewing a far off the course of this louing Comedy . . . determined to see whether it would sort to a happier end for this new actor, then it did for the old player." A couplet in Canto xlvii, spoken by "W.S.," expresses an idea suggested more than once by Shakespeare in his early works; it is not an original thought:

> She is no Saynt, She is no Nonne,
> I thinke in tyme she may be wonne.

Some see a reference here to Shakespeare's love affairs. It is certainly possible, but it is no less certainly not demonstrable.[14]

Neither Pembroke's nor Strange's played at court in the Christmas season of 1593–94, though the Queen's company did. Beginning late in December, Henslowe gave a public season of six weeks, probably at the Rose, with the Earl of Sussex's Men. Some think Shakespeare was temporarily attached to this company, since on January 24, 1594 they acted *titus & ondronicus*. It was repeated twice. Henslowe calls it new. Sussex's also gave a short Easter season in 1594 in alliance with the Queen's Men.

Soon after this, several of Shakespeare's plays got into print, though not under his name. These are: *Henry the Sixth, Part 2*, in the Bad Quarto [15] of 1594 entitled *The First part of the Contention betwixt the two famous Houses of Yorke and Lancaster; Henry the Sixth, Part 3*, in the Bad Quarto of 1595 entitled *The true Tragedie of Richard Duke of Yorke;* and *The Most Lamentable Romaine Tragedie of Titus Andronicus* in the Good Quarto of 1594. The title page of *Part 1* of *The Contention* does not specify the company that had acted it. The others mention

Pembroke's, though the title page of *Titus* lists "the Earle of
Darbie, Earle of *Pembrooke*, and Earle of *Sussex* their Seruants."
It hardly follows that because a play was once acted by a
company it must have been composed expressly for that company. Since there had been little acting in London after June,
1592, and hence no demand for new pieces, it is a reasonable
assumption that all the plays just mentioned had been written
before that date. To these earliest plays of Shakespeare should
probably be added *Henry the Sixth*, *Part 1* and *The Comedy of
Errors*, though neither was printed till the Folio of 1623 and
we have no evidence that either was ever a Pembroke play.

Against the theory that Shakespeare had been a Pembroke
man is the almost certain appearance of at least one of his
titles in the spring season of 1592 at the Rose.[16] Once again
we must conclude with a *non probatum*.[17] Shakespeare was a
leading member of the Lord Chamberlain's company by the
end of 1594. Of that there is no doubt. He may have been
connected with the same group of actors and with others at
various times between 1586 and 1594. There may have been
a period when he was free-lancing; but one or more company
connections seem probable, because he was an actor, too.
His engagement for a limited time by Pembroke's company is
a possibility.

Strange's Men seem to have had better luck than Pembroke's on their tour in 1593, though the death of their
patron, the new Earl of Derby, obliged them to find another
in 1594, and they became the Lord Chamberlain's Men. Before they turned up in London early in June, the Admiral's
company, headed by Alleyn, had begun acting under Henslowe, on May 14. Doubtless the old Strange's troupe likewise
applied to Henslowe when it got back to town. Repairs were
probably under way at the Rose; both companies went to
Newington Butts, where they played, perhaps on alternate
days, for ten performances ending on June 15, 1594. *Andronicous* was acted twice; *the tamynge of A shrowe* and *hamlet*, each
once. The last was not Shakespeare's play but an earlier
dramatization of the same story. *A Pleasant Conceited Historie,
called The taming of a Shrew* appeared anonymously in quarto

in 1594 as a Pembroke play. There are two main theories about it, the older and likelier holding that it is Shakespeare's chief source, the other that it is a Bad quarto of his play. As far as Henslowe's notation goes, the performance of June, 1594 might be of either version.

Alleyn naturally had the inside track with Henslowe, and the Admiral's went back to the Rose. The Chamberlain's Men now broke with Henslowe; Richard Burbage was their chief, and doubtless they were soon playing at his father's Theatre. They may also have acted at the Cross Keys Inn, for on October 8, 1594 Lord Hunsdon asked the Lord Mayor to permit them. Probably they wanted it for the ensuing winter. A desirable arrangement was to act in a suburban playhouse for at least half the year, and come in to a city hostelry during the winter, when audiences would less willingly put up with the discomforts of the trip to the theatrical districts. These were most serious on the way to the northern playhouses, the Theatre and the Curtain, which were reached by walking or riding. The favored method of getting over to the Rose was by using the watermen, who supplied a taxi service on the river. The Cross Keys was in the city, on the west side of Gracechurch or "Gracious" Street. It may have been the regular winter house of the Chamberlain's Men till the season of 1596–97.

If Shakespeare had been a Pembroke playwright, this was about the time he joined the Burbage forces. His transfer would have been regarded as an important feature of the general rearrangement of the companies. Others were the demise of Pembroke's and the reorganization of the Admiral's. The Chamberlain's, despite Alleyn's eminence, had the edge on their rivals. Dick Burbage was a superlative tragedian, Will Kempe was the town's favorite comedian, and Will Shakespeare was the premier dramatist. This combination made the Chamberlain's the number-one London company. They evidently purchased all plays by Shakespeare in the possession of others when they reorganized in 1594.

THE VERSE

English in Shakespeare's time had only recently become Modern English, and there were still conservatives who doubted its suitability for serious writing. Shakespeare was neither scientist nor philosopher, but a popular entertainer as well as a great artist. He delighted in words, and *Love's Labour's Lost* leaves no doubt of his intense interest in the future of the language. He employed a very large vocabulary and in his final period enjoyed playing tricks with it, and with syntax, as if to demonstrate his virtuosity. Word play he dallies with throughout his career. His profusion of puns is due no doubt partly to his own predilection and partly to his audience's relish of verbal ingenuity. Unless they are extraordinarily clever and novel, puns appeal nowadays chiefly to the unsophisticated; they are the shopworn stock-in-trade of many of our radio comedians. On the Elizabethan stage they were doubtless in their various degrees of cleverness equally palatable to the groundlings and to the wits. Many new Elizabethan words carried among their meanings the original Latin connotations, which afterwards dropped out; thus the scope for punning was even wider than it is now.

This is not the place for an essay on Elizabethan English; but the beginning reader should note that three and a half centuries have introduced many changes in pronunciation, vocabulary, and syntax. Shakespeare was a facile writer, but not a careless one; many lines that look a little obscure to us were perfectly clear to his audience. It seems more to the point here to summarize his technique as a composer of blank verse. We must not, however, lose sight of the frequent occurrence in his plays of rhymed iambic pentameter couplets and occasionally of quatrains and sonnets, nor of his greatness as a prose writer. No one has worked out a better English prose style than Shakespeare's was at the height of his career. Both verse and prose he molds to his immediate dramatic purposes, changing his style appropriately to character and situation. His mastery enabled him to vary it so widely that some critics, the "disintegrators," ascribe large

patches of the text to other pens. Shakespeare's versatility
might have given us a brilliant volume of parodies, and indeed he does occasionally parody his colleagues' styles, consciously or subconsciously. Thus the opening speech of *Henry
the Sixth* sounds for all the world like Marlowe; and parts of
Love's Labour's Lost have much the same light, quizzical touch
that distinguishes the comedies of Lyly.

Excepting its regular use for letters, proclamations, and
similar documents, there is no general principle according to
which Shakespeare turns within his plays to prose. Sometimes he uses it for low comedy or for courtly conversation,
but he also employs his very adaptable blank verse for these
or any other kinds of dialogue. His verse can be pedestrianly
expository, splendidly eloquent, or designedly rhetorical as
in the speeches of the Player King and Queen in *Hamlet;* or
it can soar to the heights of poetry. His prose is also capable
of bold poetic flights.

Blank verse had become almost mandatory for tragedy and
chronicle-history plays when Shakespeare began to write for
the stage.[18] It first came into English drama with *Gorboduc*,
the earliest "regular" English tragedy (1562).[19] Marlowe had
made the most effective use of it, investing it with color and
majestic elevation and a ringing virility well suited to his
somewhat epic tragedies. In Shakespeare's hands it became
more flexible, capable of exquisite lyricism, terrible passion,
plain and simple forcefulness, and even racy colloquialism.
But for the last of these effects he usually preferred not to
use verse at all; hence the prose of the murderers in *Richard
the Third*, I, iv. Rhyme he often employed to secure daintiness
and prettiness, as in *A Midsummer Night's Dream*, II, i, 18–31;
to set off a sententious passage, as in *Othello*, I, iii, 202–19;
to mark the close of a speech, as in *Macbeth*, I, iv, 20–21,
or of a scene, as in *Richard the Third*, I, i, 161–2; or to emphasize
asides or exits, as in *Richard the Third*, IV, iv, 15–16, 195–6.
As a rule there is more rhyme in the earlier plays than in
the later. The illustrative lines which follow are all from
Richard the Third.

"Blank" means in versification simply "unrhymed," but

so much English poetry has been written in unrhymed iambic pentameter that the term "blank verse" is restricted to that metre. Its normal line contains ten syllables, or five feet, the stresses falling on the even syllables:

And áll | the clouds | that lów'rd | upón | our house (I, i, 3).

But if all the lines in an extensive passage of blank verse were normal, the effect would be monotonous. Poets do not tick off numbers on their fingers as they compose. They feel the surge of a rhythm, and conform their expression to it with more or less regularity. Sometimes the rush of thought roughly gets the upper hand of music-making and actually dictates irregularity. A blank-verse line may vary considerably from the norm without upsetting the rhythm. Such variations add to the hearer's pleasure, just as they do in music. The best general rule is to read according to the sense, letting the stresses fall naturally.

Some of Shakespeare's words, however, were not accented by the Elizabethans as they are now. In many, accent was variable. Nor should an entire line always be read in a single breath. There is usually a pause at the end of the line, and sometimes another within it. In some verse forms, the pause near the middle of the line, called the caesura, is a regular feature. But Shakespeare, though such pauses often occur in his verse, did not compose with the caesura as such in mind, and some of his lines contain none. Nor does he always end-stop them, that is, observe a pause at the end of the line. As he grows in metrical skill, he varies his effects by frequently running the sense of a line over into the next without the slightest opportunity for a pause in reading. Since he became increasingly addicted to this trick, the ratio between "run-on" and "end-stopped" lines affords a rough test for determining the approximate positions of the plays in their chronological order. Such tests should, however, be applied with more caution than has always been exercised by metrical statisticians, for reliance on them may lead to arguing in a circle. Another criterion is the speech-ending test. As his career proceeded, Shakespeare grew fonder of ending a speech with a fraction of a line and filling it out to the required number of syllables with words by another speaker. Sometimes a line is divided among more than two speakers.

Any line of unrhymed verse derives its musical effect partly from the artfulness with which vowels and consonants are combined, and partly from the grouping of accented and unaccented syllables. With the latter consideration we are here concerned. The syllables of which a line is composed fall into sets consisting usually of one stressed and one or more unstressed syllables. Such a set is called a foot. Blank verse is unrhymed iambic pentameter. "Pentameter" means that the normal line has five feet. "Iambic" means that the normal foot consists of one stressed syllable preceded by an unstressed one.

And all | the clouds | that low'rd | upon | our house

is a perfectly regular line of iambic pentameter. We must now examine typical departures from the norm.

Common variations are lines of more or less than ten syllables. Not all lines that appear to have less are really deficient, if we recognize Elizabethan pronunciation. For example:

Then pa- | tiently | hear my | impa- | tience (IV, iv, 157),

Thus will | I drown | your ex- | clama- | tions (IV, iv, 154).

These are regular lines because the final syllable of "impatience" and of "exclamations" could be read as two syllables by the Elizabethans. The vowel in the "–ed" of the past and past participle was not always pronounced (in that case it is usually written or printed "'d"); but often it was, as in

Our bruis- | *ed* arms | hung up | for mon- | uments (I, i, 6)

and in

Envi- | ron'd me, | and howl- | *ed* in | mine ears (I, iv, 59).

Proper names are treated with great freedom. "Catesby" is regularly a dissyllable; but it probably has three syllables in

Well, let | them rest. | Come hith- | er, *Cat-* | *esby* (III, i, 157).

QUEEN ELIZABETH

from the Dillon portrait

THE FLOWER PORTRAIT OF SHAKESPEARE

THE CHANDOS PORTRAIT OF SHAKESPEARE

BEN JONSON
from the portrait ascribed to Isaac Oliver

"R," strongly pronounced, sometimes gives a word an extra syllable. "Henry" is trisyllabic (= Henery) in

So stood | the state | when Hen- | ry | the Sixth (II, iii, 16).

But sometimes "r" is so weak that it does not prevent the elision of one of two vowels separated by it. Some words are still pronounced with a varying number of syllables; here "hour" is a dissyllable:

For nev- | er yet | one hou- | r in | his bed (IV, i, 83).

Sometimes a brief pause has the metrical value of a syllable:

And help | to arm | me. ∧ | Leave me, | I say. (V, iii, 79);

But tell | me, ∧ | is young | George Stan- | ley living? (V, v, 9.)

Sometimes a superfluous syllable within the foot is to be elided or slurred. In

That no | man shall | have pri- | vate con- | ference (I, i, 86),

"conference" is a trisyllable; but here it is practically a dissyllable:

Forbear | your con- | ference with | the no- | ble Duke (I, i, 104).

Cf. the first foot of

Marry, we | were sent | for to | the just- | ices (II, iii, 46).

Elision or slurring is common in such expressions as "I had," "what is," "you will," "he is," "I am," etc. For example:

I had rath- | er be | a count- | ry serv- | ant maid (I, iii, 107).

When vowels stand unseparated by a consonant, elision or slurring is frequent; and it is not uncommon when "h," "th," or "v" intervenes:

Made glor- | ious sum- | mer by | this sun | of York (I, i, 2);

Even so, | an't please | your wor- | ship. Brak- | enbury, (I, i, 88).

Whether, in reading aloud, one is to elide or merely pronounce rapidly is for the speaker to decide. A good ear is the best guide. The first foot of the following line is probably trisyllabic, consisting not of one but of two unstressed syllables, followed by the stressed syllable:

Either thou | wilt die | by God's | just or- | dinance (IV, iv, 184).

Another test for dating a play is based on Shakespeare's increasing fondness for varying a line at the end by the addition of one or more unstressed syllables. That gives the line a double or "feminine" ending. When two additional syllables are thus employed, they are always capable of being pronounced together lightly; otherwise we should have a six-foot line. The following lines have feminine endings:

And I'll | corrupt | her man- | ners, stain | her beau | ty (IV, iv, 207);

Thy prime | of man- | hood dar- | ing, bold, | and ven | turous (IV, iv, 171).

Where a caesura falls, a metrically superfluous syllable sometimes occurs after the second or third foot. In other words, the end of the first part of the line is sometimes treated as though it were the end of the line:

Of what | you prom- | is'd me. | Well, | but what's | o'clock? (IV, ii, 113.)

Occasionally a hypermetrical syllable stands at the beginning of a line, not within the first foot:

O, | belike | his Maj- | esty | hath some | intent (I, i, 49).

On the other hand, lines are often incomplete, especially when they consist of brief exclamations, or short questions, answers, or commands:

Rich. Where is he? In his bed?
Hast. He is.   (I, i, 142–3);

Buck. Have done, have done. (I, iii, 279.)

Lengthy speeches sometimes end in an incomplete line. Apparently the poet, having concluded in a short line what he wished the character to utter, preferred leaving the line incomplete and beginning the next speech with a new line, to filling out the short line with superfluous verbiage:

Grant me this boon (I, ii, 218);

I crave your blessing (II, ii, 106).

An incomplete line may occur anywhere:

Hold me a foe — (II, i, 55).

Here, we may suppose, Shakespeare after he had written these words recognized their effectiveness as a short line and decided not to weaken their force by adding to them. Lines are sometimes incomplete because some significant action is performed, especially an exit or entrance, which may be felt as having metrical value:

I go.| | Write to | me ver- | y short- | ly (IV, iv, 428).

When the second foot might be expected, the speaker probably turns back for a moment. Lines that are apparently incomplete are often parts of regular lines distributed among two or more speakers. Such lines are capable of much variation, especially by the insertion of hypermetrical syllables both at the beginning and at the end of the words assigned to a speaker. Alexandrines (six-foot lines) are rare but occasionally occur:

Anón | expéct | him hére; | but íf | she bé | obdúr- | ate (III, i, 39);

but not all lines of twelve or thirteen syllables are Alexandrines, if scanned in accordance with the foregoing rules. Occasionally fourteeners appear, and sometimes trochaic tetrameter; and the songs employ various metres.

Besides variation in the number of syllables, Shakespeare's blank-verse line often varies the stress within the foot. A common form is the reversal of stressed and unstressed syllables, which gives a momentarily trochaic interruption to the regular iambic beat:

What, we | have man- | y good- | ly days | to see (IV, iv, 320);

My La- | dy Grey | his wife, | Clarence, | 'tis she (I, i, 64).

The strength of the stress itself varies; it is determined by the sense of the passage and the taste of the reader. Though no rule can be set up, it is evident that there are weak and strong stresses, and that, particularly in the last foot, they can usually be distinguished. In his later plays Shakespeare more freely employs the weak or light stress in this position, in harmony with his tendency to abolish the pause at the end of the line. Thus

Then curs'd she Hastings. O, remember, God (III, iii, 18)

illustrates a strong ending; while

Fairer than tongue can name thee, let me have (I, ii, 81),

That ever yet this land was guilty of (IV, iii, 3),

God bless the Prince from all the pack of you (III, iii, 4)

have weak endings. Ignorance on the part of some actors of this trick of Shakespeare's versification is responsible for grotesque blunders in the delivery of his lines. The ratio between strong and weak endings affords yet another test of the plays' chronology.

There is normally but one stress to a foot, but in practice there is some variation:

Art thou | my son? (IV, iv, 155.)

Here, whatever the number of feet may be, all four of the words might well receive equal stress. So impressive is the occasional accumulation of stresses that this line, if properly spoken, hardly seems a short one. Cf.:

Earth gápes, | héll búrns, | fíends roár, | saínts práy (IV, iv, 75);

Blúsh, blúsh, | thou lúmp | of foúl | defórm- | ity (I, ii, 57).

Until one acquires the knack of hearing through silent reading, it is best to read all dramatic or truly lyric poetry aloud. This is especially desirable in learning to appreciate Shakespeare, who wrote his lines, not to be seen and studied, but to be heard, spoken with emotional force.

Chapter 3

THE EXPERIMENTAL COMEDIES

THE COMEDY OF ERRORS

THOUGH in Falstaff he created a comic character at least the equal of any in the world's literature, one who continues to be not only witty in himself "but the cause that wit is in other men," Shakespeare is not supreme in the realm of pure comedy, where there may be something in the eighteenth century's critical bromide that he relied more on nature than on art. The freshness of his writing, recognized from the first as one of its most appealing features, gives his best work an appearance of complete freedom from artifice; and thus it lacks the designed remoteness cultivated alike by the neoclassical tragic dramatist and the playwright who tries to isolate a segment of society within the confines of a comedy of manners. In Shakespeare, comedy and tragedy are rarely far apart, and both are close to human nature. His best comedies are romantic. Like his tragedies, they tell stories and, for all their gaiety, usually skirt the brink of calamity. As comedies, they may not be so great as *The Alchemist, Tartuffe, The Way of the World, The School for Scandal,* and *Candida;* but as dramatic vehicles for poetry, wisdom, and that touch of nature which, in making the whole world kin, makes it happy in the recognition of its kinship, they do not suffer by any comparison.

Yet it took Shakespeare some time to find where his comic vein lay; and even then he remained in it only a few years, turning from the joyous comedies of happy love to the troubled themes of the realistic comedies, before closing his career with his Ninth Symphony, the dramatic romances. His earliest comedies are attempts to discover his métier. Unfortunately, not one of them can be certainly dated, and that the order in which they are here described is the right one can not be demonstrated.

128

The Comedy of Errors may be his first play, though it was not printed till 1623, in the First Folio, which gives us an excellent text. Some think that, the manuscript having been lost, the printers "copy" was assembled from the separate parts as originally written out for the actors, with the help of the "plat," the scene-by-scene abstract hung up for guidance during performance. This theory has not been generally accepted.[1] Nor does its being the shortest of Shakespeare's plays warrant our concluding that in *Errors* we are confronted with a version pared down for acting.

The accounts of the treasurer of the Chamber record payment for court performances by the Chamberlain's Men at Greenwich on December 26 and 28, 1594. Since a payment to the Admiral's is also listed for the 28th, and since on that evening the Chamberlain's were acting in London, at Gray's Inn, their second appearance at Greenwich was probably on the 27th.[2] The performance at Gray's Inn was a feature of the holiday revels there. For their second "Grand Night" Gray's had invited an "ambassador" and his retinue from another of the Inns of Court, the Inner Temple. The crowd was disorderly and too large for the hall, and the disgruntled "Templarians" withdrew. Then there was dancing;

and after such Sports, a Comedy of Errors (like to *Plautus* his *Menechmus*) was played by the Players. So that Night was begun, and continued to the end, in nothing but Confusion and Errors; whereupon, it was ever afterwards called, *The Night of Errors*.

Next evening the gentlemen of Gray's held a mock inquiry. According to its sportive findings, a sorcerer was at the bottom of the business; he "had foisted a Company of base and common Fellows, to make up our Disorders with a Play of Errors and Confusions." All this from the *Gesta Grayorum* of 1688.

Our play, then, had been written by the end of 1594; how much earlier is unknown. The punning lines (III, ii),

> Where France?
> In her forehead; arm'd and reverted, making
> war against her heir,

allude to Henry of Navarre and his long duel with the Catholic League. In 1584 the death of Anjou, Henry III's younger brother, extinguished the hopes of the house of Valois and made Navarre, a Bourbon prince, heir presumptive to the throne of France. But only a small minority held to the indefeasibility of strict hereditary right; and the League, refusing to recognize the Protestant champion, made war on him from 1585 to 1587. Henry III's instigation, late in 1588, of the murder of the League's moving spirit, the Duke of Guise, inevitably threw the King into the arms of Navarre, whose status as heir was accordingly strengthened. After the assassination of Henry III in August, 1589, Navarre was, strictly speaking, no longer heir but Henry IV of France. Since, however, he had to fight for his rights, the allusion in *The Comedy of Errors* might still have been made logically enough. Elizabeth aided Navarre with men and money. The war dragged on till July, 1593, when Henry's decision that "Paris is worth a mass" brought about the collapse of the League's efforts to exclude him from the throne. Thus, while the reference to the religious wars in France is unmistakable, it does not date the comedy for us. Suggested parallels with plays of the early nineties are insignificant. Sometime between 1584 and 1594 Shakespeare wrote *The Comedy of Errors* — of that only can we be certain; possibly its date falls about halfway between these limits.[3]

Although, under title of *The Boys from Syracuse*, a musical version, wild and free, played to critical as well as popular applause on Broadway during the season of 1938–39, Shakespeare's comedy has never, so far as we know, been really popular. A reference, however, by John Manningham [4] indicates that as late as 1602 it was still being acted, at least occasionally; and there was a revival at court in 1604.[5] No record has been found of any subsequent performance till 1734, when the Covent Garden Theatre seems to have staged a two-act adaptation called *See if you like it, or 'Tis all a Mistake*. How long after 1604 the play remained active in the repertory is therefore unknown. Down to 1642, when the Puritans closed the London playhouses, even a total absence of recorded performances does not prove that none were given. But after 1660, when acting was resumed under the patronage of the royal brothers, Charles II and the Duke of York, and diaries, stage histories, and many other documents become available, there is a strong presumption against the revival of any play of Shakespeare's that remains without contemporary mention.

From 1741, when it was acted at Drury Lane with Charles Macklin as Dromio of Syracuse, until well into the nineteenth century, *The Comedy of Errors* was played fairly often, but always in altered versions. David Garrick did not revive it; Covent Garden, the other great patent house, was its home during his long régime at Drury Lane. From 1788, when he took over the management of Drury Lane, till his retirement from the stage of Covent Garden in 1817, John Philip Kemble not only was head of the First Family of English players, he succeeded Garrick as the recognized leader of the profession. He produced his alteration of *The Comedy of Errors* at Covent Garden in 1808; it was a version of an adaptation ascribed to Thomas Hull, which had been staged at the same theatre in 1779. The chief features, which Kemble retained, are the fattening of the rôle of the Syracusan Dromio and a large infusion of sentiment in Adriana's and Luciana's scenes. Professor Odell, our chief authority on the history of Shakespearean revival, gives these changes his qualified blessing. 1790, however, had seen a new adaptation, in three acts, also at Covent Garden; it was presumably not very different from *The Twins; or, Which is Which?*, published in London in 1780 and also in Edinburgh, where it had already been performed. The efforts of the adapter, William Woods, are chiefly directed to shortening the original play and emphasizing its farcical side. Frederic Reynolds, indefatigable perpetrator of "operatic" versions, successfully brought out *The Comedy of Errors* at Covent Garden in 1819, with added musical numbers consisting of selections from other plays and poems by Shakespeare to settings lifted from Mozart, Arne, and others. There was, for example, a hunting scene in the third act, in order to introduce "When icicles hang by the wall" from *Love's Labour's Lost;* it was sung before a backing of snow-topped mountains. In the fourth act "Antipholis" of Syracuse turns up drunk at the house of the merchant Balthazar, to afford an excuse for a trio and chorus in "Come, thou monarch of the vine," from *Antony and Cleopatra.*

Shakespeare's play was restored in 1855 by Samuel Phelps at Sadler's Wells. In the long roll of Shakespeare producers his name stands among the most honorable — for his taste, his fidelity to his author, and the pious enthusiasm which led him to revive all but seven of the plays. In 1864 the Irish brothers Charles and Harry Webb were well received in the rôles of the Dromios. They acted the comedy straight through without intermission or fall of curtain. In 1883 John Sleeper Clarke, Edwin Booth's brother-in-law, played Dromio of Syracuse at the Strand. In 1878 American audiences first saw the spirited production of William Henry Crane and Stuart Robson, who acted the Dromios. But, though a "tabloid" version was in the repertory of the Globe Theatre at the New York World's Fair in the summer of 1939, the play has not held the stage well, despite revivals by repertory companies, including Sir Frank Robert Benson's and Sir Philip Ben Greet's. Both these actor-managers were devoted to Shakespeare. Countless Americans gratefully remember Greet for their first impressions, as schoolchildren, of Shakespeare on the stage; while in *My Memoirs* (1930) Benson asserts, with a proper pride, that "we were the first to achieve the notable feat of playing the whole list of Shakespeare's plays."

An early date has been urged for the composition of *Errors* on the score of its classical source. Very likely Shakespeare read Plautus in school. If he was ever a pedagogue, this comedy is probably his first surviving piece; but it seems more likely that he was already an actor when he penned it. The earliest known English translation of the source play was registered on June 10, 1594; the earliest edition known was in 1595. Shakespeare could have seen the manuscript; the translator, William Warner, dedicated his book to the Hunsdons, of whom the elder was patron of Shakespeare's company. But there is no reason to doubt that the dramatist's Latinity was equal to reading the original. In the Folio stage directions occur "Antipholis Sereptus" (*surreptus*, stolen) and, for his twin, "Antipholis Erotes" and "Errotis." Since *surreptus* appears in the Plautine Prologue, while the other adjectives may be misprints for *erraticus* or *errans* (wandering), the presumption is strengthened that Shakespeare knew his Plautus in the Latin.

From the *Menaechmi* comes the core of the plot, the confusion of twins. To it Shakespeare adds the twin servants. The second pair was doubtless suggested by another Plautine play, the *Amphitruo*, which has two sets of doubles, masters and servants, though they are not twins. Besides a number of minor details, the *Amphitruo* also supplied the theme of Act III, Scene i, the husband kept out of his house by an interloper. No English translation of this comedy is known to have existed in Shakespeare's time. The serious framework, the story of Ægeon and Æmelia, is from the old romance of *Apollonius of Tyre*, probably as told by Chaucer's contemporary, John Gower, in his *Confessio Amantis*. From these sources Shakespeare presumably worked directly. *The historie of Error* of the Paul's Boys in 1577 was probably a morality play. It is unlikely that *A historie of fferrar*, acted by Sussex's Men in 1583, has any connection with *The Comedy of Errors*.

From the mixture of blank verse, doggerel, prose, and decasyllabic verse rhymed in couplets and alternately, some have inferred the partial survival of an earlier, non-Shakespearean text. It seems more likely that Shakespeare is experimenting with style as well as genre. Others hold that the variety of metres indicates a special reworking for the performance at Gray's Inn. The better verse is supposed to be more mature writing. The theory that Shakespeare's works underwent frequent revision is open to at least two strong general objections. His steady output of new pieces could hardly have left him much time for tinkering with old ones; and if his plays were often revamped, an added burden was imposed on actors already taxed by the requirement of keeping up with new items in the repertory. It is easier to learn a new rôle than to unlearn part of one already memorized and weave in substitutions. This is not to argue that Shakespeare never rewrote. But it is very unlikely that the repertory system would allow any such wholesale revision as some believe. The conclusions of the "disintegrators," as these textual theorists have been dubbed, vary as widely among themselves as they diverge from the views of more orthodox scholars. In general, the disintegrators fall in two main groups: absolvers of Shakespeare by ascribing inferior portions of his plays to other pens, and explainers-away of harmless textual inconsistencies by hypothetical revisions which Shakespeare is alleged to have made on a very large scale both in adapting plays by other authors and in revamping from time to time earlier pieces of his own. But the various metres of *The Comedy of Errors* are probably not remains of several textual strata; they are rather tactfully adjusted to character and situation. Even the doggerel serves the dramatist's comic turn, as when the Ephesian Dromio settles the question of fraternal precedence at the final exeunt:

> We came into the world like brother and brother;
> And now let's go hand in hand, not one before the other.

Since similar effects have been applauded in the mad verses of Mr. Ogden Nash, we need not deplore nor try to explain away Shakespeare's artful appropriation of doggerel to farcical uses.

Certain stage directions, "from the Courtesan's" (IV, i, 14), "from the Bay" (IV, i, 85), "to the Priory" (V, i, 37), and "to the Abbess" (V, i, 281), recall the conventions of the old multiple setting, in which all the houses and localities are either on the stage or adjacent to it; but the frequent dispatch of the Dromios as messengers is enough to indicate that Shakespeare follows the normal Elizabethan practice of treating place impressionistically.

Though the play is a farce, it is invested with a certain dignity by its framework of romance. The comic mishaps of the two sets of twins are brought off by the author's deft manipulation of episode; there is no need of characterization in farce. But Shakespeare was incapable of the sustained callousness which marks the dramatist who deals in farce alone.

His gentleness, his sensitiveness to human pain, are always interfering. And so we have Ægeon and Æmilia handled not merely as background for their sons' misadventures, but tenderly; and Luciana is not simply Adriana's confidante. Her love story is added by Shakespeare, though he only sketches it in. He reduces and tones down the Courtesan's rôle, and the reconciliation of Adriana and her husband also departs from the source.

What the play lacks is, of course, poetry. Nor is the dialogue for the low comedians comparable to the raciness of Launce in *The Two Gentlemen of Verona*. Nowhere does the style approach the polish of *Love's Labour's Lost*. There is scarcely a touch of the sensuous beauty of *Venus and Adonis*. *Titus Andronicus*, even, has finer lines. To answer that *The Comedy of Errors* is a farce does not absolve the author, for so is *The Taming of the Shrew*. It is the stylistic poverty of *Errors* which stamps it as, in all probability, the first of Shakespeare's surviving plays. The dramatist is here concerned mainly with structural technique. The plot is neatly contrived, but he had a working model in Plautus. There is the merest trace of the romantic glow that warms his more typical work. All his histories, even the earliest, are alive with it. If the plotting of *The Two Gentlemen* is, to our taste, perfunctory in the last act, Shakespeare succeeds in the much more difficult business of making some of his puppets live as well as move.

Traces of the stock types and situations of Latin comedy continue for some time to appear in his plays, but he was never again to accept them with such docility. After Shakespeare's comedies, declares Jonson the neoclassicist, "Neat *Terence*, witty *Plautus*, now not please." For us *The Comedy of Errors* must also "antiquated, and deserted lye," not quite a member of "Natures family." If it was Shakespeare's first play, there is a certain irony in the indebtedness to Plautus of the commencing dramatist who was soon to put him in the shade.

THE TAMING OF THE SHREW

This was probably the first of those plays of Shakespeare destined to hold the stage down to our own time; but whether it was written during the experimental period or in the middle or even the late nineties no one really knows. It is not mentioned by Meres in 1598, unless it be "Love's Labour's Won." [6] Perhaps that mysterious title belongs to some play which perished before the First Folio was collected, though *All's Well that Ends Well* is a possibility. Since *Love's Labour's Lost* presents us with a group of gallants abjectly submissive to the ladies they admire, *Love's Labour's Won* may have been a companion piece. Or it could be an alternate title for a surviving play in which masculinity gets the whip hand. It may allude to Lucentio's stooping to conquer in *The Shrew*. Or, since Meres balances half a dozen comedies against as many tragedies and tragic histories, his omission of a title may have no significance. *Henry the Sixth* is not listed by him.

Metrical tests involving the proportion of weak and feminine endings, of blank verse, of rhyme, of prose, of run-on lines, and of speeches ending within a line, while by no means negligible, are not now taken so seriously as they used to be. They do not help us much here, though it is true that as Shakespeare goes on he writes blank verse more flexibly and uses more prose and less rhyme. The stock figures of the subplot and its classical origin point to an early date for *The Shrew*. Certainly the romantic note is conspicuous by its absence; the play is a double-barreled farce. The style easily surpasses *The Comedy of Errors* but is scarcely comparable to the plays of 1595-96.

No edition is known prior to the First Folio; but an anonymous play, *The taming of a Shrew*, has been tagged in a recent study as a Bad quarto [7] of Shakespeare's comedy.[8] If it is, it differs radically from the other Bad quartos. It is probably not an offshoot of Shakespeare's text but his chief source. Though Samuel Rowley has been suggested as a collaborator, efforts to discover its authorship by stylistic tests have met with no success. Nor can it be dated. The title page purports to identify it as a Pembroke company play. It contains a number of ridiculous Marlovian echoes which exclude the possibility that Marlowe wrote it. The publication in 1594 may have been an attempt to exploit the success of Shakespeare's comedy. Unfortunately, we know nothing about the original production of *The Shrew*. Henslowe's entry in June, 1594, though it specifies *A Shrew*, may refer to either piece. The first separate edition of *The Shrew* was in 1631; *A Shrew* was reprinted in 1596 and 1607.

The taming of a Shrew combines three plots. The taming story may be pure invention, though old tales have obedience tests similar to the husband's wager, wifely acquiescence in his extravagant assertions, and other episodes in the tamer's curriculum. The anonymous dramatist takes his subplot, the wooing of the younger sister, from George Gascoigne's *Supposes* (acted in 1566, published in 1573), which is in turn a translation of Ariosto's *Suppositi* (1509). The third element is the hoaxing of Christopher Sly.

That in revising the older play Shakespeare had a collaborator is the general, but perhaps erroneous, opinion. There is no reason to suppose he could not vary his style and metre at will. The collaborator, it is alleged, handled the subplot of Bianca and Lucentio, which is more complicated in *The Shrew* than in the source. In *Suppositi* the lover takes service with his prospective father-in-law, he has an elderly rival, and his servant poses as a suitor. None of these amusing features appears in the plot of *A Shrew*, where the princely wooer passes as a merchant's son and is not troubled with a competitor. His servant pretends to be a music teacher in order to keep the shrew occupied while her two younger sisters meet the hero and his friend. If, then, Shakespeare was indebted to *A Shrew* for the fusing of the two stories, he must have gone back to *Supposes* for some of the best features of his subplot. The love affair *sub rosa*, the deceived father, the clever servant, and the pedant are all of classical origin; they also appear in the *commedia dell'arte* of the Italians. As in *The Comedy of Errors*, Shakespeare is working up stock materials in deft but conventional form — another reason for inclining to an early date for *The Shrew*.

Kate and Petruchio, on the other hand, are not stock figures, and perhaps their freshness interested Shakespeare more. Certainly he writes for them with more vigor. The Sly framework is also much better done than in *A Shrew* — as far as it goes. The hoax is a variant of an old and widely current story; it appears, for example, in the *Arabian Nights*. The Sly story is continued in *A Shrew* through the play, which ends after he is left in his rags at the alehouse. He takes his experience for a dream and resolves to apply it by going home and taming his own wife. It is hard to believe that Shakespeare abandoned this logical ending after rewriting the first of the Sly framework so brilliantly. The best guess is that the Folio gives us a cut text. It is just possible that we have all the lines Shakespeare actually wrote out and that the comedians were expected to improvise.

To maintain, as Jonson did, that Shakespeare is for all time is not to say he was not of his own time. We have to take our friends as they are, and the same is true of the friendships we form with writers of earlier epochs. Shakespeare was not Ibsen. We may, if we. choose, deplore his failure to catch up the cudgels for woman's rights; but we must abstain from reading a subtlety that is not there into Kate's final speech of submission. Probably it squares with Shakespeare's opinion; but about that we must not be too positive, since if *A Shrew* is his source he did not invent its tenor. In either case, Petruchio's victory is complete. Yet we should not fail to note the delicacy with which Shakespeare treats his tempestuous heroine on her honeymoon. *The Shrew* is much less crude than the usual knockabout farce. The plot really calls for an hilarious scene of wife beating; but though the play can hardly be called elevating, Shakespeare keeps the fun on a higher plane than that. He is careful to display Kate's damnable temper when she first appears, so that Petruchio's educational program will appeal to all as no more than she deserves. In *A Shrew* this care is not exercised. Not that Shakespeare is writing to convert shrews or instruct their husbands; the object of his play is to entertain. Its principal merit is high spirits, and the sheer gaiety and extravagance of it account for its remaining in the repertory. The humor pleases by its wildness, not by richness nor by exquisiteness. Petruchio's name, by the way, should be pronounced as Shakespeare spelled it in English, not "Petrukio."

About the play's Elizabethan vogue we have little information. The Quarto of 1631 tells us it had been acted by the King's Men at the Globe and Blackfriars. There was a court performance in 1633. John Fletcher wrote a sequel, *The Womans Prize: or, The Tamer Tamed*, in which a second wife turns the tables on Petruchio. Under the Restoration, the Merry Monarch's favorite comedian, John Lacy, composed a nauseous adaptation, *Sauny the Scott*, with Grumio promoted to the leading rôle. Early in 1716 Charles Johnson made a political skit out of the Sly material. The hero of *The Cobler of Preston* is a ridiculous caricature of the humbler rebels of the '15. Johnson's piece was staged at Drury Lane on February 3. Meanwhile Christopher Bullock, star low comedian of the rival company at Lincoln's Inn Fields, had got wind of Johnson's intention and forestalled him by rushing on the stage with another *Cobler of Preston*. The next version was a two-act ballad-farce called *A Cure for a Scold*, by James Worsdale, the portrait painter and minor dramatist, acted at Drury Lane in 1735. This is a Shakespeare adaptation twice-removed, since it rests on Lacy's *Sauny the Scott*. That despicable version continued to supplant the original till 1754, when Garrick substituted a three-act alteration of his own, in which, however, he did not appear. His *Catharine and Petruchio* simplifies the subplot somewhat along the lines of *The taming of a Shrew*, though the Induction is omitted. Hannah Pritchard was the first of this long-lived version's Kates; Catherine Clive was the next. Henry Woodward, the famous light comedian, was its first Petruchio. It is hard to imagine the stately queen of tragedy, Sarah Siddons, playing Kate to John Philip Kemble's Petruchio; but she did, though not regularly. Some later Kates were Mrs. Charles Kemble, Helen Faucit, Mme. Vestris, and Isabella Glyn; while the roster of Petruchios includes, besides Charles Kemble, a knightly group of actor-managers: Sir Johnston Forbes-Robertson, Sir Frank Benson, Sir Herbert Beerbohm Tree, and Sir John Martin-Harvey. The first joint performance of Ellen Terry and Sir Henry Irving was in these rôles, in 1867.

Frederic Reynolds was responsible for an "operatic" *Shrew* at Drury Lane in 1828. It failed, and Garrick's adaptation resumed its undisputed sway. It is still occasionally acted by misguided amateurs, and was not driven from the professional stage till 1887, when Augustin Daly gave Shakespeare's comedy its first American revival, with the late John Drew as Petruchio, Ada Rehan as a superb Katherina, and that sterling veteran, Otis Skinner, then a "juvenile," as Lucentio.[9] Even the scholarly Edwin Booth, who enjoyed acting Petruchio, had used a version of Garrick's adaptation; and so did Tree, as late as 1897. Since Daly, *The Shrew* has often been played in England and the United States. It was in Benson's repertory in London and Stratford. Oscar Asche's first performance was in 1904; his Kate was Lily Brayton, his Lucentio Walter Hampden. Martin-Harvey also revived it in London, in 1913. The Old Vic has not neglected it; indeed, all the First Folio plays have been staged there. But of this and other admirable repertory organizations I shall not attempt to list all the productions. Revivals by managerial stars have usually provided the measure of a play's vogue. Yet the less conspicuous performances that a repertory company takes in its stride are often superior in merit and in the pleasure they give an auditor for whom Shakespeare's play's the thing. Edward Hugh Sothern and Julia Marlowe revived *The Shrew*, but with little success. Margaret Anglin was a fine Kate. More recently, Maurice Evans played Petruchio at Sadler's Wells, and Edith Evans Katherina at the New. Alfred Lunt and his wife, Lynn Fontanne, gave spirited performances in this country. To be sure, they overacted, but that is now the rule. *The Shrew* is farce, and farce is brutal; but there is not the slightest justification, textual or historical, for turning the rôle of Petruchio into one long riot of whip-cracking, nor indeed for introducing a whip at all.

This piece was one of the first works of Shakespeare to reach the motion-picture screen, a medium which, though it has not yet succeeded in transposing any of his plays without serious losses, seems destined to become, quite aside from its artistic possibilities, a powerful influence in keeping them before the illiterate — to whom, among the rest, their author addressed them.

THE TWO GENTLEMEN OF VERONA

None of Shakespeare's plays is more obviously experimental than *The Two Gentlemen*. Its unhappy happy ending is notorious; and its diction is a jumble of poetry a trifle too smooth (II, vii, 25–38), empty rhetoric (III, i, 4–21), brilliant raciness (IV, iv, 1–43), tedious word-catching (I, i, 70–155), and rodomontade (V, iv, 126–31). Yet it contains one of Shakespeare's most famous lyrics, "Who is Silvia?" — not among his best, but known to everyone in Schubert's lovely setting; here and there the characterization shows more of the natural touch than anything in the other experimental comedies; no longer is love merely a theme for jest nor a simple means of complicating a farcical plot; and, in Launce, Shakespeare creates the earliest of his first-rate clowns.

Aside from these merits and despite its manifest faults, *The Two Gentlemen* claims special interest because, though he has not yet shaken off the insipid influence of Lyly, it is Shakespeare's first venture into romantic comedy. Greene and Peele had done something with this Italian genre, but not much. Perhaps Shakespeare never felt quite satisfied with his own attempt. At any rate, and this may mean it had dropped out of the repertory, he quarries from *The Two Gentlemen* for later comedies. Julia and Lucetta on the suitors (I, ii) he plays over again with Portia and Nerissa in *The Merchant of Venice* (I, ii) — brilliantly. Julia's plea to Silvia for Proteus and the pathos of her speechless love for her master are handled in the Viola-Orsino-Olivia triangle of *Twelfth Night* with new depth of feeling, exquisitely blent with humor. Speed bawling for Silvia (II, i) and Launce's monologue in

II, iii are both revamped for Launcelot Gobbo in *The Merchant of Venice*, though the latter of these speeches is hardly bettered.

Meres lists *The Two Gentlemen* in 1598, and that is the only external evidence for dating it. No one doubts that it belongs among the early comedies; its imperfections label it. The somewhat perfunctory fifth act may be due to Shakespeare's haste; possibly the company was calling for a new piece in a hurry. About 1593–94 is a reasonable conjecture for the date of composition, and it may have been the first play Shakespeare gave the newly organized Chamberlain's Men. How often or how long it was acted is unknown, for no record of performance has chanced to survive till Garrick produced Benjamin Victor's adaptation in 1762. Richard Yates was the Launce and his wife the Julia; Garrick did not take a part himself. Among many changes Victor invents more matter for Launce and his ungrateful cur — as if Shakespeare had not supplied enough to insure a weakness for this play in all dog-lovers. The adaptation was acted half a dozen times in its first season and then shelved. The first recorded performance of the original comedy, apparently little altered, was at Covent Garden in 1784. In 1790 J. P. Kemble staged a Drury Lane revival; but at Covent Garden, in 1808, he used his own version of Victor's adaptation, playing Valentine himself. Neither of his attempts to revive the play met with any success. The latter was seen by Kemble's brilliant colleague, George Frederick Cooke, who says it "was, in theatrical phrase, well got up, and well acted; but dull, and without much interest." Reynolds's "operatic" version, on the other hand, had a run of twenty-nine performances; it was produced at Covent Garden in 1821. Macready's revival of the original play in 1841 was a failure. He, too, cast himself as Valentine. Under Benjamin Webster's management at the Haymarket, Charles Kean and his wife played Valentine and Julia in 1848, but the public refused to be interested. Phelps revived the play in 1857, but did not act in it. Daly produced it in New York in 1895, but his revival failed in London, though Ada Rehan was the Julia. In 1904 Mr. Granville-Barker played

Speed in J. H. Leigh's revival at the Court Theatre. Except in repertory or by amateurs, and then but seldom, the play has not, so far as I know, been offered to the twentieth-century audience since 1910, when it was acted in London and Manchester. There is, indeed, small reason why it should be.

For the text our sole authority is the Folio, which provides a good one, though there are odd features. All the characters appearing in a scene are listed at the head of it, and subsequent entrances and most exits are unmarked. Other stage directions, except final exits and exeunts, are also omitted. These textual peculiarities have been laid to the lack of a complete manuscript; the Folio text, some think, was assembled from the actors' separate parts, with aid from the plat.[10] This hypothesis may be correct, but the whole "assembly" theory is viewed with suspicion by most scholars. Such a process would multiply the chances of error, and it is doubtful whether a text so satisfactory as the Folio *Two Gentlemen* could come into being that way. Dr. McKerrow suggests that the printer's "copy" may have been a transcript made "for some classically minded amateur or patron," who preferred to see the characters listed, classical fashion, at the heads of the scenes.

The source is the story of Felix and Felismena in a Spanish pastoral romance, the *Diana Enamorada* of the Portuguese Jorge de Montemayor. The earliest complete English translation, by Bartholomew Yonge, had been made by 1582 but was not published till 1598. There is little verbal resemblance between it and the play. Earlier translations of parts of the *Diana* did not get into print. Perhaps Shakespeare read a French translation by Nicolas Colin, which went through several editions in the '70's and '80's. Perhaps he took his plot from a play that has not survived, *The history of felix & philiomena*, acted at Greenwich by the Queen's Men in 1585. In any case, the vague and even contradictory geography of his play reflects Shakespeare's rather hazy notions about northern Italy.

In the *Diana*, Felix (Proteus) sends a letter to Felismena (Julia) by her maid Rosina (Lucetta), who delivers it under

much the same circumstances as in I, ii. An amorous correspondence continues for nearly a year. Felix's disapproving
father sends him away, and Felismena follows in male attire.
She hears her former lover serenading Celia (Silvia), enters
his service as a page, becomes his confidante, and carries a
letter to the lady. From this point on Shakespeare, or an
intermediate source, changed the story. In the *Diana*, Celia,
like Olivia in *Twelfth Night* and Phebe in *As You Like It*,
falls in love with the disguised girl. Valentine is not in the
Spanish romance, nor the motif of love versus friendship, so
prominent in Shakespeare's Sonnets, Lyly's *Euphues* and *Endimion*, and many other Elizabethan works. In the romance
Celia dies of blighted love, and the unhappy Felix disap-
pears. Felismena, garbed as a shepherdess, travels far in search
of him. At last she comes on a knight hard beset by three
enemies; he disposes of one, and she kills the others. It is
Felix, and the lovers are reconciled and married.

This is the very stuff of romance, and so is Shakespeare's
play. Plot, as in *Errors* and *The Shrew*, is more important than
character, ideas, or literary polish; but now the core of the
plot is love. Shakespeare's first resort to the romantic bag of
tricks, to which he went again and again throughout the
rest of his career, provides lovers' crosses and double-crosses,
a loving maid disguised as a lad, a rope ladder and flight from
a tyrannical father, exile, outlaws in the greenwood, a sere-
nade, a rendezvous at a friar's cell, a ring for a token, attempted rape and rescue, and at last forgiveness all round and
a dash of heroics that do not quite come off.

The inexpertness of the fifth act is not in itself conclusive
evidence for an early date. Homer sometimes nods; and Shakespeare, who had composed model opening scenes of exposition
and action for *Romeo and Juliet* and *Othello*, was capable of
following the fine shipwreck which begins *The Tempest*, with
the tedious monologue of Prospero to Miranda. We must
not, however, forget that Elizabethan audiences loved the
sensational, and that even the lady's silence at "All that
was mine in Silvia I give thee" (V, iv) may not have struck
Shakespeare's contemporaries so unpleasantly as it strikes us.

How they liked the play we do not know. Certainly the dramatist is leaning too heavily on conventions — the Jack-must-have-Jill principle of patched-up happy endings, the exaltation of masculine friendship above romantic love, the passive rôle of women in courtship — still a convention, for all Mr. Shaw's valiant denial, — the speedy repentance without external motivation.

The last of these conventions is frequently employed by Shakespeare, and even here with little less plausibility than is sometimes afforded by life itself. There is no reason in human nature why Proteus should not repent, as Laertes and Leontes do. The fault lies in neglecting Aristotle's rule that what counts is not scientific possibility but artistic probability. There is no defending a play as a timeless work of art if it fails at this point. Convention was soon mastered by Shakespeare and forced to serve his turn. Here it gets the better of him. Critical ingenuity has been taxed in an effort to palliate this denouement; but while haste may have been the reason, that does not excuse the author. Nor have attempts to unload parts of the final scene onto some other dramatist met with any success. At his worst Shakespeare was capable of almost anything. He is a long way from his best in the fifth act of his first romantic comedy. It is a little comforting to reflect that even he had to learn his trade.

LOVE'S LABOUR'S LOST

When Shakespeare came up to London, the leading comic dramatist was John Lyly, the famous stylist, whose *Euphues. The Anatomy of Wyt* had made a tremendous impression in 1578. This extraordinary effort belongs to prose fiction; but the narrative is little more than an excuse for conversational essays, and the author is less interested in telling a story and having his say on a variety of topics than in displaying a coruscating command of style. It is an extremely mannered style; nothing of any artistic pretensions could be further from our conception of what good prose should be than Lyly's Euphuism, with its formal parallelism and antithesis, elaborate alliteration, and decorative allusions to unnatural natural history, classical mythology, and the lives of the Greeks and Romans. Lyly did not invent it, but the popularity of his book gave the style its name and contributed to its widespread adoption.[11]

Lyly's plays were written for performance by children's companies. They lack passion and vitality. Elegance and wit these comedies have, but they are hopelessly self-conscious and overliterary. Into them Lyly projects his Euphuistic style. It is a loving woman who speaks:

But alas, it fareth with me as with waspes, who feeding on serpents, make their stings more venomous: for glutting my selfe on the face of Phao, I haue made my desire more desperate. Into the neast of an *Alcyon* no bird can enter but the *Alcyon*, and into the heart of so great a Ladie, can anie creepe but a great Lord? There is an hearbe (not vnlike vnto my loue) whiche the farther it groweth from the sea, the salter it is; and my desires the more they swarue [swerve] from reason, the more seeme they reasonable.[12]

With the courtly audience Lyly's smart comedies had a success which could hardly continue after Kyd, Marlowe, and Shakespeare had given the public theatres robust dramas of action, passion, poetry, and full-blooded romantic or realistic characterization. Lyly's offering was prettiness, suavity, and a kind of mild charm. For the connoisseur there was the pleasure of recognizing topical hits, hearing an occasional fine song, appreciating the cleverness of word-play, and relishing the unflagging ornateness of the prose. No doubt these features of Lyly's work had a civilizing effect on the popular drama. They are all present in *Love's Labour's Lost*, which, though it contains poetic and natural touches far beyond Lyly's powers, is Shakespeare's half-emulative, half-challenging venture into the Lylyesque.

No source is known for the plot which forms its slender structure,[13] but Lyly's influence is obvious in the choice of genre and in the general tone. There is only one song, but it is one of Shakespeare's best. Word-play he reveled in, and *Love's Labour's Lost* is full of it. The future of English was to him no academic question. In this play he laughs at affectation and pedantry. He turns out a Euphuistic passage in Lyly's best manner and then, as if to prove his independence, wheels about and parodies his model. As Miss Willcock remarks,

The dominant theme of this play, as distinct from artificial and symmetrical plot, is the overwhelming event of the English language and all that had been happening to it in the last twenty years or so. In this play the great game of language is played with unfailing verve from the first Act to the last, but the fertile *use* of language by no means exhausts Shakespeare's interest in it. The play is packed with linguistic comment and allusion. . . . The bias against bookishness and University Wit . . . cannot be accidental. . . . The school of this [other] wit, this language, is the world and experience, especially the experience of love.[14]

There may be digs at persons of importance or of self-importance, but that any character is intended as a portrait or even a caricature seems unlikely. This light comedy is not a piece of propaganda. It was probably not written to attack an anti-Petrarchist group of advanced thinkers [15] nor to defend Shakespeare's patron, the Earl of Southampton, and his friends. "The school of night" (IV, iii, 255) may be no more than a misprint. If, as some believe, it refers to George Chapman's *The Shadow of Night* (1594) and to a reputedly atheistic circle interested in the new science, the allusion is in passing and not the key to an allegory.

The first edition of *Love's Labour's Lost* is the Quarto of 1598. Since the Folio was set up from it, though with numerous corrections and fresh errors, the Quarto text is our sole authority. Unfortunately, its compositor made many mistakes; but it is one of the Good quartos.

When the play was written and produced is unknown. About 1594 seems probable, chiefly because this comedy is too polished in its prose and too expert in its verse to be among the very earliest, and yet too Lylyesque to have followed *A Midsummer Night's Dream* and *The Merchant of Venice*. Long supposed to be Shakespeare's first play, partly since there is nearly twice as much rhyme as blank verse, it is now placed by some in the so-called lyrical period of 1595-96. These extremes are equally unattractive.

It is likely enough that Shakespeare wrote this piece for a special occasion, at court or at some great house. The dialogue seems aimed at a select audience, and the dearth of action distinguishes *Love's Labour's Lost* from the general run of popular comedies. The title page of the Second Quarto (1631) puts it in the repertory at the Globe and the Blackfriars, but this is not conclusive evidence. Presumably it was publicly acted; but never, so far as is known, has it been popular. The title page of the First Quarto mentions a court performance, probably in 1597. Another, before Queen Anne, was arranged for a special occasion in January, 1605.[16] It is evidently the one mentioned in the following letter, undated but endorsed "1604." According to the Old Style, "1605" would not be used till March 25. Sir Walter Cope writes to Robert Cecil, Viscount Cranborne:

I have sent and bene all thys morning huntyng for players Juglers & Such kinde of Creaturs, but fynde them hard to finde; wherefore leaving notes for them to seek me. Burbage ys come, & sayes there is no new playe that the quene hath not seene, but they have re-vyved an olde one, cawled *Loves Labore Lost*, which for wytt & mirthe he sayes will please her excedingly. And thys ys appointed to be playd to morowe night at my Lord of Sowthampton's, unless yow send a wrytt to remove the Corpus Cum Causa to your howse in Strande. Burbage ys my messenger ready attendyng your pleasure.

After this, we have to wait till 1839 for any record of a performance. In the fall of that year the brilliant actress-manager Eliza Vestris and her husband, Charles James Mathews, opened their régime at Covent Garden with *Love's Labour's Lost*. Mme. Vestris played Rosaline, but only nine performances were given. Phelps added the comedy to his string in 1857; he played Armado. Daly staged it in New York in 1874 and again in 1891; in the latter of these revivals, Ada Rehan was the Princess and John Drew the King. As far as I know, the only London productions of the present century were those of Tyrone Guthrie at the Westminster in 1932 and at the Old Vic in 1936.

The title page of the *editio princeps* claims the merit of a text "Newly corrected and augmented." This has been taken to show that Shakespeare composed at different times two versions. Some of this quarto's errors, such as the retention in Berowne's long speech (IV, iii, 289–365) of two distinct draughts of it, indicate that revisions were made, but not necessarily that they were made later than during the original composition of the play. Nor do they point to wholesale re-writing.[17]

Some argue that the First Quarto's title page, with its claim of superiority, and (since only first editions had to be registered) the absence of an entry in the Stationers' Register, point to earlier publication of a Bad quarto which has not chanced to survive. The title page of the Second Quarto (1599) of *Romeo and Juliet*, likewise published by Cuthbert Burby and likewise unregistered, makes a similar claim. The First Quarto, a Bad one, appeared two years earlier. Had no copy of it been preserved, we should call the Good quarto of '99 the first, and be none the wiser. If the case of the *Love's Labour's Lost* quarto is analogous, its compositor's blunders may, as Chambers suggests, be due to his working from a heavily corrected copy of a Bad quarto which has not survived.

An Elizabethan play that depends chiefly on verbal felicity, not to say pyrotechny, presents a special difficulty to the modern reader. Action, especially when reinforced with lively characterization, is capable of holding a reader or spectator unversed in Early Modern English idiom. But when the point lies in the jugglery of word-play or the burlesquing of an old stylistic fad, some knowledge is required of the state of our language toward the end of the sixteenth century. The more familiar one becomes with the vocabulary and syntax of Shakespeare's time, the greater one's respect for *Love's Labour's Lost*. It is a very brilliant achievement, though we may properly rejoice that Shakespeare did not continue frittering away his genius in pursuit of this particular kind of brilliance.

The slight plot is not of action but of situation, and it is neither wildly farcical nor worked up with a display of comic ingenuity. Though the situation is modified by the intrusion of love, its development is hardly romantic. As comedy, *Love's Labour's Lost* obviously differs from the rest of Shakespeare's plays. Yet though the characters are essentially mouthpieces for the author's wit, they form, as a group, the best the early comedies have to offer. The sprightly Berowne (pronounced *Buhroón*) is a worthy forerunner of Benedick. Armado struts in the long line of descent from the military braggart of Latin comedy, though, as Professor O. J. Campbell has shown, he is closer to the more refined Spanish *capitano* of the *commedia dell'arte*, relying on the "mint of phrases in his brain" instead of on the cruder boasts of such vainglorious soldiers as Sir Tophas in Lyly's *Endimion* or Captain Bobadill in Jonson's *Every Man in his Humor*. Holofernes, the pedant, is likewise out of the *commedia dell'arte*. Jaquenetta corresponds to the ill-favored wench who is often the unhappy lot of the *capitano;* Costard to another type of character, the rustic clown; Nathaniel to the parasite or *affamato*. Moth (i.e., "mote," and so pronounced) belongs with the zany of the *commedia dell'arte*, though as Armado's page he is reminiscent of Sir Tophas's Epiton.

Shakespeare does not, however, leave these types quite as he finds them. As usual, he can not refrain from humanizing; and the play is at once more poetic and more vital than any of Lyly's. The puppets almost come to life; they refuse to move strictly within their traditional grooves, and the aristocratic abstractness of the problem set by the main plot is brought down to earth by the troupe of eccentrics. Not that in making human beings of them Shakespeare invokes much sympathy for them. Like Meredith's Comic Spirit, he presides *over* the fun.

Perhaps his own entrance may be felt in the unexpected chord of seriousness that dominates the last scene for a few moments after the sharp news brought by the black-clad Marcade, and in the whimsicality of Berowne's comment,

> Our wooing doth not end like an old play:
> Jack hath not Gill,

which, however in character, pleasantly betrays a touch of
auctorial self-consciousness, completely absent from Shakespeare's best comedies. He never outgrew his virtuoso's pride
in exemplifying word mastery through word play; but never
again did he attempt to make a whole comedy out of sheer
wit.

Chapter 4

EARLY HISTORIES

THE FIRST PART OF KING HENRY THE SIXTH

DESPITE its omission from Meres's list, no one doubts that the trilogy on the reign of Henry VI is Shakespeare's earliest work in the chronicle-history form; [1] but whether *Part 1* was first composed, and even whether Shakespeare wrote all of it, are still unsolved problems. The three plays are obviously inferior in theatrical bounce to their immediate successor, *Richard the Third*, in poetry to *Richard the Second*, in humor and richness of historical coloring to *Henry the Fourth* and *Henry the Fifth*. For the most part they even fail to reach the modest level of *King John*. The trilogy embraces, then, three of the last plays the modern reader is likely to turn to; yet it contains admirable things. If an appetizer is required, let the doubter sample Jack Cade's remarks on Blackheath (*Part 2*, IV, ii, 69–90) for a taste of the same Shakespeare who was to put Utopian notions into the head of Sir John Falstaff.

The Folio is our sole authority for the text of *Part 1*, which is so varied in style that the disintegrators ascribe it to several hands. The opening speeches, for example, have a Marlovian ring:

> Hung be the heavens with black, yield day to night!
> Comets, importing change of times and states,
> Brandish your crystal tresses in the sky
> And with them scourge the bad revolting stars
> That have consented unto Henry's death.

But even the comets' crystal tresses and the proposed flagellation of the stars do not prove that Marlowe wrote the scene. It would be strange if the mighty line of *Tamburlaine* had impressed Shakespeare so little that his trial flights in serious drama showed no trace of it. There is general agreement that he wrote the choosing of the roses (II, iv), Talbot before Bordeaux (IV, ii), and perhaps Mortimer's farewell (II, v) and the rhymed Talbot scenes of Act IV. Practically everything else is disputed. Besides Marlowe, Peele and Greene have been put forward as authors or collaborators. Some believe Shakespeare touched up an old play for revival by the Chamberlain's Men in sequence with his own *Henry the Sixth, Part 2* and *Part 3*.

What the disintegrators forget is that a strangely uneven product flows oftener from a major artist's pen than from a cautious minor's. Shakespeare's working conditions must frequently have made composition a piecemeal business. Interruption of the creative glow, the demands of other affairs, shifting moods, weariness or vigor, food and drink — all these can make vast differences in the style of a writer driven hard by forces essentially nonaesthetic. Even Shakespeare's best plays are seldom executed consistently at the top of his form. Each part of *Henry the Sixth* was good enough to please the audience it was written for; the Epilogue to *Henry the Fifth* refers to the period (1422–44) covered by *Part 1*, "which oft our stage hath shown." There is no trace of popularity for any of the Henry VI plays after the 1590's.

Internal evidence for authorship is notoriously unreliable, especially at this early moment in the Elizabethan drama's development, when everyone was influencing everyone else. In this case external evidence is lacking, with a single exception: *Part 1* does appear in the Folio. Since Heminge and Condell presumably knew which pieces Shakespeare had written, a heavy burden of proof is imposed on those who would remove a Folio play from the canon. Orthodox opinion has none the less removed *Part 1*, perhaps erroneously. For it seems more likely that Shakespeare wrote this drama much as we have it, though there may be surviving passages from an old play, if one existed.[2]

That there was an old play we have no evidence whatever. Henslowe's *harey the vj* on March 3, 1592 is probably some form of this one. His calling it new may mean only that it was newly revised or even that it was new to the repertory under his management.[3] As we have seen, Nashe's allusion to spectators' tears for Talbot [4] is undoubtedly to *harey the vj*. *Part 1* has too much vitality to be Peele's or Greene's; the style is superior to Kyd's; and while there are certainly Marlowesque passages, there are others which show a freedom, a raciness, and a flexibility of versification unmatched in any of Marlowe's known works.

The orthodox view supposes that Shakespeare handled *Part 1* after *Part 2* and *Part 3*, and that the final scene was added to link it with *Part 2*. But Suffolk's love for Margaret is introduced in V, iii. The build-up for the Wars of the Roses begins in II, iv, and for Cardinal Beaufort as villain and Duke Humphrey as a kind of hero in I, iii. The scenes fall, therefore, in two main divisions: episodes in the actual plot of *Part 1*, and passages less significant for *Part 1* than for *Part 2*.

Part 1 is no model of how to plot, but two themes emerge: Talbot's feats and lamentable death in France, and the career of Joan of Arc. Eventually they are fused, and the dominant motif, as far as there is one, becomes a duel between the two champions. Both are handled with a jingo touch that flattered the patriotic audience. Of character drawing there is none save the most obvious; the author is too busy managing the too numerous strands of his plot. It is deplorable that Shakespeare saw little more in the Maid than a lustful witch, but not surprising. Why, a rereading of Mr. Shaw's great drama will make perfectly clear. Incomprehensible as seem the errors of our forefathers to the enlightened but unhistorically minded of today, they were made, and by normal, well-intentioned citizens with no taint of sadism. There is no warrant for supposing Shakespeare more clairvoyant in these matters than Holinshed; but even if he had been, an aspirant dramatist would hardly attempt to woo the public with a play showing the English getting jolly well beaten in a fair fight. Sorcery and their own dissensions explain everything. What offends the modern reader as nauseating self-righteousness was taken by the Elizabethans as a matter of course.

Talbot and Joan, to whom *Part 1* chiefly belongs, do not, however, monopolize it. Since so much of it is devoted to stating themes that involve little action till *Part 2*, it seems reasonable to suppose that Shakespeare wrote the three parts in the natural order, that of their chronology. Greene's attack [5] dates *Henry the Sixth, Part 3* not later than June, 1592. How much earlier *Parts 1* and *2* were written is impossible to say. Nashe's allusion to *Part 1* is not necessarily to the original production.

We must not expect a history to exhibit the formal excellence of a tragedy or a comedy, however the dramatist bends the facts to fit his theatrical pattern. Here the chief sources are the chronicles of Holinshed and of Halle. Talbot was actually killed in 1453; yet Joan, executed in 1431, is present when he dies in the play. Among the unhistorical episodes are the taking of Orleans after its relief by Joan, the stratagem of the Countess of Auvergne, the donning of the rose badges in the Temple garden, the interview of Richard Plantagenet with the dying Mortimer, the capture and recapture of Rouen in a single day and Fastolfe's cowardice there, Joan's enticement of Burgundy to the French side, the parley before the walls of Bordeaux (IV, ii), the enmity between York and Somerset as the cause of Talbot's plight, and Suffolk's wooing of Margaret.

Portions of the play are still good reading, as historical pageantry. For poetry and insight we must look elsewhere.

THE SECOND PART OF KING HENRY THE SIXTH

Part 2 was long supposed to be Shakespeare's revision of an anonymous play which was published in 1594 as *The First part of the Contention betwixt the two famous Houses of Yorke and Lancaster, with the death of the good Duke Humphrey: And the banishment and death of the Duke of Suffolke, and the Tragicall end of the proud Cardinall of Winchester, with the notable Rebellion of Iacke Cade: And the Duke of Yorkes first claime vnto the Crowne.* [6] This quarto was once ascribed to Marlowe; it contains not only Marlowesque passages but lines actually lifted from his known works. Kyd, Greene, Peele, Lodge, Nashe, and Drayton have also had their advocates as possible collaborators. But in *The Life and Genius of Shakespeare*, Thomas Kenny argued that *The First part of the Contention* is a Bad quarto of *Henry the Sixth, Part 2*. This study appeared in 1864, but had long been neglected when, in a series of communications to the London *Times Literary Supplement* in 1924, Professor Alexander independently proposed the same conclusion. Dr. Doran expounded this hypothesis at length in 1928. The following year saw the appearance of Alexander's *Shakespeare's Henry VI and Richard III*, and the main outlines of the Bad-quarto theory have been generally accepted.

The First part of the Contention, then, is probably a piratical acting version vamped up by actors who drew on their recollection of authorized performances in which one or more of them had played. Their motive was either to supply some fly-by-night company with the text of Shakespeare's play for use on a provincial tour, or else to capitalize on their theft by selling it to a publisher. The title page of the corresponding quarto of *Part 3* mentions Pembroke's Men; it may be that the Folio text of *Part 2* and *Part 3* was acted, though not necessarily first produced, by that company. About half the lines are much the same in both the anonymous Quarto and the Folio. The rest of the Quarto's text freely substitutes synonyms, changes word-order and inflections, wrecks metre, mangles sense, and summarizes the purport of lengthy passages in brief paraphrases. Lines are sometimes recalled out of their proper context from this and other plays. A Bad quarto is likely to betray, not the pirate actor's identity, but the rôle or rôles he had played in the authorized production, since he would remember best his own lines, and next best other speeches uttered while he was on stage. But who the reporter of this text was, remains uncertain.[7] Obviously, this sort of piracy would not have been resorted to had the company in question owned a manuscript of the play. Yet several passages in the unauthorized Quarto are practically identical with the Folio text. Very likely the Quarto, bad as it is, was used in setting up the Folio at points where something was lacking or illegible in the printer's "copy." Changes in the Third Quarto (1619) may be due to the compositor's use of a corrected First Quarto, that is, a copy brought into closer approximation to the true text by someone whose memory of the play in performance was fresher.

The textual history of *Henry the Sixth, Part 2* is further complicated by the possibility that, *after* the performances from which the imperfect memory of the pirate or pirates had compiled the text of the First Quarto, Shakespeare revised his play. If so, the Quarto would be, not the degenerate offspring of the very same text that was to appear long afterwards in the Folio, but (like the Folio) a descendant, though (unlike it) a bastard, of the original Shakespearean version now lost. Some of the Quarto's variants from the Folio may therefore be not so corrupt as they look, though they are unquestionably often wide of their mark, that is, of Shakespeare's original play.

His sources are again Holinshed and Halle. As usual, he handles history with freedom. *Part 2* covers eleven years, 1445-55. Already the future Richard III, though not as yet a Machiavel of deepest dye, interests the dramatist who is to raise the loudest voice in the chorus of his defamers. Crookback was actually in his third year when the first battle of St. Albans was fought, but that does not stop Shakespeare from assigning him prodigies of valor there.

When *Henry the Sixth, Part 2* was originally produced is unknown. It must have been by 1592, when Greene parodies a line from the companion piece, *Part 3*. McKerrow's source study points to an early date for *Part 2*, before the 1587 Holinshed came into Shakespeare's hands. This does not help us much, since some time may have elapsed before he acquired his copy. That he actually owned one can scarcely be doubted; there is ample evidence in the later histories for his use of that edition. Presumably *Part 2* was a success in the 1590's; subsequent evidence for the popularity of any part of *Henry the Sixth* is wanting.[8] In 1681, under title of *Henry the Sixth, The First Part*, the popular dramatist "little starched Johnny Crowne" adapted the first three acts of *Part 2*, with small commercial and no artistic success. This piece belongs to a series of political dramas exploiting the controversies brought to a head by the Popish Plot. The Cardinal affords Crowne a chance to indulge in "A little Vineger against the *Pope*." In 1817 Edmund Kean played the title rôle in *Richard Duke of York*, adapted, perhaps by him, largely from *Part 2*. Shakespeare's original play seems to have been revived for the first time by an unpretentious company at the Surrey Theatre in 1864.

The Quarto, that is, *The First part of the Contention*, omits about one-third of the Folio text of *Part 2*. A version based on actors' memory of performances would of course lack passages that had not been spoken in the theatre. Cutting for the early stage was less concerned than at present with preserving literary effects, and more careful about leaving the dramatic mechanism intact. Speeches now so famous that their omission would be unthinkable in any revival were ruthlessly sacrificed when Shakespeare staged his plays.

Henry the Sixth, *Part 2* opens well with a scene of really dramatic exposition. Suffolk delivers Margaret to Henry, Gloucester is set forth as a hero and the Cardinal as a villainous plotter against him, and York announces in a soliloquy his intention of fighting for the crown. The scene is expertly unified. Gloucester's animus is resentment of Suffolk's territorial concessions to Reignier; and since these are the fruit of the French marriage, the Queen's animosity is firmly linked in. Ambitious York sees his chance at the crown in the rivalry of Gloucester and the Cardinal. But this initial integrity soon goes to pieces. The first three acts are almost a little drama by themselves. The theme is the fall of Duke Humphrey, which in turn brings about the fall of Suffolk and his murder in the first scene of Act IV. The wicked Cardinal dies raving in III, iii. He is not fully developed as an adequate villain; the romance of Suffolk and Margaret is too casually handled; the virtual abandonment of Act IV to Cade's rebellion, though it inspires the best writing in the play, shatters what little unity is left; and the only threads that run all the way through, York's ambition and Margaret's opposition to it, disappear from sight for long intervals.

While there is no longer any reason to doubt Shakespeare's authorship of *Henry the Sixth, Part 2* and *Part 3* it can not be said that either of these plays is among the brightest jewels in his dramatic diadem. Yet they contain capital scenes. The chief defect of *Part 2* is inherent in the chronicle-history form. Objectivity, a great source of Shakespeare's strength in tragedy, since it checks the Romantic tendency to isolate a hero, keeps any character in *Henry the Sixth* from being much of a hero. We are absorbed in no one's fortunes throughout any of these plays nor moved to identify ourselves with the action, which is almost completely physical. In other words, *Henry the Sixth* sadly lacks spiritual values, and so it can not lay hold on us imaginatively.

THE THIRD PART OF KING HENRY THE SIXTH

The earliest text of this play is also a Bad quarto,[9] and a companion to *The First part of the Contention*. It was published in 1595, was reprinted in 1600, and along with *The First part of the Contention* appeared again in 1619 as *Part 2* of *The Whole Contention*. The title page of 1595 calls it *The true Tragedie of Richard Duke of Yorke, and the death of good King Henrie the Sixt, with the whole contention betweene the two Houses Lancaster and Yorke, as it was sundrie times acted by the Right Honourable the Earle of Pembrooke his seruants*. The textual observations on *Henry the Sixth, Part 2* also apply to the relation between the 1595 version and the Folio. So do the remarks on date and sources. Despite former theories, Shakespeare's sole authorship is now generally recognized. This Bad quarto is likewise one-third shorter than the Folio version, but in phraseology *The true Tragedie* is not so far removed from the Folio text as *The First part of the Contention* is.

The historical events covered, though with the usual liberties of combination and condensation, occurred between First St. Albans in 1455 and the death of Henry VI in 1471. It was actually the Yorkist victory at Northampton in 1460 that precipitated the settlement shown in the opening scene of the play. As usually cited, the title of 1595 is a misnomer;

for the "true tragedy" of Richard of York is over in Act I
Yet the play is more unified than its predecessor: the rise o
the Yorkist party is the constant theme.

From *Henry the Sixth, Part 1* through *Richard the Third*
there is a steady increase in the dramatist's power to mold
his materials and also in vigor, both of scene construction
and of style. That the four plays were written in their chronological order seems a reasonable inference. Of the first three,
each "plants" with a good deal of care for its immediate
successor, though each can stand alone. There is also stronger
characterization in *Part 3* than in *Part 1* and *Part 2*. Margaret
is but one of several lively portraits. King Henry is admirably
sustained; this weak and well-intentioned monarch interests
Shakespeare, and several of his speeches foreshadow the reflective discourses of Richard II. Crookback of Gloucester
carries on into *Part 3* as the gallant Yorkist champion, a
tough fighter but no fiend, till III, ii, when the dramatist,
mindful of the next play, makes him announce his sinister
intentions. After he has shown his colors, Richard is all
Machiavel; his obituary remarks over the king's murdered
corpse (V, vi) are quite of a piece with his villainous asides
and soliloquies in *Richard the Third*.

John Crowne's *The Misery of Civil-War* (1680) is an adaptation of the last two acts of *Part 2* and the whole of *Part 3*,
intended as a solemn warning to the Whigs. Theophilus Cibber staged another version, his own, in 1723, derived from
Part 2 and *Part 3*, chiefly the latter. With very few exceptions,
however, the stage history of the whole trilogy, since its
initial success, has been a blank. Even the devoted Phelps
left it alone.[10] But the Old Vic has staged it, and in 1906 Benson gave the three parts in succession at Stratford.

It can scarcely be maintained that *Part 3* is among the
wonderful works of the creative imagination; but the poetic
level sometimes rises higher than in *Part 1* and *Part 2*, and the
structural unity is better planned. The artist's powers are
waxing; he learns how to write by writing. In his next
history he is to shape his materials masterfully into superb
theatrical effectiveness and score a huge success with them

In the next but one, he takes the genre into the realm of poetry.

THE TRAGEDY OF KING RICHARD THE THIRD

With Richard Burbage as the cynical tyrant, this tragical-history was a tremendous hit. Lines like King Gloucester's, crackling with every variety of theatrical explosiveness, were something new in the experience of the London groundlings. Nor were the ears of the lowly tickled alone. Everyone has a weakness for *Richard the Third*. The original production must have electrified the hemispheres of Shoreditch and the Bankside. In *Tamburlaine*, a shoemaker's son from Canterbury *via* Cambridge had given that mimic world some lines which skyrocketed higher than the fallen spire of Paul's had ever sprung, while Shakespeare's *Richard the Third* is without poetry. But beside the baleful glare of this lurid Plantagenet the most Machiavellian of Marlowe's demidevils, hero-rogues, and men on horseback are as starlight is to sunlight; and in the devising of scenes to set off and frame a dazzling character Marlowe remained to the last a prentice dramatist. No one in the history of London had offered the public a *coup de théâtre* like Crookback, and the delighted metropolis bestowed its rewards accordingly — on author, actor, and company.[11]

How long the first vogue lasted is uncertain. There may have been a revival under the Restoration; if so, it had small success. Richard appears, still an unconscionable villain, in John Crowne's *The Misery of Civil-War*, an adaptation of *Henry the Sixth, Part 2* and *Part 3*, acted in 1680. Thomas Betterton played the title rôle in *The English Princess, or, The Death of Richard the III* (acted 1666–67), an independent, rhymed tragedy by John Caryl. But in 1700 Colley Cibber's adaptation took the stage, which it held till very recently, the longest-lived of all the acting versions of Shakespeare.[12] The famous gags, "Off with his head. So much for Buckingham" and "Richard's himself again," are pure Cibber. The adaptation begins with King Henry's reception of the news from Tewkesbury and the scene of his murder in *Henry the Sixth, Part 3*.

In general, Cibber omits scenes from which Richard is absent, and reduces the number of characters: Margaret, Clarence, and Stanley do not appear. The adapter, though his forte was the languid fop, played Richard till 1739. In 1741 Garrick chose Cibber's version for his London debut; his last appearance was in 1776, and he always outshone the Richards of his rivals, among them James Quin's. These thirty-five years, some of the poorest in the annals of English playwriting, were among the most brilliant in the stage history of *Richard the Third*. From 1783 to 1817 J. P. Kemble acted the title rôle in a manner so incongruously refined that for a time he was eclipsed by the more realistic impersonation of George Frederick Cooke, an actor of extraordinary powers, the idol of the youthful Kean. Under Kemble, Cibber's lines were pruned of some extravagances, and more attention was given to correctness of scenery and costume. Kemble's Queen Elizabeth was his sister, the great Mrs. Siddons, who had played Anne with Garrick during her first, unhappy attempt to establish herself in London.

Kemble's textual changes were preserved by Edmund Kean, who acted Richard more realistically than Kemble and more poetically than Cooke. His was the great romantic portrayal, though Junius Brutus Booth also took the part; Kean made it his own from his debut in 1814 till his death in 1833. Charles William Macready also challenged Kean; and, as in Garrick's time, London saw its two leading actors playing Richard against each other. Much of the "traditional" stage business was invented by Kean. The chief merit of Macready's revival was not (though it had its partisans) his impersonation, for which his height unsuited him, but his attempt in 1821 to restore Shakespeare's text. Though he preserved many of Cibber's most effective gags, the public was displeased and Macready reverted to Cibber's version. To Samuel Phelps, at Sadler's Wells, honor also belongs for going back to Shakespeare's text. His production in 1845 ran about a month. Then he dropped the play; and when he undertook it again, in 1862, he played the Cibber adaptation. Charles Kean also stuck to Cibber when in 1850 he staged the first of the lavishly spectacular productions, with a cast of 121; but Irving, at the Lyceum in 1877, restored Shakespeare, save for cuts, completely discarding Cibber. His conception of the title rôle was "splendidly Satanic," and he emphasized the hero-villain's intellectual pride. This production ran for three months; but Irving's subsequent revival, in 1896, had little success. By this time the second great renascence of the British drama was under way. Though still later Tree, Benson, and Martin-Harvey held to Shakespeare's text, none made much impression. The title rôle was also played, at the Old Vic, by Robert Atkins (1915) and Baliol Holloway (1925).

It is, indeed, questionable whether, except as a museum piece, *Richard the Third* is entitled to a place in the post-Ibsen theatre. It is unnecessary to read a spurious modernism into Shakespeare's tragic masterpieces or into the best of his romantic comedies to validate their claim to inclusion in the twentieth-century repertory. The former by the gorgeous and exalting sweep of their poetry, the latter by their charm and variety, and both by their poignant fidelity to human nature, have only to be adequately performed to take any audience off its feet. *Richard the Third* flourished most when the art of dramatic composition was at its two lowest ebbs in England. In comparison with the lifeless neoclassical or lachrymose and sentimental tragedies of the eighteenth century, and with the tawdry pieces bestowed upon the nineteenth-century stage by the Romantic movement, *Richard the Third* must have seemed vital and even in spots realistic.

Since, in the United States, the nineteenth century was even more barren of good dramatic writing, the play's American vogue is no less understandable. It was first performed, apparently, on March 5, 1750, in New York; it may have been acted the year before in Philadelphia. As in England, it became a stock piece. Cooke opened his American tour (1810–12) as Richard. So did Edmund Kean in 1820, and it was his chief vehicle again in 1825. J. B. Booth chose Richard to launch his American career in 1821, and it remained a favorite part till his death. His was like Kean's a romantic conception, but on a colossal scale. The Richard of Edwin Forrest, the

first American actor of genius, was a violently heroic portrayal; originally presented in 1827, it ignored the emphasis
on Richard's deformity. Charles Kean brought over his spectacular production. The play was so popular that every aspirant to theatrical laurels yearned for the title rôle. It was
acted by men, women, and children of both sexes; the most
extraordinary casting was the Bateman sisters, aged four and
six, as Richard and Richmond. Edwin Booth won his first
success as Richard in 1852 in San Francisco. His conception
changed in the course of his long career, and he gradually
modified into the wily Plantagenet the terrific ruffian of his
father and of Forrest. He rejected Cibber's text, but cut Shakespeare's to about half its original length. Cibber's version
was still used by other actors, including John McCullough
and Lawrence Barrett. Richard Mansfield restored Shakespeare
in part. John Barrymore appeared as Richard in 1920, retain-
ing a good deal of Cibber. The piece was long in the repertory
of Robert Bruce Mantell, but in Cibber's adaptation.

The first edition of the original play, the anonymous quarto
of 1597, is entitled *The Tragedy of King Richard the third. Containing, His treacherous Plots against his brother Clarence: the
pittiefull murther of his i[n]nocent nephewes: his tyrannicall vsurpa-
tion: with the whole course of his detested life, and most deserued
death. As it hath beene lately Acted by the Right honourable the
Lord Chamberlaine his seruants.*[13] The Folio text of 1623 was
set up from a copy of the Sixth Quarto (1622), but with corrections from some early manuscript. Both versions, Folio
and Quarto, present us with good texts; neither is consistently superior to the other. How to establish the true text
of this play is probably the thorniest problem that confronts
the modern editor of Shakespeare. The Folio has about 222
lines and parts of lines lacking in the Quarto. Most of the
Quarto omissions are stage cuts, but it contains about forty-
eight lines and parts of lines which do not appear in the
Folio. Some are doubtless actors' gags; but a substantial block
(IV, ii, 101-18) of the Quarto, the clock passage in Richard's
rejection of Buckingham's demand, is apparently Shakespeare's. Perhaps he wrote it in during rehearsal to point up

the scene. For the most part the two texts run parallel. They often differ by substitution of synonyms, slight inflectional changes, and altered word order. Occasionally, no doubt to shorten the acting time, the Quarto summarizes a Folio speech. Sometimes a condensation reduces the number of actors. The metre of the Quarto is less regular. The Folio usually tones down oaths, in deference to the statute of 1606 against profanity.

The relative authority of these editions has been much debated. Probably the Folio is closer to what Shakespeare actually wrote, while the Quarto gives us the play as acted in the middle nineties with such changes as were made when it went into production. Since some of these may have been Shakespeare's, we can not ignore the Quarto. Yet others are undoubtedly due to little errors made by the actors when they memorized their parts. As for the gags, for such a few of the Quarto lines appear to be, some are admirable and some are not. Did Shakespeare insert them, or are they all ad-libbing by the players? There are, besides, printer's blunders among the Quarto variants. The *editio princeps* of 1597 is none the less a Good quarto; it clearly rests on a good manuscript. But the transcript which served as the printer's copy must have been made by someone so familiar with the lines spoken on the stage that he incorporated many actor's readings. Chambers thinks he was the book-keeper, who seems to have been a combined prompter, librarian, and scribe. The modern editor should base his text on the Folio, adding the lines found only in the Quarto and adopting the Quarto's variant readings when the Folio is plainly in error. The Quarto should also be followed when its text appears to give an authorized *correction*, even though this was made in the theatre. It should not be followed when its reading looks as if it were dictated by a theatrical *exigency*. Unhappily, there is no way of being sure which is which. To follow the Folio slavishly would be to ignore the possibility of revisions by Shakespeare in the theatre. To follow the Quarto slavishly would be to include liberties taken by the players with the text he wrote.

The date of *Richard the Third* is uncertain. It may have

been composed just before or during the suspension of acting from 1592 to 1594. It is closely linked with *Henry the Sixth, Part 3;* rather early in the nineties seems the best conjecture, perhaps about 1593. The disintegrators have dallied with this play, but few now doubt that it is Shakespeare's alone.

For his materials he went again to the chronicles of Halle (1548) and Holinshed (second edition, 1587). There the Machiavellian Plantagenet lurked ready to his hand. Richard's conqueror was Queen Elizabeth's grandfather; naturally, the Tudor historians limned a black picture of the last of the Yorkist kings. Holinshed used Halle for the reign of Edward IV. For the protectorate and reign of his successor both Halle and Holinshed adopted Sir Thomas More's "history" of Richard. Halle also used the *Historia Anglica* of Polydore Vergil. Thus it was More and Vergil, through Halle and Holinshed, who gave Shakespeare the color of his portrait. Vergil had lived at the court of Henry VIII. More, Henry's chancellor, had been trained in the household of Cardinal Morton, the Ely of the play. Morton had much to do with bringing in Henry VII, under whom he was primate and chancellor. As soon as the chronicles begin to use More, Richard becomes the villain of the piece. Both More and Vergil say a bad conscience plagued him; and from the latter Shakespeare derives the dream on the eve of Bosworth and the conception of Nemesis dogging the criminal monarch to his violent end.

Yet if Shakespeare finds most of his episodes in the chronicles, he treats them masterfully and invents boldly. The play covers the years 1471–85. Fascinated as he was by the color and pageantry of great historical events, by the clash of famous personalities, and by the strange mutability of human affairs, Shakespeare heightens and intensifies everything, little hampered by sober fact. If it gets in his way, he thrusts it aside. Already in *Henry the Sixth* he had begun improvising motives and crucial scenes where history was silent. Now he makes the Yorkists' reconciliation (II, i) more dramatic by injecting Richard into it, though actually the Duke was campaigning in the North. Given the fact that Richard mar-

ried Anne, Shakespeare daringly invents the wooing scene
(I, ii). Halle says merely that Gloucester appeared to the
citizens "with a byshop on euery hand of him"; expanded,
this becomes a brilliant stroke in III, vii.[14]

Structurally, *Richard the Third* marks a bold advance, though
its unity is achieved too arbitrarily, and in his best histories
Shakespeare drastically modified the method. Marlowe's *Tamburlaine* (*c.* 1587–88) had made a sensation; episodic as it is,
the thundering hero carries it all off. Possibly this example
encouraged Shakespeare to stake everything on one dominating character. If so, he might have profited earlier in his
career. The notion that for years he was stumbling along at
Marlowe's heels is, though still orthodox, in process of being
discarded. It involves our supposing the greatest of poets so
thick-skulled that it took half a decade for the lesson of
Tamburlaine to sink in. Marlowe built his play that way
because he was a tyro. He gradually abandoned his technique,
very likely because he saw, not only that Shakespeare's was
superior, but also that it was at least equally acceptable to
those who give the drama's laws: *Henry the Sixth* was a palpable hit. Shakespeare's focus on a central character in *Richard
the Third* is better accounted for on other grounds than the
too epic structure of *Tamburlaine*. More's account is a biography. Richard's colossal wickedness, as Shakespeare saw it,
and the dramatist's intention of winding up in five more
acts his series on the Wars of the Roses, dictated, if not a
tragic form, at any rate a tragic point of view; and that entailed (as *Henry the Sixth* did not) the adoption of a hero.
Out of Shakespeare's delight in his hero-villain, and his
justifiable hope that he would fascinate the audience, grew
(in all probability) the tighter structure of this play.

Seneca, moreover, and the English Senecan drama also influenced his first essay in the tragical-historical form, as they
had already influenced the earliest of his trial flights in
tragedy. The Roman closet-playwright and his Renaissance
imitators, most notably the French Senecan, Robert Garnier,
had inspired, especially among the academic dramatists, a
tragic genre in England; while *The Spanish Tragedie* of Kyd

(*c.* 1586), Senecan but not academic, had given it a vogue which was long to affect the popular theatre. The Senecan sort of thing was more rhetorical than poetic, more gory than imaginative; but in coming to grips with the stage as a vehicle for action and passion, Kyd outdoes all his English predecessors. Far more clearly than Marlowe, Shakespeare discerned the potential effectiveness of elements in Seneca and Kyd. It is his use of them, plus a dramatist's eye for character and a poet's flair for the image-making word, both of which Shakespeare possessed from the beginning in a degree Marlowe never attained, that makes *Richard the Third*, however overemphasized its hero, so much more full-bodied a play than *Tamburlaine*. From Seneca and Kyd Shakespeare takes over the vengeance-seeking Senecan ghosts (V, iii), the set speeches (later in the same scene), and the occasional parade of stichomythia (I, ii, 192–202).

In substance, then, *Richard the Third* is chronicle history; in form it is tragedy; but in tone it is hardly more than melodrama. The hero is not merely not a good man, he is not a good hero. Macbeth is carefully built up at the outset as a noble leader of men; and though he falls into wicked courses and deserves his fate, nobility hangs round him still. His tragedy inspires awe and pity — for him and for the human race. Richard is all villain and always villain, and at the end the real hero is Richmond. The fall of Crookback can not move us deeply; he is too isolated from humanity — there is no drop of the milk of human kindness in him. Even when he wakes from his dream it is fear he feels, not remorse.

Why, then, is he so successful as a stage character? First, there is his terrific energy. Not by dazzling flights of poetry, nor by profound and awful generalizings on the common lot of men, but by eminently speakable and actable lines is Richard made intensely alive. His speeches are full of bite — an actor can get his teeth into them; and they are full of compulsion to bodily expression. And yet, all is on the surface of life; nothing comes from within. A second reason for the success of the rôle is its utter lack of subtlety. Richard is easy on the mind. Some experience in the world, the schooling of love, sensitiveness that can be wounded by wrong to others, a philosophy of history, a poet's sense of wonder, any of these is bound to increase one's capacity to receive the full effect of a great tragedy. None is required for a complete appreciation of *Richard the Third*. The young man in *Major Barbara*, whose lack of special training or even aptitude for anything under the sun does not prevent his roundly declaring that at least he knows the difference between right and wrong, would be as competent as anyone to experience this play. So broad are the strokes, so unmistakable the contrasts, that the audience is put in a flattering position of immense superiority to the action and characters. This is never the case with a true tragedy, which always deflates complacency. Tragedy makes us humble. Watching the cocksure Richard we are never moved to exclaim, "There, but for the Grace of God!" Since there is no bond of sympathy, our attitude, however reprehensible, has a touch of derision in it. And this the author intended. To it he caters in Richard's sardonic asides, when the gloating criminal brags of his cleverness. This is no tragedy of intellectual pride. By that sin fell the brightest angel, not Crookback. Richard is the comic villain of melodrama, not the right hero or hero-villain of tragedy, nor even the fiend incarnate whose Satanic malevolence, if it provokes no pity, can smite us with awe. Richard is not Satan but Machiavel. He is no forerunner of Claudius and Macbeth; he stands in the line that was to flower in Shylock, Iago, and Edmund. We relish his wickedness, serene in our confidence that the day of reckoning will come. If he were more credible, if he were one of us, we could not remain serene.

Yet, artificial as the figure is, it is a piece of conscious character portrayal, a department too neglected in *Henry the Sixth*. Margaret is also vigorously executed, if we can ignore the impossibility of her being present at all. Buckingham is badly done, wavering between a pale copy of Richard and a minor hero. Compared with what came to be his normal practice, Shakespeare's method here seems ruthless in its sacrifice of all other considerations, including all the other characters, to the portrait that forms his centerpiece. But compared with *Tamburlaine*, this play presents a brilliant gallery of realistic and individual portraits. Effective rhetoric there also is, and delightful raciness, but of poetry hardly a flash. Nor has Shakespeare anything in particular to say. There are shrewd enough comments on the ways of our species, but they are only shrewd.

All this has not deterred critics from taking the play as a mighty work of tragic art. Through the centuries their eloquence has matched the devotion of the actors. In vain Johnson and Malone raised their voices, protesting the discrepancy between its literary merits and its long triumph on the boards. Certainly it is better than *Henry the Sixth*, and if Shakespeare was ever to give us the great tragedies he had first to find a form to stage them in. As a step forward out of the messy chronicle-history form, *Richard the Third* is a hopeful sign. It is also a rattling good piece of good theatre. But that is all it is.

THE LIFE AND DEATH OF KING JOHN

This play was probably written about the same time as *Richard the Second*. No one knows which came first; possibly Shakespeare worked on them together. *Richard* is far more imaginative; the dramatist seems less interested in *King John*. Perhaps he pegged away at it when he did not feel in the right mood for the other play.[15] *John* may have been a task set by the company; in it he is making over an inferior drama of unknown authorship. Philip Faulconbridge, for example, lacks in the source the amusing personality Shakespeare gives him. The blank verse of the old play is pedestrian. There is also a good deal of undistinguished prose, rhymed couplets, and other metres, none handled with much success.

Though it is only about three hundred lines longer than Shakespeare's, the source play was printed in 1591 as a two-part drama, perhaps, as Professor Dover Wilson suggests, because a wily publisher wanted to double his profits. Each of these quartos begins with

> An old-fashioned title-page, such as presents
> A tabular view of the volume's contents.

This was the regular Elizabethan practice; as a rule it supplies, not the. author's title, but the publisher's advertisement. Thus we have *The Troublesome Raigne of Iohn King of England, with the discouerie of King Richard Cordelions Base sonne (vulgarly named, The Bastard Fawconbridge): also the death of King Iohn at Swinstead Abbey. As it was (sundry times) publikely acted by the Queenes Maiesties Players, in the honourable Citie of London. . . . The Second part of the troublesome Raigne of King Iohn, conteining the death of Arthur Plantaginet, the landing of Lewes, and the poysning of King Iohn at Swinstead Abbey. As it was. . . .* In later editions the two parts were combined. The title page of 1611 adds "Written by W. Sh."; the Quarto of 1622 boldly asserts "by W. Shakespeare." Though on stylistic grounds Peele has been put forward as the author, the evidence is unconvincing.

Shakespeare's play was not printed till the Folio of 1623. Meres lists it in 1598. Other external evidence is wanting for the date of composition, and the internal evidence is not conclusive. Probably 1594–96 is about right. The last of these years has its advocates because Hamnet Shakespeare died that summer; but, as Kittredge observes, the greatest of dramatists could have written the laments of Constance for Arthur if he had never had a son.

The Folio gives us a good text. Act II has only seventy-four lines of dialogue, after which comes the heading of Act III (modern editions, III, i, 75).[16] Since this is not a new scene, though at this point one begins in *The Troublesome Raigne*, it looks as if an original II, ii had been cut. From this and other inconsistencies of the Folio text it has been argued that Shakespeare rewrote a second time; but that hardly seems likely, though here and there changes may have been made at any moment down to the publication of the Folio.

The anonymous play covers the whole reign of John (1199–1216). Shakespeare follows suit, though at the outset he fails to link the reign with that of Richard I, and later even seems a little hazy about Arthur's parentage. While not endowed with a towering imagination, the unknown dramatist is no stickler for historical accuracy; Chatillon and the Faulcon-

bridges are invented by him. In the character of Austria he
fuses or confuses the captor of Richard I with the Viscount
of Limoges, who according to Holinshed was killed by a
bastard son of Richard's to avenge his father's death at the
siege of Limoges's castle.

Shakespeare was not content with mere revision of his
source. He adopts its plot but writes a new play. Some of the
episodes are expanded at the cost of omitting others. He tones
down the anti-Catholic bias of the original, though several
passages [17] explain well enough why the monk poisons John.
The murder is not historical. Some incidents are omitted
that in the source make somewhat clearer the Bastard's animus against the wearer of Richard's lionskin, and he finally
kills Austria on stage. Similar lapses are characteristic of
Shakespeare's handling of source materials throughout his
career. Other omissions are: the Bastard's promotion to the
dukedom of Normandy, so he may challenge Austria as an
equal; his capture of the lionskin; the seizure and rescue of
Elinor, only mentioned in *King John* (III, ii); a comic scene,
versified chiefly in Skeltonics and fourteeners, staging the
sack of Swinstead Abbey; the actual appearance of the five
moons; a long scene containing a second interview between
John and Peter the Prophet, John's reception of the news of
Arthur's death, and his decision to submit to Rome; another
showing the English lords swearing allegiance to Lewis and
the subsequent French conspiracy only reported in *King John*
(V, iv); the soliloquy of the monk who resolves to poison
the King, and his absolution in advance by the Abbot; another scene showing the death of John and of the poisoner,
who drinks first, and the Bastard's killing of the Abbot; and
the coronation of Henry III.

Despite occasional slips in coherence, Shakespeare improves
his source; but he does not make a great work of art out of it.
The strongest character is almost wholly his own contribution. To the Elizabethans, John was a Protestant hero of
sorts; the extortion of the Great Charter by the baronage
could not be expected to appeal to upholders of the Tudors'
strong monarchy. But even the admiring chroniclers were

unable to gloss over the fact that John was a cruel tyrant; and while the King is the hero of *The Troublesome Raigne*, his wickedness is plain for all sects and parties to see in the story of Arthur. As usual, Shakespeare is dispassionate when he touches controversial ideas; what fires him are the pageantry of events and the glamour of personages. Not that he is greatly fired by anything in this play. Sensitive as he always is to human rights, though nonpolitically, it looks as though he simply could not stomach John. Philip Faulconbridge as Sir Richard makes a better Plantagenet than the head of the house, and the author has a weakness for him. Nevertheless, the title rôle is an effective vehicle for an actor. *John* is poetically far below *Richard the Second;* but the best things in Richard, the hero's meditative monologues, are not worked out as drama. *John* abounds in thoroughly dramatic strokes.[18] Constance has appealed to many actresses, but her much praised lamentations are dangerously close to rant. On the whole, structure is looser than in either of the Richard plays, but tighter than in *Henry the Sixth*. It is marred by the disappearance of Constance and Elinor halfway along.

Except for the publication of the quartos of *The Troublesome Raigne*, there is no evidence that *King John* was ever popular on the early stage. It was not, apparently, revived under the Restoration. The first recorded performance was in 1737 at Covent Garden. Those were the days of the "Ladies of the *Shakspear* Club." "About the year 1737," says Murphy in his *Life of Garrick*, "a subscription was set on foot by ladies of fashion, who were tired of harlequin and all his tricks, and wished to restore Shakespeare to the stage." [19] *King John* had a modest success and continued in the repertory for several seasons. Early in 1745 Colley Cibber exploited the imminence of the Jacobite rising with a political adaptation, *Papal Tyranny in the Reign of King John*. Cibber played Cardinal Pandulph to Quin's John and Mrs. Pritchard's Constance. Five days later Garrick staged a rival production of Shakespeare's play, acting the title rôle himself and casting Macklin as Pandulph and Susanna Maria Cibber as Constance. Mrs. Cibber, sister of Dr. Thomas Arne the composer, and estranged wife of Colley Cibber's son Theophilus, was a fine contralto in oratorio (Handel composed for her) and a great tragic actress. Her Constance was considered her masterpiece. Quin afterwards appeared as John in the original play, with Mrs. Cibber, and with Spranger Barry as Faulconbridge. Garrick also essayed Faulconbridge, with small success. Other King Johns were Thomas Sheridan (Richard Brinsley's father), the accomplished John Henderson, J. P. Kemble, Edmund Kean and his son Charles, Macready, Phelps, Gustavus Vaughan Brooke, J. B. Booth, and Edward Loomis Davenport. When John McCullough played Faulconbridge in New York in 1874, he was supported in the rôle of Prince Arthur by a young actress named Minnie Maddern. Ellen Terry in her childhood took the same part in Charles Kean's revival. Famous Constances were Peg Woffington, Mary Ann Yates, Sarah Siddons (this was one of the earliest rôles of her second and victorious engagement at Drury Lane — she was immediately recognized as Mrs. Cibber's successor), Helen Faucit, Isabella Glyn, Fanny Kemble, Mrs. Charles Kean, and Helena Modjeska. In 1803 Cooke appeared in the title rôle at Covent Garden in an altered version by the Reverend Richard Valpy, headmaster of Reading School, where it had already been staged. In 1823 the production of Charles Kemble, Fanny's father and younger brother of John Philip Kemble and Sarah Siddons, ushered in the vogue of archaeological *décor:* "Every Character will appear in the precise Habit of the Period, the whole of the Dresses and Decorations being executed [by J. R. Planché] from indisputable Authorities such as Monumental Effigies, Seals, Illumined MSS. &c." The producer played Faulconbridge to the King John of Charles Mayne Young. In the title rôle Tree scored a hit in 1899; his was also an elaborate production. Lewis Waller was the Faulconbridge, and Julia Neilson the Constance. Though occasionally revived — it was in Mantell's repertory, and he gave a remarkable performance of the King — the play's popularity has long since vanished. It was most substantial under the stimulus of political storms like the '45 and the agitations for Catholic Emancipation. Certainly it is among Shakespeare's

poorer performances, though the Elizabethan Englishman
was doubtless stirred by the final lines, where the theme, as
far as there is any, is summed up:

> This England never did, nor never shall,
> Lie at the proud foot of a conqueror
> But when it first did help to wound itself. . . .
> Come the three corners of the world in arms,
> And we shall shock them. Naught shall make us rue
> If England to itself do rest but true.

THE TRAGEDY OF KING RICHARD THE SECOND

The grave beauty of this play sets it apart from all the other
histories. Since it was probably written about the same time
as *King John,* its moments of quiet but intense poetic reflection
can hardly be laid to the accident that its date falls in the
so-called lyrical period, though *A Midsummer Night's Dream*
and *Romeo and Juliet* likewise belong to the middle of the
decade, and Shakespeare was also sonneteering then. That
Richard the Second is at least not earlier than *King John* seems
likely because it is the opening play in a new tetralogy, which
continues with *Henry the Fourth* and *Henry the Fifth.* Shakespeare is careful to bring Hotspur in and to mention (V, iii)
the misconduct of Prince Hal. 1595–96 is a reasonable date for
Richard; yet in style it is very different from the three histories
which follow.[20] It is nowhere so racy nor so tingling with
sustained vitality as they usually are. Characterization is
practically restricted to Richard and his foil, Bolingbroke
the go-getter, save for a mildly comic touch in the portrait
of York. There is almost no humor elsewhere. Except in the
monologues of the stricken hero, the verse is seldom distinguished. It is not pedestrian; but its elevation is secured,
not by the development in flashing metaphor of an idea or a
passion, but by labored accumulation of too obviously "poetic" diction. Save for a few fine lines like "This precious
stone set in the silver sea," even John of Gaunt's famous
speech (II, i, 31–68) is built up rhetorical brick by brick,
not poured out in Shakespeare's best tumultuous style:

For violent fires soon burn out themselves;
Small show'rs last long, but sudden storms are short;
He tires betimes that spurs too fast betimes;
With eager feeding food doth choke the feeder.

This is tediously repetitive; and while the tribute to England strikes fire still and must have thrilled conservatives who, like the Queen, distrusted the advocates of an expansionist policy, it is constructed no less laboriously, and the speech peters out at the climax in a protest against Richard's economic program which fails to keep the chord vibrating.

The play as a whole falls between the two stools of tragedy and chronicle-history. After II, i the hero is absent till III, ii. When he reappears the pitch rises, and from then on the story of his fall is effectively told. His monologues are not in themselves very dramatic, but they reflect the meditations of a great lyric poet on the vicissitudes of life and the tyranny of death; while in the meeting of Bolingbroke and the King at Flint Castle, and in the abdication scene itself, they are successfully combined with action. The result at these moments is very moving drama. Then the play sinks again. Richard's parting from his queen misses fire; and the subplot of York and Aumerle, though quite in the chronicle-history manner, is mere padding. The King's murder is better handled; the plane is much higher than in *Richard the Third*, though the hero's violence at the end of the scene reverts to obvious theatricalism. The dramatist has still a long way to go before he is to achieve the bloody but profoundly tragic and poetic finales of *Hamlet*, *Othello*, *King Lear*, *Macbeth*, and *Antony and Cleopatra*.

The First Quarto (1597) [21] affords the most authoritative text, a good one, except for its omission of the abdication (IV, i, 154-318). This passage was not printed till the Fourth Quarto (1608). [22] The Folio text was probably set up from the Fifth Quarto (1615). [23] It corrects many errors in the passage added by the Fourth. These were very likely the result of shorthand reporting of the abdication scene in actual performance; they include omissions and mislining. Censorship either suffered or anticipated, was doubtless responsible for the deletion of this episode in the earlier quartos, and no wonder. Successful rebellion by a popular hero and the deposition and murder of a legitimate English sovereign were not welcome themes to the government of a queen who reigned under constant fear of civil and religious commotion and even of assassination. The unsettled question of the succession to her throne, while it decreased her personal danger, aggravated the general nervousness.

Of political axe-grinding Shakespeare himself was doubtless innocent, but that did not prevent the play from figuring in the rebellion of the Earl of Essex in 1601. On Saturday, February 7, the day before Essex attempted his *coup d'état*, *Richard the Second* was acted at the Globe on the behest of some of his friends.[24] Though Augustine Phillips had to testify at the Earl's trial, there is no reason to suppose that Shakespeare or any member of his company was in the confidence of the plotters.

His authorship has unsuccessfully been called in question. He may, however, have been influenced by the example of Marlowe's *Edward the Second* in choosing a weak but self-willed monarch for hero, and in arousing, first, antagonism for a frivolous tyrant, and then pity for the misery of a king. On the other hand, Marlowe's tragedy is his least poetic, and Shakespeare had long before led the way in humanizing chronicle-history drama. He had, in fact, given Marlowe a lead by dealing at length with a weak king in *Henry the Sixth*. There is no evidence that Shakespeare is making over an older play. His source is the second edition of Holinshed (1587). Here and there he may be indebted to other books; the Groom's charming lines about roan Barbary (V, v) were perhaps inspired by Froissart's account of the King's greyhound in Lord Berners's translation. Two episodes are Shakespeare's invention: the Queen with the gardeners (III, iv), and the parting of the royal lovers (V, i). *Richard the Second* does not attempt to summarize the whole reign; these events all occurred between April 29, 1398 and January, 1400. Condensation, though always a problem, is therefore not so pressing as usual. The result is the best unified of the chronicle plays, better than the somewhat specious unity of *Richard the Third*, since the method of securing it is not one of arbitrary concentration on a central figure.

The testimony of Phillips in 1601 shows that *Richard the Second* was no longer active in the repertory. An amateur performance (presumably of Shakespeare's play) was given by the ship's company on board the *Dragon*, Captain William Keeling, off Sierra Leone on September 30, 1607. The King's Men revived the play at the Globe in 1631. Late in 1680 it was staged at Drury Lane in an adaptation by Nahum Tate, which ran only two days. The government suppressed it; like Elizabeth, the brothers Stuart seem to have taken the deposition scene to heart. These were the troublous times which followed the Popish Plot, and the machinations of Shaftesbury were viewed with alarm. In a desperate attempt to stave off disaster, Tate changed the names of the characters and rechristened his version *The Sicilian Usurper*. His efforts were unavailing; but the next adapter of *Richard the Second* had a success for a couple of seasons. This was Lewis Theobald, the great editor of Shakespeare; his version appeared in 1719. The original play was elaborately staged at Covent Garden in 1738. In 1815 Edmund Kean acted in a version by Richard Wroughton; his performance was impressive, though Hazlitt found it too heroic. Vandenhoff took the title rôle at Covent Garden in 1834; and Macready, who had played the part in the provinces as a boy, appeared twice as Richard shortly before his retirement. In 1857 Charles Kean had a run of eighty-five nights in Shakespeare's play, though it was outrageously cut to make room for a pageant showing the London entry of Bolingbroke and the fallen King. Ellen Terry, who suped in this production, thought Richard one of Kean's best rôles. *Richard the Second* is among the seven Shakespeare plays avoided by the devoted Phelps. Other notable revivals were Poel's in 1899 (with Granville-Barker as Richard), Benson's in 1900, Tree's in 1903, Henry Cass's (with Maurice Evans) in 1934, and John Gielgud's in 1937. J. W. Wallack and J. B. and Edwin Booth appeared in *Richard the Second* in the United States, but it has never been a regular item in the Shakespearean repertory. Its New York run of 171 performances in 1937, admirably directed by Margaret Webster, with Mr. Evans in the title rôle, surprised everyone [25] and may have some significance for the future of our stage. The success of this the most meditative and lyrical of Shakespeare's historical plays is among the most striking of several indications that our serious theatre is about to occupy itself more often and more directly with the spirit of man.

Chapter 5

LATER HISTORIES

SHAKESPEARE's greatest comic triumph was not to be in comedy but in the comical-historical, a hybrid genre omitted by Polonius,[1] but a very important one, since Sir John Falstaff was created for it. The fat knight is gypsy king of all lovable stage rogues and literary vagabonds. Ben Jonson concedes that Shakespeare redeemed his vices with his virtues. In the eyes of most readers, Falstaff's humor redeems everything. He is a laughing philosopher, and the best example of how inspired clowning can almost reach the level of poetry.

Falstaff, indeed, actually attains it, because Shakespeare also grants him a share of his own creative imagination:

Marry, then, sweet wag, when thou art king, let not us that are squires of the night's body be called thieves of the day's beauty. Let us be Diana's Foresters, Gentlemen of the Shade, Minions of the Moon; and let men say we be men of good government, being governed as the sea is, by our noble and chaste mistress the moon, under whose countenance we steal.

Falstaff's attitude toward life is, in a way, the poet's. It is a world of beauty and of wonder that he sees, and joyously experiences as intensively as his means and years allow. He is not quite a poet (though he often speaks poetry) because, while there is spiritual capacity in him, it is repeatedly closed off by an almost doctrinaire intellectualism, far more restrictive than his sensuality. In Shakespeare it is the wicked that have the brains — not exclusively, but so brilliantly and so insistently that a certain inference about the master of ceremonies is inescapable. Intuition must have seemed to him more precious than logic. The latter Shakespeare bestows on appalling criminals like Iago and Edmund; but we can not hate Hamlet's uncle, who has an inner life and spiritual perceptions. Iago and Edmund are punished only after they have been caught; and they are not caught because their virtuous opponents are intellectually their superiors. Claudius is his own scourge, a daily one. Falstaff is no criminal; he is merely and rather mildly vicious, and with a single exception his vices injure no one but himself.

Puritans still pull a long face over him, and there is no denying that a list of his faults does not make pretty reading. Cowardice is not one of them, and the old man's day of good service at Shrewsbury entitles him, at any rate in this world of faëry, to a certain relaxation both before and after the campaign. Even with Doll Tearsheet on his knee and a gallon of sack in his belly, Falstaff is not earmarked by his creator for damnation. Who can doubt his immediate flight to Arthur's bosom? If a mightier Author than Shakespeare decides to damn him, it will be in better company than the Boar's Head ever afforded. Women and wine were not put into this world in order that the great comedians of picaresque fiction might shun them. Our severer critics want to eat their cake and keep it; they would like to have the comic recipe mixed without the breaking of any ethical eggs.

It can be done; but the result is sentimental comedy. Shakespeare gives us a great rogue, and we love him; but we need not weep into our beer over him. History marches on. Prince Hal must take the road to Agincourt. Once the Plantagenet emerges from his Eastcheap purlieus on that highway of glory, Falstaff is no longer possible. Perhaps with a tear in his eye, but certainly with a firm hand, Shakespeare writes the last scene of *Part 2;* and Falstaff he is dead, at least to royal comradeship. Like Pistol, "we must ern therefore"; but even as we mourn, we have to accept Shakespeare's evenhandedness.

> Would that in body and spirit Shakespeare came,
> Visible emperor of the deeds of Time,
> With Justice still the genius of his rhyme,

Giving each man his due, each passion grace,
Impartial as the rain from Heaven's face. . . .[2]

The unamiable exception among Falstaff's vices is financial chicanery. He cheats Dame Quickly, whose livelihood comes partly from her percentage in whores' takings. As a press officer he grafts in the usual way, though the King is not much defrauded, since the ragamuffins arrive and are led where they are peppered. As for Justice Shallow, he really asks for it. No doubt all this is reprehensible, like the simple distinctions of Robin Hood in the greenwood. But Falstaff's victims are uniformly unlovely; and Shakespeare means to evoke, not a moralistic criticism, but laughter.

Do we laugh with Falstaff, or at him? That is the question, and the answer must take into account the affection he has inspired. We adore artists who go to the trouble of pretending to be absurd and enforcing our escape into laughter's temporary freedom. When a gifted fellow creature [3] successfully makes himself a motley to the view, we are thankful that he exists. Falstaff is a great artist — that is his real vocation and that is why Hal is so fond of him. He is the perpetual card, the life of the party, the professional diner-out, the Dr. Holmes of Eastcheap. He inspires both the belly laugh and the silvery tinkle of Meredith's Comic Spirit. His are the fertility and inexhaustibility of genius. He is never caught — not till the last scene of *Part 2*, where we have the universal tragedy of the funny man. The world is not kind to artists: Agincourt is more important than lines of beauty or the explosive disintegration in a flashing phrase of a completely analyzed abstract idea. Or is it? "Truth" versus fiction, "history" versus poetry — Aristotle held other views. Was the valor of those English on St. Crispin's Day a more substantial contribution to the world's stock of memorabilia than the composition of *King Henry the Fourth*? Whether you laugh at or with Falstaff may depend on how hard you take the Agincourts.

Whether Shakespeare laughs at or with him is a simpler matter. Shakespeare does not easily laugh at anyone; that is what keeps him from the highest success in pure comedy. His mirth is commonly sympathetic, rarely derisive. It is of puppet lovers that Robin Goodfellow tinkles his "Lord, what fools these mortals be!" In more than the obvious sense, Falstaff is too solid, too much the poet, too much Shakespeare himself, to be subjected to satirical rough-handling. The author's affection for the old reprobate is plain to see even in the final scene, where he goes out of his way to give us a false clue. So Falstaff is to be reformed! He will draw an allowance from the royal purse, and eventually be recalled to court! That is sheer nonsense and opium, however gratefully we swallow it. Falstaff can never companion a king gone stark heroic. If his "conversations appear more wise and modest to the world" to a degree that warrants his reappearance within the charmed romantic circle, he will not be our Falstaff. Despite the promise of the Epilogue to *Part 2*, Shakespeare took the only possible course and killed him early in *Henry the Fifth*, not daring to let us see him even once.

It is curious that the critical debate has raged less violently over these considerations than over the special question of whether Falstaff is a coward. Misled as it was concerning the name and nature of poetry, the eighteenth century for the first three-quarters of its existence was hopelessly prosaic about him. Complacent rationalists traced the springs of his humor in his fatness and buffoonery. To their categorical blindness, Hotspur was a hero and Falstaff a coward. What they failed to perceive is that both contribute to a shrewd criticism of the proposition that war is romance. Hotspur compels admiration, even now, because, as an abstract concept, personal courage is always admirable. Yet its manifestation in a given setting of circumstance is not invariably praiseworthy. Shakespeare's admiration is qualified by Hotspur's rashness. It is not his life alone he is risking; and if he dies an honorable death, like Essex's it is not a very intelligent one. Unlike Hotspur's, Falstaff's courage is not immoderate. It is even too much the other way. But not so much as some have supposed. In the famous "honor" speech (*Part 1*, V, i,

128–44) his scepticism is expressed *in character;* that is one reason why it has been misunderstood. It is completely free from idealism, and for once there is no' touch of Falstaff's poetry. That does not mean the anatomist is quaking. He proceeds to *lead* his motley crew into the thick of it, and in *Part 2* there are repeated allusions to his gallantry. His critics miss the point that his clowning is funnier just because he is a soldier and a knight. He does his duty when it confronts him, but he is not one to go out of his way looking for it. This is the attitude of the veteran, of the professional, like Bluntschli in *Arms and the Man*, who long ago had his bellyful of fighting, retains no romantic illusions about war, is left cold by stay-at-home coinages like "the great prize of death in battle," but does his possible when the pinch comes. Fighting is all in the day's work — some days; and who but an incurable romantic like Percy, or aspirant politicians with an axe to grind like Hal, would not prefer taking his ease in his inn? "O, I could wish this tavern were my drum!" But the real drum taps. Falstaff grouses — and falls in.⁴

The First Quarto of *Part 1*, the authoritative text, appeared in 1598,⁵ the year in which Meres clumsily listed the play, without specifying the Parts, among Shakespeare's tragedies. The preceding year is usually allotted to the composition and production of *Part 1;* that is only a guess, though it is probably about right. The historical events come hard on the heels of *Richard the Second;* if that play was finished as early as the spring of 1595, *1 Henry the Fourth* may have followed in the same year or the next. However that may be, Shakespeare is obviously past his experimental period. Already he has achieved at least one of his best comedies, *A Midsummer Night's Dream*, and probably *The Merchant of Venice* as well. His prentice histories are all verse dramas and almost completely serious. In *Henry the Fourth* first appear long scenes in prose and the richest of humor. Out of the earlier epic form Shakespeare molds a genre more realistic and much more dramatic. The old seriousness is still present in the historical episodes, and their verse is supple and vigorous; but this play marks a new departure and shows the sure touch of a genius fully matured. It is a master dramatist who now composes the best of all chronicle plays.

His chief source is the second edition of Holinshed's *Chronicle* (1587); he even follows its confusion of Edmund Mortimer, fifth Earl of March, with his uncle Sir Edmund Mortimer. For a chronicle history, the play is well unified. The action runs only from Glendower's capture of Mortimer on June 22, 1402 to the execution of Worcester and Vernon on July 23, 1403. It was therefore possible to build the historical treatment wholly around the rebellion. Since Hal is to win his spurs at Shrewsbury, his Bohemian background is an integral part of the theme; and Falstaff is the main feature of that background. For Hal as prodigal, Shakespeare also used an anonymous play, *The Famous Victories of Henry the fifth*.[6] From it he took, along with other details, the name of Sir John Oldcastle, which he changed to Falstaff in the interval, whatever it was, between production and publication.[7] The historical Oldcastle was a Lollard martyr, executed for heresy in 1417. He had married an ancestress of the noble house of Brooke, Lords Cobham, which title he enjoyed in his wife's right. No doubt this influential family resented the figure he cut in the play.[8] Shakespeare makes amends in the Epilogue to *Part 2*: "for Oldcastle died a martyr, and this is not the man." The new name, though transliterated, is that of another historical figure, Sir John Fastolf, a famous commander against the French. He had already appeared in *Henry the Sixth, Part 1*, where (I, i, 131–40) he is charged with cowardice. The Folio spells his name "Falstaffe." Like Oldcastle he was a Lollard, and Gairdner thinks he was probably reared in the Norfolks' house.[9] The aspersions on his military conduct were unwarranted.

As usual, Shakespeare is pretty cavalier with the facts when he wants to heighten effects. The Prince of Wales executed with gallantry the tactical movement which decided the battle of Shrewsbury, but his rescue of his father and his spectacular combat with Sir Henry Percy are unhistorical. Hotspur was long past his youth when he fell, and who killed him is unknown. He was then thirty-nine years of age, older than King Henry, who was thirty-six. Prince Hal was sixteen, and Shakespeare reduces Hotspur to an equal age in order to emphasize the contrast between them. He was anticipated in this by Samuel Daniel's *The ciuile wars between the two houses of Lancaster and Yorke* (1595). Very likely Shakespeare read this poem, but despite occasional points of agreement it can hardly be called a source.

Upon the production of this play, Sir John Oldcastle-Falstaff leaped into fame. By 1599 the second of these surnames had become a by-word.[10] Yet, sometimes perhaps from mere carelessness and possibly now and again a little maliciously, the name of Oldcastle would not down. On March 6, 1600 a private performance of "Sir John Old Castell" by the Burbage company was a feature of the Lord Chamberlain's entertainment of Ludowic Verreyken, the Flemish ambassador. That the play was a steady drawing card in the public repertory is attested by Leonard Digges's verses, prefixed to Shakespeare's *Poems* (1640):

> And though the Fox and subtill Alchimist,[11]
> Long intermitted could not quite be mist,
> Though these have sham'd all the Ancients, and might raise,
> Their Authours merit with a crowne of Bayes.
> Yet these sometimes, even at a friends desire
> Acted, have scarce defrai'd the Seacoale fire [12]
> And doore-keepers: when let but *Falstaffe* come,
> *Hall*, *Poines*, the rest you scarce shall have a roome
> All is so pester'd.

One of the trials of Elizabethan actors, and such theatregoers as were sensitive, like Montaigne, to irritating noises, was the constant cracking and munching of nuts by the popular audience. Some prefatory verses in the Beaumont-Fletcher Folio of 1647 mention Sir John's hold on the spectators:

> I Could prayse *Heywood* now: or tell how long,
> *Falstaffe* from cracking Nuts hath kept the throng.

Unfortunately we have no such records for the Chamberlain-King's as the Henslowe papers provide for the Admiral's.

THOMAS BETTERTON

from Kneller's portrait

JAMES QUIN AS FALSTAFF
from the portrait ascribed to James MacArdell

EDMUND KEAN AS RICHARD III

from the mezzotint by Charles Turner

EDWIN FORREST

Court performances, however, got recorded because they involved official cash payments; and so we know that one or both parts of *Henry the Fourth* were played at the court of James or Charles in 1612 ("Sʳ John ffalstafe" and "The Hotspurr"), possibly about 1619 ("[Seco]nd part of Falstaff"), in 1625 ("The First Part of Sir John Falstaff"), and perhaps in 1638 ("ould Castel").[13]

Who created the rôle of Falstaff is not known. According to James Wright's *Historia Histrionica* (1699), John Lowin was much applauded in it; but he was not with the King's Men when the play was first staged. Under the Restoration, *Part 1* was among the earliest revivals. William Cartwright was the Falstaff, William Wintersell the King, the fine tragedian Charles Hart the Hotspur, and Nicholas Burt the Prince. The play remained in the hands of the King's Company (the "Old Actors") till its absorption by the Duke of York's in 1682. After that Betterton played Hotspur in his prime and Falstaff in his old age. His acting version was printed in 1700. It is seriously cut; but unlike the run of Restoration adapters, Betterton did not alter phraseology. The popularity of *Part 1* continued in the eighteenth century, though Garrick failed as Hotspur. Quin's was the chief Falstaff of that age, but Henderson's was also much admired. One or the other and sometimes both of these rôles attracted most of the leading actors through the first half of the nineteenth century. James Henry Hackett played Falstaff for forty years; no other American has had a comparable success with the part. Among the Hotspurs were J. P. and Charles Kemble, Edmund Kean, and Macready. Cooke was a remarkable Falstaff, though he says he never played the rôle to his own satisfaction. Samuel Phelps acted it at Sadler's Wells in 1846, and it became one of his stand-bys. Tree cast himself in the part for his elaborate production in 1896. It was taken by Louis Calvert in 1909 when the play was revived by Lewis Waller, who continued in the rôle of Hotspur, which he had assumed under Tree. The latter presented his own revival again in 1914. Since then the play has not been much acted. There was a New York production by the Players club in 1926, and a London revival in 1935 with George Robey as Falstaff and John Drinkwater as Henry IV. Early in 1939 Maurice Evans had a New York run of seventy-four performances as Falstaff in a spirited production directed by Margaret Webster, who added III, ii from *Part 2*.

Part 1 is by all odds the best of the histories. If it lacks the central heroic figure that gives *Henry the Fifth* a simpler unity, and if it touches but seldom the level of the lyric passages in *Richard the Second*, it is superior to both as a piece of varied yet coherent entertainment. Incomparable as Falstaff is, one star is not enough for this play. Hotspur is easy — a straight romantic rôle replete with ringing declamations. But the King requires a careful study. He is among the most interesting because among the most complex of Shakespeare's historical portraits. Henry is a reformed fox, who would like to forget the checkered past and shine, not merely as a successful ruler at home, but also as a Christian champion against the infidel. His desire to be a good king is sincere. Like most well-intentioned usurpers, he is pathetically eager to found a dynasty. His dream of a new crusade is shattered by the northern revolt, and wearily he turns to the sordid task of suppression which his own rebellion against Richard has inevitably brought upon him. The past takes its toll. Shakespeare deepens the pathos of Henry's predicament by exaggerating his age and by presenting him not alone as king but as father. His is the burden of royal loneliness made still more insupportable by the conduct of a wayward son. It is a moving scene (III, ii) in which Henry, who comes to the interview without clean hands, instructs his heir concerning the past that lies behind the glorious present, a past full of guile and blood, and tries to win him to a sense, not of filial affection — that he deems impossible, — but at least of responsibility.

The rôle of the Prince calls for versatility. He must be comedian in the taverns, hero in the field, and chastened son in the great scene of reconciliation. Shakespeare launches in this play on a trilogy which will trace the life of England's darling from its unpromising youth to its glorious conclusion on the field of victory and the steps of the French throne.

Henry V is to be the ideal ruler, patient, indefatigable, un-
daunted, unselfish. This the audience is not allowed to forget.
Hence the soliloquy, "I know you all," which ends the
second scene, a priggish speech of intolerable hypocrisy if
we take it as uttered by Hal in character. It is not Hal but
the author speaking; these are Shakespeare's sentiments and
as such they are unexceptionable — indeed, they are repeated
by Canterbury and Ely in the opening scene of *Henry the Fifth*.
It is the Prince's saying these things himself at this particular
time that grates on us — if we fail to remember that one of
the regular functions of the Elizabethan soliloquy was serv-
ing as a program note. Shakespeare is reassuring the audience:
Hal is no blind debauchee; he will show his true colors in
his own good time, and when he does he will shine all the
more for what he was. Undramatic as it may seem to us, the
device was a well-established convention on Shakespeare's
stage.

As for Hal's irresponsibility before rebellion and his father
bring him up with a round turn, it is not due to inherent
viciousness nor to dullness. It is an outlet for his most attractive youthful quality, his high spirits. We would not exchange them for the sobriety of that old young man, Prince
John of Lancaster. No doubt Hal gets drunk occasionally,
but we never see him drunk. His sexual freedoms are not
worked into the plot but merely hinted at in a rally (I, ii)
of *double-entendres* by Falstaff. Hal is engaged in sowing his
wild oats; and we are to accept his career, from Shrewsbury on,
as a reversal of the familiar case of young saint, old sinner.

THE SECOND PART OF KING HENRY THE FOURTH

"Perhaps no authour," says Dr. Johnson, "has ever in two
plays afforded so much delight." Like most sequels, *Part 2*,
which must have been conceived simultaneously with *Part 1*,
never had the success of its predecessor. There may have been
revivals at the courts of James I and Charles I [14] and at the
Globe and Blackfriars. Betterton probably produced it about
1703. An acting version ascribed to him was revived in 1720

and printed about 1721 as *The Sequel of Henry the Fourth*.[15]
This text includes an adaptation of the opening scene of
Henry the Fifth. For a while *Part 2* enjoyed some popularity.
Quin, the leading Falstaff of the eighteenth century, acted
in both plays. In 1758 Garrick acted the dying Henry IV.
There were occasional revivals in the first half of the nineteenth century. In 1804 Cooke played Falstaff. J. P. Kemble
and Macready acted the King. J. H. Hackett was the most
notable Falstaff after Cooke. In 1853 Phelps doubled Shallow
and King Henry. Since then, *Part 2* has seen the boards but
seldom, though Benson revived it, J. B. Fagan staged it at
the Court Theatre in 1921, and the Old Vic gave it in 1935.
Its absence is not surprising, for it depends on *Part 1*. Falstaff,
Hal, and the King are not carefully worked up, but taken
for granted. Falstaff, moreover, is less the poetic clown and
more the picaresque swindler; we love him still, but it was
Part 1 that made us love him. For all that, the poorer of
these plays is richer than most; and the worst that can be
said of *Part 2* is that it is not quite so good as *Part 1*.

The only quarto,[16] for most of the play the authoritative
text, appeared in 1600. The Folio makes many slight changes,
smooths up some grammatical and metrical irregularities, cuts
out profanity, adds 168 lines or parts of lines, and omits
about forty of the Quarto's. Some of the minor variants may
come from the two compositors' reading difficult copy differently. Stage directions and speech tags are revised in the
Folio. While some of its omissions are probably due to neg-
ligent typesetting, others strike out passages of doubtful propriety. Some of the Quarto's cuts are merely to shorten long
speeches; but others, Professor Schücking suggests, look as
if a censor (an official, the company, or the printer) feared
that dangerous topical applications might be made. The Earl
of Essex was in trouble in the summer of 1600 over his failure
in Ireland, and with good reason the government suspected
his loyalty.[17] One of his grievances was inability to secure
an audience with the Queen. The Quarto omits, for example,
part of the Archbishop of York's justification of the rebellion
(IV, i, 55–79), in which he gives

> the summary of all our griefs . . .
> Which long ere this we offer'd to the King
> And might by no suit gain our audience.
> When we are wrong'd, and would unfold our griefs,
> We are denied access unto his person
> Even by those men that most have done us wrong.

Several other cuts in the Quarto delete references to Richard II and his forced abdication, a ticklish subject, as we have seen.

1598 is the date usually assigned to the composition and production, since *Part 2* must closely have followed *Part 1*. In *Every Man Out of His Humor* (1599) Jonson alludes to Justice Silence (V, ii, 22) as well as to Falstaff (V, xi, 86–7). On the date and sources there is little of importance to add to the preceding section. The story of Hal's striking the Chief Justice, though it also appears in Holinshed and *The Famous Victories*, is fully told in Sir Thomas Elyot's *The Gouernour* (1531); Elyot is followed by John Stow in his *Annales*. Thence Shakespeare takes Henry IV's commendation of the judge, which Henry V quotes in the scene of reconciliation (V, ii, 108–12). Though all of *Part 1* builds up for Shrewsbury, the final scene comes after the battle; and the King's closing speech, instead of ending the part in peace, promises more action against the rebels in Yorkshire and Wales. This last scene and the Induction of Rumour provide the only interval between their defeat at Shrewsbury and Northumberland's reception of the news in the opening scene of the second play.

Part 2 is not so unified as *Part 1*; it covers eleven years, from 1403 to 1413, when Henry V was crowned. The political scenes are less dramatic because it is impossible to arouse much suspense after the crushing blow of Shrewsbury. We are impatient when Falstaff is off stage; there is no Hotspur for *Part 2*. The author himself seems a little impatient, at least in the first two acts. The comic scenes, however, are still linked with history, for Falstaff is on the King's service. With unwashed hands he grafts his way along his recruiting rounds, and in his pure and immaculate valor accepts the tame surrender of Sir John Coleville of the Dale. But the former madcap of the taverns is now, barring a single relapse, a very earnest Prince of Wales. After one scene of the old witty swordplay, his room is supplied by Bardolph and Pistol. Falstaff lacks the stimulation of Hal's brilliance in riposte, and is reduced for his themes to hardy perennials like Bardolph's fiery face and to the easy plucking of the country gander, Justice Shallow. Mistress Quickly, on the other hand, rises to new heights in *Part 2*, and hiccuping Doll is a vulgar but very comic addition to the troupe. Pistol is a triumph; his special mention on the title page of the Quarto shows that he won his place immediately.[18] Arrant coward and braggart that he is, Pistol has his share of the true Shakespeare touch; for, as Kittredge remarks, his delight in the sheer sound of words must have been characteristic of his creator. Pistol has been a great playgoer, and his diction is a garbled tissue of old-fashioned theatrical reminiscence. If he had been an actor, he would have swelled the number of Bad quartos.

With the opening of the third act the tempo of the historical scenes accelerates, to the strains of King Henry's great apostrophe to sleep; and, while Falstaff continues to bear the play's bell, the theme of father and son is movingly repeated in the last scene of Act IV. The final act is a superb example of balance between the two elements of the comical-historical. The new king's wise and manly endorsement of the Chief Justice prepares us for Falstaff's humiliation. The fat knight's captivation of Shallow evokes some acidulous etching that is almost high comedy; but Sir John is riding for a fall. It is no reflection on his intelligence that he does not know it. While he has been stealing cream in the country, great events at Westminster have passed him by. The little scene (V, iv) that intervenes between Pistol's announcement of "Africa and golden joys" and the outrageous tableau that confronts the new-crowned monarch and flaunts in everyone's face a reminder of his recent follies, is brutal but funny. To the Elizabethans it was even funnier, since they saw no occasion for sentiment in the rough handling of a poor whore. In hewing to the new royal line in the last scene of all, Shakespeare is following Holinshed and, in staging the encounter in the public street, *The Famous Victories*. There was nothing else for him, nor for Henry, to do. Hal's resolve in the soliloquy which closes I, ii of *Part 1*, is here, whether we like it or not, recalled and executed. Yet the old rogue commands our affection still, despite his King's, his Jove's, harshly truthful terms. Irrepressible to the last, he invites the man he has swindled to dinner, and there can be no doubt who is going to pay for it. Even in prison, we may be confident, Falstaff will think of something.

Like its predecessor, *Part 2* is brought to a close somewhat arbitrarily. Fair stands the wind for France. We shall see Henry there, beating the French and winning the hand of their princess. But first he broke Falstaff's heart. The actual fracture and corroboration occur off stage, a concession we are grateful for. The close of *Henry the Fourth* is no place for it; instead, Shakespeare gives us an adroit compromise between justice and mercy. Falstaff marches off to jail with colors drooping but by no means hauled down, while Harry of Monmouth faces south and dreams about the vasty fields across the narrow seas.

THE LIFE OF KING HENRY THE FIFTH

Shakespeare's historical imagination soars to its highest pitch as he takes quill in hand for this, the final chronicle-play of his unaided authorship. To it everything on the serious side of *Henry the Fourth* has been working up, and now his mind is set ablaze as he thinks of the army's greyhound leap across the Channel, the bold harrying in the heart of France, and the gathering of the storm that finally breaks on the little band of brothers but fails to shatter it and in failing makes the name of Agincourt a thing that can still stir English blood. Over the preparations, all the maneuvering, the brilliant victory itself, presides the unsleeping genius of the warrior King, "this Star of England," no longer the volatile Hal but British Harry, a sudden incarnation of Malcolm's list of the

> king-becoming graces,
> As justice, verity, temp'rance, stableness,
> Bounty, perséverance, mercy, lowliness,
> Devotion, patience, courage, fortitude.

On the whole, the English have admired cleverness and imagination in their statesmen less than tenacity and sober competence; even a steady incompetence is by many viewed with less suspicion than the unpredictable sallies of some types of genius. Shakespeare is true to the mettle of his pasture when he arbitrarily replaces the brilliance of a well-loved prince of Wales by a hard-working king's integrity, so solid that it amounts to genius. Henry V is no Harry Hotspur. But neither is he, for all his pious boasting, a stuffed shirt of a king. He is Harry Monmouth, as much man as monarch; and, though Eastcheap and the Boar's Head know him no more, he has not lost the common touch.

Henry the Fifth, then, is Drayton's "Ballad of Agincourt" dramatized, made real, made visible, as far as the limitations of that wooden O, the Globe, allowed. Shakespeare is acutely conscious of its limitations. The subject is epic; the mood is almost lyric; but everything must be trimmed down, within "the two hours' traffic of our stage," to the practicably dramatic. No wonder the poet invokes "a Muse of fire," and apologizes because ships and horses and siege guns must be visualized with the mind's eye, and the whole city of London can not be brought on stage roaring its welcome to the conquering hero. He fears lest

> we shall much disgrace
> With four or five most vile and ragged foils,
> Right ill-dispos'd in brawl ridiculous,
> The name of Agincourt.

He implores his audience to "Piece out our imperfections with your thoughts" and grant dramatist and actors full scope to work on such imaginative faculties as spectators can bring with them to a theatre. These injunctions, scattered through the Prologue and the four Choruses, constitute Shakespeare's most explicit statement of his technical theory — impressionism we call it now. He is asking for the willing suspension of disbelief and the imaginative acceptance of suggestions and symbols. It is somewhat ironical that most of the known theatrical history of this play is a tale of foolish attempts to replace Shakespeare's methods by crowding the stage with scenic lumber.

The authoritative text is the Folio of 1623. The first edition, in 1600, is one of the Bad quartos.[19] There is much omission, transposition, metrical incompetence, mislining, and printing of prose as verse. The Quarto text is much shorter; yet not all its omissions can be laid to mere cutting for the stage, since some of them wreck coherence. Synonyms and variant inflections are often substituted, and sometimes the Quarto summarizes the gist of a Folio passage. Such phenomena indicate that memory, perhaps an actor's, was an important factor at some stage of the text's transmission. The Quarto, then, appears to be an unauthorized, reduced, and corrupt rendering of the play as originally cut and performed, though occasionally its readings serve to correct Folio misprints. Among its most serious omissions are the Prologue, Choruses, and Epilogue. In the course of shortening, eleven rôles are dispensed with. This looks as if the Quarto represents an acting version arranged for a provincial tour, when any company, still more a minor one, would try to economize on traveling expenses by reducing personnel. Though many students of the text, including Pope and Johnson, have argued that the Folio gives us a literary revision of a first draft represented by the Quarto, there is little reason to doubt that, aside from the misprints, the inadvertent omission of three excellent lines preserved in the Quarto (II, i, 110-111; IV, iii, 48), and the usual half-hearted gestures of compliance with the law against profanity, we have the play in the text of 1623 substantially as Shakespeare composed it.

Special mention should be made of a difficulty in the Folio rendering of the quondam Quickly's account of Falstaff's death: "and a Table of greene fields" (II, iii); for it elicited the most famous of all textual corrections, Theobald's "and a' [i.e., 'a, he] bab[b]led of green fields." Here is emendation both sound and beautiful. Crushed by the King's coolness, the old rascal lies dying. He thinks he is a little boy again, picking flowers in the country and holding them up to smell. "For after I saw him fumble with the sheets, and play with flowers, and smile upon his fingers' ends, I knew there was but one way." No other Elizabethan, save possibly Thomas Dekker, had it in him to write like that. As the Hostess chatters on, creative impossibilities are actually accomplished in a perfect fusion of bawdy humor and the most poignant pathos. There is much blending of comic and serious in Elizabethan drama, often too much, for sometimes the ingredients simply will not mix, however justifiable the attempt on the ground that life presents them to us mingled. Here, as in Viola's near-betrayal of her love (*Twelfth Night*, II, iv), they combine into something rich and strange, that leaves us at once conscious of reality and transported into a world of wonder far beyond it.

At last we have come to a play the date of which is almost certain. "The general of our gracious Empress," whose triumphant return from Ireland would rejoice the citizens (Chorus to Act V), is the unlucky Earl of Essex. He left for the Irish war on March 27, 1599, and was back in London on September 28, but not victorious; the summer's campaign was a complete failure. Meres's *Palladis Tamia* had appeared in the fall of 1598 with no mention of *Henry the Fifth*. In all probability the play was staged at the newly built Globe in the early summer of 1599, and no doubt production had followed composition immediately.

A theory that Shakespeare had revised an early drama of his own has not won much support, though *The Famous Victories* [20] was among his sources. Like *Henry the Fifth*, it ends with the betrothal. Holinshed is again Shakespeare's principal quarry. The play is well unified, as chronicle-histories go. Parliament voted supplies for the war in 1414; Agincourt was fought on October 25, 1415; Henry and Katherine were betrothed on May 21, 1420. The remnant of the Falstaffians have no such direct bearing on the main theme as do the tavern scenes in *Henry the Fourth;* yet as a glimpse of

life among the war's lowly they contribute, like the comic
talk of the four captains and the grousing of the common
soldiers, to a more realistic picture than could be painted in
values exclusively colored by Henry's heroics. Pistol, though
no Falstaff, shoulders the main burden of comedy; he is a
great success — no routine braggart-soldier he — and he sustains and even outdoes his linguistic achievements in the
preceding play. Corporal Nym, with his "that's the humour
of it," is probably a good-natured caricature of Jonson's trick,
about this time, of drawing his characters strictly according
to their "humors," that is, the single predominating trait
or mental quirk which dictates the conduct of each. Jonson
defines his method in *Every Man Out of His Humor* (acted 1599,
printed 1600):

> As when some one peculiar quality
> Doth so possesse a man, that it doth draw
> All his affects, his spirits, and his powers
> In their confluctions all to runne one way,
> This may be truely sayd to be a Humor.

If Shakespeare had raised a laugh at his expense, Ben made a
neat return in the same play:

Mit[*is*]. . . . how comes it then, that in some one play wee see
so many Seas, Countries, and Kingdomes, past ouer with such admirable dexteritie?
Cor[*datus*]. O, that but shewes how well the Authors can trauaile
in their vocation, and out-run the apprehention of their Auditory
[i.e., audience].

In his Prologue, probably later than 1599, to *Every Man in
his Humor* (acted 1598), Ben lists the absurdities shunned by
his own play and assures the audience that no "*Chorus* wafts
you ore the seas."

The campaign in France was an abominable piece of commercial militarism, but to a patriotic Elizabethan it was
among the most brilliant episodes in English history. We
need not go back to the Renaissance to find religious sanctions
invoked for war. Once again we must make the historical
discount and accept the slaughter as chivalrous and the pious

sentiments of the blood-stained King as wholly sincere. Shakespeare is engaged in creating a work of art, not of philosophy. It is hard to believe he really supposed the French nobles the knavish fools he makes them. No doubt the vulgar portion of his audience was ready to believe it. To censure Shakespeare is to insist on his being a prophet instead of a playwright. It is the dramatist's way to heighten effects and sharpen contrasts. The theory and technique of naturalism had not been worked out when this play was written. The wonder is, not that Shakespeare fails to approach the dramatic rostrum like Bernard Shaw, but that, plots and ideas to the contrary notwithstanding, none of the great realist or naturalist writers has yet equaled him in vivid fidelity to human nature.

How often this play was acted in its own time is unknown; nor, though there was a court performance in 1605,[21] do we know how long it held the seventeenth-century stage. Apparently it was not acted under the Restoration. Roger Boyle, Earl of Orrery, wrote an independent play about Henry V, which was staged in 1664. There was another by Aaron Hill in 1723. Not till toward the middle of the eighteenth century, perhaps in 1735, certainly by 1738, did Shakespeare's take the boards again. The title rôle failed to attract many of the great actors; revivals were few and far between. In 1747 Garrick played the Chorus, in court suit, ruffles, wig, and sword, with Spranger Barry as the King and Charles Macklin as Fluellen. Later revivals staged the coronation procession lavishly. The play was advertised by J. P. Kemble in 1789 as not acted for twenty years. In 1830 Edmund Kean appeared as Henry V, a pathetic occasion, for the great actor's mind was giving way, his memory failed him, and he broke down on stage. Macready, whose first performance of this play was in 1815, produced it elaborately in 1839, restoring the long-discarded Choruses and cluttering the stage of Covent Garden with spectacular effects, among them "a moving diorama . . . depicting the voyage of the English fleet to Harfleur," and painted armies at Agincourt which, with the aid of a little stage smoke, were supposed to merge imper-

ceptibly into the ranks of the living actors. Phelps also revived
the play. Charles Kean's run of eighty-four performances in
1859 was distinguished by another spectacle, Henry's triumphant entry into London. This feature was retained by the
most successful Henry V on record, George Rignold. Kean
played the title rôle in his own production, and got around
the lack of a part for his wife by casting her as the Chorus.
At the testimonial dinner when Kean gave up his management
of the Princess's, the Duke of Newcastle, in proposing the
actor's health, maintained that his cockpit *could* hold the
vasty fields of France. Historical accuracy was now the rage,
and in pursuit of it the producers fell into a pretentious realism
still inadequate to Shakespeare's conception and most unsuited to his technique. Other notable revivals were Tree's,
Waller's, and Benson's. The piece was played by Mansfield
for a whole season. Of late its fortunes have rested almost
exclusively with British repertory companies. Recent exponents of the title rôle were Baliol Holloway (1926), Godfrey
Tearle (1934), Laurence Olivier (1937), Ivor Novello (1938).
None scored more than a modest success.

The reason is not far to seek. Since the second major renascence of the English-speaking theatre, we require our historical drama with at least a dressing of ideas. As far as *Henry
the Fifth* has any, it presents a semi-Fascist ideal. Its intellectual poverty is not compensated for by much beauty; that the
nineteenth-century revivals turned it into a vehicle for spectacle is significant. Henry's ringing speeches are superb, but
they are more rhetorical than poetic. Perhaps Shakespeare's
interest in the straight epic treatment of history had begun
to flag before he finished the play. Perhaps the inadequacy
of his medium damped his initial enthusiasm. At any rate,
though he was to take a hand in *Henry the Eighth*, he now
ends his long panorama of English history from 1398 to 1485,
abandoning a refractory genre, with which he had done all
that could be done by a dramatist to whom the telling of a
story was his first concern. In *Julius Cæsar*, written about this
time, he is working out of history into tragedy. In *Hamlet*,
only a year or two later, he storms the tragic heights.

THE FAMOUS HISTORY OF
THE LIFE OF KING HENRY THE EIGHTH

Since we are grouping the plays by genre, we have now to glance at *Henry the Eighth;* but it followed long after the other chronicle dramas, and John Fletcher probably wrote most of it. This play is very inferior to the three great comical-histories. Tragedy comes sweeping by in it, but there is too much sceptered pall, and too little coherence and cumulative dramatic force. As Henry Irving remarked, it is "a pageant or nothing."

The text was not printed till the Folio of 1623, which provides a good one. It must have been finished by the spring or early summer of 1613; for on June 29, perhaps at the first performance but certainly while the play was still new, the wadding of one of the saluting pieces (I, iv) landed on the thatched roof of the Globe. Several contemporary accounts have survived. On July 2 the diplomat Sir Henry Wotton wrote to his nephew Sir Edmund Bacon:

Now, to let matters of State sleep, I will entertain you at the present with what hath happened this week at the Banks side. The Kings Players had a new Play, called *All is true*, representing some principal pieces of the Raign of *Henry* 8. which was set forth with many extraordinary circumstances of Pomp and Majesty, even to the matting of the Stage; the Knights of the Order, with their Georges and Garter, the Guards with their embroidered Coats, and the like: sufficient in truth within a while to make greatness very familiar, if not ridiculous. Now, King *Henry* making a Masque at the Cardinal *Wolsey*'s House, and certain Canons being shot off at his entry, some of the Paper, or other stuff wherewith one of them was stopped, did light on the Thatch, where being thought at first but an idle smoak, and their eyes more attentive to the show, it kindled inwardly, and ran round like a train, consuming within less then an hour the whole House to the very grounds.

This was the fatal period of that vertuous Fabrique; wherein yet nothing did perish, but Wood and Straw, and a few forsaken Cloaks; only one man had his Breeches set on fire, that would perhaps have broyled him, if he had not by the benefit of a provident wit put it out with bottle Ale.[22]

This description fits *Henry the Eighth*, and the play is so designated by Thomas Lorkin in a letter to Sir Thomas Puckering written the day after the fire. *All is True* was evidently an alternative title; the Prologue repeatedly insists on the truth of the new piece, perhaps to emphasize its superiority to Samuel Rowley's play on the same reign, *When You See Me, You Know Me*, acted by Prince Henry's Men.

Attention was called to the metrical peculiarities of *Henry the Eighth* as early as 1758.[23] In 1850 Emerson noticed the presence of two hands,[24] independently of the first serious study, which appeared in the same year. One writes regular blank verse. The other, addicted to a profusion of feminine endings and a curious lack of co-ordination between metrical stress and emphasis according to sense, is responsible for the prodigality of hypermetrical lines which we now recognize as the hallmark of Fletcher.

> Cromwell, I charge thee, fling away ambition!
> By that sin fell the angels. How can man then
> (The image of his Maker) hope to win by it?
> Love thyself last. Cherish those hearts that hate thee. . . .
>
> (III, ii, 440–43)

Spedding, the first to claim the bulk of the play for Fletcher, credits Tennyson with the original suggestion, which is now generally accepted. There is still some dispute as to Shakespeare's share, for Philip Massinger has been proposed as collaborator, either in his stead or as a final reviser. Orthodox opinion assigns to Shakespeare I, i, ii; II, iii, iv; III, ii, 1–203; and V, i. The ascription of the remainder to Fletcher rests wholly on internal evidence; but his style is relatively easy to detect, and there can be little doubt of his responsibility.[25] There is external evidence, though late, for his collaboration with Shakespeare about this time in *The Two Noble Kinsmen*. How they worked together remains their trade secret. Very likely Shakespeare had begun *Henry the Eighth* and then, either feeling unequal to its completion or responding to his company's urgent requirement of a new play, called on his successor to aid him. At any rate, for several episodes, he starts and Fletcher finishes. It is also possible that the idea of a play of pageantry was originally Fletcher's and that, no longer associated with Beaumont, he felt the need of Shakespeare's support. Or the enterprise may have been a partnership from the first. There is not much use in speculating whether either playwright revised the other's contributions or whether they wrote up their assignments independently, though the latter seems more likely.[26]

Holinshed is again the chief source. The conspiracy against Cranmer (V, i–iii) comes from John Foxe's *Book of Martyrs*, as his *Acts and Monuments* is commonly called. Both dramatists occasionally appropriate phraseology from their sources with little alteration. The historical events run from the Field of the Cloth of Gold in 1520 (mentioned in the first scene as recent) and the arrest of Buckingham in 1521 (also in Scene i), to the attack on Cranmer, not earlier than 1540 and probably in 1544. There is much condensation and rearrangement. The christening of Elizabeth is reserved for the final scene, though it was actually in 1533. Wolsey died in 1530 and Katherine in 1536.

As the elaborate stage directions show, the play, whether or not it was so conceived, had its birth on stage as a spectacle. According to Downes, John Lowin created the title rôle and received his instructions directly from Shakespeare. Early theatrical tradition reached Downes through D'avenant and Betterton. The old prompter is frequently muddled; if we could be sure he had the facts in this instance, we should have to abandon the possibility that Shakespeare washed his hands of the play when he turned an unfinished manuscript over to Fletcher. There was a revival at the Globe in 1628, and there may have been many others before the Wars. D'avenant staged a sumptuous one in 1663, with Betterton as the King, Henry Harris as Wolsey, William Smith as Buckingham, and Mrs. Betterton as Katherine. This production

Was all new Cloath'd in proper Habits: The King's was new, all the Lords, the Cardinals, the Bishops, the Doctors, Proctors, Lawyers, Tip-staves, new Scenes. . . . Every part by the great Care of Sir *William*, being exactly perform'd . . . it continu'd Acting 15 Days together with general Applause.[27]

Pepys did not like it, perhaps because he went, on January 1, 1664, expecting "the story of Henry the Eighth with all his wives." This revival probably presented the original play, though evidently with still more emphasis on spectacular effects. Even after the appearance of John Banks's popular "she-tragedy," *Vertue Betray'd: or, Anna Bullen*, it held the boards triumphantly. There is a derisive allusion to it in *The Rehearsal* (acted 1671) when Mr. Bayes (II, v) accuses his cast of dancing "worse than the Angels in *Harry* the Eight, or the fat Spirits in *The Tempest*. I gad." Betterton was still playing the title rôle in 1709 at the Haymarket, with Theophilus Keen as Wolsey, Barton Booth as Buckingham, and the great Elizabeth Barry as Katherine.

Spectacle continued to be the chief attraction of the many revivals in the eighteenth century. In 1727 there was a special production at Drury Lane, then under Robert Wilks, Colley Cibber, and Barton Booth, in honor of the coronation of George II. Booth, Quin, and Cooke were among the actors of the title rôle. Mrs. Pritchard made a strong impression as Queen Katherine. Colley Cibber and Henderson were notable Wolseys. Theophilus Cibber claimed the credit of working in (IV, i) the ceremony of the Champion in Westminster Hall. It proved irresistible, and the coronation pantomime was actually excerpted and attached to performances of other plays.[28] The edition of 1762, "As it is Performed at the Theatre-Royal in *Drury-Lane*" under Garrick, lists 54 groups and about 140 persons in the coronation procession. There had been a long lapse when J. P. Kemble revived *Henry the Eighth* in 1788, taking the part of Cromwell himself. Afterwards he played Wolsey. The Queen was his sister, Sarah Siddons, the Tragic Muse, and the rôle was reckoned among her most effective. Yet in reviewing the latter production in 1811, the London *Times* lets the cat out of the bag. Its critic found the play

the most laborious in its construction, and the most exhausting in its effect, of any that has ever been produced by diligent servility. Processions and banquets find their natural place in a work of this kind; and without the occasional display of well-spread tables, well-lighted chandeliers, and well-rouged maids of honour, the audience could not possibly sustain the accumulated *ennui* of *Henry the Eighth*.[29]

Macready and Charles Kean both staged revivals; the latter enjoyed a run of a hundred nights. As usual, he went in for historical realism and pictorial stunts, which included the most splendid processions yet seen, a barge for Buckingham's exit to the Tower, and a motion panorama of London in the time of King Hal. He restored, however, a good deal of the text his predecessors had cut. His wife was the Queen Katherine; Fanny Kemble and Mrs. Warner also took this rôle. Both Kean and Phelps played Wolsey, as did Davenport, McCullough, and Lawrence Barrett. In the United States, Charlotte Cushman was a fine Katherine, and so was Mme. Modjeska. Wolsey was one of the eleven rôles in Edwin Booth's repertory at the height of his career. Otis Skinner was among the American King Hals. Irving came late, in 1892, to *Henry the Eighth;* it was the last of his triumphant revivals of Shakespeare. He played the Cardinal, with Miss Terry as Katherine, Forbes-Robertson as Buckingham, and William Terriss as the King. It was a superb cast, but the production was grossly pictorial. Aside from the regular overhead, and salaries that came to more than £20,000 for the run of 172 performances, it cost £11,879 1s. 10d. to mount.[30] In 1910 Tree likewise poured money into the play. This was the last of such revivals. Tree played Wolsey, Arthur Bourchier the King, Violet Vanbrugh Queen Katherine, and Henry Ainley Buckingham. Sybil Thorndike acted Katherine in 1926, and Tyrone Guthrie revived the play at Sadler's Wells in 1933 with Charles Laughton in the title rôle.

It is not among those quiescent pieces which lovers of Shakespeare are most impatient to see staged. Quite aside from its dual authorship, it is a thing of patches, though some of them are of rather fine purple. We begin with Buckingham, as if he were to cut a great figure. The first scene belongs to him; but he has only one more, and he seems too important to be sacrificed to the build-up for Wolsey. The second scene is strong enough, and Buckingham is its subject, though he does not appear; but the third and fourth are in Fletcher's lighter vein, quite failing to maintain the level on which the play begins. If Shakespeare originally planned it, Buckingham must have loomed large in the design; but in II, i Fletcher shuts up the story of his days with a sentimental swan song. Scene ii is mere preparation for the Queen's trial. As Shakespeare resumes, humor and pity are mingled in Scene iii, and there are nuggets like "And wear a golden sorrow" and "For all the mud in Egypt." Scene iv, also his, gives us the play's best drama. It is Katherine's scene, but the character of the King is masterfully painted in its all-too-human complex of lust, honor, conscience, willfulness, superstition, and almost touching eagerness for a sanction stronger than itself.

Fletcher begins Act III, and in the first scene pulls out all the pathetic stops. They were his specialty, in which, after Shakespeare's retirement, he was unapproached till the appearance of Otway. Dryden actually gives the palm for awe to Shakespeare, and for characterization to Jonson; Fletcher, he thinks, beats them both in the appeal to pity. The stronger hand takes up the reins for Scene ii, the fall of Wolsey, and drives adroitly up to the climax, with its very Shakespearean touch:

> Read o'er this;
> And after, this; and then to breakfast with
> What appetite you have.

The pathos of the fallen statesman is thereupon turned over to Fletcher; and he does so well with it that the most famous speeches in the play, Wolsey's farewell to greatness and his advice to Cromwell (III, ii, 351–72, 428–57), used to be included in all the spouter's collections of gems from Shakespeare.

The Cranmer theme is introduced in IV, i; but that scene is dominated by the coronation procession, and the next by the masque of spirits which visits Fletcher's pathetic Katherine. The first three scenes of Act V have little to do with the rest of the play; though Elizabeth's birth is announced in the first, they are devoted to the plot against Cranmer. Scene iv is only a prelude to the final scene, which once again is featured by a procession. To Cranmer's long speech predicting Elizabeth's glorious reign, an encomium of James I is necessarily and somewhat perfunctorily appended; and the play closes with a kind of benediction from King Henry, whose character as Shakespeare limned it has long before gone completely to pieces.

Chapter 6

TRIAL FLIGHTS IN TRAGEDY

THE TRAGEDY OF TITUS ANDRONICUS

FEW Shakespearean territories have been more fought over than this tragedy-of-blood; none the less it is almost certainly Shakespeare's and his alone. We start with two powerful bits of external evidence: Meres listed the play in 1598 as Shakespeare's, and Heminge and Condell put it into the First Folio. The animus behind impassioned efforts to expel it from the canon may be rehearsed in the calmly classic style of Dr. Johnson: "The barbarity of the spectacles, and the general massacre which are here exhibited, can scarcely be conceived tolerable to any audience." The answers to that are, first, that neither can bear baiting nor sewing up a pigeon's eyes so it will soar straight up till its strength gives out and it falls like a plummet to its death, and, second, that the play's success, as Johnson acknowledged, is a matter of record. Cruel sports were relished by our forefathers, and so were revenge tragedies. Lavinia's stumps are not pleasing spectacles; nor are the blood-stained cheeks of Œdipus and the blinding of Gloucester. Everything depends on how the thing is done, and it is not done very well in *Titus*. It is done better in *Lear;* but best by Sophocles, who keeps the actual mutilation off stage yet tells the audience all about it in the Messenger's long speech, till we wonder whether we can endure the return of the ruined king. Then he comes in, with the blood on his face. Well played, that moment is perfect; awe and pity move the spectator inexpressibly, yet not horribly. But *Titus Andronicus* is the merest trial flight; Shakespeare picked up Elizabethan tragedy where he found it. *The Spanish Tragedie* (c. 1586) is not milk for babes either; they hang Horatio and cut him down again, and Hieronimo bites out his own tongue. Through that popular melodrama flowed in upon the new playwright, already a better poet than Kyd, the forceful stream of Senecan influence. It was a Stygian current. All the young tragic dramatists were caught by it. Of Shakespeare's professional seniors Kyd had the soundest instinct for the stage. That in his initial tragedy Shakespeare should try to profit by Kyd's example is only what we should expect.[1] Sheridan could take pen in hand and dash off *The Rivals* for his first play, but a *King Lear* is not dashed off *in limine* by anyone.

The disintegrators find aid and comfort in an unsupported allegation by the popular playwright Edward Ravenscroft, whose adaptation, *Titus Andronicus, or The Rape of Lavinia,* though acted in 1678, was not printed till 1687:

I have been told by some anciently conversant with the Stage, that it was not Originally his [Shakespeare's], but brought by a private Author [i.e., a free lance] to be Acted, and he only gave some Master-touches to one or two of the Principal Parts or Characters this I am apt to believe,[2] because 'tis the most incorrect and indigested piece in all his Works; It seems rather a heap of Rubbish then a Structure.

Unhappily, or fortunately — whichever way you look at it — Ravenscroft's statement is worth very little. He is out to minimize his indebtedness, and this address "To the Reader" is not remarkable for candor. He boasts:

Compare the Old Play with this, you'l finde that none in all that Authors Works ever receiv'd greater Alterations or Additions, the Language not only refin'd, but many Scenes entirely New; Besides most of the principal Characters heighten'd, and the Plot much encreas'd.

This single sentence contains five misstatements of fact. Fourteen plays of Shakespeare had received more extensive alterations or additions; the language of Ravenscroft's version is comparatively little refined; only two scenes are really new characterization is virtually unchanged; the increase in plot consists of a few unimportant variations and a piling up of horrors in the final scene, which ends with the Moor simultaneously racked and burned alive in full view of the audience. The doubt Ravenscroft casts on the original authorship is probably no more reliable.

The titles inscribed in his *Diary* by Philip Henslowe are often variables. Whatever the date of *Titus Andronicus*, the play is listed inexactly there. These are the pertinent entries:[3] (1) a "ne[w]" play, "tittus & vespacia" (presumably = Vespasian), on April 11, 1592, at the Rose, by Strange's Men, subsequently sometimes entered as "titus & vespacia"; it was a hit, with six repetitions before the theatre closed on June 23. (2) A "titvs" (or "tittus" or "titus"), again by Strange's Men at the Rose, three times during the short winter season that lasted from December 29, 1592 through January. (3) A "titus & ondronicus" (or "titus & ondronicous" or "tittus & ondronicus"), marked "ne," by Sussex's Men, probably at the Rose, three times between January 24 and February 6, 1594. (4) An "andronicous," twice during the joint occupancy of Newington Butts by the Admiral's and the Chamberlain's Men from about June 5 to the 15th, 1594. All these performances were by Henslowe companies. The entry "titus & ondronicus" may be a fair index to the extent of his acquaintance with the noncommercial side of his enterprises.

Titus Andronicus was produced, then, as early as January 24, 1594. But "tittus & vespacia" raises a pretty question. Some think it was a play about the destruction of Jerusalem by Vespasian and his son Titus; that we have here another title for Shakespeare's tragedy is on the whole more likely. For an Elizabethan title, "Vespasian and Titus" would be more normal than the reverse. Moreover, in the spring of 1592 Strange's Men were also acting a "Jerusallem"; and two plays on the same subject by the same company in the same season are unlikely, though to be sure *Jerusallem* may not have dealt with the city's fall.[4] Henslowe may have got the two Tituses mixed up, and mistakenly lugged "vespacia" into the title of the Andronicus play; or Shakespeare may have had a Vespasian in it and changed the name to avoid conflicting with *Jerusallem*. We shall shortly come to another indication that there was once a character named Vespasian in *Titus Andronicus*.

Precisely what Henslowe means by "ne" is uncertain, even though he notes receipts from *elexsander & lodwicke* on January 14, 1597, "the fyrst tyme yt wasse playde," and duly marks the play "ne."[5] It is probably an elastic term, inclusive also of plays newly revised or new to Henslowe's management. Ben Jonson's gibe at *Titus*, in 1614, though "these fiue and twentie, or thirtie yeeres" is not so helpful as one could wish, establishes a presumption for a date not later than 1589.[6] That in 1594 it was not actually new is almost proved by allusions to Titus's conquest of the Goths and the offer of the crown, in an anonymous play, *A Knacke to Know a Knaue*, which Henslowe calls "ne" on June 10, 1592, though it was not printed till 1594. These references not only go to show the probable identity of *Titus Andronicus* and *tittus & vespacia*; they also strengthen the conviction that Henslowe's "ne" is not to be taken literally, and that *tittus & vespacia* may itself not have been new in 1592. Moreover, Lucius is called Vespasianus in *Eine sehr klägliche Tragœdia von Tito Andronico*, a German version printed in 1620, but presumably acted a good deal earlier by a traveling troupe of English players. The title *Titus, and Vespatian* appears in a manuscript of 1619, probably from the Revels Office, which lists plays, perhaps under consideration for court performances, including some of Shakespeare's.

The confusion of titles in Henslowe has been given too much weight by those who believe Shakespeare revised an old play. Stylistic and metrical tests have also been applied, with the usual divergent conclusions. For some years there was a curious tendency among the disintegrators to ascribe the whole of the insoluble residuum of Elizabethan drama about this time to the pretty, nerveless pen of George Peele; but no undisputed work of his encourages the supposition that he was capable of writing *Titus Andronicus*. There is much strength in this tragedy, whether or not you like its application. Not enough, perhaps, has been made of the play's share of beauty; there are many lines fragrant with such out-of-door imagery as *Venus and Adonis* abounds in. Their poetic merit is sometimes cited to support a date in 1592 or 1593. But we can not be certain when *Venus* was written, nor how good the earlier verses were that Shakespeare may have composed and thrown away; and while *Titus* rises above the unpoetic level of *The Comedy of Errors*, its tragic theme may be the reason. Comparison with the style of *Henry the Sixth, Part 1* is likewise of little value, since that play can not be dated either; but the poet who wrote the opening speech of Act II of *Titus* seems about as far along the road to Parnassus as the author of the first speech in *Henry the Sixth*. On the date of *Titus Andronicus* no one can afford to be dogmatic. My guess is about 1589; but other guessers, at least as competent, guess later.

On February 6, 1594, "a Noble Roman Historye of Tytus Andronicus" was entered in the Stationers' Register by John Danter;[7] and under title of *The Most Lamentable Romaine Tragedie of Titus Andronicus*, he published the First Quarto in that year. If the performances in January were really of a new play, it would be hard, taking into account what a moneymaker the piece had been, to understand how a Good quarto got into a publisher's hands quite so soon. For Quarto 1[8] provides the best text, except that it omits III, ii, and V, iii, 201-4. The Folio supplies these passages; elsewhere it rests on the Third Quarto. The title page of the First Quarto lists three companies that by 1594 had played *Titus:* Derby's,[9] Pembroke's, and Sussex's. It was long supposed that every copy of this edition had perished, but in 1904 one turned up in Sweden. It is now among the treasures of the Folger Shakespeare Library in Washington.

Critics have protested that Shakespeare was too refined to commit to paper the barbarities of *Titus*, as if he invented them. Turning his hand to the composition of a gory tragedy, he found his materials as well as his form in classical sources, another point in favor of an early date for this play. Tales of cruel Moors and of lustful ladies' intrigues with Moors or Negroes were widespread in Europe, but the core of Shakespeare's plot is a fusion of two ancient stories of revenge which had been used by Seneca and Ovid. From the *Thyestes* he takes the cannibalistic vengeance of Atreus; the sacrifice to the slain (I, i) was suggested by the *Troades;* and there are scraps of dialogue and ideas from other plays of Seneca. In the sixth book of his *Metamorphoses* Ovid tells the story of Philomela and Progne, mentioned in *Titus* (IV, i) as "the tragic tale of Philomel." Like the sacrifice of Alarbus, it becomes a pivot of Shakespeare's revenge plot. In Ovid the ravished and tongueless heroine contrives to identify the criminal, who, like Seneca's Thyestes, is given his child's flesh to eat. Shakespeare's hero-avenger is Titus, and when he kills his daughter he is following the classical precedent of Virginius. Indeed, Shakespeare's sources are obvious; he labels his borrowings. Thus the revolt of Coriolanus is in his mind when he describes (IV, iv) the approaching army of Lucius.[10]

Aaron is certainly a Shakespeare portrait, the first of his Machiavellian villains, and a better one than Peele or Greene ever drew, surpassing Lorenzo of *The Spanish Tragedie* and fully the equal of Marlowe's Barabas. The Moor is as wicked as any understanding gentleman of the ground could desire; but, as Kittredge remarks, even he is kept in "contact with normal human nature" by the little episode when the Nurse presents him with "his black baby." And the play has other merits — poetic flights, strong dramatic clashes, and a sounder construction than most tragedies or histories of the late eighties and early nineties can boast of.

It sadly lacks a hero who might enlist the full measure of our sympathy by accepting dramatic crucifixion for us. Every great tragedy, however local in setting, succeeds in symbolizing the defeat of man. *Titus Andronicus* is too objectively historical, even though the history is fictitious. Shakespeare's determination to write a revenge play that would make his models look tame is perfectly apparent to anyone who knows the drama of the sixteenth century. With the rashness of the talented novice, he lays everything on thick. The revenge motif itself is extraordinarily thick. One revenger and one villain, working in stout dramatic double harness, supply ample traction for a play of this type. What they can do when the reins are in an expert's hands is amply attested by the condition of the stage floor at the end of *Hamlet*. In *Titus Andronicus* Shakespeare litters the whole drama with the fruits of vengeance. The dominant theme of this revenge symphony is too freely passed about from instrument to instrument. Despite the spiritual kinship the Elizabethans felt for Rome, it is doubtful whether the sacrifice of Alarbus ever appealed to British sporting instincts. Tamora has as much reason on her side as the average heroic avenger in such plays, and no one's sympathy is going to be aroused by the slaughter of Mutius. Eventually Titus becomes *the* avenger; but though there is ample classical warrant for his technique, the play is a welter of vendettas instead of a clean-cut story of a hero's dedication to a sacred duty.

Nevertheless, and unlike *Henry the Eighth*, *Titus* is no patchwork. Except for Ravenscroft's assertion, there is no reason for connecting anyone with its authorship but Shakespeare. This tragedy came from the facile pen of a beginning playwright eager for a theatrical success, which in fact he achieved. Jonson did not couple it with *The Spanish Tragedie* for nothing. It made money for Henslowe, and was probably still active in the repertory of the King's Men in 1614 when Ben scoffed at it. The Restoration saw it but little altered by Ravenscroft, and in the eighteenth century Aaron was a favorite rôle of no less a star than Quin. About the middle of the nineteenth there was a revival by Ira Frederick Aldridge, "the African Roscius." The Old Vic staged another in 1923. No one, I think, regrets its virtual exile from the boards. But, though the youthful Burns wept over Lavinia's sorrows and wished to burn the book, the audience it was written for certainly liked it. If a decade later tastes had improved, Shakespeare did more than anyone else to raise them. Even as it stands, reeking with the blood of innocents as well as criminals, *Titus* is no further below the level of *Richard the Third* than *Hamlet* is above it.

THE TRAGEDY OF ROMEO AND JULIET

Half a dozen years had probably elapsed when Shakespeare returned to nonhistorical tragedy; but the chronicle plays had given him plenty of serious practice, and *Richard the Third* is an attempt at tragedy. What it was, about the middle of the nineties, that made him burst out into the raptures of *Romeo and Juliet* no one knows. There is a strong lyrical impulse behind this play, and behind *Richard the Second* and *A Midsummer Night's Dream*. All three were doubtless composed about the same time, though in what order is quite uncertain. To be sure, Shakespeare was a dramatist — he seems to have been capable of expressing anything; but he was a man, not a machine. It may have been love. It may have been a poet's longing to be loved. It may have been as unrelated to his inner life as we hope *Titus Andronicus* was.

Romeo and Juliet is not among the greatest tragedies; it is a pretty tale of youthful lovers' woe. Their tragedy is affecting; yet the wounds of young love, while they may leave permanent scars, are seldom mortal. Sometimes they are. Death is not, however, the inevitable outcome of such events; but from the wounds of Lear and Macbeth there is no recovery. For all that, *Romeo and Juliet* seems touched with immortality. No more solid achievement lies open to a poet than to put something universal into a form at once perfect and simple. Only the very young can be moved by this play so deeply as by *Lear* or *Œdipus;* but everyone was young once, and those who sneer at an immortal love story defile their own youth and show that maturity has failed to make them wiser. This tragedy is not symbolist; it is not like Maeterlinck's equally beautiful and more thoughtful *Pelléas et Mélisande*. Yet Romeo and Juliet are lyric expressions of one of the deepest human hopes, as well as passionate Italian children. Shakespeare is wholeheartedly for them. Mercutio's amusing ribaldry (II, i) only makes more pure and sweet the incomparable duet which follows, introduced by the brilliant and poignant modulation, "He jests at scars that never felt a wound."

For the precise date external evidence is lacking. The First Quarto was printed in 1597: *An Excellent conceited Tragedie of Romeo and Iuliet, As it hath been often (with great applause) plaid publiquely, by the right Honourable the L. of Hunsdon* [11] *his Seruants*. About two years earlier seems right for its production on stage. "'Tis since the earthquake now," says the Nurse, "eleven years"; and because London had an earthquake in 1580, some would fix the composition in 1591. Shakespeare probably had that quake in mind; but the Nurse is reckoning up Juliet's age, adding the elapsed time since her weaning. To that important event the earthquake is quite subsidiary. And the stylistic evidence, such as it is, points to about 1595.

The *editio princeps*, of 1597, is one of the Bad quartos; [12] it was followed in 1599 by a Good one, "Newly corrected, augmented, and amended." [13] Despite this claim, the Second Quarto is full of mistakes, many of which are corrected by the lucky preservation of superior readings in the unauthorized First. The Folio has no textual authority for this play, since it reprints the Third Quarto, which reprints the Second. Quarto 1 shows the stigmata of the Bad quartos; it is evidently the work of a pirate who had to rely on memory. Passages are sometimes briefly summarized and connective links left out. Metre is often mangled. There is a good deal of mislineation. Synonyms and inflectional variants are freely substituted. Some of the stage directions appear to describe action the reporter had seen at performances. A few actors' interpolations are preserved, and some lines and phrases have been transposed. Whether the thief was a player and even whether he worked alone remain doubtful; no one part stands out as better remembered than the rest. Quarto 1, then, is an imperfect version of the play as acted in the middle nineties. It is nearly eight hundred lines shorter than Quarto 2. While some of its omissions are probably due to lapses of memory, others look like stage cuts; the reporter could not reproduce passages he had never heard. Here and there, however, Quarto 2 resembles its predecessor typographically; the best explanation is that at certain points the compositor's copy for it was a corrected text of Quarto 1.

Some textual critics attribute these discrepancies to one or more revisions by Shakespeare, and they think Quarto 1 includes lines from an old drama of pre-Shakespearean authorship. This theory has not won much acceptance. It is just possible that Shakespeare began the play and then put it aside, and that when he resumed it his conception of the leading characters had changed. This possibility rests not so much on differences between the two earliest quartos as on inconsistencies within Quarto 2. To begin with, the lovers are children; afterwards they seem more mature. Except for the foreboding of the Choruses and Juliet's apprehension in the balcony scene, the first half of the play is hardly tragic at all. It belongs chiefly to Romeo, while the second half is dominated by the heroine. There is a hard problem here, especially for the actress, who must make Juliet very girlish nearly to the potion scene, where she first takes the center of the stage as a tragedy queen. Few of the actresses I have seen have been able to modulate; they play one or the other of the two Juliets straight through. Yet, though an interval in composition would account for these inconsistencies, Shakespeare may be consciously developing character; in real life trouble sometimes ends adolescence with pathetic speed. On the other hand, all these difficulties may be natural consequences of Shakespeare's dramatic treatment of the story he began with.

Its core, a wife's avoidance of an unwelcome suitor by means of a potion, is found in Greek romances. With it a tale of star-crossed lovers was subsequently combined. Masuccio of Salerno tells it in a collection of stories published at Naples in 1476. A friar performs a secret marriage. The husband kills a man and is exiled. To escape a marriage dictated by her father, the wife obtains a potion; but her message never reaches her spouse. Hearing of her supposed death he returns, attempts to open the vault from which the friar has already rescued her, and is caught and executed. The wife, who has gone to join his exile, comes back to die of grief in a convent.

About 1530 another version was published at Venice; its

author was Luigi da Porto, who says the story is true. The scene is no longer Siena, but Verona under the rule of Bartolomeo della Scala [14] — whence Shakespeare's Prince Escalus. The lovers are Romeo and Giulietta, and the reason for secrecy is the feud of the Montecchi and Capelletti. Romeo follows a cruel lady to a fiesta, where he falls in love with Giulietta. Her servant Pietro is the go-between. The friar's name is Lorenzo. It is Thebaldo that Romeo kills. Word of his wife's supposed death is brought by Pietro, the friar's agent having failed to deliver the letter. Romeo already has the poison. Before he dies in the tomb, Juliet revives. After their brief reunion the friar appears. Juliet refuses to leave her husband; she holds her breath till, with a shriek, she falls lifeless on his body. The two houses are eventually reconciled.

Among the most famous volumes of sixteenth-century fiction was the *Novelle* of Matteo Bandello, printed at Lucca in 1554. In the ninth story of Part II he tells the old tale.[15] Romeo's earlier love affair becomes more prominent. He goes masked to the Capulets', hoping that other beauties will make him forget his coy mistress. The lovers' go-between is now Giulietta's nurse. Pietro is Romeo's servant. The prospective bridegroom is Count Paris. Friar Lorenzo's message is borne by Friar Anselmo, whom the plague detains in a convent. The account of the lovers' deaths substantially follows Da Porto's.

Bandello's *novella* was one of several adapted by Pierre Boaistuau (or Boisteau) perhaps in collaboration with François de Belleforest, who afterwards added to their collection of *Histoires Tragiques*. Boaistuau's version of the lovers' story was published at Paris in 1559. It alters Bandello's ending, for Juliet wakes after Romeo's death and then kills herself with his dagger. Mercutio and the Apothecary are introduced in this redaction, though both are only sketches.

Bandello, through Boaistuau, is the source of a jog-trot poem by Arthur Broke (or Brooke), *The Tragicall Historye of Romeus and Iuliet* (1562).[16] It is a clumsy, long-winded piece; but in it the Nurse is much developed as a comic character and there are several new details, among them her acceptance of bribery, her advocacy of Paris, the despair of Romeus at the Friar's cell, and the change of the messenger's name to John. Shakespeare sometimes follows the poem very closely. It is instructive to compare IV, iii, 21–59 with Broke's lines 2361–2402:

What doe I knowe (quoth she) if that this powder shall [17]
Sooner or later then it should or els not woorke at all?
And then my craft descride as open as the day,
The peoples tale and laughing stocke shall I remayne for aye.
And what know I (quoth she) if serpentes odious,
And other beastes and wormes that are of nature venemous,
That wonted are to lurke in darke caues vnder grounde,
And commonly, as I haue heard, in dead mens tombes are found,
Shall harme me, yea or nay, where I shall lye as ded? —
Or how shall I that alway haue in so freshe ayre been bred,
Endure the lothsome stinke of such an heaped store
Of carkases, not yet consumde, and bones that long before
Intombed were, where I my sleping place shall haue,
Where all my auncesters doe rest, my kindreds common graue?
Shall not the fryer and my Romeus, when they come,
Fynd me (if I awake before) ystifled in the tombe?
And whilst she in these thoughtes doth dwell somwhat to long,
The force of her ymagining anon dyd waxe so strong,
That she surmysde she saw, out of the hollow vaulte,
(A griesly thing to looke vpon) the carkas of Tybalt;
Right in the selfe same sort that she few dayes before
Had seene him in his blood embrewde, to death eke wounded sore.
And then when she agayne within her selfe had wayde
That quicke she should be buried there, and by his side be layde,
All comfortles, for she shall liuing feere [18] have none,
But many a rotten carkas, and full many a naked bone;
Her dainty tender partes gan sheuer all for dred,
Her golden heares did stand vpright vpon her chillish hed.
Then pressed with the feare that she there liued in,
A sweat as colde as mountaine yse pearst through her tender skin,
That with the moysture hath wet euery part of hers:
And more besides, she vainely thinkes, whilst vainely thus she
    feares,
A thousand bodies dead haue compast her about,

And lest they will dismember her she greatly standes in dout.
But when she felt her strength began to weare away,
By little and little, and in her hart her feare increased ay,
Dreading that weaknes might, or foolish cowardise,
Hinder the execution of the purposde enterprise,
As she had frantike been, in hast the glasse she cought,
And vp she dranke the mixture quite, withouten farther thought.
Then on her brest she crost her armes long and small,
And so, her senses fayling her, into a traunce did fall.

Shakespeare's lines are typical of his alchemical power over
base metal. Whether Brooke's embellishments of Bandello
are entirely his own idea is uncertain, for he says that Romeo
and Juliet had already appeared in a play:

Though I saw the same argument lately set foorth on stage with
more commendation, then I can looke for: (being there much better
set forth then I haue or can dooe) yet the same matter penned as it is,
may serue to lyke good effect.

Shakespeare's major contribution is the poetry of the great
lyric passages. Next in importance is the dazzling score he
writes for Mercutio; it must have made an instantaneous hit,
for he soon tried to repeat it, no doubt for the same actor,
with Gratiano in *The Merchant of Venice*. Gaiety we are always
grateful for; in real life it is usually more welcome than
clowning, and in the theatre at least equally effective. Mercutio is among the most scintillating things Shakespeare
ever did — some of the stars have preferred this rôle to Romeo.
But it is very light for tragedy; and when, in III, i, he made
Mercutio walk the plank, Shakespeare not only strengthened
the motivation of Romeo's exile, he disposed of an awkward
problem.

It is a gorgeous gallery of Renaissance portraits that he
gives us, and he lays his color on like another Titian. Capulet
is a fine example of a proud magnate and a heavy father.
There is no better prince of cats than Tybalt on any canvas
by Velásquez. Friar Laurence demonstrates the artist's versatility — sober-strong painting that Rembrandt might have
done. The Nurse is Frans Hals at his best. The elder Pieter

Breughel might have drawn the servant groups. Romeo and Juliet are not so much painted as made of music. They are less pictorial and realistic than the others, being more abstract — they *are* love and beauty. Mercutio also goes beyond a painter's limitations. Degas can give us the dancer resting or practicing at the bar, but no painter has done justice to the ballet. Mercutio is more than a portrait, and more than a poet's words; he exists only in the moment of action on the stage — or, as John Barrymore virtually dances the rôle, on the screen.

Aside from providing poetry and brilliant characterization, Shakespeare alters Broke's version but little. He brings Tybalt to the Capulet ball, reduces Juliet's age from sixteen to fourteen, and with a regular Senecan stroke adds the corpse of Paris to the tragic spectacle at the tomb. Structurally the play is a complete success; the entertainment is varied, in the best Elizabethan style. Pathos and humor are not yet fused, but they are skilfully mingled. The opening scene is a model one, combining adroit exposition, the introduction of most of the important characters, and action that catches the attention immediately. Its turbulence is in sharp contrast with the grave Chorus which precedes it and the lyric love story that follows. Critics have found fault with Shakespeare's failure to carry through his sonnet Choruses, and advocates of the revision theory have found this inconsistency portentous. The first is an admirable prologue, sounding the tragic note like a tolling bell. The second, suggested perhaps by Broke's introductory sonnet, is inferior as a poem to the prologue; but it helps palliate Romeo's speedy falling in second love. There is no need of this device to open the remaining acts, though Shakespeare artfully reverts to it in the quatrain and couplet of the Prince's last speech.

The unity of tone is less successful, and indeed is not to be expected in Elizabethan tragedy. The atmosphere is more lighted than the "star-cross'd" of the opening sonnet implies. The awful gloom of *Lear* and *Macbeth* nowhere overcasts the bright Italian sky, Fate manifests its dread control in the mere mischance of an undelivered letter, and *Romeo and*

Juliet is more pathetic than powerful. Broke offers his poem as a warning against headstrong passion, and some of the critics have been exercised about the play's ethical purpose. Of course it has none. If nowhere else, at least here, joy is its own excuse for being. It is the idlest of critical follies to look for a tragic flaw in the lovers, or to wring a moral lesson out of their bitter deaths.

Presumably Burbage first played Romeo, but there is no evidence. The immediate popularity of the tragedy [19] seems to have continued, though records of its appearance in the repertory have not survived. How one group of readers felt about it is shown by the condition of the Bodleian Library's copy of the First Folio. It was chained to the shelves, where the boys at Oxford had access to it, and the page most worn by their leaning elbows is the one that faces the lyric scene of parting (III, v). That the play remained active on the stage is likely, for it was soon revived under the Restoration. It had been reserved for D'avenant's company; and in 1662 Sir William produced it with Harris as Romeo, Mary Saunderson as Juliet, and Betterton as Mercutio. Shortly afterward this Juliet became Mrs. Betterton. James Nokes probably played the Nurse. Betterton's prompter, John Downes, tells us that

This Tragedy of *Romeo* and *Juliet*, was made some time after into a Tragi-comedy, by Mr. *James Howard*, he preserving *Romeo* and *Juliet* alive; so that when the Tragedy was Reviv'd again, 'twas Play'd Alternately, Tragical one Day, and Tragicomical another; for several Days together.

You could pay your money and take your choice, according to your mood.

An extraordinary success was scored by Thomas Otway during the season of 1679–80 with *The History and Fall of Caius Marius*. The lovers are now Young Marius and Lavinia, and the family feud turns on the struggles of the plebeians and patricians. Betterton played the elder Marius, and "Nurse" Nokes won his permanent sobriquet. Mrs. Barry was the Lavinia; the beauteous Anne Bracegirdle succeeded her. Otway's sorry mixture of antique Roman and Renaissance banished

Romeo and Juliet from the stage until Theophilus Cibber's less outrageous version in 1744; and, though altered in phraseology, Otway's ending, with the lovers reunited a few moments before they die, was not wholly discarded till well into the nineteenth century.

In 1748 Garrick staged his own adaptation, with Spranger Barry and Mrs. Cibber in the name rôles and Woodward as Mercutio. Two years later the patent theatres played the tragedy simultaneously, in "the *Romeo and Juliet* War" — Barry and Mrs. Cibber at Covent Garden against Garrick and fair, frail George Anne Bellamy at Drury Lane, with Macklin and Woodward as the rival Mercutios. Legend hath it that one evening Miss Bellamy's utterance of the famous rhetorical question, "O Romeo, Romeo! Wherefore art thou Romeo?" was unexpectedly answered by a voice from the audience: "Because Barry has gone to the other house!" Though J. P. Kemble's was a notable revival, its text was still far from Shakespeare. In 1829 his niece Fanny made her debut, as Juliet. Under the circumstances her father, Charles Kemble, deemed it wise to forego his usual rôle and exchanged Romeo for Mercutio, in which he had a great success. Fanny, who was only nineteen, had been rushed on the stage to redeem Covent Garden, now Charles Kemble's enterprise, from imminent collapse. She took the town by storm. Credit for restoring the true text goes to the Americans, Charlotte and Susan Cushman, who in the season of 1845–46 scored a triumph in the title rôles. Early in the next season Phelps also stuck to Shakespeare's text. Since then the play has been pretty steadily before the public. Among the most radiant of the Juliets were Eliza O'Neill (whom some expected to succeed Mrs. Siddons as queen of tragedy), Helen Faucit, Adelaide Neilson, Mary Anderson, Mrs. Pat Campbell, and Viola Allen. Ellen Terry was not at her best in this rôle, and Irving was miscast. Forbes-Robertson, who calls Helena Modjeska the best Juliet he saw, was a beautiful Romeo. Some of his predecessors were both the Keans, Macready, Rignold, Edwin Booth, and Lawrence Barrett. From the days of the first professional companies in the United States, *Romeo and Juliet* has been a favorite; and its success in Germany has been constant. Of late years the tragedy has been much acted, often very well. Eva Le Gallienne, Jane Cowl, and Katharine Cornell have recently played Juliet to much applause on the American stage, where E. H. Sothern and Julia Marlowe were the last generation's favorite duo. Mantell often acted Romeo. Maurice Evans had the part in Miss Cornell's production. Among recent players of the title rôles in England were John Gielgud (he has also played Mercutio), Laurence Olivier, and Peggy Ashcroft. The Nurse of Edith Evans has been justly admired on both sides of the water.

The ambitious screen production of Metro-Goldwyn-Mayer was a gorgeous and fairly sane adaptation. The pictorial medium demands transposition, and too much antiquarian reverence would defeat its own purpose. The perfection of Shakespeare's opening was obscured by the sinful lavishness of California, but the pageantry was better than Shakespeare ever saw it done. Leslie Howard's Romeo, while thoroughly intelligent, was pretty tame and failed to follow the melodic curve of the lines; but Norma Shearer, who elected to play the girlish Juliet, gave an appealing performance. It is not likely that any Mercutio since 1595 was more exclusively composed in terms of that rôle's mercurial essence than John Barrymore's. Our screen producers have still a long way to go; but they will eventually do great things for Shakespeare and, a much more important consideration, for a public which, starving for beauty in the midst, not of God's plenty, but of Hollywood's, is above all pathetic because it knows not why it hungers.

THE TRAGEDY OF JULIUS CÆSAR

In the same season that saw the last brush strokes on Shakespeare's vast canvas of medieval English history, he turned to ancient Roman history. *The Tragedy of Julius Cæsar* is hardly a straight tragedy; and if it were, it would not be mainly Cæsar's. It falls in the tragical-historical category, and if anyone is the hero Brutus is. According to all the rules and regulations, this play should be a failure. On the contrary, it has worn extremely well. The reason must be sought, not in architectonics, nor in historical insight, but almost exclusively in its author's masterful idiom. It is a useful thing for a writer to be able to write. Shakespeare owned many masteries, not least among them his unparalleled way with words. In *Julius Cæsar* he comes close to making a play out of sheer eloquence. The speech of the characters, far more than characterization, is what brings them to life. Much of it is only rhetoric, but what rhetoric!

Meres does not mention this play in the *Palladis Tamia* of 1598. On September 21, 1599 Dr. Thomas Platter of Basel saw a "Tragedy vom ersten Keyser Julio Caesare," probably Shakespeare's, in a theatre on the Surrey side ("über d[a]z wasser"), no doubt the Globe. It was well acted, he says, had about fifteen characters, and was followed with dancing by four of the company.[20] John Weever's *The Mirror of Martyrs, or The life and death of . . . Sir Iohn Old-castle* was printed in 1601 but written "some two yeares agoe." Since the following lines from it refer to the Forum scene, 1599 or, at the earliest, late in 1598 seems a certain date for *Julius Cæsar:*

> The many-headed multitude were drawne
> By *Brutus* speach, that *Cæsar* was ambitious,
> When eloquent *Mark Antonie* had showne
> His vertues, who but *Brutus* then was vicious.

In Jonson's *Every Man Out of His Humor* (1599) Clove remarks (III, iv, 33), "*Reason long since is fled to Animals* you know," very likely an allusion to *Julius Cæsar*, III, ii, 110.

That we have no early quarto of this tragedy is strange, for it seems to have been popular. The Folio provides a good text.[21] It is much shorter than most of Shakespeare's, possibly a version cut for the stage. There are mute characters in several scenes. Brutus's reception (IV, iii) of the tidings of Portia's death, which he already knows, may be evidence of revision, though not necessarily after original composition. It is also possible that Brutus wants to show how a Roman should take stiff news, or that Shakespeare decided to score twice with the same shot.

The source is Plutarch's *Lives* — of Cæsar, Brutus, and Antonius. This famous book has helped form the minds of many remarkable men — men of action as well as poets. Henry of Navarre was brought up on it. "Plutarch is my man," said Montaigne. Lawrence of Arabia owned it. General Bonaparte added the *Lives* to his *bibliothèque du camp* when he embarked on the Egyptian adventure in 1798. Two years earlier, and nearly twenty before Waterloo, young Colonel Wesley had spent two guineas for the set he took out to India. Plutarch was a Greek of the first and second centuries; both Napoleon and Wellington read him in translation. So did Shakespeare — in Sir Thomas North's English rendering (1579) of Jacques Amyot's French version (1559). We have seen how Shakespeare turned his flame on Broke's details and fused them into the poetry of the potion scene in *Romeo and Juliet*. North's spirited prose was better stuff to work with; again and again Shakespeare preserves it almost intact.

To the Renaissance, Julius was a perennially fascinating figure, far more so, even, than he is today. Several plays had starred him before Shakespeare's, on the Continent and in England; but though the disintegrators have been extraordinarily busy with *Julius Cæsar*, we have no reason to think Shakespeare used any of its predecessors.

The original casting is unknown. No doubt the play held the stage down to the closing of the theatres in 1642. *Caesar's Tragedye* was among several pieces acted for royalty by the King's Men in 1612–13; and it was played at the court of Charles I in 1636 and 1638.[22] To its popularity on the public stage Leonard Digges testifies in commendatory verses in the 1640 edition of Shakespeare's *Poems*:

> So have I seene, when Cesar would appeare,
> And on the Stage at halfe-sword parley were,
> *Brutus* and *Cassius:* oh how the Audience,
> Were ravish'd. . . .

This play was among the few of Shakespeare's revived under the Restoration without serious adaptation. It seems to have been on the boards by 1672, with the accomplished veterans Charles Hart and Michael Mohun as Brutus and Cassius, and Edward Kynaston, who had begun his career in women's rôles, as Antony. These players were all members of the Theatre Royal. Soon after the union of the companies in 1682, Betterton took over Brutus. In his delightful *Apology*, Colley Cibber describes the great Shakespearean's impersonation:

A farther Excellence in *Betterton* was, that he could vary his Spirit to the different Characters he acted. Those wild impatient Starts, that fierce and flashing Fire, which he threw into *Hotspur*, never came from the unruffled Temper of his *Brutus* (for I have more than once seen a *Brutus* as warm as *Hotspur*): when the *Betterton Brutus* was provok'd in his Dispute with *Cassius*, his Spirit flew only to his Eye; his steady Look alone supply'd that Terror which he disdain'd an Intemperance in his Voice should rise to. Thus, with a settled Dignity of Contempt, like an unheeding Rock he repelled upon himself the Foam of *Cassius*.

The play was often acted. Genest gives the cast, a superb one, of a special subscription performance in 1707. It included the aged Betterton as Brutus, John Verbruggen as Cassius, Robert Wilks as Antony, Barton Booth as Cæsar, John Mills as Octavius, Theophilus Keen as Casca, the brilliant Mrs. Barry as Calphurnia, and beautiful Anne Bracegirdle as Portia. Magnificent acting may have been responsible for the reading public's devouring no less than six quarto editions between 1684 and 1719, when still another version appeared, purporting, probably falsely, to be an adaptation by D'avenant and Dryden.

Julius Cæsar remained a stock play throughout the careers of Wilks, who was highly esteemed as Antony, and Booth, on whom fell the mantle of Betterton's Brutus. The latter rôle was afterwards played by Quin and by Thomas Sheridan. The tragedy was occasionally revived in the age of Garrick, but not by him. Barry's rôle was Antony. The play had languished for about twenty years when, in 1812, J. P. Kemble acted Brutus in his own version, still marred by traces of the adaptation. His brother Charles as Antony and C. M. Young as Cassius made strong impressions in this revival.

Macready, already an experienced Cassius, assigned that part to Phelps in a well-cast revival in 1838, taking Brutus himself; he continued to play the latter rôle till 1851. Phelps afterwards acted Brutus. In America, J. B. Booth's rôle was Cassius. Davenport was a fine Brutus. The most famous revival in this country, seen in the seventies and eighties, presented Edwin Booth as Brutus and Lawrence Barrett as Cassius; occasionally Booth also played Cassius and Antony. John McCullough was much admired as Cassius. More recently the American theatre saw the Brutus of Richard Mansfield, the Antony of William Faversham, and the Brutus of R. B. Mantell. Meanwhile, in 1881, London witnessed the elaborate revival of the Saxe-Meiningen company, which visited the United States ten years later. Edmund Tearle offered London a modest presentation in 1892. The next production there was Tree's, in 1898; it ran over a hundred nights. Henry Ainley had a fair run in 1920; he played Antony. William Winter could write in 1915 that "few English-speaking actors have risen to distinction in tragedy without having acted *Brutus*, or *Cassius*, or *Antony*"; but leaders of the profession have not lately shown much interest in the play, though the repertory companies have been faithful to it. In 1937–38 a badly cut revival by Orson Welles and his Mercury Theatre, in modern dress and with a political bias, was enthusiastically received in New York and on the road. Most of the actor-managers have preferred plays in which one rôle has a clear lead; Tree, who played Antony, actually rearranged the text and kept the curtain tableaux to himself. The lack of a good part for an actress has also handicapped the play.

Interesting and spirited as it is, we must also recognize that *Julius Cæsar* presents no universal tragedy; it is essentially a show of Roman history. Shakespeare is working toward tragedy, hence the ghost of Cæsar. If we are sometimes impatient with Senecan materials in his plays, his half-hearted employment of the ghost in this one proves the strength of that element in Elizabethan plots. He might have done better to use it more liberally here, especially since he had classical authority for its appearance at Philippi. What unity the play has depends on "Cæsar's spirit, ranging for revenge," as Antony predicts and as Cassius acknowledges when he falls. Brutus echoes this motif when he finds the bodies of his friends:

> O Julius Cæsar, thou art mighty yet!
> Thy spirit walks abroad and turns our swords
> In our own proper entrails.

But the best Elizabethan revenge tragedies give us a good deal more of the ghost walking — and speaking. Perhaps Shakespeare was anxious to avoid the crudeness of his spirits in *Richard the Third* and meant to stake the effect on a majestic impersonation. If so, he was well advised to lean much harder on Hamlet's father and to make him very human and very vocal. Cæsar appears in only three scenes, and his ghost but once, when it speaks sixteen words in the matter-of-fact manner of a professional "hant." If Shakespeare intended Antony's prediction to strike a dominant note, he quickly mutes it with the first scene of Act IV, where we find Antony more politician than avenger. The ghost appears near Sardis, Brutus mentions its reappearance at Philippi, and he recalls it when he finds Cassius dead; that is all there is of Cæsar after the Forum scene, and it is not enough to make the play his tragedy.

Structurally the drama is so open to objection that its effectiveness on stage evidently arises from other considerations. In lieu of his usual method of close-packed compression, Shakespeare often skips. The major episodes are vigorously executed, but they fail to form a steady progression. Perhaps an uncut text gave more links and transitions. The quarrel scene is played up because it affords fine scope for the two leading actors, but it assumes a prominence out of all proportion. The piece obviously breaks in two in the middle. Our interest in Brutus does more to bridge the gap than Cæsar's ghost does. Shakespeare fails to cast the historical facts in the revenge-tragedy mold, or else deliberately chooses not to. Neither Antony nor Octavius becomes that appealing figure, the sorely tried avenger consecrated to a great task. They remain Antony and Octavius, famous persons from the pages of Roman history. Nor is Brutus much more satisfactory. He is not the hero-villain whose fall inspires awe, nor the eager hero who fully commands our sympathy. For one thing, Cæsar dwarfs him at first. For another, Shakespeare's touch is less sure than usual; he seems not quite certain what to make of Brutus. No doubt in "This was the noblest Roman of them all" he formulates the impression he wishes to leave with us. But we have also seen Brutus through the eyes of Cassius, and there is more than a hint of the stuffed shirt about him. Shaw calls him the perfect Girondin, doomed by the coarser Antony and Octavius, "who at least knew the difference between life and rhetoric." Cassius is the best piece of character drawing — the genuine radical and drive-wheel of revolution. Antony is for the company's "juvenile" — a straight and sure-fire rôle, embellished with splendid recitatives and arias.

Besides faulty structure and the blurred outlines of the chief character, the absence of ideas mars the play. If it is a play, and not an empty pageant, it is a political play; but Shakespeare has little to say. Platitudes in republican and in Fascist style are enunciated with equal neatness; yet whether Shakespeare thought Cæsar admirable or comic is still debated. We see him near his end, like Napoleon in 1812, infatuated, impervious to common sense, addicted to a kind of calm boasting no less symptomatic than the frenzies of some later dictators. Sir Thomas Elyot in *The Gouernour* (ed. 1531, fol. 117) had already psychographed him: "beinge nat able to sustaine the burden of fortune, and enuienge his owne felicitie, [he] abandoned his naturall disposition, and as it were beinge dronke with ouer moche welth, sought newe wayes howe to be aduanced, aboue the astate of mortall princes." Shaw has noticed that Shakespeare's view of a Cæsar "not even Plutarchian" owes something to the tradition of stage conquerors established by Marlowe's Tamburlaine; and Kittredge remarks that the Cæsarian dialect accords with the strutting conqueror set up as early as 1553 in the Latin tragedy of

Julius Cæsar by Muretus (Marc Antoine Muret), while the more-than-mortal pose, which Cassius finds so irritating, reflects the ancient doctrine that the gods first plunge into blind folly those whom they would destroy. "Hence! Wilt thou lift up Olympus?" This is not what President Franklin D. Roosevelt once called the "ugly truculence" of the dictators; it is ugly complacency, no whit less ugly because it has its comic side. Yet Cæsar, though pompous, is dignified, and he dies in the grand manner. Perhaps Shakespeare was a little puzzled by him, as Napoleon, but not Wellington, can puzzle us now. The Duke could raise both arms as he left the mess table the night of Waterloo and exclaim to his staff, "The hand of God has been over me this day!" He could also tell Creevey, "By God! I don't think it would have been done if I had not been there!" The first of these observations is more pious than mystical, and the second is neither. But the Emperor can not believe his eyes when he sees his massed columns recoiling from infantry strung out in line, and his squadrons riding helplessly around the squares. For, not in the end but toward the end, the Cæsars all arrive at the conviction that divinity is in them.

Even if Shakespeare had no political opinions to voice, he might have made his play more poetic. He adopted for it an admirably simple, straightforward style. But the verse is rarely suggestive; and when it soars, it soars with rhetorical eloquence. That these internecine struggles afford a glimpse of humanity's ignorant armies clashing in the night, that the wreckage of noble lives has aught of mystery or warning to mankind, this play gives never a hint. Relatively cold and unaffecting, Dr. Johnson calls it.

> And all their passionate hearts are dust,
> And dust the great idea that burned
> In various flames of love and lust
> Till the world's brain was turned.

So sings Masefield after *The Tragedy of Pompey the Great*, and his play has already enforced that idea upon us. It is a poet's idea, but it is not Shakespeare's in *Julius Cæsar*.

Yet his tragedy is an excellent play, and a better one than *Pompey*. Why? At every turn and from whatever angle it is approached, we are driven back upon its speeches as speeches. For to list its weaknesses is only to recognize how it rises above them. Attempt to formulate its details in a politico-philosophical pattern and it goes to pieces, dissolves to a thing of shreds and patches, to be shared out according to the whims of the disintegrators. But considered as a stirring pageant of the collapse of republican Rome, it hangs together well enough and its title is not a misnomer. It is not a superlative work of the creative imagination, but it is a remarkable example of imaginative reconstruction. And it is capital entertainment. I commend it to Hollywood, for here is a piece that cries for the screen. On the stage it rides to success on the wings of some of the best orations in English. But a great play requires something more than able speechmaking. Better than any stage, the screen could bring its processions and mob and battle scenes up to the level of the dialogue. A superb opportunity awaits the camera that shoots the crowd while Antony is talking, and films the shifting tides of Philippi. A master of motion-picture art may yet give *Julius Cæsar* all the stage can give it and in addition a tragic direction that Shakespeare may have felt but did not quite succeed in communicating.

Chapter 7

HIS BEST COMEDIES

A MIDSUMMER NIGHT'S DREAM

WHEN I am asked for a definition of poetry, I think of Titania and Oberon of the Midsummer-Night's Dream." This pretty saying is often attributed to Poe.[1] If he had uttered it, we should have an interesting index to his taste and its limitations. For while the beauties of this play are exquisite, they are works of craftsmanship, not of high artistic purpose and belief. It is a delightful entertainment, very likely written for marriage festivities at some great house, no one knows whose; and into it, as into its companion pieces, *Romeo and Juliet* and *Richard the Second*, the composer, now about thirty, poured a ravishing lyricism. But the tenderness of his greatest comedies is absent from the *Dream*, which lacks his usual solid underpinning, rock-hewn from the facts of life. It is not that this play is fantastic; so is *The Tempest*, a drama both more poetic and more humane. The *Dream* is a little too romantic (in the worst sense), too glittering with poetic tinsel, and as essentially trivial as a good many of Poe's own verses.

That, I must own, is not the orthodox view of this unique comedy; and I hasten to dodge the objurgations of the irate reader by subscribing my allegiance to it, this side idolatry. The unconfessed, and, let us hope, often subconscious aim of all Criticism with a big C is to rationalize the critics' likes and dislikes. It is a rare soul among them who has the candor to admit he adores what he disapproves of. Nowhere more than in Shakespeare commentary has this amiable weakness resulted in cant and hypocrisy. The critic knoweth in his heart that the psychological department of his endeavors is vanity. The creative process remains inscrutable. In the play before us, the lovers' mishaps are only to be laughed at. Stately Theseus and his bride are only gilded framework. We only delight in Bully Bottom; we do not love him. And the coldly brilliant fairies, though they are the best of their species, lay no hold on mortal affection. These objections would lack all force if the play were either plain farce or comedy of manners. Heaven forbid the social approach to drama from adopting a neosentimental route and eventually giving up catastrophe-tickling for its indifference to pain and humiliation, or the explosion of ideas because someone may get hurt! If it is anything, *A Midsummer Night's Dream* is a romantic comedy with farcical episodes. Unfortunately, each of these elements obscures the other.

What, then, are the reasons that dispose us to admire this *olla-podrida* of a play, whose absurdly incongruous ingredients (fairies from British folklore hobnobbing with legendary Greeks) please separately without quite blending into something new and rich and strange? Why, it is a good show, as Dr. Johnson remarked, though not precisely in those terms. Why, it runs the gamut from enameled prettiness to slapstick. Why, it has, if any play ever had, that indefinable thing called charm — it defines, not poetry, but charm. But do honest reasons like these bring us a whit nearer the heart of the mystery? The day the critic unlocks that door he can throw the key away and address the remainder of his life to composing masterpieces of his own. Let us therefore not be ashamed to like this play for what it is, the best of the lowest order of romantic comedy, far below such triumphs as Portia, the fourth act of *Much Ado*, and the whole of *Twelfth Night*. All these creations vibrate with the pulse of humanity; but not the *Dream*, which on the other hand fails to transport us into a true realm of faëry. However frequented by the little people, the wood near Athens has no practicable communications with otherworldliness, and *A Midsummer Night's Dream* remains neither high fantasy nor mundane truth.

Yet what an amazing performance it is, all the more amazing when we pause to reflect that the same hand drew Puck and Jack Falstaff! Shakespeare here displays another sparkling facet of his genius, and the spectator who is not entranced must be defective in more than one of his senses. This play is not intended to move us, except to laughter and perhaps a caught breath at the beautiful speaking of a perfect line. A reader can find the going harder. His attempt should be to reconstruct imaginatively an Elizabethan eye-and-ear show, with all the actors' grace, gorgeous silks and satins, the slimness of young boys, dancing in profusion, melting harmonies from lute and woodwind, fresh treble voices — all by London's leading producing unit. Libretto by Shakespeare.

The date (*c.* 1595) rests on the tenuous evidence of metre and style, for we have certainly to go on only Meres's mention of the title in 1598. There is no reason to suppose that in (V, i, 52–3),

> The thrice three Muses mourning for the death
> Of Learning, late deceas'd in beggary,

Shakespeare alludes to the demise of any particular poet. But Titania's meteorological report (II, i, 88–114) probably reflects the long spell of unseasonable weather which marked the three years from 1594 to 1596.

In a sense the *Dream* belongs among the experimental comedies, though its charm and the adroitness with which the author drives an unruly four-in-hand narrative team put it in a higher category. Shakespeare has not yet quite found his comic métier; he still faces several ways. The plot seems to be original; its elements are, however, traceable, and among them are certain materials and a deft but shallow treatment of them which the poet immediately abandoned as he went on to press home the human issues raised in his more truly romantic comedies. From the "errors" and cross-purposes of Latin farce, refined by the graceful influence of Lyly, are derived the intrigues and recriminations of the lovers, an uninteresting quartet, whom he does not trouble himself to characterize. Lysander and Demetrius are as alike as two peas in a pod. Hermia is short, dark, fiery; Helena tall, fair, gentler. But the contrast is perfunctory and superficial, for the girls are sisters under their skins, the dominant trait of each being her intention of getting her man. The puppets of farce regu-

larly dance to the tune of plot. Treat them realistically, and
we begin to think of other strings — the cords that bind —
and laugh less thoughtlessly. Hermia's terror on waking from
her dream (II, ii) is a mere joke. We do not share her fear,
nor her pain, but echo Robin's sallies about mortals' folly
and Cupid's knavery. Shakespeare could have made these lovers plausible; desiring a farcical effect, he deliberately chose
otherwise.

As for Theseus and Hippolyta, he had probably met them
in Chaucer's "The Knightes Tale"; and North's translation
of Plutarch, which he was soon to use for *Julius Cæsar*, includes a life of Theseus. The court interlude of the workingmen burlesques the familiar story of Pyramus and Thisbe,
which Shakespeare presumably read in Ovid as a schoolboy.
The fairies he had known from infancy in old wives' tales
and peasant lore, though the names of Oberon and Titania
were not English. The former is a dwarf-magician in the Old
French romance of *Huon de Bordeaux*. Shakespeare may have
found him in Berners's translation, but Oberon had already
appeared on the London stage. Greene's *The Scottish Historie
of Iames the fourth* (*c.* 1590) introduces him as fairy king, and
a *hewen of burdoche* [2] was thrice acted by Sussex's Men in the
short winter season of 1593–94. Ovid gives in his *Metamorphoses* the beautiful name "Titania" to Diana (III, 173) and
to Circe (XIV, 438). Shakespeare takes it over directly; Golding, to whose version he had resorted for *Venus and Adonis*,
translates "Titan's daughter" and "Circe." But Robin Goodfellow, the Puck, was an experienced hand in English folklore. Reginald Scot's *The discouerie of witchcraft* (1584) describes
him, and doubtless he had been seen by more than one old
Warwickshire biddy who had never laid eyes on Scot's book
and could not have read it if she had. Scot also has a version
of the ass-head story; it is an ancient tale, appearing in Apu-
leius and available in William Adlington's translation as
early as 1566. To the peasantry the fairies were uncanny, not
aesthetic; that we picture them now as diminutive and benevolent is due to Shakespeare.

The First Quarto, of 1600, is the authoritative text, though it is far from perfect.[3] It does not mark acts and scenes; evidently the play was originally performed without interruption. The Folio breaks it into acts. At the end of the third, a stage direction is added: "They sleepe all the Act." Here "act" has been taken to mean an interval between the third and fourth; but there would be no point to a stage direction prescribing what the actors should do during an intermission, when the curtains would close off the inner stage. Certainly they were not expected to recline on the outer platform while the performance was suspended. This direction means simply that the lovers continue asleep during the intervening action, until the horns wake them at IV, i, 141. Some think Shakespeare revised the play once or even twice, others that it was a piece of political propaganda, in its original state overflowing with allegory and satire. There is some evidence, but not enough, to support the former of these hypotheses; for the second there is no evidence at all.

As usual, there is little clue to the comedy's Elizabethan popularity. If it was written for a noble lord, and if Theseus, more Renaissance than Grecian, was intended for a flattering portrait of the patron, the compliment to the "fair Vestal, throned by the West" (II, i, 155–64) encourages belief in the likelihood that Elizabeth saw the first performance. The piece was doubtless soon put on the public stage. Record of a revival at the court of James in 1604 has survived in a letter from Dudley Carleton to John Chamberlain: "On New yeares night we had a play of Robin goode-fellow." Under the Commonwealth, when the drama was banned, farcical scenes from regular plays were sometimes excerpted, adapted, and performed. One of the drolls, as they were called, was separately printed in 1661 and again in Francis Kirkman's collection, *The Wits; or, Sport upon Sport* (ed. 1672–73) as *The Merry conceited Humours of Bottom the Weaver*. *A Midsummer Night's Dream* was revived as early as 1662, apparently with small success. Pepys pronounced it "the most insipid ridiculous play that ever I saw in my life." The Restoration did well by several of the tragedies; but Shakespeare's more fragile comedies could not raise their drooping heads till the romantic dew, well past the turn of the century, began moistening the neoclassic dust-bowl. To revive *A Midsummer Night's Dream* took, as we shall see, even longer. Pepys's is the only allusion to Restoration performance prior to *The Fairy-Queen*, the famous operatic version with music by Henry Purcell, perhaps the greatest of English composers. It was produced at Dorset Garden in 1692.[4] In 1716 the gifted musician Richard Leveridge made a little "Comick Masque," burlesquing Italian opera, out of the rehearsal and performance of "Pyramus and Thisbe." As an afterpiece, it was a hit at Lincoln's Inn Fields. In 1723 Charles Johnson's *Love in a Forest* was acted at Drury Lane. This is an adaptation of *As You Like It*, with the addition in Act V, while Rosalind is off stage changing her clothes, of the Pyramus and Thisbe interlude. In 1745 the interlude served a German composer, John Frederick Lampe, for his expanded version of Leveridge's skit, played at Covent Garden. Ten years later Garrick omitted the workingmen, but used the lovers, in *The Fairies*, another musical version. Yet another was staged at Drury Lane in 1763 by the elder George Colman. It left out practically the whole of the fifth act. This piece lasted only a single evening; parts of the wreckage were salvaged in *A Fairy Tale*, an afterpiece in more senses than one. The line of pseudo-operatic [5] versions and perversions runs on into the next century. Reynolds was responsible for a spectacular and profitable one, which J. P. Kemble produced in 1816. The music was by Henry Bishop, whose charming setting of "Lo, here the gentle lark" is still beloved of coloratura sopranos. Hazlitt damns this revival with characteristic gusto in a disillusioned review which might be weighed with profit by some recent producers.

The spirit was evaporated, the genius was fled; but the spectacle was fine. It was that which saved the play. — Oh, ye scene-shifters, ye scene-painters, ye machinists and dress-makers, ye manufacturers of moon and stars that give no light, ye musical composers, ye men in the orchestra, fiddlers and trumpeters and players on the double drum and loud bassoon, rejoice! This is your triumph; it is not ours: and ye full-grown, well-fed, substantial, real fairies . . . we shall believe no more in the existence of your fantastic tribe.[6]

But the protest went unheeded, and 1833 saw a two-act after-piece, presumably compiled from earlier musical versions.

A long step in the right direction was made by Charles Mathews and his brilliant wife, Eliza Vestris, when they took over the management of Covent Garden, with a lavish, drastically cut, but otherwise fairly faithful revival of the *Dream*, staged during their second season, in 1840. J. R. Planché was the adapter and designer. Meanwhile, in 1827, there had been a splendid revival in Berlin, supervised by the aged Romantic and Shakespearean, Ludwig Tieck. It was for this production that Mendelssohn wrote his graceful music. Samuel Phelps's modest revival at Sadler's Wells in 1853 was eulogized for its fidelity to the play's dreamlike charm. He played Bottom, one of his best rôles. This production is sup-posed to be Phelps's masterpiece. In 1856 Charles Kean's severely cut version, in which he did not appear, had a run of 150 nights. The Puck was a little girl named Ellen Terry; she made her first entrance rising on a mushroom. Subsequent revivals have been numerous in England, Germany, and the United States. Laura Keene produced the *Dream* in 1859 in New York. She played Puck herself; but while a girl child may be tolerated in the rôle, a grown woman is an abomina-tion, though this casting is only too common. A boy or an athletic youth is best. Augustin Daly, who, despite his ad-diction to cutting and rearranging, did a great deal for the romantic comedies, staged the *Dream* several times. In 1888 his Helena was Ada Rehan; Otis Skinner and John Drew played Lysander and Demetrius, and James Lewis was Bottom. A later Lysander of Daly's was John Craig, who, like many another manager of a stock company, offered, during his long tenure of the Castle Square in Boston, numerous excellent revivals of Shakespeare. Among the alumni of Daly's com-pany were Fay Templeton (Puck), Effie Shannon and Kitty Cheatham (Titania), Tyrone Power (Quince), and Maxine Elliott (Hermia). In 1889 Benson made his managerial debut in London with a spectacular revival. Others were staged by Tree in 1900 and Otho Stuart in 1905. Benson played Lysander; Tree, Bottom. In Stuart's production, the Bottom was Asche;

the Oberon was Walter Hampden. Arthur Bourchier played Bottom for Tree in 1911; this revival was full of pictorial silliness — there were actually real rabbits in the wood. Granville-Barker's production in 1914 — his fairies were oriental beings with gilded faces — attempted by violent distortion to achieve a dreamlike mystery. The Helena was Lillah McCarthy; the Bottom, Nigel Playfair; the Theseus, Baliol Holloway, eventually (like Sir Nigel) a manager on his own account. This revival was by many roundly condemned; Winter, for example, objected to "gilded steam-radiator raiment."

For generations, repertory companies and amateurs have staged the play. Of all Shakespeare's romantic comedies this is the one most obviously adaptable to motion-picture technique; but the screen version by Max Reinhardt was an artistic failure. Several rôles were hopelessly misconceived and miscast; and the director, despite some toothsome bits of fairy prettiness, made the old mistake of smothering the play's delicacy with quantity. This revival was a glaring case; but in general the movies, when they attempt to play Shakespeare, seem to be about where the legitimate stage was a century ago. The aim should be, not to astound by an overlavish use of newly invented material accessories, but to employ every possible accessory with a single eye to furthering, more effectively than was possible till now, the communication of an incomparable artist with an audience that awaits him in larger numbers than he has ever played to before.

THE MERCHANT OF VENICE

None of Shakespeare's plays identifies him more certainly as a man of his own day and age, for *The Merchant* is as Elizabethan as sack and sugar. Its wildly romantic plot has small relevance to life, but that does not keep the dramatist from one of his most brilliant expositions of his knowledge of the human heart. The bond story has an anti-Semitic edge, and in recent years many secondary schools have wisely removed the play from the curriculum; but its anti-Semitism is of a different stripe from the cold-blooded political variety which

disgraces our unhappy times. Shakespeare simply accepts the
Jews as a notoriously bad lot; he constructs no fantastic
theorems about them, he invents no slanders, he fabricates
no documents, he proclaims no pogrom. But his conception
can not be whitewashed by comparing Shylock with Aaron,
Iachimo, Angelo, Claudius, Edmund, Macbeth, Richard III,
and Don John. True, all these are villains; but he also painted
benevolent Moors, Italians, Viennese, Danes, Britons, Scots,
and English. Though the Don was the national enemy, he
even has one fairly admirable Spaniard. He never drew a
noble Jew. To require that of him would be to insist on his
being very far ahead of his time. It is highly remarkable and
to his credit that Shylock is thoroughly human, being neither
a Machiavellian like Marlowe's Barabas nor the fiend in
human form of some earlier theorists in anthropology. But
he is a hateful and sinister creature, and he is moved by racial
malice as well as mercantile competition.

> You may as well go stand upon the beach
> And bid the main flood bate his usual height . . .
> As seek to soften that — than which what's harder? —
> His Jewish heart.

I do not see how a Jew can read *The Merchant of Venice* without
pain and indignation. It is a tribute to the comprehensiveness
of a great race that some of Shakespeare's warmest admirers
and most learned students have been Jews.

The authoritative text, a good one though with some
typographical oddities, is the First Quarto, of 1600.[7] Professor Wilson has ably demonstrated the probability that abbreviated speech tags in the "copy" were misread and resulted
in "the three Sallies." Solanio and Salerio are Shakespeare's;
but Salarino appears to be the typesetter's creation, and should
be omitted, as a separate character, from editions and revivals. Theories that Shakespeare merely rewrote an old drama
and that he subsequently made a further revision have not
won much credence.

The dates of composition and production can not be fixed
precisely. Except when the theatres had to shut down, there

was such a steady demand for new plays that performance, it is safe to assume, normally followed writing at once. *The Merchant* was entered in the Stationers' Register on July 22, 1598, as "the Marchaunt of Venyce or otherwise called the Jewe of Venyce"; and it is mentioned later in the same year by Meres.[8] Gratiano's Pythagorean allegation (IV, i) that Shylock's soul was once a wolf's has been taken to refer to the execution on June 7, 1594, of the Queen's physician, Roderigo Lopez, a converted Jew from Spain, who was accused, probably falsely, of conspiring to poison her. Though *lupus* and "Lopez" are not very dissimilar in sound, a connection like this could hardly be made in the theatre even by the quickest-witted auditor. It is very unlikely that Shakespeare intended any. About 1596 is probably right for *The Merchant*, which obviously flows from a more seasoned pen than the earlier comedies. Chambers cites, moreover, two epistolary references in the fall of that year, to a "St. Gobbo," evidently Robert Cecil, later Earl of Salisbury.[9]

Several ancient stories are combined in this play. The casket plot, as it is now called, was originally casketless. It is an old tale, with many variants, in which a suitor has to pass a test in order to win a wife who in the earliest versions is a fairy or magician. The choice of caskets is an oriental theme; when it got attached to the wife-winning story is unknown, but the date was relatively late. As a moral tale, illustrating the great truth that inward substance is better than outward show, the casket-choosing had appeared in several books Shakespeare may have got hold of: the *Speculum Historiale* (XV, 10) of Vincent of Beauvais, the *Legenda Aurea* of Jacobus de Voragine,[10] the *Decameron* (X, 1) of Boccaccio, the *Confessio Amantis* (V, 2273–2434) of John Gower, and the *Gesta Romanorum*, edited in English translation by Richard Robinson. In the *Gesta* is a version combining the casket motif with a tale of how a feminine chooser wins an emperor's son for a husband.

The pound-of-flesh story is likewise old and widespread. Doubtless Shakespeare knew it in the ballad of *The Crueltie of Gernutus* (probably earlier than 1590), which resembles some details in the play, and perhaps in Lazarus Piot's translation, *The Orator*, from the *Histoires Tragiques* of Alexandre van den Busche, commonly called Sylvain. The ninety-fifth declamation in *The Orator* (1596) is a speech by the Jew; it resembles Shylock's argument before the Duke, but priority is uncertain.

The wife-winning at Belmonte (without the caskets), the lover's older friend (here his godfather), the pound of flesh, the lady as lawyer, and the final fillip of Shakespeare's plot, the ring episode, are all in the story of Gianetto told by Ser Giovanni Fiorentino in his *Il Pecorone* late in the fourteenth century. It was not printed till 1558, and no English translation is known earlier than the play. The elopement of Jessica is not in the Florentine writer's tale; that is probably Shakespeare's invention, though suggested by Abigail, the Jew's daughter in Marlowe's *The Jew of Malta*. In Fiorentino the suitor's test is to stay awake all night in the lady's bed, despite her attempt to drug him. Gianetto fails twice, and the lady confiscates his ships and goods. He wins the third time.

The names of Shylock and Jessica are probably Biblical in origin. The former seems to be the Hebrew *shalach*, translated "cormorant" in Leviticus 11:17 and Deuteronomy 14:17. "Cormorant" for usurious rapacity occurs in contemporary plays; Shakespeare has "cormorant belly" in *Coriolanus*, I, i, 125, where a mutinous citizen complains of patrician usury. Jessica may be derived from *Jesca*, a form of *Iscah* (Genesis 11:29), "she that looketh out." Shylock warns her against clambering to the casements (II, v), but "for all this" Launcelot advises her to "look out at window"; and that is what she does, to the salvation of her soul, in the next scene.

That the adroit and dramatic interweaving of these narratives was wholly Shakespeare's work is uncertain. For in *The Schoole of Abuse* (ed. 1579, fol. 22ᵛ), Stephen Gosson lists among the exceptions to his general condemnation of the stage "The Iew . . . showne at the Bull [Inn] . . . representing the greedinesse of worldly chusers, and bloody mindes of Usurers." Whether this play, about which nothing else survives, had already combined the bond and casket elements, or whether its themes had nothing to do with Shakespeare's, no one knows. At any rate, the stories are joined so neatly in *The Merchant* that many commentators have failed to perceive which one is subordinate.

The bond plot is more striking and, realistically considered, even more "remov'd," as Rowe says of both plots, "from the Rules of Probability": the law of the trial scene is a very romantic kind of law. The main structural unit is the casket plot, that is, the winning of a wife by means of an irrational test. Learned attempts have been made to rationalize it; we are assured that any properly educated Renaissance young gentleman would have gone straight to the leaden box. There is no need thus to endorse the sagacity of Portia's father. This is romantic stuff, and the third try usually wins in a fairy tale. Morocco's argument is as sound as Bassanio's, though the contrast of inward beauty with outward dross is more dramatic than Portia's picture in the golden chest could be. This part of the play doubtless delighted its first audience more than it often does now. For there have been many charming Portias; but as Ellen Terry, queen of them all, testifies from her own experience, an even tolerable Bassanio is extremely rare. Ordinarily the rôle is assigned to a stick of a lad with a classic profile and a good leg, and does not get acted. The earliest production for which we know the cast relegated Shylock to the low comedian and gave Bassanio to the star, Thomas Betterton, no less, old as he then was and although in other plays he had abandoned the heroes for character parts. It is the casket not the bond plot that opens and that closes the drama; much more time is assigned to it, and we are done with the bond in the fourth act. *The Merchant* has been dubbed by one critic "a colossal dramatic failure"; but if you can forget its distortion on stage and take it as a romantic comedy about a strange wooing, with the bond plot an ominous cloud that briefly overcasts a bright Italian sky, then the fifth act, though minus Shylock, clicks perfectly into place. But you must also imagine a Bassanio with brains as well as calves, and a voice that gives to "In Belmont is a lady richly left" all its thrilling lyricism and joins at the casket scene in a duet with Portia very different from the orchard duet of Romeo and Juliet but not much inferior to that immortal music. Bassanio and Portia are less ecstatically lyric; but they are more human, and they express nuances unknown to the children of Verona.

There are, indeed, a number of historical adjustments to make. The hundred-per-cent American or true-blue British heart may scorn Bassanio's avowal that he seeks money as well as love. No Elizabethan was troubled by this frankness. The conversion of Jessica was likewise above reproach. A faithless reader of our day may be unperturbed about a future state; but our forefathers, who considered themselves transients but immortals, had a right to some concern about their destination. To renounce her people's errors and embrace the only true faith was the best action of which a Jewish maiden was capable, and a mere matter of robbing a father of his jewels and ducats was trivial in comparison. Indeed it was positively commendable, since to deprive a Jew of money was to draw his fangs. On our stage Jessica seems a horrid little cat; to the prentices in the yard she was as good as a sermon. Gratiano kicks Shylock when he is down; and, unless we are subscribers to the totalitarian ideology, we think he behaves disgustingly. We may be confident the Elizabethans were delighted with him. He is a gay sequel to Mercutio, though like most sequels nowhere near so good. We wonder why Antonio is sad; no one wondered in that theatre. He says he is sad because he is sad; it is idle to invent external reasons, when every Elizabethan knew that if you had too much black bile it was your hard luck. Antonio is sad and subdued because he is not to be the hero, but a passive personage, the title giver, the hero's friend and the object of the villain's attack. He must not be allowed to steal the stage, even at his own trial. Old Gobbo is a dainty character bit; I once saw E. E. Clive play a whole company off the stage in it. His son is the least successful of the major clowns, in fact, rather a nuisance. There had to be a part for Will Kempe. Launcelot is not a motley Fool, even though Shylock calls him patch; he is a moronic serving-boy. The courting princes are brilliantly executed, especially the noble and glamorous Morocco. Was Shakespeare already meditating a Moorish hero? He had already imagined his ideal heroine, and Portia is just that made flesh. Beauty she has, and as much brain as beauty, and as much sheer maddening feminine charm as brain, and as much depth as charm, and a heart how high and loving! Shakespeare's loves are his secret, for all his more than a century of sonnets. One can only hope for him that he drew Portia from the life.

In *The Jew of Malta* Marlowe had scored such a success that his play of *Judenhass* long remained in the repertory of the Admiral's Men. It is quite possible that Shakespeare, now committed to romantic comedy, conceived the idea of injecting the bond plot into the wooing story in order to provide his company with a competing vehicle. He knew Marlowe's play well, and his own contains many similarities, including some verbal borrowings. Betrayal of the Jew by his daughter is a striking feature of both. It is unnecessary to suppose that Shylock ran away with his author, though such things can happen. Very likely the character grew on him — he is always humanizing — and "Hath not a Jew eyes?" (III, i, 61–76) is a superb example of his power to go out of himself. It is certainly not an apologetic for Judaism; Shylock merely gets, as everyone does, his day in the Shakespearean court. The *point* of the speech is not humanity but vindictiveness, and there follows immediately the diatribe on the stolen ducats. We take our Shakespeare so hard nowadays that these almost farcical speeches are recited by our actors with all the solemnity of a Hebrew prophet cursing in C major. They even roll up their eyes and pump out a huge chest tone at "a wilderness of monkeys." Of course this phrase, like many others of Shylock's, is comic. He is thoroughly malevolent — Shakespeare gives him an aside, immediately upon Antonio's entrance (I, iii), which reveals his wickedness at the outset — yet he is not the appalling but the semifarcical villain, the comic butt, as Stoll calls him. Played no doubt in a big nose and with countless shrugs and grimaces, the part was essentially different, even from an Iago or an Edmund, still

more from a Claudius. It is much like the villain's rôle in Vic
torian melodrama, who plots, gloats, curses, and ha-ha's his
way through to the final scene, when he is exposed, foiled
disgraced, and ridiculed, till he expires, leaves town, or at
best slinks off stage with a futile imprecation. But a Shakespeare, not a Boucicault, composed Shylock's lines; and the
result is, not an heroic part, but from start to finish one of
the best character rôles ever written.

Who created it is unknown; the expanded version of an
elegy on the death of Burbage names it among his parts, but
this addition is one of Collier's forgeries. A court revival is
recorded on February 10, 1605.[11] For nearly a century there
after no performance is known. This state of affairs is not
conclusive evidence against a play's retention in the repertory
but quite possibly the initial vogue of The Merchant, if it was
inspired by some special circumstance, did not long continue
Stage history has, as we shall see, something to contribute
to the interpretation of Hamlet's character; but the possi
bility of a very long hiatus in the acting of Shylock precludes
similar reliance on the earliest performance of which interpre
tive details have survived. For light on Shylock we are re
stricted to the fact that for three centuries it had been illegal
for Jews to reside in England, to the conventional handling
of Jews in Elizabethan literature and on the Elizabethan stage
to Shakespeare's references to the race in other plays, and
above all to examination of the score of The Merchant. Hap
pily — from a scholastic if not from a social point of view —
there is no disagreement among these; and, the Romantic
critics and their surviving disciples to the contrary notwith
standing, they are decisive for an unheroic Shylock.

The earliest performance we know anything about was of
an adapted version, The Jew of Venice, by George Granville
first Baron Lansdowne, in 1701. It held the stage forty years
The quarto, also of 1701, is prefaced with an apology for
undertaking the improvement of a piece so objectionable in
its original form. Granville's remarks encourage the supposi
tion that The Merchant had long been absent from the boards
His adaptation is sufficiently contemptible, but Shylock's

character is not altered in the slightest particular. He was played by the famous comedian Thomas Dogget, with Betterton as Bassanio and the charmer Anne Bracegirdle as Portia. It is to Dogget's interpretation that Rowe refers in the preface to his edition (1709):

but tho' we have seen that Play Receiv'd and Acted as a Comedy, and the Part of the *Jew* perform'd by an Excellent Comedian, yet I cannot but think it was design'd Tragically by the Author. There appears in it such a deadly Spirit of Revenge, such a savage Fierceness and Fellness, and such a bloody designation of Cruelty and Mischief, as cannot agree either with the Stile or Characters of Comedy.

There speaks, not only the critic of a new dawn, but also the sentimental Augustan dramatist. As an object of ridicule Shylock became intolerable to an age of enlightenment, which proceeded to transmogrify him. In 1741 Charles Macklin electrified London with a revival of Shakespeare's play in which he acted Shylock as a heavy villain, with no taint of farce, and elicited from Pope the well-known epigram on

the Jew
That Shakespeare drew.

With great difficulty Macklin had prevailed on the management of Drury Lane to stage the original play and let him do Shylock his own way. He concealed his intentions and merely walked through the part at rehearsals. The surprise and triumph were complete, and he continued to act the rôle for half a century.

Ever since that epoch-making revival, *The Merchant* has been pretty constantly before the public. Garrick staged it but did not act in it. He opened his management at Drury Lane with it on September 15, 1747. Macklin was the Shylock and Kitty Clive the Portia. For this occasion Dr. Johnson wrote his famous prologue, with the oft quoted lines:

The Drama's Laws the Drama's Patrons give
For we that live to please, must please to live.

In the trial scene the roguish Clive was actually allowed to indulge in imitations of the best-known barristers of the day. Peg Woffington and Mrs. Yates were also famous eighteenth-century Portias. The next important Shylock was John Henderson, whose performance J. P. Kemble thought the greatest single effort he ever saw. Henderson died young in 1785, but his half-dozen of Shakespeare impersonations were long remembered. He seems to have followed Macklin's lead; but Cooke's Shylock, which made a tremendous impression at the turn of the century, introduced a note of pathos. J. P. Kemble's production in 1803 was strongly cast, with the manager as Antonio, Cooke as Shylock, Charles Kemble as Bassanio, and Mrs. Siddons as Portia. J. P. had previously essayed Shylock without much success; he later resumed the part.

Even more dramatic than Macklin's debut as Shylock was Edmund Kean's in 1814. After a dog's life as a strolling player, Kean had been engaged by Drury Lane but given nothing to do. Desperately poor and snubbed by his fellow actors, he believed in himself and insisted, in accordance with his contract, that he would act only in leading rôles and that he would begin with "Shylock or nothing." At the single rehearsal allowed him he restrained himself, as Macklin had done; and no one suspected the powers he was about to unleash. He stepped on the stage for Shylock's first entrance that evening an unknown. He left it after the trial scene with the audience in the hollow of his hand, and the rôle was pre-eminently his for the rest of his life. He made Shylock a romantic hero, murderous but volcanically majestic in his racial fanaticism and the fury of his passion. He played in a black wig, discarding the traditional auburn. Junius Brutus Booth also played the part as the fiery representative of a race. Portia was among the earliest rôles of Fanny Kemble.

The acting versions of the eighteenth and early nineteenth centuries were severely cut, and there were musical interpolations, especially for Lorenzo and Jessica. Macready's fine revival in 1841 abandoned these flourishes but still left out Morocco and Aragon. He played a lofty, idealistic Shylock.

The two princes were restored in the next major production, Charles Kean's, in 1858. Like his father, he acted Shylock; his wife, the former Ellen Tree, was his Portia. Charles Kean seems to have been the first to go in for the bridges, gondolas, and carnival crowds which still, though on a smaller scale, distract audiences from the play. At the Prince of Wales's in 1875 those sterling actor-managers Squire Bancroft and his wife, Marie Wilton, turned from cup-and-saucer drama to *The Merchant of Venice*. They failed dismally, though it was on their stage that Ellen Terry made her first appearance as Portia, one of her very greatest rôles. Not even her radiance could counteract Charles Coughlan's failure as Shylock. It had, however, full scope in Irving's revival, first seen in 1879. This was the most famous of his Shakespeare productions. It ran for two hundred and fifty performances. Shylock was probably Irving's best rôle; he played the Jew as a proud aristocrat. For this revival the *décor* was happily on a scale less lavish than was his custom, and it was less pedantically archaeological. Shylock was also a favorite rôle of Edwin Booth. This great American actor was a lifelong student of Shakespearean score, and Shylock was not the only character of which he modified his first conception. Booth began to play the Jew in his father's romantic vein, but afterwards changed to the depiction of bitter hatred. Daly produced *The Merchant* in New York, in 1875, with E. L. Davenport as Shylock. Later on the Portia was Ada Rehan. Among other Portias Mme. Modjeska shone; and other notable American Shylocks were McCullough, Barrett, and Mansfield. Recent revivals have been frequent. Successful Portias were Julia Marlowe, Viola Tree, Violet Vanbrugh, and Edith Evans; while Benson, Bourchier, William Poel, Tree, Greet, Maurice Moscovitch, Holloway, E. H. Sothern, R. B. Mantell, Walter Hampden, Otis Skinner, and George Arliss all played Shylock. In recent years the sentimentalizing of the rôle touched its nadir in the production of David Warfield. This Shylock was a good old Jewish paterfamilias, with only amiability in his heart till Jessica's elopement warped his nature. The bond with Antonio was honestly executed in "a merry sport."

The play's future in our theatre seems less certain now than it did a few years ago. Lovers of Shakespeare and of common decency must unite in hoping that the time will come when the hatreds of these years will seem to nations rededicated to civilization and freedom only a dreadful and inexplicable dream. Then an effective revival of *The Merchant* might be staged without on the one hand fanning the hideous flames of racial animosity, or, on the other, attempting to allay them by distorting the play.

MUCH ADO ABOUT NOTHING

"As it truly is," groans Bernard Shaw's Shakespeare; and certainly this play is not written around an idea. That romantic comedy is a bastard genre is an arguable proposition; but if you allow the genre, *Much Ado* is a great play; and even if you don't, it is too good to rule out. If this is not comic art, our definition had better be revised.

Much Ado was one of four plays entered in the Stationers' Register on August 4, 1600, with the note "to be staied." It was entered again on the 23rd, without the restriction. What the staying entry signifies no one knows.[12] The Folio reprints the sole quarto (1600), which provides the better text, though here and there the Folio makes corrections. There are some queer things in the Quarto. A mute character, "Innogen," Leonato's wife, appears only in the entrance directions of I, i and II, i; and there are other directions that make little sense. Both generic and actors' names are occasionally used for speech tags. Thus Dogberry is sometimes "Constable," "Andrew" (i.e., Clown), and "Kemp." There is, however, no reason to think that these and other inconsistencies must have resulted from a rewriting of the play. Nor is revision indicated by the dramatist's failure to make as clear as he might the assignation of Borachio with Margaret and the pairing off in II, i. Few have accepted a recent contention that alleged "verse fossils," that is, lines surviving from a hypothetical original play in verse, are embedded in the Benedick-Beatrice scenes. A reader who would like to amuse

ELLEN TERRY AS PORTIA

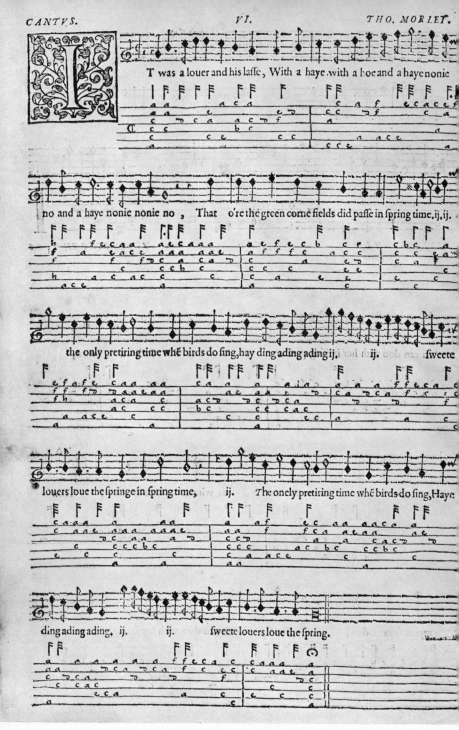

THOMAS MORLEY'S SETTING OF ''IT WAS A LOVER AND HIS LASS''

As You Like It, V, iii

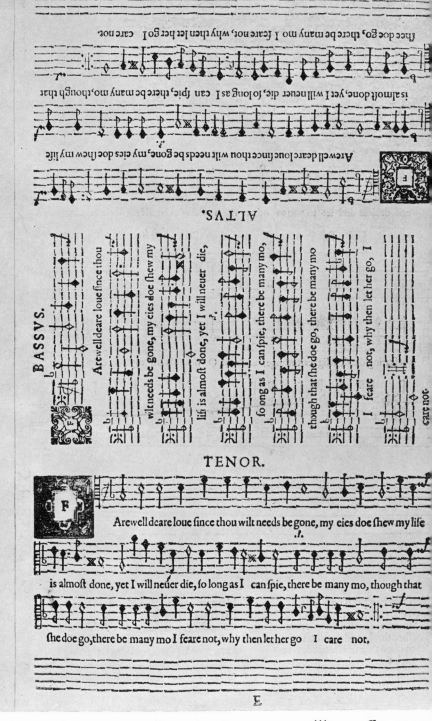

"FAREWELL, DEAR LOVE" — *TWELFTH NIGHT*, II, iii, 110 ff.

from Robert Jones's *The First Booke of Songes or Ayres*

THE CHURCH SCENE OF *MUCH ADO ABOUT NOTHING*

Ellen Terry as Beatrice (left), Forbes-Robertson as Claudio (at steps), Irving as Benedick (right center); from Forbes-Robertson's painting of Irving's production

himself by refuting this theory may turn to almost any book of sinewy old conventional English prose with the certainty of finding blank-verse lines galore.

The art with which Shakespeare combines the three plot and character groups would be enough to demonstrate his technical mastery, even if we were disposed to withhold full credit for similar deftness in *The Merchant of Venice*. The harmonizing of three tones is no less remarkable. The main plot, the wooing of Hero, is highly romantic; the Benedick-Beatrice scenes constitute Shakespeare's nearest approach to the gayer sort of comedy of manners; and the Dogberry group furnish the highest order of low comedy, a brilliantly literary low comedy.

The Hero tale is at least as old as the Greek romances of about A.D. 400. Bandello tells it as the twenty-second of his *Novelle* (1554), and it is retold with embellishments in the third volume of Belleforest's *Histoires Tragiques*. No English translation that Shakespeare might have used is known.[13] In Bandello, a young girl of Messina named Fenicia (Hero), daughter of Lionato de Lionati is engaged to Timbreo di Cardona (Claudio), a favorite of King Piero of Aragon (Don Pedro). She is also loved by Timbreo's friend, Girondo (only partly corresponding to Don John), who hires an accomplice (functionally corresponding in part to Don John) to help him break off the match. The accomplice slanders Fenicia; and Timbreo is tricked when he sees a servant (Borachio), dressed like a gentleman, entering a palace window supposedly for a nocturnal assignation. No confederate is needed within, since the family's apartments are on the other side. Timbreo sends a messenger to break the engagement and accuse Fenicia, in her parents' presence. Lionato remains unconvinced of his daughter's guilt. Fenicia swoons, apparently to death. Her recovery is concealed, a coffin is buried, and an epitaph asserting her innocence is placed on the tomb. Meanwhile she lives secluded in the country house of an uncle (Antonio). Timbreo repents; so does Girondo, who begs his friend to kill him. There is a general reconciliation, and Timbreo promises to refrain from marriage (as does Leontes in

The Winter's Tale) unless a bride is proposed by Lionato. A long interval elapses, after which Lionato easily deceives his prospective son-in-law. Timbreo fails to recognize "Lucilla," though he notices her resemblance to his lost love. They marry, the bride's identity is disclosed, she forgives the past, and Girondo weds her younger sister Belfiore. All's well that ends well, and the end is a dance.

In Cantos iv–vi of the *Orlando Furioso* (1516), Ariosto had given the tale literary currency before Bandello. Among a number of changes, he varies the plot with an additional twist, which, directly or indirectly, Shakespeare took over, perhaps from Sir John Harington's translation (1591).[14] Ariosto's lovers are named Ariodante and Genevra. The latter's maid, who is in love with the contriver of the slanderous trick, impersonates her mistress and thus ensures its success. Another feature of this version, also absent from Bandello's, is the challenge of the heroine's betrothed to a trial of her chastity by combat. In 1590 Edmund Spenser's redaction of this story was published (*Faerie Queene*, II, iv, 17–36); he includes the maid's masquerade, but not the challenge.

Ariosto's romantic narrative was dramatized in London as early as 1583, when *A historie of Ariodante and Geneuora* was acted at court by "mʳ Mulcasters children," the boys of the Merchant Taylors School. Their play has not survived. Some have conjectured that a "matter of Panecia," in the Revels Office accounts, for a play of 1574, also lost, is a mistake for *Fenicia*. This is possible, but unlikely.[15] Jakob Ayrer of Nuremberg wrote a *Comedia Von der schönen Phaenicia* (*c.* 1595?), but its source is Belleforest and it did not influence Shakespeare. Nor did I. I. Starter's Dutch dramatization of Bandello, *Timbre de Cardone ende Fenicie van Messine*. It is, indeed, quite unnecessary to hypothecate an intermediary play between Shakespeare's and his sources, direct or translated, in Bandello and Ariosto.

Benedick and Beatrice are his own creation; and so is Dogberry, whose name still passes current for a thick-witted limb of the law. Aubrey, with what truth no one knows, but certainly with some inaccuracy, asserts that

The Humour of . . . [*sic*] the Constable in a Midsomersnight's
Dreame [*sic*], he happened to take at Grendon in Bucks [16] wch is
the roade from London to Stratford [17] and there was living that
Constable about 1642 when I first came to Oxon. Mr Jos: Howe is of
y^t p[a]r[i]sh and knew him. Ben Johnson and he did gather Humours
of men dayly where ever they came.

No doubt they were both expert snappers-up; and if the constable of Grendon never sat for Dogberry's portrait, it is
likely enough that somewhere one or more of his peers did.
It is a keen stroke of poetic irony that Dogberry's bungling
fingers untangle the main plot — and a clever means of
keeping us in suspense, since we are far from confident that,
even though truth cries in the streets, anyone is going to
listen.

> God, moving darkly in men's brains,
> Using their passions as his tool,
> Brings freedom with a tyrant's chains
> And wisdom with the fool.[18]

This thought is not actually expressed by Shakespeare; but
no doubt he had at least a mordant moment over the reflection, probably a favorite of his, that the logical faculty is
not likely to save the world in our time.

The winter of 1598–99 almost certainly saw the original
production. For Meres's *Palladis Tamia* does not mention
Much Ado, and his dedication is dated October 19, 1598; while
Will Kempe, whose name got into Dogberry's speech tags,
probably left the company fairly early in 1599. How popular
the play was in the public theatre is uncertain. The Quarto
of 1600 stands alone.[19] It is not likely that Kempe had made
Dogberry too much his own; Armin, his successor, seems to
have played that rôle. There was a revival at court during
the betrothal and marriage festivities (1612–13) of the Princess Elizabeth and the Elector Palatine. The performance was
evidently well received, for it was repeated, King James himself attending the second time.[20] According to verses by Leonard Digges in the 1640 edition of Shakespeare's *Poems*, the
play was high in favor just before the Puritans closed the
theatres:

let but *Beatrice*
And *Benedicke* be seene, loe in a trice
The Cockpit Galleries, Boxes, all are full.

Though it was formally reserved for the Duke's Company, *Much Ado* was not revived under the Restoration. In 1662, however, Benedick and Beatrice were injected by D'avenant into *The Law against Lovers*, a mangled version of *Measure for Measure*, which seems to have held for a few years a modest place in the repertory. *Much Ado* was staged at Lincoln's Inn Fields in 1721 under John Rich's management. Little is known about this revival, which did not succeed in re-establishing the original comedy. For in 1737 *The Universal Passion*, by the Reverend James Miller, took the boards at Drury Lane. This unexciting piece, which had some success, combines *Much Ado* with Molière's *La Princesse d'Élide*. *Much Ado* itself was revived at Covent Garden in 1739. The celebrated Hannah Pritchard played Beatrice there in 1746. Two years later Garrick produced the comedy, acting Benedick himself to Mrs. Pritchard's Beatrice. The play had a run of eight performances and with one exception was revived at least once each season during Garrick's tenure of Drury Lane. He was evidently an incomparable Benedick. The rôle was afterwards played by both J. P. and Charles Kemble; the latter was reckoned Garrick's true successor in this part. Mrs. Siddons appeared as Beatrice at Bath in 1779, but Mrs. Abington's success was much greater. Macready and Charles Kean also staged revivals; both played Benedick, the latter to his wife's Beatrice. Phelps revived the play, but did not act in it. Benedick was one of Edwin Booth's regular rôles. Modjeska was a sparkling Beatrice. Irving's production, first presented in 1882, was by some considered his finest Shakespearean effort. Though he played Benedick, with Forbes-Robertson as Claudio, those who remember this revival have little to say about the men, reserving their superlatives for the bewitching Beatrice of Ellen Terry, "more enchanting," says Harold Child, "even than her Portia." Subsequent productions have been fairly numerous, more so in England than in the United States; but, though Daly also revived the play, none has made a comparable impression. Among the more notable were the Benedick and Beatrice of George Alexander and Julia Neilson in 1898, of Oscar Asche and Ellen Terry in 1903, and of Tree and his daughter Viola in 1905.

It is not that the faked death of Hero and her subsequent acceptance sight unseen lay too heavy a stress on the willing suspension of disbelief. In many of Shakespeare's plays romantic conventions are quite as difficult to swallow, but we accept them. Nor is it that Claudio's easy credence of calumny and Shakespeare's alteration of the source in order to stage the rejection at the altar make the hero of the main plot unattractive. There is no point in introducing slander unless the hero is to believe it; the scene of rejection is intensely dramatic, and it is held and followed through like a long but closely knit act in a modern play. A good actor càn readily make Claudio's youth, grief, and bewilderment sympathetic. His lament (IV, i, 101–109) is a good tenor aria. Leonato's rôle, which till now has looked like a minor one, affords a player splendid scope in the same scene. The barrier to our appreciation, whether or not we are conscious of it, is the inadequacy of the villain. In the source, sexual jealousy provides strong motivation; and even in the play the illegitimacy of Don John would, like Edmund's, be accepted by an Elizabethan audience as fully explanatory of his malevolence. He has, moreover, a courtier's envy of Claudio. It is not, even for us, so much inadequacy of motive as inadequacy of characterization. Iago and Edmund are plausible because they *exist*. Not that they are psychologically analyzed; but they speak with a copious and compelling idiom, each in his own unique way. And Othello is plausible because Iago is. Don John, on the contrary, is too taciturn for a good stage villain. Perhaps Shakespeare intentionally mutes him in order not to turn a romantic comedy into a tragedy.

As a comic tour de force Benedick and Beatrice are far from being cater-cousins to Alceste and Célimène or to Mirabel and Millamant, for Shakespeare is not so easy as usual on those rare occasions when he essays pure comedy. But however they fail to meet Continental standards of politesse, those who speak the English tongue are likely to find only sheer delight in their merry use of it. If these characters are, as a French critic calls them, a pair of barbarians trying to be witty, then we Americans and British are all tarred with the same stick. Beatrice is the next heroine after Portia, whom she much resembles, being a bolder projection of Portia's liveliest qualities, without her capacity for resignation. The new woman and her independence were much under discussion; Beatrice insists, a little too much if you feel that way about it, on her status as a human being. If the eighteenth-century heroine was merely the object of male lust, and the nineteenth, in a natural revulsion, the torchbearer of propriety, Shakespeare's girls, despite the gush they evoked from Victorian commentators, were born in a younger day. They are usually high-spirited creatures, intellectually at least the equals of his men. They are not arid, they are not cold; and in the great church scene Beatrice and, with her, Benedick are not merely swept gloriously out of the eddies of an intrigue plot into the main romantic current, their true natures are disclosed and deepened — to them, as well as to us. If before we have only suspected that Beatrice has a great heart, now we know it; and Benedick's, like many another man's, takes noble fire from hers. With the best intentions in the world he has gone at the problem (IV, i, 148) like a lawyer's clerk. Beatrice handles the question of guilt or innocence illogically but soundly — because she is a great woman. And then they pass, for a moment, to their own affair and their wonderful *duettino*, so strange, so characteristic, so tartly dramatic, and just as full of deeply tender love as Juliet's for Romeo and Portia's for Bassanio.

Shakespeare's fourth acts are sometimes a vale of preparation between two peaks of exaltation. This one contains in the first scene one of the strongest things in his special kind of comedy, and in the second the best clownish scene in English. In both his touch is perfectly sure. As the final act unrolls the romantic plot, prettily if a trifle ponderously, toward its reconciling end, we are not denied a last glimpse of him who, though he wots not of it, has already been indelibly writ down an ass; while the witty lovers are as much in love as ever, and gayer and wittier than ever, in their new-found happiness. They may not please the Gaul, who needs them not, having Molière's matchless creations at his disposal; but it is clear that Shakespeare is very pleased with them. So all goes merry as a marriage bell. Nothing clouds a summer sky. The pipers strike up. Everybody dances. Of Don John we are not even to think "till tomorrow," and in romantic comedy that never comes.

AS YOU LIKE IT

Shakespeare was not an apt inventor of titles; Beaumont and Fletcher, Dekker, Jonson, and Middleton all had a superior knack. Too many of Shakespeare's neither epitomize the center of interest nor stir the imagination. "As You Like It," like "What You Will," seems to enjoin the reader to name the thing himself — call it anything you please — take it as you please. It is not a good title; but at least it arouses curiosity, and that appears to be its sole function. Mr. Shaw's guess that it was meant to convey the author's disgust at having to write romantic instead of problem comedies is probably wide of the mark. As You Like It is the closest Shakespeare comes to an English pastoral, and he is thinking more of the Warwickshire Arden [21] than of the Ardennes in northeastern France. Yet he was not one to let geography stand in his way; and so, when the plot requires her, the hungry lioness lurks there.

This play was one of four "staied" in the Stationers' Register on August 4, 1600.[22] Meres does not list it. Since Much Ado must have been produced in the winter of 1598–99, As You Like It was probably written in 1599 and certainly not later than rather early in 1600. Marlowe's posthumous Hero and Leander, completed by George Chapman, was published in 1598; from it Shakespeare quotes (III, v, 81–2):

> Dead shepherd, now I find thy saw of might,
> 'Who ever lov'd that lov'd not at first sight?'

It is likely, however, that he had long known Marlowe's part of the poem in manuscript. In this same year of 1598 two plays on Robin Hood were produced by the Admiral's Men, *The Downfall of Robert, Earle of Huntington*, by Anthony Munday, and *The Death of Robert, Earle of Huntington*, by Munday and Chettle. Perhaps it was company rivalry that turned Shakespeare's thoughts to a comedy of the greenwood.

"It was a lover and his lass" (V, iii) appeared in 1600 with a setting by the great composer Thomas Morley, in *The First Booke of Ayres. Or Little Short Songs;* but the play seems not to have been printed until the Folio of 1623. At any rate, no surviving quarto is known. Disintegrators have excavated alleged verse fossils [23] and argue that these identify a textual substratum of Shakespeare's original version, which they date in 1593. That the actor-dramatist was forever tinkering with his earlier work is extremely unlikely, and the theory that the Folio *As You Like It* is a rewriting has won little acceptance. Nor is there any reason to believe that Shakespeare did not compose the entire piece.

Its source is *Rosalynde. Euphues golden legacie* (1590), a novel by Thomas Lodge. Rosader (Orlando), oppressed by his brother Saladyne (Oliver), attacks the servants when they try to tie him up. Saladyne agrees to restore Rosader to his rightful station, but on the death of the wrestler bars the door to his brother. With a party of friends Rosader breaks it down, and they feast in the hall. He is on the point of assaulting Saladyne when Adam Spencer appeases them. Saladyne catches Rosader asleep, has him chained to a post, and spreads the news that he is mad. Adam informs Rosader of the slander and unlocks his fetters, leaving him still chained in appearance. Saladyne's guests accept his story and bait the supposed lunatic. Rosader and Adam attack them, killing some and expelling the rest. The sheriff arrives to arrest Rosader, but with Adam he escapes to the Forest of Arden. From this point Shakespeare follows Lodge with little change, except the introduction of several new characters: that small cog in the plot, the good Le Beau; Audrey, William, and Sir Oliver Martext; Jaques, of whom more hereafter; and Touch

stone, one of Shakespeare's most engaging Fools, probably
the first part he wrote for Robert Armin, whom the company
had brought in to replace Kempe. Not a great deal is known
about Armin; that he was a rare one is clear from the terms
in which Shakespeare composes for him. He had himself some
reputation as a writer. His coming was a great thing for the
poet, who at once lifts the Fool from loutish stupidity to the
plane of wise folly. Touchstone is an eccentric, but shrewd
and clever, as Jacques immediately recognizes. He is a professional, not a defective.

Shakespeare's only important further deviation from the
plot of *Rosalynde* is that he does not finish off the usurping
duke by death in battle. The tone of the play is, however,
quite different. It bubbles with merriment. Rosalind, so ar-
dently and tenderly in love, is nevertheless of all the romantic
heroines the most humorous.[24] The novel is practically humorless; and though there are love lyrics scattered through
its prose, Lodge's touch is a little heavy and his style Euphuistic.[25] On the other hand, a novelist has all the time in the
world; an Elizabethan dramatist had two hours. Considering this inexorability, the conversions at the end of the play
are not too abrupt; but Saladyne's is much less so in the
novel. Lodge's source was the pseudo-Chaucerian *Tale of
Gamelyn*, unprinted till 1721. Manuscripts must have been
fairly numerous. It is possible but unlikely that in several
minor differences from *Rosalynde* Shakespeare is following
this fourteenth-century tale.

Professor O. J. Campbell has noticed that *As You Like It*
contains in Jaques Shakespeare's comment on the efforts of
certain contemporaries, among them Jonson and more particularly Marston, to make the drama a vehicle of satire.
Nondramatic satire was enjoying a new vogue, and the turn
of the century saw several of the most gifted of the playwrights frittering away their energies in the War of the
Theatres.[26] There seems to be little personal caricature in
Shakespeare's works; and indeed his many hits at such universal foibles as feminine affectation and volubility, or extravagance in dress, masculine as well as feminine, are for the

most part good-humored, not savage. Evidently he did not
care for the direction in which his colleagues were taking
the drama; at any rate, he did not emulate them.

But Jaques is nothing if not satirical, and the question is
do we laugh at or with him? He is not the malcontent type;
compared with, say, the verbal acidity of the deposed duke
in Marston's *The Malcontent* (?1604), the crustiness of Jaques
is positively genial. Jaques is the melancholy man; and melancholy, like the Byronic pose of the next romantic outpour-
ing, was fashionable and almost expected of any young man
of sensibility. Jaques is not young; as Campbell shows, he
wears his melancholy with a difference. It is derived from
experience, a past which, like that of many intellectuals, has
imposed a rationalistic divorce upon the emotional life and
idealism; till the logical Jaques, finding himself in the brave
new world of Arden, also finds himself completely at a loss
there. His is the tragedy of the man who becomes aware in
middle life that he has lost the capacity for love and wonder.
That is the priceless thing. Life without it is death in life.
Jaques is burned out, and the lovers' raptures [27] are beyond
his wisdom's reach. So is the noble speech of the banished
Duke on the uses of adversity. Jaques is the logician in
search of Nature, a pre-1929 realist in search of America and
the Emerson he adored in boyhood. At least he retains a
certain curiosity, but he is only a thinker. At the end of the
play he is characteristically off on a new scent. "There is much
matter to be heard and learn'd" from "convertites" — from,
that is, persons who have had, or think they have had, an
overwhelming spiritual experience. His curiosity is charming;
unfortunately, some things can not be acquired at second hand.

How well men on the threshold of the new age liked this
very Elizabethan play is unknown, and so is the original
casting. That Shakespeare played Adam [28] is quite possible
but can not be substantiated. No more can a performance at
Wilton before King James in 1603.[29] *As You Like It* appears in
"A Catalogue of part of His Ma^tes^ Servants Playes as they
were formerly acted at the Blackfryers & now allowed of to
his Ma^tes^ Servants," at the Theatre Royal in Drury Lane.[30]

This document is undated but seems to belong to 1669. It affords no ground for supposing that the comedy had remained active in the pre-Wars repertory, since of the plays named in this and other lists half, including *As You Like It*, apparently remained on the shelf. The eighteenth century was well under way before the first faint glow of renascent romanticism afforded light enough to see Shakespeare's more delicate comedies by. The first to be staged for many years was *As You Like It*, in an insipid version by Charles Johnson called *Love in a Forest*, with infusions from *A Midsummer Night's Dream*, *Much Ado about Nothing*, *Richard the Second*, and *Twelfth Night*. It was acted at Drury Lane in 1723, with Colley Cibber as Jaques, who falls in love with Celia! Wrestling being a "low" sport for a gentleman, Charles and Orlando fight with rapiers. Johnson aimed, laudably enough,

> The Sce[n]e from Time and Error to restore,
> And give the Stage, from SHAKESPEAR one Play more.

Touchstone, Phebe, Corin, Audrey, William, and Sir Oliver Martext are all omitted from this version.

The original comedy was revived at Drury Lane in 1740, perhaps as Odell suggests, through the influence of Charles Macklin. For this production Thomas Arne wrote the fine settings, still familiar, of "Blow, blow, thou winter wind," and "Under the greenwood tree." Quin played Jaques; the Rosalind was Mrs. Pritchard; the Celia, Mrs. Clive. Eventually Macklin himself assumed the part of Touchstone. Once back on the boards, the play was often acted during the rest of the eighteenth century, though Garrick never appeared in it. Dora Jordan, that incomparable daughter of Thalia, as Cole calls her, was the most famous of the Rosalinds; but there were many others, among them Peg Woffington, "Perdita" Robinson (charmer of the future George IV), Mrs. Yates, and the tragedy queen Mrs. Siddons. It is difficult to imagine the overpowering Sarah in this breeches rôle; but she had essayed it in the provinces before her London triumphs, and was ill-advised enough to repeat it in the metropolis. For once she was outplayed by a rival, and she speedily abandoned Rosalind to Mrs. Jordan. Of Mrs. Siddons's performance an unkind critic alleged that a lady wept throughout, being under the impression that she was witnessing Rowe's *Jane Shore!* Barry, Henderson, and Cooke all played Jaques. In the nineteenth century there were, according to Winter, at least sixty notable revivals. J. P. Kemble acted Jaques to Charles Kemble's Orlando. Operatic versions were inescapable. For one of two staged at Covent Garden in 1824, Bishop composed the music. Mme. Vestris played Rosalind in 1825. Macready revived Shakespeare's comedy at both the great theatres — at Covent Garden in 1837, at Drury Lane in 1842. He acted Jaques. James Anderson opened his management of the latter house in 1850 with *As You Like It*. Charles Kean, who assumed the rôle of Jaques, also produced the play. Phelps took the same part at Sadler's Wells in 1857. Among the famous Rosalinds were Charlotte Cushman, Helen Faucit, Isabella Glyn, Anna Cora Mowatt, Laura Keene, Ellen Tree, Adelaide Neilson, Helena Modjeska, Mary Anderson, Mrs. Pat Campbell, and Ada Rehan. Miss Rehan played in Daly's revival, to the Orlandos of John Drew and John Craig, the Celia of Henrietta Crosman, and the Touchstone of James Lewis. Miss Crosman later took the leading rôle, as did Julia Neilson, Julia Arthur, Lily Brayton, Viola Allen, Julia Marlowe, Margaret Anglin, and Edith Evans. Max Montesole was an exquisite Touchstone when Henry Jewett produced the play in Boston in 1915. Neither Madge Kendal nor Lily Langtry was particularly successful as Rosalind. No doubt Ellen Terry would have eclipsed everyone. She never got the chance; Irving did not revive this comedy. Among the Orlandos were Forbes-Robertson, Alexander, and Henry Ainley. Asche, Holloway, and Playfair acted Jaques. The present century has seen many admirable productions, not least the unpretentious English film starring Elisabeth Bergner, with Laurence Olivier as Orlando. There is every prospect that the popularity of this fresh and dainty play will continue — as long as men sicken of city streets and dream, in one fashion or another, of an Arden woodland, where Nature is kind to those who trust her, and Charity and Love find out the way.

TWELFTH NIGHT, OR WHAT YOU WILL

This much loved comedy, as merry as the holiday night it is named for, is relatively free from vexatious problems. You may even write your own title, if you don't like the author's: call it what you will. Its text is not one of the battlegrounds; the sole basis is the First Folio, which is particularly good for this play. The date, it is true, can not be fixed with certainty. The writing was finished before February 2, 1602, when John Manningham of the Middle Temple notes in his *Diary:*

At our feast wee had a play called 'Twelue Night, or What You Will,' much like the Commedy of Errores, or Menechmi in Plautus, but most like and neere to that in Italian called *Inganni*.[31] A good practise [i.e., trick] in it to make the Steward beleeve his Lady widdowe was in love with him, by counterfeyting a letter as from his Lady in generall termes, telling him what shee liked best in him, and prescribing his gesture in smiling, his apparaile, &c., and then when he came to practise making him beleeue they tooke him to be mad.

Evidently the piece was new to Manningham, but his reference provides only the later limit of composition. *Twelfth Night* is not mentioned by Meres in 1598, presumptive but not conclusive evidence for a subsequent date. Since *Much Ado* was pretty clearly written in the fall or winter of 1598–99 and *As You Like It* in '99 or early in 1600, there was hardly time for *Twelfth Night*, which has obvious affinities of style and tone with the latter, before 1600. But 1601, and even early in 1602, are possibilities. Virginio Orsini, Duke of Bracciano, was in London in the winter of 1600–1601; possibly the visit of this Italian grandee suggested the name of Shakespeare's Dalmatian duke.[32] The snatches of song in II, iii, 110–21 are inspired by the lyric "Farewell deare loue since thou wilt needs be gone" in Robert Jones's *The First Booke of Songes or Ayres*, printed in 1600. Presumably the "new map with the augmentation of the Indies" (III, ii, 85) is the one made about 1598–99 by Emerie Molyneux. About 1600–1601 is a reasonable date for *Twelfth Night*.[33]

In *Riche his Farewell to Militarie profession* (1581), a tale "Of Apolonius and Silla" is told by Barnabe Riche. Silla (Viola) falls in love with Duke Apolonius (Orsino) of Constantinople, when he visits her father's court at Cyprus; but he is indifferent. Determined to win him, she follows him to Constantinople. She is escorted by the servant Pedro, who passes as her brother Silvio (Sebastian). The master of the ship tries to force his attentions on her, and she considers suicide. This expedient proves unnecessary, for the ship is wrecked. Separated from Pedro, she gets ashore on a chest full of money and the captain's clothes. As Silvio she enters the Duke's service and in his behalf woos the young widow Julina (Olivia), who falls in love with her. Supposing that his sister has eloped with Pedro, Silvio goes in search of her. He reaches Constantinople, where Julina sees him and, such is their resemblance, takes him for Silla. Reproached for his coldness, he accepts the situation; but after spending one night with Julina, he sets out again. To the Duke's importunities Julina, now pregnant, replies that she is betrothed. Hearing that she has received Silvio, the Duke assumes that his own servant is responsible for his rejection and imprisons Silla, who still maintains her disguise as Silvio. Julina pleads for the prisoner, her betrothed as she supposes. The Duke threatens Silla with his rapier, insisting on fulfillment of the obligation to Julina. To the latter Silla now reveals her identity and also her amorous design in leaving home. Julina informs the Duke, who has an immediate change of heart. He marries Silla, and Julina is disconsolate. The story of Silla's adventures is widely circulated. When Silvio hears it he returns to Constantinople. Everything is clear at last, and he marries the widow.

Riche's narrative is a free adaptation, either directly or through Belleforest's *Histoires Tragiques*, of the thirty-sixth story in Part II of Bandello's *Novelle*. Bandello seems to have derived it from *Gl'Ingannati*, a Sienese comedy of about 1531, perhaps by Alessandro Piccolomini, certainly by some member of the academy of the Intronati. In a Latin adaptation entitled *Lælia* it was acted at Queens' College, Cambridge, in 1595. Shakespeare's source is Riche's version; but he also repeats situations he had used in earlier plays, especially *The Two Gentlemen of Verona*, whose Julia, though her predicament is the same, is very inferior to Viola. The subplot of Olivia's household and the gulling of Malvolio appears to be his own invention.

The original cast can only be conjectured; but doubtless Armin played the gay rôle of Feste and sang, besides his mocking verses about the old Vice, the three exquisite lyrics, "O mistress mine," "Come away, come away, death," and "When that I was and a little tiny boy." Feste is the most elegant of the Fools, and he speaks only the truth when he says he wears not motley in his brain. He is a professional, earning his subsistence in the Lady Olivia's service by a life of impersonation. He is as sane as Tom Killigrew, dramatist and theatrical patentee, who held the formal appointment of jester to Charles II and on several occasions took full advantage of it. As usual, evidence bearing on the play's early vogue is slight, but one can hardly suppose it was not received with enthusiasm. There were court revivals in 1618 and 1623, the latter recorded under the title *Malvolio*. A squinting construction by Leonard Digges in 1640 points to continued popularity:

> let but *Beatrice*
> And *Benedicke* be seene, loe in a trice
> The Cockpit Galleries, Boxes, all are full
> To heare *Maluoglio* that crosse garter'd Gull.

When the theatres reopened under Charles II the play was speedily revived by D'avenant. It was his second Shakespearean venture, *Hamlet* being the first. Very likely his choice of *Twelfth Night* was also dictated by its success on the pre-Wars stage. The youthful Betterton, who had first played the Dane a month before, now showed his versatility in the rôle of Sir Toby. The Sir Andrew was Henry Harris, second man of the Duke's Company. The Malvolio was Thomas Lovel, a minor actor; and Feste, unhappily, was entrusted to Cave Underhill, who was to have a long career as an exponent of loutish parts. The only other character mentioned by John Downes, whose *Roscius Anglicanus* is our authority for this revival, is Olivia, played by Ann Gibbs. The acting text has not survived. Downes says the play was a "mighty Success," and the references of Pepys show it held the stage. He saw it at least three times and never liked it: "a silly play, and not related at all to the name or day." Its popularity, coupled with Downes's failure to list the Viola, Orsino, Sebastian, and Antonio, points to its being a violently altered version, with the romantic plot either omitted or greatly reduced. The age was indifferent to romantic charm, while the foolery of the knights and the ridicule of the precise Malvolio were well within the scope of the Restoration audience.

A stupid adaptation by William Burnaby,[34] *Love Betray'd; or, The Agreable Disappointment*, was staged at Lincoln's Inn Fields in 1703. It was revived at least once, in 1705. Shakespeare's comedy seems to have been shelved till 1741, when it was produced at Drury Lane with Macklin as Malvolio, Harry Woodward, afterwards among the most famous of light comedians, as Sir Andrew, Hannah Pritchard as Viola, and Kitty Clive as Olivia. Since then it has held the stage, though it is not a vehicle for a star. When one part is played up at the expense of the rest, distortion results, as in E. H. Sothern's interesting but sentimentalized Malvolio. This rôle is no better than Feste, Sir Toby, or Viola; while Orsino, Sir Andrew, Olivia, and Maria are all attractive secondary parts. *Twelfth Night* was acted throughout the age of Garrick, but the great little man did not cast himself in it. Famous Violas were, besides Mrs. Pritchard, Peg Woffington, Dora Jordan, Mrs. Yates, and Ann (Mrs. Spranger) Barry. Henderson and J. P. Kemble played Malvolio. In 1820 the insatiable adapter Frederic Reynolds made a pseudo-opera out of *Twelfth Night*. With music by Bishop, it had a good run. Charlotte and Susan Cushman appeared as Viola and Olivia in 1846. Two years later Mrs. Charles Kean (as Ellen Tree she had long played the rôle) scored a hit as Viola in a production by her husband, who revived the play again in their first repertory season (1850) at the Princess's. Another charming Viola was Adelaide Neilson. A notable Malvolio was Phelps. In 1865 Kate Terry doubled the rôles of Viola and Sebastian, an expedient not unknown in our day. J. B. Buckstone was her Sir Andrew. Irving also acted Malvolio, in 1884, to Ellen Terry's Viola; but this revival made little impression. Daly's was more successful; the version was a bad one, but Ada Rehan, the Viola of his final production of *Twelfth Night* (1893–94), captivated both New York and London. James Lewis played Sir Toby. Another perversion of the play was used by W. H. Crane and Stuart Robson when they starred as the two knights in New York in 1881. Also in the United States, Helena Modjeska played Viola to enraptured audiences. Julia Marlowe triumphed in this breeches part. So did Viola Allen, in 1904; her Orsino was John Craig. Other Violas of the American stage were Edith Wynne Matthison, Annie Russell, Margaret Anglin, and Jane Cowl. Miss Anglin's production was graced by the admirable impressionistic scenery of Livingston Platt. Her Feste was Max Montesole. If Armin played the rôle as well as he, Shakespeare must have been delighted. Benson and Tree (both acted Malvolio, the latter to his daughter's Viola) staged fine revivals, in 1900 and 1901; since their day there have been many. Granville-Barker's was presented in 1912, with Ainley as Malvolio, Leon Quartermaine as Sir Andrew, and Lillah McCarthy as Viola. In 1916 Ben Greet played Malvolio in the production of Lilian Baylis at the Old Vic. More recently, Baliol Holloway made a strong impression in the same rôle. Certainly the unrealistic theme has been no barrier to modern liking.

As usual, the play's core is a romantic plot, not so wild as some, but sufficiently improbable. And, as usual, Shakespeare invests its characters with such humanity that we accept it. The love story of Viola and Orsino is handled with the utmost delicacy. It is she who most attracts us, and she ranks next to Portia and Beatrice among the heroines of the comedies — unless you like her and Rosalind better. Neither Viola nor Rosalind is quite the nobly enchanting woman; but Viola burns with a flame so intense and so pure, while Orsino is so dulled by masculine obtuseness, that, as the situation between them threatens to duplicate the story of the maid whose history was a blank because she never told her love, Viola's suffering suggests what countless women have had to endure with head held high, and their little representative in doublet and hose makes a powerful demand on our sympathy. Yet how deliciously comic the scene is, too! Orsino is so near the great prize — and so far. We would call out to him, as Leonardo wished to exclaim to all men, "Open your eyes!" And Viola, true to her code but true also to her heart, turns (II, iv, 82 ff.) from humor to stabbing pathos and back again with a tact so exquisite, and so sure a finger on the pulse of the audience, that this passage of less than fifty lines is of itself enough to knock into the absurdest of cocked hats the neoclassic rule prescribing the "strict separation" of tragedy and comedy.

Any dramatic treatment of Riche's story required on the Elizabethan public stage a subplot that at the very least might serve to distract occasionally from the main narrative and allow it to elapse with adequate speed. It was a happy thought to create a household of eccentrics, not around the Duke, who is to be lapped in flowers and music, but at Olivia's, whither our masquerading heroine must proceed in line of duty and get involved with them. Merriment is the order of the day there, and of the night as well — oddly enough, since Olivia secludes herself to grieve. But Shakespeare makes it all plausible, and Sir Toby is not one to brood over anything. He is the most admirable of sots because he is the merriest, and Sir Andrew the best of simpletons because he makes such an effort to be merry. Maria and Fabian are the sprightliest attachés that ever livened up a house of mourning. And Feste is the very essence of foolery — a man who is wise enough to accept the fact that this is the direction his genius takes, and to go along with it. "God give them wisdom that have it; and those that are fools, let them use their talents." As that profound thinker Quinapalus pertinently remarks, "Better a witty fool than a foolish wit." How much better, Feste proceeds to demonstrate — with

perfect lucidity. For no sooner has he established himself
with the audience (I, v) as the cleverest of Fools, than Malvolio comes on. "Sometimes he is a kind of Puritan." Shakespeare does not directly indict the sect through the cross-
gartered one, but it becomes clear at once that Malvolio is
definitely against cakes and ale. He is against Fools, too, and
"these wise men that crow so" at them — like some outraged contemporary looking down his nose at you and me,
my dear reader, because we are fond of Chaplin, Ed Wynn,
W. C. Fields, or the brethren Marx, or Feste. Malvolio,
totally without the saving grace, damns himself by condemning it. He is sick of self-love, like a "humors" character
out of Ben Jonson.[35] In his conceit he sets himself up against
the world's gaiety in general, and the fun at Olivia's in particular. Needless to say, gaiety wins — at any rate, in a romantic
comedy it does.

The play ends with love triumphant and joy not much
confined by the presence of Orsino and Olivia. Everyone leaves
the stage except Feste, and then he sings the plaintive little
song which gently wafts the audience back from the Illyrian
shore: — When I was a child no one minded my capers, but
maturity entailed a sobering-off process. Matrimony proved
more realistic than romantic, and even in old age I found
I still got drunk when I took too much. It is an old world
and is not going to suspend its inexorable laws for the likes
of you and me. But never mind, the play is over. Come again.
We aim to please. — And Feste prances out, tossing off the
world's burden with a "that's all one." But in real life the
cakes and ale were put away, the king's crown went down,
the stage itself went down, the Puritans won. Feste's song is
not, of course, a prophecy; it is a reminder, and a transition
from a world of faëry to the marshy Bankside lane outside
the door of the Globe. For us it is a clue to what the Master
of Ceremonies, the Feste of Festes, must himself have been
thinking. It is the epilogue to the last and greatest of his
joyous romantic comedies. He is to write more comedies, but
very different ones, with a great deal in them that is far from
joyous. And he had already set his feet, or was about to

set them, on the *via dolorosa* of supreme and heart-shaking tragedy.

THE MERRY WIVES OF WINDSOR

Introducing the Folio of 1623, Heminge and Condell fail to disclose the principle on which the plays are arranged. Yet the order must have been carefully considered. Comedies first, for the book was designed to sell. Not yet had publishing separated from the retail book trade. A Jacobean buyer leafed through the volumes at a stationer's stall, chose what appealed to him, bought the sheets, and had them bound in accordance with his taste and purse. The Folio leads off with *The Tempest,* and the reasons seem clear. It was the most recent of the plays wholly written by Shakespeare, it was greatly liked, it had not been printed before, and it belonged to the new popular genre of dramatic romance. If this guess is right, it seemed desirable to display in the opening pages samples of all of Shakespeare's kinds of comedy. For the second selection not popularity but novelty was decisive. *The Two Gentlemen of Verona* had probably long before been dropped from the repertory, and it too had never been printed. The third play is *The Merry Wives;* and I take it the publisher placed this comedy well forward for the same reason that dictates its inclusion in this chapter — because Falstaff is in it. *Measure for Measure* stands next, illustrating another comic department; on the whole it is the strongest of the more realistic comedies. Then come the Latinate farce of *The Comedy of Errors,* the great romantic comedy of *Much Ado,* the unique *Love's Labour's Lost,* and *A Midsummer Night's Dream,* also unique. The six plays which follow lump the rest of the romantic comedies, another early farce, another realistic comedy, another dramatic romance. The chronicle plays follow historical chronology, but the arrangement of the tragedies at least begins on the same principle as the comedies. The position of *Troilus and Cressida* is, as we shall see, fortuitous. *Coriolanus* was intended to lead, since it was the latest of the completed tragedies. Immediately after it, stands the earliest of them, *Titus Andronicus.* Next comes the ever-popular love

tragedy of *Romeo and Juliet*. There my theory stops; for there
is no discernible principle, nor any need of one, in the order
of the remaining plays.

For *The Merry Wives* the Folio provides the authoritative
text. The first edition, in 1602, is a Bad quarto,[36] piratical
and corrupt. It was entered in the Stationers' Register on
January 18, 1602, as "An excellent and pleasant conceited
commedie of Sir John ffaulstof and the merry wyves of Winde-
sor." The thief depended on his memory, which completely
failed him for several scenes and for many passages in others.
He transposes speeches and even scenes, brings in lines from
other dramas, most notably from *Henry the Fourth*, and generally plays hob with style and sense. Probably, as Dr. Greg
has shown, this traitor had acted the Host, whose part, while
not perfect, agrees more closely than the rest with the Folio
text.

The Quarto's stage directions are fuller than the Folio's,
where exits are noted only at the ends of scenes and, with a
single exception, each scene is headed by a list of all the
characters appearing in it. This last peculiarity may be a
blundering attempt, certainly not the author's, at the neoclassical method of scene division.[37] It was Jonson's regular
practice. Some think these features indicate the assembly of
the Folio text from the various players' parts with the aid
of a plat, but this theory is not much favored now. The
Quarto's stage directions reflect the reporter's imperfect memory of what he had seen. A good deal has been made, as
evidence for rewriting, of a discrepancy in the domestic arrangements of Dr. Caius. In the Folio he has a large room
with a smaller one, a "Closset," behind it. This establishment becomes in the Quarto a "Counting-house" with a
"stall." But the difference proves nothing about an alleged
earlier form of the play. The stage may have been set that way,
or the reporter may be mixed up. Among the scenes omitted
by the Quarto is William's Latin lesson, which Chambers
thinks was either completely beyond the thief's powers or
intended only for court performance "where it would please
Elizabeth's pedantry." Ford's pseudonym in the Quarto is

the appropriate one of "Brooke," which the Folio alters to
"Broome," no doubt in deference to the Brooke family and
the memory of the late Lord Chamberlain, who had died on
March 5, 1597.[38]

That the Folio reproduces the text precisely as it left Shakespeare's desk is not likely, but that it represents a radical
revision of an earlier version is even less likely. As it stands,
its allusions to an off-stage horse-stealing episode (IV, iii,
v, vi) are somewhat sketchy. Alleging that they are to meet
at court a nonexistent German Duke, three Germans who
have been living for a week at the Garter Inn trick the Host
into letting them make off with three of his horses. Bardolph,
who rides behind one of these rogues, evidently to bring back
the nags, is pitched off near Eton. It is possible, as Professor
Wilson contends, that more was made of this affair when the
play was first acted. The conclusion that *The Merry Wives* was
originally a bourgeois drama imitative of Italian intrigue
comedy has not been generally adopted. According to this
theory, originally set forth by Fleay, "the gelyous comodey"
marked "ne" by Henslowe on January 5, 1593, is the earliest
version of *The Merry Wives*.[39] Unhappily, our knowledge of
this piece is confined to Henslowe's record. Professor Wilson
thinks the deceived lover was originally not Falstaff but a
kind of "Joseph Surface amorist," with a Euphuistic tongue,
and that a series of abridgments and revisions intervened between its pristine form and its metamorphosed appearance as
The Merry Wives. It is true that Falstaff sometimes speaks
(e.g., II, ii, 247-50) in a glib conventional idiom that lacks
his usual flavor. But hasty composition is more likely to be
responsible than that these speeches, which after all are very
few, are survivals from a non-Shakespearean play.

The thief's precise quotation, in the Quarto (sig. F2^r), of
the line "What is the reason that you use me thus?" from
Hamlet (V, i, 312), has been taken to indicate 1600-1601 as
the earlier limit for the date of *The Merry Wives*, since *Hamlet*
was probably produced then. Yet the line may also have
occurred, in precisely this form, in the pre-Shakespearean
Hamlet; and (as Kittredge observes) the expression is common-

place, anyway. There is nothing whatever to indicate where the action of the comedy is supposed to cut into Falstaff's story as we have it in *Henry the Fourth* and *Henry the Fifth*. The plot is therefore no help in determining the play's date. Its registration in 1602 gives us the later limit. It is not mentioned by Meres in 1598. It ought to be later than *Henry the Fourth*, since Nym now has his corporal's stripes, as in *Henry the Fifth*. That he would be promoted for the French war is likelier. With *Henry the Fifth* definitely in Shakespeare's mind when he wrote *Part 2* of its predecessor, it seems probable that he would go straight on with King Harry before turning aside to show Falstaff without him. Some have thought that after composing the moving scene in which the old reprobate's death is narrated,[40] the dramatist could not have brought himself to write another play, a farcical one, about him. It seems probable that the creative force which went under the name of William Shakespeare was made of sterner stuff. Falstaff continued to play the "roaring boy" on Gadshill long after Quickly heard him cry out "God, God, God!" three or four times. There is as much against that as against his travels in the buck-basket. No hint in *The Merry Wives* suggests that he is out of the King's favor. Indeed his appearance so near Windsor Castle is evidence to the contrary; and it is likely enough that Shakespeare, having broken his promise and disappointed the Falstaff fans by keeping him out of *Henry the Fifth*, yielded to a general as well as a royal demand and served him up in a play of his own.

For this is Falstaff's play, and he is the same Falstaff, though there is nothing in it to suggest that he was ever Oldcastle.[41] In the dedicatory epistle to his adaptation, *The Comical Gallant* (1702), the well-known critic John Dennis asserts that the original "pleas'd one of the greatest Queens that ever was in the World. . . . This Comedy was written at her Command, and by her direction, and she was so eager to see it Acted, that she commanded it to be finished in fourteen days." These statements appear more than a century after the fact, but we have no reason to suppose Dennis was inventing. Such, apparently, was the current tradition, which may have reached him through D'avenant and Dryden. It squares well enough with some internal evidence of hasty composition. That the play is largely in prose may be significant. Only seven years later, Rowe is either writing very loosely or tapping the same tradition when he says that Elizabeth "was so well pleas'd with that admirable Character of *Falstaff*, in the two Parts of *Henry* the Fourth, that she commanded him to continue it for one Play more, and to shew him in Love." It does not tax the powers of credulity to believe that Elizabeth wanted to see Falstaff again — probably everyone did. And she was not one to let her wishes languish unexpressed.

But, we are told, this is not the same Falstaff — it is not Falstaff at all: in *Henry the Fourth* he always comes out on top; here, he is everybody's dupe. But in *Henry the Fourth* he does not come out on top at the end, though the contrast is in general just. There is, however, this unimpeachable bond of identity — he is still genial, still lovable in his rascality. Even at Herne's Oak, and while he is yet black and blue from the fairy pinches, his whimsical acceptance of his discomfiture is simply charming. Not even a Welsh preacher can talk him down; Falstaff has the last word, and a good one, with the honest busybody Sir Hugh. Page invites him to a posset; and if Ford is still waspish, he is soon shown up for as big a fool as anyone, comes off his high horse, and approves the proposal to "laugh this sport o'er by a country fire."

Falstaff is bound to come a cropper in this play. The theme invites it, and perhaps the motif of the biter bit was inevitable. Whether or not at the dictation of the Virgin Queen, Shakespeare is to display the fat knight in a comedy of amorous intrigue and jealousy. Now, obviously it will not do to write another romantic comedy. Not even Shakespeare can create a Forest of Arden or vast Illyrian shore that will give Falstaff room enough to play Orlando or Orsino. The piece, then, is to be an intrigue comedy. In Malvolio, Shakespeare had already studied a humor in Jonson's best manner. Ford is the jealous man, like Jonson's Kitely in *Every Man in his Humor*.

he is not the normal man made jealous, like Othello, who is much more typical of Shakespeare's way of drawing character. Falstaff in "love" is fated to be ridiculous. Of course Shakespeare does not really try to convince us he is in love; Ford's purse is as strong a magnet as the merry matrons' charms. The fun comes, as it does in *Henry the Fourth*, from the discrepancy between Falstaff's claims and his performances, and his merry way of acknowledging it. Considering Ford's folly and the ability of the ladies to take care of themselves, Falstaff's objects, seduction and swindling, can shock only those for whom art as well as life is overwhelmingly real and unvaryingly earnest. Sir Hugh is such an one, and he retains our respect to the end. What Falstaff retains is even better than that.

No source of Shakespeare's plot is known or needed, though the wanton wife who hides a successful lover and the chaste wife who plays a trick on her would-be corrupter are the heroines of very old tales. Concealment, or even elopement from a cruel father, in tubs or laundry (or bread) baskets was nothing new in either literature or life.

While this play is more like Jonson's humors comedies than is usual with Shakespeare, the satirical note is, even here, scarcely audible. Satire and caricature were not Shakespeare's line, as his contemporaries (if not all his commentators) well knew. On this point John Davies of Hereford is explicit:

> Some others raile; but, raile as they thinke fit,
> Thou hast no rayling, but, a raigning Wit.

What an eye, none the less, Shakespeare had for human foibles, and what an engaging way of exploiting them without malice! *The Merry Wives* is genially Jonsonian, not only in the humors of Ford and Nym, but also in Dr. Caius, exemplar of the comic Frenchman who for centuries has been rolling them in Britannia's aisles, and in Slender, nonpareil of ninnies. Thy rôle, Cousin, is too like thy name; by these gloves, thou deservest five acts all thine own. For thou art one of those minor stars of Shakespeare more refulgent than the suns of other writers.

Some think topical references play a large part in the entertainment. That a London audience would be expected to identify Justice Shallow as Sir Thomas Lucy, Shakespeare's old enemy, if that is what he was, is incredible.[42] That it could identify, or that Shakespeare could have intended, the countryman come to court as Gardiner, the Bankside J. P.,[43] is even less credible. Nym is certainly not a satirical portrait of Jonson, though his obsession with humors raises repeated laughs at a new fad, not merely in Jonson's plays but everywhere.[44]

There is probably a topical hit in the Quarto's version of a passage which appears as follows in the Folio (IV, v, 77–81):

Haue a care of your entertainments: there is a friend of mine come to Towne, tels mee there is three Cozen-Iermans, that has cozend all the *Hosts* of *Readins*, of *Maidenhead;* of *Cole-brooke*, of horses and money.

Corrupt as it is, the Quarto seems to preserve the original form of a joke which in the Folio's "cousin-germans" has dwindled into a mere pun and a stale one at that:

Now my Host, I would desire you looke you now,
To haue a care of your entertainments,
For there is three sorts of cosen garmombles,
Is cosen all the Host of Maidenhead & Readings.

In 1592 Frederick, Count of Mömpelgart, who succeeded in the following year to the ducal throne of Württemberg, visited England and was received by the Queen at Reading. It has been alleged that he had some trouble about posthorses; but there seems to be no evidence that he did, though he accepted, as was his due, a warrant for their use gratis. Mömpelgart was eager to receive the greatly prized honor of the Garter, and afterwards wrote the Queen from Germany about it. She put him off with a plea that the number of the Order was fixed and that others had prior claims on vacancies. In 1595 he sent an envoy, J. J. Breuning von Buchenbach, to press his request. Breuning, who was also commissioned to buy horses, had some difficulties with English dealers. The

Duke was at last elected, on April 23, 1597; but the costly insignia were not sent over to him. His pursuit, first of election, and then of the trinkets betokening it, was too anxious to be entirely dignified. In 1598 he dispatched an embassy to thank the Queen for admission to the Order; he protested in 1599 that the insignia had not been forthcoming; in 1600 he sent a third mission to demand them. His name may have become a standing joke, at any rate in court circles; it was apparently good for a laugh when Shakespeare wrote *The Merry Wives*. Investiture was not, as a matter of fact, granted till the first year of James. Elizabeth called the German "our cousin Mömpelgart," and that the Quarto's "cosen garmombles" is a punning reference is generally agreed. "Garmombles" means "confusion." Nothing in the play, however, suggests that the Duke had any connection with the horse thieves. That was merely their story, and there is no valid argument in the business for advancing the date of *The Merry Wives*.

It is likely enough that the first performance was at court. Windsor Castle would have been an appropriate place for it, and the Queen was there in the summer of 1601. There is a complimentary reference (V, v, 65 ff.) to the Order and its famous motto. But no payment for a play is recorded, and speculation is useless. That Falstaff carried the comedy to success in the public theatre can not be doubted, but the only early performances recorded are court revivals in 1604 and 1638.[45] It was produced by Killigrew's company soon after the theatres reopened in 1660. While Pepys disliked it, and it failed to become one of the Theatre Royal's stand-bys, it was acted fairly often. It lacks the delicate charm which the Restoration found cloying in the romantic comedies. Dennis's *The Comical Gallant: or The Amours of Sir John Falstaffe*, an abominable vulgarization, was acted at Drury Lane in 1702. It deservedly failed. Shakespeare's play was revived about three years later, and again at Lincoln's Inn Fields with Quin as Falstaff. He played the rôle long and well, and the comedy has held the stage ever since. Garrick did not act in *The Merry Wives*; but during his reign at Drury several of the best players appeared in it, among them Woodward as Slender and Hannah Pritchard and Fanny Abington as Mrs. Ford. Henderson was a capital Falstaff. J. P. Kemble acted Ford to Cooke's Falstaff in 1804. Twenty years later the play fell, as was inevitable, into the hands of Reynolds, who made another of his pseudo-operas; the music was composed by Bishop. With Mme. Vestris as Mrs. Page, this was the most successful of all their Shakespearean ventures. Jointly with Charles Mathews, however, Vestris staged a fairly faithful version in 1839, though there was still too much of Bishop's music. To Charles Kean in 1851 goes the honor of freeing the play from its operatic flourishes. In the same year the distinguished American Falstaff, J. H. Hackett, showed London his very successful production; he had already acted the rôle for twenty years. At the Gaiety Theatre in the Christmas season of 1874, burlesque was suspended in favor of an elaborate revival of *The Merry Wives* with Phelps as Falstaff and music by Arthur Sullivan. Forbes-Robertson, then a beginner, was the Fenton. Augustin Daly produced the play three times. Among his comedians were Fanny Davenport and Ada Rehan as Mrs. Ford, John Drew as Ford, Otis Skinner and John Craig as Page, and Charles Fisher as Falstaff. Other notable American Falstaffs were William Evans Burton and W. H. Crane. Tree's first production of Shakespeare was *The Merry Wives* in 1889. He staged it afresh in 1902 with Madge Kendal and Ellen Terry (Mrs. Page) in the title rôles. When he brought it to New York in 1916, Edith Wynne Matthison and Henrietta Crosman played them. James K. Hackett produced the comedy in the same year, with Thomas A. Wise as Falstaff and Viola Allen and Miss Crosman as the merry wives.

That the present century has seen so much more of Falstaff in this play than in *Henry the Fourth* can only be deplored. For *The Merry Wives* is not among Shakespeare's greatest comedies if, as I hope we do, we want poetry from him, even in comedy. Yet in few humors plays is there a more amusing collection of oddities and whimsies. In an excellent American revival the late Minnie Maddern Fiske shocked some of the unco' guid when, to employ the quaint terminology of the English, she cocked a deliberate snook at her admirable associate Otis Skinner in the rôle of Falstaff. It was a high-spirited gesture for the lady dean of our stage, but it was quite in the right key. For, above all, *The Merry Wives* has the inestimable merit of gaiety. Shakespeare was never to pluck that string straight through a whole play again.

Chapter 8

REALISTIC COMEDIES

THE TRAGEDY OF TROILUS AND CRESSIDA

Thus it is entitled in the Folio of 1623, but the Quarto calls it a history, not a tragedy. By the threefold division it must be reckoned a comedy,[1] but fundamentally distinct from the sort of thing we have just been considering. It belongs in a group for which no satisfactory title has been invented. "Problem comedies" some have called them, yet they are not thesis plays. "Gloomy comedies" will hardly do for *All's Well*. "Bitter comedies" implies a contrast between them and the sweetness of the three great romantic comedies, but it seems unlikely that *All's Well* tasted bitter to the Elizabethans. "Realistic comedies" is open to the objections that they long antedate the rise of realism in the current sense, that they are, in fact, highly romantic, and that they do not present a picture of contemporary English life. Yet they all show, as their great predecessors do not, the influence of the realistic direction which Jonson had given to comedy. He was speedily followed by Middleton; and even a natural Elizabethan like Dekker soon sheered away, as a Jacobean, from the sunlit isles of pure romance. With Dekker, the new mode flowered in a masterpiece, *The Honest Whore*, which takes him far beyond the gay fake realism of *The Sho[e]makers['] Holiday*.

In Shakespeare the result is less happy. He is at his best when he is most poetic and most idealistic, since in him the ideal is never divorced from the humane and he abhorred an unillustrated abstraction as much as nature abhors a vacuum. The most damaging difference between the three realistic comedies and their predecessors is not that the plots, characters, or ideas of the three are either feeble or sordid, but that they lack, for the most part, the life-blood of great drama — poetry. If Shakespeare had been able to transfuse it into any one of them, he might like Dekker have scored his greatest comic triumph. Even as it stands, *Measure for Measure* is almost a great play — it is thoughtful, strong, and full of humanity. All it lacks is poetry, which Shakespeare may have been unable to supply because he was at the same time assaulting the supreme heights of tragedy and was unwilling or unable to divert the main strength of his resources to operations on a minor front. Or it may be that he wrote these comedies to supply his company with something in the popular realistic vein, could not put his heart into them, and never felt quite at home in them.

The new group is not a series of studies; these are not comedies of ideas; the core is still romance. But the old gaiety has vanished. The unquestioning assumption of the golden lads and girls that life was made for love is replaced by a troubled attitude toward sex. The poet seems less confident than formerly that our emotions and instincts are on the whole pretty decent. Of itself this is proof neither of moral decay nor of professional collapse, and too much should not be made of the change. Nothing biographical explains it or can be laid to it. We must, however, even at the risk of being dubbed reactionary, admit the possibility of some connection here between life and literature. Guesses like the following are only guesses, but an unsupported conjecture may chance to be right.

At the height of his passion Troilus expresses a deep-seated mistrust of woman's sincerity and faith.

"O that I thought it could be in a woman —
As, if it can, I will presume in you —
To feed for a[y]e her lamp and flames of love;
To keep her constancy in plight and youth,
Outliving beauty's outward with a mind
That doth renew swifter than blood [i.e., passion] decays."

In the mouth of Ulysses or any other character . . . such a sentiment would not surprise: coming from Troilus, the passionate lover, it exercises a curiously barren effect, reducing his dramatic vitality, for such conviction of disillusionment is hardly natural in a young and inexperienced lover. The general and deeper truth of poetry here seems suddenly to have given way before the intrusion of some strong personal feeling or experience of the poet, bitterly realized in himself or vividly expressed in the fortune of a friend.[2]

It may be so. On the other hand, this speech is quite as likely to be one of Shakespeare's many sacrifices of consistency in the interest of dramatic effectiveness. It may be simple foreboding, to prepare the audience. It may be intended merely to heighten the contrast between Cressida's professions and her conduct. Against the biographical explanation is the poet's simultaneous work in other genres. It is possible that the realistic comedies overlap the great romantic ones. They certainly run side by side with tragedies.

There is, none the less, a different tone in these three comedies. It is not a question of new ideas; the same ideas recur in the tragedies. There they smite us with a realistic force far more penetrating because impelled by poetry. Lear on the essential nature of man (III, iv) is bitter but sublime. Achilles on a similar theme (III, iii) is only bitter. The conclusion seems reasonable that as Elizabeth's reign drew toward its end Shakespeare was subject to the same urge as Jonson and Marston, though he did not respond so powerfully. The close of an epoch also brought him face to face with middle age, and an Elizabethan felt a great deal older at forty than we do. Evidently Shakespeare had things he wanted to say, things that could not be said in romantic comedy without shattering its fragile charm. Not that he writes any play in order to expound his views. But views he had; and, his facility in expression being what it was, they were bound to get expressed. In the four great tragedies he achieves his perfect medium, but he often says the same things in these comedies. Perhaps he thought at first that he was going on with the same rich vein he had been following since *The Merchant of Venice*, only cutting deeper. A man can be a very great genius and remain quite at sea concerning the relative merits of his works. To him they are all parts of the grand design at which he labors, fragments perhaps, but authentic fragments, of the thought he is trying to utter. It is your minor artist who coolly reads over what he has written and with unerring judgment consigns most of it to the only flame he knows. That is why a minor poet's books are often more even in their excellence, such as it is, than a major's. There is no mystery about the appearance, at the height of Shakespeare's powers, of a number of inferior works. It is merely another indication, though of course not sufficient in itself, of the existence of a first-rate creative force, in this case working under external pressure as well as the thrust of its own genius.

Troilus and Cressida was entered in the Stationers' Register on February 7, 1603, "as yt is acted by my lord Chamberlens Men." Its publication was delayed till 1609, when, after re-entry in the Register, two issues [3] of the first edition appeared in quarto. The first issue professes to print the play "As it was acted by the Kings Maiesties seruants at the Globe." The second omits this claim, adds to the title "Excellently expressing the beginning of their loues, with the conceited wooing of Pandarus Prince of Licia," and includes an anonymous preface by "A neuer writer, to an euer reader": "Newes. Eternall reader, you haue heere a new play, neuer stal'd with the Stage, neuer clapper-clawd with the palmes of the vulger, and yet passing full of the palme comicall." [4] Probably, then, this play, if it had been acted at all, had seen only private performance.[5] The precise relation of the Folio text to the Quarto is uncertain. Both are good, though each omits a few lines and there are many variants. On the whole the Quarto seems somewhat more authoritative. Two copies of the First Folio have survived with a cancelled leaf bound in by mistake. On its *recto* is printed the last page of *Romeo and Juliet;* on the *verso, Troilus and Cressida* begins. Evidently the play's place in the Folio is not the one originally contemplated. Pollard suggests that some difficulty in obtaining publishing rights from the owner of the Quarto may have been responsible. Probably *Troilus and Cressida*, which was to have come next after *Romeo and Juliet*, was withdrawn from the project. It was finally inserted, virtually without pagination and very likely at the last moment, between the histories and the tragedies.

As for the date of composition, the registration in 1603 gives us one limit, but the earlier is quite uncertain. An allusion in the prologue (lines 22–24) to another, Jonson's armed and arrogant one to *Poetaster* (probably produced in the spring of 1601), is useless, for the *Troilus and Cressida* prologue may easily be later than the play. It does not appear in the Quarto. The tone of this comedy indicates a date after *Twelfth Night* and *The Merry Wives*, that is, about 1601–1602. But that is not proof. Late in 1600 is a possibility, or even earlier. In any case, *Troilus and Cressida* seems likely to have preceded *Poetaster*. Jonson's ridicule, in its uproariously funny trial scene, of Marston's penchant for outlandish importations into his crabbed vocabulary might have deterred Shakespeare or anyone else from indulging in the extraordinary profusion of unusual, strained, Latinized, and highfalutin expressions with which *Troilus and Cressida* abounds. Marston had been experimenting for two or three years with similar diction. Shakespeare, always intensely interested in words as words, may have consciously followed suit. Certainly this style, in both Marston and Shakespeare, comes at times perilously close to affectation. It is often downright precious, though no doubt an actor could deliver a resounding effect with Troilus's agonized outburst (V, ii) when Cressida makes her exit, pledged to Diomedes:

> *Ulysses.* All's done, my lord.
> *Troilus.*   It is.
> *Ulysses.*   Why stay we then?
> *Troilus.* To make a recordation to my soul
> Of every syllable that here was spoke.
> But if I tell how these two did coact,
> Shall I not lie in publishing a truth?
> Sith there is yet a credence in my heart,
> An esperance so obstinately strong,
> That doth invert th' attest of eyes and ears,
> As if those organs were deceptious functions,
> Created only to calumniate.
> Was Cressid here?

Ulysses answers drily, "I cannot conjure, Trojan," perhaps in allusion to the blighted lover's bombast as well as to his own inability to have called up a spirit in Cressida's likeness. In one respect, however, this exchange is very typical of Shakespeare, who loves to score twice whenever he can. Troilus's first speech gives the actor a fine opportunity in the suppressed style, and that makes the full voice which follows all the more effective.

Though textual geologists have been busy with this play, there is no reason to doubt that, with the possible exception of the epilogue, it is all Shakespeare's or that the text we have is, substantially, the only one that ever existed. Attempts have been made to link *Troilus and Cressida* with the War of the Theatres.[6] Some think that in the strong, though far from subtle, comic rôle of Ajax, Jonson is caricatured, and in Thersites Marston. It is very unlikely. Whatever the animus behind them, the stage blows in the contestants' plays left the recipients in no doubt of whom they were meant for. If this play is Shakespeare's contribution, he pulled his punches.

The first ten books of the *Iliad* had been published in Arthur Hall's translation in 1581. Two more, the eleventh and eighteenth, were among the eight of Chapman's first batch in 1598. There was also available a complete translation in French. But Shakespeare's picture of the Trojan War, whether or not he had read Homer, could not escape modification from its medieval coloring. Troy was one of the great themes of romance, which grafted onto it the chivalric code, both of arms and of love; and Renaissance literature is full of redactions and allusions that Shakespeare must have known. And indeed the code itself, hollow and hypocritical though it had become, survived in Tudor life. Great lords still tilted, a contrast with the realities of warfare no less amazing than the discrepancy between Shakespeare's romantic plots and the humanity of his characterization. Though Sidney died in their best tradition, the Earl of Essex might have learned how to live more successfully if he could have forgotten the heroes of the romances. As Professor Lawrence has noted,

Essex sticking a pike into the gate of Lisbon and daring any of the besieged Spaniards to break a lance in favor of his mistress is of a piece with Shakespeare's Hector challenging (I, iii) for his lady's beauty's sake. The graces and absurdities of the old code of courtly love were practiced by Elizabeth's highborn or high-flown courtiers. To the aged Queen, wrinkled as she was, Essex and Raleigh played the amorous rôle in good set terms. That there was a conventional rhythm, with centuries of art behind it, made their insistence on her physical charms somewhat less ridiculous. Shakespeare thinks of the Homeric figures in terms, not of Greek vases, but of living models as well as of medieval story. Hence the flowery chivalric speeches, now boastful now courteous; hence the knightly armor; hence the stylized pattern of love.

Greeks and Trojans had appeared on the English stage throughout the sixteenth century, Troilus and Pandarus among them. All good Englishmen sympathized with the Trojans, for the British nation was supposed to owe its foundation to Brutus, great-grandson of Æneas. No dramatic source, however, is known for Shakespeare's play. He had probably read John Lydgate's early fifteenth-century *The Sege of Troye* and William Caxton's *The Recuyell of the Historyes of Troye* (1475), both derived from the thirteenth-century *Historia Destructionis Troiae* of Guido delle Colonne, who adapts his Latin prose account from the great twelfth-century *Le Roman de Troie* of Benoît de Sainte-More, apparently the inventor of the Troilus and Cressida story. In his *Il Filostrato* Boccaccio develops it as a tale of love. Boccaccio's poem is the main source of the most artistic treatment, medieval or modern, the story has yet received, Chaucer's *Troilus and Criseyde*, which Shakespeare had certainly read. Chaucer is gentle with the frail heroine. There is nothing puritanical about his commentary. Even when she yields to Diomedes, Chaucer sees a woman's very human weakness and has only pity for her. Her sin is not against our ethical code, such as it is, but against the code of courtly love, against love itself. But in *The Testament of Cresseid* the Scottish poet Robert Henryson adds to Chaucer's highly analytical narrative a final chapter on the heroine's miserable end, with trimmings of poetic justice and a partial infusion of Christian morality. According to Henryson, Diomedes deserts her; and, as "sum men sayis," she falls to the dreadful trade of camp prostitute. O fair Cresseid, he exclaims, what a fate was thine!

> To change in filth all thy Feminitie,
> And be with fleschlie lust sa maculait,
> And go amang the Greikis air and lait
> Sa giglotlike, takand thy foull plesance!

Making her way to her father's "kirk," she blasphemes against Venus and Cupid and is punished with a loathsome malady, which appears in the symptoms of leprosy. Reduced to beggary, she is sitting at the edge of the highway when Prince Troilus rides by and, such are the ravages of the disease, fails to recognize the gay lady he has loved. Yet something in her face reminds him of Cresseid, and he tosses down his purse. She dies of a broken heart.

That Shakespeare accepted this account of her fate and this view of her character is evident from allusions in two earlier plays. For Henryson's version lies behind Pistol's proposal (*Henry the Fifth*, II, i) of a marriage between Corporal Nym and Doll Tearsheet, "the lazar kite of Cressid's kind," and Feste's observation (*Twelfth Night*, III, i) that "Cressida was a beggar." It was apparently the source of another play, of 1599, the *Troilus and Cressida* of Chettle and Dekker. Henslowe records payments for this drama, the appearance of which possibly imposed a set task on Shakespeare, since his company may have pressed him for a competing piece. Its text has not survived, but there is a fragment of a plat [7] probably belonging to it, with the stage direction "Enter Cressida, wth Beggars." Henryson's poem had long been ascribed to his master Chaucer; it was printed in editions of the elder poet from 1532 on.

Unless his aim is frankly to burlesque and he achieves it with both humor and good taste, it is hard to forgive a writer who takes a beautiful theme and degrades it, especially when he seeks the reward of those who inspire the thoughtless laughter of a shallow cynicism. But though there has been much critical dispute regarding his object, Shakespeare is guiltless on both counts. His tone is often derisive, but in no sense is the play a burlesque. If we laugh, it will be rather thoughtfully. To put the worst aspect first, Thersites is undeniably a foul-mouthed cynic and totally without a clown's customary gaiety. Pandarus is an appalling, but certainly a comic, portrait of impotent and prematurely senile lechery. Ajax is a brainless athlete, and Menelaus merely the stock Elizabethan cuckold, always good for a laugh in the old theatres. Achilles betrays his country for love of the Trojan Polyxena, though Shakespeare did not invent this intrigue; and he dallies lustfully with young Patroclus. But the name of Pandarus had acquired its meaning long before Shakespeare drew him. It is strange how critics have followed the lead of Thersites in distorting the portraits of the Greek and Trojan worthies, as if he were Shakespeare's sole mouthpiece. Thersites is unmistakably the clown's rôle; presumably Armin created it. Cressida was already a drab in Henryson, and she is not altogether strumpet in the play. It is true that Achilles slays his heroic opponent unchivalrously; but before a British audience of those days it would not do for Hector to fall in a fair fight — it takes the whole corps of Myrmidons to dispose of him. Despite Thersites's snarling, Ulysses and Nestor are attractive characters. So are Hector, Agamemnon, and Æneas. Paris is by no means degraded, nor is Helen. Naturally, the Greeks have something to say about what she has cost them, and Diomedes is bitter about her "bawdy veins." But her liaison with Paris, while it is not handled with any special tenderness, is treated with sufficient dignity. Even Diomedes, a mere cog in the plot, is cited by some commentators as an example of Shakespeare's blackening of character. Actually, of course, he is hardly characterized at all. Patroclus, however the affection of Achilles has passed beyond normal bounds, is not restricted to effeminacy in love and is not effeminate at all in war. On the other hand, the realistic trend is plain and needs no emphasis here. It is a far cry from Touchstone and Feste to Thersites. It is even farther from Rosalind and Viola to Cressida. Professor Stoll remarks of the young lovers in the romantic comedies that they "keep their distance both in fact and in thought, as, when . . . of one accord, in life they seldom do." That they do not in this play indicates again that we are not wide of the mark in calling it realistic.

And indeed, given Henryson's poem, Shakespeare's very choice of theme marks a turn away from idealistic romance. Lust, not love, is the subject of the main plot, as anyone can see from IV, ii, where the dramatist unmistakably indicates the plane on which the principals proceed. They give themselves completely away, both of them, and both before and after, even without the running comment of the *tertium quid*. For Troilus, who is Hotspur in love, there is at least the excuse of ignorance. He is passionate, uninstructed, and inexperienced. There is a touch of the tragic about him. But Cressida, though she is a coquette not without charm, is more whore than coquette and more wanton than charming. Neither to Troilus nor to Diomedes is hers the yielding of innocence or of headlong passion — or even of generosity; it is a thoroughly sensual surrender. Her emotional outburst at the end of IV, ii. when she learns she must leave the youth who has just possessed her, has almost the right passionate ring. For the moment, as in her soliloquy at the end of I, ii and again in IV, iv, we are asked to believe in the sincerity of her feeling. But actually Shakespeare is here abandoning consistency in order to make still more effective the contrast with her speedy relapse upon the neck of Diomedes.[8] If she is to be a perpetual symbol, not so much of infidelity as of fickleness, she must think and show herself strongly attached to Troilus before she leaves town for camp. Hence his reiteration of "Be true." As soon as she reaches the tents, the wisest Greek promptly sums her up for us — if, like Troilus, we are green enough to need it.

The first recorded performance was of Dryden's version in 1679, entitled *Troilus and Cressida, or Truth Found Too Late*. It was strongly cast, with Betterton as Troilus, the sprightly comedian Tony Leigh as Pandarus, Henry Harris as Ulysses,

William Smith (who eventually succeeded Harris as Betterton's second) in the rôle of Hector, the popular Cave Underhill as Thersites, Mary Lee as Cressida, and Mrs. Betterton
as Andromache. The piece was no great hit, but there were
occasional revivals. In his old age Betterton played Thersites.
Dryden's adaptation was produced the year after *All for Love*
had shown that he was through with Heroic drama. For him
Troilus and Cressida is a tragedy: Cressida becomes a model
heroine, faithful and true, her flirtation with Diomedes being
innocent of desire and only her father's means of securing help
in getting back to Troy. Even the yielding to Troilus is
sanctified by her exaction of an unwilling promise from Pandarus that "the holy Priest Shall make us one for ever!"
Troilus's reception (IV, ii) of the news that Cressida must
leave Troy is improved by Dryden, who at Betterton's suggestion wrote in an admirable scene of quarrel and reconciliation between him and Hector. The final act is much altered.
As a bitter-ender at the war council Troilus has a touch of
Drawcansir: "And when I breathe, methinks my nostrills
hiss!" He fights his rival and gets him down. Cressida pleads
for the Greek's life, thus confirming Troilus's disbelief in her
innocence, which Diomedes belies. To convince her beloved,
Cressida kills herself, a stale expedient, as Sir Walter Scott
remarks. But at least Dryden gives the play an ending.[9] Diomedes, an out-and-out scoundrel, is killed by Troilus; but
Achilles storms in with the Myrmidons. "All the Trojans
dye upon the place, *Troilus* last"; and the tragedy ends with
the usual caveat to the Whigs on the dangers of "homebred
Factions." Dryden's is probably the better piece for the stage,
though Cressida, if too naughty in Shakespeare, is in Dryden
too much the other way.

As a candidate for revival, *Troilus and Cressida*, along with
Titus Andronicus, *The Two Noble Kinsmen*, and *Henry the Sixth*,
has long stood at the bottom of the poll. Munich saw it in
1898, Berlin in 1904, and London in 1907. William Poel, gallant enemy of the upholstered revival of Shakespeare, staged
it, uncut, in London and Stratford in 1912 and 1913. The Old
Vic did its devoir in 1923. There was a revival in 1932 at

Cambridge, England, and another by the Players club in New York. Neither seems to have afforded much reason to question the wisdom of the actor-managers of the eighteenth and nineteenth centuries who let the play alone.

That its theatrical history is meager is not strange. Even if we chance to be of that dwindling band who began their Greek in impressionable high school years, these alleged Argives of Shakespeare leave us cold. We met the real, that is to say the romantic, ones with Homer for our guide. And if we did not, the name of Achilles or of Hector can not of itself stir us much. Nor are their characters built up for us and made convincing and fascinating by the earlier acts of the play. We are expected to take their stature on trust, like Cæsar's, but with less reason. Shakespeare himself does not warm up to them. He is in a reflective mood, and neither delighted with the possibilities of a good story nor in love with a character. Naturally, he communicates little to us, except ideas. And it is not out of talk about ideas that his successful plays are made.

Cressida is also painted too flat, without a third dimension behind her. Like Evadne in Beaumont and Fletcher's *The Maides Tragedy*, she has no history. Neither of these wantons is accounted for. Boy meets girl. Plot employs heroine. That is all we know on stage and all we need to know. But Shakespeare rarely operates on that principle. Compare his Cressida with his Cleopatra to see how artfully he makes the Egyptian live. As a book to be read, *Troilus and Cressida* suffers, even more than it might in the theatre, from the poverty of the characterization. Nor is plot better managed. There is too little comedy to the square foot. It comes in heavy doses instead of crackling an accompaniment or permeating the texture of the play, which could have been a tragedy, but is not. Structurally shaky, like the histories, it is too little concerned with the principals and too much, as was doubtless inevitable, with exhibiting famous Greeks and Trojans. Hence III, i; for we must view the face that launched the ships.

The test of enjoyment as a book is best sustained by the

style. Shakespeare is very style-conscious in this play, often trying for an effect in Marston's manner by using a queer word. The rhetoric, though the foolish trick of hendiadys is worked to death, is often excellent. If one happens to be politically minded, the play makes excellent reading, and not alone for such purple patches as Ulysses on Degree (I, iii, 75–137) and Time (III, iii, 145–90). Now and again, for it is Shakespeare's, but not often, comes the flash and stab of poetry. They must part, says Troilus (IV, iv),

> And suddenly, where injury of chance
> Puts by leave-taking, justles roughly by
> All time of pause, rudely beguiles our lips
> Of all rejoindure, forcibly prevents
> Our lock'd embrasures, strangles our dear vows
> Even in the birth of our own labouring breath.
> We two that with so many thousand sighs
> Did buy each other, must poorly sell ourselves
> With the rude brevity and discharge of one.
> Injurious Time now with a robber's haste
> Crams his rich thiev'ry up, he knows not how.
> As many farewells as be stars in heaven,
> With distinct breath and consign'd kisses to them,
> He fumbles up into a loose adieu,
> And scants us with a single famish'd kiss,
> Distasted with the salt of broken tears.

ALL'S WELL THAT ENDS WELL

If Shakespeare had not sent Bertram and Helena to bed together, there would be no compelling reason against the inclusion of this play among the romantic comedies or the dramatic romances; and "shocking," "revolting," and "corrupt" might have lain dormant in the vocabularies of its critics. Despite the substantial difference between that odd nuptial couch and the veil of decorum in the joyous comedies, it is possible to exaggerate the bedlessness of the earlier plays. Their heroines are sweet and pure, but not cold. Like Helena, they sometimes converse with a frankness unknown to the "nice girl" of Victorian convention. Lysander proposes to pass the night on the same pillow; and Hermia, though she loves him, insists on

> Such separation as may well be said
> Becomes a virtuous bachelor and a maid.

Portia hears Gratiano's broadest witticism, and it is not nominated in the score that the pearl of heroines is offended by it. She is herself afterwards remarkably pleasant on the privileges she expects to grant the wearer of a certain ring. The merry Beatrice goes out of her way to protest that though she has just "put down" Benedick he shall not do the same by her, lest she "prove the mother of fools" — as if there could be any danger of that! Rosalind is playful with her Orlando on "your wive's wit going to your neighbour's bed." Of them all Viola is most devoured by "the terrible lion of loving"; she is never in a mood to jest about love. She burns with a steadfast flame of passion so intense, and she is so pierced with her double sorrow, that her mind is far too occupied as well as too pure to anticipate connubial joys with sensual imagery.

Yet the bed trick in *All's Well* and in *Measure for Measure* has thrown many an unhistorically minded critic into curious fits. To the Elizabethans, we may be sure, there seemed nothing immodest about it, especially since the condition was imposed on Helena by her husband, and in *Measure for Measure* is suggested by the virtuous Duke. In both dramas, the trick is played by a wronged woman whose affection has remained unaltered. By means of it Helena's marriage to the man she loves is consummated; it is a brilliant marriage for her and a lucky one for him. It was in a later age, when the old romances were no longer human nature's daily food, that it occurred to anyone to question whether the ending is really a happy one. The convention under which Shakespeare was writing prescribed, and still prescribes in fiction designed for the unsophisticated, that when the thing ends on the right joyous note, whether of happy bells or of Mendelssohn's march or of a long kiss that symbolizes them, the story is over. Certainly there is no trace of irony or scepticism in Shakespeare's handling of this very romantic plot.

His source is the ninth story of the third day of Boccaccio's *Decameron*, the tale of Beltramo di Rossiglione and Giglietta di Nerbone. No doubt Shakespeare read the translation in William Painter's *The Palace of Pleasure* (vol. I — 1566), for the inhabitants of Siena are called "Senois" by Painter (fol. 99), and "Senoys" in the First Folio. The king is less prominent in the *novella;* he drops out after the marriage. The girl who helps the heroine arrange the bed trick is well rewarded and does not accompany her to France. Giglietta (Helena) lacks neither money nor kinsfolk. It is the king who suggests rewarding her with a husband. She does not return to claim him till after she has given birth to twin boys. The fifth-act confusion over the second ring and the proposal of a second marriage for Bertram are added by Shakespeare in order to heighten suspense to the very end. The delightful Countess, "the most beautiful old woman's part ever written," Mr. Shaw calls it (though she is not *very* old), is Shakespeare's own; and so are Lafew, Lavatch, and Parolles. Neither the "Healing of the King" nor the deserted wife's "Fulfilment of the Tasks," as Professor Lawrence terms them, was invented as a narrative motif by Boccaccio. Both are old and widespread in Asiatic as well as European story. They regularly redound to the heroine's credit, proving her devotion, her cleverness, and her courage. The husband is usually quite charmed with the outcome.

All's Well was not published till the Folio of 1623, the text of which is for this play far from satisfactory. It may have been cut. About 1602 is the best guess at the date of composition, but it is scarcely more than a guess. Perhaps *All's Well* was written hastily about that time, in response to the company's need of a new comedy, while Shakespeare's mind was chiefly absorbed by one or more of the great tragedies. This hypothesis and dating would account for the quasi-realistic handling of the romantic story, for the lack of poetry, for the mixture of prose and verse, for the thinness of the plot, and for the somewhat perfunctory treatment of certain episodes. But anything worth calling evidence is completely wanting, and various scholars have adopted various dates and theories. Some think the play is the *Love's Labour's Won* listed by Meres in 1598.[10] Others hold the Folio text a revision by Shakespeare of an earlier work by him or someone else. Lafew's "Lustick! as the Dutchman says" (II, iii, 47) very likely alludes to a character who is free with this word in an anonymous play, *The Weakest goeth to the Wall*. It was printed in 1600; but since no one knows how long before that it had been acted, there is nothing decisive about the reference, if indeed it be an allusion to the play and not to Dutchmen in general.

Nothing at all is known of the comedy's reception on the Elizabethan boards. The first recorded performance was at the minor theatre of Goodman's Fields in 1741. From then on it was occasionally acted there and at the great patent houses. It had ten performances at Drury Lane in 1742, with Peg Woffington as Helena. The Parolles was Theophilus Cibber, but Harry Woodward became that part's leading exponent and played it for thirty years. Macklin acted Lavatch. In 1756 Mrs. Pritchard, who had previously played Helena, appeared as the Countess. J. P. Kemble revived *All's Well* in 1794; he played Bertram to Dora Jordan's Helena. Charles Kemble acted Bertram twice in 1811. A pseudo-operatic version was staged at Covent Garden in 1832. Phelps produced Shakespeare's comedy in 1852, playing Parolles himself. Daly revived it in New York; and in 1916 Benson staged it at Stratford, where it was also revived in 1922. Lilian Baylis produced it at the Old Vic in 1921, when the Parolles of Ernest Milton was praised.

To modern readers Bertram's character has been the great stumbling block, but that is inherent in the plot, if we are to be wholeheartedly for Helena. Shakespeare means that we shall be, and so he makes Bertram stupid and even vicious in his rejection of her, although in Boccaccio he is neither and his motive is the understandable one of aversion to a marriage beneath his rank. Helena, noble creature that she is, needs not in the eyes of this generation the defense which, despite the admiration of Coleridge and Hazlitt, had till quite recently to be put up for her. She is utterly without and above feminine artifice. The methods by which she backs the skittish Bertram between the thills of matrimony are, like her dangerous ministry to the King, more intellectual than temperamental, more boldly masculine than reliant on the wiles of sex. She employs no lures, no coquetries; she does not try either to dazzle or to enchant; she refrains from turning on the full force of her charm. But before the first scene is half over she has won our sympathy completely by her passionate, reckless soliloquy of desperate love: — "I think not on my father," though we are confident she loved him deeply:

> What was he like?
> I have forgot him. My imagination
> Carries no favour in't but Bertram's.
> I am undone! There is no living, none,
> If Bertram be away.

Her conduct throughout is, for a heroine of old romance, in complete harmony with this declaration. Hers is a love like Viola's, and it carries her even farther — in miles and in expedients. So she goes to Paris; but when her great moment comes, only to shame her, and Bertram roundly replies, "I cannot love her, nor will strive to do't," she wins us all the more by her dignity in pain:

> That you are well restor'd, my lord, I'm glad.
> Let the rest go.

Shakespeare is artful for her. It is the King who presses the reluctant youth, not she. After that come solemn oaths and an awful sanction, and she has, according to the older view of such matters, not only rights but duties. That the King should dictate a marriage is not in the least surprising; it was a commonplace in life as well as in fiction. That it was, makes Helena's choice of a reward still less open to objection.

As for Bertram, if he had recognized his happiness when it met him, there would be no play. He is even more obtuse than Orsino, whom we prefer because he speaks poetry. But

Bertram was not, presumably, a hateful specimen to the
Elizabethans. He is immature; he is misguided by Parolles;
he makes mistakes of his own. He sees the light at the end
very suddenly — as men sometimes do in real life, as is customary in romantic plots that wind up with a change of
heart (it is no less abrupt in Boccaccio), as is more or less
necessary in a play that must conform to a strict time limit,
and as is more acceptable in a drama than in other forms
of fiction because an audience *witnesses* the hero's revulsion
of feeling and in the theatre seeing is believing, provided the
acting is all it should be. The unexpected appearance of the
woman he has injured shocks Bertram, we must suppose,
out of his wayward humor into his true self; and with his
eager promise to love her "ever, ever dearly" Shakespeare's
audience was doubtless completely satisfied.

If we are not, even after making the historical discount,
the reason is probably the scarcity of poetry. This may be
due to haste or some lack of interest; it is probably not the
result of the author's having gone sour. Mere style, when it
drips from Shakespeare's pen, can create the romantic haze
or fairy mist through which an absurd plot will loom up
as inevitable. As usual, he is telling a story. In this comedy
he tells little else. And he does not tell it with his usual
charm. *All's Well* transports us no farther than along the
beaten tracks of France and Italy; we touch at no Illyrian
shore, we wander in no Arden glades. Instead of a languishing
Duke all "canopied with bow'rs," or a composer of verses
published by the trees of the forest, or any of the other young
lovers who succeed in being gloriously ardent without kissing,
we have for hero a boy aristocrat as ambitious as they come
and hard with the hardness of the youngster who has yet
both to win his spurs and to prove himself with women. He
takes to war as to his native element; and he assumes, like
any young blood without a poetic side, that one learns what
women are by commencing rake. Bertram, in contrast with
the lovers of the romantic comedies, provides an additional
warrant for calling this one, at least relatively, realistic.
Neither his blindness nor his attempt on Diana endear him,

yet it is hard to see why he should be singled out for universal denunciation. *All's Well* is not a recent work, and in older fiction the hero is often expected to make a few mistakes before he straightens out and settles down. Compared with the young gentlemen of the eighteenth-century novel, Bertram is, save of course for a deficiency of sensibility, almost a model youth. It is perhaps regrettable that Shakespeare failed · to invent some scene in which the recreant husband might help an old lady across the street or throw his purse to a deserving beggar or perform some other good turn that would prove him the owner of a heart of gold at least the equal of Tom Jones's. Aptitude for war, however, went a long way toward establishing a romantic hero. He is, moreover, a count and a protégé of the King of France. He does the right thing in the end. The play's title clinches the argument against its detractors.

To be sure, no one is obliged to like it. But if one can bring oneself to accept the romantic plot, the effort is worth making, for the play repays reading. It is a little thin, as Elizabethan dramas go, there being no subplot, unless we count the exposure of Parolles. But its tone, while not gay, is not depressing; on the contrary, it is lofty and exhilarating. The absurdity of calling it sordid becomes obvious with the reflection that every one of the feminine characters is decent through and through. Two of them are very noble women — not Helena alone, for the Countess is fully her equal, a great lady and a true lady, as charming old Lafew is the true gentleman. Lavatch is not among the greatest of the clowns; he is coarser and less merry, but his wit comes from the same mint. Like Feste, he is perfectly sane and a jester by profession. Parolles is a variation on that familiar theme, the braggart captain — and what a variation! One might think that by this time Shakespeare and Jonson, to mention no others, had put this veteran figure through all possible comic hoops; but Parolles, however he marches to the wars in the column that stretches back through the *commedia dell'arte* to the ancient comedy of Rome, and however he is like Pistol in his poltroonery and his complete innocence of the saving grace of humor, is not Pistol. He is Parolles. Each is unique; each speaks his own language. Parolles was "dressed," of course, in the most extravagant costume the wardrobe afforded. Before he spoke a word, his first entrance doubtless raised a mighty laugh, in which, if he so elects, the reader is still privileged to join.

MEASURE FOR MEASURE

On December 26, 1604 "A play Caled Mesur for Mesur" was acted at court.[11] Aside from Meres's failure to mention it in 1598, this is the only evidence for the date of composition. So 1604 is the favored year, though we must put a *circa* in front of it. The piece obviously belongs with the realistic comedies, but that it was new when the holiday performance was given is only an assumption. It was not printed till 1623, and the text then provided by the Folio is unsatisfactory. Perhaps it had been cut. Stage directions are scanty. There is much mislining of verse. But the disintegrators' theories are steadily losing ground, and their contentions have failed to convince most scholars that *Measure for Measure* is not entirely from Shakespeare's pen.

The chief source is George Whetstone's *The . . . Historye, of Promos and Cassandra*, a two-part play published in 1578. Whetstone dramatizes a *novella* of Giovanni Battista Giraldi (commonly called Cinthio), another of whose stories was used by Shakespeare, probably also about 1604, for *Othello*. Though Cinthio wrote on the same subject the tragicomedy of *Epitia*, that play was not printed till 1583, and Whetstone's indebtedness is to Cinthio's *novella*, the fifth in the eighth decade of his *Hecatommithi* (1565). The theme was common enough in Renaissance fiction, but there is a good chance that Cinthio may have based his tale on an actual occurrence near Milan in 1547. *Promos and Cassandra* was still unacted when, in 1582, with a few new details afterwards taken over by Shakespeare, Whetstone tells the story again in *An Heptameron of Ciuill Discourses*.

In Cinthio's *novella*, Juriste (Angelo) virtually promises to marry Epitia (Isabella) as well as to free her brother. There is no bed trick. Epitia yields, but her brother is actually beheaded. In Cinthio's dramatic version, however, the jailer substitutes a condemned criminal and deceives the Governor. Whetstone independently makes the same change, a fine warning to those source hunters whose calculations never include the possibility that two minds may conceive a single thought. He also follows Cinthio's *novella* in marrying Isabella to the doomed Governor by the sovereign's command, and in revoking his death sentence at her request. Mariana and the bed trick are Shakespeare's addition.[12] Perhaps a part was wanted for another boy; at any rate, the distressed heroine is rewarded with a much finer marriage than falls to her lot in the source. It is not that Angelo is too far beneath her in integrity. His repentance, if abrupt like Claudio's, is like his in being sincere.

The bed trick in *Measure for Measure* has a somewhat different status from the one in *All's Well*, Angelo not being married to Mariana but only "affianced to her by oath." It can not be used to explain away Shakespeare's premarital relations with Anne Hathaway, for the betrothal of Angelo was no bar to his desertion of the lady. There is nothing automatic about this bed trick. It depends on the Duke as *deus ex machina*. He predicts that "it *may* compel him to her recompense," and then sees to it that it does — by the flat order "Go take her hence and marry her instantly." Angelo has just been exposed, and he has asked for the death penalty. The Duke has him on the hip. Not that the disposal of the case has any standing in equity. As Lawrence remarks,

The law and authority in these pieces is romantic law and authority. ... Shakespeare used dukes and friars when the peculiar powers and opportunities afforded by their station would help his narrative. He did not bother himself about the strict legality or rationality of their actions. What they suggest or decide has in his plays the binding force of constituted and final authority, and was so understood by his audiences.

As for Isabella, she is no Helena; yet she is a high-minded girl, sexually still unawakened, but with a potential fund

of passion in her nature, as she shows in her pleadings with
Angelo, Claudio, and the Duke. Like Helena, she is much
more sober than the gay young things of the romantic comedies; yet she has heart as well as principles and dignity. She
will grace a throne and learn to love its occupant, whose
virtue is not qualified by the deviousness of his administrative
methods. These are dictated by plot, not built into the Duke's
character, which is wholly noble. He plays a more active
part in Shakespeare's drama than in its predecessors. With
Isabella and the benevolent Provost, we cling to him and
his goodness as the only hope of an equitable solution of the
tangled situation, which Shakespeare complicates still further
in the final scene. If the Duke were to act sooner, throwing
off his disguise and dispensing justice instead of stage-manag-
ing, like the sovereign in *All's Well*, a grand theatrical finale
of prolonged suspense, he would, as Lawrence observes, save
Isabella and Claudio much suffering. But then (the words
have to be repeated in Shakespeare criticism), there would
be no play. "No, he knows what is expected of him as a
stage Duke." "Give me your hand," he commands the novice
not yet a votarist, "and say you will be mine." At moments
like these, when all the affairs of the comedy are being rapidly
wound up, silence always indicates consent.

> Dear Isabel,
> I have a motion much imports your good,
> Whereto if you'll a willing ear incline,
> What's mine is yours, and what is yours is mine.

A more importunate proposal by one so mighty to one who
had so recently put all her thoughts on no earthly bridegroom
would be in poor taste. This is no moment for a passionate
declaration, and the Duke knows it. He is an understanding
person, and we are assured by these lines that his wooing
will be gentle and will succeed.[13]

As in *All's Well*, there is no subplot worthy the name.
Instead, we have once more a comic band recruited chiefly
from the lower elements of the population. Like the God of
Abraham Lincoln, Shakespeare must have been fond of the

common people, however he distrusted their political sagacity. At any rate he created them in large numbers, and in
this play he is remarkably tender with their ignorance and
folly, and indeed with their wickedness. In using them to
exhibit the prevailing licentiousness of the city, he is following Whetstone's secondary plot. Lucio is functionally similar
to Parolles, since his discomfiture is the nearest we come to
a subplot. But how much merrier he is! Pompey is a rather
amiable reversion to the clownish servant. He is not a Fool,
and he is more humorous than witty. Dogberry lives again
for a few moments in Elbow. In Angelo we have one of Shakespeare's most fascinating portraits. His self-analysis, the contrast between his uncontrollable desires and the gravity of
his aspect, "Wherein (let no man hear me) I take pride,"
and the acid-etched delineation in him of a too common type
of the successful man, would put this play, even if it were
not preoccupied with sex, into the category of the more
realistic comedies. Angelo has every appearance of being
studied from the life. Happy the blithe or sensitive man who
has never been obliged as a subordinate to deal with this
kind of self-righteous, humorless, pseudojudicial stiffness,
whether genuine or assumed. It is a type of character frequently advanced to executive positions, where it enjoys
tyrannizing over less successful, more decent men. For natures like Angelo's are subject to a powerful emotional drive,
though such a man tries to conceal it or attempts to turn his
passions into the sole channel of ambition. The mask of
gravity often impresses and deceives trustees and other ap-
pointing officials. Shakespeare is deceived by no one; he has
Angelo's number — that is, he sees through men of his stamp.
Bagehot remarks that "the entire character of Angelo . . . is
nothing but a successful embodiment of the pleasure, the
malevolent pleasure, which a warm-blooded and expansive
man takes in watching the rare, the dangerous and inanimate
excesses of the constrained and cold-blooded."

As a whole, the play, so strongly conceived, just misses
what it takes to make a work of fiction live greatly. That is
an injection of poetry, which the dramatist either preferred

to reserve for his tragedies or thought unsuited to the new kind of comedy. But he surpasses this drama's two companion pieces by allowing his natural flow of sympathy to warm and invigorate it. The title means, of course, an eye for an eye, a tooth for a tooth, the same fate for Angelo that Claudio is supposed to have suffered. But, as with the next group of comedies, the dramatic romances, *Measure for Measure* ends with mercy for everyone, even the callous Barnardine.

In his *Roscius Anglicanus*, the old prompter John Downes lists among the minor pieces in the repertory of the Duke's company from 1661 to 1665 Sir William D'avenant's *The Law against Lovers*, an adaptation of *Measure for Measure*, adorned by "Benedict" and Beatrice from *Much Ado* and the latter's small sister Viola, who obliges from time to time with song-and-dance turns. Benedict is Angelo's brother, Beatrice his ward and Julietta's cousin. The bed trick is omitted. Angelo is only testing Isabella's virtue; he has already pardoned Claudio. In a new fifth act Benedict leads a revolt against his brother. The Duke finally appears, forgives everyone, and bestows Beatrice on Benedict and Isabella on Angelo. In accordance with the dictates of decorum, Lucio's character is "elevated," and Pompey, Froth, and Elbow are missing, except for the little colloquy with the executioner. Claudio is nobly ready to die, but Julietta asks Isabella to save him. Her mouth is stopped by the suggestion that she might play the substitute's part in the bed trick. Pepys thought well of this piece. The casting is unknown.

Nearly forty years later, in the last season of the seventeenth century, Betterton's seceding troupe at Lincoln's Inn Fields staged another adaptation, a pseudo-operatic one à la *Fairy-Queen*, arranged by the eminent critic and defender of Shakespeare, Charles Gildon. It was entitled *Measure for Measure, or Beauty the Best Advocate*. This version proved fairly successful, and was revived for a benefit as late as 1706. Betterton played Angelo to the Isabella of Anne Bracegirdle. Gildon preserves a good deal of D'avenant, dispensing however not only with Benedick and Beatrice but with almost all the low-comic scenes and characters. He restores Mariana, who is Angelo's deserted wife. Claudio and Juliet are also a proper wedded pair; but the ceremony was secret, and the cruel Angelo refuses to wait for the arrival of a wedding certificate from the absent priest. Plot is reduced to lowest terms to make room for the four-part masque on Dido and Æneas with music by Purcell. Escalus presents it as a palace entertainment.

Shakespeare's play was revived by John Rich in 1720, though in what form is doubtful. Quin played the Duke. The low-comic characters came back at Drury Lane in 1738; Mrs. Cibber was the Isabella. She and Quin were seen in this comedy fairly often. It remained active in the repertory, though Garrick never appeared in it. Mrs. Pritchard and Mrs. Yates played Isabella. Woodward was the Lucio. There was a superbly cast revival at Covent Garden in 1803 with Cooke as Angelo, J. P. Kemble as the Duke, and Mrs. Siddons as Isabella. Under Kemble the play continued to hold a modest place. He retained a fair amount of the low comedy, and nothing that is not Shakespeare's. Phelps, in 1846, also revived the play. Adelaide Neilson first acted Isabella in London in 1876; she had already played the rôle in this country. Mme. Modjeska also acted Isabella here. Long neglected, the comedy was presented in 1906 by Otho Stuart, with Oscar Asche as Angelo, Lily Brayton as Isabella, and Walter Hampden as the Duke. Tyrone Guthrie's production at the Old Vic in 1933 had Charles Laughton and Flora Robson in the chief rôles. He staged it again, with a new cast, in 1937, when the Duke of Stephen Murray was warmly praised. Surely the time is ripe for an American revival of this strong play, which might take on a new lease of life in a theatre which is not shocked by candor about sex.

Chapter 9

THE FOUR GREAT TRAGEDIES

THE TRAGEDY OF HAMLET, PRINCE OF DENMARK

No comparable work of art has been so much discussed as this tragedy. Every man, the saying goes, thinks he could run a newspaper and play Hamlet. But while the reefs of journalism are strewn with the wreckage of great papers, we have Macready's word for it that in this title rôle "a total failure is of rare occurrence." Hamlet is part of the inner life of every literate member of the English-speaking race who has an inner life, while the Germans long ago took the Prince to their bosoms. Something deep in the northern breeds responds *de profundis* to Hamlet's cry. Vachel Lindsay's "Edwin Booth in California" tells how in his salad days

> The youth played in the blear hotel.
> The rafters gleamed with glories strange.
> And winds of mourning Elsinore,
> Howling at chance and fate and change . . .
> Disturbed the new-built cattle-shed,
> The street, the high and solemn range.
> The while the coyote barked afar
> All shadowy was the battlement.
> The ranch-boys huddled and grew pale,
> Youths who had come on riot bent. . . .
> A haunted place, though new and harsh!
> The Indian and the Chinaman
> And Mexican were fain to learn
> What had subdued the Saxon clan.
> Why did they mumble, brood, and stare
> When the court-players curtsied fair
> And the Gonzago scene began? . . .

Our adorable Prince is not, however, an exclusive cultural property of the North. Hamlet's predicament has appealed to the general conviction of mankind that, as Arthur Schnitzler entitled another great drama, a human life is The Lonely Way. That is one reason why *Hamlet* is the most popular tragedy ever composed. Every great tragedy is the tragedy of the Life of Man. Somehow the dramatist must bridge the abyss between his own lonely way, formulated in terms of the peculiar trials of an individual hero on a mimic stage, and the experience and aspirations of those diverse personalities which, momentarily united as an audience in a mimic theatre, are all actors on the stage where every man must play a part. The tragedy of *Hamlet, Prince of Denmark* is the most successful bridge ever built.

The other reason for its popularity is the variety of the entertainment. This play has everything. While the Italian and French theatre took during the Renaissance the well-graded neoclassical highway, studded with those cautionary notices, the Rules, English drama rambled along as fancy inclined. One of the Rules — it was known as Strict Separation — forbade mixing tragic and comic. The Continent produced excellent humorless tragedies, and the neoclassical road led eventually to the masterpieces of Racine. But in the theatre of life, tears and laughter are strangely mingled; and Shakespeare, who for all his addiction to sensational plots was a realist in handling human nature, puts tragic possibilities into his comedies, and relieves the most austere of his tragedies with wit and even clowning. *Hamlet* is not the most austere of them. The hero's pretended madness opens the door to bold sallies of satire, caricature, and broad fun. Dr. Johnson rightly declared that these should "cause much mirth."

Though it was invented or adapted in primitive Germanic times, no one knows precisely when or where the Hamlet saga originated. It is retold in François de Belleforest's *Histoires Tragiques*, the source of the Elizabethan dramatizations. Belleforest, whose story appeared in the seventies but had to wait till 1608 for an English translation, got it from the *Gesta Danorum* of the Danish writer Saxo Grammaticus. This

work was composed, in Latin, about 1200 and first printed
in 1514. In the French version, the King has killed his brother
openly, and Hamlet feigns madness while biding his time.
Doubtful whether his nephew is really mad, the King resolves to murder him if he is shamming. A fair damsel and a
spy attempt, without success, to find out. The Queen repents
and becomes her son's confidante. Hamlet's revenge is complete. He burns the feasting hall and with it the courtiers,
kills the King, and takes the throne. Eventually he falls in
battle with another uncle.

Shakespeare probably produced his play in 1600 or early
in 1601.[1] But according to Henslowe's *Diary*, a *Hamlet* had
been performed at Newington Butts as early as June 11, 1594,
and no doubt before that, since Henslowe fails to mark the
piece "ne[w]." Thomas Lodge, in his *Wits Miserie, and the
Worlds Madnesse* (1596), alludes (p. 56) to "the Visard of y^e
ghost which cried so miserally at ye Theator like an oister
wife, *Hamlet, reuenge.*" This points to a performance by Shakespeare's company, the Lord Chamberlain's Men, at their own
house, the Theatre; but in his play the Ghost does not actually
say "Hamlet, revenge." Before Shakespeare took up the
theme, then, it had been acted on the London stage. The
author of the *Ur-Hamlet* (that is, the pre-Shakespearean drama)
may have been Thomas Kyd, whose *The Spanish Tragedie*
(*c.* 1586) resembles Shakespeare's play at many points. In a
prefatory epistle to Robert Greene's *Menaphon*, Tom Nashe
takes occasion in 1589 to jeer at the imitators of Seneca. In
English translation "read by candle light," says Nashe,
Seneca "yeeldes manie good sentences, as *Bloud is a begger*,
and so foorth: and if you intreate him faire in a frostie morning, he will affoord you whole *Hamlets*, I should say hand-
fulls of tragical speaches." Evidently the old *Hamlet* was
built on the Senecan model.[2]

Shakespeare's play was first printed in 1603, "As it hath
beene diuerse times acted by his Highnesse seruants in the
Cittie of London: as also in the Vniuersities of Cambridge
and Oxford, and else-where." An attempt was made by the
company to prevent publication; for it was doubtless at their

behest that James Roberts had entered the play, probably
with no intention of publishing it, in the Stationers' Register
on July 26, 1602, "as yt was latelie Acted." Presumably the
company hoped that formal registration would deter the
unauthorized publisher from proceeding. The piratical First
Quarto differs widely from the authorized editions which
followed. It omits some indispensable passages, paraphrases
others, transposes speech order, often echoes lines from other
scenes, introduces unauthentic stage directions and actors'
gags, and in general mangles both meaning and poetry. This
sorry text has been taken by some for the old *Hamlet* and by
others for Shakespeare's first revision of it. Pious actors have
even produced it, nonsense and all — a misguided labor of
love. A more likely theory, now generally accepted, regards
this edition as a Bad quarto,[3] a debased text of Shakespeare's
play, sold to the publishers by one of the company's hirelings.
Though he may have doubled in other rôles, he seems to
have played Marcellus, whose speeches agree pretty well
with the better texts. This unimportant but traitorous player
must have lacked a manuscript of the play; as best he could,
he drew on his memory. When that failed him completely,
he either gave up a speech as a bad job or filled in, sometimes
with lines of his own, sometimes with scraps recalled from
elsewhere in *Hamlet* and even from other plays. Once, at least,
he must have had some sort of access to the manuscript; he
was unable to copy it, but he had time enough for jotting
down the gist of certain speeches. For he frequently supplies
— very badly, it is true — the drift of passages that were
probably never spoken on Shakespeare's stage.

Having studiously avoided them for several years, I once
tried to reconstruct scenes of *The Winter's Tale* from my unsupported recollection of an undergraduate revival in which
I played Leontes. The result was similar to the Bad quartos,
save that I wove in no scraps from other scenes or plays.
Except for cuts, I could reproduce fairly well the speeches of
my old rôle; the cues of Leontes were also well remembered.
Lines of other characters in scenes I played in were often
garbled and sometimes quite lost, yet I could give their up-

shot, more or less metrically. But only the most striking phrases were recalled with any accuracy from passages occurring when Leontes was off stage.

Some, however, of the divergences in the First Quarto of *Hamlet* stamp it as more than a mere debased version of the play preserved by the Second Quarto and the First Folio. A few of the characters have different names, the Queen not only repents but offers to aid her son's revenge, and the confrontation scene with Ophelia comes before the first interview with Rosencrantz and Guildenstern. Probably the First Quarto rests, though very corruptly, on the acting version used at the Globe when Shakespeare's play was making its initial hit. The text of an Elizabethan drama was not static, though few now believe that Shakespeare was constantly revamping his work. No doubt he made alterations during rehearsals and sometimes even after a play had won its place in the repertory. And actors will gag their lines, as he protests in Hamlet's advice to the Players. Shakespeare may have revised his original version more thoroughly during the six months which followed publication of the First Quarto, when a new outbreak of the plague forced a closing of the theatres.

The Second Quarto, the most authoritative edition, "enlarged to almost as much againe as it was, according to the true and perfect Coppie," appeared late in 1604,[4] though some copies of it carry the date 1605. It represents the version on the stage of the Globe at that time, though not all the text was actually spoken. Despite the notable success of Maurice Evans's uncut revival, nearly all Shakespeare's plays have proved too long for the endurance of most audiences; they were certainly cut then as well as now. Only *Antony and Cleopatra* exceeds *Hamlet* in length. Why Shakespeare, who almost lived in the theatre, habitually wrote in excess of its requirements is a pretty question. Of the other dramatists, only Jonson (who had literary ambitions) regularly goes beyond the two-hour limit. My own theory, not generally accepted, rests on contemporary testimony to Shakespeare's facility as a writer and talker. Probably he let himself go poetically, well aware that his play would be hammered into shape in rehearsal. No one ever knew more about stage technique than he; presumably he directed his plays himself and did his own theatrical trimming. We have no reason to suppose he wrote any of them with an eye to eventual publication.

The Second Quarto gives us the longest text, more than two hundred lines longer than the First Folio gives, though it omits about eighty-five of the Folio's lines. There are many compositor's blunders, but not so many actual misreadings as seems at first glance; for many words, like "*horrowes* me with fear and wonder," for the Folio's "harrowes," are mere spelling variants and do not even indicate pronunciation differences. The Second, then, is one of the Good quartos. Later quartos successively reprint each other, and even the "players quartos" (1676–1703) are Second Quarto derivatives in so far as they stick to unadapted lines.

The First Folio also provides an excellent text, though like the Second Quarto it is not complete. Some of its omissions are stage cuts required by the play's extraordinary length. Its source was probably a transcript of a copy of the Second Quarto once used as a prompt book. A general rule can not be formulated to cover all points at which the two good texts differ. For some Folio variants the transcriber is doubtless responsible, for others the compositor; some are certainly corrections. Every editor of *Hamlet* is obliged to draw on both editions; even the text of the New edition, for all its editor's advocacy of the Second Quarto, departs from it frequently.

One other version must be mentioned, *Der bestrafte Brudermord: oder, Prinz Hamlet aus Dännemark.* The manuscript of this *Fratricide Punished* dates only from 1710, but it is probably a corrupt descendant of a version of Shakespeare's play used by some English company touring Germany. Such a troupe played *Hamlet* at Dresden in 1626. Many attempts have been made to utilize the German text for solution of the problems we have been considering. But while it resembles the First Quarto at certain points, at others it is closer to the true text. At still others it departs radically from Shakespeare's play, from which, however, it probably stems, rather than from

he *Ur-Hamlet*. For the interpretive critic, its most interesting
feature is Hamlet's categorical mention of his stepfather's
guards. They are not specified by Shakespeare, but may be
taken for granted.

To list the famous men who have played Hamlet would be
to call the roll of the most illustrious British and American
actors of four centuries, and then we should have to add
celebrated names from many other nations, especially Germany. The original Prince was Burbage. On his death Joseph
Taylor took the part. The play was revived in 1661 at Lincoln's
Inn Fields by Sir William D'avenant, who made a version
structurally intact, except for cuts, but grievously altered in
diction. *Hamlet* has held the boards ever since. Betterton was
D'avenant's Prince, and he continued in the rôle throughout
his long and honorable career. His last recorded performance
was in 1709, when he was over seventy, and Steele (*Tatler*,
no. 71) praised his portrayal of "a young man of great expectation, vivacity, and enterprise." Probably no Hamlet
ever went beyond Betterton's in tragic elevation. "When,"
said Barton Booth, "I acted the Ghost with Betterton, instead of my awing him, he terrified me. But divinity hung
round that man!"[5] Editions of the D'avenant version in 1676,
1683, 1695, and 1703 also testify to the constant popularity
of the tragedy. Robert Wilks succeeded Betterton. Garrick
was not the only Hamlet of his time; but from 1742 to 1776
it was one of his most successful parts. Among his Ophelias
were Kitty Clive, Susanna Cibber, and Maria Macklin. Mrs.
Pritchard often played the Queen. Charles Macklin was First
Gravedigger. Toward the end of Garrick's career he arranged
a version which left out the Gravediggers, omitted Ophelia's
funeral, and radically altered the final scene. Others who
played the title rôle were Spranger Barry, Thomas Sheridan,
and John Henderson.

John Philip Kemble was the first of the great actors to reject the Romantic misconceptions; he played Hamlet heavily,
though with restraint. Cooke was not a remarkable Hamlet.
The Prince of Edmund Kean, who first undertook the rôle
in 1814, was of course extremely Romantic. Others who

played Hamlet were Forrest, Charles Kemble, J. B. Booth
Macready, Charles Kean, G. V. Brooke, Phelps, Charles Fech
ter, Davenport, Barry Sullivan, McCullough, and Tommaso
Salvini. Irving first appeared as the Prince in 1874. Eller
Terry was an appealing Ophelia. Meanwhile Edwin Bootl
had acted Hamlet in the United States and in England. His
scholarly yet poetic portrayal must have been among the
greatest. Tree, first seen as the Prince in 1892, was a senti
mental Hamlet. Forbes-Robertson's performances, which be
gan in 1897, were perhaps too quiet, but they were very
beautiful. Since then, notable Hamlets have been Wilson
Barrett, Benson, H. B. Irving, Martin-Harvey, Sothern, Man
tell, John Barrymore, Hampden, John Gielgud, and Maurice
Evans. Mr. Gielgud followed an earlier success at the Old
Vic, under the direction of Maurice Browne, with a record
breaking run on Broadway in the season of 1936–37. On
October 12, 1938 Mr. Evans began another remarkable New
York run with an uncut production. Despite the requirement
of a long intermission for dinner, and a conception of the
title rôle which in its determination not to be Romantic went
to the other extreme and gave us a chatty young gentleman
instead of a tragic prince, this revival soon established itself
among the season's hits. There were ninety-eight performances in New York alone. There have also been — this is
true of many of these plays — admirable revivals by less
famous actors, especially in repertory. Thus one of the best
all-round productions I have seen was John Craig's at the
old Castle Square in Boston. Craig played Hamlet to the
Ophelia of his gifted wife, Mary Young, with magnificent
impressionistic scenery by Livingston Platt and a brilliant
supporting cast which included William Carleton (the best
Claudius in my experience), Irving Pichel (Laertes), Donald
Meek (First Gravedigger), and a beginner named Alfred Lunt
as Player King.

On no character in either history or fiction has opinion
varied more widely than on Hamlet; but no one seems to
have thought there was anything queer about him till toward
the end of the eighteenth century, when the Romantics began

seeing their own moody selves mirrored in the play, and fell in love with the reflection. Henry Mackenzie, the Edinburgh Man of Feeling, seems to have been the earliest of the obscurantists. For Burbage's conception of the title rôle we have no external evidence. We may suppose it embodied Shakespeare's. No doubt Taylor did not radically depart from it; and since his performance was seen by D'avenant, and since D'avenant coached Betterton, the chain of stage tradition is uncommonly strong. Betterton, probably as great a Shakespearean as ever lived, we know played Hamlet as a manly and active prince. There is no hint of a Hamlet Problem in Charles Johnson's allusion to Shakespeare in the Prologue to *Love in a Forest* [6] at Drury Lane in 1723:

> The Hero, Courtier, Patriot, and the Man,
> Form in one Character his pious *Dane*.

But the Romantics' sense of personal frustration was read into the play by Scottish philosophers and by Goethe and Coleridge; and the baseless notion was invented of Hamlet the self-deceived, the irresolute, the man of sensibility too refined for this wicked world. It still obscures the play for many readers, though not as a rule for audiences.

Of course Hamlet is thoughtful. No one denies that, nor does it make him a whit less representative of the Renaissance man. His reflections on death are

the voice of a Renaissance grown middle-aged, when the confident bombast of a Tamburlaine is no longer possible. . . . It is not Hamlet alone who speaks, just as it is not Hamlet alone who holds a skull. The English Renaissance was becoming contemplative, and its contemplation was led more and more, like Hamlet's, to death.[7]

Shakespeare's was a reflective mind, and (this is probably even more to the point than a changing *Zeitgeist*) he was growing older. Given the requirement of the soliloquies as arias for the leading actor, world-weariness and to-be-or-not-to-be were natural, indeed almost inevitable, themes. What we must guard against is taking those speeches exclusively as guides to Hamlet's character.

There is really no mystery at all, except as every manifestation of genius is mysterious. Granted a reasonable degree of sensitiveness to art, anyone can perceive the play as Shakespeare wrote it who will take the trouble to learn how to read Elizabethan dramatic score. To read score accurately involves, first, the mastery of Elizabethan English, which is further from our own than it looks, and, second, an understanding of dramatic technique in general and of Elizabethan technique in particular. Unfortunately, a grip on idiom and technical principles is not to be acquired without some study, while it is an amiable weakness of our race that everyone wants to give his views on *Hamlet*, whether or not he can read it. Shakespeare can certainly be enjoyed without this mastery; he can not be comprehended without it. Not that he can be fully comprehended even then; that would take another Shakespeare. Exactly as Mr. Toscanini brings himself by repeated study of the score closer to Beethoven's intentions, the modern scholar seeks with reverence and humility, not to justify a philosophy nor to turn Shakespeare into a contemporary, but to learn from the score itself, that is, from the text of the plays, studied in the light of all that can be learned about literature and about life in their times, what Shakespeare actually wrote and how he intended his audience to take it.

The theatre is a temple of conventions, and among those which Shakespeare built into *Hamlet* were the avenger's assumption of madness while biding his time (that is in the source and in many other revenge plays) and his self-reproach for inaction. Hamlet is not mad for a single moment; he is playing mad. As for the morality of personal vengeance, however abhorrent the concept we must accept it in the play as Hamlet's sacred duty, just as we must accept the Ghost who urges it. At the outset the Prince is depressed by his father's death, by his uncle's election to the throne,[8] and by his mother's remarriage. Under the circumstances, his melancholy is not excessive. Not till he meets the Ghost has he the slightest inkling that his uncle has committed murder and his mother adultery. She has no knowledge of her present

JOHN PHILIP KEMBLE AS HAMLET

from a portrait by Lawrence

In their tables, before they come to the play, as thus:
Cannot you ſtay till I eate my porrige? and, you owe me
A quarters wages: and, my coate wants a culliſon:
And, your beere is ſowre: and, blabbering with his lips,
And thus keeping in his cinkapaſe of ieaſts,
When, God knows, the warme Clowne cannot make a ieſt
Vnleſſe by chance, as the blinde man catcheth a hare:
Maiſters tell him of it.

  players We will my Lord.
  Ham. Well, goe make you ready. *exeunt players.*
  Horatio. Heere my Lord.
  Ham. *Horatio*, thou art euen as iuſt a man,
As e're my conuerſation cop'd withall.
  Hor. O my lord!
  Ham. Nay why ſhould I flatter thee?
Why ſhould the poore be flattered?
What gaine ſhould I receiue by flattering thee,
That nothing hath but thy good minde?
Let flattery ſit on thoſe time-pleaſing tongs,
To gloſe with them that loues to heare their praiſe,
And not with ſuch as thou *Horatio*.
There is a play to night, wherein one Sceane they haue
Comes very neere the murder of my father,
When thou ſhalt ſee that Act afoote,
Marke thou the King, doe but obſerue his lookes,
For I mine eies will riuet to his face:
And if he doe not bleach, and change at that,
It is a damned ghoſt that we haue ſeene.
Horatio, haue a care, obſerue him well.
  Hor. My lord, mine eies ſhall ſtill be on his face,
And not the ſmalleſt alteration
That ſhall appeare in him, but I ſhall note it.
  Ham. Harke, they come.
  Enter King, Queene, Corambis, and other Lords. (a play?
 King How now ſon *Hamlet*, how fare you, ſhall we haue
 Ham. Yfaith the Camelions diſh; not capon cramm'd,
                  feede

A BAD QUARTO PAGE: *HAMLET*, 1603

Compare the garbled version of Hamlet's long speech to Horatio with
the more authentic text opposite.

Nay, doe not thinke I flatter,
For what aduancement may I hope from thee
That no reuenew haft but thy good fpirits
To feede and clothe thee, why fhould the poore be flatterd?
No, let the candied tongue licke abfurd pompe,
And crooke the pregnant hindges of the knee
Where thrift may follow fauning; dooft thou heare,
Since my deare foule was miftris of her choice,
And could of men diftinguifh her election,
S'hath feald thee for herfelfe, for thou haft been
As one in fuffring all that fuffers nothing,
A man that Fortunes buffets and rewards
Haft tane with equall thanks; and bleft are thofe
Whofe blood and iudgement are fo well comedled,
That they are not a pype for Fortunes finger
To found what ftop fhe pleafe : giue me that man
That is not paffions flaue, and I will weare him
In my harts core, I in my hart of hart
As I doe thee. Something too much of this,
There is a play to night before the King,
One fcene of it comes neere the circumftance
Which I haue told thee of my fathers death,
I prethee when thou feeft that act a foote,
Euen with the very comment of thy foule
Obferue my Vncle, if his occulted guilt
Doe not it felfe vnkennill in one fpeech,
It is a damned ghoft that we haue feene,
And my imaginations are as foule
As *Vulcans* ftithy; giue him heedfull note,
For I mine eyes will riuet to his face,
And after we will both our iudgements ioyne
In cenfure of his feeming.
  Hor. Well my lord,
If a fteale ought the whilft this play is playing
And fcape detected, I will pay the theft.

    Enter Trumpets and Kettle Drummes, King, Queene,
            Polonius, Ophelia.
  Ham. They are comming to the play. I muft be idle,

EDWIN BOOTH AS HAMLET

husband's crime, though of her innocence Hamlet is not certain till her surprise clears her when he brings the accusation just after the death of Polonius.

Temporary inaction is a condition of the revenge tragedy; vengeance comes at the end of the play, and the dramatist's task is to motivate the delay. Up to the "Mousetrap," the play within the play, Hamlet's delay is motivated by doubt whether it is "an honest ghost." Every Elizabethan knew the Devil could assume the form of a ghost, give a fictitious account of murder to a relative of the deceased, and by inciting the survivor to the slaughter of an innocent man secure the would-be avenger's damnation. Hamlet believes he has talked with his father's spirit, but not till he has verified the Ghost's story by staging the play which breaks down the King's nerve has he a moral right to act. "The spirit that I have seen May be a devil. . . . The play's the thing." He is a very young man; this is the first time he has been called on to make a momentous decision. He accepts his task courageously; but, like anyone still on the threshold of life, he is not yet entirely sure of himself. He is troubled by sordid thoughts about sex, all the more because the haste of his mother's remarriage inclines him to cynicism about women. He loves Ophelia, but accepts dismissal because she is a woman and under her father's thumb. There is only one possible confidant for the avenger, Horatio, though Shakespeare artfully keeps most of the confidential sessions off stage in order not to interfere with one of the most appealing features of this play, the hero's loneliness.

Immediately after the "Mousetrap" scene Hamlet finds Claudius on his knees, apparently in prayer. Here another convention is utilized by the dramatist, who is not yet ready to end his play. The revenge code, in literature at any rate, required destruction of soul as well as body. If the King is at peace with God and Hamlet kills him, his soul will be saved. The Prince postpones his vengeance, not because he is weak, but because he is strong enough to wait till he can make it complete. In the next scene he kills Polonius, whom he supposes to be the King. That puts Claudius on guard, and Hamlet has no chance to strike again until the final scene, when he consummates his revenge at the first opportunity he has had to obtain full vengeance after obtaining certain knowledge of his uncle's guilt. Much of the critical confusion arose from failure to recognize the greatness of Claudius, who is often played by an inferior actor, with the part cut to ribbons. He is really a magnificent character, a foeman well worthy of Hamlet's steel; and on the seventeenth-century stage many more of his lines were preserved than is now customary.

Hamlet certainly chafes at his enforced delay, but he gives us plenty of action. He sets the trap for Claudius, he kills Polonius, we learn how he foils Rosencrantz and Guildenstern and boards the pirate ship; and at the end of the tragedy, which is the proper place, he avenges his murdered father, though he comes short, as all men must, of the full measure of his hopes, since he fails to win the throne and falls in the moment of victory. No one in the play suggests that Hamlet is weak or dull except the Prince himself and his father. The latter's reproach in the closet scene is of no moment: the Ghost knows he is an honest ghost. The Romantic case rests on the two soliloquies of self-reproach at the end of II, ii and of IV, iv. These are elocutionary arias in the conventional vein of heroic avengers never accused by critics of undue delay. Both close with the author's assurance to his audience that the revenge will come at the proper time. And one of them ("How all occasions") was omitted in the Bettertonian *Hamlet*, while the other ("O, what a rogue") was drastically reduced in length, both cuts being in all probability similar to those on Shakespeare's stage.

This view of Prince Hamlet as ardent, masculine, and heroic, as a gallant boy playing out a lone hand for revenge and a throne against a great opponent, does not depreciate him.[9] On the contrary. He is a man of action but not, like Laertes, of unscrupulous action. He is also a sensitive and reflective person, often saddened or irritated by the sorry scheme of things; but those qualities no more frustrate him than Sidney's fineness kept him from being his age's beau idéal. The last speech of an Elizabethan tragedy is normally delivered by the character of highest rank left alive, and it affords the author his final opportunity to make everything clear. Such speeches have almost the authority of a program note. Fortinbras orders a soldier's funeral, endorses the royal promise of Hamlet's character, and says nothing whatever about the tragedy of a spirit inadequate to the burden life has laid upon it.

Hamlet, though he is shaped for love and friendship and delight in the world's beauty, accepts, not without bitter protest, a difficult and dangerous mission, and prosecutes it while life is in him. The human cry in the protest endears him to us, makes us feel that he is one of us; while the pluck with which he carries on fills us with pride in the capacity of our kind to endure while we must and press forward when we may to such victory as we can win and the ultimate defeat that is the lot of Man.

THE TRAGEDY OF OTHELLO, THE MOOR OF VENICE

Othello is unlike the others; it has even been called Shakespeare's most modern play. No throne is at stake, as in *Hamlet*, *King Lear*, and *Macbeth;* this is essentially a domestic tragedy, even though we have the usual background of war and statecraft. The hero is not, like Macbeth, driven into his fatal course by an ungovernable trait of his own character; nor does he wage war against a powerful adversary, as Hamlet does. He does not act at once upon the theme of the play; till toward its close he is acted on, and by an enemy; and the field of action is, throughout most of the drama, the hero's mind. The structure is less loose-jointed than usual. All this has led some to call *Othello* the most perfect work of art in existence.

The relatively tight construction has made the duration of the action a puzzle to some of the critics. The elaborate timetables given in editions of Shakespeare are a fine example of wasted time. When the author wishes to impress us with the rapidity of the action, he drops short-time hints into the dialogue; when he wants us to know that matters are proceeding slowly, he gives us long-time hints. This principle is all that is required to solve every "problem" of time in Shakespeare. Whenever we need to know anything more specific, the dramatist always tells us — specifically.

Othello was performed at court on November 1, 1604,[10] probably soon after Shakespeare wrote and produced it publicly. Burbage acted the title rôle. There was no edition till 1622,[11] the year before the earliest collection of Shakespeare's works, the First Folio. Both the Quarto and the Folio afford good texts, apparently derived from a common original; and, since each omits some lines, both must be used by the modern editor. There are many variant readings; on the whole the Folio is probably a little closer to what Shakespeare wrote.

Othello seems to have held the stage from the very first. So scanty are the records which preserve the dates when Jacobean plays were acted, that even a scattering of them is presumptive evidence of steady performance. We know that *Othello* was acted in 1610, 1612–13, 1629, 1635, and (probably) 1636. According to James Wright's *Historia Histrionica* (1699), Burbage's successor, Joseph Taylor, played Iago, and a Caroline King's Man, Eliard Swanston, Othello. The play was one of the first revivals under the Restoration; it was acted without "improvement." By the end of 1660 Margaret Hughes had made her debut at Vere Street as Desdemona — probably the first appearance on the London stage of a professional English actress. Nicholas Burt and Walter Clun seem to have been the earliest Restoration Othello and Iago. To the second of these parts the accomplished Michael Mohun soon fell heir; while Charles Hart, a sterling tragedian, one of the few surviving players from before the Civil Wars, moved up from Cassio to the title rôle. The latter was taken over with great success by Betterton after the union of the patent companies in 1682, and the play remained a stock piece throughout his career. Anne Bracegirdle was his Desdemona. Wilks and Booth played Othello early in the eighteenth century. Colley Cibber, Macklin, Henderson, and Cooke were Iagos. Garrick failed in both rôles, but Quin and Barry were successful Othellos. . Famous nineteenth-century exponents of the title rôle were J. P. Kemble, Edmund and Charles Kean (it was one of Edmund's greatest rôles), Brooke, Forrest, Macready, Fechter, J. B. Booth, Ira Aldridge ("the African Roscius"), E. L. Davenport, Phelps, Salvini, McCullough, Thomas Cooper, Lawrence and Wilson Barrett, Edwin Booth, and Irving. The last two were also famous but quite different Iagos. According to Ellen Terry, an appealing Desdemona, Irving rightly emphasized the pose of soldierly bluffness, while Booth was the snake in the grass; but Winter says that was only when he was alone. Booth was never satisfied with his performance; yet those who saw him could not forget the malignant glare with which he coldly swept the audience after a soliloquy. Through the generosity of Irving, these great actors appeared together in London in 1881, alternating in the two rôles. Among other notable Iagos of the last century were Edmund Kean, Davenport, Fechter, J. B. Booth, Brooke, Phelps, and Lawrence Barrett. The tragedy was beautifully produced by Forbes-Robertson in 1902. He played Othello, to the Desdemona of his wife, Gertrude Elliott, and the Emilia of Lena Ashwell. Other revivers in London were Tita Brand (1905), Lewis Waller (1907 — his Iago was H. B. Irving), Giovanni Grasso (1910 — in Italian), Tree (Othello, 1912), Matheson Lang (1920, Othello to Bourchier's Iago), Charles Warburton (1920), J. B. Fagan (1921: Godfrey Tearle, Othello; Basil Rathbone, Iago), Maurice Browne (1930: Paul Robeson, the well-known Negro baritone, Othello, to the producer's Iago); Ernest Milton (1932 — he played the title rôle), Henry Cass (1935: Othello, Abraham Sofaer; Iago, Maurice Evans), Tyrone Guthrie (1938: Othello, Ralph Richardson; Iago, Laurence Olivier). *Othello* was in the repertory of R. B. Mantell, who acted now one now the other of the two leading rôles; but an American revival is now long overdue, despite the failure of Walter Huston's recent attempt.

The source of *Othello* is an allegedly true *novella* in the *Hecatommithi* (1565) of Giovanni Battista Giraldi, who was usually called Cinthio. There seems to have been no intermediate version. The Italian story gave Shakespeare only his plot, and not all of that. The Ensign (Shakespeare's "Ancient," Iago — in Cinthio none of the characters is named except "Disdemona") is not actuated by professional jealousy of the Captain (Cassio), but by his desire for the Moor's wife. He thinks she is in love with the Captain. The latter's dismissal, the wife's appeal for his reinstatement, and the stolen handkerchief are all in Cinthio. In her husband's presence Disdemona is bludgeoned by the Ensign with a stocking filled with sand, and then they pull down the ceiling to supply an explanation of her death. Distracted with grief, the Moor cashiers the Ensign, who thereupon accuses him of murder. Torture of the Moor fails to elicit confession. He is sentenced to exile and eventually killed by avenging relatives of his wife. He never learns that she was innocent. The Ensign likewise maintains silence when on another accusation he too is put to the torture, under which he dies. His complicity in the murder is disclosed by his wife after his death.

Upon this sensational story Shakespeare lavishes all his art of characterization. "Honest" Iago becomes the best of all the unscrupulous villains of drama, but Shakespeare keeps him thoroughly human and plausible. Coleridge, it is true, calls the soliloquy which closes Act I "the motive-hunting of a motiveless malignity." This not only ignores the expository function of the soliloquy, but discounts the professional jealousy, explicitly mentioned in the opening scene and elsewhere. It also discounts the sexual jealousy, which Shakespeare takes over from his source, adding Iago's suspicion of Othello with Emilia, though he subordinates Iago's passion for Desdemona. Both motives are powerful incentives in real life; and while the second is despicable in this case, the first is not wholly ignoble. As far as Shakespeare lays the facts before us, Iago's claim to promotion is stronger than Cassio's. This does not, of course, justify his behavior; but there is nothing in the play to indicate that Iago sees at the outset where his vague notion of making trouble is going to lead him. The amazing success of his improvised plans encourages his self-confidence and his contempt for his dupes, but involves him more deeply than he has expected. In the end he finds himself fighting for his life. Horrible, therefore, as Iago's villainous course proves to be, we begin the play not completely out of sympathy with him. As the drama unfolds he speedily forfeits this claim, though he is still an agreeable villain, on account of the pungency of his general observations, many of them as sound as pungent, and his humorous way of putting them. Not till the end is in sight, and "the pity of it" becomes almost unbearable, do we find ourselves regarding him with unqualified horror.

Critics have searched for a tragic flaw in Othello, something to justify his miserable end, on the theory that to present the fall of an innocent man is, as Aristotle holds, incapable of arousing and purifying the emotions of pity and fear. Pity is uppermost in this tragedy, all the more because, humanly speaking, Othello is blameless. He is set before us, in his first appearances, as noble and calm. In his dying speech he describes himself as "one not easily jealous," and that is clearly the impression Shakespeare wishes to leave. Othello is a normal man, and the play is not a study of the passion of jealousy. Why, then, does the magnanimous hero fail so wretchedly?

It has been argued that the plot is absurd on the face of it, that such a person as Othello would not act upon unsupported allegations. Thomas Rymer (d. 1713), the neoclassical bloodhound, bays at this drama, calling it "a Bloody Farce, without salt or savour," and suggesting as an apt title the "Tragedy of the Handkerchief." Perhaps it would be dubious as a novel; but a play, if not necessarily another story, is a very different way of telling a story. Once more we must consider certain conventions of the theatre which was Shakespeare's narrative medium.

Neither villainy nor gullibility needed on the Elizabethan stage the motivation we expect in a contemporary psychological novel. Disease and social maladjustment were not familiar concepts of the cause of crime. How a criminal's mind worked was not a question necessarily to be asked of an artist in fiction, as it is now. Back of the Shakespearean villain lay centuries of English stage-villainy: there was the Devil of the medieval mystery plays; there was Judas, most incomprehensible of villains; there were the bad angels of the morality plays — no motivation was needed for them; there was the Vice of the later moralities and interludes, the mischief-making mainspring of every plot, who neither required nor received any accounting for; and there were the sinister Italian scoundrels of more recent drama, men with the weasel words of Machiavelli on their lips, as the Tudor age misunderstood Machiavelli, or desperate Dons, like Lorenzo in *The Spanish Tragedie*, whose wicked designs are scarcely motivated at all. For an audience habituated to the machinations of a villain as essential to the plot of a serious play, a study of the cause of his antisocial conduct was as little called for as a rehearsal of the reasons why a hero was a normal man or a good man. All the dramatist had to do was exhibit his hero and villain; the audience did the rest.

As for gullibility, while the villain may or may not be foiled in the end, there is no point in introducing him unless at least one important character is going to be at least temporarily taken in by him. In a plot like that of *Othello* it is the hero's business, as a character in the play, to be deceived. The only objection to that must be on the ground of whether Shakespeare has made the deception plausible in the theatre. To that question the best answer is a matter of fact. Audiences do not consider and never have considered the central situation in the least absurd: Nor have many readers. Our inquiry should, therefore, not be "Has Shakespeare succeeded?" but "How has he succeeded?"

He succeeds, in the first place, by emphasizing Othello's simplicity, his ignorance of city life, and his humility. He is a professional soldier, bred in the camp, unversed in Venetian subtleties. He is touchingly humble when he thinks of how he differs from Desdemona in age, in social background, and in race. He is older; though he claims royal descent, only his military prowess gives him his precarious standing in Venice; and, while he is not a Negro, he is a Moor and therefore "black" to the Venetians.

Iago, on the other hand, is a native son, and wise in the ways of the world. His wisdom, we discover, is more limited than either he or Othello thinks it is. But the General is not alone in being duped by "honest Iago." Everyone, up to the very last, succumbs to his charm and his pose of bluff, outspoken soldierliness. Cassio and Roderigo are as easily led by the nose as the hero is. To make Othello's credulity plausible, Shakespeare creates the most accomplished of villains. Thus he motivates his principal characters in profuse excess of what his audience demanded. Again and again, in this study, the technical conditions and conventions under which Shakespeare wrote must be cited to illuminate his methods. But while they help us to understand the plays, they do not account for them. We have in *Othello* a superb example of the generosity of great creative power.

In the second place, whatever one may conclude about the plausibility of the deception, considered as a paradox in character, the noble Othello being eventually moved to commit certain acts that are not like him, Shakespeare has taken pains to make every step in Iago's scheming and every response of Othello to it plausible *at the moment*. In the theatre, where incessant attention is required of the audience, as it is not of a reader, a convincing whole can be created out of a series of plausible moments. The hearers do not ask, "Can this happen?" — the artifice of the dramatist persuades them it is happening. They *see* it happen. To conclude that Shakespeare fails to accomplish this in *Othello* is to conclude that the chain is weaker than its weakest link.

Not only to Othello and Iago does Shakespeare give the full measure of his incomparable characterization. Cassio and Roderigo are also drawn with great care, so that what they do seems in harmony with what they are. Desdemona is less interesting than Queen Gertrude or Lady Macbeth or any of Lear's three daughters; but she is far from being the mouselike creature sometimes depicted on the stage, though her tragedy is only corollary to Othello's. She is a high-spirited Venetian aristocrat; the most interesting thing about her is her willingness to break her social mould and follow Othello.

That gives her dignity, which she carries well. Shakespeare chooses to invest her at the end with little more than pathos, though that is very poignant. She, too, is blameless. It is idle to argue that the dramatist renders her poetic justice because she lies about the handkerchief. The lie is trivial, she supposes; and what she supposes affords the only ground on which to judge her. It is a telling stroke of irony that the handkerchief, so .insignificant in itself, becomes to Othello a symbol of his wife's infidelity as well as an important link in the chain by which Iago leads him on.

The play, then, is more pathetic than terrible, and Othello is less Everyman than Macbeth, Lear, and Hamlet. Yet the misery of his end, so unnecessary, so at variance with his noble nature, is not wanting in mystery and awe. His dying speech is a lamentation over the debacle of good intentions, and a cry of protest against the inexplicability of it all. He has been "not easily jealous, but, being wrought, *Perplex'd* in the extreme." Nothing is more tragic than the unanswerable "How has this come about? Why must this be so?" which humanity is always asking when it is too late. Did Shakespeare once throw a pearl away, richer than all his tribe? No one, except a poet, can feel the full force of this tragedy who has never had to ask himself whether that is what he has done.

THE TRAGEDY OF KING LEAR

This is the grandest, the most titanic of Shakespeare's plays, perhaps of all plays. The scarcely bridled scope of the several actions, the poet's superb disdain of neat and formal patterns, the torrential allusiveness of a style which, despite its indirectness, hits harder than the simpler idiom of *Hamlet* and *Othello*, the lurid passions of Lear's enemies, his own mistakes and helpless recognition of them, the wild storm that shatters his last defenses — all these combine to produce an overpowering effect of resistless and mysterious and on the whole evil energy, against which human resources can not prevail. Yet it is not the gates of hell that quite prevail.

Lear's weary flesh succumbs to the unbearable stress of existence; but his death follows a spiritual regeneration which endows this stern tragedy with much the same strangely triumphant note that Beethoven wished his music to sound for the sons of men.

Lear was well known to the Elizabethans when Shakespeare, probably in 1605 or 1606, produced his play, with Burbage in the chief rôle. According to the entry in the Stationers' Register, it was acted "before the kinges maiestie at Whitehall vppon Sainct Stephens night at Christmas Last," that is, on December 26, 1606. Two other bits of evidence point to 1605–1606 as the date of composition. The "late eclipses" (I, ii) may be those of September and October, 1605. Edward Sharpham's *The Fleire* (registered on May 13, 1606) imitates, in idea and phrase, the disguised Kent's offer (I, iv) of his services. Whether *King Lear* preceded or followed *Macbeth* is uncertain.

Lear's story is told in Holinshed's *Chronicle*, in Warner's *Albions England* (III, xiv), in Spenser's *The Faerie Queene* (II, x, 27–32), by John Higgins in *The First parte of the Mirour for Magistrates* (fols. 47–54), and by Gerard Legh in *The Accedens of Armory* (fols. 164–6). Behind them all lies Geoffrey of Monmouth's twelfth-century *Historia Regum Britanniæ*, in which the three daughters of an old folk tale current in Asia as well as Europe are assigned to the legendary Lear of pre-Roman Britain. Doubtless Shakespeare had read Holinshed's account. From Spenser he probably derived Cordelia's name. He may have read any or all of the other versions; the evidence is not conclusive. He was not the first to dramatize the subject. An anonymous play, *The True Chronicle History of King Leir*, was acted as early as 1594, when Henslowe records performances. Though it was entered that spring (May 14) in the Stationers' Register, the first known edition appeared in 1605 as "lately acted." Possibly Shakespeare's play had already been produced, and the publication of *King Leir* was designed to exploit its success. Or it may be that a revival of the old play and the printing of its text gave Shakespeare his idea. There is no way of telling.

The nondramatic versions end quite differently from Shakespeare's: Cordelia restores Lear's crown and wears it after his death. The sons of Goneril and Regan finally dethrone her, and she kills herself in prison. The old play closes with the restoration of Lear. It is hardly Shakespeare's source. Probably he knew it in some form, and he may have begun with the intention of rewriting it. If so, he soon abandoned it; for, though he is indebted to earlier treatments for his main plot, he handles the materials with the boldest independence. His constant borrowing of narrative outlines was the usual thing in those times; it would not have occurred to anyone that this practice implied any lack of inventiveness. That Shakespeare was a very original writer becomes evident the moment comparisons are instituted. Had it seemed to him desirable to think up unfamiliar plots, no doubt he would have done so — profusely.

The Gloucester subplot he takes from the story of a Paphlagonian king in Sidney's *Arcadia* (II, x). In attaching it to the story of Lear, he crowds his canvas dangerously but successfully. Filial gratitude and ingratitude are the themes of both plots; yet instead of obscuring each other, each intensifies the other. They are, moreover, combined with great skill, chiefly through Edmund, whose villainy is an important factor in the chief as well as the minor plot.

Among the books that helped form Shakespeare's mind was Florio's translation of Montaigne's essays. Several of the play's reflective speeches are based on Montaigne's ideas.

The First Quarto of *King Lear* [12] was entered in the Stationers' Register on November 26, 1607, and published in 1608. It has survived in several states, corrected and uncorrected sheets having been bound up in various combinations. The First Folio supplies a text regarded by most scholars as more authoritative, but it omits about three hundred lines preserved in the Quarto. Though it lacks about one hundred of the Folio's lines, the Quarto also supplies many superior readings. Both versions seem to be derived from a common original, which included all the text we have, except the Fool's prophecy at the end of III, ii; this speech, preserved

only in the Folio, is probably a gag. Palpable errors in the
Quarto and certain typographical peculiarities, such as the
mislining of verse and the printing of verse as prose, favor
the theory that the Quarto rests on an unauthorized shorthand report; but the question of its origin has not been
settled.[13]

How successful *King Lear* was at the Globe and Blackfriars
we do not know. Sir William D'avenant staged it soon after
Charles II was restored, and this production had at least one
revival, in 1675. Betterton probably took the title rôle. D'avenant's was the last presentation of the original play for a
century and a half; for in 1681 appeared the most notorious
of all the Restoration perversions of Shakespeare, Nahum
Tate's *The History of King Lear*. Tate considered the original
"a Heap of Jewels, unstrung and unpolisht."

'Twas my good Fortune to light on one Expedient to rectifie what
was wanting in the Regularity and Probability of the Tale, which
was to run through the whole A *Love* betwixt *Edgar* and *Cordelia*. . . .
This renders *Cordelia*'s Indifference and her Father's Passion in the
first Scene probable. It likewise gives Countenance to *Edgar*'s
Disguise, making that a generous Design that was before a poor
Shift to save his Life. . . . This Method necessarily threw me on
making the Tale conclude in a Success to the innocent distrest
Persons.

Tate also played up Edmund's amours with Goneril and
Regan, and he left out the Fool.

Betterton acted Tate's Lear till within a few months of his
death in 1710. Then Barton Booth inherited it. Quin also
played it. Garrick's was probably the greatest Lear of all.
In the words of Macklin, "the little dog made it a *chef
d'oeuvre*." He produced a modified version of Tate, with substantial restorations. Addison had protested against Tate's
changes, but Dr. Johnson defended some of them. J. P. Kemble preserved more of Tate than Garrick had. Barry and
Cooke were other Lears of this epoch. Edmund Kean also
acted in a version of Tate's version; in 1820 he had a run
of twenty-six performances. In 1823 he restored the tragic

ending; but after three appearances he reverted to Tate. To Macready belongs the honor of scrapping Tate; in 1838 he produced Shakespeare's play, Fool and all, though with some structural dislocations. Phelps followed, in 1845, with a revival which kept the original order of the scenes and cast a man as the Fool — Macready had assigned the part to an actress, as did Charles Kean in 1858. Other notable productions were those of Forrest (one of the greatest of Lears), J. B. and Edwin Booth, Salvini, McCullough, and Irving, though the last was most distinguished by the beautiful Cordelia of Ellen Terry. Irving's version was a mutilation; according to Bernard Shaw, "the numerous critics who had not read the play" could not follow the story of Gloucester. *King Lear* has not held the twentieth-century boards so well, though the title rôle was movingly acted for American audiences by Robert B. Mantell, and London saw the Lears of Benson, Norman McKinnel, Russell Thorndike, and William Devlin. The time is ripe for another revival — if there is an actor of the requisite passion and largeness of mind. A merely pictorial impersonation will not carry a player through the rôle of King Lear.

Fantastic interpretations abound. To one critic this is an allegory of the murder of Darnley, the unfortunate husband of Mary Queen of Scots. Others hold that Shakespeare takes pen in hand to expose the hollowness of Stuart pretensions to divine right, by showing us an absolute monarch who behaves like a fool and finally goes stark mad, if indeed he is not insane to begin with. Such critical whimsicalities ignore the prime importance of narrative in Shakespeare's plays. His greatest contemporary was apparently stimulated to compose by an idea; Jonson often writes his play around an idea. Shakespeare seems normally to have begun with a story. Before he is through telling it we are likely to be enthralled by the splendor of his poetry, the humanity of his characters, and the wisdom of his reflections on life in general; but the narrative remains the central fact in the structure. We shall not go wrong with this play if we remember that Shakespeare is telling the story of a mythical king. We must accept the myth, just as we accept it in one of Wagner's operas. Neither the remoteness nor the romantic handling of the episodes need blind us to the underlying truths of characterization and commentary.

In the first scene Shakespeare exemplifies his impressionistic method of handling a realistic problem embedded in fairy-story material. His source lays down a romantic situation; it is inherently unrealistic: the daughter who loves Lear best is to refuse to speak her love. This has led some of the literal-minded to maintain that Cordelia's guilt in suppressing the truth makes her death a piece of poetic justice. Certainly Cordelia ought to please her father; it is not much he asks of her. At this point the dramatist, whose medium, being the flesh and blood of actors, involves *per se* a realism not demanded of the other arts, is proceeding over thin ice. He gets across it by giving his audience an impression at variance with the literal facts. In two asides Cordelia assures us of her love before she is asked to voice it. Lear's response to her refusal is sharp and inconsiderate. The language in which he disowns her is extravagant. An audience always likes a courtier who stands up to a monarch, and so Kent's espousal of Cordelia's cause inclines us all the more to sympathize with her. Lear is so patently wrong in resenting Kent's advice that the moral issue of Cordelia's silence is successfully obscured. The comment of France is palliative:

> Is it but this — a tardiness in nature
> Which often leaves the history unspoke
> That it intends to do?

Finally, the wicked daughters sum up the situation at the end of the scene. Their remarks condemn the King's action, but revive our sympathy for him, since their tone is unpleasantly hostile to him as well as callous toward their sister. All this, we may be sure, is artfully contrived on Shakespeare's part. It works. We are sorry for Cordelia and also for Lear, which is exactly what the author wishes.

As for Lear himself, he is in this opening scene unwise, vehement, and irascible. If he were not, there would be no play. But his wilfulness is not in the least like madness, nor at all lacking in plausibility, considering that he is not only an absolute but a fairy-tale sort of monarch. There is a species of critic who is always looking for trouble. If a character goes mad everything he says throughout the play is raving. If he is the villain of the piece, everything he says is sinister. We are certainly not expected to agree with the judgments of Goneril and Regan on Lear's mental stability, any more than we agree with Goneril's characterization of his knights, whose conduct on stage fails to substantiate her charges. Lear makes two imprudent decisions, but neither is evidence of senile dementia. His speeches, while overstrained in tone, are logical in structure. And when at last his mind does give way, it is only temporarily.

The cause is twofold: physical exposure to the elements after an intense emotional upheaval, too protracted for the endurance of an old man's nerves. It is in a condition of intolerable sorrow that he goes out to meet the storm, on which both dialogue and stage directions lay repeated emphasis. His mental anguish is even more terrible than the elements, against which his preoccupation with grief sustains him for a while. He withdraws from the physical onslaught too late. Enfeebled by it, he can not withstand the gibbering of the disguised Edgar; it is when "Poor Tom" runs out of the hovel (III, iv) that Lear becomes, not mad, but delirious, as the subsequent diagnosis of the doctor shows (IV, iv, vii). This excellent physician prescribes rest and quiet; and nature, Lear's own sound nature, asserts itself and pulls him through to complete physical and mental recovery. If it were not so, the tragedy would be vastly less effective. The catastrophe is inexpressibly moving because it is after heartbreaking trials have actually been borne that the survivor perishes just as he reaches the haven of rest. No sentences in all drama are more affecting than the simple speeches in which the reunion with Cordelia is accomplished and then ruthlessly broken by a malevolence which, though it operates through human agencies, is invisible and unassailable. What depths of despair Shakespeare had known it is idle to inquire. That he had known them, no experienced reader of *King Lear* and *Macbeth* can doubt.

Beginning, then, with a fantastic story, Shakespeare makes of it the most deeply affecting of his tragedies, till at the end the plot itself, almost unmanageable to start with and a little unmanageable in the fourth act (where each of the two actions cries for more development than the dramatist has time for), becomes a perfect instrument for the larger issues of character, idea, and tone. Chiefest of the sacrifices is the most endearing of Shakespeare's Fools, who does not appear in earlier versions of the story. He is not a "half-witted lad," but a crackbrained man of experience, though of course much younger than Lear. What becomes of him we are never told, for "my poor fool is hanged" (V, iii) refers to Cordelia. Perhaps this silence is an artistic blemish. But it is in line with the fierceness of the tragic sweep. The Fool does his best to rally his master's spirits; yet he never quite understands what the matter is, and it is hard to conceive how he could figure effectively in the catastrophe without distracting us from Lear's and Cordelia's woe.

The play calls for an accomplished cast; it abounds in first-rate rôles. Edmund is almost as good as Iago, though he is a colder-blooded villain, acting solely from self-interest, a businessman of villainy, lacking (save for his bastardy) anything like Iago's touch of justifiable resentment for past wrongs. Edgar, with his disguises, is the kind of rôle a versatile player revels in. So is Kent. As for the women, each a full-length portrait in her own right, Goneril the brazen and Regan the subtle are equally wicked and painted with equal power. Cordelia is a masterpiece of much in little. Lear's outbursts, like "O, reason not the need" (II, iv), are beyond all praise; yet we can praise them. But Cordelia's "And so I am! I am!" and "No cause, no cause" (IV, vii) leave us speechless. Criticism has not yet got completely free from the old notion that Shakespeare's genius was wild, enormously effective, but not quite under control. No artist has ever been able to let himself go more successfully. Minor poets achieve restraint with revealing ease. Shakespeare is master of both effects, and there is no better example than Cordelia of his ability to govern his unequaled imagination.

Few artists of the first rank have been distinguished for complacence — or complaisance. Men of talent in whom these qualities predominate often succeed as Society painters, kept poets, professors, officials of museums and foundations, members of academies, bearers of titles, wearers of ribbons. The hardest thing for laymen to grasp about art seems to be that it springs from a way of life and an attitude of mind, and that technique while indispensable is secondary. The artist is harried. He makes war. He does not always hope to right what is wrong, but he protests the wrong. He is likely to be a good hater — if only of human stupidity because it does not know how to recognize beauty. Great poets are our champions. They challenge divine justice as well as human. Shakespeare was a court dramatist, but he never developed the soul of one. If he wrote no plays of propaganda, it was because the tragedy of living seemed to him more terrible than the fate of institutions and the conflict of personalities. *King Lear* is his most ringing protest for stricken humanity. At the height of the storm (III, iv) the hero exclaims with a pity he never knew before:

> Poor naked wretches, wheresoe'er you are,
> That bide the pelting of this pitiless storm,
> How shall your houseless heads and unfed sides,
> Your loop'd and window'd raggedness, defend you
> From seasons such as these? O, I have ta'en
> Too little care of this! Take physic, pomp;
> Expose thyself to feel what wretches feel,
> That thou mayst shake the superflux to them
> And show the heavens more just.

At the height of *his* tragedy (IV, i) the protagonist of the other plot, not out of the physical pain that has left him sightless, but in a moment of reflection afterwards, quietly utters the awful lines,

> As flies to wanton boys are we to th' gods.
> They kill us for their sport.

DAVID GARRICK AS KING LEAR
from a mezzotint by James MacArdell after the painting by Benjamin Wilson

SARAH SIDDONS

from her portrait as the Tragic Muse by Reynolds

The play closes on an even quieter note. Lear dies perfectly sane, and more noble than he lived, in a strange peace that is of his own making. But we have not forgotten those speeches.

THE TRAGEDY OF MACBETH

Macbeth, the shortest of Shakespeare's tragedies, is the most uneven of the great ones. Yet eleven of its twenty-eight scenes are at least the equal of any in dramatic literature; and there are several speeches which for concentrated tragic force are hardly to be matched. They establish this play among the most powerful efforts of the human mind. Perhaps more perfect tragedies have been composed; no one ever wrote a greater.

It was very likely produced about 1606, though external evidence is lacking. There is a pretty clear reference to the banquet scene, in Beaumont's *The Knight of the Burning Pestle* (V, i, 19–29), probably staged about 1607. Metrical and stylistic tests indicate 1605–1606 for *Macbeth*. Certainly the highly figurative style is post-*Othello*, like that of *King Lear*. Shakespeare may have turned to a Scottish theme for his royal patron's sake. The ancestors of the Stuart monarch appear in the show of kings which follows the apparitions in IV, i. James's interest in witchcraft was well known, and he conformed to the royal custom of "touching" for scrofula.

Macbeth was not separately printed till late in the century. The First Folio is thus our only authority. With certain exceptions it gives us a good text, apparently based on a prompt copy. It does not, however, reproduce the play as Shakespeare wrote it, but an acting version, perhaps cut down, and almost certainly altered at two points by another writer. The text we have could be played in about two hours, the normal length of Elizabethan performances. As we have seen, Shakespeare habitually wrote in excess of it. Some have argued that a number of the short lines show where cuts have been made, but we have no reason to think that if Shakespeare happened to complete a thought in a line of less than ten syllables he felt compelled to pad it out to the usual length.

It is more likely that he was in a terser mood when he wrote this play and that even in its original form it was shorter than the other tragedies. The most dramatic scenes are remarkably crisp; it is hard to believe their effectiveness due to theatrical cutting. There are, to be sure, points at which it is easy to accept the possibility, for example, Lady Macbeth's soliloquy in III, ii. But there is no evidence that this speech was ever longer. Moreover, if the cutting was extensive it was for the most part done with great skill, but badly in IV, iii, when Malcolm and Macduff confer in England. Even as the play stands, a reduction is needed here; not because this scene is uninteresting, but because it slows down the action beyond the requirement of suggesting a long interim before we return to Scotland. *Macbeth* is more nearly a one-man play than any of the others; behind IV, iii, much of which is in Holinshed, may lie the need of giving the company's second actor, in the rôle of Macduff, and the juvenile, in Malcolm, more opportunities than their parts elsewhere allow.

The Folio's stage directions for the death of Macbeth are inconsistent, which indicates that we are not dealing with an unaltered text; but there is no evidence in the appearance of the Third Murderer (III, iii), who is certainly not Macbeth, nor in Lady Macbeth's allusion (I, vii) to a previous conversation in which her husband broached the subject of the murder. The last is an expository touch which gives the illusion of more planning than Shakespeare wishes actually to stage. Macbeth and his wife are spiritually in tune; they love and understand each other without speaking everything out. The murder is first discussed, though without uttering the word itself, in I, v, the idea having originally entered Macbeth's mind in the first of his long asides in I, iii. Speculation concerning a previous discussion is absurd; if it had taken place before the play opens, Shakespeare would have told us.

On the other hand, it is reasonably certain that Hecate is an interpolation by another author, very likely Thomas Middleton, in whose *The Witch* are preserved the songs specified in stage directions of *Macbeth* (III, v, and IV, i). The whole of

II, v, with its jaunty metre and its subordination of the
Weird Sisters to the prettified Hecate, was almost certainly
not in the original play; and the same is true of the speeches
in IV, i which immediately precede the song and the witches'
dance. These features are *divertissements* alien to the tone of
the play; they were further expanded in Sir William D'avenant's adaptation of *Macbeth*, which turns it into an "opera,"
with music, dancing, and "flyings" by the witches, all keenly
relished by Samuel Pepys and his contemporaries. There is,
however, nothing against Shakespeare's authorship of III, vi
(the expository conversation of Lennox and another lord) or
any other passage. Coleridge rejected the sleepy Porter, except for the one magical phrase about "the primrose way to
th' everlasting bonfire." But the Porter's appearance allows
for the passing of time, gives the company's low comedian
his chance to do a turn, slacks off the emotional tension between two strong scenes, and consists of several cleverly
phrased topical hits that no doubt evoked guffaws from the
audience. On our own stage, the flavor of the jests being un-
intelligible to most of the auditors, the Porter's invariable
success is due to the actor's drunken clowning; actually, of
course, the Porter is not drunk — this is the morning after.

The source of *Macbeth* is *The Historie of Scotland* in Holinshed's *Chronicles*. There Shakespeare found the Weird Sisters,
not real witches, but supernatural beings which have temporarily assumed human form. He retains that conception
and uses them to create the grim atmosphere of his play.
According to Holinshed, "the common opinion was, that
these women were either the weird sisters, that is (as ye
would say) the goddesses of destinie, or else some nymphs or
feiries." This identifies them as the Norns of Scandinavian
mythology, and in the play they stand for Fate or Destiny.
Yet they are not abstractions nor personifications, but objec-
tive characters of the drama, just as much so as the ghosts
of the elder Hamlet and of Banquo, or the Furies in the *Eu-
menides* of Æschylus. Their powers of prophecy and the embodiment in them of omnipresent forces of evil do not prevent
Shakespeare from giving us a clear impression that *Macbeth*

is a tragedy of free will. The hero can not prevent wicked thoughts from entering his mind, but he has the power to expel them if he chooses. He does expel them, for a while at the end of I, iii; but he welcomes their return at the end of I, iv, when the promotion of Malcolm implies the assent of the nobles to his eventual succession to the throne.

Not that this is a philosophical play. It is not a discussion of anything. It is the tragedy of a normal man who becomes a criminal. Macbeth is carefully set forth, before his first appearance, as admirable. Even after he embarks on his career of crime, he is no casehardened brute:

> I cannot strike at wretched kerns, whose arms
> Are hir'd to bear their staves.

Goaded by ambition, he chooses the wrong course. But his eyes are open, and he is too imaginative to suppose, until the prophecies of IV, i delude him, that he will not have to pay a price. His inherent nobility, his share of the milk of human kindness, his capacity for mental suffering, make the fall of this royal murderer extraordinarily moving. *Macbeth* too, is a successful bridge from author to audience, as it could not be if Macbeth were not a normal man but a thug. In the fourth and fifth acts Shakespeare adroitly detaches our sympathy sufficiently to align us on Malcolm's side, but not sufficiently to make us gloat over the hero-villain's dreadful collapse.

The period is the eleventh century. For it Holinshed used Hector Boece's *Scotorum Historiæ* (Paris, 1526), which in turn incorporates earlier writings. In the most dramatic of his scenes Shakespeare is scarcely indebted at all. He takes over the rebellion and a foreign invasion, historically three separate campaigns, and transfers to the murder of Duncan certain details of the murder of the earlier King Duff by Donwald, lieutenant of the castle at Forres, whose wife persuaded him to the crime. Among these are the prodigies mentioned in II, iv, the king's largesse, the drugging of the attendants, and their slaughter the next morning. It was King Kenneth, a brother and successor of Duff, who was struck with terror

and sleeplessness by a voice that reproached him for murdering his nephew, Duff's son. Shakespeare carries the Weird
Sisters through, as the source does not; in Holinshed one of
the prophecies of IV, i is made by wizards and the others by
an ordinary witch. In the source, Duncan is an easygoing and
ineffective monarch, dependent on the strong arm of Macbeth
for the preservation of order. After the murder, Macbeth rules
justly for ten years; then, worried over the prophecy about
Banquo's descendants, he turns into a cruel tyrant and his
subjects finally rebel.

The original cast is unknown.[14] Betterton played the title
rôle in D'avenant's operatic version, with his wife as Lady
Macbeth, and incidental music by Matthew Locke. There
was singing, dancing, and aerial frisking about on wires by
the witches. Pepys saw this show at least four times; he
praises especially the "divertisement . . . which is a strange
perfection in a tragedy." The play held the stage throughout
Betterton's career, though Mrs. Betterton was succeeded by
Elizabeth Barry. The witches were played by men. After
Betterton's death Macbeth was acted by John Mills. He was
not the equal of Robert Wilks or Barton Booth, who took
over Betterton's other great parts. D'avenant's version continued, however, to be played frequently, till in 1744 Garrick
restored most of the original text. His Lady Macbeth was
Hannah Pritchard; it was her greatest rôle (though she had
not read the rest of the play), as Macbeth seems to have been
one of his greatest. Other Macbeths of the time were Quin,
Barry, Henderson, Cooke, and Macklin. The last of these
actors came to the part in his old age; he mounted the play,
in 1773, with Scottish costumes.

J. P. Kemble's production retained some of D'avenant's
additions; its chief merit was Mrs. Siddons's Lady Macbeth,
probably the most powerful performance in the history of the
rôle. Sheridan Knowles told Edwin Forrest that when she
played the sleepwalking scene, "Well, sir, I smelt blood! I
swear that I smelt blood!" Kemble misguidedly staged the
banquet scene without actually bringing on Banquo's ghost
— as much a *dramatis persona* as anyone. This fancy has been

followed by other producers, but happily not by all. Macready's revival likewise kept the amplified witch scenes, and so did Edmund Kean's. Phelps abolished them in 1847, but Charles Kean restored them. Irving had two long runs in *Macbeth*, but the part was unsuited to him. Other famous players of the guilty Thane were Forrest, Davenport, Rignold, McCullough, both Booths, Lawrence Barrett, Salvini, Benson, Tree, Forbes-Robertson, Bourchier, Mantell, Sothern, James K. Hackett, Ainley, and Hampden — till quite recently, the play has always been before the public. Among the Lady Macbeths were Charlotte Cushman, Mme. Modjeska, Mrs. Warner, Ellen Terry, Mrs. Campbell, Violet Vanbrugh, Julia Marlowe, and Sybil Thorndike. A New York production in 1928, with Lyn Harding and Florence Reed in the chief rôles, and settings by Gordon Craig, won critical esteem. Nevertheless, while dozens of actors have delighted us as Hamlet, no one has for generations made a comparable impression as Macbeth.

This unhappy state of affairs must be laid, but not astrologically, to the stars, for *Macbeth* presents no such array of great characters as *King Lear*. It is sustained by the hero, chiefly assisted by Lady Macbeth and the witches. To what extent the principal rôles are intended to present a contrast in masculinity and femininity who shall say? We may, however, be confident that, although Ellen Terry was censured for her intensely feminine portrayal, Lady Macbeth is no hulking virago scourging a reluctant husband into the initial crime. Certainly she hastens his decision, and it may be that without her he would never have disregarded the considerations against it. But though in the source she is ambitious on her own account, she does not utter a word to that effect in the play. In her simple feminine way, she conceives that a straight line is always the shortest distance between two points. She has an almost innocent confidence in logic and in her own adroitness. Macbeth, on the other hand, endowed with a more comprehensive mind and an extraordinary visual imagination, realizes from the first that murdering Duncan is not so simple as that. He is a soldier, tried in battle; yet

he knows that "but this blow" is not all that will be required. The driving power is none the less his. When his wife
taunts him (I, vii) and he replies,

> Prithee peace!
> I dare do all that may become a man.
> Who dares do more is none,

he is reacting directly to her aspersions on his courage. The
player sometimes rolls up his eyes and strikes a noble attitude
at "man," but this speech is not an expression of superior
morality. It is a plain statement that he is equal to anything
short of bestiality.

His wife's nerves prove unequal to the strain. Shaken by
Duncan's resemblance to her father, she maintains at a fearful
cost her poise during the discovery, till fainting brings momentary relief. After that she is a broken woman, well aware
when we next learn (III, ii) how she is standing up under the
stress of their guilt that

> Naught's had, all's spent,
> Where our desire is got without content.

From this point on Macbeth formulates his plans alone. At
the banquet she rallies her forces as best she can, but despair-
ingly. And when we next see her, in the amazing sleepwalking
scene, she is completely shattered. After that she is to her
husband only a memory of what she was, and in the final
speech we are told that, "as 'tis thought," she has evaded
the burden of her reflections by suicide.

But Macbeth goes doggedly on. His mind is tougher. His
nerves harden. In the fifth act he is dying daily. His suffering
is appalling because, unlike the Queen, he can not find sur-
cease in madness. He is conscious of every turn of the screw.

> I have liv'd long enough. My way of life
> Is fall'n into the sere, the yellow leaf.

And when at last he knows his wife is dead, he can only
mutter that the end was bound to come, that every day brings
death to someone, and that our life is only

a walking shadow, a poor player,
That struts and frets his hour upon the stage
And then is heard no more. It is a tale
Told by an idiot, full of sound and fury,
Signifying nothing.

The triumph of Malcolm does not erase these lines. When they are pronounced they mean a great deal more than the end of a hero. For behind the puny figure of the actor of an hour fall in the endless legions, dead, living, and to come. There is no escaping that vista of pain — when Macbeth cries out because innocent sleep has left him for ever; when he groans, "Blood will have blood"; when he sums up the meaning of existence in that one terrible word, "nothing."

Chapter 10

LAST TRAGEDIES

THE TRAGEDY OF ANTONY AND CLEOPATRA

S HAKESPEARE's first permanent success in tragedy dramatized a famous love story; in the last of his most remarkable tragedies he turns to another. *Antony and Cleopatra* comes close to making a fifth with the four greatest; what keeps it from being another *Macbeth* is a certain retreat from universalization. It was inherent in the theme. Antony and Cleopatra are too well known to be ideal tragic figures:[1] they resist the symbolizing tendency of all serious and poetic drama. When Dryden lays hands on the old clay he molds this heroine into Woman in Love, but she is no more Cleopatra. In Shakespeare she is that identical dusky Egyptian (as he supposed her to be), and none other. He holds us with a tale of a grand passion, told powerfully and with a good deal of sympathy, which does not obscure the dramatist's judgment that Antony has made a mess of his life. But the play is half pageant. Before their tragedies are over, Hamlet, Othello, Lear, and Macbeth all stand for suffering and aspiring or bewildered Man. Not that they are handled expressionistically; they are individualized to the end. But by the generalizing speeches they are made to utter they insist that their agonies are not theirs alone. Antony comes nearer to that sublimation than Cleopatra does, except in her dying speech; but it is chiefly her play, and, however Shakespeare adorns and vivifies her, she always remains the celebrated historical figure. That is what keeps this tragedy below the plane on which the great four move. Yet, as the engaging Enobarbus says of its heroine, it is none the less a wonderful piece of work, which to leave unseen would discredit your travel in the realms of gold. The sheer scale of it, the mass of material manipulated, sets it beside *Lear* as proof of the largeness of the poet's grasp, even though he is content with the loose organization of the chronicle-history form. Shakespeare had all and more of the power of Rubens to plan the canvas hugely and fill it full of vitality. *Antony and Cleopatra* is his longest play.

It was apparently not printed till the Folio of 1623, which provides a fairly good text. The title had, however, been entered in the Stationers' Register on May 20, 1608. Presumably the entry refers to Shakespeare's play, though his name is not mentioned and no edition seems to have ensued. About 1606–1607 is a likely date for its composition; but the evidence consists only of the probability that *Lear* and *Macbeth* fall in 1605–1606, and a development beyond those plays in metrical freedom and stylistic subtlety.[2] Shakespeare's source is Plutarch's Life of Antonius.[3] North's translation is vigorous and imaginative prose. Shakespeare transmutes it into magnificent poetry, but he often preserves phrases and vivid and visual details.

Nothing is known of the play's reception on the Jacobean and Caroline boards. Under the Restoration it was reserved for the King's Company, but not acted. Sir Charles Sedley's *Antony and Cleopatra* (1677) is independent of Shakespeare's. Dryden's *All for Love: or, The World well Lost* (1678) is also a new play, but frankly "Written in Imitation of *Shakespeare*'s Stile." Its dialogue is often reminiscent, though structurally it is a neoclassical affair, a fifth-act tragedy with all three unities strictly adhered to. It opens after Actium, with Antony in the Heroic vein, conventionally torn 'twixt love and honor. Cleopatra's pretty throat is cut on the altar of decorum; for Dryden makes her the puppet of a ruling passion, her unwavering devotion to Antony. *All for Love* long held the stage. When in 1759 Garrick revived Shakespeare's tragedy and played Antony to Mrs. Yates's Cleopatra, he had a run of six nights, not bad for those times; but the public still preferred Dryden. J. P. Kemble staged the original play in 1813; he added a good deal from *All for Love*, as well as a grand spectacle of the battle of Actium and at the end "an Epicedium" with music by Bishop. The stage has seldom seen a costlier funeral. Neither the manager nor Mrs. Siddons appeared in this production, though they had played Dryden's lovers in 1788. *All for Love* was professionally acted as late as 1838. Macready played Antony, in 1833, in a lavishly pictorial revival of Shakespeare's text, with infusions from Dryden. The last traces of *All for Love* were cleaned out by Phelps in 1849. His Cleopatra was Isabella Glyn. In 1865 Charles Calvert staged *Antony and Cleopatra* in Manchester. He played Antony and was well received. London revivals in 1867, 1873, and 1890, the last by Lily Langtry, failed to please. In 1897 the title rôles were performed by Louis Calvert and Janet Achurch. Benson's repertory company revived the play in 1900. Tree produced it elaborately in 1907. Constance Collier played Cleopatra to his Antony; the Enobarbus was Lyn Harding. The title rôles were assumed at the Old Vic in 1925 by Baliol Holloway and Edith Evans. On the American stage, George Vandenhoff appeared as Antony in 1846, Edward Eddy in 1859, the elder Joseph Wheelock in 1877, and the late Frederick B. Warde in the same year to the Cleopatra of Rose Eytinge. In 1889 there was a magnificent revival in New York by Kyrle Bellew and Cora Potter. It ran for fifty-seven performances. In 1908 E. H. Sothern and Julia Marlowe failed in their production. However interesting these and the very few subsequent efforts have proved, *Antony and Cleopatra* simply is not a piece for our pictorial stage, even though most of its known history is a record of grossly spectacular treatment. Forty-two scenes were no inconvenience in an Elizabethan theatre, though the play must have been severely cut even there; in ours they are impossible unless the producer is content with impressionistic settings or none at all. Of all Shakespeare's dramas this is the one in direst need of transposition to the motion-picture screen.

Julius Cæsar had been greatly liked; its success must have encouraged Shakespeare to return to the vein of Roman tragi-history. He accepts as an historical fact the story of Antony's infatuation and ruin, and does not philosophize over it. What happens to Antony in Egypt is obvious; the poet does not need to underscore it. He was no professed moralist, though that does not mean his works are devoid of ethical value. He was perhaps not sufficiently positive about the exact location of the boundary line that zigzags between right and wrong, nor so clear on the nature of the *summum bonum* as Robert Browning on the one hand and Bernard Shaw on the other. Possibly he was too experienced. Certainly he was too imaginative. Every Roman in the play knows Antony is losing the world and condemns him for it. Shakespeare lets the condemnation stand. And yet . . .

Unlike Dryden, he adds no subtitle of endorsement, but Cleopatra is described and exhibited in terms equally vigorous with the censure of Antony. She is a coquette, as Cressida is, but quite dissimilarly to the Trojan an overwhelming personality and an artist. So she rules the play as well as Antony's destiny; and her play, unlike Cressida's, is not in any moment a dissertation. Men do not willingly talk politics with Cleopatra, though she has mastered the art of governing them. Her majesty, whether for good or evil, eclipses Antony's, great captain and lover though he be; and to her rightly goes the whole of the fifth act. He dies for love, but she mostly for love and yet a little for *la haute politique*.

> O, couldst thou speak,
> That I might hear thee call great Cæsar ass
> Unpolicied!

In the end Antony is wholly hers.

> I am dying, Egypt, dying; only
> I here importune death awhile, until
> Of many thousand kisses the poor last
> I lay upon thy lips.

That she loves him is indubitable, but not as Juliet loves her Romeo, not as the heroines of the romantic comedies love. When Antony turns ship at Actium he submerges his identity. She, never. Yet he has her heart, more of it than Julius ever had. Dying, he might exclaim with Edmund, "Yet, Antony was belov'd!" And by a Cleopatra! Certainly that is some-

thing to show for a life. Precisely how much Shakespeare
thought it was he nowhere tells us, neither in this play nor
in any other of his works, despite the sonnet lines,

> For nothing this wide universe I call
> Save thou, my rose; in it thou art my all.

For Cleopatra he writes one of his best death scenes, by
far the finest he gives her sex. It is incomparable because we
are already convinced that Cleopatra is a very great woman
and because the poet reaches the height of his lyric powers
in her dying speech. With

> Give me my robe, put on my crown. I have
> Immortal longings in me,

begins a strain of immortal music. It is a music that only
Cleopatra could sing; it is not the voice of young love but
of mature and deliberate passion.

> Give me some music! music, moody food
> Of us that trade in love.

Every aspect of her fascination is in that last speech, full of
longing to put off this corruptible, but heavy with the world
of sense in which she has lived and loved. The juice of Egypt's
grape is not absent from her thought, nor the homage Antony
will pay her noble act, nor a woman's revenge on the unlov-
ing Cæsar, nor a sparkle of coquetry with a greater enemy
than he:

> If thou and nature can so gently part,
> The stroke of death is as a lover's pinch,
> Which hurts, and is desir'd.

De contemptu mundi is among the themes, as is usual at the
end of the great tragedies; but Cleopatra is still ardent, even
as she picks up the asp, for her hero's heavenly kisses. There
are also piercing yet homely touches, like Lear's over Cordelia, to remind us that this dying queen is a fellow mortal:

> Peace, peace!
> Dost thou not see my baby at my breast,
> That sucks the nurse asleep?

The broken phrases with which she yields her breath reveal, in a final flash of simple poetry, yearnings hitherto unexpressed and perhaps unfelt. Now she wants Love's Peace. It is the same desire to which Richard Wagner gave its supreme musical expression in the motif in *Tristan und Isolde:*

> As sweet as balm, as soft as air, as gentle —
> O Antony!

This is completely disarming. Even the Roman of Romans, that enemy of the East, the severe, censorious Cæsar, pronounces in his final summary no moral judgment, but a benediction that actually includes a few crisp words of pity.

From what source, more profound than Plutarch, more fruitful than Holinshed and all the *novelle*, did Shakespeare learn the facts that went to the making of this dying speech of Cleopatra? The discipline of love? Perhaps. We must not assume it. For the well of a poet's knowledge is near the hidden springs of power.

THE TRAGEDY OF CORIOLANUS

"Not worth a damn," said Irving of this tragedy, the last Shakespeare completed. The actor was thinking of its effectiveness on the stage; but as an imaginative effort it falls so far below the level of *Antony and Cleopatra* that some believe the immense activities of 1600–1607, and especially the strain laid on the dramatist's nerves by the tremendous emotions of the great tragedies, had drained him dry of creative energy, or even that his mind was near collapse. Others invent an illness to account for the interval of comparative mediocrity between the best tragedies and the dramatic romances. *Coriolanus* is certainly not up to Shakespeare's standard, but the finest poet must be allowed his off seasons. Jonson had them; some of his failures are bracketed by masterpieces. Possibly Shakespeare had already said what he felt moved to say in the great tragedies, and ground out this one with no inner compulsion driving him. He seems to be merely going through the motions. He stakes out a plot ending in a hero's fall, and it is a plot full of dramatic situations. But the vital thing is missing; the play lacks poetry, both in the conception of the characters and in the execution of their speeches.

Small wonder, then, that of late its stage history has been almost a blank. The eighteenth century, however, did not insist on poetry in art. In the arid neoclassical soil the play found a new life, especially at moments when the actual political scene was favorable to a warning against either mob rule or the man on horseback. How *Coriolanus* was received at the Globe, the Blackfriars, or the Stuart court is unknown.[4] In the winter of 1681–82 a foolish adaptation by Nahum Tate failed at Drury Lane. *The Ingratitude of a Common-Wealth: Or, the Fall of Caius Martius Coriolanus* was intended "to set the *Parallel* nearer to Sight" between the meddlesome Tribunes and "the busie *Faction* of our own time," the Whigs, and "to Recommend Submission and Adherence to Establisht Lawful Power, which in a word, is 𝕷𝖔𝖞𝖆𝖑𝖙𝖞." As if to anticipate Dr. Johnson's objection that Shakespeare's last act has too little "bustle," Tate packs his with surprise and violence. Volumnia, Virgilia, and Young Martius turn up in Corioli. Aufidius, though he is mortally wounded, threatens to ravish his rival's wife before her husband's eyes. Virgilia is brought in; but she too is dying, from a self-inflicted wound, and the sight is too much for Aufidius. He promptly expires; and so, after a farewell passage with Coriolanus, does she. Nigridius, a villainous Roman renegade, gloatingly informs the stricken hero that he has killed Menenius and put Young Martius to the torture. Volumnia rushes in with the boy under her arm, his limbs all broken. At the end of a conventional mad scene she snatches a weapon, kills Negridius, and runs off. Young Martius has a pathetic dialogue with his father before both die.

A new adaptation by John Dennis, *The Invader of His Country: or, The Fatal Resentment*, was acted in 1719. To some extent it was inspired by the rebellion of '15. It is a dull piece, which deservedly failed. The original play was revived at Lincoln's Inn Fields in 1720. James Thomson's posthumous *Coriolanus*, staged four years after the '45, is not an alteration but a new work. Quin and Peg Woffington played the chief rôles in it. In 1754 Shakespeare's tragedy was produced at Drury Lane, with Mrs. Pritchard as Volumnia but without Garrick, in an effort to steal the thunder of a mongrel version, perhaps by Thomas Sheridan, in preparation at Covent Garden and shown there a month later. This adaptation was patched together from Shakespeare and Thomson. Sheridan played the title rôle. J. P. Kemble's revival in 1789 was another hybrid; but his stately style was well suited to Coriolanus. He often acted the part, to the Volumnia of Mrs. Siddons, which seems to have been one of her most impressive rôles. On the other hand, the physique of Edmund Kean, who first assumed the title rôle in 1820, was too slight for it, and he had small success. He stuck to Shakespeare's text, but the wisdom of this was disputed by some of the critics. Meanwhile Cooke had also played Coriolanus. Macready staged the play lavishly in 1838, in a fairly faithful version; but he made little impression as the hero. Phelps added *Coriolanus* to his series in 1848, and there were other mid-century revivals by less famous players. James Anderson played Coriolanus at Drury Lane in 1851, and afterwards in the United States. G. V. Brooke assumed the rôle in 1863 in Dublin. Irving came late to this tragedy, in 1901. He failed; both he and Miss Terry were hopelessly miscast. Benson was another Coriolanus; his Volumnia was Genevieve Ward, who took the part again at the Old Vic in 1920. Other Volumnias were Charlotte Cushman and Isabella Glyn. Among those who played Coriolanus on the American stage were Forrest, Edwin Booth, Lawrence Barrett, McCullough, and Salvini. A production at the Old Vic in 1938 failed to convince the critics that the piece has a strong claim to revival.

Coriolanus was not printed till the Folio of 1623. The text is very faulty, with much mislineation and misprinting. The mistakes seem chiefly due to lack of clarity and precision in the copy; yet nothing suggests that, such as it was, it was not authentic.

The date is uncertain. Conclusive external evidence is nonexistent. Cominius's encomium, "He lurch'd all swords of the garland" (II, ii, 105), may be echoed in Jonson's *Epicoene* (V, iv, 224-5), "you haue lurch'd your friends of the better halfe of the garland"; but "lurch" meaning "rob" and "garland" meaning "prize" were too common to make a connection certain. *Epicoene* was produced in 1609. In the same year appeared Robert Armin's poem *The Italian Taylor, and his Boy*. In its preface occurs a figurative expression about throwing a cap at the horns of the moon, an image which is perhaps less likely to be of his own coinage than borrowed from *Coriolanus* (I, i, 216-17). Metrical and stylistic tests point to a date later than *Antony and Cleopatra* and before *Pericles*. About 1608 is reasonably safe.

Shakespeare's source is again North's translation of Plutarch, in this case the Life of Coriolanus.[5] The fable of the belly and its members (I, i, 99 ff.) appears, in a longer version than Plutarch's or Livy's (II, 32), in William Camden's *Remaines . . . Concerning Britaine* (1605-sig. Cc 4^r). Very likely Shakespeare had read it in all three of these authors.

There is a curious lack of energy in the last of the Roman tragedies. Not in the style, which though unpoetical is forceful; nor in the episodes, which are lively; but in the whole conception. Once more Shakespeare rests content with the chronicle-history form. He uses Plutarch much as he had used Holinshed and Halle. But even in *Macbeth*, still more in the other great tragedies, he had found a better way of plotting. In *Coriolanus* he frankly takes the line of least resistance. There is, as Stoll observes, a lack of "constructive mechanism." The tragedy is without Fate and without a competent villain. Awe and mystery are absent. Aufidius is totally inadequate, either as a cause of the hero's fall or as a *modus operandi*. The real cause is of course psychological, the pride of Coriolanus being his fatal flaw. But the tragedy is not worked out psychologically; there is little analysis and no internal struggle, save over the question of whether to spare Rome. Shakespeare follows the facts laid down in his source — that is all; and the last of his Roman protagonists does not interest or move him sufficiently to induce him to inquire into the springs of conduct. Here is none of that lavish invention of motives which animates the plays based on the English chronicles. Nor does he take pains to enlist our sympathy for the man. Coriolanus is a bonny fighter and a dutiful son. A few touches in his relations with his wife and child or with Menenius might have cracked the marble shell within which he has his statuesque being, and then we might become really anxious about him. Shakespeare does not provide them.

Though Coriolanus is ruined by political tactlessness, the tragedy is in no sense a political play. That the people is a great beast the author assumes; but there is no political exposition or debate, such as we have in *Troilus and Cressida*. By and large, Shakespeare's own opinions must have been well over on the Hamiltonian side, but there is better evidence for that in other plays. Here patrician contempt is inherent in the plot. Had the Conscript Fathers been Jeffersonians, there would be no play. There is not much of a play, anyhow. The dramatic machine is assembled; it seems ready to run. But something has happened to the battery; the spark is missing, ignition fails.

THE LIFE OF TIMON OF ATHENS

The first three acts of this tragedy, according to those who have seen it, act even worse than they read. With the opening of the fourth the piece suddenly begins to move. The cause is the propulsive bursts of energy in Timon's misanthropic tirades, hurled at society out of a bitter despair much like Lear's, though with far less of self-contempt. Yet they fail to save the play. In *King Lear* we are speedily made aware of the hero's greatness. Timon's folly may be quantitatively less, but it is certainly more trivial and consequently ineffective as a ground of dramatic action. The Athenian spendthrift, however generous in his ostentation, fails during the first half of the play to convince us that his is a large and comprehensive mind. Abdications are not unknown in history; but Timon is a fool, not about love, not about empire, but about money. Perhaps his fall could stir the emotions of a susceptible millionaire.

As drawn and constituted, this figure has neither Lear's capacity for suffering nor his provocation. There is not character enough; he is insufficiently equipped with a past and too confined to a single quality in the present. He gives all to false friends; Lear gives to his nearest and dearest, and love goes with the gift. The betrayal of Timon is almost a matter of course: it would surprise us if he were not betrayed. Filial ingratitude is something else. Like many a philanthropist, this Grecian lord remains, after all his generosity, chiefly distinguished by the ownership of money. Despite the profusion of his complaints, he is almost inarticulate. We never feel we really know him. He lashes out with the fury of a wounded animal, and then creeps away to die in a dark place. He has one faithful servant; but why this expansive spirit, as at the outset we take Timon to be, has run his course through life without acquiring family or any true friends, we are not informed. Shakespeare might have made this the tragedy of a lonely heart, but did not. To make it a tragedy of ingratitude would require effective marshaling of the ungrateful, and there is no one in *Timon* remotely resembling in vigor Cordelia's wicked sisters. "Without boldness," says Delacroix, "and indeed without extreme boldness, there are no beauties." Whether or not that is true of art in general, it is certainly true of tragedy. The possibility of success was unfortunately narrowed when Shakespeare decided to leave the Timon theme in the conventional groove of, not ingratitude, but misanthropy. Lear's tragedy is more exalted as well as more pitiful because he is a father and was a king.

Thomas Shadwell had the right idea when he involved the Timon of his adaptation with two women, one true, one false. In Shakespeare's play the (largely unhistorical) doings of Alcibiades and the menace to Athens are insufficiently connected with the central plot. Timon's tragedy is merely personal. Yet the play is not a domestic tragedy. To insist that it is neither one thing nor the other, and not even good red

herring, is not to canonize Aristotle. A painter is supposed
to make up his mind before he begins whether he is going
to do a portrait, a still life, or a landscape; and though there
are successful exceptions, and there is always room for a new
genre that can prove its case, on the whole a play had better
be some kind of play.

The style of this one is extremely uneven, and the mixture
of prose and verse is distinctly queer. Indeed for long stretches
style is not present at all. Theories of divided authorship and
of revision by or of Shakespeare are inevitable, numerous,
and irreconcilable. It can not yet be maintained that a scholarly consensus is in sight; but the present tendency is to accept
the play as Shakespeare's alone. That it fully embodies his
conceptions is, however, very unlikely. The most authoritative opinion now holds that he never finished it. He may
have intended to turn some of the prose into verse and to
polish up the bad verse. It is not impossible that he was
accustomed to block in his plays with a rough-and-ready
mixture of prose and irregular verse and then, having worked
out the action and the cross-fire of the dialogue, turn the
speeches into his usual style of blank verse or carefully wrought
prose. One can not suppose that, style aside, he was satisfied
with either characterization or structure. The former is tame,
the latter at several points inconsistent. Why he quit work
on this play is not worth even a guess. That he did so is little
more than a guess.

His return to North's Plutarch for *Antony and Cleopatra* was
natural. As he read, he came once more on the Lives of Coriolanus and Alcibiades; and the Life of Antonius outlines Timon's story. Evidently Shakespeare saw two more plays in
these materials. Coriolanus may have bored him long before
the dovecotes in Corioli were subjected to their final flutter;
and Timon, save in his social diatribes, bores everyone, not
excluding, apparently, the author.

If the date could be established even approximately, we
might be able to guess at the reason why the piece was
abandoned. The only evidence is from the general tone and
mood and statistical tests of metre and style. These indicate

1605–1608; but a conclusion resting on such considerations is never certain and often involves arguing in a circle. Perhaps *Timon* was Shakespeare's next effort after *Coriolanus;* perhaps it was earlier, a failure from the years of great tragedy, begun and tossed aside in an interval between two masterpieces. If it was written before *Lear*, Shakespeare could hardly have meant to go back to it after he had expressed the best things in it incomparably better. Some are confident that *Timon* betrays a pathological condition, of which the first symptoms are visible in *Coriolanus*. It is certainly possible that the artist was ill or tired and his powers flagging, but inferences from unfinished work are always risky. Any poet is entitled to spoil paper without having a scholar conjure theories out of the wastebasket.

The only early text of *Timon* is the Folio of 1623. Evidently the "copy" for it was irregular. Possibly there were confusing marginal additions; at any rate, a great deal of mislineation resulted and much printing of prose as verse and of verse as prose. *Troilus and Cressida* was to have followed *Romeo and Juliet* in the Folio. When it was withdrawn,[6] *Timon* was substituted. Perhaps the publication of *Timon* had not originally been contemplated, simply because it was unfinished work, never acted. If so, the need of something to take the place of *Troilus* may have swayed the decision to include it.

Besides Plutarch's Lives of Antonius and Alcibiades in North's translation, Lucian's *Timon the Misanthrope* was used by Shakespeare. He probably read this sparkling dialogue in a Latin or French translation; the chances are against his knowing Greek. The faithful steward and the mock banquet are in neither Lucian nor Plutarch. Lucian is the source of an anonymous comedy which has both these features; it was doubtless written for an academic audience, probably at least a decade earlier than Shakespeare's play. It had not been printed; but that Shakespeare had read this manuscript *Timon* or had seen or heard of a performance is perhaps more likely than that both dramatists hit independently on details so striking or derived them from some common source unknown to us.

No contemporary performance of *Timon of Athens* is on record. Nor was the play separately published till 1734, except in Shadwell's adaptation, which ran through many editions and held the stage for over sixty years. *The History of Timon of Athens, the Man-Hater*, produced at Dorset Garden in 1678, is on the whole the best or at any rate the least objectionable of the Restoration versions of Shakespeare. Subsequently furnished with music by Purcell, it became toward the end of the century one of the most popular tragedies in the London repertory. Shadwell praises the "Masterly strokes" of the original; "Yet I can truly say, I have made it into a Play." The claim is well founded. Shadwell's Timon has a mistress, Evandra (originally played by Mrs. Betterton), and a fiancée, the shallow Melissa. When his ruin is disclosed, Melissa throws him over and goes back to an old admirer, none other than Alcibiades. Timon's steward is also disloyal. But Evandra offers her savings and shares the exile. News of the treasure brings Melissa out in a vain attempt to win Timon back. He dies on stage and Evandra commits suicide. Melissa tries to make up with Alcibiades, who spurns her. He announces the overthrow of the Four Hundred, and a messenger brings the news of Timon's death. Among eighteenth-century players in Shadwell's adaptation were Quin as Apemantus, whose rôle is fattened, and Mrs. Pritchard as Melissa. Another version, part Shadwell and part Shakespeare, was published in 1768; it was the work of James Dance, whose stage name was James Love. His Falstaff at Drury Lane was much admired. His play met with some liking at Richmond, but apparently he did not venture it in London.

A new adaptation by the arch sentimentalist, Richard Cumberland, had small success at Drury Lane in 1771. Garrick did not act in it; Barry had the title rôle. Like Shadwell, Cumberland perceived the need of a domestic interest; but his Evanthe, Timon's daughter, is a poor substitute for the faithful mistress. Still like Shadwell, Cumberland uses the added feminine character to tie in the Alcibiades subplot; Evanthe and the general are in love, and Timon's last action is the joining of their hands. New attempts to make the play go down with the public were undertaken by Thomas Hull in 1786 (Mrs. Inchbald was the Melissa, but the piece was "coldly received") and by George Lamb in 1816. Edmund Kean played Timon in the second of these versions, which was somewhat more successful and closer to Shakespeare than the first. An adaptation by Nathaniel Harrington Bannister was staged in 1839 in New York. In 1851 Phelps gave at Sadler's Wells the first recorded performance of the original play. It was repeated some forty times within four months. Subsequent productions have been few. Charles Calvert revived it at Manchester in 1876, and Benson at Stratford in 1892. Under J. H. Leigh at the Court Theatre the play had a short London run in 1904. The repertory of Frederick Warde in this country in 1910 included *Timon*. The intrepid Shakespeareans at London's Old Vic revived it in 1922, and Ernest Milton played the title rôle at the Westminster in 1935.

Chapter 11

HIS DRAMATIC ROMANCES

XCEPT the last, which is only partly Shakespeare's, the plays of the final group are heavily spiced with wickedness; but their lines are not bitter in the mouth, like many in the realistic comedies. The poet is spinning us tales of the far away or long ago, replete with all the violence to life and probability of the old romances, yet sweetened by endings whose happiness is more than conventional. Gladness and peace mark the close of each. His enthusiasm for the great ideal of reconciliation has led many to conclude that some private happiness had swept from his mind the doubts and lacerations of the tragic period. It may be so.[1] If, however, we recognize that, alike in tragedy, realistic and romantic comedy, and dramatic romance, Shakespeare is primarily engaged in giving theatrical form to narrative, it is easy to see that without evil there could be no artistic good. Even in *As You Like It* murder threatens. If there is less pain in *The Tempest*, there is no indication that Shakespeare thought he had solved the Problem of Evil. Suffering is at least recollected in all the plays of the final group. In *Cymbeline* and *The Winter's Tale* its pangs are not for old, unhappy, far-off things; there is enough to turn whole acts into tragedy.

Nevertheless, there is a difference in tone. That Jack has Jill at last, and such a charming Jill, had sufficed in the great comedies near the turn of the century; but the best of the dramatic romances end on a deep note of joy. They are young lovers in the romantic comedies, which give the theme of boy meets girl the most exquisite treatment it has received. Pericles, Leontes, and Prospero come into port after more extensive voyaging. They are older, possibly even wiser. At any

rate, their wisdom has been won under the bludgeoning of
experience; it is not intuitive like Rosalind's. The serenity
they achieve is all the more impressive because they have
been storm-beaten longer. With this group of calmly happy
plays *Pericles* belongs in subject, in structure, and in tone.

The authoritative text is the First Quarto, which appeared
in 1609: [2]

The Late, And much admired Play, Called Pericles, Prince of Tyre.
With the true Relation of the whole Historie, aduentures, and
fortunes of the said Prince: As also, The no lesse strange, and worthy
accidents, in the Birth and Life, of his Daughter Mariana [*sic*]. As
it hath been diuers and sundry times acted by his Maiesties Seruants,
at the Globe on the Banck-side. By William Shakespeare.

But the *editio princeps* is full of errors, and is usually reckoned
among the Bad quartos. Much verse is printed as prose and,
however it is arranged, refuses to scan. The edition was apparently unauthorized; it looks like a reported text, reconstructed from an imperfect transcript in shorthand. Almost
certainly it omits a good deal. [3]

The play was not included in the First Folio (1623), nor
in the Second (1632), nor in the first issue (1663) of the Third.
The title page of the Third Folio's second issue (1664) announces:

And unto this Impression is added seven Playes, never before
Printed in Folio. *viz*. Pericles Prince of *Tyre*. The *London Prodigall*.
The History of *Thomas* L[d]. *Cromwell*. Sir *John Oldcastle* Lord *Cobham*.
The *Puritan Widow*. A *York-shire* Tragedy. The Tragedy of *Locrine*.

With the exception of *Pericles*, there is no reason to suppose
that Shakespeare had a hand in any of these plays. [4]

The textual problems of *Pericles* are inseparable from questions of date and authorship. "A booke called. The booke
of Pericles prynce of Tyre" was registered on May 20, 1608
by Edward Blount, but he did not publish it. The play was
seen by Zorzi Giustinian sometime during his residence in
England as Venetian ambassador, from January 5, 1606 to
November 23, 1608. A novel by the obscure playwright George
Wilkins appeared in 1608, entitled *The Painfull Aduentures of*

Pericles Prince of Tyre. Being The true History of the Play of Pericles, as it was lately presented by the worthy and ancient Poet Iohn Gower. The prefatory "Argument" refers to the excellent performance given "vnder the habite of ancient *Gower* the famous English Poet, by the Kings Maiesties Players." 1607–1608 seems a likely date for the completion of *Pericles*, but nothing precludes an earlier one.

The problem of authorship has not been solved; but there is general agreement on relieving Shakespeare of any responsibility for the first two acts, save possibly an occasional touch. The prevailing opinion holds that most of Acts III, IV, and V is his, including the brothel scenes and the Gower choruses of those acts. The rude octosyllabic verse of Gower's speeches has led some to deny that Shakespeare wrote them; but, like the dumb shows, they produce a designedly archaic effect. As for the first two acts, no one knows who composed them or whether the play as we have it was the fruit of collaboration, of independent revision by Shakespeare, or of abandonment by him of unfinished work he had lost interest in to the extent of turning it over to some minor author for completion. There is not enough evidence to warrant even a tentative conclusion.

The plot is a *rifacimento* of the old and very popular romance of Apollonius of Tyre. Where the dramatist got the name of Pericles is uncertain; possibly it was suggested by the maritime adventures of Prince Pyrocles in Sidney's *Arcadia*. The appearance of Chaucer's contemporary, John Gower, is a tacit acknowledgment of the play's source in his *Confessio Amantis* (VIII, 271–2008), which for this story follows the account of the twelfth-century chronicle, *Pantheon*, of Godfrey of Viterbo. Godfrey's Latin verse redaction is based in turn on the *Historia Apollonii Regis Tyri*, apparently a work of the fifth or sixth century but presumably derived from some lost Greek romance. *Pericles* also draws on another English version, *The Patterne of Painefull Aduentures* by Laurence Twine. This work was registered in 1576; two editions have survived, one undated, the other of 1607. Twine's source is the *Gesta Romanorum*. The authors of *Pericles* follow now

Gower, now Twine; but each dramatist embroiders the plot
with details of his own.

In his *Painfull Aduentures*, Wilkins is clearly attempting to
capitalize on the success of the play. He frankly lifts a good
deal from it and also from Twine. Presumably he had the
text of *Pericles* before him. He wrote *The Miseries of Inforst
Mariage* for the King's Men in 1607; perhaps they allowed
him access to the manuscript of *Pericles*. Some think he was
the author of the first two acts, but the general opinion is
against this. That his book preserves the gist of a few passages missing from the play quarto is rather likely.

Since the seventeenth century, *Pericles* has not been a favorite with either readers or theatregoers; but it was originally
a hit. To its drawing power there is an allusion in the anonymous *Pimlyco. Or, Runne Red-Cap* (1609):

> (As at a *New-play*) all the Roomes
> Did swarme with *Gentiles* mix'd with *Groomes*,
> So that I truly thought all These
> Came to see *Shore* or *Pericles*.

It seems to have maintained a place in the repertory. Records
have chanced to survive of a court performance in 1619 and
a public one at the Globe in 1631; while in 1660, when the
theatres reopened, *Pericles* was staged at once by the company
of young players at the Cockpit in Drury Lane, where Betterton began his great career. Downes mentions particularly his
success in the title rôle. Apparently he dropped it when he
went under D'avenant's management. *Pericles* remained on the
shelf till 1738, when it was taken in hand by none other than
George Lillo, author of the epoch-making bourgeois tragedy
The London Merchant: or, The History of George Barnwell. His
three-act version, *Marina*, is restricted to the heroine's life,
from her flight and capture by the pirates to the final reunion.
Act II is devoted to the quarrel and mutual assassination of
Leonine and Philoten, daughter of the now deceased Cleon
and Dionyza; it is Philoten's jealousy which inspires the plot
against Marina.

The next recorded revival was by Phelps in 1854. His almost

invariable practice was to produce Shakespeare unaltered; but he was afraid of the choruses and, along with some minor changes, omitted Gower as presenter, though he wove in some of the expository lines. This revival was a success, largely because of its scenic splendor. This, too, was not characteristic of Phelps's methods; at the moment, he was in desperate competition with the lavish spectacles of Charles Kean. On the last voyage, to the temple, the ship "seems to glide along the coast" as "an admirably painted panorama slides before the eye." There were processions, banquets, and dances; and the rendezvous at Ephesus was appointed by Diana from a chariot in the clouds. *Pericles* was revived at Munich in 1882, and it was in Benson's repertory at Stratford. The Old Vic staged it successfully in 1921, under the direction of Robert Atkins.

The critics used to hold their noses over this play, chiefly on account of the brothel scenes. These are undeniably far from pleasant, in spots; but the purity, still more the *winning* purity of Marina, is rendered much more effective by the baseness of the Bawd and her commercial associates. It is, in fact, with the brothel scenes that the play begins to lift above the merely narrative and the conventionally romantic. Marina's stand is not taken in the style of the lily maid of Victorian sentiment, who would rather drown than be rescued by a gentleman inconsiderate enough to have pulled off his trousers. There is nothing insipid or affected in Shakespeare's conception; Marina has strength, character, and that flaming intensity required by any work of art that aspires to be more than merely decorative. Acts I and II stumble along; their author has no notion of how and where, along the linear continuity of narrative, to seize and fortify the key dramatic positions. As Shakespeare takes hold of Act III, the tension tightens with the bold use of contrast (the babe and the storm), the sailor talk (with its foretaste of *The Tempest*'s opening scene), the elegiac lines of Pericles ("A terrible childbed hast thou had, my dear"), and such vivid, suggestive phrases as "belching whale" and "humming water."

From then on, almost every scene is capable of bringing
off a brilliant dramatic effect: the pale princess reviving on
the Ephesian beach, the parting of Pericles from the child
in Tharsus, the capture of Marina, her purchase, her triumph
over the lust of Lysimachus and Boult, and in the last act
the long, stately climax and final dawn of reunion. I am not
sure that, with some amendment of the first two acts, a reckless reviver of *Pericles* might not find himself with a hit on
his hands. It is really a noble play, though the lack of a
dominating rôle might prove fatal to it. It would be amusing
to see both our self-appointed and our official censors squirm,
and take under advisement whether to forbid the acting of a
Shakespeare play. It might even prove educational to bring
them face to face with the important truth that purity is
most attractive when it refuses to pretend that evil does not
exist.

CYMBELINE

Of all the completed plays of Shakespeare's unaided authorship, this seems to me the poorest. The nine lines of "Hark,
hark! the lark," now inseparable from Schubert's perfect
setting, and the first stanza of "Fear no more the heat o' th'
sun," have more of Shakespeare's genius in them than all
the tedious plot, characters, and sentiments in a lump. What
unmitigated bores the principal characters are, except the
good Belarius! Of course he is a bore, too, but the nice old
bore, like Friar Laurence, who inspires a tepid affection as
well as respect. For the rest, the Devil take them! Cymbeline
is every inch not a king. Cloten is uncertain whether to provide a rôle for the clown, the first heavy, or the leading juvenile. Posthúmus Leonatus, the principal tenor, is simply
incredible; compared with him, Beaumont and Fletcher's Philaster is positively a hero, and they give him more effective
arias to sing. The mountain princes, though mere bundles of
instinct, are fairly amusing cubs; but they are a poor substitute for Nature's dwarfs in the folk tale, and theirs is a fake
primitivism since Papa Belarius is always on the job baby-
tending his Noble Savages. Philario is a cipher. Iachimo is

little more; and Shakespeare's failure to characterize him wrecks the play, as a comparable Iago would have wrecked *Othello*. Caius Lucius is just another imperturbable empire-builder. Pisanio and Cornelius, those bright vague angels of good works, are as characterless as the villain.

"We come now to Imogen," as Mrs. Jameson says — the beloved of Swinburne and many a gentle pulpiter. And, needless to state, of Mrs. Jameson. Far be it from me to deny that she is all a heroine should be, except interesting. She is a very fine girl and she loves her odd spouse very much, though with a curious admixture of a "pudency so rosy" that it more enkindles him than recommends her to this day and generation. It is such phases that raise doubts concerning Shakespeare's experience. Once, at least, he must have been *enchanted* by a woman; but whether he had ever known the flame which makes the most intense passion the most pure is by no means certain. Imogen, though she is chaste and affectionate, does not support the theory that he had. How the Regency sentimentalists and right-thinking Victorians adored her! She is, of course, a clumsily or carelessly executed Snow-White.

Now art's Snow-Whites, Micaelas, and Paminas are pretty regularly put in the shade by wicked stepmothers, Carmens, and Queens of the Night. The lyric soprano, indispensable to the plot (since there is no sense in hanging up a cage without a canary inside it), is often so boring, even to the composer, that his repressions find relief in writing for the sinister dramatic soprano, whom he favors with such dazzling arias that, although she has to perish and leave the hero in the arms of virtue, she dies happy because she has had so much fun. But of the malevolent great lady in *Cymbeline* we can only wonder what even a feeble-minded monarch saw in her. Two courses are open to the dramatist who gets sufficiently interested in Snow-White to try to save her from boredom's oblivion or eclipse by Hecate. One is to make her an almost abstract symbol of beauty or young love, and that is what Walt Disney did in his exquisite film. The other is to move in precisely the opposite direction, individualizing her, making

her a very charming but very human girl; and that is what
Shakespeare ordinarily does with a romantic heroine.

But not here. He seems to be writing *Cymbeline* half asleep.
I have never seen it acted, and perhaps the right sort of
dreamy performance could create a romantic haze through
which the vicissitudes of its plot might prove alluring. But
I doubt it, and strongly suspect that the elder critics who
exhaust their superlatives over Imogen were vamped in their
youth by some pretty actress who played her. "To remark,"
remarks Dr. Johnson, "the folly of the fiction, the absurdity
of the conduct, the confusion of the names and manners of
different times, and the impossibility of the events in any
system of life, were to waste criticism upon unresisting im-
becility, upon faults too evident for detection, and too gross
for aggravation." Johnson's salvo is not quite on the target.
For the trouble with this play is mainly that Shakespeare
lets poetry and artful characterization alone, and confines
his attention almost exclusively to plot. The two magical
touches, already mentioned, indict all the rest. The vision
of V, iv cries for the application of poetry — and does not
get it. So, of course, we are told that Shakespeare did not
write it. The argument is worthless, since the unsuccessful
lyricism of the vision is no farther below his standard than
the play as a whole.[5] That my sentiments are shared by many
lovers of Shakespeare I have no doubt; but the prevailing
note of the critics is one of praise and, for Imogen, of ecstasy.

It is not, *pace* Johnson, that the nearly fatal wager will not
do; for this is old romance, and part of it is sheer fairy tale.
Shakespeare no more intends Posthumus for a cad than Bassanio, and the wager itself is no harder to swallow than the
love test thought up by King Lear. We have seen how in-
geniously the dramatist contrives to make Cordelia's silence
acceptable; but in *Cymbeline* he votes himself a holiday from
the exacting requirements of art. As in *Othello*, he leans hard on
the tried principle of the calumniator credited. But Othello's
ignorance of Venetian society is not matched by the court-
reared Posthumus, nor Iago's brilliance as an inventive genius
and extraordinarily attractive personality by Iachimo's merely

functional existence. Iago and Iachimo are both pivots in the plot. The former functions to perfection because he has been artfully forged and tempered by the great observer of human nature. Iachimo functions imperfectly because, though he is correctly placed in the mechanism, he is not well made.

Cymbeline was first published in the Folio of 1623, which, despite numerous misprints, provides a good text. The date of composition has not been fixed. The general opinion favors *c.* 1609–10, but the only evidence is internal — metrical and stylistic tests, similarity of subject and tone to the other dramatic romances, and the lifting from the same sources of several details in both *Cymbeline* and *The Winter's Tale*.[6]

Shakespeare took the ancient British historical setting from Holinshed's *Chronicle*, which ultimately rests for Cymbeline on Geoffrey of Monmouth's twelfth-century *Historia Regum Britanniæ*. This king is the early first-century Cunobelinus of Roman historians. Geoffrey tells of his two sons; but Belarius and the kidnapping are fictitious, though the trio's exploits in the lane are adapted from Holinshed's account of the Battle of Loncart between the Scots and the Danes.[7] Posthumus, Cloten, and the wicked Queen's attempt on her stepdaughter's life are all invented by Shakespeare. The wager on Imogen's chastity is an old motif, which appears in many versions; Shakespeare uses Boccaccio's *Decameron* (II, 9). In this *novella* the wager is made at a gathering of Italian merchants in a Parisian inn. Bernabò, the husband, is a Genoese; the would-be seducer is Ambruogiuolo, of Piacenza. The latter does not present himself to Zinevra, the wife; he is convinced by her reputation in Genoa that he has no chance of succeeding, and secures the introduction of his chest by bribing a dependent. The scene in the bedchamber is essentially as in Shakespeare, but without the dramatist's vivid detail. Bernabò is easily deceived by the slander and sends a servant to kill his wife on her way to their country house, where he orders her to meet him. The servant spares her, takes her dress to show his master, and leaves her some of his own clothing. At this point Shakespeare ceases to follow Boccaccio. Zinevra eventually enters the service of the Soldan of Egypt. In the end

Ambruogiuolo is confronted with Bernabò and frightened into a confession. Husband and wife are reconciled. The villain is smeared with honey, tied to a stake, and stung to death by wasps and flies. Shakespeare probably found the primitive milieu of Belarius in *The Rare Triumphes of Loue and Fortune* (printed in 1589). The romantic caves are common enough, but the lovers of this anonymous play are Fidelia and Hermione; hence "Fidele," and the name of Leontes's Queen in *The Winter's Tale.*

Nothing whatever is known about the fortunes of *Cymbeline* on the Jacobean boards. Its first recorded performance was on January 1, 1634 at the court of Charles I, when it was "Well likte by the kinge." The next was in Tom Durfey's adaptation, *The Injured Princess, or The Fatal Wager,* acted in 1682. Neither the cast nor the reception it met with is known. Durfey's major changes are simplification of the last act (the vision is among his omissions) and the addition of a new character, Pisanio's daughter, who is accused of conniving at the flight of "Eugenia" from court. By way of punishment this blameless creature is turned over to a drunken friend of Cloten's for raping. Pisanio saves her by killing him, but is thereupon disarmed and deliberately blinded by Cloten. It was probably this version that was acted at Lincoln's Inn Fields in 1720 and at Covent Garden in 1738; but in 1740 Theophilus Cibber played Posthumus in a text which apparently discarded Durfey's contributions. In 1746 the leading rôles were taken by Lacy Ryan and Hannah Pritchard. An altered version was staged in 1759. The adapter was William Hawkins, formerly a Professor of Poetry at Oxford; his object was to improve the play by Aristotle's light, but the public showed little gratitude for the illumination. Garrick revived *Cymbeline* in 1761. For a decade no year passed at Drury Lane without at least five performances, and for five years more there were never less than two or three each season. Garrick originally played Posthumus, but soon dropped out of the cast. William Powell succeeded him. Samuel Reddish, who afterwards took over the rôle, was much admired in it. Mrs. Yates and Mrs. Barry were the leading Imogens. Garrick's text was fairly faithful, for those days, though it contains many minor alterations. Another warmly praised Posthumus was John Henderson. Elizabeth Young was his Imogen. It is no accident that the palmy days of *Cymbeline* came after sentimentalism had triumphed.

J. P. Kemble revived the play in 1806; he acted Posthumus for thirty years. Cooke was the "serpent-like" Iachimo of this production. Others who shone in the hero's rôle were J. B. Booth in 1817, and Edmund Kean in 1823. Neither continued in it for long, though in 1837 Booth played Iachimo in Boston. In 1827 Charles Kemble, who acted Posthumus, made one of his splurges in "historical accuracy," with scenery, costumes, and properties studied from relics of ancient Britain. Besides distracting the audience from the play, this sort of thing is hopelessly misguided for most of Shakespeare's dramas, and especially for *Cymbeline*, whose courtiers often talk and behave like gentlemen (in the technical sense) at the court of James. Young, who had acted Iachimo to Kean's Posthumus, appeared in the latter rôle in 1829. Macready made his first appearance in it in 1811, when he was eighteen. He subsequently revived the play several times, with small success. Samuel Phelps's production was in 1847. He played Posthumus to enthusiastic applause; Dickens actually sent him a letter, not merely of congratulation, but of thanks. Others who undertook the part were Charles Kean, G. V. Brooke, Walter Montgomery, George Rignold, Edward Compton, John H. Barnes, and Otis Skinner. Several of these actors — obvious exceptions are the first named and the last — are little remembered now; I mention them to emphasize the frequency with which *Cymbeline* used to be played. Among the Imogens were Dora Jordan, Sarah Siddons, Helen Faucit (the most famous of them), Adelaide Neilson, Helena Modjeska, and Julia Marlowe.

Irving revived *Cymbeline* in 1896. The Imogen of Ellen Terry was lauded to the skies, but the play failed. Irving's version cuts the text drastically. It was originally prepared by William Winter, who modestly observes that it was "fairly coherent." Irving, who told him that except for Imogen *Cymbeline* "isn't

worth a damn for the stage," slashed Winter's version still
further, to the point of unintelligibility. He had, indeed,
little desire to stage the play, and did so only to give Miss
Terry a chance at the heroine. He played Iachimo, with
"emphasis on the villain's contrition." In 1906 Viola Allen's
Imogen was admired. Of late years, though it has occasionally
been revived, especially by repertory companies, not much
has been done with this play. Lewis Casson and Sybil Thorndike staged it in 1923; they played Aviragus and Imogen. A
London production in 1937 was chiefly notable for a new fifth
act by Bernard Shaw. It is only a brilliant trifle; but, for once,
it really is "Better than Shakespear."

THE WINTER'S TALE

It is deplorable that *The Winter's Tale* is so seldom revived,
for this dramatic romance affords a delightful and comprehensive entertainment. By themselves, the first three acts almost constitute a complete tragedy; and then we remove to
that marvelous maritime province of Bohemia for an act of
the most agreeable pastoralism in English drama. No sooner
do we meet Autolycus — like Falstaff one of those poet-
rogues securely above all comparisons because they have to
be taken on their own lyrical terms — than we are absorbed
in the society of Cloud-cuckoo-land; and the sorrows of our
Sicilian friends are forgotten, as we sometimes forget the blows
of fate in the first movement of the symphony while the orchestra is playing the scherzo. Shakespeare has not forgotten;
and each theme (except the plaintive little motif of Mamil-
ius) is restated, and all are combined, in the magnificent
counterpoint of the fifth act. Once more, reconciliation becomes the final subject, summed up in the breathless climax
when the audience, artfully instructed to respond through the
emotions of Leontes, thrills to his wondering cry, "O, she's
warm!" And the queenly statue takes his hand and steps
down to the level of her adoring court, of which we spectators
are now a part; while the radiant young lovers are blest, and
the sharp-tongued, warm-hearted Paulina, properly forbidden

to wing off like an old turtle-dove "to some wither'd bough,"
is united by her king with the sterling Camillo, "an hon
ourable husband," Leontes calls him, which is putting i
mildly.

If there were any who thought after *Cymbeline* that Shake
speare had emptied his quiver, *The Winter's Tale* (provided
we are dating it correctly) gave sufficient proof to the con
trary. It is a play of abundant energy, written toughly, and
brilliant with unique characters. Shakespeare is not repeating
himself, he is not played out, his invention is still peerless
Varied as the drama is, there is no lack of unity, for the tone
throughout is one of mature confidence in human nature
Few plays offer such a galaxy of lovable personages. Even
the impulsive Leontes is lovable in his wholehearted con
trition; and his wicked petulance in the beginning only em
phasizes the goodness of all who surround him. This is a
court to belie all the gibes of former plays, and to offer an
example of idealism at hopeless variance with the Jacobean
facts. Camillo, Antigonus, and indeed all the lords, are *good*
The shepherds are *good*. So, considering that he is cast in the
rôle of heavy father, is Polixenes, who is not to be censured
for leaving Sicilia. His life, in this world of absolute mon
archy, is explicitly forfeit. There are times, as the Duke of
Marlborough knew in his youth, when departure, though
by a window, is best, even for the guilty partner. Polixenes
is innocent; it would be natural to suppose that, the irritating
object once removed from sight, Leontes's jealousy would
subside. Above all, the plot requires his flight. And Autolycus,
while littered under Mercury, is not out to make a name for
himself in the annals of crime. He modestly sees himself as
no big shot, but the merest snapper-up of inconsiderable
trifles, and (not very realistically, to be sure) commends
himself with assurance to the affections of the audience. A
lovable rascal, if there ever was one; and of that there is no
possible probable shadow of doubt — in art. Nor in life,
either. This may be sad. It is certainly true. If the reader
thinks otherwise, his experience has been unduly limited.
Autolycus and the three women are the best testimony that

Shakespeare is still at the full tide of his powers. Perdita is scored for so ravishingly that an actress with any looks at all may be confident that half the congregation will be in love with her by the end of Act IV. Paulina is the feminine equivalent of Kent in King Lear; such characters, true as steel but free of tongue, especially with kings, an audience takes to its heart. And Hermione, so high-minded, so spirited, so dignified in her anguish, is perfection in her queenliness and womanliness.

The play is, moreover, replete with effective dramatic situations, which Shakespeare brings off in the grand manner. Such is the opening episode — Leontes torn between his normal instincts and tigrish jealousy, playing with the boy while his wife and his friend go on with their innocent chatter. Such is the opening of the second act, when the enraged King bursts in upon the quiet little scene of Hermione with her child. Such is the other major episode of that act, Paulina's invasion of the tormented monarch's privacy. The trial scene in Act III is dominated by the women — first by Hermione and then by Paulina; it is one of the best-acting trial scenes in drama. Then, after the chorus which bridges the wide gap of time, we revert to the pure romantic for an act of exquisite charm and humor, before returning to Leontes in his noble sorrow. Structurally, the only serious blemish is the tedious preparation of the fifth act for its one great scene. For a while the play moves far too slowly, especially in Scene ii, the expository conversation of the walking gentlemen. But the last scene is worth waiting for — remembering, of course, that the genre is dramatic romance and that we are not to be rude enough to inquire into Paulina's ways and means of keeping the Queen so long perdue. It is proof of the chapel scene's strength that, although Hermione speaks only once after she leaves the stage in the third act, hers is the compelling rôle.

Why, then, do we see the play so seldom? I am afraid one reason is the reluctance of a leading actress to play a part which contains only seven lines after Act III. Perhaps stellar ladies are afraid of eclipse by Perdita's *jeune-fille* charms. If so,

there is something wrong with their instincts; creatures such
as these lack a true vocation for the stage, and know little
of its history. Any actress worth her salt would, perhaps
not sell her soul, but certainly pawn it, for a chance to play
Hermione in the trial scene. And if then she plays well
enough, like Mrs. Siddons she will have the audience at her
feet once more the moment Paulina pulls open the curtain
in the chapel scene.

Leontes is not an heroic rôle, but he offers a very human
one. The actor has a fine chance to rant and rave before the
trial, and then to win the audience with a good display of
repentance. His character has baffled some of the commentators. God knows why. Had they never once been unreasonable
themselves? Obviously, Leontes is not Othello. He is not a
normal man led into crime by a villain, but neither is he
congenitally jealous and tyrannical. He is a young king; this
is the first time he has ever gone off the reservation. His
courtiers, evidently accustomed to expect only the best from
him, are puzzled; but they are so little afraid of him that they
remonstrate in terms which, as he aptly observes, would cost
them their heads were he the tyrant Paulina calls him
Leontes illustrates the terrible potentialities of a fit of irrita-
tion. Not that Shakespeare is preaching on a text; he is telling
a story. Leontes flies into a jealous rage; that is the fact, and
the Elizabethan dramatist was not required to parade a psychological theory. Petulance, the pique of an imperious youth
his will as yet uncrossed, seems to be what Shakespeare has
in mind. It is inspired by Hermione's success in persuasion,
after Leontes's own appeals have failed to change his friend's
mind. His jealousy of her triumph begins like a man's anger
when the family dog refuses to obey him but comes immediately at his wife's command. It passes, naturally enough,
though of course most unwarrantably, into suspicion that
there is something behind Polixenes's yielding. Time's winged
chariot always hovers near the dramatist, whom we must
allow to proceed more rapidly than life or a novel usually
does. As Leontes meditates on his suspicion it becomes an
idée fixe, a "humor," to be cured only by a shock.

The sole textual authority for this play is the First Folio.
'or the precise date of composition there is no evidence.
There was a court performance on November 5, 1611.[8] Plainly
The Winter's Tale belongs in the final group; metre, style, and
one agree on that. Jonson's masque of *Oberon, the Faery Prince*
vas performed at Whitehall on January 1, 1611; Prince Henry
vas among the courtly players. It had a chariot drawn by
wo white bears, but the man-eating bear in *The Winter's
Tale* (III, iii) may not have been inspired by them. A likelier
possibility (it is no more) resides in the dancing satyrs (IV,
v); "one three of them . . . hath danc'd before the King,"
and there were satyrs in *Oberon*. Early in 1611 is the generally
favored date for *The Winter's Tale*, but it is a conjectural date.

Shakespeare's source for the main plot is Greene's *Pandosto.
The Triumph of Time* (1588). The hero of this novel is the
original of Leontes; but he is king of Bohemia, and so the
pastoralism is properly Sicilian. His motivation bears small
resemblance to that of Leontes; for Pandosto's psychic states
are first a "melancholy passion" with which he has long
been afflicted, then "doubtfull thoughts," next a "secret
mistrust," and at last a "flaming Iealousie." Shakespeare
makes other important changes. In Greene the queen actually
dies, and the child is cast adrift at sea. Eventually Pandosto
falls in love with his own daughter, Fawnia, the supposed
shepherdess, who is in love with Dorastus (Florizel). The
truth comes out; but Pandosto, though he is glad to learn
that the child has survived, grows remorseful, relapses into
his old melancholy, and kills himself. Autolycus and the
Shepherd's son, a gay rôle for the clown, are Shakespeare's
invention. So are Paulina and Antigonus. The final effect,
the supposed statue coming to life, may have been suggested
by the story of Pygmalion; Shakespeare was familiar, of
course, with Ovid's version (*Metamorphoses*, X, 243 ff.). But
Hermione is not a statue, and that Shakespeare was the first
to hit upon this unrealistic but rather obvious stroke seems
unlikely.

The Winter's Tale was one of fourteen plays acted for the
Princess Elizabeth and the Elector in 1612–13. There were

also court performances in 1618, possibly in 1619, in 1624, and in 1634. On the last of these occasions the record adds "likt." The rest is silence, till the minor theatre of Goodman's Fields revived the play in 1741, with Henry Giffard and his wife in the major rôles. Covent Garden took it up the following season; Hannah Pritchard, afterwards a superb Hermione, played Paulina. There, also, appeared *The Sheep-Shearing: or, Florizel and Perdita*, in 1754, ascribed to McNamara Morgan; this afterpiece was made into an operetta in 1761. Meanwhile, in 1756, Garrick had mounted his own version at Drury Lane, in a double bill with his *Catharine and Petruchio*. He played Leontes to the Hermione of Mrs. Pritchard; but these rôles were drastically reduced, and the adaptation was subsequently styled *Florizel and Perdita*. Mrs. Cibber was the Perdita, Woodward the Clown, and Richard Yates the "Autolicus." Garrick's adaptation draws chiefly on Acts IV and V of the original. In 1771 Covent Garden staged a more faithful version, but soon withdrew it in favor of Garrick's. "Perdita" Robinson gained her sobriquet at Drury Lane in 1779. Mrs. Yates was a great Hermione. Shakespeare's play was restored with a fair degree of fidelity by J. P. Kemble in 1802. The manager played Leontes to the Hermione of Mrs. Siddons. Their handsome younger brother, Charles Kemble, was the Florizel. Macready, who had acted Leontes as early as 1815, revived the play in 1837 with Helen Faucit as Hermione. In 1845 Phelps staged it virtually intact. His Hermione was his comanager, Mary Amelia Warner. This brilliant actress afterwards revived several of Shakespeare's plays at the Theatre Royal, Marylebone. She opened her régime there in 1847 with *The Winter's Tale*. Charles Kean's lavish production, in 1856, ran 102 nights. His wife played Hermione; little Ellen Terry was the Mamillius. Manchester saw the Leontes of Charles Calvert, and there were also revivals in the United States; Edwin Booth's came in 1871. The Saxe-Meiningen troupe took the play to London in 1881. In the fall of 1887 it began a run at the Lyceum which extended nearly through the season; the American actress Mary Anderson doubled the rôles of Hermione and Perdita, to the Leontes of Forbes-Robertson.

Her example was afterwards followed in the United States by Viola Allen. H. B. Irving acted Leontes in 1895; the Autolycus was Ben Greet. Tree staged the play in 1906 (with Ellen Terry as Hermione — Tree did not appear), Louis Calvert (in New York) in 1910, and Granville-Barker in 1912. In the last of these revivals Lillah McCarthy played Hermione; Henry Ainley acted Leontes; the Clown was Leon Quartermaine. The piece was in Benson's repertory and in the Old Vic's.

An American revival is long overdue, and the peculiar availability of this romantic and varied entertainment ought to insure its eventual adaptation to the art of the motion picture. Here is ample opportunity for a gorgeous treatment of court and pastoral scenes, while the exposure of the babe on the Bohemian seashore could be handled far more effectively on screen than on stage. And, for once, the happy ending beloved of Hollywood's patrons could be left to the original author.

THE TEMPEST

This is the flower of dramatic romances, in its way as fine and beautiful a work as anything Shakespeare ever wrote. Long extremely popular in the theatre, it failed to survive the rise of nineteenth-century realism and materialism. With the recent collapse of confidence in the machine as civilization's greatest achievement and in the lavish use of mechanical accessories as essential to the effective staging of Shakespeare, the time is ripe for a great revival of *The Tempest*. For the thing requisite above all other things, whether to produce Shakespeare or to enjoy him, is imagination; and in this play that is what he supplies — as freely as ever. Some of his works are more terrible in their intensity, some more exquisite in their grace and humor; none is a bolder record of the power of the poetic mind.

It passes, indeed, from conceptions broad and inclusive in their humanity to explorations and experiments beyond the limitations of our species — to Caliban, only half human but sufficiently a man to be capable of thought and of development — to Ariel, who owns nothing human and can therefore never be more than Ariel. Shakespeare was an artist, not a philosopher nor an historian of ideas; but this does not mean, as some have supposed, that he had no mind or that thought was foreign to it. Let him who doubts its intellectual powers reread *King Lear*. Like every major artist, Shakespeare received the world, passed it through his genius, and, as Emerson says, "uttered" it in new forms. In *The Tempest* the scheme of things entire is under the consideration of a great mind. Naturally, the conclusions are not expressed in mathematical symbols but in artistic symbols. One creator surveys the work of another. On the whole, he seems to find it good, though his warmest enthusiasm is reserved for that portion of it known as human nature. He is not presumptuous enough to offer a specific endorsement of the authoritative though possibly biased conclusion arrived at on the sixth day; like Beethoven, he modestly restricts himself to composing the finale of a Ninth Symphony. With *Pericles* and *The Winter's Tale* this last great drama unites, not in a paean to worldly pleasure or content or happiness or even hope, but in an Ode to Joy, comparable only to that other Titan's.

I choose the last word deliberately, for that is what the youth from Stratford had become. In *The Tempest* the whole thing is under perfect control every moment. The composer is so certain of what he wants and of precisely how to get it from his actors and from his audience that, of all his dramatic scores, *The Tempest* most successfully combines the boldest freedom with the most delicate tact. Once more, as in *The Winter's Tale*, he tells a fascinating story, invents some of his most enchanting characters, and offers an entertainment of extraordinary variety. There is roaring comedy, if that is what you like best in a comedy; and in drawing Trinculo and Stephano the pencil flies fast but does not repeat itself. There is an idyllic little love story, though Miranda is not so strong a character as Shakespeare usually makes of his heroines. She is, however, entirely adequate to her rather passive rôle in the plot; and Shakespeare does not push her, as, to the detriment of her best interests, he pushes Imogen.

The Neapolitans and Milanese talk like the cleverest courtiers at Whitehall, and good old Gonzalo-Belarius (II, i, 147 ff.) has read and understood Florio's translation of Montaigne. The spirit masque also reflects a current fashion at court. All these contribute to our pleasure; but it is in Prospero, Caliban, and Ariel that the matchless imagination finds its fullest scope. "Shakespeare alone," says Delacroix, "could make spirits talk." Prospero is so evidently Master of the cosmic Revels that he has been subjected to all sorts of auto-biographical and symbolistical interpretations. None convinces; but as he wrote Prospero's renunciation of his art (V, i, 33 ff.), Shakespeare may have thought of his own creative accomplishment and of his retirement. At any rate, *The Tempest* is very likely his last play, except for his share in *Henry the Eighth* and *The Two Noble Kinsmen.*

The sole authority for the text is the First Folio. About 1611 is the generally accepted date of composition. The play was acted at court on November 1 of that year;[9] and, while the source of the plot is unknown,[10] Shakespeare took some details of the storm and of the island from the actual adventures of Sir George Somers on the Virginian voyage in 1609–10. Somers's fleet of nine sail was dispersed by a terrific gale on July 24, 1609. All made Jamestown except the flagship, the *Sea Adventure*, which sprang a leak. On July 28 they ran her ashore on the Bermudas, without loss of life. The castaways, who included Sir Thomas Gates, Lieutenant-General of the Virginia Company, wintered on the islands, built two pinnaces, and reached Jamestown the following spring. Gates sailed for England in July, 1610, and arrived in September with the first report of the Bermudan adventure. It was the subject of Sylvester Jourdan's *A Discovery of the Barmudas, otherwise called the Ile of Divels* and of the anonymous *A True Declaration of the estate of the Colonie in Virginia.* Both were published before the close of the year 1610. Shakespeare had probably read these narratives and also a letter by William Strachey. Both Jourdan and Strachey had sailed in the *Sea Adventure.* The latter wrote his account in the summer of 1610. It was not printed till 1625, when it appeared as *A true reportory of the wracke and redemption of Sir Thomas Gates Knight* in Samuel Purchas's *Hakluytus Posthumus, or Purchas his Pilgrimes* (part iv, pp. 1734–58); but no doubt the letter reached England with Gates and circulated in manuscript.

The first scene of *The Tempest* is impressionistic, but the nautical terminology is so precise that Shakespeare's seamanship has been much discussed. There is, however, no reason to think he had been a sailor. Part of his business as a dramatist was to pick up the lingo of every trade. He appears to have talked with men in all walks of society, seamen included. As far as the evidence of the plays goes, he had till now been strangely insensitive to the exploits of the English voyagers; it can not be said that he is remarkably sensitive even in *The Tempest*. His imagination is fired by the fancy of an ocean-girt Never-never-land, not by the spectacle of the English colors planted in the soil of a new continent. There is a powerful argument in this fact against the theory that he was a facile imitator, responsive to the slightest flaws of fashion's breezes, and childishly eager to work in a topical reference at every opportunity.

Once again the chief defect is the poet's failure to avoid tedious exposition, as in the long narrative of I, ii. Some attribute it to his revising an earlier form of the play, but this theory has met with little acceptance. For once, perhaps after a friendly wrangle with Jonson, perhaps because he had gone to the other extreme in *The Winter's Tale*, Shakespeare determined to bow to the neoclassical fetish of the unities. The rules of time and place are strictly observed, though the subplot, the conspiracy against Alonso, slightly mars the unity of action. It is a commendable deviation, both because it helps fill out the drama and because it brings the island peace into effective contrast. Prospero's exposition is indispensable if we are to have unity of time and place, but the necessity does not account for the boredom. Shakespeare is taking things a bit easy at this point, confident that he has riveted the attention of the audience with the brilliant opening scene.

The Tempest was acted again at court in 1612–13 as part of the festive program for the betrothal and wedding of Princess Elizabeth and the Elector. That it won and held a place in the public repertory is probable. Its revival under the Restoration, at Lincoln's Inn Fields in 1667, was in an adaptation by D'avenant and Dryden. The former added Miranda's counterpart, a man who has never seen a woman, and this necessitates a sister for Miranda — one of those prurient Restoration maidens in desperate need of a psychiatrist. Some comic additions for the sailors were largely composed by D'avenant, and he revised Dryden's contribution, which was by far the larger share. Besides Hippolito and Dorinda, the new characters are an unpleasant sister for Caliban and a sweetheart for Ariel — anyone can see that these improvements give the play a truly classical balance! The part of Prospero is drastically reduced; and "the wild and savage character" of Caliban, as Sir Walter Scott protests, "is sunk into low and vulgar buffoonery." The tone of the play is completely altered; the adaptation's initial success rested on scenic magnificence and licentious innuendo. In 1674 the D'avenant-Dryden version was made by Thomas Shadwell into an "opera," which means that, besides further musical and scenic embellishment, mechanical effects were multiplied. The text remained, however, essentially as Dryden had left it. Purcell wrote the music. We have to wait till 1746 for a revival of the original comedy; it failed to displace the popular perversion. Garrick appeared in neither, but under his management *The Tempest* was often played at Drury Lane. A new operatic version was produced there in 1756; Garrick prepared the libretto, and John Christopher Smith composed the music. But the following year saw the play acted "as written by Shakespear."

J. P. Kemble, however, went back to Dryden in 1789, though he made some restorations. In 1821 Reynolds and Bishop presented another operatic version, with Macready as Prospero. In 1838 Macready staged the original comedy himself; and, though he felt impelled to replace the dialogue of the opening scene with a mechanical shipwreck, the D'avenant-Dryden follies were thenceforth seen no more. Helen Faucit was the Miranda of this production. Phelps gave twenty-two performances of Shakespeare's play in 1847. Ten years later Charles Kean cut ruthlessly to make room for spectacular effects. He played Prospero and enjoyed a run of eighty-seven nights. Benson staged the play in 1900, Leigh in 1903, and Tree in 1904. They all cast themselves as Caliban. Since then, although in 1921 Viola Tree played Juno in her own production (she had played Ariel in her father's), there has been little revival of *The Tempest* except in repertory and by amateurs, who have been remarkably faithful to it. To predict its future on our stage would be risky indeed; but a renewal of life may be in store for it on the screen. Some day an enlightened director will set sail from the Californian shore and make a wonderful motion picture out of it.

THE TWO NOBLE KINSMEN

The only external evidence that Shakespeare had a hand in this inferior play is on the title page of the Quarto (1634): "The Two Noble Kinsmen: Presented at the Blackfriers by the Kings Maiesties servants, with great applause: Written by the memorable Worthies of their time; Mr. John Fletcher, and Mr. William Shakspeare. Gent." [11] The truth of this ascription has not been demonstrated; it is, indeed, incapable of proof, and there is some evidence against it. Heminge and Condell did not include the play in the Shakespeare Folio (1623). It *was* included in the Second Beaumont-Fletcher Folio (1679), though not in the First (1647). On October 31, 1646, twelve years after its original entry, the Stationers' Register, recording an assignment of the publishing rights, lists it, along with two other plays, by "Mr Flesher."

These considerations are not decisive. There is now fairly general agreement that a good deal of the piece is from Shakespeare's pen, although some favor Massinger, an uninspired but far from ineffective dramatist, to whose imitation of Shakespeare these critics believe are due the passages which are clearly not Fletcher's but which, while almost Shakespearean, do not have quite the true ring, as they call it. Beaumont is another candidate, though few have taken his nomination seriously. Internal evidence, stylistic and metrical, is always risky; for no test has yet been devised that will reject imitative composition, and those who profess ownership of an ear infallibly delicate for distinguishing the "overtones" of individual poetic expression are as capable of being fooled as the art experts who accept fake Rembrandts or assign a carefully planted torso to a pupil of a pupil of Praxiteles. Such as it is, however, the internal evidence supports the hypothesis that Shakespeare's is the non-Fletcherian hand in *The Two Noble Kinsmen*. And the conclusion is further buttressed by the strong probability that he collaborated with Fletcher about the same time in *Henry the Eighth*, and by the possibility of their collaboration in the lost play of *Cardennio*.[12]

It is reasonably certain that two playwrights wrote this dramatic romance. Whoever they were, it presents a case of close collaboration, and not of completion by one poet of another's unfinished work. Fletcher is easier to spot than Shakespeare,[13] and there can be little doubt that he wrote II, ii-vi; III, iii-vi; IV, i, ii; V, ii. But I, v and III, ii might easily be either dramatist's; I think the chances favor Fletcher. Those who become seriously agitated, not to say acrimonious, over this question are less inspired by the value of the two scenes, which is negligible, than by the importance of demonstrating the merits of their systems of detection. If, as seems probable, the other coauthor is Shakespeare, to him may fairly confidently be assigned the bulk of I, i-iv; III, i; V, i, iii, iv. This division accounts for everything except the prose scenes of the Jailer, Wooer, and Daughter (II, i), and of the same trio with the addition of the Doctor (IV, iii). These may be Shakespeare's, since Fletcher usually avoids prose. No one knows who wrote the songs. "Roses, their sharp spines being gone" is perhaps likelier to be Fletcher's than Shakespeare's. The author of the prologue and epilogue is also unknown; they may be later than the play. Nothing excludes the possibility that the collaborators revised each other's work. Every scene may be a joint effort; and to attempt anything more than a rough partition would be, as

Kittredge says, to go "beyond the scope of sane criticism."
Nor should we neglect the possibility of a third hand. Twenty-
one years intervened between production and publication. We
may have the original text; but it is much more probable that,
even if no one made an actual revision, some changes had crept
in. Eloquence is therefore out of order in dealing with this
play. For my part, I find no difficulty in refraining from it.

The authoritative text is provided by the Quarto, an excellent one. The source is "The Knightes Tale" of Chaucer, which
in turn is derived from Boccaccio's *Teseide*. The dramatists
follow Chaucer pretty closely, though the subplot of the
Jailer's lovelorn Daughter is an addition. In "The Knightes
Tale" Palamon escapes by drugging the jailer; to have a woman
in the case is dramatically an improvement.[14] The date is probably 1613; production must have been later than February 20,
for the morris dance in III, v introduces (lines 122–32) a
group of characters from the Second Antimasque of Beaumont's *The Masqve of the Inner Temple and Grayes Inne*, which
was acted at Whitehall on that date. It had a pedant, a May
lord and his lady, a chambermaid and a servingman, a host
and a hostess, a clown, a Fool, and not one Bavian but two
— a "Hee Baboone" and a "Shee Baboone."

Nothing is known of the play's reception. There may have
been a court revival in 1619.[15] In 1664 D'avenant produced his
love-and-honor adaptation entitled *The Rivals*. Betterton
played Philander (Palamon); Harris, Theocles (Arcite). The
subplot is "elevated"; the Jailer becomes a Provost, and
Celania, his now socially acceptable daughter, is finally married to Palamon. The unities are subserved by dropping the
sorrowful Queens and the Theban scenes of Act I. This piece
had some success; it was still being acted in 1667.

The speedy disappearance from the stage of *The Two Noble
Kinsmen* is not a cause for lamentation, but it ought to be
included in editions of Shakespeare as well as of Fletcher.
No one is obliged to like it; few do. For one thing, there is
almost no poetry in it, and less characterization than poetry.
Spectacular effects are more important than is usual in Shakespeare, and stage directions are correspondingly elaborate.

It seems probable that in this play we have Shakespeare's last dramatic writing. The best of it, the vigorous invocation of the deities (V, i), is not particularly dramatic. However substantial Shakespeare's contribution, he never gets control of the piece, which in tone remains his colleague's. Palamon and Arcite are one more pair of Fletcherian tenors. The play clearly belongs with the dramatic romances. True, one of the heroes has a horse fall on him, and conveniently expires; but, such is the absurdly mathematical aesthetics of the plot, this is felt as a relief by all concerned, since it simplifies the arithmetical problem for Emilia, who could obviously be happy with either, were tother dear charmer away. As for the nameless little flower of the jail, she could be happy with anyone, and only exists to go mad in white satin. Such interest as the authors succeed in generating comes out of the vicissitudes of romantic narrative and the childish pleasure of being kept in the dark about which of the knightly cousins will draw which destiny.

> See how the Fates their gifts allot;
> For A is happy, B is not.

Death, or Emilia? It is something like the lady-or-the-tiger plot, and about as serious. Shakespeare put no heart into this play; and a few well-chosen tears by that graceful mourner, John Fletcher, do not suffice to endow it with humanity. Shakespeare is a gifted storyteller; his plot is usually the central fact of his play; but never is it near the springs of his greatness. When, as in *Cymbeline* and *The Two Noble Kinsmen*, he leaves the play to the mercy of its plot, he fails.

I could think of no better way of closing my account of Shakespeare's life than by quoting Ben Jonson's estimate of what it accomplished. Let his namesake, also among the best Shakespeareans, have the last word now. It is strictly applicable to Shakespeare's failure in *The Two Noble Kinsmen*, and no less to his victorious life, which was one of as much triumph as any hero or artist can possibly hope for, and as inexorably

doomed as every man's. There is a kind of grim propriety in
the imperfections of this final work of his wonderful hand.
It smells of mortality. But because he was a great artist as
well as a man, his mortal had put on immortality and his
corruptible had put on incorruption. That had happened a
decade earlier — as he had hoped, though not in the form
his hopes had taken. Whether he knew that death was already swallowed up in victory, and whether if he knew it
he was any happier for knowing it, are unsolved mysteries,
rather unimportant ones. For, however our hearts go out to
our benefactors, the seed is more than the sower, the work
than the life, the book than the poet. That is the world's
verdict, though it may not always be the artist's. *Vox mundi,
vox dei*, perhaps. For the world, Dr. Johnson expertly sums
up the conclusion of the whole matter: "*Shakespear*'s Excellence is not the Fiction of a Tale, but the Representation
of Life; and his Reputation is therefore safe, till Human
Nature shall be changed."

NOTES

NOTES

ITLE PAGE. Quotation from the *Journal* (May 15, 1824) of Eugène Delacroix, leader of the Romantic movement in French painting. "What makes men of genius, or rather makes what they do, is not new ideas; it is that idea, by which they are possessed, that what has been said has not yet been said enough."

CHAPTER 1

PAGE 3. Nor have any authenticated **relics** survived, except four legal documents and possibly one or two books, to be mentioned later in connection with Shakespeare's signatures. The nearest things to authentic portraiture are: (1) the limestone half-length statue, usually called the bust, on the monument in the Stratford church; and (2) the Droeshout engraving, prints of which appear on the title pages of the earliest collected editions, the four Folios. The chances are overwhelmingly against either's having been executed from life. — **The monument** was erected at least as early as 1623, when Leonard Digges mentions it in verses composed for the First Folio. In a diary written in interleaved almanacs, the famous Warwickshire antiquarian Sir William Dugdale ascribes it in 1653 to "Gerard Johnson." (*The Life, Diary, and Correspondence of Sir William Dugdale*, ed. William Hamper, London, 1827, pp. 99, 512.) This craftsman — sculpture in northern Europe was then in the hands of artisans rather than artists — was a son of Gheerart or Garratt Janssen, an immigrant from Holland, whose business in Southwark was carried on by his sons after his death in 1611. Their shop was near the Globe Theatre; no doubt the sculptor had often seen the poet, but whether his reliance was wholly on memory is unknown. The monument itself, though to present taste pretty ornate, is a more than respectable job in the Jacobean style. The bust is something else. "Porkbutcher" and "pudding-face" are typical epithets of outraged bardolaters. But it was presumably acceptable to the family; and the proportions of the skull agree with those of the Droeshout engraving, the derivation of which is probably independent. The statue's face is so rigid that some students of the poet's iconography believe Johnson could only have worked from a death mask. The best authority rejects this view, at least as compulsory, and denies the authenticity of a mask that turned up in Mainz. In regular monumental fashion the carving of the head minimizes detail; doubtless this was supplied with the brush, when the bust was colored, as was then customary. Dugdale's *The Antiquities of Warwickshire* (1656) prints an engraving of the monument (sig. Mmm 2ᵛ [p. 520]); and his sketch, from which the engraver worked, is extant. Since, as M. H. Spielmann shows, to found a case on the fidelity of seventeenth-century engraving is to abandon it, and since

prints in Dugdale of other monuments reveal similar discrepancies, we
can only conclude, not that the Dugdale plate depicts an original state
of the bust, since altered, but rather that incompetent draftsmanship,
imperfect memory, or plain heedlessness played him and his engraver
false. — The monument was **repaired** in 1749, chiefly with the proceeds
of a benefit performance of *Othello* given on Sept. 9, 1746 by John Ward,
grandfather of the great Mrs. Siddons. His strolling company had been
playing Stratford since May. The advertisement says the monument
"Is through length of Years and other accidents become much impair'd
and decay'd." A letter by Ward on Dec. 3, 1748, now in the Folger
Shakespeare Library along with papers of the Rev. Joseph Greene, then
headmaster of the Stratford Free School, agrees with them in suggesting
that local disputes had caused the delay. As Mrs. C. C. Stopes, who had
seen these MSS, observes in *Shakespeare's Environment*, the details are not
entirely clear. Apparently the £12 10s. on hand was insufficient. The
following announcement was "publish'd Nov^{br}. 20th 1748. In Stratford
Church": "I am desir'd to give notice, that on Friday next, there will
be a meeting at the Market-Hall in Stratford, of those persons who
Contributed for ye repairing of Shakespear's Monument; In order to
resolve upon a proper Method of repairing & beautifying the Monument
aforesaid." According to a letter written long afterward by Greene, the
work cost about £16. In a draft of another letter, dated Sept. 27, 1749,
Greene writes: "In repairing the whole, (which was done by contribution of ye Neighbourhood early in ye current year) Care was taken, as
nearly as cou'd be, not to add to or diminish what ye work consisted of,
& appear'd to be when first errected: And really, except changing y^e
Substance of ye Architraves from white Alabaster to white Marble,
nothing has been done but Supplying with ye Original Materials whatsoever was by Accident broken off; reviving the old Colouring, and
renewing the Gilding that was lost." According to J. O. Halliwell-
Phillipps (*Outlines*, I, 283), the pen, right forefinger, and part of the
right thumb were missing, were restored, and had to be replaced again
in 1790, when a quill was inserted in lieu of the original lead pen. According to Spielmann, the colors of the bust had been renewed in 1649.
Neither of these writers mentions any authority for his assertion. Renewal of the lost lead pen with a real pen and the fracture of the first
two fingers of the right hand are the (variant) details of F. W. Fair-
holt's undocumented account in Halliwell-Phillipps's *Works of Shakespeare* (1853-65), I, 234-7. In 1793, at the instigation of the great
scholar Edmond Malone, the bust was given a coat of white paint.
This was removed in 1861 and replaced by the present colors, which
follow such traces of the originals as were still discernible. Their
probable accuracy is indicated by a surviving picture of the monument
before the repairs of 1749. It was painted by John Hall, the Bristol
limner to whom they were entrusted. Greene alludes to Hall's painting

the monument as it was before restoration. Drafts of projected agree-
ments in the Greene papers relating to the scope of the repairs emphasize the requirement of fidelity to the original. It is therefore probable
that Shakespeare was auburn-haired and hazel-eyed, as well as prematurely bald. — What **the Folio engraver** worked from is likewise
unknown. Copies of the First Folio contain prints of his clumsy effort
in two states, the later showing retouching of the copper plate. The
frontispiece of the present volume reproduces one of the few examples
of the earlier state, or "proof" as it is sometimes called. The plate was
cut by Martin Droeshout, a third-generation London Fleming. Some
of the experts think he followed a line drawing, "with perhaps delicate
flat washes of colour," made when the poet was twenty years younger
than he is in the Johnson bust. Droeshout was fifteen when Shakespeare
died and only twenty-two when the Folio appeared. His engraving was
therefore early work. Its lack of promise was prophetic; he never had
much success. The probability that the engraving at least approximates
fidelity to the subject is evident from accompanying lines "To the
Reader" by Ben Jonson:

> "This Figure, that thou here seest put,
>   It was for gentle Shakespeare cut;
> Wherein the Grauer had a strife
>   with Nature, to out-doo the life:
> O, could he but haue drawne his wit
>   As well in brasse, as he hath hit
> His face; the print would then surpasse
>   All, that was euer writ in brasse.
> But, since he cannot, Reader, looke
>   Not on his Picture, but his Booke."

Yet this encomium falls short of proof, since the verses are conventional. — Claims of authenticity have been made for many **other pictures,** some of which are genuine early paintings — of other persons.
With the exception of these, all the other alleged portraits are either
fakes or derivations from the bust or the Droeshout engraving, usually
with idealizing variations. The Stratford Memorial's Flower portrait
(so called from the name of the discoverer and donor) was said by a
former owner to have been handed down in the Shakespeare family.
It bears the date 1609; but neither date nor early ownership can be verified, though the work may be seventeenth-century. Some have taken
it for the original of Droeshout's plate, but Spielmann demonstrates
that the painter followed the second state of the engraving. The Chandos
portrait (named for a former owner) limns a more poetic face, though
it looks Italian rather than British. Tradition attributes this painting
to Richard Burbage, the tragedian. It was pretty certainly once owned
by the Caroline poet laureate Sir William D'avenant, and according to
eighteenth-century tradition by Joseph Taylor, the Jacobean actor.

But its earliest history is only traditional, and its dissimilarities to the work of Johnson and Droeshout stamp it as an example, not of life study, but of wishful painting. — There is no more to be gained by waxing eloquent against the stolid features of the **two earliest portraits** than by rhapsodizing over the noble forehead both exhibit. According to the poet himself,

"There's no art
To find the mind's construction in the face."

More than half a century after Shakespeare's death, Aubrey says he was handsome and well shaped; but it is possible that the best of poets did not look the part. It is no less possible that his face was lit with a spiritual fire quite beyond the poor powers of the two men on whom fell the heavy responsibility of perpetuating his features. Fortunately a better artist than they arranged for his own survival by erecting a monument more durable than any painter, sculptor, or architect has offered emperor or millionaire:

"Not marble nor the gilded monuments
Of princes shall outlive this pow'rful rhyme."

2 PAGE 4. No further reference will be made in these pages to the whimsical notion that Francis Bacon wrote Shakespeare's works. Space forbids, and anyway the favorite in the anti-Stratfordian steeplechase is now the seventeenth Earl of Oxford. The layman may rest assured that, however extravagantly these interesting entries have been backed by amateurs, no responsible scholar has ever put any money on either horse. (For a concise account of the mania, with bibliography, see J. M. Robertson, "The Bacon-Shakespeare Theory," *Encyclopædia Britannica*, 14th ed., XX, 447–8.)

3 PAGE 5. She had also visited Warwick and Kenilworth in 1572. He may have seen the public celebrations both times.

4 PAGE 5. The poet signs himself "Shakspere" and "Shakspeare" (see S. A. Tannenbaum, *Problems in Shakspere's Penmanship*); but London documents, the First Folio, most of the quartos, and the subscription of the dedicatory epistles of *Venus and Adonis* and *Lucrece* use "Shakespeare," sometimes hyphened. The derivation of the name is uncertain. Professor Leslie Hotson has discovered two references to residents of Stratford named John Shakespeare who were there a few years before the poet's father appears. (London *Times*, July 6, 1935, pp. 13–14.)

5 PAGE 5. *Agricola.* — William Shakespeare's uncle Henry, another survivor, died hard pressed by creditors in 1596 and was buried at Snitterfield.

6 PAGE 6. Thus his friend and fellow antiquarian Anthony à Wood, author of *Athenae Oxonienses*, who was much indebted to his researches. It is easy to be irritated with Aubrey, but these epithets are too severe.

7 PAGE 6. The original letter is in the Folger Shakespeare Library. It is jocosely signed "John at Stiles" and addressed to "Mr Southwell," the writer's "Dr Cousin." Someone, presumably the recipient, en-

dorsed the letter "From Mr Dowdall." Neither writer nor recipient
has been identified. — In *Henry the Sixth, Part 2*, an early play, Shakespeare introduces a butcher and makes many allusions to the trade.
These prove nothing, but it seems odd that the following lines should
appear in a serious speech (III, ii) on the death of Duke Humphrey:

> "Who finds the heifer dead, and bleeding fresh,
>   And sees fast-by a butcher with an axe,
>   But will suspect 'twas he that made the slaughter?"

8 PAGE 7. L. Hotson, London *Times*, Nov. 22, 1930, p. 13.

9 PAGE 7. From whom part of the Shakespeare farm was leased.

10 PAGE 8. Shakespeare's two elder sisters, Joan and Margaret, died in infancy. He was probably not survived by any of his three brothers, none
of whom, with the possible exception of Gilbert, seems to have left
issue. Gilbert (probably d. 1612) was two and a half years younger;
Richard (d. 1613), ten years. Edmund, sixteen years younger than
William, became an actor; he was buried on Dec. 31, 1607 at St. Saviour's, near the Globe Theatre. Nothing is known of his career. Anne
Shakespeare (d. 1579) was seven and a half years younger than her
famous brother. Their father was buried at Stratford on Sept. 8, 1601,
and their mother on Sept. 9, 1608. Another sister Joan (d. 1646), five
years younger than the poet, married William Hart, a hatter. Her
descendants are still living; some of them occupied part of the Henley
Street house till 1806.

11 PAGE 8. "Johannes" is of course a slip for "Johannis." — If Shakespeare
died on April 23, 1616 in his fifty-third year, as the tablet on the monument in the Stratford church declares, the limits for his birthday are
April 24, 1563 and April 23, 1564. The first mention of April 23,
St. George's Day, the traditional date, appears to be a manuscript note
by the antiquarian William Oldys about the middle of the eighteenth
century, in a copy of Gerard Langbaine's *An Account of the English
Dramatick Poets* (1691). Oldys gives the year as 1563. The late antiquary
E. I. Fripp argues for the 22nd.

12 PAGE 9. Though in the same year he went bail in the amount of £10 at
Coventry for a fellow citizen of Stratford. The record calls him a glover.
(E. I. Fripp, *Minutes and Accounts*, IV, 1–2.) — He had a long quarrel
with one William Burbage (otherwise unknown), to whom he had
leased a house. Hotson (London *Times*, Dec. 29, 1926, p. 6) gives details
of litigation in the Court of Common Pleas. In 1582 John was ordered
by arbitrators to release Burbage from the agreement and pay him £7.
He was still refusing payment in 1592, when an entry describes him as a
glover. — Also in 1592, his name appears in a list of persons unlawfully
absenting themselves from monthly attendance at church. For nine of
them, including John Shakespeare, an excuse is offered: "it is say'd"
they "coom not . . . for feare of processe for Debtte." This is explicit
enough, though it has been conjectured that the real reason was re-

cusancy. John Whitgift, who became Archbishop of Canterbury in 1583, had occupied the See of Worcester since 1576; he had been diligent against nonconformists. Some have jumped to the conclusion that John Shakespeare was a Puritan; others argue that he was a Catholic. There is no evidence; neither his nor his son's religious convictions, if any, are known. (See, however, for the theory that the former was a staunch Protestant and not in financial straits at all, E. I. Fripp, *Shakespeare Studies*, pp. 81–98.) John must have been at least an outward conformist when he took the oaths of municipal office.

13 PAGE 11. It remained in the family's possession till 1838. The only evidence for Anne's age is the inscription on her grave beside her husband's: she died "the 6th day of August: 1623 being of the age of 67 yeares." That she was the Richard Hathaways' daughter can not be proved, but she is presumably the "Agnes" mentioned in Richard's will. It is a curious fact (though it is not proof of an unhappy marriage) that Shakespeare goes out of his way in *Twelfth Night* (II, iv) to utter the following untactful opinion:

"Let still the woman take
An elder than herself: so wears she to him,
So sways she level in her husband's heart."

14 PAGE 12. When, in all likelihood, the license was actually issued. The registry date was probably copied from the applicant's sworn allegation, which along with the bond was a prerequisite to the dispensation. Which of the interested parties actually went to Worcester and procured the license is unknown. — The bridegroom's given name is not spelled out in either of these documents. Writers of the Secretary script freely employed symbols of contraction. Throughout my quotations I expand these into the full forms.

15 PAGE 12. The late antiquary Richard Savage favored St. Martin's in the Corn Market, Worcester, where he found that two leaves which might have contained the record had been cut out of the register. He suspected an unscrupulous collector. (E. I. Fripp, *Shakespeare, Man and Artist*, I, 190, n. 5.)

16 PAGE 12. That is, six months after the parents married. Happily the day is over when the biographer need feel obliged to dodge the obvious conclusion that Shakespeare was Anne's lover before he was her husband. If anyone is severe enough to think hardly of the poet on that account, the privilege is his. If anyone is naive enough to think worse of the plays and poems, he had better close this book and seek another guide. The hypothesis that there had been a formal betrothal, preceding and permissive of cohabitation, is a well-meant effort to whitewash a name too great to stand in need of it. The obloquy which conventionally followed such anticipations of the marriage ceremony is expressed by Shakespeare himself in *The Tempest*, IV, i, 15–31. (For the contrary view see J. S. Smart, *Shakespeare: Truth and Tradition*, pp. 75–9.)

17 PAGE 12. Susanna married John Hall, a well-known physician, on June 5, 1607. She died in 1649. Her one daughter, who became ten years after her grandfather's death Mrs. Thomas Nash and later Mrs. and subsequently Lady (wife of Sir John) Bernard, died in 1670 without issue. No other legitimate descendant of William Shakespeare was then alive. There is no evidence that he had illegitimate offspring, but see pp. 71–2.

18 PAGE 12. "Hamnet" and "Hamlet" appear in Stratford records interchangeably. Shakespeare's son was buried at Stratford on Aug. 11, 1596. Judith Shakespeare married Thomas Quiney on Feb. 10, 1616. She was buried in Stratford on Feb. 9, 1662. None of her three sons survived her. None left issue. The eldest, who died in infancy, was born seven months after his grandfather's death and named Shakespeare.

19 PAGE 12. See p. 9, above.

20 PAGE 13. See p. 6, above.

21 PAGE 16. *Outlines*, II, 286.

22 PAGE 17. On May 22, 1592, in London, a William Shakespeare lent £7 to John Clayton, yeoman, of Willington, Bedfordshire. Payment of the debt was forced by legal action in 1600. The probability that the lender was not the poet is strengthened by Hotson's discovery of a Bedfordshire William Shakespeare. (London *Times*, Nov. 22, 1930, p. 13.)

23 PAGE 18. A publisher normally entered his book in the register of the Stationers' Company shortly before issuing it. His right to it was thus protected, since all the private publishers were supposed to be members of the Company.

24 PAGE 19. *Amores*, I, xv, 35–6. Marlowe translates:
> "Let base conceited wits, admire vilde things,
> Faire Phœbus leade me to the Muses springs."

25 PAGE 20. Chettle's book was entered in the Stationers' Register on Dec. 8, 1592. — "*Facetious* grace" is probably what he wrote; but at least two copies have "fatious," just possibly for "featous," "featous" = elegant, polite. But this is doubtless the meaning of "facetious," too. Cf. Lat. "facetus."

26 PAGE 21. For the suspension and various theories of how Shakespeare employed his enforced leisure, including a hypothetical love affair, see Chap. 2, "Early Companies and Theatres," pp. 113, 115–116, above.

27 PAGE 24. The first literary mention of Shakespeare by name.
> "Yet *Tarquyne* pluckt his glistering grape,
> And *Shake-speare*, paints poore Lucrece rape."

28 PAGE 27. It is impossible to strike an accurate ratio between purchasing power then and now. For most commodities money went a great deal farther. See A. V. Judges, "A Note on Prices in Shakespeare's Time," in H. Granville-Barker and G. B. Harrison's *A Companion to Shakespeare Studies*, pp. 382–4.

29 PAGE 34. G. L. Kittredge, "The Man Shakespeare," *Shakespeare Association Bulletin*, XI (1936), 173.

30 PAGE 37. For further discussion of these years, see Chapter 2, "Early Companies and Theatres," pp. 106–18, above.

31 PAGE 40. See p. 21, above; and Chapter 2, "Early Companies and Theatres," pp. 113, 115, above.

32 PAGE 41. The Theatre was built in 1576 and the Curtain, in the same district, the year after. Both were operated by the Burbages. Their rival was the Rose, owned by Philip Henslowe, the house of the Lord Admiral's Men. It stood on the Bankside, just south of the Thames and west of London bridge. See the present volume's endpapers.

33 PAGE 42. See Chapter 7, "As You Like It," p. 259, above.

34 PAGE 43. Shakespeare's brothers probably predeceased him; and when Edward Capell notes the same tradition in 1774, he calls the narrator merely a relation of Shakespeare's. Capell connects this tradition with the lameness mentioned in Sonnet 37. This might quite well have been temporary or even figurative; certainly Shakespeare was not lame when he played the rôles of kings. And Sonnet 89 cites lameness as contrary to fact.

35 PAGE 47. "A golden silver-headed tilting-spear, pointing upwards, within a broad black band in a golden shield, the band extending from the upper right-hand corner of the field down and to the left [according, that is, to heraldic terminology, which reverses left and right]. Above the shield and resting on it is a silver and gold helmet in profile, with visor closed, supporting a gold and silver wreath of six convolutions, the helmet and shield being invested with a gold and silver mantle with golden tassels. Resting on the wreath is a white falcon with both wings spread and pointing upwards, supporting in one claw a silver-headed golden spear pointing upwards. Above the timbre or crest is a scroll bearing the motto, 'Non Sans Droict.'" (S. A. Tannenbaum, *The Shakspere Coat-of-Arms*, New York, 1908, pp. 17–18.) Some think Ben Jonson jeers at the motto, "Not without right," in *Every Man Out of His Humor* (III, iv, 86). After some jokes about the coat of arms purchased by the clownish countryman Sogliardo, Puntarvolo suggests the motto "Not without mustard," as appropriate to the boar's head of the arms.

36 PAGE 54. There are twenty short poems in *The Passionate Pilgrim*. The last six are introduced by a separate title page as "Sonnets To sundry notes of Musicke," without the settings and without mention of Shakespeare. See Rollins's New Variorum edition of the *Poems* for the debate on authorship. General opinion is at present as follows. (There is some confusion in numbering the poems, since some editors have split XIV and XX. I follow Rollins and Kittredge.) Where the verdict is "author unknown," Shakespeare remains, of course, a possibility.

I, II. Shakespeare's Sonnets 138 and 144, with minor variants.

III, V, XVI. Shakespeare's, from *Love's Labour's Lost* (IV, iii, 60–73; IV, ii, 109–22; IV, iii, 101–20).

XII ("Crabbed age and youth"). Author unknown. This song has been extravagantly admired by some; it seems pretty lame to me. It appears with four additional stanzas in the earliest surviving edition of Thomas Deloney's *The Garland of Good Will.* Whether it was in earlier editions is unknown; the first was not later than 1596.

VII, X, XIII, XIV, XV, XVII, XVIII. Author unknown.

IV, VI, IX, XI (all on Venus and Adonis). Probably by Bartholomew Griffin, since the quartet is homogeneous and XI had appeared in his *Fidessa* (1596).

XIX. Four stanzas (with variants) from Marlowe's "The passionate Sheepheard to his loue," and one from "The Nimphs reply to the Sheepheard," later ascribed to Raleigh.

VIII, XX. Richard Barnfield's, from his *Poems: In diuers humors* (1598).

37 PAGE 56. In *Diaphantus, or the Passions of Love.*

38 PAGE 58. T. W. Baldwin (*The Organization and Personnel of the Shakespearean Company*) has made an exhaustive study of the company's receipts. He estimates (pp. 167–70) that Shakespeare's average annual income from all theatrical sources was probably under £25 a year down to 1594, toward £50 to 1599, and about £110 to 1608, after which acting was more or less interrupted for two seasons by a new outbreak of the plague. After the retirement to Stratford, Baldwin calculates an income as housekeeper of from £60 to £70. He thinks that even an unusually good year never brought Shakespeare more than £175 from the theatre. An income of upwards of £150 was then a pretty good one.

39 PAGE 59. In his *The History of the Worthies of England*, 1662. When this note was written is unknown, but it was probably at least a quarter of a century after Shakespeare's death.

40 PAGE 59. Probably written some years after the play, which was produced in 1598.

41 PAGE 60. Cf. *Henry the Sixth.*

42 PAGE 60. Cf. *Henry the Fifth.*

43 PAGE 60. From the "hut," whence such properties were lowered onto the stage.

44 PAGE 61. For Henslowe at the Rose, see Chapter 2, "Early Companies and Theatres," pp. 109, 111–13, 116, 117–18, above.

45 PAGE 65. The first of these was at Wilton, where James spent several weeks. At this great house, the Earl of Pembroke's countryseat, the poet-historian William Cory alleged the existence, toward the end of the nineteenth century, of a letter in which Lady Pembroke told her son "to bring James I from Salisbury to see *As You Like It;* 'we have the man Shakespeare with us.'" Cory seems, however, not to have seen the letter himself; and even if there was one, it may have been a forgery.

(*Extracts from Letters and Journals*, ed. F. Warre Cornish, 1897, p. 168.)

46 PAGE 65. The Master of the Revels was a subordinate of the Lord Chamberlain. He had charge of entertainments at court and general supervision of the actors, including censorship of plays. New pieces had to be approved by him in advance of performance. This lucrative post was held by Edmund Tilney from 1579 till his death on August 20, 1610. After James's accession he seems to have delegated his authority to his nephew and deputy, Sir George Buck, who succeeded him.

47 PAGE 66. Similar records for 1611–12 and 1638 have also been disputed. The question has been ably debated on both sides. For a sceptical conclusion, see S. A. Tannenbaum, *Shakspere Forgeries in the Revels Accounts*, 1928. Cf. W. W. Greg, *Review of English Studies*, V (1929), 344–58; A. E. Stamp, *The Disputed Revels Accounts*, 1930; and Dr. Tannenbaum's rebuttal, *More about the Forged Revels Accounts*, 1932. The problem is complicated by the discovery among Edmond Malone's papers, after his death, of a sheet containing a list of plays with dates of performance at court in 1604–5. The Malone Scrap tallies with the disputed Revels list. If the Scrap's authenticity were certain, it would settle the question, since it would antedate the alleged forgeries. Tannenbaum concludes that the disputed accounts are a fabrication by the learned scholar and notorious forger, John Payne Collier.

48 PAGE 66. See, for example, *The Tempest*, IV, i, 60 ff.

49 PAGE 68. This play, Jonson's best tragedy, did not please the public. In a way he throws down a gage to Shakespeare, for it embodies his conception of how Roman history should be handled on the stage.

50 PAGE 69. Sly and Fletcher died in 1608, and Armin in 1615. For an important note on the livery lists see T. W. Baldwin, "Shakespeare's Company," London *Times Literary Supplement*, Feb. 8, 1934, p. 92. See also his *The Organization and Personnel of the Shakespearean Company*, chap. II. With this may be compared Chambers's views, *William Shakespeare*, vol. i, chap. III, and vol. ii, pp. 77–87. Chambers suggests as a third new sharer (implied by the payment to twelve Grooms in August, 1604) Samuel Crosse, otherwise unknown, whose name appears in the Folio of 1623 between Lowin's and Cooke's, and assigns him an early death in order to make room for Tooley, presumably a member by 1605. As Phillips's successor, Baldwin proposes Robert Gough, certainly a member by 1619. His name is fourth from the end in the Folio roster. Chambers inclines to Samuel Gilburne as Phillips's successor and Gough's predecessor. Gilburne had been Phillips's apprentice and is remembered in the will to the extent of "fortye shilings, and my mouse colloured velvit hose, and a white taffety dublet, a blacke taffety sute, my purple cloke, sword and dagger, and my base viall."

51 PAGE 70. A pleasant conjecture has it that Shakespeare improved his

French in conversation with the Mountjoys. That *Henry the Fifth*, III, iv reflects his sojourn in Silver Street seems unlikely; the date of that play and the vulgarity of the passage warrant the hope and strengthen the conviction that the origin of these jokes must be sought elsewhere.

52 PAGE 71. On the consequent litigation, of minor importance, see E. K. Chambers, *William Shakespeare*, II, 122-7.

53 PAGE 72. *Remarks and Collections of Thomas Hearne*, ed. C. E. Doble (Oxford Historical Society), II, 228. — Sir William D'avenant was born in 1606. He died, poet laureate and theatrical proprietor, in 1668.

54 PAGE 73. Unless the Revels account is forged. See pp. 65-6, and p. 394, n. 47, above.

55 PAGE 73. Some, like Chambers (*William Shakespeare*, I, 85-6), ascribe the decline to the mental strain of the tragic period, culminating in an illness, perhaps a nervous breakdown, that left *Timon* unfinished. ·

56 PAGE 74. In H. Granville-Barker and G. B. Harrison's *A Companion to Shakespeare Studies*, p. 258.

57 PAGE 76. See Chapter 5, "Henry the Eighth," p. 200, above.

58 PAGE 77. See p. 14, above.

59 PAGE 77. See, however, the opinion of E. I. Fripp, *Shakespeare, Man and Artist*, p. 812 and n. 4.

60 PAGE 79. Dr. Tannenbaum, who brings to the problem the advantage of specialization both in Shakespeare studies and in medicine, points out that an attack of angina pectoris is likelier than a fever to have followed the merry meeting.

61 PAGE 79. The latter part of this sentence probably means that if he received an invitation to join in debauchery he wrote and excused himself with the polite fiction that illness prevented acceptance. — This note occurs on a scrap of ms. (not in Aubrey's Life) in the Bodleian Library.

62 PAGE 81. The precise intention of this clause is uncertain. For a detailed analysis, see S. A. Tannenbaum, *Problems in Shakspere's Penmanship*, chap. V, "Shakspere's Will."

63 PAGE 81. By Dowdall. See p. 6, and pp. 388-9, n. 7, above.

64 PAGE 81.   "Good frend for Iesvs sake forbeare,
                    To digg the Dvst encloased heare!
                    Bleste be yᵉ man yᵗ spares thes stones,
                    And cvrst be he yᵗ moves my bones."

Dowdall is the first to record the tradition that Shakespeare composed these lines "a little before his Death." They are cut on the stone slab, not the original one, which covers the grave. The purpose of the injunction was to prevent the transfer of the bones to the adjacent charnel house (no longer extant) on some future occasion when a new claimant of the honor of burial inside the church might require the space. The warning sufficed; the remains have never been disturbed.

65 PAGE 81. With the possible exception of a copy of the first edition of Florio's translation of Montaigne's *Essays*, now in the British Museum, mentioned below in connection with signatures, "Notes to Chapter 11," page 414, note 4.

66 PAGE 82. For the contemporary and subsequent allusions to Shakespeare, see J. Munro, *The Shakspere Allusion-Book*, and E. K. Chambers, *William Shakespeare*, vol. II, Appendices A, B, and C.

67 PAGE 82. These monuments know not how to die. — Though it was printed in 1627 with *The Battaile of Agincovrt*, I add Drayton's reference in his "To Henery Reynolds," since Drayton, like Jonson, was an eminent poet who knew Shakespeare well:

> "And be it said of thee,
> *Shakespeare* thou hadst as smooth a Comicke vaine,
> Fitting the socke, and in thy naturall braine,
> As strong conception, and as Cleere a rage,
> As any one that trafiqu'd with the stage."

68 PAGE 85. Or Phoenix, a new theatre, in Drury Lane, built after Shakespeare's death.

CHAPTER 2

1 PAGE 89. As Frank Vernon insists in *The Twentieth Century Theatre* (London and Boston, 1924), p. 16.

2 PAGE 90. See W. J. Lawrence, *The Physical Conditions of the Elizabethan Public Playhouse*, pp. 11–12.

3 PAGE 91. For amusing accounts see Chap. VI of Thomas Dekker's *The Gull's Horn-Book*, 1609, often reprinted, and the Induction to Jonson's *Cynthias Revels*.

4 PAGE 98. The extent to which title and scene boards were used in the public theatres is uncertain. The former announced the play; the latter helped the audience recognize a change of scene or the direction of near-by localities. Both were sometimes used at court and in the private theatres.

5 PAGE 103. Quarto 1, sig. A4.

6 PAGE 106. R. W[illis], *Mount Tabor. Or Private Exercises of a Penitent Sinner* (1639), pp. 110–11.

7 PAGE 112. On "ne," see Chapter 6, "Titus Andronicus," p. 210, above.

8 PAGE 112. See p. 19, above.

9 PAGE 113. The "plat" or "plot" was a scene-by-scene abstract of the play. Hung up for guidance during performance, it told at a glance who was on. For facsimiles of surviving ones, see W. W. Greg, *Dramatic Documents*.

10 PAGE 113. This permission was solemnly granted at a meeting of the Privy Council on May 6, 1593; both the Lord Admiral and the Lord Chamberlain were present. (J. R. Dasent, *Acts of the Privy Council of England*, XXIV, 212.)

11 PAGE 113. For a full exposition of the theory that Shakespeare's whole career was with the Strange-Chamberlain actors see T. W. Baldwin, *The Organization and Personnel of the Shakespearean Company.*

12 PAGE 114. Usually quoted as "iij." For the correction see T. W. Baldwin, *Modern Language Notes,* XL (1925), 343–9. A facsimile of Kyd's letter forms the frontispiece of F. S. Boas's edition of Kyd's *Works.*

13 PAGE 115. Henslowe got some of his dates wrong. For the corrections see *Henslowe's Diary,* ed. W. W. Greg, II, 46, 324–7.

14 PAGE 116. For an ingenious argument see L. Hotson, *I, William Shakespeare,* pp. 53–70. The couplet may echo *Titus Andronicus,* II, i, 82–3.

15 PAGE 116. By a Bad quarto (with a capital B) is meant, not necessarily a badly printed text, but a defective and unauthorized one. Most scholars now believe that as a general rule a Bad quarto came into existence through the treachery of a minor actor who had once belonged to the company that owned the play. For his new associates, or for a piratical publisher, he reconstructed the text as best he could from memory. On the features of the Bad quartos of Shakespeare, see, for example, Chap. 4, "The Second Part of King Henry the Sixth," pp. 155–7, above, and Chap. 9, "Hamlet," pp. 308–9, above. For the now generally accepted theory that the *Contention* plays are not Shakespeare's sources but degenerate derivatives from the true text, i.e., Bad quartos, see Peter Alexander, *Shakespeare's Henry VI and Richard III.*

16 PAGE 117. See pp. 112, 113, above.

17 PAGE 117. For an exposition of the Pembroke theory see Peter Alexander, *Shakespeare's Henry VI and Richard III.* Some have concluded that on the failure of Pembroke's company Shakespeare transferred to Sussex's and thence to the Chamberlain's. See J. O. Halliwell-Phillips, *Outlines,* I, 122, II, 329–30; and E. K. Chambers, *Elizabethan Stage,* II, 129–30.

18 PAGE 120. The following pages on metrics are reprinted in slightly modified form, with the generous permission of Messrs. D. C. Heath and Company, from my edition of *King Richard the Third* in their Revised [American] Arden Shakespeare. Except as indicated, all the illustrative lines are from that play.

19 PAGE 120. Admired by Sidney, who, like most of the Elizabethan critics, was so impressed with neoclassical theory that he failed to perceive that a great new art was flowering. Renaissance England, in contrast with Italy and France, had no dramatic criticism of importance.

CHAPTER 3

1 PAGE 129. Cf. on *The Two Gentlemen of Verona,* p. 143, above.

2 PAGE 129. It is, however, just possible that they played at Greenwich on the *afternoon* of the 28th. — For the Inns of Court, see p. 45, above.

3 PAGE 130. Chambers hazards the guess that *the gelyous comodey* marked "ne" by Henslowe on Jan. 5, 1593 may be *Errors*. (On Henslowe's *Diary* see p. 112, above.) T. W. Baldwin ([American] Arden ed., pp. xi–xvi), finding no reference to *Errors* in Henslowe's lists, concludes, on the assumption that Shakespeare was one of Strange's Men, that it must be dated before the autumn of 1590. His further argument, based on the "geography" of the play and the company's occupancy of the Theatre or Curtain on the site of Holywell Priory, has not been widely accepted, though his date for *Errors*, late in 1589, is an attractive one. See also Baldwin's *William Shakespeare Adapts a Hanging* (Princeton, 1931).

4 PAGE 130. See Chapter 7, "Twelfth Night," p. 263, above.

5 PAGE 130. According to a disputed Revels list. See pp. 65–6, and p. 394, n. 47, above.

6 PAGE 136. For Meres, see pp. 51–2, above.

7 PAGE 136. Cf. above, p. 397, note 15.

8 PAGE 136. P. Alexander, "The Taming of a Shrew," London *Times Literary Supplement*, Sept. 16, 1926, p. 614.

9 PAGE 140. The original play had been revived, however, by Benjamin Webster at the Haymarket in 1844, and by Samuel Phelps at Sadler's Wells in 1856. Phelps played Sly. Webster, who played Petruchio, entrusted the designing of the revival to J. R. Planché; they attempted to simulate the Elizabethan manner by using a draped stage and scene boards.

10 PAGE 143. On the plat, see p. 396, n. 9, above.

11 PAGE 146. George Pettie's *A petite Pallace of Pettie his Pleasure* (1576) seems to have been the most influential work.

12 PAGE 146. *Sapho and Phao* (1584), III, iii, 100–108.

13 PAGE 146. Though, as Abel Lefranc points out, the framework may have been suggested by a diplomatic mission of Catherine de' Medici, Queen-Mother of France, to Henry of Navarre at Nérac in 1578. She was accompanied by her daughter, Navarre's estranged wife, Marguerite de Valois, a princess of France. The negotiations had to do with the sovereignty of Aquitaine and the money which the King of France owed Navarre. There ensued, to put it mildly, a brilliant social season, which Shakespeare may have heard of from some traveler. From 1589 to 1593 (see p. 130, above) Navarre was fighting for the French throne, and as a Protestant hero was much admired in England. The Maréchal de Biron (afterwards the subject of a tragedy by Chapman) was the most famous of his generals. The Duc de Longueville, Governor of Normandy, was also on the Huguenot side. So were the Duc de Mercade and the Marquis de la Mothe; but the Duc de Mayenne (whence "Dumain") was a brother of the head of the Catholic League, the Guise himself.

14 PAGE 147. Gladys D. Willcock, *Shakespeare as a Critic of Language*, pp. 8–9.

15 PAGE 147. For Petrarchism, see pp. 28–30, above.

16 PAGE 148. According to a disputed Revels account. See pp. 65–6, and

p. 394, n. 47, above. — For Cope's letter, see *Reports of the Historical Manuscripts Commission*, III (1872), 148.

17 PAGE 149. There is a similarly mistaken preservation of a canceled passage in V, ii, 826–31. For the theory that Shakespeare rewrote his play, see J. D. Wilson, "The Copy for *Love's Labour's Lost*, 1598," in the New edition, pp. 97–130.

CHAPTER 4

1 PAGE 152. On the form in general, see p. 38, above; and on Meres, pp. 51–2, above.

2 PAGE 153. For a theory involving several hands, see E. K. Chambers, *William Shakespeare*, I, 290–2.

3 PAGE 154. See Chapter 6, "Titus Andronicus," p. 210, above.

4 PAGE 154. See p. 19, above.

5 PAGE 155. See pp. 18–19, above.

3 PAGE 155. Separately reprinted in 1600, and (with some change) in 1619 as *Part 1* of *The Whole Contention betweene the two Famous Houses, Lancaster and Yorke.* . . .

7 PAGE 156. Someone who had played Suffolk and Cade in *Part 2* has been proposed, and Warwick and Clifford in *Part 3*. Chambers suggests the prompter, working perhaps with a plat, which would give him the Quarto's unusually full stage directions. On the Bad quartos, cf. p., 397 n. 15, above.

3 PAGE 157. In the Prologue to *Every Man in his Humor*, printed in 1616 and probably written some years earlier but still in the Jacobean era, Jonson scoffs at various types of plays, among them such as

"with three rustie swords,
And helpe of some few foot-and-halfe-foote words,
Fight ouer *Yorke*, and *Lancasters* long iarres [jars, i.e., quarrels]."

9 PAGE 159. Technically, however, an octavo.

10 PAGE 160. Phelps staged all Shakespeare's plays except *1, 2,* and *3 Henry the Sixth, Richard the Second, Titus Andronicus, Troilus and Cressida*, and *The Two Noble Kinsmen*.

11 PAGE 161. With the kind consent of Messrs. D. C. Heath and Company, the following paragraphs on stage history are substantially from my edition, the Revised [American] Arden, 1933.

12 PAGE 161. For summaries see Alice I. P. Wood, *The Stage History of Shakespeare's King Richard the Third*, or H. Spencer, *Shakespeare Improved*.

13 PAGE 164. Later quartos, all carrying the author's name, appeared in 1598, 1602, 1605, 1612, 1622, 1629, and 1634. Once a play got into print, reprintings are prima-facie evidence of popularity; but, as Chambers observes, the enterprise of the owner of the copyright, such as it was, is a factor of importance. Failure to reprint is not prima-facie evidence of unpopularity.

14 PAGE 167. For a full discussion of the sources, see G. B. Churchill *Richard the Third up to Shakespeare.* It is unlikely that Shakespeare's play was influenced by Thomas Legge's *Richardus Tertius,* acted at St. John' College, Cambridge, at least as early as 1580; or by the anonymou *The True Tragedie of Richard the Third,* printed in 1594 as a Queen's Men' play.

15 PAGE 170. Cf., however, on *Richard the Second,* p. 175, above.

16 PAGE 171. Modern editors change the Folio's I, ii to II, and place th 74 lines of Folio's II at the beginning of III, i.

17 PAGE 172. I, i, 48–9; III, iii, 6–13; III, iv, 171–3; IV, ii, 141–2.

18 PAGE 173. E.g., III, iii, 19 ff., where John's speeches are replete with op portunities for the player. The interview with Hubert arouses suspense advances the plot, and builds up the King's character. His long an sinuous approach to his wicked proposal is too subtle for Hubert, wh fails to get the point. John's next speech, the monosyllable "Death," gives a brilliant effect of contrast and shock.

19 PAGE 173. See G. C. D. Odell, *Shakespeare from Betterton to Irving,* I, 26c and Arthur Murphy, *Life of Garrick,* II, 159.

20 PAGE 175. Arguments for a more precise dating rest on parallels wit Samuel Daniel's *Ciuile wars between . . . Lancaster and Yorke* (1595) an on a letter (endorsed Dec. 7, 1595) from Sir Edward Hoby to Sir Rober Cecil inviting him to supper "& K. Richard [shall] present him self to your vewe"; but there is really no evidence. I follow Chambers' transcription of Hoby's letter, which is calendared in *Hist. MSS. Com mission, Cecil MSS.,* V (1894), 487.

21 PAGE 176. Later quartos appeared in 1598 (two editions), 1608, 1615 and 1634. As Pollard notes, this is the only play of Shakespeare's tha went into three editions in two years.

22 PAGE 176. Surviving copies of Q₄ differ in the title page. The earlier give the title simply as "The Tragedie of King Richard the second," an repeats the older quartos' mention of the Chamberlain's Men. To ad vertise the restoration of the censored passage and to bring the descrip tion of the acting up to date, a new page was substituted in later copie of Q₄, adding to the title: "With new additions of the Parliamen Sceane, and the deposing of King Richard, As it hath been lately acte by the Kinges Majesties seruantes, at the Globe." Whether the deposi tion was acted when the play was originally staged is uncertain. Cen sorship of performances was in the hands of the Master of the Revels to print a play required a license from the Archbishop of Canterbur or the Bishop of London.

23 PAGE 176. The Third is also a possibility.

24 PAGE 177. See pp. 64–5, above. That it was Shakespeare's play is almos certain. (Nevertheless, there were others: the anonymous *The Life an Death of Iacke Straw,* 1593, and the anonymous ms. *1 Richard the Secon or Thomas of Woodstock* — Malone Society, 1929. — The alleged descrip tion by Dr. Simon Forman of a King's Men play on the earlier years of Richard's reign is probably a forgery: see page 411, note 14, below.) The Elizabethans saw an analogy between the Queen and Richard II; her flatterers were called, by courtiers who lacked the entrée to the inner circle, "Richard II's men." In 1599 appeared a prose history of *The First Part of the Life and raigne of King Henrie the IIII* by Dr. (afterward Sir) John Hayward, with a dedicatory epistle to Essex; it was suppressed as seditious, and the author went to the Tower for it. According to an undated abstract of the evidence against Essex, he was accused of encouraging Hayward's book, with its dangerous dedication, and of liking and frequently attending "the playing thereof." It seems probable that the play in question was *Richard the Second*, but it is uncertain whether these charges were brought when the Earl was under examination in the summer of 1600 for his mismanagement of the Irish command, or later. In the eyes of the government he aspired to the rôle of Bolingbroke, and he was executed on Feb. 25, 1601. On Aug. 4 Elizabeth remarked to William Lambarde, Keeper of the Tower, "I am Richard II. know ye not that?" And then she complained of a tragedy acted "40^{tie} times in open streets and houses." The last of these specifications may reflect her indignation at the staging of the offensive piece within the city, where the King's Men were very likely playing in the winter seasons when *Richard the Second* was originally produced. On Feb. 18 the Chamberlain's Men were represented at the conspirators' trial by Augustine Phillips, who testified that a bonus of forty shillings offered by the Earl's friends had overcome the company's reluctance to revive a play "so old & so long out of vse." "Old" is not of much significance; in theatrical parlance it means simply "not new," and a new play is and was not new for very long.

25 PAGE 179. Its success continued on the road during the season of 1937–38.

<h2 style="text-align:center">CHAPTER 5</h2>

1 PAGE 180. See *Hamlet*, II, ii, 415 ff.

2 PAGE 182. Vachel Lindsay, "Litany of the Heroes."

3 PAGE 182. Harpo Marx, for example.

4 PAGE 184. This view was first suggested by Maurice Morgann in *An Essay on the Dramatic Character of Sir John Falstaff*, 1777. For the ablest exposition of the contrary opinion see E. E. Stoll, "Falstaff," *Shakespeare Studies*, pp. 403–90. There is a good deal of logic on Stoll's side, and his argument advances on parallel lines with his admirable handling of Hamlet and Shylock, to name but two of his many brilliant studies. Yet, however one would like to go along with him for the sake of the neatness of the whole pattern, the score itself forbids; and all "historical" criticism must rest on score reading.

5 PAGE 184. Subsequent quartos are dated 1599, 1604, 1608, 1613, 1622, 1632, and 1639—eloquent testimony to Falstaff's popularity. (But cf. p. 399, n. 13, above.) Each reprints its predecessor. The First Folio reprints Q5. The only serious difference between Q and F is that oaths are excised in the latter. The Folger Shakespeare Library has a four-leaf fragment of an earlier edition than Q1, which adds the italicized word in "How the *fat* rogue roar'd" (II, ii, 118).

6 PAGE 185. *The Famous Victories* had belonged to the old Queen's Men, according to the title page of the first surviving edition, 1598. Since it was entered in the Stationers' Register in 1594, there may have been an edition in that year. Possibly the printing in 1598 was inspired by the success of Shakespeare's play. The Admiral's Men were acting a *harey the v* in 1595–6; this piece, which has not survived, may have been likewise inspired; but it is likelier that Shakespeare began his trilogy on the same theme to provide the Chamberlain's Men with a competing vehicle.

7 PAGE 185. See "my old lad of the castle" (*Part 1*, I, ii, 47) and the speech-tag "*Old.*" in Q 1600 of *Part 2* (I, ii, 137). In 1599–1600 the Admiral's Men acted a two-part drama, by Michael Drayton and others, on the historical Oldcastle. It was a reply to the slanderous portrait in *Henry the Fourth;* the Prologue to *Part 1* declares:

> "It is no pamperd glutton we present,
> Nor aged Councellor to youthfull sinne,
> . . . . let faire Truth be grac'te,
> Since forg'de inuention former time defac'te."

Despite Shakespeare's change to "Falstaff," numerous allusions to "Oldcastle" show that the part had been played under that name long enough to impress the public mind.

8 PAGE 185. The seventh Lord Cobham was lord chamberlain in 1596–7. See p. 48, above.

9 PAGE 185. Cf. *2 Henry the Fourth*, III, ii, 27–9.

10 PAGE 186. See, for example, the allusion of the Countess of Southampton, p. 53, above.

11 PAGE 186. Jonson's *Volpone* and *The Alchemist*.

12 PAGE 186. At the Blackfriars.

13 PAGE 187. The last of these entries has been questioned by S. A. Tannenbaum, *Shakspere Forgeries*, p. 60 (facsimile on p. 98). Cf. pp. 65–6, and p. 394, n. 47, above.

14 PAGE 189. For the record, see p. 187, above.

15 PAGE 190. To Mr. Henry N. Paul of Philadelphia I am indebted for some observations that have reversed my previously expressed opinions on Betterton's revival and the version of *c.* 1721.

16 PAGE 190. Evidence (but not conclusive) against popularity on the stage. See p. 399, n. 13, above. In the case of *2 Henry the Fourth* the problem is complicated, as we shall see, by the likelihood of political censorship.

17 PAGE 190. See pp. 64–5, 177; and pp. 400–01, n. 24, above. The Quarto was entered in the Stationers' Register on Aug. 23, 1600. It is unnecessary to assume that it was not published till after the Earl's rebellion on Feb. 8, 1601 (1600, O.S.). For Schücking's article see Bibliography, and cf. Hart's study.

18 PAGE 192. *The Second part of Henrie the fourth, continuing to his death, and coronation of Henrie the fift. With the humours of Sir Iohn Falstaffe, and swaggering Pistoll. As it hath been sundrie times publikely acted by the right honourable, the Lord Chamberlaine his seruants. Written by William Shakespeare.*

19 PAGE 195. See p. 397, n. 15, above. Q₁ seems to have been reprinted independently by Qq₂,₃ (1602, 1619). Q₃ was falsely dated 1608; it is one of ten plays published in 1619 by William and Isaac Jaggard and Thomas Pavier. A letter of the lord chamberlain on May 3 had ordered the Stationers' Company to print none of the King's Men's plays without their consent. Since some of the ten are dated 1619, it seems likely that, on learning of the chamberlain's ukase, the publishers altered the dates of the remainder in order to palm them off as earlier editions. For summary and bibliography see E. K. Chambers, *Willliam Shakespeare*, I, 133-7.

20 PAGE 196. See p. 185, and p. 402, n. 6, above.

21 PAGE 198. Recorded in a disputed Revels account. See pp. 65-6, and p. 394, n. 47, above.

22 PAGE 200. *Reliquiæ Wottonianæ*, third ed., "with large *Additions*" (London, 1672), pp. 425-6. Ben Jonson mentions the fire in his "Execration upon Vulcan"; probably he was in the audience. See, for other allusions, E. K. Chambers, *Elizabethan Stage*, II, 419-23. Two of them enlarge Wotton's one hour to two.

23 PAGE 201. By Richard Roderick, in Thomas Edwards's *The Canons of Criticism*, from the sixth edition of which (1758) Roderick's notes are reprinted in the *New Shakspere Society Transactions*, ser. I, part i (1874), appendix, pp. 66*-68* [*sic*].

24 PAGE 201. "Shakespeare; or, The Poet," *Representative Men, Works*, Centenary ed., IV, 195-6.

25 PAGE 201. There remains, of course, the very remote possibility that Shakespeare wrote the whole thing. He might have begun it in his own style and then have picked it up again and completed it in Fletcher's — out of curiosity to see what he could do with the new popular mannerisms (his may have been to the last a virtuoso's pride), or just for the devil of it.

26 PAGE 202. Cf. p. 76, above. It is none the less true that there are many lines which might be either Shakespeare's or Fletcher's. Neither poet is quite himself in this play.

27 PAGE 202. John Downes, *Roscius Anglicanus* (London, 1708), p. 24.

28 PAGE 203. W. R. Chetwood, *A General History of the Stage* (London, 1749), p. 68, says this spectacle was given seventy-five times its first season.

29 PAGE 204. Oct. 21, 1811, p. [3].

30 PAGE 204. Austin Brereton, *Life of Irving*, II, 167–8.

CHAPTER 6

1 PAGE 208. Cf. pp. 167–8, above.

2 PAGE 208. Note Ravenscroft's admission of uncertainty.

3 PAGE 209. Cf. pp. 111–13, 116–17, above.

4 PAGE 209. Some would identify *Jerusallem* with *Part 1* of *Godfrey of Bulloigne with the Conquest of Jerusalem*, entered in the Stationers' Register on June 19, 1594; its further identity with Heywood's *The Foure Prentises of London, With the Conquest of Jerusalem* has also been suggested. See A. M. Clark, *Thomas Heywood: Playwright and Miscellanist* (1931), pp. 24–6; and cf. E. K. Chambers, *Elizabethan Stage*, III, 340–41.

5 PAGE 210. He proceeds to mark it "ne" *again* on Feb. 11. See *Henslowe's Diary*, ed. W. W. Greg, I, 45, 50, 51.

6 PAGE 210. Everyone uses Jonson's figures for dating *The Spanish Tragedie*. On his gibe, see p. 37, above.

7 PAGE 211. It has been suggested that this entry refers to a prose history, the first surviving and indeed known edition of which was published about the middle of the eighteenth century. It is more likely, but by no means certain, that it refers to the play.

8 PAGE 211. Later quartos appeared in 1600 and 1611. Among the MSS of the Marquis of Bath at Longleat is a single sheet on which (1) two passages from the play are copied; with (2) a three-line link, in part adapted and in part not to be found in any of the printed texts; and (3) a drawing, with seven figures, of Tamora pleading to Titus for her sons. For a facsimile see E. K. Chambers, *William Shakespeare*, I, opp. p. 312; and for an extensive analysis, J. Q. Adams's facsimile ed. of Q_1, pp. 31–40. The MS has penciled annotations which Adams attributes to the scholar-forger J. P. Collier. He concludes that while the MS itself is no forgery, it must, despite the inscribed date 1595, be later than the Quarto of 1611 and perhaps than the First Folio, and thus has no textual value. The MS is signed by Henry Peacham, but Adams and Greg consider the drawing superior to examples of Peacham's known work.

9 PAGE 211. See p. 111, above.

10 PAGE 212. It is possible, of course, that he did not invent his pseudo-historical personages. A Byzantine emperor of the twelfth century, Andronicus Comnenus, and a Georgian queen, Thamar, may have been brought together in some tale Shakespeare had come upon. (See Bibliography, under "Dibelius" and "Granger.") Some believe the chapbook (see p. 404, n. 7) is an edition or version of Shakespeare's direct source. That this "History" antedates the play has not, however, been demonstrated.

11 PAGE 215. See p. 111, above.

12 PAGE 215. See p. 397, n. 15, above.

13 PAGE 215. Later quartos are dated 1609, n.d., and 1637.

14 PAGE 217. That is, in the early years of the fourteenth century. A history of Verona (1594-6) by Girolamo de la Corte actually gives 1303 for the lovers' deaths.

15 PAGE 217. His source is Da Porto, but he may have used a poem on *Giulia e Romeo* (Venice, 1553). It purports to be the work of a lady named Clitia; Gherardo Bolderi may be the author. A few details in this work are closer to Bandello than to Da Porto.

16 PAGE 217. A prose translation of Boaistuau's version appears in vol. II (1567) of William Painter's *The Palace of Pleasure*, but Shakespeare's source is Broke. Coincidence in a few details between the tragedy and another, Luigi Groto's *La Hadriana* (1578), has led some to conclude that both Groto and the author of a play mentioned by Broke used some lost Italian version, and that Shakespeare knew the lost play. It seems more likely that resemblances between Shakespeare and Groto are fortuitous. True, the parting lovers in *La Hadriana* hear a nightingale and Juliet declares it was that bird and not the lark when Romeo talks of going. In both plays an adviser attempts to comfort the grieved father with conventional optimism. These are fair samples of the similarities. We can hardly suppose that either poet was incapable of inventing them.

17 PAGE 218. The original prints each line as two.

18 PAGE 218. Companion.

19 PAGE 221. See pp. 41, 52, and cf. p. 86, above.

20 PAGE 224. G. Binz, "Londoner Theater und Schauspiele im Jahre 1599," *Anglia*, XXII (1899), 456-64. Platter continues with a brief account of the theatre and other amusements. Chambers (*Elizabethan Stage*, II, 364-6) gives the German text and a translation.

21 PAGE 224. For Jonson's reference to III, i, 47-8 ("Know, Caesar doth not wrong, nor without cause / Will he be satisfied"), see pp. 60-61, above. He is probably misquoting, without a text before him. Some have taken his words to prove the Folio text a revision, but that is erecting a tall edifice on a slight foundation. It is, however, quite possible that Shakespeare incorporated a suggestion from Ben at this point.

22 PAGE 225. For an argument against the validity of these Revels accounts, see S. A. Tannenbaum, *Shakspere Forgeries*, pp. 58, 60; and cf. pp. 65-6, and p. 394, n. 47, above.

CHAPTER 7

1 PAGE 232. For what Poe really wrote — it included mention of Prospero and *The Tempest*, — see the "Letter to B—," preface to *Poems*, 1831, or *Southern Literary Messenger*, II (1836), 501-3. The Letter has often been reprinted, e.g., *Works*, ed. Stedman and Woodberry (1914), X, 146-55. Furnivall seems to be responsible for the currency of the misquotation.

2 PAGE 235. Also spelled "burdockes."

3 PAGE 236. Published by Thomas Fisher, as *A Midsommer nights dreame*. The "Roberts" Quarto, a reprint, also dated 1600, was printed in 1619. See, for the misdating and its motive, p. 403, n. 19, above. The First Folio reprints Q_2.

4 PAGE 237. See my *Shakespeare Improved*, pp. 318–24. The *Dream* has been distressingly subject to repeated and stupid alteration. *The Fairy-Queen* was full of marvels, including a twelve-foot fountain, swans that swam and then turned into fairies and danced, Juno drawn by peacocks with practicable tails (they spread), Chinese soloists on the theme of the happy because primitive existence led by their romantic compatriots, and a monkey ballet. The nineteenth century did fearful things to the *Dream;* but it was left to the twentieth, at the Hollywood Bowl in 1922, to work in the goddesses of Olympus, the Great Lovers of the World, and Tom Mix and his pony Tony.

5 PAGE 237. These pieces were not real operas, such as Verdi was later to compose, with libretti based on Shakespeare's plays but molded to the composer's purposes. They were badly cut and garbled versions of the plays, with many interpolated and often unsuitable lyrics.

6 PAGE 237. *Examiner*, Jan. 22, 1816, p. 44.

7 PAGE 240. Published by Thomas Heyes as *The most excellent Historie of the Merchant of Venice. With the extreame crueltie of Shylocke the Iewe towards the sayd Merchant, in cutting a iust* [i.e., exact] *pound of his flesh: and the obtayning of Portia by the choyse of three chests.* Q_2 was published by William Jaggard in 1619, misdated 1600 and ascribed to the press of James Roberts. For the motive, see p. 403, n. 19, above. The First Folio reprints Q_1. A third quarto appeared in 1637 and a fourth in 1652.

8 PAGE 241. It was entered again, by Heyes, with "Consent of master Robertes" on Oct. 28, 1600 without the alternative title, as "A booke called the booke of the merchant of Venyce." Dr. Greg suggests that the redundancy points to the use of the prompt book itself. It may be so; but a scribe, preparing a copy for the printer, may have made the same mistake the Register does.

9 PAGE 241. See T. Birch, *Memoirs of the Reign of Queen Elizabeth*, II, 185, 204.

10 PAGE 241. His surname appears in various spellings. The caskets figure in the legend "De Sancto Barlaam" (cap. 176, in the edition of 1555 at Lyons).

11 PAGE 246. For an attack on the authenticity of the document in question, see pp. 65–6 and p. 394, n. 47, above.

12 PAGE 250. For the theories, see E. K. Chambers, *Elizabethan Stage*, III, 188–91.

13 PAGE 251. Miss Henrietta C. Bartlett (*Mr. William Shakespeare*, p. 92) cites Joseph Warton as quoting the mention by Bishop Thomas Tanner of an English edition of Bandello by "W.W." in 1580.

14 PAGE 252. Harington mentions a verse translation of the fifth canto, in which this episode occurs, by George Turberville. Nothing more is known of it.

15 PAGE 252. See G. L. Kittredge, ed., *Complete Works of Shakespeare*, p. 160.

16 PAGE 253. Aubrey adds marginally: "I thinke it was Midsomer night that he happened to lye there."

17 PAGE 253. A little off the direct road, Chambers notes.

18 PAGE 253. John Masefield, *The Tragedy of Pompey the Great*, appended verses.

19 PAGE 253. Cf. p. 399, n. 13, above.

20 PAGE 253. The *Benedicte and Betteris* of the second payment to Heminge on the Privy Council's warrant, also dated May 20, 1613, is certainly *Much Ado*. See p. 76, above. Prince Charles, who saw the first of these performances and probably the second as well, afterwards wrote the alternative title in his copy of the Second Folio.

21 PAGE 257. See p. 5, above.

22 PAGE 257. See p. 250, above.

23 PAGE 258. See pp. 250–51, above.

24 PAGE 259. Stoll observes of the love stories in the romantic comedies: "Merriment serves also another purpose, characteristic of great art, that of substitution and suggestion. It replaces the voluptuous and luscious." *Shakespeare's Young Lovers* (London, New York, etc., 1937), p. 52.

25 PAGE 259. On Euphuism, see pp. 145–6, above.

26 PAGE 259. See p. 63, above.

27 PAGE 260. Orlando does not recognize Rosalind in the garb of "Ganymede." The disguise convention is in complete control.

28 PAGE 260. See pp. 42–3, above.

29 PAGE 260. See pp. 393–4, n. 45, above.

30 PAGE 260. A. Nicoll, *Restoration Drama*, pp. 315–16.

31 PAGE 263. There was more than one play thus entitled, but Manningham probably means *Gl'Ingannati*. See p. 264, above. His *Diary* was edited by J. Bruce for the Camden Society in 1868; see p. 18.

32 PAGE 263. A few years later the house of Bracciano was to provide John Webster with the subject of his tragic masterpiece, *The White Divel*, in which Virginio appears as the child Giovanni.

33 PAGE 263. **An air** entitled "O mistress mine" was published, but without words, in Thomas Morley's *The First Book of Consort Lessons* in 1599. It is often cited as evidence for dating *Twelfth Night* earlier; but both Canon Fellowes and Mr. Noble are doubtful whether it was intended for Shakespeare's words (II, iii). Certainly it does not fit them perfectly. (In Morley's *The First Booke of Ayres. Or Little Short Songs*, 1600, there is an air, no. VIII, for a lyric beginning "Misteresse mine well may you fare." The unique copy is in the Folger Shakespeare Library. The words are completely independent of Shakespeare.) One would like to know whether the great composer was the poet's friend. They lived for a time in the same parish, St. Helen's, Bishopsgate. Shakespeare loved music; he must have loved Morley's. — Nor is there evidence for the date in the play's **Persian allusions**. "A pension of thousands to be paid from the Sophy [Shah]" (II, v, 197) *may* refer to the Persian adventure of Sir Anthony Sherley. Accompanied by his younger brother Robert, he set out from Venice in 1598 and reached the court of Abbas the Great. By April of 1601, having returned via Russia and Germany, he was back in Rome, where Will Kempe seems to have met him. Robert Sherley remained in Persia; he did not see England till 1611. *A True Report* of the journey was suppressed in 1600 but reissued the year following. Also in 1601 appeared William Parry's *A new and large discourse*. Parry was a follower, detached from the party in Germany with dispatches for London, where he arrived in September, 1600. No doubt tall tales of the Sherleys' adventures were in circulation; but the allusion in the play may have nothing to do with the Sherleys. The well-known traveler and commercial adventurer Anthony Jenkinson had visited the Shah's court in 1562. He brought home a glowing account of its wealth. He lived till 1611, honored and famous, the recognized English authority on Central Asia. Long before the Sherleys, other Englishmen had followed up his pioneer investigations of the Persian market. See E. P. Shirley, *The Sherley Brothers* (Chiswick, 1848), and *Stemmata Shirleiana* (2nd ed:, London, 1873), pp. 272–87; *The Three Brothers* (London and Edinburgh, 1825); F. Babinger, *Sherleiana: I. Sir Anthony Sherley's persische Botschaftreise* (Berlin, 1932); E. D. Ross, *Sir Anthony Sherley and his Persian Adventure* (London, 1933); S. C. Chew, *The Crescent and the Rose* (New York, 1937), chaps. v, vi, vii; and B. Penrose, *The Sherleian Odyssey* (Taunton, England, 1938), chaps. iv, v, vi, ix, x. The novice in Sherleiana should begin with Professor Chew's authoritative and fascinating book. Part II of Ross's reprints four seventeenth-century narratives, including Parry's, George Manwaring's (he was another of Anthony Sherley's companions), and *A True Report*.

34 PAGE 266. Called Charles by most historians of the theatre and, alas, by me in *Shakespeare Improved*, where his version is described. See F. E. Budd, *The Dramatic Works of William Burnaby*, London, 1931.

35 PAGE 269. See p. 197, above.

36 PAGE 271. See p. 397, n. 15, above. — Q₁ was reprinted in 1619, as part of the enterprise which led to the misdating of several quartos. (See p. 403, n. 19, above.) Q₃ (1630) reprints the Folio text.

37 PAGE 271. Cf. p. 143, above.

38 PAGE 272. Cf. p. 185, above.

39 PAGE 272. See pp. 397–8, n. 3, above.

40 PAGE 273. *Henry the Fifth*, II, iii. See pp. 195–6, above.

41 PAGE 273. Cf. p. 185, above.

42 PAGE 276. Cf. pp. 14–15, above.

43 PAGE 276. See pp. 48–9, above.

44 PAGE 276. Cf. p. 197, above.

45 PAGE 277. On the authenticity of those records see pp. 65–6 and p. 394, n. 47, above.

CHAPTER 8

1 PAGE 280. It can not be a tragedy, for the hero is preserved alive, a sadder but also a wiser youth. "Troilus does not fail; Cressida fails him, but that failure rather strengthens the fibre of his nature, as Coleridge saw, so that . . . after the death of Hector he comes forward as the leader of the Trojans." ("Troilus and Cressida," London *Times Literary Supplement*, May 19, 1932, pp. 357–8.) This is apt, though possibly overstated. Troilus is no Marchbanks, and the Problem of Evil is not to be solved by talking about strengthened fibres.

2 PAGE 282. *Ibid*. Cf. p. 289, above.

3 PAGE 283. That is, both were printed from the same setting of type, but changes were made before the second was printed. In this case the title leaf was cut away and a new double leaf was pasted in to carry the title page and the advertisement.

4 PAGE 283. It is easy to believe that a "never writer" penned this effusion; but the testimony to Shakespeare's popularity is important. His comedies "are so fram'd to the life, that they serue for the most common Commentaries, of all the actions of our liues shewing such a dexteritie, and power of witte, that [this is certainly an overstatement] the most displeased with Playes, are pleasd with his Commedies." The dull, he continues, who "by report" are attracted to the theatre, feel "an edge of witte set vpon them" by these works. "So much and such sauored salt of witte is in his Commedies, that they seeme (for their height of pleasure) to be borne in that sea that brought forth *Venus*. . . . And beleeue this, that when hee is gone, and his Commedies out of sale, you will scramble for them, and set vp a new English Inquisition. Take this for a warning, and . . . refuse not, nor like this the lesse, for not being sullied, with the smoaky breath of the multitude. . . ."

5 PAGE 283. Another possibility, advocated by W. W. Lawrence, is that the play had failed at the Globe. Hence it is not presented in book form as a stale piece already familiar in the theatre, but as a new one which ought to appeal to intellectual readers. J. Q. Adams, on the other hand, thinks the publishers had assumed that the play had been acted and, having learned the contrary at the last moment, hastened to advertise its complete novelty.

6 PAGE 285. See p. 63, above.

7 PAGE 287. Reproduced by W. W. Greg, *Henslowe Papers*, p. 142, and also in his *Dramatic Documents*.

8 PAGE 289. It is just such considerations that impel Dryden to praise the decorum of Jonson's characters, at the expense of Shakespeare's, in his essay on "The Grounds of Criticism in Tragedy" prefaced to his adaptation of *Troilus and Cressida*.

9 PAGE 290. Shakespeare could not have given it such a finale — the Troilus-Cressida story was too familiar, and the English theatre too young. If he intended to dramatize the heroine's punishment, he left it for another play. Perhaps he had thought of it, but found no encouragement to proceed with a sequel. The play we have is built on the structural plan of the histories. For example, the Trojan lords come in from battle in I, ii, but in I, iii we hear of "this dull and long-continu'd truce." Disintegrators take such inconsistencies for evidence of divided authorship or of revision; but while the quoted phrase is a bit abrupt as a long-time hint, it is regular chronicle-history technique, and the scene has already run for 261 lines when it is spoken. *Troilus and Cressida* begins epically, as the prologue states, *in medias res*,

"starting thence away
To what may be digested in a play."

Some of the critics forget that even Shakespeare could not get everything into a two-hour digest. There is no reason to suppose (though many have made the assumption) that the battle scenes (V, iv-x) are not Shakespeare's. Dryden could violate the old story — he could even violate Shakespeare's play. But the Elizabethans would have been as puzzled by Cressida's suicide and Troilus's immediate fall as we should be by a play about Napoleon ending with his death at Waterloo in a hand-to-hand fight with Wellington. I am bound to add that there is little agreement on Shakespeare's play among scholars. Some consider Troilus an idealist. Some even think that Cressida "is touched for a moment with his own bright clear flame."

10 PAGE 295. See pp. 51-2, above.

11 PAGE 299. On the authenticity of this record see pp. 65-6, and p. 394, n. 47, above.

12 PAGE 300. On the bed trick in general, see pp. 292-4, above. Some critics of this play, too, have had hysterics over it. "Procuress" and "rancid in her chastity" epitomize one estimate of Isabella.

13 PAGE 301. This is not the general opinion, which holds that Shakespeare leaves the marriage in doubt.

CHAPTER 9

1 PAGE 307. The evidence is far from conclusive. *Hamlet* is not mentioned in Meres's *Palladis Tamia* (1598). Gabriel Harvey noted in a copy of Chaucer (ed. Speght, 1598): "The younger sort takes much delight in Shakespeares Venus, & Adonis: but his Lucrece, & his tragedie of Hamlet, Prince of Denmarke, haue it in them, to please the wiser sort." (*Gabriel Harvey's Marginalia*, ed. G. C. Moore Smith, Stratford, 1913, p. 232.) Harvey also noted that "The Earle of Essex much commendes

[William Warner's] Albions England." The Earl was executed on Feb. 25, 1601; and while it is possible, it is not likely that Harvey would thus have used the present tense shortly after that event. The dates of Meres's book and of the Earl's death give us reasonably safe limits for the production of *Hamlet*.

2 PAGE 307. See pp. 167–8, above. Nashe also alludes to scribblers who leave "the trade of *Nouerint* whereto they were borne" (Kyd's father was one of the scriveners, often copyists of legal documents beginning "Noverint") and to "the Kidde in *Æsop*"; but while Kyd is probably a butt of Nashe's satire, there is nothing in the passage that implies his responsibility for a *Hamlet*.

3 PAGE 308. See p. 397, n. 15, above.

4 PAGE 309. Later quartos were published in 1611, n.d., and 1637.

5 PAGE 311. Thomas Davies, *Dramatic Miscellanies*, III, 32.

6 PAGE 313. See p. 261, above.

7 PAGE 313. Theodore Spencer, *Death and Elizabethan Tragedy*, pp. 234–5.

8 PAGE 314. That the throne is elective is certain, though the point has been disputed.

9 PAGE 316. A. Ralli's *A History of Shakespearian Criticism* summarizes many other theories about Hamlet. So does A. A. Raven's *A Hamlet Bibliography*. A. C. Bradley's *Shakespearean Tragedy* presents an elaborate interpretation which still has its admirers. J. D. Wilson's more ingenious than cogent *What Happens in Hamlet* has attracted much attention, as have H. Granville-Barker's *Hamlet* (the third volume of his *Prefaces*) and L. L. Schücking's *The Meaning of Hamlet*.

10 PAGE 318. Unless the Revels account is a forgery. See pp. 65–6, and p. 394, n. 47, above. A performance in 1636 has been questioned on similar grounds.

11 PAGE 318. It was entered in the Stationers' Register on Oct. 6, 1621. Later quartos appeared in 1630, 1655, 1681, 1687, 1695, and 1705; all of these I have examined. Jaggard also lists quartos in 1670, 1674, 1697, and 1701, as altered or edited by Dryden; but I can find no trace of them.

12 PAGE 326. Later quartos were published in 1619 (title page, 1608) and 1655. On the misdating of Q2, see p. 403, n. 19, above.

13 PAGE 327. Inconsistencies in the textual peculiarities indicate, in Miss Doran's opinion, that Shakespeare had gone back over his play and developed some of its features far beyond his original intention, and that these expansions, rather than a shorthand reporter's blunders, are responsible for the confusion. The case has been ably argued on both sides (see Bibliography), but remains in doubt. A more recent study rejects both views and declares for the superior authority of the Quarto.

14 PAGE 337. The account of a performance seen at the Globe in 1611 by Dr. Simon Forman is probably one of the forgeries of John Payne Collier. (See S. A. Tannenbaum, *Shaksperian Scraps*, pp. 1–35.)

CHAPTER 10

1 PAGE 341. For summaries of the many plays about them, beginning with Estienne Jodelle's in 1552, see Furness's New Variorum edition of *Antony and Cleopatra*, pp. 507–83. Dryden's *All for Love* is reprinted on pp. 409–72.

2 PAGE 342. The appearance in 1607 of a new edition of Samuel Daniel's *Certaine Small Workes*, with a revised text of his *Cleopatra*, has been cited as evidence for the date of Shakespeare's tragedy. Daniel's play was first printed in 1594, and an edition in 1605 remained unaltered by the changes of 1607. But these were not necessarily inspired by Daniel's having seen a performance of *Antony and Cleopatra*. (See Bibliography, under "Schütze.")

3 PAGE 342. Cf. p. 225, above.

4 PAGE 347. The assignment of the title rôle to Burbage in the expanded version of the elegy on his death is one of the fabrications of J. P. Collier.

5 PAGE 349. See p. 225, above.

6 PAGE 353. See pp. 283–4, above.

CHAPTER 11

1 PAGE 356. Cf. pp. 73–4, above. But see also C. J. Sisson, *The Mythical Sorrows of Shakespeare*.

2 PAGE 357. There were two editions in 1609, and reprints in 1611, 1619, 1630, and 1635. The first two editions are known as the "Enter Gower" and "Eneer Gower" quartos; the misprint occurs in the third line of sig. A2^r, and the edition distinguished by it is believed to be the later, though this has not been proved. There are numerous other variants.

3 PAGE 357. "Having completed an exhaustive examination of the extant *Pericles*, I can report that all the various kinds of corruption found in it have their parallel in other bad versions." L. Kirschbaum, "A Census of Bad Quartos," *Review of English Studies*, XIV (1938), 25.

4 PAGE 357. **Other ascriptions.** On quarto title pages or in booksellers' catalogues many other plays were ascribed to Shakespeare. With the exception of *The Two Noble Kinsmen*, general opinion is now strongly against his authorship of any of these pieces, among which *Edward the third*, *The Merry Devill of Edmonton*, *Faire Em*, *Mucedorus*, and *Arden of Feversham* have had persistent advocates. For a review of the whole subject and the texts of fourteen plays, see C. F. T. Brooke's *The Shakespeare Apocrypha*. — **Cardennio.** A lost play, "The History of Cardennio, by M^r. Fletcher. & Shakespeare," was registered by Humphrey Moseley on Sept. 9, 1653. There are records of two court performances in 1612–13. Moseley's ascription opens a possibility, although it is not decisive of Shakespeare's authorship. In 1612 was published Thomas Shelton's translation of Cervantes's *Don Quixote;* in it the author or authors of the play had evidently found the story of Cardenio and Lucinda. In 1727 a play by the brilliant Shakespearean scholar Lewis Theobald was produced at Drury Lane; it was entitled *Double Falshood; or, The Distrest Lovers,* and it dramatizes the same tale. This play, published the following year, purports to be an adaptation of one by Shakespeare which had allegedly survived in several manuscripts, one of them transcribed by John Downes, the Restoration prompter. Theobald mentions a tradition that the poet had presented the original manuscript to an illegitimate daughter. All this is sufficiently implausible; but, by working backward from Theobald's version, attempts have been made to hypothecate the original play and determine its authorship. For the view that *Cardennio* was another joint work by Fletcher and Shakespeare, see G. Bradford, "The History of Cardenio by Mr. Fletcher and Shakespeare," *Modern Language Notes,* XXV (1910), 51-6; W. Graham, "The Cardenio-Double Falsehood Problem," *Modern Philology,* XIV (1916), 269-80, and *ibid.* (1917), p. 568; and especially E. H. C. Oliphant, "Double Falsehood: Shakespeare, Fletcher, and Theobald," *Notes and Queries,* ser. 12, vol. v (1919), pp. 30-32, 60-62, 86-8, and *The Plays of Beaumont and Fletcher,* pp. 282-302. Obviously, efforts to distinguish the contributions of collaborating authors are very risky when the only text is an adapted one. The question is still open. The conclusion, held by many, that Theobald perpetrated a fabrication is weakened by his presumptive ignorance of the recorded performances and of the registration. On the other hand, though he said he had several manuscripts of the original play, he never printed it; and no one else seems to have seen any of them, neither when he was bringing out his adaptation nor since. Perhaps he had one or more old manuscripts and persuaded himself, or was convinced by an earlier fabricator's annotations, that Shakespeare was the author. — **Sir Thomas Moore.** The British Museum has a manuscript (Harleian 7368) entitled *The Booke of Sir Thomas Moore.* ("Booke" means prompt or official copy, the text submitted for "allowance" to Edmund Tilney, Master of the Revels.) This presumably unacted play dramatizes the rise and fall of the martyred chancellor. The original draft was written by a single hand. Whether Tilney saw the text in this form or after alteration is disputed. He found much fault, and objected by means of notes and marks of deletion. The manuscript also contains, in five hands, several added passages, one of which is believed by some scholars to have been composed and written in by Shakespeare about 1593 or 1594. It occupies three pages, which contain the first part of the scene (ed. Brooke, II, iv, 1-172) in which Sheriff More persuades the rebellious citizens to surrender. There is general agreement that the original hand is Munday's; Hand A (of the additions), Chettle's; and Hand E, Dekker's. Possibly Hand B is Heywood's. Kyd has been suggested for Hand C, but this has been warmly disputed.

The most heated controversy is over Hand D. Pollard, Greg, Wilson, and others are confident that it is Shakespeare's; Tannenbaum is sure it is not. Proponents have proceeded argumentatively on independent but "converging" lines, as they regard them — "palæographic, orthographic, linguistic, psychological." Paleographically, the ascription rests, not on allegations of the identity of Hand D with the extant signatures unquestionably Shakespeare's, but on the hypothesis that these, all of them belonging to 1612 or later, are in a hand which is the natural development of Hand D in the *Moore* addition of nearly twenty years before. In this department I am no expert; but, on the face of it, the unquestioned signatures being only six, and Hand D not being an unusual type of sixteenth-century English penmanship, the proposition laid down by the advocates of Shakespeare's authorship obviously labors under an extremely heavy burden of proof, in my opinion a heavier burden than they have been able to sustain. (See below.) — **Signatures.** Contrary to the popular impression, there is no evidence that Shakespeare was not a good penman. The illegibility of his signatures to the novice arises from the fact that, like most writers of the time, he continued to use the Old English or Secretary hand he had learned in school, a style more like the present German script than like the Italian hand now universally employed in penning English. The six certain signatures appear on his deposition in Belott's suit against Mountjoy, on the conveyance and on the mortgage of the Blackfriars house, and on each of the three sheets of his will. On the third sheet he prefixed his signature with the phrase "By me." No other scrap of handwriting is certainly his. Among the numerous alleged signatures, two in books have been certified by some experts and rejected by others. "W^m Sh^r," "W^m Sh^e," or "W^m Sh^{re}" appears on the title page of a copy of Ovid's *Metamorphoses* (in the Bodleian Library at Oxford) printed at Venice by Aldus in 1502. There is also a note signed "T.N. 1682" declaring that "W. Hall who sayd it was once Will. Shakesperes" gave him the volume. The authenticity of this signature is generally doubted. Tannenbaum makes out a strong claim, though there is some dissent, for the "Willm Shakspere" in a copy (in the British Museum) of Florio's translation of Montaigne's essays. — **Sir Thomas Moore, again.** Fortunately the disagreement of the experts who have dealt with Hand D of *Moore* does not, in this particular trial, involve the rope or electric chair. It is not, however, of slight importance, since in his New edition of Shakespeare's plays Professor Dover Wilson attempts to solve many textual problems on the assumption that we have, not merely six or seven signatures, but three pages of play manuscript in Shakespeare's hand. From a literary point of view they might well be his. It is doubtful whether any other dramatist known to be writing in 1593 or 1594 was capable of them. Unfortunately, that Shakespeare *could* have been the author does not prove he *was*. There remain the possibilities of imitation, of authorship by some unknown, of authorship by someone whose known works came later. It is, moreover, quite possible that the *Moore* manuscript is itself later. (See Bibliography, under "Textual Matters.") Shakespeare had no patent of monopoly on its blend of stalwart adherence to law and order with a good-humored treatment of personalities in the mob which threatens them. Upholders of his authorship believe that censorship was expected, since the play's hero was done to death by Elizabeth's father. Shakespeare, they think, was asked to inject a "loyal" passage, condemning rebellion and eloquently supporting the crown's authority. The ascription must, however, stand or fall chiefly on its paleographical merits. On the whole, the chances seem to be against the addition's being his. See, to list but a few of the studies in which the problem is tackled, the editions of: C. F. T. Brooke (*Shakespeare Apocrypha*, 1908), J. S. Farmer (photographic facsimile, 1910), and W. W. Greg (carefully edited type-facsimile, 1911); supporting Shakespeare's authorship: E. M. Thompson's *Shakespeare's Handwriting* (1916), *Shakespeare's Hand in The Play of Sir Thomas More* by A. W. Pollard *et al.* (1923), and Greg's "Shakespeare's Hand Once More" London *Times Literary Supplement*, Nov. 24, 1927, p. 871, Dec. 1, 1927, p. 908; and for the contrary opinion: S. A. Tannenbaum's *The Booke of Sir Thomas Moore* (1927), *Shakspere and Sir Thomas Moore* (1929), *An Object Lesson in Shaksperian Research* (1931), and "More about The Booke of Sir Thomas Moore," *Publications of the Modern Language Association of America*, XLIII (1928), 767–78.

5 PAGE 363. V, iv, 30–92, the rhymed portion of the vision, does seem pretty bad, even for Shakespeare at his worst. For a guess, these verses could be the work of a composer who thought he had literary as well as musical gifts. Who made the setting is unknown. If any part of the vision is an interpolation by another pen, this is it; but the chances are Shakespeare wrote the whole thing, in response to the current demand which evoked the angels in *Henry the Eighth* and the "revels" in *The Tempest*.

6 PAGE 364. An alleged account of the play by Dr. Simon Forman is probably a forgery. Cf. p. 411, n. 14, above.

7 PAGE 364. *Chronicles*, ed. 1807–8, V, 242–3.

8 PAGE 371. Unless the Revels account recording it is a forgery. See pp. 65–6, and p. 394, n. 47, above. An alleged account of a performance seen by Dr. Simon Forman is probably a forgery. Cf. p. 411, n. 14, above.

9 PAGE 375. According to a disputed document. Cf. p. 394, n. 47, above.

10 PAGE 375. There are analogous details in the German comedy of *Die Schöne Sidea*, printed in 1618, but written by Jakob Ayrer, who died in 1605. (For the German text, with English translation, see A. Cohn, *Shakespeare in Germany*, pp. 4–75; Furness gives a translation, New Variorum ed. of *The Tempest*, pp. 325–41.) They include a princely magician, his beautiful daughter, his familiar spirit, and his enemy's son. The last is in love with the daughter, his sword is restrained by enchantment, and he has logs to carry. The storm and the island are not in Ayrer's play, which is fundamentally unlike *The Tempest* and certainly no source. The common features were doubtless picked up independently by the two dramatists from some old tale or fable. None, however, has been discovered.

11 PAGE 378. The entry in the Stationers' Register on Apr. 8, 1634, with the same ascription, is derived, of course, from the manuscript which served as the printer's copy.

12 PAGE 379. See pp. 412–13, n. 4, above.

13 PAGE 379. See p. 201, above.

14 PAGE 380. In 1566 Queen Elizabeth saw at Oxford a lost academic play on Palamon and Arcite by Richard Edwardes. A *palamon & arsett*, either the same or another lost play, is mentioned by Henslowe in 1594. Whether Shakespeare knew anything about these performances can not be determined.

15 PAGE 380. Cf. p. 210, above.

BIBLIOGRAPHY

KEY TO ABBREVIATIONS

Anglia   Anglia Zeitschrift für englische Philologie (Halle)
Archiv   [Herrig's] Archiv für das Studium der neueren Sprachen (Braun-
             schweig)
ELH   ELH, a Journal of English Literary History (Baltimore)
E studien   Englische Studien (Leipsig)
E studies   English Studies (Amsterdam)
JEGP   Journal of English and Germanic Philology (Urbana)
Library   The Library: Transactions of the Bibliographical Society (Lon-
             don)
MLN   Modern Language Notes (Baltimore)
MLR   Modern Language Review (London)
MP   Modern Philology (Chicago)
Neophil   Neophilologus (Groningen)
NQ   Notes and Queries (London)
PMLA   Publications of the Modern Language Association of America
             (Menasha)
PQ   Philological Quarterly (Iowa City)
RES   Review of English Studies (London)
SAB   Shakespeare Association Bulletin (New York)
SJ   Jahrbuch der deutschen Shakespeare-Gesellschaft (Weimar)
SP   Studies in Philology (Chapel Hill)
TLS   Times Literary Supplement (London)

BIBLIOGRAPHY

REMARKS

From that portion which I have read of the vast and constantly increasing accumulation of books and articles, I select the merest handful. Many landmarks of scholarship are omitted because they are now more interesting as monuments than reliable as guides. Of recent works I have not attempted to sift out the best. Certain admirable performances are not mentioned, even though they constitute important additions to our knowledge or syntheses of it, because they will lead a new student less directly to the core of the problems; and the Index fails to give the names of many scholars whose contributions are, in intrinsic merit, superior to some of those listed.

In the bibliographies of the several plays I have particularly sought to include such special studies as will most readily establish this contact. Further references will be found in the footnotes of most of these, and that the more important recent editions should always be consulted goes without saying. I think I have listed all the works to which I am consciously indebted. To a few I am not indebted at all, except for their effect in fortifying contrary convictions. On some points no short cut can be offered, and every serious reader will have to decide for himself who is right or has made the best guess. For fuller bibliographies, see the second section under "General," below. Aside from acknowledgment, the purpose of this one is to indicate where to begin widening the circle of reading.

General

EDITIONS

The first collected edition (it includes all the surviving plays except *Pericles* and *The Two Noble Kinsmen*, but not the poems) appeared (a single volume) in folio in 1623. The

First Folio was reprinted, with some anonymous editorial revision and of course further corruptions, in 1632, 1663 (second issue of F₃ in 1664 with seven additional plays, none now generally accepted as Shakespeare's except *Pericles*), and 1685 (F₄ also includes the seven additional plays). Facsimiles of all four of the Folios were published by Methuen and Company, London, 1904–10; a facsimile of F₁ was issued by the Oxford University Press in 1902, ed. S. [L.] Lee.

Dates of early publication of the separate plays and poems have already been given in text and notes. Under the supervision of F. J. Furnivall, forty-three volumes of photo-lithographic facsimiles of various quartos (of the plays, the poems, and certain source plays) were executed by W. Griggs and C. Praetorius, London, 1880 *et seq.* These replaced the earlier Ashbee facsimiles, but they are far from satisfactory. Excellent collotype facsimiles are *Pericles* (1609), Oxford, 1905; *Richard II* (1598, Q₃), London, 1916; *Hamlet* (1603), Cambridge, 1931; *Titus Andronicus* (1594), New York and London, 1936; *Hamlet* (1604), San Marino, 1938. For collotype facsimiles of the poems, see below, under "1. Life," "Poems." A new series of collotype facsimiles of twenty-one play quartos has been announced by the (English) Shakespeare Association, London.

The following eighteenth-century editions require notice more for their historical importance than as essential guides for today's student. They were the work of: Nicholas Rowe (1709, with biography and illustrations, and in 1710 a seventh volume with the poems; second edition, "1709," perhaps pr. 1710 — see R. B. McKerrow, "Rowe's Shakespeare, '1709,'" *TLS*, March 8, 1934, p. 168; 3rd. ed., 1714), Alexander Pope (1723–5 — of little merit; 2nd ed., 1728), Lewis Theobald (1733, important and often reprinted — he had already made a brilliant contribution with *Shakespeare Restored*, 1726), Thomas Hanmer (1744), William Warburton (1747), Samuel Johnson (1765, with invaluable glosses and critical observations, often reprinted), Edward Capell (1768, valuable), Samuel Johnson and George Steevens (1773, important and often reprinted), Edmond Malone (1790; but this great scholar's work is best consulted in the Malone-Boswell Variorum, 1821). Of subsequent editions I list a small and miscellaneous lot, for various reasons. (See also, under "Textual Matters," "McKerrow": "Prolegomena.")

MALONE-BOSWELL VARIORUM. E. Malone and J. Boswell, eds. London, 1821. 21 vols. Begun by Malone, who bequeathed his papers to the son of Johnson's biographer. Often called the Third Variorum. Still among the most useful eds. Includes biography and history of the stage. (Previous variorum editions were I. Reed's revisions of Johnson-Steevens, also in 21 vols., in 1803 and in 1813).

CAMBRIDGE. W. G. Clark and W. A. Wright, eds. (1st vol. by Clark and J. Glover.) Cambridge (England), 1863-6. 9 vols. 2nd ed., 1867; 3rd, 1891-3. Useful only for textual work. The Globe one-vol. ed. (eds. Clark and Wright, 1864) gives the Cambridge text. As a text it is inferior to Kittredge's and to Neilson's, but the Globe is still standard for line numbering.

NEW VARIORUM. H. H. Furness *et al.*, eds. Philadelphia and London, 1871-. In progress. The most useful of all editions, not in coming to conclusions, but in presenting materials for study, though the earlier volumes are now sadly out of date. The original editor was succeeded by his son, the late H. H. F., Jr. The edition is now going forward under the supervision of the Modern Language Association of America, with J. Q. Adams as general editor. The following volumes have appeared: A&C, AYLI, Cor, Cym, Ham (2 vols.), 1H4, John, JC, Lear, LLL, Mac (revised, 1903), MV, MND, MAN, O, Poems (not Sonnets), R3, R&J, Temp, TN, WT.

ARDEN. W. J. Craig and R. H. Case, general eds. London, 1899-1924. 39 vols. Uneven, like all editions for which the several volumes are prepared by a variety of editors; but usually offers helpful annotation.

NEILSON. W. A. Neilson, ed. Boston and New York, 1906. An excellent one-volume edition. Portions of the introductions are now out of date.

TUDOR. W. A. Neilson and A. H. Thorndike, general eds. New York and London, 1911-13. 40 vols. The Neilson text in a handy reading edition with critical matter by various scholars.

[AMERICAN] ARDEN. Boston, etc., 1915-. In progress. 28 vols. issued. Originally an English edition, the Warwick. For the most part of no textual interest; but some of the original volumes were uncommonly well annotated, and a number of those which have recently been re-edited are important. Does not yet include AW, 123H6, MM, MW, Per, Poems, TS, Titus, TNK.

YALE. W. L. Cross and [C. F.] T. Brooke, general eds. New Haven, etc., 1917-27. 40 vols. Another handy reading edition.

NEW. A. Quiller-Couch and J. D. Wilson, eds. (now the latter alone), with notes on stage history by H. Child. Cambridge (England),

1921–. In progress. The most provocative edition ever published. Brilliant, occasionally cogent, often unconvincing. Yet even those who distrust the editor's theories and methods await with impatience the appearance of the successive volumes. Thus far these give the comedies (except *Troilus and Cressida, Pericles,* and *The Two Noble Kinsmen*), *Hamlet, King John,* and *Richard II.*

KITTREDGE. G. L. Kittredge, ed. Boston, etc., 1936. The best one-volume edition. Includes an admirable glossary. (The first volumes of another edition by Kittredge, a play to a volume, with commentary, have now been issued by the same publisher. The text is the same. The commentary is very valuable.)

BIBLIOGRAPHIES

BARTLETT, HENRIETTA C. Mr. William Shakespeare: original and early editions of his quartos and folios, his source books and those containing contemporary notices. New Haven and London, 1922.

BARTLETT, HENRIETTA C., AND POLLARD, A. W. A census of Shakespeare's plays in quarto, 1594–1709. New Haven and London, 1916. Revised and extended ed., by Miss Bartlett, New Haven and London, 1939.

CRAIG, H. Recent literature of the English renaissance. SP, XXIII (1926), *et seq.,* April no. Often with useful summaries. A fuller continuation of the bibliography begun by T. S. Graves, *ibid.,* XIX (1922).

EBISCH, W., AND SCHÜCKING, L. L. A Shakespeare bibliography. Oxford, 1931. Relatively short, well classified and indexed.

—— Supplement for the years 1930–1935 to A Shakespeare Bibliography. Oxford, 1937. Others, it is hoped, will follow.

GREENHILL, J., HARRISON, W. A., AND FURNIVALL, F. J. A list of all the songs & passages in Shakspere which have been set to music. New Shakspere Society publications, ser. VIII, no. 3. Revised ed. London, 1884.

GREG, W. W. A list of English plays written before 1643 and printed before 1700. London, 1900.

—— A list of masques, pageants, &c. supplementary to A List of English Plays. London, 1902.

HALLIWELL-PHILLIPPS, J. O. A calendar of Shakespearean rarities, drawings and engravings formerly preserved at Hollingbury Copse, near Brighton. Second ed., E. E. Baker, ed. London, 1891. These items are now in the Folger Shakespeare Library, Washington, D.C.

HERFORD, C. H. A sketch of recent Shakespearean investigation, 1893–1923. London, etc., 1923.

JAGGARD, W. Shakespeare bibliography: a dictionary of every known issue of the writings of our national poet and of recorded opinion thereon in the English language. Stratford-on-Avon, 1911.

LEE, S. [L.], AND CHAMBERS, E. [K.] A Shakespeare reference library. Second ed. London, 1925. A selection of fifteen pages.

MODERN HUMANITIES RESEARCH ASSOCIATION. Annual bibliography of English language and literature. Cambridge (England), 1920, *et seq.* See, under "Sixteenth Century," "Shakespeare." Very useful, but usually two years in arrears.

POLLARD, A. W. Shakespeare folios and quartos: a study in the bibliography of Shakespeare's plays, 1594-1685. London, 1909.

POLLARD, A. W., AND REDGRAVE, G. R. A short-title catalogue of books printed in England, Scotland, & Ireland, and of English books printed abroad, 1475-1640. London, 1926.

TANNENBAUM, S. A. Shakspere and his contemporaries: a classified bibliography. SAB, IV (1929), *et seq.* The January number carries the bibliography for the preceding year. Its speedy appearance adds to its value. See also II (April, 1927), 7-14; and III (April, 1928), 1-21. Prior to 1936 the title varies.

THE YEAR'S WORK IN ENGLISH STUDIES. London, 1921, *et seq.* See under "Shakespeare." Selective, with comments. Very useful, though tardy in appearance. The first number covers 1919-20.

CRITICISM

BABCOCK, R. W. The genesis of Shakespeare idolatry, 1776-1799: a study in English criticism of the late eighteenth century. Chapel Hill, 1931.

BAGEHOT, W. Shakespeare — the man. The works and life of Walter Bagehot. London, 1915. I, 218-61. Deserves to be better known.

BAILEY, J. [C.] Shakespeare. English heritage series. London, etc., 1929. Often illuminating in its critical observations.

BAKER, G. P. The development of Shakespeare as a dramatist. New York, 1907. On his technique as a playwright.

BOAS, F. S. Shakspere and his predecessors. London, 1896.

BRADLEY, A. C. Shakespearean tragedy: lectures on Hamlet, Othello, King Lear, Macbeth. Second ed. London, 1905. A brilliant performance, still valuable for its application of devastating logic to the theories of others, but often misleading on account of failure to approach the plays historically and theatrically. Other essays on Shakespeare appear in Bradley's *Oxford Lectures on Poetry* (London, 1909), pp. 245-393.

CHAMBERS, E. K. Shakespeare: a survey. London, 1925. Short critical introductions to the several plays.

COLERIDGE'S SHAKESPEARE CRITICISM. T. M. Raysor, ed. Cambridge, 1930. 2 vols. Coleridge never published it. There are several cheap reprints of various versions, but none gives so close an approximation as this to what Coleridge actually wrote or said.

DRAKE, N., ed. Memorials of Shakespeare; or, sketches of his character and genius, by various writers. London, 1828. Contains some important criticism not included by Smith.

EMERSON, R. W. Shakspeare; or, the poet. Works. Centenary ed. Boston,

1903–4. Vol. IV, representative men. Pp. 187–219. An idealist's appreciation and warning.

GRANVILLE-BARKER, H. From Henry V to Hamlet. Aspects of Shakespeare, being British Academy lectures. Oxford, 1933. Pp. 49–83. A revision of the lecture separately published in 1925.

—— Prefaces to Shakespeare. London, 1927, 1930, 1937. 3 vols., subtitled first series, second series, and third series: Hamlet. Of special value because the author is able to supplement his scholarship from his own experience as dramatist, actor, and producer.

—— Shakespeare's dramatic art. A companion to Shakespeare studies. Ed. H. Granville-Barker and G. B. Harrison. Cambridge (England), 1934. Pp. 45–87.

HAZLITT, W. Characters of Shakespear's plays. Complete works. Centenary ed. P. P. Howe, ed. London, 1932–4. IV, 165–361. [First ed. 1817.] Also reprinted in cheaper eds. In the same volume, see also "On Mr. Kean's Iago," pp. 14–17; "On Posthumous Fame, — Whether Shakspeare Was Influenced by a Love of it?", pp. 21–4; "On the Midsummer Night's Dream," pp. 61–4. See also vol. XXI, General Index, under the titles of the several plays, for references to other comments by Hazlitt.

HUNT, L. Critical essays on the performers of the London theatres, including general observations on the practise and genius of the stage. London, 1807.

ISAACS, J. Shakespearian criticism . . . from Coleridge to the present day. A companion to Shakespeare studies. Ed. H. Granville-Barker and G. B. Harrison. Cambridge (England), 1934. Pp. 300–304.

—— Shakespearian scholarship. A companion to Shakespeare studies. Ed. H. Granville-Barker and G. B. Harrison. Cambridge (England), 1934. Pp. 305–24.

KITTREDGE, G. L. Shakspere: an address. Cambridge and London, 1916. The best short introduction to the historical approach.

LAMB, C. On the tragedies of Shakespeare, considered with reference to their fitness for stage representation. The Works of Charles and Mary Lamb. Ed. E. V. Lucas. London, 1903–5. I, 97–111.

LAWRENCE, W. W. Shakespeare's problem comedies. New York, 1931. Important.

LOUNSBURY, T. R. Shakespeare as a dramatic artist. New York, 1901. Especially valuable for eighteenth-century criticism.

MACKAIL, J. W. The approach to Shakespeare. Oxford, 1930. Contains suggestive critical notes.

MARRIOTT, J. A. R. English history in Shakespeare. London, 1918. A valuable study of the chronicle-history plays.

NICOLL, A. Studies in Shakespeare. London and New York, 1928. On the four great tragedies.

RALEIGH, W. Shakespeare. London and New York, 1907. Valuable for critical freshness and freedom from cant.

——, ed. Johnson on Shakespeare: essays and notes selected and set forth with an introduction. London, New York, etc., 1916.

RALLI, A. A history of Shakespearian criticism. London, 1932. 2 vols. Summaries of the chief critical works in English, German, and French.

RAYSOR, T. M. The study of Shakespeare's characters in the eighteenth century. MLN, XLII (1927), 495–500. See also under "Coleridge," above.

SCHÜCKING, L. L. Character problems in Shakespeare's plays: a guide to the better understanding of the dramatist. New York and London, 1922. A translation, with some modification, of *Die Charakterprobleme bei Shakespeare:* Leipsig, 1919; 2nd ed., 1927. Independent, but similar to Stoll in approach. See review by K. Young, PQ, I (1922), 228–34.

SHAW, [G.] B. Dramatic opinions and essays. New York, 1907. 2 vols. Includes reviews of Shakespeare revivals, and observations *passim*.

SMITH, D. N., ed. Eighteenth century essays on Shakespeare. Glasgow, 1903.

—— Shakespeare criticism: a selection. Oxford, 1916. From Ben Jonson to Carlyle.

STOLL, E. E. Art and artifice in Shakespeare: a study in dramatic contrast and illusion. Cambridge (England), 1933.

—— Poets and playwrights: Shakespeare, Jonson, Spenser, Milton. Minneapolis, 1930.

—— Shakespeare studies: historical and comparative in method. New York, 1927. Of first-rate importance. See also Stoll's separate studies of *Hamlet* and *Othello*, under "9. The Four Great Tragedies."

—— Shakespeare's young lovers. London, New York, and Toronto, 1937.

SWINBURNE, A. C. A study of Shakespeare. London, 1880. Rhapsodic but brilliant. Reprinted in *The Complete Works of Algernon Charles Swinburne*, ed. E. Gosse and T. J. Wise (London and New York, 1926–7), XI, 1–222. See also *Four Plays* (originally appeared 1902–14), *ibid.*, pp. 223–66.

TILLYARD, E. M. W. Shakespeare's last plays. London, 1938. Suggestive.

VAN DOREN, M. Shakespeare. New York, 1939. A poet's appreciation, often original and suggestive, of Shakespeare's poetic style in the plays. Curiously lacking in appreciation of the poems — in only one of the sonnets (no. 71) does Shakespeare "achieve that kind of excellence which is interesting to criticism." The beautiful simplicity with which many of the couplets close the sonnets (e. g., no. 30) is condemned as "out of step" with the quatrains.

WARNER, B. [E.], ed. Famous introductions to Shakespeare's plays by the notable editors of the eighteenth century. New York, 1906.

WENDELL, B. William Shakspere: a study in Elizabethan literature. New York, 1894. Vigorous and independent criticism.

WILLIAMS, C. The English poetic mind. Oxford, 1932. Contains a long chapter on "The Cycle of Shakespeare," a very suggestive one, though limited by inadequate recognition of Shakespeare's theatrical medium.

YOUNG, K. Samuel Johnson on Shakespeare: one aspect. University of Wisconsin studies in language and literature, XVIII (Madison, 1923), 146–

226. Johnson as originator of the "historical or genetic method" in Shakespeare criticism, with a review of previous efforts.

—— Shakespeare skeptics. North American review; CCXV (1921), 382-93.

TEXTUAL MATTERS

ALBRIGHT, EVELYN M. Dramatic publication in England, 1580-1640: a study of conditions affecting content and form of drama. Modern Language Association of America monograph series, II. New York and London, 1927. Chapters on control of companies, censorship, ownership of plays, sources of printed texts, and publishing conditions. See W. W. Greg's review, RES, IV (1928), 91-100; the author's reply, ibid., pp. 193-202; and the reviewer's rejoinder, ibid., pp. 202-4.

ARBER, E. A transcript of the registers of the company of stationers of London, 1554-1640. Vols. I-IV, London, 1875-7; vol. V, Birmingham, 1894.

BALD, R. C. 'Assembled' texts. Library, 4th ser., XII (1932), 243-8. Sceptical of Wilson's theory.

BLACK, M. W., AND SHAABER, M. A. Shakespeare's seventeenth-century editors, 1632-1685. New York and London, 1937.

BYRNE, MURIEL ST. C. Elizabethan handwriting for beginners. RES, I (1925), 198-209.

CHAMBERS, E. K. The disintegration of Shakespeare. Aspects of Shakespeare, being British Academy lectures. Oxford, 1933. Pp. 23-48. A cogent attack on it. Originally published in 1924.

—— William Shakespeare: a study of facts and problems. Oxford, 1930. 2 vols. See chaps. iv, "The Book of the Play" (I, 92-125); v, "The Quartos and the First Folio" (I, 126-67); vi, "Plays in the Printing-House" (I, 168-204); vii, "The Problem of Authenticity" (I, 205-42); viii, "The Problem of Chronology" (I, 243-74).

CHAMBERS, R. W. Some sequences of thought in Shakespeare and in the 147 lines of Sir Thomas More. MLR, XXVI (1931), 251-80.

DAM, B. A. P. VAN. Textual criticism of Shakespeare's plays. E studies, VII (1925), 97-115. Critical of Wilson's methods.

FÖRSTER, M. Shakespeare and shorthand. PQ, XVI (1937), 1-29. Argues that stenography best accounts for the corrupt texts.

GOLLANCZ, I., and others. Studies in the first folio, written for the Shakespeare Association. London, 1924.

GREG, W. W. Dramatic documents from the Elizabethan playhouses. Oxford, 1931. 2 vols. Reproductions and commentary.

—— The first folio and its publishers. Studies in the first folio, written for the Shakespeare Association. London, 1924. Pp. 129-56.

—— The function of bibliography in literary criticism illustrated in a study of the text of King Lear. Neophil., XVIII (1933), 241-62.

—— Principles of emendation in Shakespeare. Aspects of Shakespeare, being

British Academy lectures. Oxford, 1933. Pp. 128–201. Originally published in 1928.

——, ed. The book of Sir Thomas More. Malone Society reprints. London, 1911.

——, ed. Two Elizabethan stage abridgements: The Battle of Alcazar & Orlando Furioso. Malone Society reprints. London, 1922. Expounds theory of reconstruction of texts from memory.

HUNTER, M. Act- and scene-division in the plays of Shakespeare. RES, II (1926), 295–310. Thinks Shakespeare wrote in acts and scenes. Cf. J. D. Wilson, "Act- and Scene-Divisions in the Plays of Shakespeare: A Rejoinder to Sir Mark Hunter," RES III (1927), 385–97; W. W. Greg, "Act-Divisions in Shakespeare," RES, IV (1928), 152–8; and E. E. Willoughby, "The Heading, Actus Primus, Scæna Prima, in the First Folio," ibid., pp. 323–6.

KINNEAR, B. G. Cruces Shakesperianae: difficult passages. London, 1883.

KIRSCHBAUM, L. A census of bad quartos. RES, XIV (1938), 20–43.

LEO, F. A. Verzeichnis noch zu erklärender oder zu emendierender text-lesarten in Shakespeare's dramen. SJ, XX (1885), 149–70. Lists cruces.

LOUNSBURY, T. The text of Shakespeare: its history from the publication of the quartos and folios down to and including the publication of the editions of Pope and Theobald. New York, 1906.

MATTHEWS, W. Shorthand and the bad Shakespeare quartos. MLR, XXVII (1932), 243–62; XXVIII (1933), 81–3. Concludes that existing systems would be impracticable for reporting plays. For other reviews of this subject by Matthews, see Library, 4th ser., XV (1935), 481–98, and JEGP, XXXIV (1935), 483–510.

MCKERROW, R. B. The Elizabethan printer and dramatic manuscripts. Library, 4th ser., XII (1932), 253–75. Thinks printer's copy was likely to be "an author's rough draft much corrected."

—— An introduction to bibliography for literary students. Oxford, 1927. Indispensable. What the student needs to know about how Elizabethan books were made.

—— Printers' & publishers' devices in England & Scotland 1485–1640. London, 1913.

—— Prolegomena for the Oxford Shakespeare: a study in editorial method. Oxford, 1939. A masterly exposition of textual principles, introductory to a forthcoming edition.

——, ed. A dictionary of printers and booksellers in England, Scotland and Ireland, and of foreign printers of English books 1557–1640. London, 1910.

POLLARD, A. W. The foundations of Shakespeare's text. Aspects of Shakespeare, being British Academy lectures. Oxford, 1933. Pp. 1–22. Originally published in 1923. Contains a modifying postscript.

—— Shakespeare folios and quartos: a study in the bibliography of Shakespeare's plays, 1594–1685. London, 1909. Important not only as a contribution but also as the inspiration of an important trend in recent scholarship.

—— Shakespeare's fight with the pirates and the problems of the transmission of his text. Second ed. Cambridge (England), 1920. Important.

—— Shakespeare's text. A companion to Shakespeare studies. Ed. H. Granville-Barker and G. B. Harrison. Cambridge (England), 1934. Pp 263–86.

POLLARD, A. W., GREG, W. W., THOMPSON, E. M., WILSON, J. D., AND CHAMBERS R. W. Shakespeare's hand in the play of Sir Thomas More. Cambridge (England), 1923. For titles of other works, supporting or attacking, see p. 415, n. 4, above.

PRICE, H. T. Towards a scientific method of textual criticism for the Elizabethan drama. JEGP, XXXVI (1937), 151–67. A cogent caveat against some current applications of certain stylistic and metrical tests to problems of authorship and revision.

RHODES, R. C. Shakespeare's first folio: a study. Oxford, 1923.

SCHÜCKING, L. L. Das datum des pseudo-shakespeareschen Sir Thomas More. E studien, XLVI (1913), 228–51. Argues for 1604–5.

—— Shakespeare and Sir Thomas More. RES, I (1925), 40–59. Favors date in 1601–2 and rejects Shakespeare's authorship. Cf. G. B. Harrison, "The Date of Sir Thomas More," RES, I (1925), 337–9; A. W. Pollard, "Verse Tests and the Date of Sir Thomas More," ibid., pp. 441–3; and D. C. Collins, "On the Date of Sir Thomas More," RES, X (1934), 401–11.

SIMPSON, P. The bibliographical study of Shakespeare. Oxford Bibliographical Society proceedings and papers, I (Oxford, 1927), 19–53.

—— Proof-reading in the sixteenth, seventeenth, and eighteenth centuries. London, 1935.

SISSON, C. J. Bibliographical aspects of some Stuart dramatic manuscripts. RES, I (1925), 421–30.

TANNENBAUM, S. A. The Booke of Sir Thomas Moore: a bibliotic study. New York, 1927. For titles of other works, supporting or attacking the theory that three pages are in Shakespeare's hand, see p. 415, n. 4, above.

—— The handwriting of the renaissance, being the development and characteristics of the script of Shakspere's time. New York, 1930.

—— How not to edit Shakspere: a review. PQ, X (1931), 97–137. Critical of Wilson's methods. Cf. H. T. Price, Beiblatt zur Anglia, XLI (1930), 104–9.

—— Problems in Shakspere's penmanship, including a study of the poet's will. New York, 1927. See also titles of other works by Tannenbaum, p. 415, n. 4, above.

—— Reclaiming one of Shakspere's signatures. SP, XXII (1925), 392–411. Supports authenticity of the "Montaigne" signature. Reprinted, "radically revised," in Tannenbaum's *Problems in Shakspere's Penmanship*, pp. 159-78.

—— Two new Shakspere autographs (?). SAB, VII (1932), 113. Mentions "two alleged Shakspere" signatures at the Folger Shakespeare Library.

TAYLOR, G. C. The date of Edward Capell's Notes and Various Readings to Shakespeare, volume II. RES, V (1929), 317-19. Supports the authenticity of the signature in Florio's Montaigne.

THOMPSON, E. M. The autograph manuscripts of Anthony Munday. Transactions of the Bibliographical Society [London], XIV (pr. 1919), 325-53.

—— Handwriting. Shakespeare's England. Oxford, 1917. I, 284-310.

—— Shakespeare's handwriting: a study. Oxford, 1916.

—— Two pretended autographs of Shakespeare. Library, 3rd ser., VIII (1917), 193-217. In copies of Ovid and Florio's Montaigne.

WILLOUGHBY, E. E. The printing of the first folio of Shakespeare. Oxford, 1932.

WILSON, J. D. Textual introduction. The Tempest. Ed. A. Quiller-Couch and J. D. Wilson. Cambridge (England), 1921. See also the textual introductions to subsequent volumes of the New edition; and Wilson's *The Manuscript of Shakespeare's Hamlet and the Problems of its Transmission*, Cambridge (England), 1934.

—— Thirteen volumes of Shakespeare: a retrospect. MLR, XXV (1930), 397-414. Supplementary to the textual introduction to the New *Tempest*.

BACKGROUND

ADAMS, J. Q. Hill's list of early plays in manuscript. Library, New ser., XX (1939), 71-99.

——, ed. Chief pre-Shakespearean dramas. Boston, etc., 1924. An anthology.

ALLEN, J. W. English political thought 1603-1660. Vol. I, 1603-1644. London, 1938.

—— A history of political thought in the sixteenth century. London and New York, 1928. See pp. 447-94 for Machiavelli.

ANON. Elizabethan decoration: patterns in art and passion. TLS, July 3, 1937, pp. 485-6.

BANG, W., ed. Materialen zur kunde des älteren englischen dramas. Louvain, 1902-14. 44 vols. Texts, concordances, and other aids to study. For the continuation, see "Vocht," below.

BARNARD, E. A. B. New links with Shakespeare. Cambridge (England), 1930.

BIRCH, T. Memoirs of the reign of Queen Elizabeth from the year 1581 till her death. London, 1754. 2 vols. Valuable for correspondence of Anthony Bacon.

BLACK, J. B. The reign of Elizabeth, 1558-1603. Oxford history of England, VIII. Oxford and New York, 1936.

BOAS, F. S. Shakspere and his predecessors. London, 1896. Pp. 1–88 trace the development of English drama before Shakespeare.

—— University drama in the Tudor age. Oxford, 1914.

BROOKE, C. F. T., ed. The Shakespeare apocrypha: being a collection of fourteen plays which have been ascribed to Shakespeare. Oxford, 1918. With valuable introduction, notes, and bibliography.

—— The tudor drama. Boston, etc., 1911. A survey.

BUSH, D. Mythology and the renaissance tradition in English poetry. Minneapolis, 1932.

BYRNE, MURIEL ST. C. Elizabethan life in town and country. Second ed. London, 1934.

—— The social background. A companion to Shakespeare studies. Ed. H. Granville-Barker and G. B. Harrison. Cambridge (England), 1934. Pp. 187–218.

CHAMBERS, E. K. The Elizabethan stage. Oxford, 1923. 4 vols. An encyclopedic treatment of entertainments at court, control of the stage, companies, theatres, staging, plays, and playwrights. Index to the four volumes and to *William Shakespeare* compiled by Beatrice White, Oxford, 1934.

CHEW, S. C. The crescent and the rose: Islam and England during the renaissance. New York, 1937. Includes many valuable notes on Shakespeare's plays.

CHEYNEY, E. P. A history of England from the defeat of the Armada to the death of Elizabeth. New York, 1914–26. 2 vols.

COLLINS, A., ed. Letters and memorials of state, in the reigns of Queen Mary, Queen Elizabeth, King James. London, 1746. 2 vols. Often referred to as *Sydney Papers*.

CRAIG, H. The enchanted glass: the Elizabethan mind in literature. New York, 1936. A valuable introduction to the intellectual background.

DAVIES, G. The early Stuarts, 1603–1660. Oxford history of England, IX. Oxford and New York, 1937.

DOBRÉE, B. Shakespeare and the drama of his time. A companion to Shakespeare studies. Ed. H. Granville-Barker and G. B. Harrison. Cambridge (England), 1934. Pp. 243–61.

DYER, T. F. T. Folk-lore of Shakespeare. New York, 1884.

FAIRCHILD, A. H. R. Shakespeare and the arts of design (architecture, sculpture, and painting). University of Missouri studies, vol. XII, no. 1. Columbia, 1937.

FARMER, J. S., ed. Tudor facsimile texts. London, 1907–13. 184 vols. Facsimiles of printed and manuscript plays.

FARNHAM, W. The medieval heritage of Elizabethan tragedy. Berkeley, 1936.

FELLOWES, E. H. The English madrigal composers. Oxford, 1921.

FROUDE, J. A. A history of England from the fall of Wolsey to the defeat of the Spanish armada. London, 1856–70. 12 vols.

GARDINER, S. R. History of England from the accession of James I. to the outbreak of the civil war, 1603–1642. New ed. New York, etc., 1894–6. 10 vols.

GILBERT, A. H. Seneca and the criticism of Elizabethan tragedy. PQ. XIII (1934), 370–81.

GREEN, A. W. The inns of court and early English drama. New Haven and London, 1931.

HARINGTON, J., et al. Nugæ antiquæ: being a miscellaneous collection of original papers, in prose and verse. Ed. T. Park. London, 1804. 2 vols.

HARRISON, G. B. An Elizabethan journal, being a record of those things most talked of during the years 1591–1594. London, 1928.

—— A second Elizabethan journal, being a record of those things most talked of during the years 1595–1598. London, 1931.

—— A last Elizabethan journal, being a record of those things most talked of during the years 1599–1603. London, 1933.

—— The national background. A companion to Shakespeare studies. Ed. H. Granville-Barker and G. B. Harrison. Cambridge (England), 1934. Pp. 163–86.

—— Shakespeare at work: 1592–1603. London, 1933. Admittedly "sheer guess-work" at many points, but interesting for its emphasis on current events. Published in New York as Shakespeare under Elizabeth.

HOTSON, L. I, William Shakespeare, do appoint Thomas Russell, esquire. New York, 1938. Notes on contemporaries of Shakespeare, especially Russell (mentioned in his will).

JUDGES, A. V., ed. The Elizabethan underworld: a collection of Tudor and early Stuart tracts and ballads telling of the lives and misdoings of vagabonds, thieves, rogues and cozeners, and giving some account of the operation of the criminal law. London, 1930. Includes several pieces by Greene and Dekker.

LEE, S. [L.] The French renaissance in England: an account of the literary relations of England and France in the sixteenth century. Oxford, 1910.

MADDEN, D. H. The diary of Master William Silence: a study of Shakespeare & of Elizabethan sport. New ed. London, New York, etc., 1907.

MAIR, G. H., ed. [Thomas] Wilson's Arte of Rhetorique, 1560. Oxford, 1909.

MALONE SOCIETY, COLLECTIONS OF THE. Oxford, 1907–. Relating to drama.

MALONE SOCIETY REPRINTS, THE. W. W. Greg, general ed. London, 1907–. Careful reprints of Elizabethan plays.

MILLS, L. J. One soul in bodies twain: friendship in Tudor literature and Stuart drama. Bloomington, 1937.

MUNRO, J. The Shakspere allusion-book: a collection of allusions to Shakespeare from 1591 to 1700. 2 vols. London, 1909. Reissued, 1932.

NAYLOR, E. W. Shakespeare and music, with illustrations from the music of the 16th and 17th centuries. New ed. London, 1931. [1st ed. 1896.]

NEALE, J. E. Queen Elizabeth. London and New York, 1934.

NICHOLS, J. The progresses and public processions of Queen Elizabeth. London, 1823. 3 vols.

—— The progresses, processions, and magnificent festivities of King Jame
the First. London, 1828. 4 vols.

POTTER, G. R. Elizabethan verse and prose (non-dramatic). New York, 1928
An anthology.

POWELL, C. L. English domestic relations, 1487-1653. New York, 1917.

PRAZ, M. Machiavelli and the Elizabethans. Proceedings of the British
Academy, XIV (1928), 49-97.

PUTTENHAM, GEORGE. See Willcock, Gladys D.

SCHELLING, F. E. Elizabethan drama 1558-1642: a history of the drama in
England from the accession of Queen Elizabeth to the closing of the
theaters, to which is prefixed a résumé of the earlier drama from its
beginnings. Boston and New York, 1908. 2 vols.

—— Elizabethan playwrights: a short history of the English drama from
mediæval times to the closing of the theatres in 1642. New York and
London, 1925.

—— The English chronicle play: a study in the popular literature environing
Shakespeare. New York and London, 1902.

—— English literature during the lifetime of Shakespeare. Revised edition.
New York, 1927.

—— Foreign influences in Elizabethan plays. New York and London, 1923.

SCOT, REGINALD. The discouerie of witchcraft. London, 1584. This important
treatise has been edited by M. Summers, London, 1930.

SHAKESPEARE'S ENGLAND: an account of the life & manners of his age. Oxford, 1916. 2 vols.

SISSON, C. J. Le goût public et le théâtre élisabéthain jusqu'à la mort de
Shakespeare. Dijon [1922].

—— Lost plays of Shakespeare's age. Cambridge (England), 1936. Contains
much information on the relation of the drama to contemporary life,
and on the jig.

SMALL, R. A. The stage-quarrel between Ben Jonson and the so-called poetas-
ters. Breslau, 1899.

SMITH, G. G., ed. Elizabethan critical essays. Oxford, 1904. 2 vols.

SPENCER, H., ed. Elizabethan plays: written by Shakespeare's friends, colleagues, rivals, and successors. Boston, 1933. An anthology.

SPENCER, T. Death and Elizabethan tragedy: a study of convention and
opinion in the Elizabethan drama. Cambridge, 1936.

SPINGARN, J. E. A history of literary criticism in the Renaissance. Second ed.
New York, 1908.

STOW, J. A survey of London. Reprinted from the text of 1603. Ed. C. L.
Kingsford. Oxford, 1908. 2 vols.

SYMONDS, J. A. Shakspere's predecessors in the English drama. London, 1884.

TAWNEY, R. H. The agrarian problem in the sixteenth century. London,
New York, etc., 1912.

TAYLOR, H. O. Thought and expression in the sixteenth century. New York,
1920. 2 vols.

HOMPSON, E. N. S. The controversy between the Puritans and the stage. Yale Studies in English, XX. New York, 1903.

RAILL, H. D., ed. Social England: a record of the progress of the people in religion laws learning arts industry commerce science literature and manners from the earliest times to the present day. Second ed. London and New York, 1894-7. Vol. III; vol. IV, pp. 1-202.

REVELYAN, G. M. England under the Stuarts. London and New York, 1904.

UPPER, F., JR. The Shaksperean Mob. PMLA, XXVII (1912), 486-523. Shakespeare's views were conventional.

OCHT, H. DE, ed. Materials for the study of the old English drama. Louvain, 1927-. Continues W. Bang's *Materialen*.

WARD, A. W. A history of English dramatic literature to the death of Queen Anne. Revised ed. London and New York, 1899. 3 vols.

VELLS, H. W. Elizabethan and Jacobean playwrights. New York, 1939. Treats Shakespeare's work, along with that of the others, according to genre, on the theory "that the plays are even more clearly typified by theatrical convention than by the individuality of their authors."

VELSFORD, ENID. The fool: his social and literary history. London, 1935.

VILLCOCK, GLADYS D., AND WALKER, ALICE, eds. The arte of English poesie by George Puttenham. Cambridge (England), 1936.

VILLIAMS, SARAH, ed. Letters written by John Chamberlain during the reign of Queen Elizabeth. Camden Society, no. 79. London, 1861.

VILSON, F. P. The plague in Shakespeare's London. Oxford, 1927.

VILSON, THOMAS. See Mair, G. H.

VINWOOD, R. Memorials of affairs of state in the reigns of Q. Elizabeth and K. James I. London, 1725. 3 vols. Contemporary letters and state papers.

VRIGHT, L. B. Middle class culture in Elizabethan England. Chapel Hill, 1935.

1. Life

GENERAL STUDIES

ADAMS, J. Q. A life of William Shakespeare. Boston and New York, 1923. The best general study of Shakespeare on the biographical plan.

HAMBERS, E. K. William Shakespeare: a study of facts and problems. Oxford, 1930. 2 vols. An invaluable encyclopedia of Shakespeare scholarship, distinguished by comprehensiveness and caution.

RIPP, E. I. Shakespeare, man and artist. London, 1938. 2 vols. Rambling, credulous, not always up to date, and often capricious in its conclusions, but full of antiquarian lore.

ALLIWELL-PHILLIPPS, J. O. Outlines of the life of Shakespeare. Seventh (finally revised) edition, 1887. The foundation of all subsequent Lives.

EE, S. [L.] A life of William Shakespeare. Fourteenth ed. London and New York, 1931. First published in 1898; revised and enlarged in 1915. Eds. 1922 and 1925 contain some new matter; ed. 1931 has a few posthumous corrections and addenda. Long the standard Life, and (though superseded by Chambers and Adams) still valuable.

HANDBOOKS

ALDEN, R. M. A Shakespeare handbook. Revised and enlarged by O. J Campbell. New York, 1932. Includes a good deal from the sources o the best plays.

ALEXANDER, P. Shakespeare's life and art. London, 1938. Contains an excellent outline of the life and original observations of value on Shakespeare as an artist.

BROOKE, [c. F.] T. Shakespeare of Stratford: a handbook for students. New Haven and London, 1926. Rigorously documentary.

CHAMBERS, E. K. A short life of Shakespeare, with the sources. Abridged by Charles Williams from Sir Edmund Chambers's William Shakespeare A Study of Facts and Problems. Oxford, 1933.

GRANVILLE-BARKER, H., AND HARRISON, G. B., eds. A companion to Shakespeare studies. Cambridge (England), 1934. Essays by British scholars on various aspects. The more important are herein cited separately.

LAMBERT, D. H. Cartae Shakespeareanae: Shakespeare documents: a chronological catalogue of extant evidence relating to the life and works of William Shakespeare. London, 1904.

LAMBORN, E. A. G., AND HARRISON, G. B. Shakespeare: the man and his stage London, 1923.

NEILSON, W. A., AND THORNDIKE, A. H. The facts about Shakespeare. Revised ed. New York, 1931.

PARROTT, T. M. William Shakespeare: a handbook. New York, etc., 1934 An especially readable brief account.

SPECIAL BIOGRAPHICAL CONTRIBUTIONS

FOR THEATRICAL ITEMS see below, under "2. Medium."

ALLEN, D. C., ed. Francis Meres's Treatise on Poetrie. University of Illinois studies in language and literature, vol. XVI, nos. 3–4. Urbana, 1933 A critical edition. Allen has also edited a facsimile of the original o 1598, for Scholars' Facsimiles & Reprints, New York, 1938.

ANGELL, PAULINE K. Light on the dark lady: a study of some Elizabethan libels. PMLA, LII (1937), 652–74. Attacks the identification of Avisa as Mrs. Davenant.

BAKER, O. In Shakespeare's Warwickshire and the unknown years. London 1937. Attempts to trace Richard Shakespeare's and Mary Arden's ancestry, supports John Shakespeare's literacy, suggests that the poet may have been the Willm Shakeshafte mentioned in the will (1581) of Alexander Houghton of Lea, Lancs., describes numerous antiquities, etc.

BROOKE, [c. F.] T. Shakespeare's moiety of the Stratford tithes. MLN, XL (1925), 462–9. Cf. E. K. Chambers, *William Shakespeare*, II, 125–7.

sDAILE, [KATHARINE A.] Shakespeare's monument: a family of sculptors. London *Times*, Aug. 6, 1928, p. 13. On the inferiority of Gerard's work to that of other members of the family.

AIRCHILD, A. H. R. The Stratford bust. Shakespeare and the arts of design. University of Missouri studies, vol. XII, no. 1 (Columbia, 1937), pp. 90–96.

RIPP, E. I. Master Richard Quyny, bailiff of Stratford and friend of William Shakespeare. London, 1924.

— Shakespeare studies, biographical and literary. London, 1930.

— Shakespeare's haunts near Stratford. Oxford and London, 1929.

— Shakespeare's Stratford. London, 1928.

—, ed. Minutes and accounts of the corporation of Stratford-upon-Avon and other records 1553–1620. Publications of the Dugdale Society, I, III, V, X. London, 1921, 1924, 1926, 1929.

RAY, J. W. Shakespeare's marriage, his departure from Stratford, and other incidents in his life. London, 1905. Important.

REENWOOD, G. [G.] The Stratford bust and the Droeshout engraving. London, 1925. Critical of Spielmann's conclusions.

ALES, J. W. London residences of Shakespeare. Athenæum, March 26, 1904, pp. 401–2. Confirms Malone's statement that Shakespeare lived on the Bankside, and reports the assessments in St. Helen's parish.

ARRISON, G. B., ed. Willobie his Avisa 1594, with an essay on Willobie his Avisa. London and New York, 1926. Thinks *Lucrece* was taken as an attack on Raleigh and that "his followers," perhaps Matthew Roydon, wrote *Avisa* to ridicule Southampton and his friends, among them Shakespeare. Rejects the identification of the heroine with Mrs. Davenant.

OTSON, L. Shakespeare versus Shallow. Boston, 1931. Reports the trouble with Wayte on the Bankside, suggests an original for Shallow, and advocates an earlier date for *The Merry Wives*.

AW, E. P. A. Shakespeare as a groom of the chamber. London, 1910.

EE, S. L. Stratford-on-Avon: from the earliest times to the death of Shakespeare. New and revised ed. London and Philadelphia, 1907.

ALONE, E. An inquiry into the authenticity of certain miscellaneous papers and legal instruments. London, 1796. Mentions documents establishing Shakespeare's residence in Southwark.

ARCHAM, F. William Shakespeare and his daughter Susannah [Running title: William Shakespeare and his family]. London, 1931.

ERES, FRANCIS. See Allen, D. C.

ETHERCOT, A. H. Sir William D'avenant: poet laureate and playwright-manager. Chicago, 1938.

HODES, R. C. The Stratford monument. TLS, May 7, 1925, p. 316. Advances the dubious theory that the colors painted over in 1793 were no older than 1769.

SSON, C. [J.] Marks as signatures. Library, 4th ser., IX (1928), 1–37. Doubts John Shakespeare's literacy.

—— The mythical sorrows of Shakespeare. Annual Shakespeare lecture o
the British Academy. London, 1934.

SMART, J. S. Shakespeare: truth and tradition. London, 1928. Polemical bu
valuable.

SPIELMANN, M. H. The portraits of Shakespeare. The Works of William Shake
speare. Stratford town ed. Stratford, 1904–7. X, 373–98. States tha
the monument but not the bust (except two broken fingers on th
right hand) was repaired in 1649. I find no evidence for repairs i
1649.

—— The portraits of Shakespeare. Encyclopædia Britannica, 14th ed., XX
448–52.

—— Shakespeare's portraiture. Studies in the first folio. London, 1924
Pp. xxxv, xxxvi, 1–52. Amply illustrated. The most authoritativ
study. Separately issued in 1924 as The Title-Page of the First Folio.

STOPES, CHARLOTTE C. Shakespeare's environment. London, 1914.

—— Shakespeare's family, being a record of the ancestors and descendant
of William Shakespeare, with some account of the Ardens. Londo
and New York, 1901.

—— Shakespeare's Warwickshire contemporaries. New ed. Stratford-upon
Avon, 1907.

TANNENBAUM, S. A. A new study of Shakspere's will: reprinted from Studie
in Philology (XXIII, 117–141), augmented with three pages of note
and additions. Baltimore, 1926.

—— Problems in Shakspere's penmanship, including a study of the poet'
will. New York, 1927.

—— The Shakspere coat-of-arms. New York, 1908.

—— Was William Shakspere a gentleman?: some questions in Shakspere'
biography determined. New York, 1909. The application of 1596 fo
arms was granted.

WALLACE, C. W. The newly discovered Shakespeare documents. Universit
studies of the University of Nebraska, V (Lincoln, 1905), 347–56.

—— Shakespeare and his London associates as revealed in recently dis
covered documents. University studies of the University of Nebraska
X (Lincoln, 1910), 261–360. Includes the Belott-Mountjoy papers.

EDUCATION AND READING

ANDERS, H. R. D. Shakespeare's books: a dissertation on Shakespeare's read
ing and the immediate sources of his works. Berlin, 1904.

ATTWATER, A. L. Shakespeare's sources. A companion to Shakespeare studies
Ed. H. Granville-Barker and G. B. Harrison. Cambridge (England)
1934. Pp. 219–41.

BALDWIN, T. W. A note upon William Shakespeare's use of Pliny. Essays i
dramatic literature: the Parrott presentation volume. Ed. H. Craig
Princeton, 1935. Pp. 157–82.

BAYNES, T. S. What Shakespeare learnt at school. Shakespeare studies and essay on English dictionaries. London and New York, 1894. Pp. 147–249.

BOSWELL-STONE, W. G., ed. Holinshed's Chronicle as used in Shakespeare's plays. London, 1896. Reprinted, I. Gollancz, ed., Shakespeare Classics, London, 1907.

BROOKE, C. F. T., ed. Shakespeare's Plutarch. London, 1909. 2 vols.

BUSH, D. Notes on Shakespeare's classical mythology. PQ, VI (1927), 295–302.

CARTER, T. Shakespeare and holy scripture, with the version he used. London, 1905.

CLARKSON, P. S., AND WARREN, C. T. A comparative and critical analysis of Shakespeare's law. Daily record (Baltimore), April 20, 1937, p. 3. A systematic refutation of the claims of Lord Campbell and others for Shakespeare's legal proficiency, based on a comparative study of Shakespeare and other dramatists of the time, about half of whom use legal expressions more freely than he. The authors, lawyers themselves, have collected some 3700 passages.

GOLDING, ARTHUR. The. XV. Bookes of P. Ouidius Naso, entytuled Metamorphosis, translated oute of Latin into English meeter. London, 1567. Reprinted, ed. W. H. D. Rouse, London, 1904.

GREEN, H. Shakespeare and the emblem writers; an exposition of their similarities of thought and expression. Preceded by a view of emblem-literature down to A.D. 1616. London; 1870.

HALLE, EDWARD. The vnion of the two noble and illustre families of Lancastre & Yorke. London, 1548. Reprinted, London, 1809.

HART, A. A new Shakespearean source-book. Shakespeare and the homilies: and other pieces of research into the Elizabethan drama. Melbourne, London, etc., 1934. Pp. 9–76. Concludes that Shakespeare "outdoes every other important dramatist of his time" in indicating his acceptance of monarchical divine right, the duty of passive obedience, and the importance of political order; and suggests that he imbibed these ideas from homilies which the government required the clergy to read to their congregations.

HAZLITT, W. C., ed. Shakespeare's library: a collection of the plays, romances, novels, poems, and histories employed by Shakespeare in the composition of his works. Second ed. London, 1875. 6 vols. Partly based on J. P. Collier's ed. of 1843.

HOLINSHED, RAPHAEL. Chronicles of England, Scotland, and Ireland. London, 1577. 2 vols. Second ed., 1587. Reprinted, London, 1807–8. 6 vols. (See also Boswell-Stone and Nicoll.)

LEACH, A. F. English schools at the Reformation, 1546–8. London, 1896.

LUCAS, F. L. Seneca and Elizabethan tragedy. Cambridge (England), 1922.

MACCALLUM, M. W. Shakespeare's Roman plays: and their background. London, 1910.

NICOLL, A. AND JOSEPHINE, eds. Holinshed's Chronicle as used in Shakespeare's plays. London, Toronto, and New York, 1927.

NOBLE, R. S. H. Shakespeare's Biblical knowledge and use of the Book of Common Prayer, as exemplified in the plays of the first folio. London and New York, 1935.

OVID. See Golding, Arthur.

PAINTER, WILLIAM. The palace of pleasure: Elizabethan versions of Italian and French novels from Boccaccio, Bandello, Cinthio, Straparola, Queen Margaret of Navarre, and others. Ed. J. Jacobs. London, 1890. 3 vols.

PLUTARCH. See Brooke, Hazlitt, and Skeat.

PRAZ, M. The English emblem literature. E studies, XVI (1934), 129-40.

ROOT, R. K. Classical mythology in Shakespeare. Yale Studies in English, XIX. New York, 1903.

SANDYS, J. E. Education. Shakespeare's England. Oxford, 1917. I, 224-50.

SHACKFORD, MARTHA H. Plutarch in Renaissance England, with special reference to Shakespeare. [Wellesley] 1929.

SKEAT, W. W., ed. Shakespeare's Plutarch. London, 1875.

STARNES, D. T. Shakespeare and Elyot's Governour. University of Texas studies in English, VII (Austin, 1927), 112-32.

STOW, J. Annales, or, a generall chronicle of England. Begun by Iohn Stow: continved and augmented . . . vnto the end of this present yeere, 1631. By Edmvnd Howes, gent. London, 1631. [First ed. of Stow's *The Chronicles of England*, 1580; first ed. of *The Annales of England*, 1592.]

TAYLOR, G. C. Shakespeare's debt to Montaigne. Cambridge, 1925.

WATSON, F. The English grammar schools to 1660: their curriculum and practice. Cambridge (England), 1908.

POEMS

ALDEN, R. M., ed. The sonnets of Shakespeare, from the quarto of 1609, with variorum readings and commentary. Boston and New York, 1916.

ARCHER, C. Thou and you in the sonnets. TLS, June 27, 1936, p. 544. On possible inferences from the lack of consistency.

BROOKE, [C. F.] T., ed. Shakespeare's sonnets. London and New York, 1936. A brilliant (and, as such things go, a reasonable) attempt to read them as autobiography. The ablest study on the Southampton hypothesis.

BROWN, C. [F.], ed. Poems by Sir John Salusbury and Robert Chester. Bryn Mawr, 1913. Reissued by the Early English Text Society (London, 1914), extra ser., CXIII. Concludes that "The Phoenix and the Turtle" was written at Salusbury's request in behalf of Chester, his protégé, to further the success of his volume. Chester's poem, Brown thinks, celebrates the marriage of Salusbury and Ursula Stanley, and their daughter Jane is the Phoenix. Shakespeare's poem differs from the rest in its consistently funereal tone; the allegory is not apropos, which indicates that he was not a personal friend of Salusbury.

——, ed. Venus and Adonis, The Rape of Lucrece, and other poems. Tudor ed. New York, 1913.

BUSH, D. Mythology and the renaissance tradition in English poetry. Minneapolis, 1932. Chap. VII, Shakespeare: Venus and Adonis and The Rape of Lucrece; and Bibliography, p. 339.

DÜRNHÖFER, M. Shakespeares Venus und Adonis im verhältnis zu Ovids Metamorphosen und Constables Schäfersgesang. Halle, 1890. Shakespeare's alleged indebtedness to Constable is, however, now scouted; and H. E. Rollins (TLS, Oct. 1, 1931, p. 754) argues that "The Sheepheards Song" was composed by Chettle, later than the date of Venus. Dürnhöfer is also wrong in denying that Shakespeare used Golding's translation of Ovid. See my "Shakespeare's Use of Golding in Venus and Adonis," MLN, XLIV (1929), 435-7.

EWIG, W. Shakespeare's Lucrece. Eine litterarhistorische untersuchung. Anglia, XXII (1899), 1-32, 343-63, 393-455. A comprehensive study. Chap. 2, on sources (pp. 9-32), concludes in uncertainty as to whether Shakespeare read Livy and Ovid. First published separately, in dissertation form, Halle, 1899.

FAIRCHILD, A. H. R. The Phœnix and Turtle: a critical and historical interpretation. E studien, XXXIII (1904), 337-84. Thinks the poem connected with the Court-of-Love genre and indebted to Chaucer's The Parlement of Foules.

FORT, J. A. A time scheme for Shakespeare's sonnets, with a text and short notes. London, 1929.

FURNESS, MRS. H. H. A concordance to Shakespeare's poems: an index to every word therein contained. Philadelphia, 1874.

GALINSKY, H. Der Lucretia-stoff in der weltliteratur. Sprache und kultur der Germanisch-romanischen völker, III. Breslau, 1932. From the Greek and Roman historians to the present century.

GOLDING, ARTHUR. The. XV. Bookes of P. Ouidius Naso, entytuled Metamorphosis, translated oute of Latin into English meeter. London, 1567. Reprinted, ed. W. H. D. Rouse, London, 1904.

HARRISON, G. B. The mortal moon. TLS, Nov. 29, 1928, p. 938. Attempts to date Sonnet 107 in 1596. See B. M. Ward's objection, ibid., Feb. 8, 1934, p. 92; and other correspondence, ibid., Jan. 25-Apr. 19.

HUGHES, M. Y. Kidnapping Donne. Essays in criticism. By members of the department of English, University of California. Second series. Berkeley, 1934. Pp. 59-89.

JOHN, LISLE C. The Elizabethan sonnet sequences: studies in conventional conceits. New York, 1938. Includes a good summary of the early history of the sonnet.

LEE, S. [L.], ed. The Passionate Pilgrim. Oxford, 1905. A collotype facsimile, with introduction.

——, ed. Shakespeare's Lucrece. Oxford, 1905. A collotype facsimile. On the earlier treatments of the theme, and sources, see pp. 9-23.

——, ed. Shakespeare's Sonnets. Oxford, 1905. A collotype facsimile, with introduction.

——, ed. Shakespeare's Venus and Adonis. Oxford, 1905. A collotype facsimile. See pp. 14–36 for Lee's learned but exaggerated account of earlier treatments of the theme and Shakespeare's indebtedness to them.

MACKAIL, J. W. A Lover's Complaint. Essays and studies by members of the English Association (Oxford, 1912), III, 51–70. Thinks the Rival Poet is imitating Shakespeare.

—— Shakespeare's sonnets. Lectures on poetry. London, New York, etc., 1911. Pp. 179–207. A general study.

MATTINGLY, G. The date of Shakespeare's sonnet cvii. PMLA, XLVIII (1933), 705–21. Concludes that 1603 is indicated by the line generally agreed to offer most hope for dating any of the sonnets: "The mortal moon [Elizabeth] hath her eclipse endur'd." Reviews the arguments for other dates.

NEWDIGATE, B. H. The Phoenix and Turtle: was Lady Bedford the phoenix? TLS, Oct. 24, 1936, p. 862. Repeats the proposal made in his edition of Jonson's Poems (Oxford, 1936). See Newdigate's supplementary letter, TLS, Nov. 28, 1936, p. 996. The identification is attacked by R. W. Short, TLS, Feb. 13, 1937, p. 111; see Newdigate's rejoinder, Feb. 20, 1937, p. 131.

PEARSON, LU E. Elizabethan love conventions. Berkeley, 1933. On Petrarchism in England, the sonnet cycles, anti-Petrarchism, and Shakespeare's relation to both schools.

POOLER, C. K., ed. Shakespeare's poems: Venus and Adonis, Lucrece, The Passionate Pilgrim, Sonnets to Sundry Notes of Music, The Phoenix and Turtle. Arden Shakespeare. London, 1911.

——, ed. Sonnets. The works of Shakespeare. Arden ed. London, 1918.

ROBERTSON, J. M. The problems of the Shakespeare sonnets. London, 1926. Reviews the theories. Pp. 257–81 give Robertson's conclusions, which include rejection of Shakespeare's authorship of some of the poems.

—— Shakespeare and Chapman: a thesis of Chapman's authorship of A Lover's Complaint, and his origination of Timon of Athens, with indications of further problems. London, 1917. Cf. H. D. Sykes's review, MLR, XIII (1918), 244–50.

ROLLINS, H. E., ed. The poems: Venus and Adonis, Lucrece, The Passionate Pilgrim, The Phoenix and the Turtle, A Lover's Complaint. New variorum ed. Philadelphia and London, 1938.

TUCKER, T. G., ed. The sonnets of Shakespeare, edited from the quarto of 1609. Cambridge (England), 1924.

WELLS, H. W. A new preface to Shakspere's sonnets. SAB, XII (1937), 118–29. Attacks Lee's theory of their complete artificiality. Thinks they are "realistic" and mark Shakespeare's divorce from the Platonic school of English poetry.

WYNDHAM, G., ed. The poems of Shakespeare. London, 1898. The introductory essay is reprinted in Wyndham's *Essays in Romantic Literature*,
ed. C. Whibley (London, 1919), pp. 237–388.

2. *Medium*

THE STAGE TO 1642

ADAMS, J. C. The staging of The Tempest, III, iii. RES, XIV (1938), 404–19.
Contains notes on the structure of the stage. See, especially, on the
heavens. Cf. the same writer's articles (suggestive though undocu-
mented) in *Theatre Arts Monthly*, XX (1936), 812–18, 896–904. Cf.
TLS, Feb. 15, 1936, p. 159, and further correspondence, Feb. 22, 29,
May 23, 30.

ADAMS, J. Q. The housekeepers of the Globe. MP, XVII (1919), 1–8.

—— Shakespearean playhouses: a history of English theatres from the beginnings to the Restoration. Boston, etc., 1917.

——, ed. The dramatic records of sir Henry Herbert, master of the revels,
1623–1673. New Haven and London, 1917.

——, ed. Macbeth. Boston, 1931. Pp. 293–8. Questions authenticity of Forman's notes on Shakespeare. Cf. under "Tannenbaum," below.

ALBRIGHT, V. E. The Shaksperian stage. New York, 1909.

ALEXANDER, P. Shakespeare's Henry VI and Richard III. Cambridge (England), 1929. See especially, in A. W. Pollard's introduction, pp. 7–28;
and Alexander's "The First Period," pp. 193–215.

ARBER, E. A transcript of the registers of the company of stationers of London, 1554–1640. Vols. I–IV, London, 1875–7; vol. V, Birmingham,
1894.

BAKER, G. P. The development of Shakespeare as a dramatist. New York,
1907.

BALDWIN, T. W. The organization and personnel of the Shakespearean company. Princeton, 1927.

—— Posting Henslowe's accounts. JEGP, XXVI (1927), 42–90.

BASKERVILL, C. R. The Elizabethan jig and related song drama. Chicago,
1929.

BRAINES, W. W. The site of the Globe playhouse in Southwark. Second ed.
London, 1924.

CAMPBELL, LILY B. Scenes and machines on the English stage during the
Renaissance. Cambridge (England), 1923.

CHAMBERS, E. K. The Elizabethan stage. Oxford, 1923. 4 vols. An encyclopedic treatment of entertainments at court, control of the stage, companies, theatres, staging, plays, and playwrights. Index to the four
volumes and to *William Shakespeare* compiled by Beatrice White, Oxford, 1934.

—— The medieval stage. Oxford, 1903. 2 vols.

COHN, A. Shakespeare in Germany in the sixteenth and seventeenth centuries
an account of English actors in Germany and the Netherlands and (
the plays performed by them during the same period. London, 1865.

COWLING, G. H. Music on the Shakespearian stage. Cambridge (England)
1913.

DAVIES, W. R. Shakespeare's boy actors. London, 1939. On the women'
rôles "with reference to the potentialities of the boy actor." This stud
is also of some importance critically.

DEKKER, THOMAS. The guls horne-booke. London, 1609. Chap. VI. Fre
quently reprinted; e.g., ed. R. B. McKerrow, London, 1904.

DENT, E. J. Shakespeare and music. A companion to Shakespeare studies
Ed. H. Granville-Barker and G. B. Harrison. Cambridge (England)
1934. Pp. 137–61.

FEUILLERAT, A. Documents relating to the office of the revels in the tim
of queen Elizabeth. Materialen zur kunde des älteren englischen dramas
ed. W. Bang, XXI. Louvain, 1908.

GRAVES, T. S. The court and the London theatres during the reign of Eliza
beth. University of Chicago dissertation. Menasha, 1913. Thinks th
court stage more influential than the inn yards or the construction o
public theatres.

GREG, W. W. Dramatic documents from the Elizabethan playhouses: stag
plots: actors' parts: prompt books. Oxford, 1931. 2 vols. Reproduction
and commentary.

——, ed. Henslowe papers, being documents supplementary to Henslowe'
Diary. London, 1907.

——, ed. Henslowe's diary. London, 1904–8. 2 vols.

HARBAGE, A. Elizabethan acting. PMLA, LIV (1939), 685–708. Argues tha
it was "formal," not "natural."

HART, A. Shakespeare and the homilies: and other pieces of research into th
Elizabethan drama. Melbourne, 1934. Pp. 77–153 analyze the length
of Elizabethan plays.

HILLEBRAND, H. N. The child-actors: a chapter in Elizabethan stage history
Urbana, 1926.

ISAACS, J. Production and stage-management at the Blackfriars theatre
London, 1933.

KELLY, F. M. Shakespearian costume for stage and screen. London, 1938
With nine plates and ninety-three line drawings. Pp. 100–115 offe
special suggestions on the several plays.

LAW, E. P. A. More about Shakespeare "forgeries." London, 1913. In re
buttal of objections to *Some Supposed Shakespeare Forgeries.*

—— Some supposed Shakespeare forgeries: an examination into the authen
ticity of certain documents affecting the dates of composition of severa
of the plays. London, 1911.

LAWRENCE, W. J. The Elizabethan playhouse and other studies. Stratford
upon-Avon, 1912.

—— The Elizabethan playhouse and other studies. Second series. Stratford-upon-Avon, 1913.

—— Old theatre days and ways. London, etc., 1935.

—— The physical conditions of the Elizabethan public playhouse. Cambridge, 1927.

—— Pre-Restoration stage studies. Cambridge, 1927.

—— Those nut-cracking Elizabethans: studies of the early theatre and drama. London, 1935.

LEA, KATHLEEN M. Italian popular comedy: a study in the commedia dell'arte, 1560–1620, with special reference to the English stage. Oxford, 1934. 2 vols. A. Nicoll's review (*Year's Work in English Studies*, XV, 169–70) should be noted.

LINTHICUM, M. C. Costume in the drama of Shakespeare and his contemporaries. Oxford, 1936.

MARCHAM, F. The king's office of the revels 1610–1622. London, 1925. Gives facsimiles of the fragments relating to proposed performances in 1619.

MURRAY, J. T. English dramatic companies 1558–1642. London, 1910. 2 vols.

NICOLL, A. The development of the theatre. New ed. London, 1937.

—— Stuart masques and the renaissance stage. London, 1937.

NUNGEZER, E. A dictionary of actors and of other persons associated with the public representation of plays in England before 1642. New Haven, 1929.

REYNOLDS, G. F. Some principles of Elizabethan staging. Chicago, 1905. 2 vols. Reprinted from *MP*, II, 581–614; III, 69–97. Exposes the weakness of the "alternation" theory of staging.

—— What we know of the Elizabethan stage. MP, IX (1911), 47–82. An important summary.

RHODES, R. C. The stagery of Shakespeare. Birmingham, 1922. Inferences from the quartos' stage directions.

SISSON, C. J. The theatres and companies. A companion to Shakespeare studies. Ed. H. Granville-Barker and G. B. Harrison. Cambridge (England), 1934. Pp. 9–43.

STAMP, A. E. The disputed revels accounts, reproduced in collotype facsimile, with a paper read before the Shakespeare Association. London, 1930.

STEELE, MARY S. Plays and masques at court during the reigns of Elizabeth, James and Charles. New Haven and London, 1926.

TANNENBAUM, S. A. The Forman notes on Shakspere. Shaksperian scraps and other Elizabethan fragments. New York, 1933. Pp. 1–35. A cogent argument against their authenticity.

—— More about the forged revels accounts. New York, 1932.

—— Shakspere forgeries in the revels accounts. New York, 1928.

THALER, A. Minor actors and employees in the Elizabethan theater. MP, XX (1922), 49–60.

—— Shakspere to Sheridan: a book about the theatre of yesterday and today. Cambridge and London, 1922. Useful information on the commercial methods of the theatres.

—— Shakspere's income. SP, XV (1918), 82–96.

—— The traveling players in Shakspere's England. MP, XVII (1920), 489–514.

THORNDIKE, A. H. Shakespeare's theater. New York, 1916. The standard work.

WALLACE, C. W. The children of the chapel at Blackfriars, 1597–1603. London, 1908.

WELSFORD, ENID. The court masque, a study in the relationship between poetry and the revels. Cambridge (England), 1927.

WRIGHT, L. B. Will Kemp and the commedia dell'arte. MLN, XLI (1926), 516–20. Suggests that Shakespeare may have been influenced through Kempe's contacts with Italian players at home and abroad.

STAGING SINCE 1642

ADAMS, J. Q. The dramatic records of Sir Henry Herbert, master of the revels, 1623–1673. New Haven and London, 1917.

ALGER, W. R. Life of Edwin Forrest, the American tragedian. Philadelphia, 1877. 2 vols.

ARCHER, W. William Charles Macready, London, 1890.

BAKER, D. E., REED, I., AND JONES, S. Biographia dramatica, or a companion to the playhouse. London, 1812. 3 vols. (sometimes bound in 4 vols.).

BOADEN, J. Memoirs of Mrs. Siddons, interspersed with anecdotes of authors and actors. London, 1893. [1st ed. 1827. 2 vols.] Incredibly windy, but more of a general stage history than the other biographies of Mrs. Siddons, and a more detailed report of her acting by one who saw it.

—— Memoirs of the life of John Philip Kemble, esq., including a history of the stage from the time of Garrick to the present period. London, 1825. 2 vols.

BRERETON, A. The life of Henry Irving. London, etc., 1908. 2 vols.

CHILD, H. Revivals of English dramatic works, 1901–1918, 1926. RES, III (1927), 169–85.

—— Revivals of English dramatic works, 1919–1925. RES, II (1926), 177–88.

—— The Shakespearian productions of John Philip Kemble. London, 1935.

—— The stage-history of The Tempest. In the New edition of that play, ed. A. Quiller-Couch and J. D. Wilson. Cambridge (England), 1921. Similar accounts for the various plays appear in the subsequent volumes of the New ed.

CIBBER, C. An apology for the life of Colley Cibber, written by himself. Ed. R. W. Lowe. London, 1888. 2 vols.

CLARKE, ASIA B. The elder and the younger Booth. Boston, 1882.

COLE, J. W. The life and theatrical times of Charles Kean, F.S.A., including a summary of the English stage for the last fifty years. Second ed. London, 1859. 2 vols.

DAVIES, T. Dramatic miscellanies: consisting of critical observations on several plays of Shakespeare . . . as represented by Mr. Garrick and other celebrated comedians. London, 1784. 3 vols.

DOWNES, J. Roscius anglicanus, or an historical review of the stage from 1660 to 1706. London, 1708. Facsimile reprint, ed. J. Knight, London, 1886. Also edited, with copious notes, by M. Summers, London, 1927.

DUNLAP, W. Memoirs of George Fred. Cooke, esq. London, 1813. 2 vols.

FFRENCH, YVONNE. Mrs. Siddons: tragic actress. London, 1936.

FITZGERALD, P. The Kembles: an account of the Kemble family, including the lives of Mrs. Siddons, and her brother John Philip Kemble. London, n.d. [1875?] 2 vols.

—— A new history of the English stage: from the Restoration to the liberty of the theatres, in connection with the patent houses. London, 1882. 2 vols.

GENEST, J. Some account of the English stage, from the restoration in 1660 to 1830. Bath, 1832. 10 vols.

HILLEBRAND, H. N. Edmund Kean. New York, 1933.

IRVING, H., AND MARSHALL, F. A., eds. The works of William Shakespeare. London, 1906. 14 vols. This edition of the Irving Shakespeare contains valuable sketches of stage history.

KIRKMAN, J. T. Memoirs of the life of Charles Macklin, esq., principally compiled from his own papers and memorandums. London, 1799. 2 vols.

KNIGHT, J. David Garrick. London, 1894.

LINTON, C. D. Shakespeare on the London stage from Irving to Gielgud. Unpublished master's thesis, Johns Hopkins University, 1939. I am indebted to this careful study for a number of performances which have not, so far as I know, been listed elsewhere.

MACMILLAN, D. Drury lane calendar, 1747–1776. Compiled from the playbills and edited with an introduction. Oxford, 1938.

MALLOY, J. F. The life and adventures of Edmund Kean, tragedian: 1787–1833. London, 1888. 2 vols.

MURPHY, A. The life of David Garrick, esq. London, 1801. 2 vols.

NICOLL, A. A history of Restoration drama, 1660–1700. Second ed. Cambridge (England), 1928.

—— A history of early eighteenth century drama, 1700–1750. Cambridge (England), 1925.

—— A history of late eighteenth century drama, 1750–1800. Cambridge (England), 1927.

—— A history of early nineteenth century drama, 1800–1850. New York and Cambridge (England), 1930. 2 vols.

ODELL, G. C. D. Annals of the New York stage. New York, 1927–. In progress.

—— Shakespeare from Betterton to Irving. New York, 1920. 2 vols. A valuable and lavishly illustrated survey.

PHELPS, W. M., AND FORBES-ROBERTSON, J. The life and life-work of Samuel Phelps. London, 1886.

[RALPH, JAMES.] The case of our present theatrical disputes, fairly stated. London, 1743. Mentions encouragement of revivals by the ladies of the Shakespear Club.

SPENCER, H. Shakespeare improved: the Restoration versions in quarto and on the stage. Cambridge and London, 1927. Includes a history of the Restoration stage.

WATSON, E. B. Sheridan to Robertson: a study of the nineteenth-century London stage. Cambridge, 1926.

WINTER, W. Life and art of Edwin Booth. New ed. New York and London, 1894.

—— Shakespeare on the stage. [First series.] New York, 1911. Though unreliable for the seventeenth century, Winter's three volumes are valuable for later performances. They are, however, extremely crotchety.

—— Shakespeare on the stage. Second series. New York, 1915.

—— Shakespeare on the stage. Third series. New York, 1916.

LANGUAGE AND VERSE

ABBOTT, E. A. A Shakespearian grammar. New ed. London, 1872. Includes a section on metrics.

ALDEN, R. M. The punctuation of Shakespeare's printers. PMLA, XXXIX (1924), 557–80. Takes issue with Simpson.

BARTLETT, J. A new and complete concordance or verbal index to words, phrases, & passages in the dramatic works of Shakespeare, with a supplementary concordance to the poems. London and New York, 1894.

BAUGH, A. C. A history of the English language. New York and London, 1935. Chap. VIII.

BAYFIELD, M. A. A study of Shakespeare's versification, with an inquiry into the trustworthiness of the early texts, an examination of the 1616 folio of Ben Jonson's Works, and appendices including a revised text of Antony and Cleopatra. Cambridge (England), 1920. Thinks abbreviated forms such as "o' th' best" should be expanded if we are to hear the verse aright.

BRADLEY, H. Shakespeare's English. Shakespeare's England. Oxford, 1917. II, 539–74.

CHAMBERS, D. L. The metre of Macbeth: its relation to Shakespeare's earlier and later work. Princeton, 1903. An illuminating study.

DAVIES, CONSTANCE. English pronunciation from the fifteenth to the eighteenth century: a handbook to the study of historical grammar. London, 1934. Pp. 1–18, 70–123.

FIEDLER, H. G. A contemporary of Shakespeare on phonetics and on the pronunciation of English and Latin: a contribution to the history of phonetics and English sounds. M.H.R.A.: annual bulletin of the Modern Humanities Research Association, no. 15 (1936), pp. 1–21.

FLEAY, F. G. On metrical tests applied to Shakespeare. In: C. M. Ingleby. Shakespeare the man and the book: being a collection of occasional papers. London, 1877–81. 2 vols. Vol. II, occasional papers on Shakespeare: being the second part of Shakespeare the man and the book, pp. 51–141. Includes Fleay's revised tables.

FRIES, C. C. Shakespearian punctuation. Studies in Shakespeare, Milton, and Donne. University of Michigan publications, language and literature, I (1925), 65–86. A cogent attack on the theory that the punctuation of the original texts was "dramatic" and independent of syntax.

GORDON, G. [s.] Shakespeare's English. Oxford, 1928. A lecture of 21 pages.

HOSKINS, JOHN. Directions for speech and style. Ed. H. H. Hudson. Princeton, 1935. See also under "Osborn."

INGLEBY, C. M. See Fleay, F. G.

MCKNIGHT, G. H. Modern English in the making. New York and London, 1928. Chaps. V–XI.

NARES, R. A glossary; or, collection of words, phrases, names, and allusions to customs, proverbs, etc. New ed., by J. O. Halliwell [-Phillips] and T. Wright. London, 1872. 2 vols.

NEW ENGLISH DICTIONARY on historical principles. Oxford and New York, 1888–1933.

ONIONS, C. T. A Shakespeare glossary. Second ed. Oxford, 1919.

OSBORN, LOUISE B. The life, letters, and writings of John Hoskyns, 1566–1638. New Haven, 1937. Pp. 103–66 reprint *Directions for Speech and Style*, with a critical introduction.

PRICE, H. T. Towards a scientific method of textual criticism for the Elizabethan drama. JEGP, XXXVI (1937), 151–67. For some sensible observations on metrics, see pp. 155–60.

SAINTSBURY, G. A history of English prosody from the twelfth century. London and New York, 1906–10. II, 3–204.

SCHMIDT, A. Shakespeare-lexicon. Revised by G. Sarrazin. Berlin, 1902. 2 vols.

SIMPSON, P. Shakespearian punctuation. Oxford, 1911. Attempts to demonstrate "dramatic" rather than grammatical punctuation. No longer generally accepted.

SPURGEON, CAROLINE F. E. Shakespeare's imagery and what it tells us. New York and Cambridge (England), 1935. Interesting for its collections, but despite wide acceptance fundamentally unsound in its inferences.

STOKES, F. G. A dictionary of the characters and proper names in the works of Shakespeare. London, 1924.

SUGDEN, E. H. A topographical dictionary to the works of Shakespeare and his fellow dramatists. Manchester, London, and New York, 1925.

TILLEY, M. P. Elizabethan proverb lore in Lyly's Euphues and Pettie's Petite Pallace with parallels from Shakespeare. University of Michigan publications, language and literature, vol. II. New York and London, 1926.

VIËTOR, W. Shakespeare's pronunciation. (I, phonology; II, reader.) Marburg and London, 1906–7. 2 vols.

WILLCOCK, GLADYS D. Shakespeare and Elizabethan English. A companion to Shakespeare studies. Ed. H. Granville-Barker and G. B. Harrison. Cambridge (England), 1934. Pp. 117–36.

WYLD, H. C. A history of modern colloquial English. Second ed. London, 1920.

ZACHRISSON, R. E. The English pronunciation at Shakespeare's time as taught by William Bullokar. Skrifter utgivna av Kungl. Humanistiska Vetenskaps-Samfundet i Uppsala, 22:6. Uppsala and Leipzig, 1927.

3. *Experimental Comedies*

THE COMEDY OF ERRORS

GAW, A. The evolution of The Comedy of Errors. PMLA, XLI (1926), 620–66. Thinks Shakespeare rewrote *The Historie of Error* of 1577 and 1583.

GREG, W. W., ed. Gesta Grayorum, 1688. Malone Society reprints. London, 1914.

LEA, KATHLEEN M. Italian popular comedy. Oxford, 1934. 2 vols. See I, 434–42, for connections with the *commedia dell'arte*.

ROUSE, W. H. D., ed. The Menaechmi: the original of Shakespeare's Comedy of Errors: the Latin text together with the Elizabethan translation. Shakespeare classics. London, 1912.

TANNENBAUM, S. A. Notes on The Comedy of Errors. SJ, LXVIII (1932), 103–24. A trenchant criticism of the New edition. Argues that the compositor had a Shakespeare holograph before him.

THE TAMING OF THE SHREW

ALEXANDER, P. The taming of a shrew. TLS, Sept. 16, 1926, p. 614. Argues that *A Shrew* is a Bad quarto of *The Shrew*.

ASHTON, FLORENCE H. The revision of the folio text of The Taming of the Shrew. PQ, VI (1927), 151–60. Contends that bibliographical evidence shows the text to be a revision of an old play.

BOAS, F. S., ed. The taming of a shrew, being the original of Shakespeare's Taming of the Shrew. Shakespeare classics. London, 1908. There is also a Griggs facsimile, London, 1886.

CUNLIFFE, J. W., ed. Supposes and Jocasta: two plays translated from the Italian, the first by Geo. Gascoigne, the second by Geo. Gascoigne and F. Kinwelmersh. Boston and London, 1906.

DAM, B. A. P. VAN. The taming of a shrew. E studies, X (1928), 97–106.

Suggests that the text is a stenographic report of a performance improvised by actors in imitation of *The Shrew*.

KUHL, E. P. The authorship of The Taming of the Shrew. PMLA, XL (1925), 551–618. Argues for Shakespeare's sole authorship.

SYKES, H. D. The authorship of The Taming of a Shrew, The Famous Victories of Henry V, and the additions to Marlowe's Faustus. Sidelights on Elizabethan drama. London, 1924. Pp. 49–78. Argues for Samuel Rowley's partial authorship of *A Shrew*.

THE TWO GENTLEMEN OF VERONA

CAMPBELL, O. J. The Two Gentlemen of Verona and Italian comedy. Studies in Shakespeare, Milton, and Donne. University of Michigan publications, language and literature, I (1925), 49–63. Calls attention to the conventions of Italian comedy, concludes that the source was "some thoroughly Italianate play," minimizes the originality of Shakespeare's contribution to the development of Elizabethan romantic comedy, and ascribes the unsatisfactory denouement to the hasty retention of conventional material "in its original stiff caricature of reality."

HARRISON, T. P., JR. Concerning Two Gentlemen of Verona and Montemayor's Diana. MLN, XLI (1926), 251–2. Rejects the theory that Shakespeare used the play of *Felix and Philiomena*.

—— Shakespeare and Montemayor's Diana. University of Texas studies in English, no. 6. Austin, 1926. Pp. 72–94.

HAZLITT, W. C., ed. The shepherdess Felismena. Shakespeare's library. London, 1875. I, 275–312.

PARKS, G. B. The development of The Two Gentlemen of Verona. Huntington library bulletin, no. 11 (Cambridge, 1937), pp. 1–11. Examines the confusions in designations of place, and proposes the dubious theory that the travel element was an addition to the original version.

TANNENBAUM, S. A. The New Cambridge Shakespeare and The Two Gentlemen of Verona. SAB, XIII (1938), 151–72, 208–23. Textual and interpretive notes.

LOVE'S LABOUR'S LOST

CAMPBELL, O. J. Love's Labour's Lost re-studied. Studies in Shakespeare, Milton, and Donne. University of Michigan publications, language and literature, I (1925), 3–45. Important.

CHARLTON, H. B. The date of Love's Labour's Lost. MLR, XIII (1918), 257–66, 387–400. Argues for 1592.

GRANVILLE-BARKER, H. Love's labour's lost. Prefaces to Shakespeare. First series. London, 1927. Pp. 1–49.

KIRSCHBAUM, L. Is The Spanish Tragedy a leading case? Did a bad quarto of Love's Labour's Lost ever exist? JEGP, XXXVII (1938), 501–12. Thinks "there is almost no probability" that a lost Bad quarto preceded Q_1.

LEFRANC, A. Sous le masque de William Shakespeare: William Stanley, VIᵉ comte de Derby. Paris, 1918–19. II, 17–103. Fantastic in its main thesis, but valuable for its suggestion of the meeting at Nérac as a possible source.

SORENSON, F. The masque of the Muscovites in Love's Labour's Lost. MLN, L (1935), 499–501. Shows that the Gray's Inn Revels of 1595 are valueless for dating the play.

SPENS, JANET. Notes on Love's Labour's Lost. RES, VII (1931), 331–4. Critical of the New edition's handling of the Rosaline-Katherine confusion.

TAYLOR, R. The date of Love's Labour's Lost. New York, 1932. Argues for 1596.

WILLCOCK, GLADYS D. Shakespeare as a critic of language. London, 1934. Important.

YATES, FRANCES A. A study of Love's Labour's Lost. Cambridge (England), 1936. An ingenious argument for the play's topicality, but on the whole unconvincing.

4. Early Histories

HENRY THE SIXTH

ALEXANDER, P. Shakespeare's Henry VI and Richard III. Cambridge (England), 1929. Generally accepted as proving 1 Contention and True Tragedy Bad quartos, not source plays. Also holds that 1 Henry the Sixth is Shakespeare's. See reviews by [C. F.] T. Brooke, JEGP, XXIX (1930), 442–6, and R. A. Law, "Shakespeare's Earliest Plays," SP, XXVIII (1931), 631–8.

CHAMBERS, E. K. Actors' gag in Elizabethan plays. TLS, March 8, 1928, p. 170.

DENNY, C. F. The sources of 1 Henry VI as an indication of revision. PQ, XVI (1937), 225–48. Argues that Halle and Holinshed vary so little that one author would not have used both, and that the use of both therefore points to a reviser's hand.

DORAN, MADELEINE. Henry VI, Parts II and III: their relation to the Contention and the True Tragedy. University of Iowa humanistic studies, vol. IV, no. 4. Iowa City, 1928. Expounds the Bad-quarto theory, though doubtful of piracy.

THE FIRST PART OF THE CONTENTION. London, 1594. Reprinted in Shakespeare's library, ed. W. C. Hazlitt (London, 1875), V, 379–520. There is also a Praetorius facsimile, 1889.

GAW, A. The origin and development of 1 Henry VI in relation to Shakespeare, Marlowe, Peele, and Greene. University of Southern California studies, ser. 1, no. 1. Second ed. Los Angeles, 1927. Concludes that Marlowe, Peele, and two others collaborated on harey the vj, that

Shakespeare first revised it in 1594, and that about 1599 he gave the play its present form.

GREER, C. A. The place of 1 Henry VI in the York-Lancaster tetralogy. PMLA, LIII (1938), 687–701. Thinks Shakespeare revised an earlier play but disputes the assignment of the revision to as late a date as 1600.

—— The York and Lancaster quarto-folio sequence. PMLA, XLVIII (1933), 655–704. Argues against the Bad-quarto theory.

GREG, W. W. Henry VI and the Contention plays. PMLA, L (1935), 919–20. Critical of Greer.

KENNY, T. The life and genius of Shakespeare. London, 1864. Pp. 277–367. On 1 Contention and True Tragedy as Bad quartos.

KING, LUCILLE. Text sources of the folio and quarto Henry VI. PMLA, LI (1936), 702–18. Concludes that a lost play based on Halle was the source of both F and Q.

—— 2 and 3 Henry VI — which Holinshed? PMLA, L (1935), 745–52. The Folio texts show that Shakespeare used the edition of 1587.

—— The use of Hall's Chronicles in the folio and quarto texts of Henry VI. PQ, XIII (1934), 321–32. Shows use of Halle as well as Holinshed.

MCKERROW, R. B. A note on Henry VI, Part II and The Contention of York and Lancaster. RES, IX (1933), 157–69. Argues that, while practically all the history in Q_1 is in 1577 Holinshed, Q_3's revision of the genealogy of II, ii is based on 1587 Holinshed, and that 1 Contention stems from an earlier version of 2 Henry VI than is given by F.

—— A note on the bad quartos of 2 and 3 Henry VI and the folio text. RES, XIII (1937), 64–72. Suggests (anticipated by Miss Doran) that the virtual identity of certain passages in Qq and F is due to use of Qq by the F compositor when his "copy" was defective. Agreement of a Good text and a Bad Q may therefore mean, not the confirmation of the Good text's reading, but the presence of the same Bad text in both editions.

—— 2 Henry VI. and The Contention — a correction. RES, IX (1933), 316.

THE TRUE TRAGEDY OF RICHARD DUKE OF YORKE. London, 1595. Reprinted in Shakespeare's library, ed. W. C. Hazlitt (London, 1875), VI, 1–105. There is also a Praetorius facsimile, 1891.

RICHARD THE THIRD

ALEXANDER, P. Shakespeare's Henry VI and Richard III. Cambridge (England), 1929. Shakespeare is the sole author of Richard the Third.

BABCOCK, R. W. An introduction to the study of the text of Richard III. SP, XXIV (1927), 243–60. Suggests that Q 1597 may be "an actor's imperfect version."

CHURCHILL, G. B. Richard the third up to Shakespeare. Berlin, 1900.

LAMB, C. G. F. Cooke in Richard the Third. Works, ed. E. V. Lucas. London,

1903. I, 36–8, 398–9. Contains some shrewd comments on the characte
of Richard.

PATRICK, D. L. The textual history of Richard III. Stanford University an
London, 1936. An interesting introduction to the textual problem

WOOD, ALICE I. P. The stage history of Shakespeare's King Richard the Third
New York, 1909.

KING JOHN

FURNIVALL, F. J., AND MUNRO, J., eds. The troublesome reign of king
John: being the original of Shakespeare's Life and Death of King John.
Shakespeare classics. London, 1913. Also reprinted in the New Variorum
King John, ed. H. H. Furness, Jr., 1919, pp. 471–537; and in Praetorius
facsimiles, 1888.

HARRISON, G. B. Shakespeare's topical significances: I. King John. TLS
Nov. 13, 1930, p. 939. Dates composition in the summer of 1596 but
ignores the likelihood that the alleged "topical significances" are at
variance with Shakespeare's reduction of the anti-Catholic element of
The Troublesome Raigne.

SYKES, H. D. The troublesome reign of king John. Sidelights on Shakespeare. Stratford-upon-Avon, 1919. Pp. 99–125. Tries to demonstrate
Peele's authorship.

WILSON, J. D. Introduction. King John. Cambridge (England), 1936. Pp. vii–
lxi. Thinks Shakespeare first rewrote *The Troublesome Raigne* in 1590
and revised it again in 1594 for the Chamberlain's Men.

RICHARD THE SECOND

ALBRIGHT, EVELYN M. Shakespeare's Richard II and the Essex conspiracy.
PMLA, XLII (1927), 686–720. Argues that the play "bespoken" by
the friends of Essex was Shakespeare's, that it contains many topical
allusions, and that a MS of Hayward's *Henrie the IIII* was among Shakespeare's sources.

—— Shakespeare's Richard II, Hayward's History of Henry IV, and the
Essex conspiracy. PMLA, XLVI (1931), 694–719. Defends her earlier
article and attacks Heffner's.

BOAS, F. S. Hamlet & Richard II on the high seas. Shakespeare & the universities, and other studies in Elizabethan drama. Oxford, 1923. Pp. 84–
95. Supports the authenticity of Keeling's performances.

FRIJLINCK, WILHELMINA P., ed. The first part of the reign of king Richard
the second, or Thomas of Woodstock. Malone Society reprints. London,
1929.

HEFFNER, R. Shakespeare, Hayward, and Essex. PMLA, XLV (1930), 754–80.
Attacks Miss Albright's first article. Argues that the identification of
Elizabeth with Richard II was based on Hayward's *Henrie the IIII*,
that when Essex was examined in 1600 he was accused of having seen

a dramatization of Hayward's book, and that there is no connection between *Richard II* and either Hayward or Essex.

KUHL, E. P. Shakespeare and Hayward. SP, XXV (1928), 312–15. Suggests that Hayward borrowed from Shakespeare.

POLLARD, A. W., ed. A new Shakespeare quarto: the tragedy of King Richard II . . . 1598 . . . in facsimile. London, 1916. Pp. 5–102 constitute a valuable introduction to textual problems.

SMITH, R. M. Froissart and the English chronicle play. New York, 1915. Pp. 143–57 argue that Shakespeare is indebted to Samuel Daniel's *Ciuile wars*. For a sweeping acceptance of far-flung "sources," see the Introduction to the New ed. of *Richard II* (1939).

5. Later Histories

HENRY THE FOURTH

BAESKE, W. Oldcastle-Falstaff in der englischen literatur bis zu Shakespeare. Palaestra, L. Berlin, 1905.

BOWLING, W. G. The wild Prince Hal in legend and literature. Washington University studies, XIII (1925–6), humanistic ser., pp. 305–34.

DRAPER, J. W. Sir John Falstaff. RES, VIII (1932), 414–24. Examines his character as an army officer.

THE FAMOUS VICTORIES OF HENRY THE FIFTH. The earliest known quarto, 1598, a facsimile. Ed. P. A. Daniel. London, 1887. Also reprinted in J. Q. Adams's *Chief Pre-Shakespearean Dramas*.

GAIRDNER, J. On the historical element in Shakespeare's Falstaff. Studies in English history. Edinburgh, 1881. Pp. 55–77. On Falstaff, Oldcastle, and Fastolf. An admirable essay, critically as well as historically.

HART, A. Was the second part of King Henry the Fourth censored? Shakespeare and the homilies, and other pieces of research into the Elizabethan drama. Melbourne, etc., 1934. Pp. 154–218. An independent and more elaborate investigation, differing in some details, but reaching the same general conclusions as Schücking.

KNOWLTON, E. C. Falstaff redux. JEGP, XXV (1926), 193–215. Gives a useful bibliography of the debate.

LAW, R. A. Structural unity in the two parts of Henry the Fourth. SP, XXIV (1927), 223–42. Argues that the core of *Part 1* is a conflict between Hal and Hotspur, and of *Part 2* another, in morality style, between Falstaff and the Chief Justice for the soul of Hal.

MORGAN, A. E. Some problems of Shakespeare's Henry the Fourth. London, 1924. Argues that both Parts are abridged versions and that the earlier Oldcastle form of the play was almost wholly in verse and based on a still older play on which *The Famous Victories* was also based.

MORGANN, M. An essay on the dramatic character of sir John Falstaff. London, 1777. Reprinted, ed. W. A. Gill, London, 1912.

POLLARD, A. W. The variant settings in II. Henry IV. and their spellings. TLS, Oct. 21, 1920, p. 680. A bibliographical study of Q 1600.

SCHÜCKING, L. L. The quarto of King Henry IV., Part II. TLS, Sept. 25, 1930, p. 752. Suggests political reasons for censorship of the Quarto text.

STARNES, D. T. More about the prince Hal legend. PQ, XV (1936), 358–66. Cites three more versions of Hal's clash with the Chief Justice.

STOLL, E. E. Falstaff. Shakespeare studies. New York, 1927. Pp. 403–90.

HENRY THE FIFTH

CRAIG, H. The relation of the first quarto version to the first folio version of Shakespeare's Henry V. PQ, VI (1927), 225–34. Argues that the Folio is a revision of the Quarto.

THE FAMOUS VICTORIES OF HENRY THE FIFTH. The earliest known quarto, 1598, a facsimile. Ed. P. A. Daniel. London, 1887. Also reprinted in J. Q. Adams's *Chief Pre-Shakespearean Dramas*.

NICHOLSON, B. The relation of the quarto to the folio version of Henry V. Transactions of the New Shakspere Society, 1880–2. Part I, pp. 77–102. Argues that the Quarto is a first draft and the Folio a literary revision.

OKERLUND, GERDA. The quarto version of Henry V as a stage adaptation. PMLA, XLIX (1934), 810–34. Concludes that the Quarto is a shortened stage version based on a piratical copy of the authentic MS, which was subsequently somewhat revised.

POLLARD, A. W., AND WILSON, J. D. The stolne and surreptitious Shakespearian texts: Henry V (1600). TLS, March 14, 1919, p. 134. Argues for an intermediate play between *The Famous Victories* and *Henry V*, revised by Shakespeare before 1593, and for the origin of the Quarto in a piracy of an abridgment of that revision acted by Lord Strange's Men.

PRICE, H. T. The quarto and folio texts of Henry V. PQ, XII (1933), 24–32. Critical of Miss Simison.

—— The text of Henry V. Newcastle-under-Lyme, 1920. Rejects the Pollard-Wilson hypothesis of an intermediate play. Argues that the Folio gives us what Shakespeare wrote for the Globe production in 1599, and that the Quarto piracy is the work of a shorthand reporter and a traitorous actor who supplied the text of his rôles. See Pollard's review, *MLR*, XVI (1921), 339–40.

RADOFF, M. L. Influence of the French farce in Henry V and The Merry Wives. MLN, XLVIII (1933), 427–35. The French lesson in *Henry V* and the Latin examination in *The Merry Wives* may be imitations.

ROMAN, E., ed. King Henry V. Parallel texts of the first and third quartos and the first folio. Marburg, 1908.

SIMISON, BARBARA D. Stage-directions: a test for the playhouse origin of the first quarto Henry V. PQ, XI (1932), 39–56. Supports the theory that the quarto represents a stage abridgment.

STOLL, E. E. Henry V. Poets and playwrights: Shakespeare, Jonson, Spenser, Milton. Minneapolis, 1930. Pp. 31-54.

SYKES, H. D. The authorship of The Taming of a Shrew, The Famous Victories of Henry V, and the additions to Marlowe's Faustus. Sidelights on Elizabethan drama. London, etc., 1924. Pp. 49-78. Thinks Samuel Rowley is the author.

HENRY THE EIGHTH

ALEXANDER, P. Conjectural history, or Shakespeare's Henry VIII. Essays and studies by members of the English Association, XVI (Oxford, 1931), 85-120. Pp. 100-119 argue against Fletcher's hand in the play.

FARNHAM, W. E. Colloquial contractions in Beaumont, Fletcher, Massinger, and Shakespeare as a test of authorship. PMLA, XXXI (1916), 326-58. Concludes that the non-Fletcherian portions of *Henry VIII* are by Shakespeare, not Massinger.

LAWRENCE, W. J. The stage directions in King Henry VIII. TLS, Dec. 18, 1930, p. 1085. See letters by R. C. Rhodes and P. Alexander, *TLS*, Jan. 1, 1931, p. 12.

MAXWELL, B. Fletcher and Henry the Eighth. Manly anniversary studies in language and literature. Chicago, 1923. Pp. 104-12. Argues that stylistic tests indicate that Fletcher, if he wrote some of the scenes, was revising another's work or was himself modified by a collaborator.

NICOLSON, MARJORIE H. The authorship of Henry the Eighth. PMLA, XXXVII (1922), 485-502. Argues that Shakespeare had planned a tragedy rather than a history, and that Fletcher inconsistently completed it in the new style of "oratory, and spectacles, and sentiment, and tears."

OLIPHANT, E. H. C. The plays of Beaumont and Fletcher: an attempt to determine their respective shares and the shares of others. New Haven and London, 1927. Pp. 302-16. Thinks Massinger revised the play.

—— The plays of Beaumont and Fletcher: some additional notes. PQ, IX (1930), 7-22. See pp. 12-13 for doubt as to Massinger's hand.

SPEDDING, J. On the several shares of Shakspere and Fletcher in the play of Henry VIII. New Shakspere Society transactions, ser. I, part i (1874), appendix, pp. 1-18. Reprinted from *Gentleman's Magazine*, Aug., 1850, pp. 115-23. The original ascription to Fletcher. See also *Transactions*, *ibid.*, pp. 18-24 for an independent study by Hickson and notes by Fleay and Furnivall.

SYKES, H. D. King Henry VIII. Sidelights on Shakespeare. Stratford-upon-Avon, 1919. Pp. 18-47. Thinks it is an early work of Massinger and Fletcher. See B. Maxwell's devastating review, *MP*, XXIII (1926), 365-72.

THORNDIKE, A. H. The influence of Beaumont and Fletcher on Shakspere. Worcester, 1901. See especially pp. 22-8, 35-44.

6. Trial Flights in Tragedy

TITUS ANDRONICUS

ADAMS, J. Q., ed. Shakespeare's Titus Andronicus: the first quarto: 1594. Reproduced in facsimile from the unique copy in the Folger Shakespeare Library. New York and London, 1936. With a valuable introduction.

BAKER, H. Induction to tragedy: a study in a development of form in Gorboduc, The Spanish Tragedy and Titus Andronicus. University (Louisiana), 1939. Attempts to minimize Senecan influence.

BOLTON, J. S. G. The authentic text of Titus Andronicus. PMLA, XLIV (1929), 765–88. Argues for the authority of Q_1. See also Bolton's supplementary notes, MLN, XLV (1930), 139–41. On the improvisations of the compositor of Q_2, who worked from a damaged copy of Q_1, see also R. B. McKerrow's independent study, "A Note on Titus Andronicus," Library, 4th ser., XV (1934), 49–53, and cf. Adams's facsimile ed., pp. 20–28.

—— Titus Andronicus: Shakespeare at thirty. SP, XXX (1933), 208–24. Thinks Shakespeare was carefully revising an older play.

CHAMBERS, E. K. The first illustration to Shakespeare. Library, 4th ser., V (1925), 326–30. Peacham's drawing and text. Cf. Adams's facsimile ed. of Q_1, pp. 31–40.

CLARK, ELEANOR G. Titus and Vespasian. MLN, XLI (1926), 523–7. Denies a connection between Titus Andronicus and tittus & vespacia.

COHN, A. Shakespeare in Germany. London, 1865. Pp. 156–235 give in parallel columns the German text and an English translation of the Tragædia von Tito Andronico.

CRAWFORD, C. The date and authenticity of Titus Andronicus. SJ, XXXVI (1900), 109–21. Thinks Shakespeare the sole author, and the play not earlier than 1593.

DIBELIUS, W. Zur stoffgeschichte des Titus Andronikus. SJ, XLVIII (1912), 1–12. Sets forth a Byzantine origin for Titus and Tamora.

FULLER, H. DE W. The sources of Titus Andronicus. PMLA, XVI (1901), 1–65. Concludes that Aran en Titus, a Dutch play by Jan Vos (1641), and the German Tragædia von Tito Andronico (in Englischen Comedien und Tragedien, 1620) are based on two separate English plays, which he supposes to be Henslowe's tittus & vespacia and titus & ondronicus, and that Shakespeare's Titus Andronicus is a rehash of both. The plots of the German and Dutch plays are summarized by Fuller in parallel columns with Shakespeare's plot. Fuller also considers the evidence of a program of a performance in 1699 of another German play about Titus Andronicus: Raache gegen Raache (Revenge versus Revenge). See G. P. Baker's supplementary article "'Tittus and Vespacia' and 'Titus and Ondronicus' in Henslowe's Diary," PLMA, XVI (1901), 66–76.

GRANGER, F. Shakespeare and the legend of Andronicus. TLS, April 1, 1920, p. 213. Suggests as Shakespeare's source a Byzantine account of Andronicus Comnenus. See R. W. Bond's sceptical comment, April 15, p. 239; and letters by Granger and J. Rose, April 29, p. 272; by Bond, May 6, p. 284; by Granger, May 13, pp. 302–3; and by Bond and H. Davey, May 27, p. 335.

GRAY, A. K. Shakespeare and Titus Andronicus. SP, XXV (1928), 295–311. Supports the argument that Shakespeare rewrote an old play, and gives parallels with *Venus and Adonis* and *Lucrece*.

GRAY, H. D. The authorship of Titus Andronicus. Flügel memorial volume. Leland Stanford Junior University publications, university ser., no. 21. Palo Alto, 1916. Pp. 114–26. Argues that Shakespeare was the original author and that "un-Shakespearean" passages are revisions by Greene and Peele. Attacked by [C. F.] T. Brooke, "Titus Andronicus and Shakespeare," *MLN*, XXXIV (1919), 32–6; and defended by Gray, "Titus Andronicus Once More," *ibid.*, pp. 214–20. Gray withdraws his theory in "Shakespeare's Share in Titus Andronicus," *PQ*, V (1926), 166–72.

PARROTT, T. M. Shakespeare's revision of Titus Andronicus. MLR, XIV (1919), 16–37. Argues that Shakespeare's work is confined to a superficial revision of an old play, and attempts to distinguish his share. See W. W. Greg's criticism, "Titus Andronicus," *ibid.*, pp. 322–3; and H. D. Gray's "The Titus Andronicus Problem," *SP*, XVII (1920), 126–31.

RHODES, R. C. Titus and Vespasian. TLS, April 17, 1924, p. 240. Asserts that it must have dealt with the destruction of Jerusalem. See letters by W. W. Greg, May 1, p. 269; by J. S. Smart, May 8, p. 286; by Greg, May 15, p. 304; by Rhodes, May 22, p. 322; by J. M. Robertson, May 29, p. 340; and by Smart, June 5, p. 356.

ROBERTSON, J. M. An introduction to the study of the Shakespeare canon. London, 1924. Denies Shakespeare's authorship of *Titus*. Cited here as an example of the extreme school of "disintegration." Like Robertson's work in general, ingenious but fantastic.

ROMEO AND JULIET

ALLEN, B. S. Tom Coryat and Juliet's balcony. PMLA, XLVIII (1933), 945–8. Argues that, since the Italian balcony was unknown in sixteenth-century England, Juliet appears at a window.

DAM, B. A. P. VAN. Did Shakespeare revise Romeo and Juliet? Anglia, LI (1927), 39–62. Attacks the revision theory.

DANIEL, P. A., ed. Romeus and Iuliet, Arthur Brooke: Rhomeo and Iulietta, William Painter. New Shakspere Society transactions, ser. 3, part i, (1875). Reprints, with a valuable introduction on sources, including a synopsis of Groto's play. Broke and Painter are also reprinted in *Shakespeare's Library*, ed. W. C. Hazlitt, I, 57–260, and the former in

Brooke's Romeus and Juliet, ed. J. J. Munro, Shakespeare classics, London 1908.

FULLER, H. DE W. Romeo and Juliette. MP, IV (1906), 75–120. Argues that the Dutch play of *Romeo en Juliette* (*c.* 1630) by Jacob Struijs was derived from the lost English play.

GRANVILLE-BARKER, H. Romeo and Juliet. Prefaces to Shakespeare. Second series. London, 1930. Pp. 1–66.

HJORT, GRETA. The good and bad quartos of Romeo and Juliet and Love's Labour's Lost. MLR, XXI (1926), 140–46. Attacks the theory of Wilson and Pollard.

HUBBARD, F. G., ed. The first quarto edition of Shakespeare's Romeo and Juliet. University of Wisconsin studies in language and literature, no. 19. Madison, 1924. Gives a modernized text of Q1 and makes an unconvincing attempt to show that this edition was no piracy.

JONAS, M., ed. Romeo and Juliet: a photographic reproduction of Luigi da Porto's prose version of Romeo and Giulietta dated 1535, being the original source. . . . With a literal translation into English from the Italian. Also a photographic reproduction of the 1539 edition. London, 1921.

LAW, R. A. On Shakespeare's changes of his source material in Romeo and Juliet. University of Texas studies in English, no. 9 (Austin, 1929), pp. 86–102.

MOORE, O. H. Bandello and Clizia. MLN, LII (1937), 38–44. Bolderi's influence on Bandello.

—— Shakespeare's deviations from Romeus and Juliet. PMLA, LII (1937), 68–74. Argues from Shakespeare's agreement "in at least four or five instances exclusively with Luigi da Porto" that he was not dependent on the Bandello-Boaistuau-Broke line of transmission. It may be so, but the deviations from Broke are such as would probably be at least considered by any dramatist handling this plot.

STOLL, E. E. Romeo and Juliet. Shakespeare's young lovers. London, New York, and Toronto, 1937. Pp. 1–44. "The emotional situation is justified . . . not by analysis and realism, but by stage management, by poetry, by the fitness of the situation in the world that the poet has created."

WILSON, J. D., AND POLLARD, A. W. The stolne and surreptitious Shakespearian texts: Romeo and Juliet, 1897. TLS, Aug. 14, 1919, p. 434. Argues that Q1 is an abridged version of Shakespeare's first revision of an older play, eked out by what a pirate could remember of a later version.

JULIUS CÆSAR

AYRES, H. M. Shakespeare's Julius Cæsar in the light of some other versions. PMLA, XXV (1910), 183–227. An important study, showing how Cæsar was endowed "with a strut" in pre-Shakespearean drama.

BROOKE, C. F. T., ed. Shakespeare's Plutarch. Shakespeare classics. London, 1909. Vol. I, containing the main sources of Julius Caesar.

BUSH, D. Julius Caesar and Elyot's Governour. MLN, LII (1937), 407–8. Suggests Elyot as a source of Cæsar's *hybris*.

DELIUS, N. Shakespeare's Julius Caesar und seine quellen im Plutarch. SJ, XVII (1882), 67–81. A scene-by-scene account.

GRANVILLE-BARKER, H. Julius Cæsar. Prefaces to Shakespeare. First series. London, 1927. Pp. 51–132.

MACCALLUM, M. W. Shakespeare's Roman plays and their background. London, 1910. Roman plays in the 16th century, pp. 1–72; Shakespeare's treatment of history, pp. 73–94; Plutarch, pp. 95–119; Amyot, pp. 119–41; North, pp. 141–67; *Julius Cæsar*, pp. 168–299, 628–30, 644–7.

MORSBACH, L. Shakespeares Cäsarbild. Studien zur englischen philologie, LXXXVIII. Halle, 1935. Thinks it is Cæsar's, not Brutus's play, and that Shakespeare was an admirer.

OLIPHANT, E. H. C. The plays of Beaumont and Fletcher: an attempt to determine their respective shares and the shares of others. New Haven and London, 1927. An exercise in disintegration. Thinks Shakespeare revised an old play, probably by Marlowe, and that parts of *Julius Cæsar* were afterwards altered by Beaumont. Unconvincing.

PARROTT, T. M. The academic tragedy of Caesar and Pompey. MLR, V (1910), 435–44. Includes a list of the plays on Julius Cæsar.

—— Marlowe, Beaumont, and Julius Caesar. MLN, XLIV (1929), 69–77. An able attack on Oliphant's theory.

ROBERTSON, J. M. The origination of Julius Cæsar. The Shakespeare canon [part I]. London, 1922. Pp. 66–154. This study, if I follow it aright, argues that Marlowe, under the stimulus of his association with Kyd, wrote a three-part play. Part 1 was revived by the Admiral's in 1594 as *Cæsar and Pompey*. In 1595 Part 2 was probably revised for them by Chapman, Drayton, and perhaps Heywood, as Part 2 of *Cæsar*. Part 3 was revised for them in 1602, as *Cæsar's Fall*, or *The Two Shapes*, by Drayton, Dekker, Middleton, Munday, and Webster. Part 1 was afterwards reworked by Chapman as *Cæsar and Pompey* [Parrott dates this play conjecturally in 1612–13]. Parts 2 and 3 were acquired by Shakespeare's company, and sometime after 1602 he revised Parts 2 and 3. "Either about 1607 or after Shakespeare's death" Jonson probably compressed Parts 2 and 3 into *Julius Cæsar*. "We may surmise" that Shakespeare originally presented Julius quite adequately; Jonson saw to it "that Cæsar was duly minimised." This fantastic hypothesis is cited here only as an example of the lengths to which disintegrators will go.

SHAW, G. B. Better than Shakespear. Preface. Three Plays for Puritans. London, 1900.

7. Best Comedies

A MIDSUMMER NIGHT'S DREAM

CHAMBERS, E. K. The occasion of A Midsummer Night's Dream. A book of homage to Shakespeare. Ed. I. Gollancz. London, 1916. Pp. 154–60. Cf. Chambers's *William Shakespeare*, I, 358–9. Inclines to the wedding of the Earl of Derby and Elizabeth Vere (Jan. 26, 1595) or that of Thomas Berkeley and Elizabeth Carey (Feb. 19, 1596).

LATHAM, M. W. The Elizabethan fairies: the fairies of folklore and the fairies of Shakespeare. New York, 1930.

LITTLEDALE, H. Folklore and superstitions: ghosts and fairies: witchcraft and devils. Shakespeare's England. Oxford, 1917. I, 516–46.

SIDGWICK, F. The sources and analogues of A Midsummer Night's Dream. Shakespeare [classics]. London, 1908.

SPENCER, H. A nice derangement: the irregular verse-lining in A Midsummer Night's Dream, act V, sc. i, ll. 1–84. MLR, XXV (1930), 23–9. Rejects Wilson's conclusion that the mislining indicates later expansion by Shakespeare, and suggests that (if we must have a theory) the mislined passages are likelier to be stage cuts. See Wilson's reply, *ibid.*, pp. 29–31, and my rejoinder, *ibid.*, XXXI (1936), 393–5.

THE MERCHANT OF VENICE

BASKERVILL, C. R. Bassanio as an ideal lover. Manly anniversary studies in language and literature. Chicago, 1923. Pp. 90–103.

CARDOZO, J. L. The background of Shakespeare's Merchant of Venice. E studies, XIV (1932), 177–86.

—— The contemporary Jew in Elizabethan drama. Amsterdam, 1925.

CLARKSON, P. S., AND WARREN, C. T. A comparative and critical analysis of Shakespeare's law. Daily record (Baltimore), April 20, 1937, p. 3. Includes an expert study of "law" in *The Merchant of Venice*.

DAM, B. A. P. VAN. The text of The Merchant of Venice. Neophil., XIII (1927), 33–51. Critical of Wilson's edition. Argues that Q_1 "was printed from Shakespeare's autograph . . . adapted for the stage."

DRAPER, J. W. Usury in The Merchant of Venice. MP, XXXIII (1935), 37–47.

FURNESS, H. H., ed. The merchant of Venice. New variorum ed. Philadelphia, 1888. See pp. 288–319 for sources in the ballad, *Il Pecorone*, the *Gesta Romanorum*, and Sylvain.

GOLLANCZ, I. Bits of timber: some observations on Shakespearian names — Shylock; Polonius; Malvolio. A book of homage to Shakespeare. Ed. I. Gollancz. London, 1916. Pp. 170–78.

GRANVILLE-BARKER, H. The merchant of Venice. Prefaces to Shakespeare. Second series. London, 1930. Pp. 67–110.

SISSON, C. J. A colony of Jews in Shakespeare's London. Essays and studies by members of the English Association, XXIII (Oxford, 1938), 38–51. Concludes they were not oppressed if they conformed politically and religiously.

OLL, E. E. The maidens of Shakespeare's prime. Shakespeare's young lovers. London, New York, and Toronto, 1937. Pp. 45–84. On Portia, Beatrice, Rosalind, and Viola.

— Shylock. Shakespeare studies. New York, 1927. Pp. 255–336. A sound, if somewhat doctrinaire, exposition of the anti-Romantic interpretation. Appeared originally in JEGP, X (1911), 236–79. See also Stoll's "Shakespeare's Jew," *Univ. of Toronto Quarterly*, VIII (1939), 139–54.

ALLEY, H. R. Shakespeare's portrayal of Shylock. Essays in dramatic literature: the Parrott presentation volume. Ed. H. Craig. Princeton, 1935. Pp. 213–42. Sceptical of the existence of Elizabethan anti-Semitism. Thinks Shylock a consistently drawn villain, not comic, though humanized.

OLF, L. Jews in Elizabethan England. Jewish Historical Society of England transactions, XI (1924–7), 1–91. Lists the Marranos or converted Jews in Elizabethan England. They were few.

RIGHT, CELESTE T. Some conventions regarding the usurer in Elizabethan literature. SP, XXXI (1934), 176–97.

MUCH ADO ABOUT NOTHING

ALDWIN, T. W. Shakespeare's jester: the dates of Much Ado and As You Like It. MLN, XXXIX (1924), 447–55. Relates the dates to Kempe's withdrawal from the Chamberlain's Men and his replacement by Armin.

ENNETT, M. L. Shakespeare's Much Ado and its possible Italian sources. University of Texas studies in English, no. 17 (Austin, 1937), pp. 52–74. Concludes that Shakespeare used neither Bandello nor Belleforest directly, that Harington is the chief source, and that nothing about this play suggests that Shakespeare could read Italian. The argument is weakened by misconceptions as to which episodes constitute the core of the plot; these are in Bandello, not Ariosto. Suggestions that Benedick and Beatrice originate in a note of Harington's recommending amiability in marriage, and that the original of Dogberry is Ariosto's knight-errant Rinaldo, are unconvincing.

RNESS, H. H., ed. Much ado about nothing. New variorum ed. Philadelphia, 1899. See pp. 296–326 for sources in Ariosto, Spenser, and Bandello.

AW, A. Is Shakespeare's Much Ado a revised earlier play? PMLA, L (1935), 715–38. A cogent refutation of Wilson's argument for rewriting, and an able indictment of several features of the New edition in general.

AGE, NADINE. My lady disdain. MLN, L (1935), 494–9. Beatrice is not antimatrimonial, but discriminating; not a "romantic dream," but the Renaissance "free" woman.

—— The public repudiation of Hero. PMLA, L (1935), 739–44. A defence
of the play and the characters "in the light of Elizabethan culture and
ideals."

AS YOU LIKE IT

CAMPBELL, O. J. Jaques. Huntington library bulletin, no. 8 (Cambridge
1935), pp. 71–102. Goes too far in ascribing to Shakespeare refinements
of characterization based on the physiological humors, but brilliantly
illuminating on the relation of the play to the current trend of
satire.

FINK, Z. S. Jaques and the malcontent traveller. PQ, XIV (1935), 237–52.
Rejects Stoll's view. Points to parallels between Jaques and the
melancholy returned-traveler of the '90's.

LODGE, T. Lodge's Rosalynde, being the original of Shakespeare's As You
Like It. Shakespeare classics. Ed. W. W. Greg. London, 1907.

SKEAT, W. W., ed. The tale of Gamelyn. 2nd ed., revised. Oxford, 1893.

STOLL, E. E. Jaques, and the antiquaries. MLN, LIV (1939), 79–85. Attacks
Campbell's article and the intrusion of "Elizabethan text book physi-
ology or psychology" in the interpretation of Shakespeare's characters

—— Shakspere, Marston, and the malcontent type. MP, III (1906), 281–303.
Dating Marston's The Malcontent 1600 (against the general opinion for
1604), argues that Jaques is a malcontent and that he shows Marston's influence.

THORNDIKE, A. H. The relation of As You Like It to Robin Hood plays.
J[E]GP, IV (1902), 59–69.

TWELFTH NIGHT

DRAPER, J. W. Olivia's household. PMLA, LXIX (1934), 797–806. Social
aspects of the play.

HARRISON, T. P., JR. Shakespeare and Montemayor's Diana. University of
Texas studies in English, no. 6. Austin, 1926. Pp. 103–15.

MUESCHKE, P., AND FLEISHER, JEANETTE. Jonsonian elements in the comic
underplot of Twelfth Night. PMLA, XLVIII (1933), 722–40. On Sir
Andrew and Malvolio.

RICHE, BARNABE. Apolonius and Silla. Reprinted by H. H. Furness, ed.
Twelfth Night (new variorum ed., Philadelphia, 1901), pp. 328–39.
Also ed. M. Luce (Shakespeare Classics), London and New York,
1912.

THE MERRY WIVES OF WINDSOR

BRUCE, J. D. Two notes on The Merry Wives of Windsor. MLR, VII (1912),
239–41. On the meaning of "garmombles."

CAMPBELL, O. J. The Italianate background of The Merry Wives of Windsor.
Essays and studies in English and comparative literature by members

of the English department of the University of Michigan (Ann Arbor, 1932), pp. 81–117. Accepts the revision theory, but argues that Falstaff was originally the pedant of Italian comedy.

CROFTS, J. Shakespeare and the post horses: a new study of the Merry Wives of Windsor. Bristol (England), 1937. An elaborate but unconvincing attempt to reconstruct the history of the play.

GREG, W. W., ed. Shakespeare's Merry Wives of Windsor, 1602. Oxford, 1910. A type facsimile of the Bad quarto, with a bibliographical introduction.

HOTSON, L. Shakespeare versus Shallow. Boston, 1931. Reports the discovery of Shakespeare's trouble with Wayte, thinks Gardiner and Wayte caricatured in Shallow and Slender, and argues for early in 1597 as the date of *The Merry Wives*. See reviews: *TLS*, Oct. 1, 1931, p. 749, and comment by T. W. Baldwin, *ibid.*, Oct. 8, 1931, p. 778; and S. A. Tannenbaum, *New York Times*, Oct. 18, 1931, sect. 3, p. 2.

KLARWILL, V. VON. Queen Elizabeth and some foreigners, being a series of hitherto unpublished letters from the archives of the Hapsburg family. London, 1928. See pp. 357–423 for Breuning's account of his mission.

LEA, KATHLEEN M. Italian popular comedy. Oxford, 1934. See II, 431–3, for plot parallels to *The Merry Wives* in the *commedia dell' arte*.

POLLARD, A. W., AND WILSON, J. D. The stolne and surreptitious Shakespearian texts: The Merry Wives of Windsor. TLS, Aug. 7, 1919, p. 420. Sets forth a theory of revision, which is expanded and modified in Wilson's New ed.

RADOFF, M. L. Influence of the French farce in Henry V and The Merry Wives. MLN, XLVIII (1933), 427–35. The Latin examination in *Merry Wives* and the French lesson in *Henry V* may be imitations.

RYE, W. B. England as seen by foreigners in the days of Elizabeth and James the first: comprising translations of the journals of the two dukes of Wirtemberg in 1592 and 1610, both illustrative of Shakespeare. London, 1865.

SCHÜCKING, L. L. The fairy scene in The Merry Wives in folio and quarto. MLR, XIX (1924), 338–40. On the contradiction concerning the impersonator of the fairy queen.

8. *Realistic Comedies*

TROILUS AND CRESSIDA

ADAMS, J. Q. Timon of Athens and the irregularities in the first folio. JEGP, VII (1907), 53–63. A bibliographical account of the temporary withdrawal of *Troilus* and the substitution of *Timon*. Cf. E. E. Willoughby, *The Printing of the First Folio*, pp. 46–50.

ALEXANDER, P. Troilus and Cressida, 1609. Library, 4th ser., IX (1928),

267–86. Concludes that the Folio text was set up from a quarto whic
had been corrected from a manuscript giving an earlier draft.

[ARMIN, ROBERT.] The fool and the ice: a brief account of a singular adven
ture. Ed. J. O. Halliwell-Phillipps. London, 1883. From Armin's Foo
Vpon Foole, or Six Sortes of Sottes (1600), according to the text of *A Ne
of Ninnies*, 1608. The editor thinks that "The fool slides o'er the ic
that you should break" (*Troilus*, III, iii, 215) refers to an inciden
witnessed by Armin prior to joining the Lord Chamberlain's Men
It seems not unlikely, but there is no evidence here for the date of th
play. Armin's story may also be found in *E Studien*, XXX (1902
47–8, and in Halliwell-Phillipps's *Outlines*, I, 321–3.

BARKER, E. A Shakespeare discovery. Spectator, April 2, 1937, pp. 615–
Thinks Ulysses's speech on Degree is derived from the first two chapte
of Sir Thomas Elyot's *The Gouernour*. Barker asserts, as a professor o
the subject, that I, iii "contains more political science . . . than I hav
ever taught or am likely to teach."

BOYLE, R. Troilus and Cressida. E studien, XXX (1902), 21–59. Thinks th
love story is early and the "Ulysses story" later work of Shakespeare'
and that Marston added the "Hector story."

BROOKE, [C. F.] T. Shakespeare's study in culture and anarchy. Yale review
XVII (1928), 571–7. Thinks *Troilus and Cressida* a subtle study of th
effect of environment on character and Shakespeare's "most defini
realization of the social forces operative . . . at the end of Quee
Elizabeth's reign."

CAMPBELL, O. J. Comicall satyre and Shakespeare's Troilus and Cressid
San Marino, 1938. See pp. 185–234 for a dubious interpretation of th
play as a "comicall satyre," like Jonson's *Every Man Out, Cynthi.
Revels*, and *Poetaster*.

GORDON, R. K., ed. The story of Troilus, as told by Benoît de Sainte-Maur
Giovanni Boccaccio, (translated into English prose), Geoffrey Chauce
and Robert Henryson. London, 1934.

GRIFFIN, N. E. Un-Homeric elements in the story of Troy. JEGP, VII (1907
32–52.

GUHA, P. K. The problem of Shakespeare's Troilus and Cressida. Dac
University bulletin, IX (London, Bombay, etc., 1926), 23–41. Argue
that there is no lack of unity, since both the love and the camp plo
illustrate "the unmanning influence of the woman on the man."

HARRISON, G. B. Shakespeare's topical significances: II. The earl of Esse
TLS, Nov. 20, 1930, p. 974. Thinks that Ulysses's speech on Degre
(III, iii, 145–90) would remind an audience of Essex, that the sulk
Achilles satirizes him, and that the play was therefore "performe
privately before an anti-Essex audience, either in the summer of 159
or else about two years later when Essex and his followers were brewir
treason."

HENDERSON, W. B. D. Shakespeare's Troilus and Cressida yet deeper in i tradition. Essays in dramatic literature: the Parrott presentation volume. Ed. H. Craig. Princeton, 1935. Pp. 127–56. Thinks Lydgate was the chief source of humanist ideas and that the play sets forth a "philosophy of values.",Thersites is derived from Homer; but Armin joins the company, and Erasmus's "wise fool" enters Shakespeare's thinking.

HENRYSON, R. The testament of Cresseid. The poems of Robert Henryson. Ed. G. G. Smith. Scottish text society. Edinburgh and London, 1906–14. III, 3–24.

LAWRENCE, W. W. Shakespeare's problem comedies. New York, 1931. Pp. 1–31, 122–73.

ROLLINS, H. E. The Troilus-Cressida story from Chaucer to Shakespeare. PMLA, XXXII (1917), 383–429.

STEIN, ELIZABETH. Caxton's Recuyell and Shakespeare's Troilus. MLN, XLV (1930), 144–6. Thinks Shakespeare must have used Caxton.

TANNENBAUM, S. A. A critique of the text of Troilus and Cressida. SAB, IX (1934), 55–74, 125–44, 198–214. Concludes that "Shakspere's manuscript (A), in a crude state, disfigured . . . was copied by a scribe (B) who added some stage-directions of his own; subsequently Shakspere revised his manuscript (A), and then another scribe (C) made another copy, adding his own stage-directions and making his own mistakes." B's version became the "copy" for Q, and C's for F.

TATLOCK, J. S. P. The siege of Troy in Elizabethan literature, especially in Shakespeare and Heywood. PMLA, XXX (1915), 673–770. Thinks Shakespeare revised, with little interest in his work, an older play, which Heywood also used for his Iron Age. (General opinion now regards Heywood's play as later and indebted to Shakespeare's.)

TAYLOR, G. C. Shakespeare's attitude toward love and honor in Troilus and Cressida. PMLA, XLV (1930), 781–6. Thinks the play cynical, but insists that there is much realism in the romantic comedies, too.

ULRICI, H. Ist Troilus und Cressida comedy oder tragedy oder history? SJ, IX (1874), 26–40. Concludes it is a comedy.

YOUNG, K. The origin and development of the story of Troilus and Criseyde. Chaucer Society. London, 1908.

ALL'S WELL THAT ENDS WELL

BOYLE, R. All's Well that Ends Well and Love's Labour's Won. E studien, XIV (1890), 408–21. Thinks All's Well a revision of Love's Labour's Won, the rhymed passages and some of the prose being survivals.

LAWRENCE, W. W. Shakespeare's problem comedies. New York, 1931. Pp. 32–77.

PAINTER, WILLIAM. The palace of pleasure. Ed. J. Jacobs. London, 1890. See I, 171–9, for the 38th story, "Giletta of Narbon." Also reprinted in W. C. Hazlitt, Shakespeare's Library, III, 140–51.

MEASURE FOR MEASURE

BUDD, F. E. Material for a study of the sources of Shakespeare's Measure for Measure. Revue de littérature comparée, XI (1931), 711–36. Lists the various versions of the story, with summaries, and notes that the treatment, especially in the plays, tends to avoid a tragic ending.

—— Rouillet's Philanira and Whetstone's Promos and Cassandra. RES, VI (1930), 31–48. Thinks Whetstone used this French play as well as Cinthio.

CHAMBERS, R. W. The Jacobean Shakespeare and Measure for Measure. Annual Shakespeare lecture of the British Academy. London, 1937. Denies the play is evidence of disillusionment.

DURHAM, W. H. Measure for Measure as a measure for critics. Essays in criticism. By members of the department of English, University of California. First series. Berkeley, 1929. Pp. 111–32. Reviews the critical opinions.

FAIRCHILD, H. N. The two Angelo's. SAB, VI (1931), 53–9. Thinks the Angelo of Acts I and II is a harsh precisian tempted beyond endurance and a development of Whetstone's magistrate, while in the last three acts we have a smooth rascal, "the result of the introduction of the Mariana plot."

K., L. L. The plot of Measure for Measure. NQ, July 29, 1893, pp. 83–4. On Cinthio's possible source in real life.

LAWRENCE, W. W. Shakespeare's problem comedies. New York, 1931. Pp. 78–121.

SUDDARD, SARAH J. MARY. Measure for Measure as a clue to Shakespeare's attitude towards puritanism. Keats, Shelley, and Shakespeare: studies and essays in English literature. Cambridge (England), 1912. Pp. 136–52.

WHETSTONE, GEORGE. Promos and Cassandra. Ed. J. S. Farmer. Tudor facsimile texts. London, 1910.

WILSON, R. H. The Mariana plot of Measure for Measure. PQ, IX (1930), 341–50. Thinks it a late insertion.

9. Four Great Tragedies

HAMLET

BOWERS, F. T. The audience and the revenger of Elizabethan tragedy. SP, XXXI (1934), 160–75.

CORBIN, J. The Elizabethan Hamlet: a study of the sources, and of Shakspere's environment, to show that the mad scenes had a comic aspect now ignored. London, 1895.

CREIZENACH, W., ed. Tragoedia der bestrafe brudermord, oder: prinz Hamlet aus Dännemark. Deutsche national-literatur, XXIII (Die schauspiele der englischen komödianten, Berlin and Stuttgart, n.d.), 147–86. The play is translated in the New Variorum *Hamlet*, II, 121–42; and, in parallel columns with the German text, in A. Cohn's *Shakespeare in Germany*, pp. 236–303.

GOLLANCZ, I., ed. The sources of Hamlet. Shakespeare classics. London, 1926. Belleforest's version is given with the English translation of 1608 on pp. 164–311.

GRANVILLE-BARKER, H. Prefaces to Shakespeare. Third series: Hamlet. London, 1937.

GRAY, H. D. The reconstruction of a lost play. PQ, VII (1928), 254–74.

GUTTMAN, SELMA. The fencing bout in Hamlet. SAB, XIV (1939), 86–100.

HART, A. H. The vocabulary of the first quarto of Hamlet. RES, XII (1936), 18–30. Supports the Bad-quarto hypothesis.

JONES, H. M. The king in Hamlet. University of Texas bulletin, comparative literature series, no. 1. Austin, 1921 [dated 1918].

KIRSCHBAUM, L. The date of Shakespeare's Hamlet. SP, XXXIV (1937), 168–75. Argues that we can not depend on Harvey's marginalia, that the play could not have been completely written before 1601, and that it was produced before 1602.

LAVATER, LEWES. Of ghostes and spirites walking by nyght. Ed. J. D. Wilson and May Yardley. Oxford, 1929. [First ed. 1572.] The standard Protestant treatise. Valuable for the demonological background of the play. An appendix treats the Catholic position.

LAWRENCE, W. W. Hamlet and the mouse-trap. PMLA, LIV (1939), 709–35. Critical of Wilson's views.

LEWIS, C. M. The genesis of Hamlet. New York, 1907. "Kyd's Hamlet does most of the deeds . . . and Shakespeare's Hamlet thinks most of the thoughts."

MALONE, K. Etymologies for Hamlet. RES, III (1927), 257–71. The origin of the name.

—— The literary history of Hamlet: I the early tradition. Anglistische forschungen, heft 59. Heidelberg, 1923.

MCGINN, D. J. A new date for Antonio's Revenge. PMLA, LIII (1938), 129–37. Argues that Shakespeare, not Marston, initiated the revived vogue of revenge tragedy.

PARROTT, T. M., AND CRAIG, H., eds. The tragedy of Hamlet, a critical edition of the second quarto, 1604, with introduction and notes. Princeton, 1938. See review by W. W. Greg, RES, XV (1939), 208–13.

PYLES, T. Rejected Q_2 readings in the New Shakespeare Hamlet. ELH, IV (1937), 114–46. Supports the correctness of Q_2 and criticizes Wilson's departures from it.

RAMELLO, G. Studi sugli apocrifi Shakespeariani: the tragicall historie of Hamlet prince of Denmarke, 1603. Turin, 1930. Thinks Q_1 and Q_2 are derived from the same version.

RAVEN, A. A. A Hamlet bibliography and reference guide 1877–1935. Chicago, 1936.

SHAKESPEARE'S HAMLET: the first quarto 1603: reproduced in facsimile from the copy in the Henry E. Huntington Library. Cambridge, 1931.

SPENCER, H. Seventeenth-century cuts in Hamlet's soliloquies. RES, IX (1933), 257–65.

STOLL, E. E. Hamlet. Art and artifice in Shakespeare. Cambridge (England), 1933. Pp. 90–137.

—— Hamlet: an historical and comparative study. Minneapolis, 1919. Important.

—— Hamlet and The Spanish Tragedy: quartos I and II: a protest. MP, XXXV (1937), 31–46. Thinks *The Spanish Tragedie* modeled on the *Ur-Hamlet*. Argues that Q_1 rests in part on the latter.

STONE, G. W., JR. Garrick's long lost alteration of Hamlet. PMLA, XLIX (1934), 890–921. Concludes that this version is better than it has been painted. Compares the cuts with those of earlier stage versions. Reprints Garrick's fifth act.

THORNDIKE, A. H. The relations of Hamlet to contemporary revenge plays. PMLA, XVII (1902), 125–220.

WALDOCK, A. J. A. Hamlet: a study in critical method. Cambridge (England), 1931. A useful review.

WILSON, J. D. The manuscript of Shakespeare's Hamlet and the problems of its transmission. Cambridge (England), 1934. 2 vols. Inconsistent in applying the bibliographical method, but valuable. A sounder contribution than the author's edition of the play or his volume of commentary.

—— What happens in Hamlet. Second ed. Cambridge (England) and New York, 1937. More ingenious than cogent.

OTHELLO

BENTLY, G. E. The diary of a Caroline theatergoer. MP, XXXV (1937), 61–72. Lists a performance of *Othello* in 1635.

GIRALDI, G. B., (CINTHIO). Hecatommithi. Venice, 1566. Deca terza, novella VII. Reprinted, with translation, in the New Variorum *Othello*, pp. 376–89.

HART, A. The date of Othello. TLS, Oct. 10, 1935, p. 631. Cites possible echoes of *Othello* in the Bad *Hamlet* quarto and concludes the former was written not later than 1602.

RYMER, THOMAS. A short view of tragedy; It's Original, Excellency, and Corruption. With some reflections on Shakespear, and other practitioners for the stage. London, 1693. See pp. 86–146 for the famous attack on *Othello*.

STOLL, E. E. Othello. Art and Artifice in Shakespeare. Cambridge (England), 1933. Pp. 6–55. See also pp. 56–76.

—— Othello: an historical and comparative study. Minneapolis, 1915. Important.

TILLOTSON, G. Othello and The Alchemist at Oxford in 1610. TLS, July 20,

1933, p. 494. The letter which mentions these performances indicates that Desdemona was movingly played.

KING LEAR

ATKINSON, DOROTHY F. King Lear — another contemporary account. ELH, III (1936), 63–6. Brings forward Gerard Legh's *The Accedens of Armory* as a possible source.

DAM, B. A. P. VAN. The text of Shakespeare's Lear. Louvain, 1935. Argues for the superiority of Q_1, and attacks the theories of Miss Doran, Chambers, and Greg. A stimulating study, weakened by the author's fixed idea that English blank verse lacks flexibility. See Miss Doran's review, MP, XXXIV (1937), 430–3.

DORAN, MADELEINE. Elements in the composition of King Lear. SP, XXX (1933), 34–58.

—— The quarto of King Lear and Bright's shorthand. MP, XXXIII (1935), 139–57. A convincing argument against the shorthand theory as far as Bright's system is concerned. There were, however, other systems.

—— The text of King Lear. Palo Alto and London, 1931.

GRANVILLE-BARKER, H. King Lear. Prefaces to Shakespeare. First series. London, 1927. Pp. 133–231.

GREG, W. W. The function of bibliography in literary criticism illustrated in a study of the text of King Lear. Neophil., XVIII (1933), 241–62. Defends the theory of a shorthand origin of Q_1. Incidentally an admirable introduction to the bibliographical method of textual criticism.

—— King Lear — mislineation and stenography. Library, 4th ser., XVII (1936), 172–83. Reiterates the argument for a shorthand origin of Q_1.

LAW, R. A. On the date of King Lear. PMLA, XXI (1906), 462–77. Argues for a date earlier than May, 1605.

LEE, s.[L.], ed. The chronicle history of king Leir: the original of Shakespeare's King Lear. Shakespeare classics. London, 1909.

PERETT, W. The story of King Lear from Geoffrey of Monmouth to Shakespeare. Berlin, 1904.

PERKINSON, R. H. "Is this the promis'd end?" E Studien, LXXIII (1939), 202–11. "Whatever inevitability the conclusion possesses is the result of Shakespeare's art."

SYKES, H. D. The pre-Shakespearean King Leir. Sidelights on Shakespeare. Stratford-upon-Avon, 1919. Pp. 126–42. Attempts to prove Peele's authorship.

MACBETH

CHAMBERS, D. L. The metre of Macbeth: its relation to Shakespeare's earlier and later work. Princeton, 1903.

KITTREDGE, G. L. Witchcraft in old and New England. Cambridge, 1929.

KRÖGER, E. Die sage von Macbeth bis zu Shakespere. Palaestra, XXXIX. Berlin, 1904.

STOLL, E. E. Macbeth. Art and artifice in Shakespeare. Cambridge (England), 1933. Pp. 77–89.

10. Last Tragedies

ANTONY AND CLEOPATRA

BROOKE, C. F. T., ed. Shakespeare's Plutarch. Shakespeare classics. London, 1909. Vol. II, containing the main sources of Antony & Cleopatra and of Coriolanus.

GRANVILLE-BARKER, H. Antony and Cleopatra. Prefaces to Shakespeare. Second series. London, 1930. Pp. 111–233.

MACCALLUM, M. W. Shakespeare's Roman plays and their background. London, 1910. On *Antony and Cleopatra*, pp. 300–453, 648–56. For an analysis of the earlier portion of this book, on general topics, see above, under "6. Trial Flights in Tragedy," "Julius Cæsar."

SCHÜTZE, J. Daniels Cleopatra und Shakespeare. E studien, LXXI (1936), 58–72. Argues that Daniel's changes do not alter the essentially academic nature of his play, that all may be accounted for as the fruit of Daniel's rereading of Plutarch, that they are not indicative of Shakespeare's influence, and that they do not provide evidence for dating Shakespeare's play.

SHAW, G. B. Better than Shakespear. Preface [to his *Caesar and Cleopatra*]. Three Plays for Puritans. London, 1900. Objects "to making sexual infatuation a tragic theme."

STOLL, E. E. Cleopatra. Poets and Playwrights. Minneapolis, 1930. Pp. 1–30. A cogent defence of the character against Schücking's charge of inconsistency.

STONE, G. W., JR. Garrick's presentation of Antony and Cleopatra. RES XIII (1937), 20–38.

CORIOLANUS

BRADLEY, A. C. Coriolanus. Proceedings of the British Academy, 1911–1912 (London, 1912), pp. 457–73. Interpretive notes. Reprinted in Bradley's A Miscellany (London, 1929), pp. 73–104.

BROOKE, C. F. T., ed. Shakespeare's Plutarch. Shakespeare classics. London, 1909. Vol. II, containing the main sources of Antony & Cleopatra and of Coriolanus.

MACCALLUM, M. W. Shakespeare's Roman plays and their background. London, 1910. On *Coriolanus*, pp. 454–627, 631–43, 657–9. For analysis of earlier portions on general topics, see above, under "6. Trial Flights in Tragedy," "Julius Cæsar."

TIMON OF ATHENS

ADAMS, J. Q. Timon of Athens and the irregularities in the first folio. JEGP VII (1907), 53–63. Concludes that they have no bearing on the problem of authorship. See also listing of this article under "8. Realistic Comedies": "Troilus and Cressida."

—— The Timon plays. JEGP, IX (1910), 506-24. Beaumont and Fletcher's moral interlude *The Triumph of Time*, the ms. *Timon*, and Shakespeare's tragedy.

BOND, R. W. Lucian and Boiardo in Timon of Athens. MLR, XXVI (1931), 52-68. Thinks Shakespeare more indebted to Lucian than to Plutarch and that he drew heavily on Boiardo's *Timone*. Reprinted in *Studia Otiosa: Some Attempts at Criticism* (London, 1938), pp. 75-105.

BRADLEY, A. C. King Lear and Timon of Athens. Shakespearean tragedy. Second ed. London, 1905. Pp. 443-5, 477-80. Indicates points of resemblance. Dates *Timon* between *King Lear* and *Macbeth*.

DELIUS, N. Ueber Shakespeare's Timon of Athens. SJ, II (1867), 335-61. Thinks Shakespeare revised an old play.

DRAPER, J. W. The theme of Timon of Athens. MLR, XXIX (1934), 20-31. Thinks it is usury.

FLEAY, F. J. On the authorship of Timon of Athens. New Shakspere Society's transactions, ser. 1, no. 1 (1874), pp. 130-51. Thinks the "non-Shakespearean" portions are later than the rest.

HAZLITT, W. C., ed. Timon [the ms. comedy]. Shakespeare's Library. London, 1875. VI, 389-484.

PARROTT, T. M. The problem of Timon of Athens. Shakespeare Association papers, no. 10. London, 1923. Thinks a third writer revised an unfinished play by Shakespeare to which Chapman had made additions.

ROBERTSON, J. M. Shakespeare and Chapman: a thesis of Chapman's authorship of A Lover's Complaint and his origination of Timon of Athens, with indications of further problems. London, 1917. Thinks Shakespeare revised Chapman. See, especially, pp. 123-81.

SYKES, H. D. The problem of Timon of Athens. Sidelights on Elizabethan drama. London, 1924. Pp. 1-48. Thinks Shakespeare revised a play by Middleton and Day.

WECTER, D. Shakespeare's purpose in Timon of Athens. PMLA, XLIII (1928), 701-21. Thinks the original author was Shakespeare but that the play was partly rewritten by someone else. Believes Shakespeare's real theme was the Earl of Essex.

WENDLANDT, W. Shakespeare's Timon von Athen. SJ, XXIII (1888), 107-92. Argues that Shakespeare was the sole author.

WILLIAMS, S. T. Some versions of Timon of Athens on the stage. MP, XVIII (1920), 269-85.

WRIGHT, E. H. The authorship of Timon of Athens. Columbia University studies in English. New York, 1910. A careful study, arguing that unfinished work by Shakespeare was taken in hand by some inferior writer.

11. Dramatic Romances

PERICLES

BAKER, H. T. The relation of Shakspere's Pericles to George Wilkins's novel The Painfull Adventures of Pericles, Prince of Tyre. PMLA, XXIII (1908), 100–18. Thinks Shakespeare revised Wilkins, whose source was two old plays, about Pericles and about Marina. Attacks Fleay's theory.

BOYLE, R. Pericles. E studien, V (1882), 363–9. Thinks Shakespeare, Wilkins, and William Rowley wrote portions.

DELIUS, N. Ueber Shakespeare's Pericles, Prince of Tyre. SJ, III (1868), 175–204. Thinks Shakespeare revised George Wilkins.

FLEAY, H. G. On the play of Pericles. New Shakspere Society's transactions, ser. 1, no. 1 (1874), pp. 195–209. Concludes that Shakespeare originally dramatized the Marina story, as it appears in the last three acts, without Gower and the brothel scenes, but left his play unfinished, the rest being supplied by Wilkins and Rowley.

GARRETT, R. M. Gower in Pericles. SJ, XLVIII (1912), 13–20. Argues that the choruses are Shakespeare's and constitute a careful experiment.

GRAVES, T. S. On the date and significance of Pericles. MP, XIII (1915), 545–56. Offers an ingenious but unconvincing argument for a performance late in 1606 or early in 1607, with a diplomatic object.

GRAY, H. D. Heywood's Pericles, revised by Shakespeare. PMLA, XL (1925), 507–29. Thinks Heywood, not Wilkins, wrote Acts I and II, the choruses, the brothel scenes, and the "substratum" of the scenes Shakespeare revised.

HASTINGS, W. T. Exit George Wilkins? SAB, XI (1936), 67–83. Concludes that prior to Twine's version of 1607 Shakespeare revised a complete earlier play, not by Wilkins, whose novel was "faked up mainly" from Twine in hope of profiting from public interest in the play.

—— Shakspere's part in Pericles. SAB, XIV (1939), 67–85. An argument for Shakespeare's revision of an earlier play, and an analysis of his contributions.

HAZLITT, W. C., ed. Shakespeare's library. London, 1875. IV, 179–392. Reprints Gower, Twine, and Plutarch's "Pericles."

LEE, S.[L.], ed. Shakespeares Pericles. Oxford, 1905. A collotype facsimile, with introduction.

SMYTH, A. H. Shakespeare's Pericles and Apollonius of Tyre: a study in comparative literature. Philadelphia, 1898. An account of the various versions of the romance. An appendix reprints that of the *Gesta Romanorum*.

SPIKER, SINA. George Wilkins and the authorship of Pericles. SP, XXX (1933), 551–70. Rejects Wilkins's authorship. Holds that his novel follows the play.

ʏKES, H. G. Wilkins and Shakespeare's Pericles, Prince of Tyre. Sidelights on Shakespeare. Stratford-upon-Avon, 1919. Pp. 143–203. Argues that Wilkins's novel rests on the play, which he himself had drafted, the choruses and Acts I and II remaining as he'wrote them, while the other acts were hastily revised by Shakespeare.

ʜOMAS, D. L. On the play Pericles. E studien, XXXIX (1908), 210–39. Rejects Wilkins's authorship, but thinks parts of the play are by an earlier hand than Shakespeare's, possibly Thomas Heywood's.

CYMBELINE

ʀANVILLE-BARKER, H. Cymbeline. Prefaces to Shakespeare. Second series. London, 1930. Pp. 234–345.

ʜAZLITT, W. C., ed. Shakespeare's library. London, 1875. II, 177–210. Reprints sources in Boccaccio and Holinshed. See also the New Variorum Cymbeline, pp. 455–81, for Boccaccio and notes on other versions.

ʜNIGHT, G. W. The vision of Jupiter in Cymbeline. TLS, Nov. 21, 1936, p. 958. Argues that Shakespeare wrote it.

ʟAWRENCE, W. W. Shakespeare's problem comedies. New York, 1931. Pp. 174–205. Argues that Posthumus is better than the impression he makes, and that the play mixes the genres of romance and "problem" comedy. Originally published as "The Wager in Cymbeline," PMLA, XXXV (1920), 391–431.

ʜCKEITHAN, D. M. The debt to Shakespeare in the Beaumont-and-Fletcher plays. Austin, 1938. Concludes that Shakespeare led the way in the dramatic romances.

ʜE RARE TRIUMPHS OF LOVE AND FORTUNE. London, 1589. Reprinted in R. Dodsley's Old Plays (ed. W. C. Hazlitt, 1874), VI, 143–243.

ʜAW, [G.] B. Cymbeline refinished: a variation. London mercury and bookman, XXXVII (1938), 373–89. Shaw's new fifth act, with a critical foreword.

ʜORNDIKE, A. H. The influence of Beaumont and Fletcher on Shakspere. Worcester (Massachusetts), 1901. Dates Philaster before Cymbeline, and argues that in his dramatic romances Shakespeare is imitating Beaumont and Fletcher. This theory is losing ground.

THE WINTER'S TALE

ʜAIRCHILD, A. H. R. The Hermione statue. Shakespeare and the arts of design. University of Missouri studies, vol. XII, no. 1. Columbia, 1937. Pp. 71–6.

ʜREENE, ROBERT. Greene's Pandosto, or Dorastus and Fawnia, being the original of Shakespeare's Winter's Tale. Shakespeare classics. Ed. P. G. Thomas. London, 1907.

ʟANCASTER, H. C. Hermione's statue. SP, XXIX (1932), 233–8. Finds closest parallels to the statue motif in seventeenth-century French plays, which may have been influenced by the same story Shakespeare knew.

TANNENBAUM, S. A. Ralph Crane and The Winter's Tale. Shaksperian scraps and other Elizabethan fragments. New York, 1933. Pp. 75–86. Concludes that the compositor's copy may have been Shakespeare's manuscript.

—— Textual and other notes on The Winter's Tale. PQ, VII (1928), 358–67.

TAYLOR, G. C. Hermione's statue again (Shakspere's return to Bandello). SAB, XIII (1938), 82–6. Thinks *Much Ado about Nothing* and its source in Bandello contain the essential features of the statue coming to life.

THE TEMPEST

CAWLEY, R. R. Shakspere's use of the voyagers in The Tempest. PMLA, XLI (1926), 688–726. See also Cawley's *The Voyagers and Elizabethan Drama*, Boston and London, 1938.

CHAMBERS, E. K. The integrity of The Tempest. RES, I (1925), 129–50. Critical of Wilson's theories of revision.

COHN, A. Shakespeare in Germany in the sixteenth and seventeenth centuries. London, 1865. Pp. xviii–lxxi, 4–75. On Ayrer's *Die Schöne Sidea*, with text.

GRAY, H. D. Some indications that The Tempest was revised. SP, XVIII (1921), 129–40.

—— The sources of The Tempest. MLN, XXXV (1920), 321–30. Thinks they are certain Italian scenarios.

LAWRENCE, W. J. The masque in The Tempest. Fortnightly review, new ser., CVII (June, 1920), 941–6. Thinks it was interpolated for a court performance immediately after the betrothal of the Princess Elizabeth.

LEA, KATHLEEN M. Italian popular comedy. Oxford, 1934. See II, 443–53 for possible connections with the *commedia dell'arte*.

STOLL, E. E. The Tempest. PMLA, XLVII (1932), 699–726. Denies the existence of "any allegory, or symbolism, or even 'veiled biography.'"

TANNENBAUM, S. A. How not to edit Shakspere. PQ, X (1931), 97–137. Consists chiefly of notes on *The Tempest*.

WILSON, J. D. The meaning of The Tempest. Newcastle upon Tyne, 1936. Defends the play against Lytton Strachey's charge ("Shakespeare's Final Period," in *Books and Characters*) that it is the fruit of Shakespeare's boredom. Thinks the "conversion" of Prospero shows that Shakespeare was at the end "no prophet upon the heights, but a penitent on his knees."

THE TWO NOBLE KINSMEN

BOYLE, R. On Massinger and The Two Noble Kinsmen. New Shakspere Society transactions, ser. I, no. 9 (London, 1884), 371–99. Argues for Massinger's authorship of the non-Fletcherian portions.

BRADLEY, A. C. Scene-endings in Shakespeare and in The Two Noble Kinsmen. In: A miscellany. London, 1929. Pp. 218–24. Supports Shakespeare's authorship of the non-Fletcherian portions.

BROOKE, C. F. T. The Shakespeare apocrypha. Oxford, 1918. Pp. xl–xlv incline to Massinger's authorship of the non-Fletcherian portions. Pp. 307–48 reprint the play. Pp. 432–5 contain notes.

CRUICKSHANK, A. H. Massinger and The Two Noble Kinsmen. Oxford, 1922. Ascribes the play to Fletcher, Shakespeare, and some hack. Denies Massinger's authorship. Thinks Shakespeare's was confined to II, i; IV, iii; and possibly "much of Act V."

—— Philip Massinger. Oxford, 1920. Pp. 92–104. Rejects Massinger as a collaborator.

FARNHAM, W. E. Colloquial contractions in Beaumont, Fletcher, Massinger, and Shakespeare as a test of authorship. PMLA, XXXI (1916), 326–58. Concludes (on pp. 352–7) that the non-Fletcherian passages of TNK are by Shakespeare, not Massinger or Beaumont.

GRAY, H. D. Beaumont and The Two Noble Kinsmen. PQ, II (1923), 112–31. Offers a complicated theory of authorship.

HART, A. Shakespeare and the vocabulary of The Two Noble Kinsmen. Shakespeare and the homilies. Melbourne, etc., 1934. Pp. 242–56. Concludes that Shakespeare wrote Act I; Act III, Scene i; and all of Act V except Scene ii.

HICKSON, S. The shares of Shakespeare and Fletcher in The Two Noble Kinsmen. New Shakspere Society's transactions, ser. I, no. 2 (London, 1874), appendix, pp. 25*–65* [sic]. With notes by Fleay and Furnivall.

LAWRENCE, W. J. New light on The Two Noble Kinsmen. TLS, July 14, 1921, p. 450. Thinks Fletcher was the sole original author and that Massinger partly revised the play for revival. See objections by A. H. Cruickshank and rejoinder by Lawrence: TLS, Aug. 11, p. 516; Aug. 25, p. 548; Sept. 1, p. 564; Sept. 8, p. 580.

LITTLEDALE, H., ed. The two noble kinsmen. New Shakspere Society, ser. II, no. 8. London, 1876. The standard edition, annotated.

OLIPHANT, E. H. C. The plays of Beaumont and Fletcher: an attempt to determine their respective shares and the shares of others. New Haven and London, 1927. Pp. 325–48. Admits Beaumont as well as Shakespeare and Fletcher. Includes a review of various theories.

SPALDING, W. A letter on Shakspere's authorship of The Two Noble Kinsmen; and on the characteristics of Shakspere's style and the secret of his supremacy. Ed. J. H. Burton. New Shakspere Society, ser. VIII, no. 1. London, 1876.

SPENCER, T. The two noble kinsmen. MP, XXXVI (1939), 255–76. Thinks Fletcher's share "much better theatre than Shakespeare's."

SPRAGUE, A. C. Beaumont and Fletcher on the restoration stage. Cambridge, 1926. On D'avenant's The Rivals, see pp. 28–9, 129–37.

SYKES, H. D. The two noble kinsmen. Sidelights on Shakespeare. Stratford-upon-Avon, 1919. Pp. 1–17. Cites parallel passages in support of the ascription to Massinger of the non-Fletcherian portions.

INDEX